P9-DTM-641

# CRYPTOGRAPHY:

An Introduction to Computer Security

I said it in Hebrew - I said it in Dutch -
I said it in German and Greek:
But I wholly forgot (and it vexes me much)
That English is what you speak!

from *The Hunting of the Snark*
Lewis Carroll

'What does it mean by *speak, friend and enter?*' asked Merry.
'That is plain enough,' said Gimli. 'If you are a friend, speak the
password, and the doors will open, and you can enter.'
'Yes,' said Gandalf, 'these doors are probably governed by words ...'

from *The Lord of the Rings*
J. R. R. Tolkien

*To Bozena, Alicja, Luke, Pawel and Ralph*

**PRENTICE HALL**
**ADVANCES IN COMPUTER SCIENCE SERIES**
Editor: Richard P. Brent

# CRYPTOGRAPHY:
## An Introduction to Computer Security

Jennifer Seberry

*University College*
*The University of New South Wales*
*Australian Defence Force Academy*

Josef Pieprzyk

*University College*
*The University of New South Wales*
*Australian Defence Force Academy*

PRENTICE HALL

New York   London   Toronto   Sydney   Tokyo

Printed and bound in Australia by Impact Printing, Brunswick, Vic.

3 4 5 93 92 91
ISBN 0 7248 0274 6 (paperback)
ISBN 0-13-194986-1 (hardback)

**National Library of Australia**
**Cataloguing-in-Publication Data**

Seberry, Jennifer, 1944–
    Cryptography : an introduction to computer security.

    Bibliography.
    Includes index.
    ISBN 0 7248 0274 6.

    1. Computers—Access control. 2. Cryptography.
    I. Pieprzyk, Josef, 1949–    . II. Title.

005.8

**Library of Congress**
**Cataloguing-in-Publication Data**

Seberry, Jennifer, 1944–
    Cryptography : an introduction to computer security/by Jennifer
    Seberry and Josef Pieprzyk.
        p.   cm.
    Bibliography: p.
    ISBN 0-13-194986-1
    1. Computers—Access control. 2. Cryptography.
    I. Peiprzyk, Josef, 1949–    . II. Title.
QA76.9.A25S37 1989
005.8—dc19                                                87-27026
                        68696                                  CIP

Prentice Hall, Inc., *Englewood Cliffs, New Jersey*
Prentice Hall Canada, Inc., *Toronto*
Prentice Hall Hispanoamericana, S.A., *Mexico*
Prentice Hall of India Private Ltd, *New Delhi*
Prentice Hall International, Inc., *London*
Prentice Hall of Japan, Inc., *Tokyo*
Prentice Hall of Southeast Asia Pty Ltd, *Singapore*
Editora Prentice Hall do Brasil Ltda, *Rio de Janeiro*

 PRENTICE HALL

A division of Simon & Schuster

# CONTENTS

# PREFACE

The first electronic computers were built during the Second World War to help with cracking codes. They used various components originating from many sources, some of which themselves arose from the need for security, (e.g. the mercury delay lines used in radar were later used for high speed computer memory).

The first computers were physically massive and it was estimated that not more than ten would be needed to do all the ballistic calculations and code breaking that would ever be needed.

Soon it was realized that computers had a vast role to play in commercial data processing and weather forecasting which would have a tremendous impact on the average citizen.

The advent of the transistor led to smaller computers and faster speeds. The race into space prompted even greater miniturization with integrated circuitry and chips.

At that time, most computers were still used in physically secure environments and programs were processed as batch jobs. Both these enviroments have security advantages but are inefficient in the use of both computing power and the rapidly increasing need for communications.

Today we have a world-wide interlocking communications network which lets me sit at my terminal and send messages, on an average day, to three or four different continents, to carry out my personal business, to undertake various research projects, to write a book or to run computer programs on a vast number of different computers.

Governments and private firms keep enormous amounts of data on people, products, commodities, and processes, all of which have needs for security and privacy protection.

This book started out as a set of lecture notes given to third year undergraduate applied mathematics students at the University of Sydney. Interest was so great that the notes rapidly evolved to be given to first honours year and then third year computer science students. Thus, this book is intended to meet the needs of an upper level undergraduate or early masters level course.

We could not cover all of cryptology or all of computer security. It is a vast field with many different applications and requirements. We have set it against our knowledge, now, but researchers are still finding better algorithms, better protocols, better equipment and flaws in those that have been previously devised.

The original notes were prepared on the VAX within the Department of Computer Science, at The University of Sydney. We are grateful to the numerous students who pointed out errors in the text and solutions. Having taught the course in some form for several years, we were able to simplify much of the mathematics to make it accessible to a students with less of a mathematical background. The book can still be read by these students by skipping Chapter 2.

Later parts of the notes were prepared on the Pyramid 90X at the Department of Computer Science, University College, The University of New South Wales, Australian Defence Force Academy, Canberra. These notes were handed over to Mr Ray Loyzaga under whose expert hand the final version was produced.

We are especially grateful to Terry Jones Jr, Susy Deck, Ralph Gyoery, Leisa Condie, Hugh McGuinness, Michael Newberry, Gary Finkelstein, Thomas Hardjono, Elizabeth Hardjono and Lawrie Brown for their comments, corrections and the use of their programs.

# 1

# INTRODUCTION

Security of information results from the need for private transmission of both military and diplomatic messages. This need is as old as civilization itself. The ancient Spartans, for instance, enciphered their military messages. For the Chinese, merely writing down the message made it private, for few could read Chinese characters. The first communication channels were very simple and they were arranged using trustworthy messengers. The security of such an arrangement depended on both the messenger's reliability and his/her ability to keep out of situations where the disclosure of the message might take place.

Due to the invention of computer systems and the introduction of nation-wide computer networks, the twentieth century has drastically changed the range of protection issues. At the earliest stage of computer system development, physical security along with a suitable staff selection policy was sufficient to ensure security. But this became insufficient and inflexible after the advent of time-sharing computer systems with many terminals dispersed over a large geographic area.

Many protection issues of both time-sharing computer systems and computer networks are strictly related to the protection of communication channels which not only connect terminals to corresponding computers but create communication networks among host computers as well. Due to the natural attributes of any channel, we have a communication medium that is accessible to eavesdroppers so physical security is useless. The only way to enforce protection in communication channels is by the application of cryptography.

On the other hand, coexistence of many user programs which share the same computer resources sometimes causes illegal information leakages. Therefore, the access control mechanism of a computer must ensure correct interaction between different user programs (processes). If, however, an illegal access attempt takes place, this access must be forbidden and the operating system must record the attempt.

In general, security of both time-sharing computer systems and computer networks consists of three components:

- security of computing centre(s);
- security of terminals;
- and security of communication channels.

Protection of computing centres needs many different security countermeasures. First of all, centers must be protected from any possible natural disasters like flood, fire, earthquake, etc. Also the building must be protected against outside activity like terrorist attacks, eavesdropping, etc. All these countermeasures can be viewed as external

1

security. Internal security, however, includes protection measures used inside the computer system (like a secure access control mechanism, illegal access attempt monitoring system, user identification mechanism, etc.) and others applied outside the computer like the proper selection of staff, physical protection of computer components, a suitable backup strategy, etc. Experience shows that terminals are the most vulnerable parts of any computer system. Most illegal access attempts are initiated just via terminals. To minimize the chance of successful illegal activity, terminals have to be tamper-proof, and placed in secure buildings (this enforces the partial physical security).

Cryptography is used to protect information to which illegal access is possible and where other protective measures are inefficient. Thus it can be applied to protect communication channels and physical databases.

The primitive operation at the disposal of cryptography is *encryption*. It is a special computation that operates on messages, converting them into representation that is meaningless for all parties other than the intended receiver. Transformations effected on messages are so intricate that it is beyond the means of an interloper to undo the process. Almost without exception all modern cryptosystems rely upon the *difficulty* of reversing the encryption transformation as a basis for secure communication.

The encryption algorithm is chosen from a family of invertible transformations known as the *general system, cryptosystem*, or simply *system*. The parameter that selects the particular transformation from the family is called the *enciphering key*, or simply the *key*. The cryptosystem may take any of several forms, say a set of instructions, a piece of hardware or a program, one of which is selected by the enciphering key.

Formally, a cryptosystem is a single parameter family of invertible transformations,

$$E_K \; ; \; K \in \mathbf{K} \tag{1.1}$$

where $\mathbf{K}$ is the *keyspace*, which is of finite length. If $M$ is the *message space* and $C$ is the *cryptogram* or *ciphertext space*, then the system must have the following properties:

- enciphering algorithm

$$E_K : \mathbf{M} \to \mathbf{C}$$

for any fixed encryption key $K \in \mathbf{K}$, is an invertible transformation of the message space into the cryptogram space, i.e. $E_K(M) = C$ where $M \in \mathbf{M}$ and $C \in \mathbf{C}$;

- there is an inverse algorithm $E_K^{-1} = D_K$ called the decryption algorithm

$$D_K : \mathbf{C} \to \mathbf{M}$$

such that $D_K(C) = D_K[E_K(M)] = M$;

- the keys should uniquely define the enciphered message,

$$E_{K_1}(M) \neq E_{K_2}(M) \;\; \text{if} \; K_1 \neq K_2$$

Cryptography deals with the design and analysis of systems that provide secure communications or resist *cryptanalysis*. A system is said to be *compromised* via cryptanalysis if it is possible to recover the original message, the *plaintext*, from the *ciphertext*, the encrypted plaintext, without knowledge of the key used in the encryption algorithm. Cryptanalysis is a highly specialised facet of applied mathematics drawing from such disciplines as probability theory, number theory, statistics and algebra. The skilful cryptanalyst must be well-versed in each of these fields and have the ability to assimilate them. Cryptanalysts also make use of secondary information about the system such as the nature of its algorithms, the communication language, the context of the messages and the statistical properties of the plaintext language (i.e. its redundancy).

Cryptanalysis is a system identification problem and the goal of cryptography is to build systems that are hard to identify. An ideal system is one that has a flat distribution for all statistical properties of the cipher, implying that the redundant qualities of the natural language have been obscured.[1]

The 'noisy channel' problem is analogous to the problem of secure communications in cryptography — the noise corresponding to the enciphering transformation and the received message as the ciphertext. The role of the sender, though, is to make the recovery of the original message as difficult as possible, if not impossible. Cryptographers seek to devise encryption techniques that produce ciphertext that cannot be distinguished from purely random bit strings by an opponent.

> The statistical communication channel of the coding/decoding model has been replaced by a game theoretic channel; nature has been replaced by an intelligent opponent.[2]

It is not sufficient, though, that a cryptosystem be able to thwart cryptanalysis alone. It should frustrate any and all aims of unauthorized parties attempting to subvert the integrity of a supposedly secure channel.

The typical aims of an opponent may be summarized as follows:

1. to determine the content of message $M$;
2. to alter message $M$ to $M'$ and have $M'$ accepted by the receiver as a message from the transmitter of $M$;
3. to initiate communications to a receiver and have the interloper posing as an authorized transmitter.

Traditionally, the first of these aims, known as the *privacy problem*, has consumed the greater portion of cryptographers' attention. But as electronic communication has acquired a more ubiquitous presence in public and private spheres alike, circumventing the latter two of the aims has gained overwhelming importance in system design. Foiling these aims is known as the *problem of authentication* and the *problem of dispute*.

Security is directly related to the *difficulty* associated with inverting encryption transformation(s) of a system. The protection afforded by the encryption procedure can be evaluated by the uncertainty facing an opponent in determining the permissible keys used. Shannon [SHAN49] characterized a system that has *perfect security* with the following property: if an opponent knows $E$ (the encryption transformation) and has an

---

1. There are two main methods of uniformly distributing the redundant characteristics of a natural language. First through *diffusion*, which spreads the correlations and dependencies of the messages over substrings as long as feasible so as to maximize the unicity distance. The second approach is *confusion*, where the functional dependencies of the related variables are made as complex as possible so as to increase the time needed to analyze the system.

2. [SIMM79b], p. 315. Game theory is a mathematical theory that deals with the general features of competitive situations, placing particular emphasis on the decision-making process of the adversaries.

arbitrary amount of cipher, he/she is still left with a choice between all messages from the message space when attempting to recover the corresponding plaintext for some ciphertext. Let $P_C(M)$ be the probability that a message $M$ was sent given that $C$ was received, with $C = E(M)$. Then perfect security is defined as:

$$P_C(M) = P(M)$$

where $P(M)$ is the probability that message $M$ will occur. Let $P_M(C)$ be the probability of receiving ciphertext $C$ given that $M$ was sent. Then $P_M(C)$ is the sum of the probabilities $P(K)$ of the keys that encipher $M$ as $C$:

$$P_M(C) = \sum_{K, E_K(M) = C}^{K} P(K)$$

where $\mathbf{K}$ means across the space of $\mathbf{K}$. Usually there will only be one key $K$ that satisfies $E_K(M) = C$. A necessary and sufficient condition for perfect secrecy is that for every $C$,

$$P_M(C) = P(C)$$

This means that the probability of receiving ciphertext $C$ is independent of encrypting it with plaintext $M$. Perfect secrecy can only be assured if the length of the key is as long as the message sent, and the cardinality of the key space is the same as that of the message space. These conditions ensure that the uncertainty of the key and cipher are maintained and maximized.[3]

The opponent is faced with at least as much uncertainty with respect to the message as he or she is with the key.[4] Being in possession of $C$ adds no information to the task of recovering $M = D_K(C)$. Systems that are based on Shannon's equivocation are *unconditionally secure*, meaning that the system will resist cryptanalysis even in the presence of infinite computing power. The security of such systems is derived directly from statistical uncertainty. If $H_C(K)$, the entropy of the key (see Chapter 2) never approaches zero for any message length, then the cipher is considered unconditionally secure.

Shannon assumed in devising his perfect ciphers that opponents had access to unlimited computing power. It is far from unreasonable though, to believe that any single opponent, or cartel of opponents, is in possession of inexhaustible computing resources. Such security measures as warranted by Shannon would appear to be excessive, for what they are guarding against is not a tangible threat. With this in mind, modern cryptosystems look beyond uncertainty and unicity distances to establish a basis of security and, in particular, the *work factor*, the ratio of the complexity of cryptanalyzing a system to decryption, is taken as a strong indication of a system's security. Security can be cited in terms of the number of person/computer years needed to break the system. The subtle distinction can be drawn between perfect secrecy and *cryptosecrecy*, the first

---

3. Ciphers that could not be shown to have perfect secrecy but did not disclose sufficient information to allow the key to be determined, Shannon called *ideally secret*. By not revealing more information than the unicity distance, these systems were effectively unbreakable.

4. The only such system is the *one time pad*. The key used is a non-repeating stream of random bits, and discarded after each transmission. A separate key is used for each transmission as two ciphertexts encrypted with the same key could be correlated.

being asymptotically defined while the latter appeals to the concept of intractability. Even though the threats that a cryptosystem must resist can be listed as above, there does not exist, at present, any general method or algorithm that can *prove* a cryptosystem is cryptosecure. Designers have come to rely upon *certification* by cryptanalysts, who with considerable zest attempt to compromise the system using *ad hoc* and heuristic measures, as an indication of a *system's* security. History has repeatedly shown that systems purported by their inventors to be unbreakable were demonstrated to be far less secure than thought after being handed over to be scrutinized by cryptanalysts. Though certification is inexact and without the elegance of mathematical proof, it has remained the acid test for substantiating the claim that a system is secure. It is hoped that complexity theory will provide the necessary theoretical tools to establish and construct provably secure cryptosystems. If this was to eventuate, then cryptography would relinquish its reputation as an art and assume the properties of an exact science.

There are several criteria, so-called *attacks*, used to determine the adequacy of a prospective cryptosystem. A *ciphertext-only attack* is where a system is attempted to be compromised by examining encrypted messages, or cipher, and referring to related secondary information. Any system whose security cannot weather a ciphertext-only attack is considered inadequate and totally insecure. A *known-plaintext attack* is when a system is attempted to be compromised with the cryptanalyst being in possession of plaintext and its corresponding ciphertext. If a system can withstand a known-plaintext attack, this is taken as a reasonable indication that the system is secure[5]. There is a third attack that accords to cryptanalysts a set of circumstances so favorable, that compromization under this attack is not considered a realistic indication of a system's innate ability to resist being broken. An attack when the cryptanalyst can submit an unlimited amount of plaintext and obtain the corresponding ciphertext is called a *chosen-plaintext attack*. A system that avoids compromization when subjected to a chosen-plaintext attack is certainly secure.

It should be realized that a system's security does not depend on the concealment of its encryption transformation or algorithm. Generally these algorithms will be available for all to examine and study, which is known as *Kerckhoff's principle*.[6] When $E$ is revealed, a very difficult or *inefficient* method is also revealed to compute the inverse of $E$. Given the ciphertext $C$, the cryptanalyst can examine the message space exhaustively until an $M$ is found such that $E(M)=C$. Whenever a key of finite length is employed, it can always be theoretically compromised through direct search methods. The success of such an attack depends upon the work factor associated with the cipher, i.e. the minimal number of computations needed to invert the system. It should be noted that the unicity distance indicates the number of characters needed to determine the key, but it makes no comment on the *complexity* of this task. A system can disclose more ciphertext than its unicity distance considers safe but still may remain cryptosecure.

Let us consider a further definition of security that has been appealed to as a basis for endorsing sound cryptosystems. A system is *computationally secure* if the task of inverting $E$ is *computationally infeasible* or *intractable*. This sounds very similar to the properties of **NP** problems (given in section 2.2), and more recent system designs are

---

5. In 1977 the NBS accepted the DES system on the basis of it resisting a known plaintext attack.

6. [SIMM00], p. 5.

based on an encryption transformation where the best known deterministic algorithm to invert the transformation has exponential complexity. Problems that are characterized by computational difficulty that exceeds **NP** are not suited to cryptography as their associated encryption and decryption algorithms are too slow.

Systems that rely on computational security to isolate the key and thus thwart compromization are assuming that even though cryptanalysis is *achievable* in a finite number of steps, the amount of resources *required* to invert the system and the stock of resources at the disposal of the cryptanalyst are so disproportionate that for all practical purposes the system is singular.[7] Shannon systems resist compromization because the cryptanalyst does not have enough *information*, whereas in computationally secure systems the cryptanalyst does have enough information to resolve the equivocation of the system but does not have enough *time* to complete it.[8] The equivocation of the system has been effectively reduced to zero, but practically has remained undiminished due to the complexity involved.

Diffie and Hellman [DIHE76a] introduced the concept of computationally secure cryptosystems in 1976 and while such systems have better prospects for commercial application than Shannon systems, they 'do not however provide a complete solution to the basic problem of the design of provably secure cryptosystems'.[9] If **P≠NP** can be proven, then systems based on intractable problems can also be proven secure, under a computational definition of security. With the **P≠NP** contention unresolved, complexity theory can only furnish an upper bound on the time taken to cryptanalyze a computationally secure cryptosystem.

Perfect systems resist inversion through ignorance while imperfect systems are based on the belief that compromization is beyond the economic means of any interloper. Another essential difference between the two systems is that the former can be proven secure whereas the security of the latter can only be suspected at this point in time. Though totally secure, Shannon systems place restrictions on the key, its length and frequency of replacement, that make such systems impractical for frequent communications between a large number of users. Cryptosystem designers have endeavored to find procedures that magnify the uncertainty of a small key, as if it were a key of much greater length and associated uncertainty. The *true key* is said to be modified to the *pseudo key* with the security of the system relying on the infeasibility of determining the true key from the pseudo key, and such systems will be discussed in the next sections. It should be stressed that at present complexity theory lacks the adequacy to demonstrate the infeasibility of any cryptographic problem.

---

7. 'With current technology, the practical limit on the number of operations a cryptanalyst can perform is between $2^{50}$ and $2^{60}$ ... and the practical limit on the number of memory cells he can use is between $2^{25}$ and $2^{35}$', [SCSH79].

8. This can be illustrated by an example from Lakshmivarahan [LAKS83], p. 53. Let the key be 128 bits long and an exhaustive search requires decryption of $2^{128} \approx 10^{38}$. Excluding leap years there are only $3.15 \times 10^7$ seconds in a year. If it is assumed that decryption with a distinct key can be performed in $10^{-1}$ seconds, then in a year $3.15 \times 10^{16}$ unique keys can be tested, and to exhaust the entire message space would require at least $3.17 \times 10^{21}$ years.

9. [LAKS83], p. 53.

# 2
# BACKGROUND THEORY

## 2.1 Mathematical methods

The mathematics needed to understand the concepts and algorithms of elementary cryptography is not particularly deep or difficult but as some readers may have come to study the area from a non-mathematics background we are going to introduce all the ideas we need.

Those readers with a good mathematical training may wish merely to browse through this section or pass over it completely. Those who need more mathematical background should consult a book on elementary number theory such as Vinogradov [VINO61].

### 2.1.1 Modular arithmetic

Modular arithmetic is often introduced in school as 'clock arithmetic'. Fourteen hours after 3 pm is 5 am the next morning.

Simply,

$$14 + 3 \equiv 5 \pmod{12}$$

or

$$14 + 3 = 1 \cdot 12 + 5$$

The notation $a \equiv b \pmod{n}$ is said as '$a$ is congruent to $b$ modulo $n$'. It holds for integers $a$, $b$ and $n \neq 0$ if and only if

$$a = b + kn \quad \text{for some } k$$

Hence $n|(a - b)$ which is said as '$n$ divides $(a - b)$'.

If $a \equiv b \pmod{n}$, $b$ is called a residue of '$a$ modulo $n$'. In our example $17 \equiv 5 \pmod{12}$ and 5 is a residue 17 modulo 12. A set $\{r_1, r_2, \ldots, r_n\}$ is called a complete set of residues mod $n$ if for every integer $a$, exactly one $r_i$ in the set satisfies that $a \equiv r_i \pmod{n}$. For any modulus $\{0, 1, \ldots, n - 1\}$ forms a complete set of residues mod $n$. For $n = 12$ the set of complete residues is $\{0, 1, \ldots, 11\}$.

We usually prefer to use $b \in \{0, \ldots, n - 1\}$ but sometimes an integer in the range $b \in \{-\frac{1}{2}(n - 1), \ldots, \frac{1}{2}(n - 1)\}$ is more useful.

Note:

$$-12 \pmod 7 \equiv -5 \pmod 7 \equiv 2 \pmod 7 \equiv 9 \pmod 7 \equiv \ldots \text{ etc.}$$

Now the integers modulo $n$ with addition and multiplication form a commutative ring with the laws of associativity, commutativity and distributivity holding. In fact we can either reduce modulo $n$ and then do the operations or do the operations and then reduce modulo $n$, since reduction modulo $n$ is a homomorphism from the ring of integers to the ring of integers modulo $n$.

So,

$$(a \pm b) \pmod{n} \equiv [a(\bmod\, n) \pm b(\bmod\, n)] \pmod{n}$$

and

$$(a * b) \pmod{n} \equiv [a(\bmod\, n) * b(\bmod\, n)] \pmod{n}$$

*Example*

The rule of 'casting out nines' relies on adding all the digits of a number. If they add to 9 ultimately, then the original number was divisible by 9.
For example,  is 46909818 divisible by 9?

The sum of the digits is $4 + 6 + 9 + 9 + 8 + 1 + 8 = 45$ and the sum of these digits is $4 + 5 = 9$ so the number is divisible by 9. The method relies on the fact that:

$$
\begin{aligned}
10 &\equiv 1(\bmod\, 9) \\
10^2 &\equiv 10(\bmod\, 9) * 10(\bmod\, 9) \\
&\equiv 1(\bmod\, 9) \\
10^3 &= 10^2(\bmod\, 9) * 10(\bmod\, 9) \\
&\equiv 1(\bmod\, 9)
\end{aligned}
$$

.
.
.

etc.

So the integer,

$$
\begin{aligned}
a_1\, a_2\, \ldots\, a_m \,(\bmod\, n) \\
\equiv a_1 \times 10^{m-1} + a_2 \times 10^{m-2} + \ldots + a_m(\bmod\, n) \\
\equiv a_1 + a_2 + \ldots + a_m \,(\bmod\, n)
\end{aligned}
$$

where $a_i$; $i = 1, \ldots, m$, are successive digits of the integer.     □

*Example*

We illustrate how these rules can help.

$$3^{12} \pmod{7} \equiv (3^2(\bmod\, 7))^6 \equiv (2(\bmod\, 7))^6 \equiv 1(\bmod\, 7)$$

Note though $2^{5(\bmod\, 3)}(\bmod\, 3) \equiv 1$  but $2^5 \pmod{3} \equiv 2$.     □

Because many encryption algorithms are based on exponentiation mod $n$ we give here a 'C' algorithm for fast exponentiation (Figure 2.1). It should be noted that most implementations of 'C' do not allow the numbers to be very large. A slow but accurate method to circumvent the problems can be found on UNIX™ by using *bc* or *dc*.

| *Fast exponentiation* |
| Algorithm *fastexp(a, z, n)* |

```
/* fastexp - return a^z (mod n)
*/
#include <stdio.h>
int fastexp(a, z, n)
int a, z, n;
{
    int x = 1;

    while (z) {
        while (z % 2==0) {
            z /= 2;
            a = ((a % n)*(a % n)) % n;
        }
        z--;
        x = ((x % n)*(a % n)) % n;
    }
    return (x);
}

main()
{
    int a, z, n;

    printf("Calculates a^z (mod n), please enter a, z, n : ");
    scanf("%d %d %d", &a, &z, &n);
    printf("result = %d\n", fastexp(a, z, n));
}
```

**Figure 2.1** Fast exponentiation in 'C'

Suppose $a$, $z$ and $n$ are $k$-bit integers. Letting $z_{k-1}, \ldots, z_1, z_0$ denote the binary representation of $z$, the algorithm processes the bits in the order $z_0, z_1, \ldots, z_{k-1}$ (i.e. from low to high order) squaring when the bits are 0, and multiplying and squaring when they are 1. In a hardware implementation of the algorithm, these bits could be accessed directly, omitting the computations $z \bmod 2$, $z$ div 2 and $z - 1$.

Let $T$ be the running time of the algorithm. Because each 0-bit gives rise to one multiplication and each 1-bit gives rise to 2 multiplications (except the leftmost 1-bit which gives 1 multiplication), the number of multiplications is bounded by:

$$k + 1 \leq T \leq 2k + 1$$

where $k = \lfloor \log_2 z \rfloor$ (round down the nearest integer). This is linear in the length of $z$. The expected number of multiplications for all $z$ of length $k$ is $1.5\,k + 1$. By comparison a naive algorithm performs $z - 1$ multiplications, which is exponential in the length of $z$.

*Example*

Suppose we wish to find $7^5$ (mod 9). We first note 5 is $z = 101$ in binary. Now the rightmost digit of $z$ is 1. So,

$$a = 7 \text{ and } x = 7$$

Since the second rightmost digit is zero, we square $a$ but do not multiply it onto $x$:

$$a = 7^2 = 49 \equiv 4 \;(\text{mod } 9), \text{ and } x = 7$$

The leftmost digit of $5 = z$ is 1, so we square $a$ and multiply it onto $x$ to get the result,

$$a = 7^4 \equiv 4^2 = 16 \equiv 7 (\text{mod } 9), \text{ and } x = 7^5 \qquad \square$$

*Remark*

This fast exponentiation is not suitable for 'large' numbers and special care must be taken.

## 2.1.2  Discrete logarithms

The inverse problem to that of finding powers of numbers in modular arithmetic is that of finding the *discrete logarithm* of a number. Specifically we wish to find $x$ where,

$$a^x \equiv b (\text{mod } n)$$

*Example*

Find $x$, $y$ if $3^x \equiv 4 \;(\text{mod } 13)$ and $2^y \equiv 3 \;(\text{mod } 13)$. Consider, $3^1 \equiv 3$, $3^2 \equiv 9$, $3^3 \equiv 1$, $3^4 \equiv 3$, ... $(\text{mod } 13)$ which clearly has no solution.

On the other hand, for $2^y \equiv 3 (\text{mod } 13)$,

$$2^1 \equiv 2, \; 2^2 \equiv 4, \; 2^3 \equiv 8, \; 2^4 \equiv 3, \; 2^5 \equiv 6, \; 2^6 \equiv 12, \; 2^7 \equiv 11$$
$$2^8 \equiv 9, \; 2^9 \equiv 5, \; 2^{10} \equiv 10, \; 2^{11} \equiv 7, \; 2^{12} \equiv 1 \;(\text{mod } 13)$$

So $y = 4$. $\qquad \square$

*Example*

To solve,

$$3^x \equiv 4 \;(\text{mod } 14)$$

we first note that $14 - 1 = 13$ has no factors. So we must try the seven even powers of 3 and quickly find that:

$$3^2 = 9, \; 3^4 = 11, \; 3^6 = 1 \;(\text{mod } 14)$$

so there are no solutions. $\qquad \square$

Finding discrete logarithms is generally a **hard** problem. We discuss this further after discussing arithmetic in Galois fields later in this section.

## 2.1.3  Computing inverses

Unlike ordinary integer arithmetic, sometimes modular arithmetic has inverses. So given $a \in \{0, n-1\}$ there may be a unique $x \in \{0, n-1\}$ such that,

$$ax \;(\text{mod } n) \equiv 1$$

For example,

$$3 \cdot 7 \ (\text{mod } 10) \equiv 1.$$

We write $gcd(a, n)$ for the **greatest common divisor** of $a$ and $n$. So $gcd(6, 3) = 3$ but $gcd(6, 5) = 1$.

**Lemma:**    *If $gcd(a, n) = 1$ then,*

$$ai \ \text{mod } n \neq aj \ \text{mod } n, \qquad 0 \leq i < j < n, \ i \neq j$$

**Proof:** We proceed by contradiction. Assume $ai \equiv aj \ (\text{mod } n)$. But this means that:

$$n \mid a \ (i{-}j)$$
$$\Rightarrow i{-}j \equiv 0 \ (\text{mod } n) \text{ since } gcd(a, n) = 1$$
$$\Rightarrow i \equiv j$$

which is a contradiction.    □

So $ai \ (\text{mod } n)$, $i = 0, 1, \ldots, n{-}1$ when $gcd(a, n) = 1$ is a permutation of $0, 1, \ldots, n{-}1$.

For example, if $a = 3$ and $n = 7$ then,

$$3i \ (\text{mod } 7), i = 1, 2, \ldots, 6 \text{ is } 0, 3, 6, 2, 5, 1, 4$$

just a permutation of the set $\{0, 1, \ldots, 6\}$. This is not true when $gcd(a, n) \neq 1$. For example, if $a = 2$, $n = 6$ then,

$$2i \ (\text{mod } 6), i = 0, 1, \ldots, 5 \text{ is } 0, 2, 4, 0, 2, 4$$

*Remark*

The same problem mentioned before arises if $a$ and $n$ are 'large' numbers and special care must be taken.

**Theorem:** *If* $gcd \ (a, n) = 1$, *then* $a^{-1}$, $0 < a^{-1} < n$, *exists such that,*

$$a \cdot a^{-1} \equiv 1 (\text{mod } n)$$

**Proof:** $ai \ (\text{mod } n)$ is a permutation of $0, 1, \ldots, n{-}1$ so there exists $i$ such that $a \cdot i \equiv 1 (\text{mod } n)$.    □

| Algorithm $gcd(a, n)$ |
|---|
| ```
begin
  g₀ := n;
  g₁ := a;
  i := 1;
  while gᵢ !≠ 0 do
  begin
    g_{i+1} := g_{i-1} mod gᵢ;
    i := i + 1
  end;
  gcd := g_{i-1}
end
``` |

**Figure 2.2** Euclid's algorithm for computing the greatest common divisor
```

A **reduced set of residues** is a subset of the complete set of residues relatively prime to $n$.

*Example*

The complete set of residues modulo 10 is:

$$\{ 0, 1, 2, 3, 4, 5, 6, 7, 8, 9 \}$$

but of these only 1, 3, 7, 9 do not have a factor in common with 10, so the reduced set of residues modulo 10 is $\{1, 3, 7, 9\}$.

The elements that have been excluded to form the reduced set are '0', the multiples of '2' and the multiples of '5': 1, 4 and 1 elements respectively, leaving,

$$10 - 1 - 4 - 1 = 4$$

elements in the reduced set.    ☐

In general the reduced set of residues for a product of primes $mn$ has $(m-1)(n-1)$ elements.

*Example*

The complete set of residues modulo 11 is:

$$\{ 0, 1, 2, 3, \ldots, 10 \}$$

Of these, only one element, '0', is removed to form the complete set of residues which has,

$$11 - 1 = 10$$

elements.    ☐

In general for a prime, $n$, the reduced set of residues has $n-1$ elements.

*Example*

The reduced set of residues modulo 27 is:

$$\{ 1, 2, 4, 5, 7, 8, 10, 11, 13, 14, 16, 17, 19, 20, 22, 23, 25, 26 \}$$

which has 18 elements.

The number 18 is obtained by noting the reduced set of residues; modulo 3 has 2 elements "1" and "2" and all the elements are :

$$3i + 1 \text{ or } 3i + 2, \ 0 \leq i \leq 8$$    ☐

In general for a prime power, $n^r$, the reduced set of residues has:

$$(n - 1)\, n^{r-1}$$

elements.

The **Euler totient function** $\phi(n)$ is the number of elements in the reduced set of residues. This is tabulated in Table 2.1.

**Table 2.1** Euler's totient function

| $n$ | *Reduced set* | $\phi(n)$ |
|---|---|---|
| $n$ prime<br>$n^2$ ($n$ prime) | $\{1, 2, \ldots, n-1\}$<br>$\{1, 2, \ldots, n-1, n+1,$<br>$\ldots, 2n-1, 2n+1,$<br>$\ldots, n^2-1\}$ | $n-1$<br>$n(n-1)$ |
| .<br>.<br>.<br>$n^r$ ($n$ prime) | .<br>.<br>.<br>$\{1, 2, \ldots, n^r-1$<br>— multiples of<br>$n < n^r\}$ | .<br>.<br>.<br>$(n^r-1) - (n^{r-1}-1)$<br>$= n^{r-1}(n-1)$ |
| $pq$ ($p,q$ prime)<br>.<br>.<br>.<br>$\prod_{i=1}^{t} p_i^{e_i}$ ; ($p_i$ primes) | $\{1, 2, \ldots, pq\text{-}1$<br>— multiples of $p$<br>— multiples of $q\}$<br>.<br>.<br>. | $(pq-1) - (q-1) - (p-1)$<br>$= (p-1)(q-1)$<br><br><br>$\prod_{i=1}^{t} p_i^{e_i-1}(p_i-1)$ |

**Theorem:**    (Euler's Generalization). *Let $gcd(a, n) = 1$ then*

$$a^{\phi(n)} \bmod n = 1$$

**Proof:** Let $R = \{r_1, \ldots, r_{\phi(n)}\}$ be a reduced set of residues modulo $n$, $0 < a < n$, $1 \le i \le \phi(n)$. Then $\{ar_1, ar_2, \ldots, ar_{\phi(n)}\}$ is a permutation of $R$.

Thus,

$$\prod_{i=1}^{\phi(n)} r_i = \prod_{i=1}^{\phi(n)} ar_i = a^{\phi(n)} \prod_{i=1}^{\phi(n)} r_i \equiv a^{\phi(n)} (\bmod\, n) \prod_{i=1}^{\phi(n)} r_i$$

Hence $a^{\phi(n)} \equiv 1 \ (\bmod\, n)$.    □

**Fermat's Theorem:**    *Let $p$ be a prime and suppose the $gcd\ (a, p) = 1$ then*

$$a^{p-1} \ (\bmod\, p) \equiv 1$$

For our later understanding of the important Rivest–Shamir–Adelman algorithm, we need to study why finding inverses in modular arithmetic can in practice take a very long time to compute.

**Algorithms to find $a^{-1}$ (mod $n$).**

1. Search through $1, \ldots, n-1$ until an $a^{-1}$ is found such that $a \cdot a^{-1} \ (\bmod\, n) = 1$.
2. If $\phi(n)$ is known then use **fastexp**.

$$a^{-1} \equiv a^{\phi(n)-1} (\bmod\, n)$$

to get the answer.
3. If $\phi(n)$ is not known we can use an extension of Euclid's algorithm (Figure 2.3).

$$\textit{Algorithm inv}(a, n)$$

```
{Return x such that ax mod n = 1,
    where 0 < a < n}
begin
    g₀ := n; g₁ := a;
    u₀ := 1; v₀ := 0;
    u₁ := 0; v₁ := 1;
    i := 1;
    while gᵢ ≠ 0 do ''gᵢ = uᵢn + vᵢa''
    begin
        y := gᵢ₋₁ div gᵢ;
        gᵢ₊₁ := gᵢ₋₁ - y * gᵢ;
        uᵢ₊₁ := uᵢ₋₁ - y * uᵢ;
        vᵢ₊₁ := vᵢ₋₁ - y * vᵢ;
        i := i + 1
    end;
    x := vᵢ₋₁;
    if x ≥ 0 then inv := x else inv := x + n
end
```

**Figure 2.3** Euclid's algorithm extended to compute inverses

*Example*

Use Euclid's algorithm to find $gcd(5, 23)$. Now,

$$23 = 4 \cdot 5 + 3$$
$$5 = 1 \cdot 3 + 2$$
$$3 = 1 \cdot 2 + 1$$
$$2 = 2 \cdot 1 + 0$$

Then $gcd(5, 23) = 1$.

Use Euclid's algorithm to find $gcd(6, 22)$. Now,

$$22 = 3 \cdot 6 + 4$$
$$6 = 1 \cdot 4 + 2$$
$$4 = 2 \cdot 2 + 0$$

Then $gcd(6, 22) = 2$.

This process is now modified to find inverses.

*Example*

Find the inverse of 5 modulo 23. Now,

$$
\begin{aligned}
3 \quad &= 23 - 4 \cdot 5 \\
2 \quad &= 5 - 1 \cdot 3 & &= 5 - 1 \cdot (23 - 4 \cdot 5) & &= 5 \cdot 5 - 1 \cdot 23 \\
1 \quad &= 3 - 1 \cdot 2 & &= 23 - 4 \cdot 5 - 1 \cdot (5 \cdot 5 - 1 \cdot 23) & &= 2 \cdot 23 - 9 \cdot 5
\end{aligned}
$$

So,

$$1 \equiv -9 \cdot 5 \pmod{23}$$

and $-9 \equiv 14 \pmod{23}$ gives $5^{-1} \equiv 14 \pmod{23}$.    □

*Example*

Find the solution of $11x = 1 \pmod{26}$.

Now,

$$4 = 26 \pmod{11} \qquad\qquad 4 = 26 - 2 \cdot 11$$
$$3 = 11 \pmod{4} \qquad\qquad 3 = 11 - 2 \cdot 4$$
$$\qquad\qquad\qquad = 11 - 2(26 - 2 \cdot 11)$$
$$\qquad\qquad\qquad = 5 \cdot 11 - 2 \cdot 26$$
$$1 = 4 \pmod{3} \qquad\qquad 1 = 4 - 3$$
$$\qquad\qquad\qquad = (26 - 2 \cdot 11) - (5 \cdot 11 - 2 \cdot 26)$$
$$\qquad\qquad\qquad = -7 \cdot 11 + 3 \cdot 26$$

So,

$$x = -7 = 19 \text{ and } 19 = 11^{-1} \pmod{26}$$    □

**Algorithm to find inverses:**  To solve,

$$ax = b \pmod{n}$$

first solve,

$$ay = 1 \pmod{n}$$

then find,

$$x = yb$$

*Example*

To solve

$$5x \equiv 9 \pmod{23}$$

We first solve,

$$5y \equiv 1 \pmod{23}$$

obtaining $y = 14$ and thus $x = 14 \cdot 9 \equiv 11 \pmod{23}$.    □

**Theorem:** *If $g = gcd(a, n)$ and $g \mid b$, ($b \equiv 0 \pmod{g}$) then $ax = b \pmod{n}$ has $g$ solutions*

$$x \equiv \left[ \left[ \frac{b}{g} \right] x_0 + t \left[ \frac{n}{g} \right] \right] \pmod{n} \quad \text{for } t = 0, \ldots, g-1$$

*where $x_0$ is the solution to,*

$$\left[ \frac{a}{g} \right] x \equiv 1 \left[ \bmod \left[ \frac{n}{g} \right] \right]$$

*otherwise it has no solution.*

**Proof:** If $ax \equiv b \bmod n$ has a solution in $[1, n-1]$ then $n \mid (ax-b)$. Now $g \mid n$, $g \mid a \Rightarrow g \mid b$ must hold.  Hence,

$$\left\lfloor\frac{a}{g}\right\rfloor x \equiv 1 \left(\bmod \left\lfloor\frac{n}{g}\right\rfloor\right)$$

has a unique solution $x_0$ in $[1, \frac{n}{g} - 1]$. Thus $x_1 \equiv \frac{b}{g}x_0 \left(\bmod \frac{n}{g}\right)$ is a solution of,

$$\left\lfloor\frac{a}{g}\right\rfloor x \bmod \left\lfloor\frac{n}{g}\right\rfloor \in \left[1, \frac{n}{g}-1\right]$$

therefore $\frac{a}{g}x_1 - \frac{b}{g} = kn$ for some integer $k$.

Multiplication by $g$ gives,

$$ax_1 - b = k'n$$

so $x_1$ is a solution of $ax = b$ (mod $n$). But any $x$ in $[1, n{-}1]$ such that $x \equiv x_1 \left(\bmod \frac{n}{g}\right)$ is also a solution. So all solutions are:

$$x = x_1 + t\left\lfloor\frac{n}{g}\right\rfloor \qquad t = 0, \ldots, g{-}1 \qquad \qquad \square$$

*Example*

Suppose we wish to solve $9x \equiv 6$ (mod 12). We note $g = gcd(9,12) = 3$ and 3 divides 6 so there are three solutions. We first solve:

$$3x_1 = 2 \;(\bmod\; 4)$$

by finding the solution to:

$$3x_0 = 1 \;(\bmod\; 4)$$

Now $x_0 = 3$ and so $x_1 = 3{\cdot}2 = 6 = 2$ (mod 4). Thus the three solutions are:

$$x = 2 + t \cdot 4, \qquad t = 0, 1, \text{ and } 2$$

That is x = 2, 6 and 10.   $\qquad \qquad \square$

We are now going to develop a powerful cryptographic tool called the **Chinese Remainder Theorem**. First we note:

**Theorem:** *Let* $p_1, \ldots, p_r$ *be pairwise relatively prime. Further let* $n = p_1 p_2 \ldots p_r$. *Then,*

$$f(x) \;(\bmod\; n) \equiv 0 \quad \textit{iff} \quad f(x) \;(\bmod\; p_i) \equiv 0 \quad (i{=}1,2, \ldots,r)$$

**Proof:** The $p_i$ are pairwise relatively prime so if,

$$f(x) = kn = k{\cdot}p_1{\cdot}p_2{\cdot} \ldots {\cdot}p_r$$
$$\Rightarrow p_i\,|\,f(x) \text{ for any } i \qquad \qquad \square$$

Hence to solve,

$$ax = b \pmod{n}$$

we need to solve the system of congruences:

$$ax \equiv b \pmod{p_i}, \text{for } i=1, \dots, r$$

**Theorem** **(Chinese Remainder Theorem):** *Let $p_1, \dots, p_r$ be pairwise relatively prime, where $n = p_1 \cdot p_2 \cdot \dots \cdot p_r$. Then the system of congruences,*

$$x = x_i \pmod{p_i}; \quad i = 1, \dots, r$$

*has a common solution in $[0, n{-}1]$.*

**Proof:** For each $i$, $gcd\left(p_i, \dfrac{n}{p_i}\right) = 1$. Therefore there exists a $y_i$ such that:

$$\left[\frac{n}{p_i}\right] y_i \equiv 1 \pmod{p_i}$$

Also,

$$\left[\frac{n}{p_i}\right] y_i \equiv 0 \pmod{p_j} \quad \text{for } j \neq i \text{ and } p_j \mid \frac{n}{p_i}$$

Let $x = \left[\displaystyle\sum_{i=1}^{r}\left[\frac{n}{p_i}\right]y_i x_i\right] \bmod n$. Then $x$ is a solution of $x = x_i \pmod{p_i}$ because,

$$x = \frac{n}{p_i} \, y_i \, (x_i) = x_i \pmod{p_i} \qquad \qquad \square$$

*Example*

Solve two equations $x \equiv 1 \pmod 5$ and $x \equiv 10 \pmod{11}$ to find a solution modulo 55.

First consider:

$$\frac{55}{5} y_1 = 1 \pmod 5 \text{ or } 11 y_1 = y_1 = 1 \pmod 5 \implies y_1 = 1$$

| *Algorithm* $crt(n, p_1, \dots, p_r, x_1, \dots, x_r)$ |
|---|
| ```
{return x ∈ [0, n - 1]
  such that x mod p_i = x_i (1 ≤ i ≤ t)}
begin
  for i := 1 to t do
    y_i := inv((n/p_i) mod p_i, p_i);
  x := 0;
  for i := 1 to r do
    x := [x + (n/p_i) * y_i * x_i] mod n;
  crt := x
end;
``` |

**Figure 2.4** An algorithm to find a solution to system of congruences using the Chinese Remainder Theorem
```

$$\frac{55}{11}y_2 = 1 \ (\text{mod } 11) \quad \text{or} \quad 5y_2 = 1 \ (\text{mod } 11) \Rightarrow y_2 = 9$$

Now the congruences become:

$$11 \cdot y_1 \cdot 21 \equiv 21 \equiv 1 = x_1 \ (\text{mod } 5)$$
$$5 \cdot y_2 \cdot 21 \equiv 21 \equiv 10 = x_2 \ (\text{mod } 11)$$

Thus,

$$\begin{aligned}
x &= \frac{55}{5}y_1 \, x_1 + \frac{55}{11}y_2 x_2 \\
&\equiv 11 \cdot 1 \cdot 1 + 5 \cdot 9 \cdot 10 \\
&\equiv 11 + (44+1)10 \\
&\equiv 11 + 10 \\
&\equiv 21 \ (\text{mod } 55)
\end{aligned}$$

□

*Example*

Find $7^{-1} (\text{mod } 65)$, that is we must solve,

$$7x \equiv 1 \ (\text{mod } 65)$$

We note $65 = 5 \cdot 13$ and solve,

$$7x \equiv 1 \ (\text{mod } 5) \text{ to find } x_1 = 3$$
$$7x \equiv 1 \ (\text{mod } 13) \text{ to find } x_2 = 2$$

We use the Chinese Remainder Theorem to solve,

$$x = x_1 = 3 \ (\text{mod } 5) \text{ solution } 3$$
$$x = x_2 = 2 \ (\text{mod } 13) \text{ solution } 2$$

Now we find $y_1$ and $y_2$ such that,

$$(65/5) \, y_1 = 13 \cdot y_1 \equiv 1 \ (\text{mod } 5) \text{ implies } y_1 = 2$$

and

$$(65/13) \, y_2 = 5 \cdot y_2 \equiv 1 \ (\text{mod } 13) \text{ implies } y_2 = 8$$

Finally this gives,

$$\begin{aligned}
x &= (65/5) \, x_1 \, y_1 + (65/13) \, x_2 \, y_2 \\
&= 13 \cdot 3 \cdot 2 + 5 \cdot 2 \cdot 8 \\
&= 28 \ (\text{mod } 65)
\end{aligned}$$

So,

$$7^{-1} = 28 \ (\text{mod } 65)$$

□

## 2.1.4  Computing in Galois fields

If $p$ is prime then $a \in [1, p-1]$ is relatively prime to $p$ and so $a^{-1}$ is unique.

Hence for $p$ prime we have a **finite field** called the Galois field GF($p$). Arithmetic

**Table 2.2** The multiplication and addition tables for GF(5)

| × | 1 2 3 4 | | + | 0 1 2 3 4 |
|---|---------|---|---|-----------|
| 1 | 1 2 3 4 | | 0 | 0 1 2 3 4 |
| 2 | 2 4 1 3 | | 1 | 1 2 3 4 0 |
| 3 | 3 1 4 2 | | 2 | 2 3 4 0 1 |
| 4 | 4 3 2 1 | | 3 | 3 4 0 1 2 |
|   |         | | 4 | 4 0 1 2 3 |

modulo $p$ is more powerful than ordinary integer arithmetic because we have division. Real arithmetic is not generally applicable to cryptography because information is lost through round-off errors (or truncation with integer division). Thus we find many ciphers are based on arithmetic in GF($p$) where $p$ is a large prime.

The Galois field GF(5) has elements 0, 1, 2, 3, 4 and is described by the multiplication and addition tables (see Table 2.2).

This is a field because multiplication, division, addition and subtraction are well defined. There is an identity element for addition, '0', and multiplication, '1', there are unique inverses and the associative, distributive and commutative laws hold.

Another type of Galois field in cryptography is based on arithmetic modulo $q$ over polynomials of degree $n$ ($q$ is prime). These fields, denoted GF($q^n$), have elements that are polynomials of degree $n - 1$ (or lower) of the form,

$$a(x) = a_{n-1}x^{n-1} + \ldots + a_1 x + a_0$$

where the coefficients are integers modulo $q$. Each element $a(x)$ is a residue modulo $p(x)$ where $p(x)$ is an irreducible polynomial of degree $n$ (i.e. $p$ cannot be factored in polynomials of degree $<n$). Arithmetic on the coefficients is done modulo $q$ and the highest power of $x$ is $n-1$ so we reduce modulo some $p(x)$.

The Galois field GF($2^3$) has elements 0, 1, $x$, $x+1$, $x^2$, $x^2+1$, $x^2+x$, $x^2+x+1$. These elements are often written in other ways but they must always be subject to a cubic equation (in GF($q^n$) the elements are subject to an equation of degree $n$) which is used to construct the multiplication table. In GF($2^3$) we illustrate, using $x^3 = x+1$, the multiplication and addition tables (see Table 2.3).

To produce these without using the exclusive 'and' for multiplication and the exclusive 'or' for the polynomial reduction we note,

$$a = x^2 + 1$$

so,

$$a^2 = x^4 + 1$$

but we reduce, using $p(x) = x^3+x+1$ so $x^3 = x + 1$ (in binary),

$$a^2 = x(x^3) + 1 = x(x+1) + 1 = x^2 + x + 1$$

*Example*

Multiply the following polynomials in GF($5^3$) modulo $x^3-1$:

$$a(x) = x^2 + 4x + 2$$
$$b(x) = 2x^2 + 3x + 1$$

**Table 2.3** The multiplication and addition tables for $GF(2^3)$

| × | 1 | $x$ | $x+1$ | $x^2$ | $x^2+1$ | $x^2+x$ | $x^2+x+1$ |
|---|---|---|---|---|---|---|---|
| 1 | 1 | $x$ | $x+1$ | $x^2$ | $x^2+1$ | $x^2+x$ | $x^2+x+1$ |
| $x$ | $x$ | $x^2$ | $x^2+x$ | $x+1$ | 1 | $x^2+x+1$ | $x^2+1$ |
| $x+1$ | $x+1$ | $x^2+x$ | $x^2+1$ | $x^2+x+1$ | $x^2$ | 1 | $x$ |
| $x^2$ | $x^2$ | $x+1$ | $x^2+x+1$ | $x^2+x$ | $x$ | $x^2+1$ | 1 |
| $x^2+1$ | $x^2+1$ | 1 | $x^2$ | $x$ | $x^2+x+1$ | $x+1$ | $x^2+x$ |
| $x^2+x$ | $x^2+x$ | $x^2+x+1$ | 1 | $x^2+1$ | $x+1$ | $x$ | $x^2$ |
| $x^2+x+1$ | $x^2+x+1$ | $x^2+1$ | $x$ | 1 | $x^2+x$ | $x^2$ | $x+1$ |

| + | 0 | 1 | $x$ | $x+1$ | $x^2$ | $x^2+1$ | $x^2+x$ | $x^2+x+1$ |
|---|---|---|---|---|---|---|---|---|
| 0 | 0 | 1 | $x$ | $x+1$ | $x^2$ | $x^2+1$ | $x^2+x$ | $x^2+x+1$ |
| 1 | 1 | 0 | $x+1$ | $x$ | $x^2+1$ | $x^2$ | $x^2+x+1$ | $x^2+x$ |
| $x$ | $x$ | $x+1$ | 0 | 1 | $x^2+x$ | $x^2+x+1$ | $x^2$ | $x^2+1$ |
| $x+1$ | $x+1$ | $x$ | 1 | 0 | $x^2+x+1$ | $x^2+x$ | $x^2+1$ | $x^2$ |
| $x^2$ | $x^2$ | $x^2+1$ | $x^2+x$ | $x^2+x+1$ | 0 | 1 | $x$ | $x+1$ |
| $x^2+1$ | $x^2+1$ | $x^2$ | $x^2+x+1$ | $x^2+x$ | 1 | 0 | $x+1$ | $x$ |
| $x^2+x$ | $x^2+x$ | $x^2+x+1$ | $x^2$ | $x^2+1$ | $x$ | $x+1$ | 0 | 1 |
| $x^2+x+1$ | $x^2+x+1$ | $x^2+x$ | $x^2+1$ | $x^2$ | $x+1$ | $x$ | 1 | 0 |

$$
\begin{aligned}
a(x)\,b(x) &= 2x^4 + 11x^3 + 17x^2 + 10x + 2 \\
&= 2x^4 + x^3 + 2x^2 + 2 \quad \text{(reduction of coefficients)} \\
&= 2x + 1 + 2x^2 + 2 \quad \text{(reduction of exponents)} \\
&= 2x^2 + 2x + 3 \pmod{x^3 - 1}
\end{aligned}
$$
$\square$

## 2.1.5  Computer application

We are especially interested in the fields $GF(2^n)$. Here the coefficients are 0 and 1. Thus the polynomial $a(x)$ can be represented as an $n$-tuple:

$$a_{n-1}, a_{n-2}, \ldots, a_1, a_0$$

and each of the possible $n$-bit vectors corresponds to a different element in $GF(2^n)$. For example, 11001 corresponds to $x^4 + x^3 + 1$ in $GF(2^5)$.

Computing in $GF(2^n)$ is more efficient in space and time than computing in $GF(p)$ where $p$ is prime. It is possible to represent many more elements in $GF(2^n)$ than in $GF(p)$ using exactly the same space. This is important in cryptographic applications where security depends on the size of the field.

We observe that arithmetic is more efficient in $GF(2^n)$ than $GF(p)$. We can:

1. add by using the **exclusive or**:
$$u + v \bmod 2 = u \oplus v = \begin{cases} 0 & u = v \;\; \text{both bits the same} \\ 1 & u \neq v \end{cases}$$

2. subtract in the same manner:
$$u - v \;(\bmod 2) = u \oplus v$$

3. multiply bits by taking the boolean **and**:

$$u \times v = u \text{ and } v$$

*Example*

Let,

$$a = 10101$$
$$b = 01100$$

then,

$$c = a + b = 11001 \qquad \square$$

By comparison if we regard $a$ and $b$ as the binary representations of 21 and 12, to add or multiply together the binary numbers and reduce mod 31 (N.B. $21+12 = 33$ and $21 \times 12 = 252 \equiv 4$ (mod 31)) we have to perform carries during the process, then divide the result by 31 and keep the remainder.

Mostly in working with $GF(2^n)$ the results of multiplication must be reduced by the irreducible polynomial associated with the field.

*Example*

Let $a = 101$, find $a^2$ in $GF(2^4)$ by using the irreducible polynomial $p(x) = x^3 + x + 1$ (1011 in binary):

$$a \times a = 0101 \times 0101 = 0111 \qquad \square$$

## 2.1.6 How to divide and find inverses in $GF(2^n)$

To divide $b$ by $a$ in $GF(2^n)$ modulo $p(x)$ we find $a^{-1}$ (by using our previous algorithms) and hence find,

$$ba^{-1} \pmod{p(x)}$$

Now every binary vector of length $n$, except 0, is relatively prime to $p(x)$ regardless of $p(x)$. Thus the number of residues relatively prime to $p(x)$ is $\phi(p(x)) = 2^n - 1$ (extending Euler's totient function to polynomials).

Thus,

$$a^{-1} = a^{\phi(p(x))-1} \bmod p(x) = a^{2^n-2}$$

or using the extended Euclid algorithm, with arithmetic in $GF(2^n)$.

*Example*

Let $a = 100$ and $p(x) = 1011$ in $GF(2^5)$.
One way to invert $a(x) = x^2$ modulo $p(x) = x^3 + x + 1 = 0$ is to let $k(x) = (ex^2 + fx + g) = a^{-1}(x)$ so that:

$$1 = a(x)a^{-1}(x) = a(x)k(x) = x^2(ex^2 + fx + g) \; (modulo \; x^3 + x + 1)$$

We then solve the linear equations obtained by noting,

$$1 = ex^4 + fx^3 + gx^2 = ex(x+1) + f(x+1) + gx^2 \quad \text{(since } x^3 = x + 1\text{)}$$

Thus,

$$1 = f, \ e = g, \ f = e$$

and,

$$a^{-1}(x) = h(x) = x^2 + x + 1 \quad \text{giving } a^{-1} = 111$$

Alternatively, using addition in $GF(2^4)$ to do the calculations, we get:

$$
\begin{aligned}
a^{-1} \quad &= 100^{2^3-2} \ (\text{mod } 1011) &\quad \text{where} \quad & 100^2 = & 10000 \oplus 10110 = 110 \\
&= 100^6 \ (\text{mod } 1011) \\
&= 100^4 \cdot 100^2 \ (\text{mod } 1011) &\quad \text{and} \quad & 110^2 = & 10100 \oplus 10110 = 010 \\
&= 010 \cdot 110 \ (\text{mod } 1011) \\
&= 1100 \ (\text{mod } 1011) &\quad \text{and} \quad & 1100 = & 1100 \oplus 1011 = 111 \\
&= 111
\end{aligned}
$$

We observe that computation in $GF(2^n)$ is often desirable for the following reasons:

1. Algorithms for computation in $GF(2^n)$ exist that are suitable for parallel implementation.
2. Polynomial arithmetic in $GF(2^n)$ is more efficient as nothing is carried and there is no need to divide by the modulus in order to perform addition or subtraction.
3. The cost of the hardware depends on choice of modulus. It is known we can use $p(x) = x^n + x + 1$ for $n = 1, 3, 4, 6, 7, 9, 15, 22, 28, 30, 46, 60, 63, 127$ as in these cases we have the appropriate theoretical results to justify use.
4. These polynomials $p(x)$ are good because of the long string of zeros.
5. A fast implementation in $GF(2^{127})$ is known (developed by researchers at the University of Waterloo[MULL83]).

## 2.1.7  A metaview of the mathematical background

We shall see that one of the major advantages of public key cryptosystems is their straightforward mathematical description compared with the involved opaque description of secure secret key systems such as the Data Encryption Algorithm (DEA or DES) or Fast Data Encipherment Algorithm (FEAL) [SHMI87].

Public key schemes are based on a class of functions known as one-way trapdoor functions, derived from a class of computationally difficult problems termed **NP**(non-deterministic polynomial) problems (see [WILL82]). Private secret key schemes, in contrast, rely on a series of substitution and transposition operations, called involution, which are very complex to analyze mathematically. Although no conclusive proofs have yet been obtained, Brassard [BRAS79a] has shown that, for both the RSA and the Diffie-Hellman key distribution schemes, if a successful cryptanalytic attack is possible in polynomial time then it would imply that **NP** = **Co-NP**, a result that is regarded as improbable at present, and is thus indicative of the probable security of these schemes. For the definitions of **NP** and **Co-NP** see section 2.3.1.

Much work has been done in the last decade on the problem of calculating discrete logarithms in various finite fields, and its cryptographic significance. Pohlig and Hellman [POHE78] present a new algorithm for computing discrete logarithms in a field GF($p$) with time complexity $O(\ln^2 p)$ if $p - 1$ has only small prime factors. This compares favourably with previous algorithms which require $O(\sqrt{p})$ complexity in both time and space. The paper concludes that such fields should thus be avoided in cryptographic applications.

Hellman [HELL80b] reports a new algorithm by Adleman [ADLE79] which can compute discrete logarithms in a field GF($p$) with the same time complexity as for factoring, namely:

$$O(e^{\sqrt{k \ln p \ln \ln p}})$$

Hellman then describes an extension to this algorithm which permits it to be used in fields of the form GF($p^m$) with the same complexity. Adleman's algorithm is, however, criticized by Herlestam [HERL83] from a number theoretic point of view. Herlestam concludes that it contains several algebraic traps which appear to be hard to circumvent, and that the presupposed abundance of so-called round numbers will not be at hand in the computationally interesting cases. Wells [WELL84] derives an explicit polynomial form for logarithms in a field GF($p$) where the coefficients have a surprisingly simple form. He then shows that this polynomial must have at least $p - 2$ non-zero coefficients and that its evaluation would be much slower than other algorithms known for computing discrete logarithms. This is further evidence of the difficulty of this problem.

Finite fields of the form GF($2^p$) have been studied specifically with respect to the discrete logarithm problem, since it is much more efficient to perform arithmetic in these fields than in GF($p$), and several recent implementations of the Diffie-Hellman Public Key Distribution System (PKDS) have exploited this. However recent developments have shown this to be an inadvisable choice. Herlestam [HERL81] mentions a new heuristic algorithm which suggested that the problem may be simpler in these fields than previously thought. Coppersmith [COPP84] outlines in detail a new algorithm with an asymptotic running time of $O(e^{cn^{1/3} \ln^{2/3} n})$. This gives a dramatic improvement for moderate sized fields such as GF($2^{127}$) and makes (barely) possible calculations in fields of size around GF($2^{400}$). This algorithm involves an initial precomputation stage whereby a table is built of linear equations relating logarithms of the various irreducible polynomials of moderate degree. This step is fairly expensive, but need be done only once per field. Then for each logarithm that needs to be calculated this table is used to search for a linear relationship among these terms. This step is relatively fast. A practical implementation of an earlier version of this algorithm in the field GF($2^{127}$) is described in Mullin [MUNE84] on the HEP supercomputer. The initial table building stage took about seven hours; subsequent computation of a specific logarithm took several seconds. By using some advances suggested by Coppersmith, it should be possible to reduce these times considerably.

El Gamal [ELGA84a] presents a new algorithm for computing discrete logarithms in the field GF($p^2$). It is distinguished from the previous algorithms by Adleman and Coppersmith in that they were for fields GF($p^m$) in which $p$ was fixed and $m$ was growing, whereas here the reverse is true, namely $m$ is fixed as 2, and $p$ is growing. The algorithm is similar to that of Coppersmith, and has a running time of:

$$O\left(e^{(1+\delta)\sqrt{48 \ln p \ln \ln p}}\right)$$

A comprehensive overview of the status of the discrete logarithm problem is given by Odlyzko [ODLY84a]. It commences with a discussion of a number of possible algorithms, including the inefficient ones. It then proceeds to introduce the most powerful general purpose algorithm known today, the index-calculus algorithm, and analyzes its asymptotic performance. Some dramatic improvements in its performance in fields of the form GF $(2^n)$ have been made recently by Coppersmith; these are discussed in detail in this paper. Then a number of technical improvements are discussed, which, although they don't affect the asymptotic performance substantially, can result in significant practical improvements in these algorithms. The performance of this algorithm in the fields GF $(p)$ where $p$ is prime is then presented. Finally the implications of these algorithms for cryptography are given. Odlyzko concludes that the field GF $(2^{127})$, which has been used in several current systems (see [BERK79], [YIPE82]), is very insecure and should be avoided. Depending on the level of security required, he concludes that in fields GF $(2^n)$, $n$ should be no smaller than 800, and preferably larger than 1500; and these values should be carefully chosen. In fields GF $(p)$ where $p$ prime, $p > 2^{500}$ should be more than adequate, and $p > 2^{1000}$ should be sufficient even when extreme security is required. These fields GF $(p)$ appear at present to offer the same level of security as an RSA scheme with modulus of size $p$.

The problem of factoring large integers is one of the oldest problems in number theory. It has taken on new significance recently with the advent of public key cryptosystems whose security rests on the practical impossibility of factoring large integers. Several major advances in the state of the art in factoring have been made in the last decade or so. The current best algorithms are the Continued Fraction algorithm developed by Morrison and Brillhart [MOBR75], the Quadratic Sieve developed by Pomerance [POME84], the Monte Carlo method developed by Pollard [POLL75], and Brent [BREN80], and variants of one of these. A popular overview of the various algorithms used to factor integers is given in Williams [WILL84], which includes simple examples illustrating each of the algorithms described. A more detailed introduction to these algorithms is provided by Dixon [DIXO84].

The general technique used to factor large numbers is as follows:

- First, use trial division to locate any small prime factors ( $<10$ ).
- Then run a number of strong pseudo-prime tests on the remainders to indicate whether they are probably prime or composite, and depending on the results either:

  - look for proofs of primality (see next section); or
  - use one of the advanced factoring algorithms to attempt to locate factors.

In more detail the advanced factoring algorithms are:

- Pollard's Monte Carlo Algorithm — described in Pollard [POLL75], and in Brent [BREN80].
- Continued Fraction Algorithm — first practically implemented by Morrison and Brillhart in 1975 [MOBR75].
- Pomerance's Quadratic Sieve — the most recently proposed algorithm, and the one on which the fastest known factoring algorithms in use (at the Sandia National

Laboratories) are based. It was originally described in Pomerance [POME84], and a status report of its use at Sandia is given in [DAHO84].

Poet [POET85] discusses the design of special VLSI hardware to assist in the implementation of Morrison and Brillhart's continued fraction algorithm ([MOBR75]). The techniques used to introduce parallelism into the algorithm are discussed, along with the design of the resultant computing engine to perform the algorithm. The paper concludes that by stretching silicon technology to the limit a 140 digit number could be factorized, and hence that the 200 digit number proposed for use in Rivest-Shamir-Adleman (RSA) schemes has a good safety margin for security.

Testing an integer for primality is a key requirement needed in the use of public key schemes. Much work has been done on this problem recently, and near polynomial-time algorithms have now been developed. It thus appears at this time, that primality testing is significantly easier than factorization. A survey and overview of the recent developments in primality testing is given by Pomerance [POME81], who outlines the various algorithms in use. Nearly all of these make use of strong pseudo-prime tests, which if failed prove that the integer is definitely composite. By doing a large number of such tests, and by extracting information from them, the range of possible factors of a number can be severely limited. This range may then be exhaustively searched to prove that the number is prime. An analysis of a couple of pseudo-prime tests in practical use is given in Bond [BOND84].

The key papers on primality testing are: Solovay [SOST77], Couvreur [COUV82], Adleman [ADPO83], Adams [ADSH82], and Kurtz [KURT86].

Recently there has been a significant amount of interest in the construction of cryptographically secure pseudo-random number generators. Such generators are 'good' in the sense that they pass all probabilistic polynomial-time statistical tests. Some such generators have been proved to be as computationally difficult to calculate as factoring. Several papers have outlined such generators, and have shown that the RSA encryption function is such a generator. The papers are: Vazirani and Vazirani [VAVA84], Akl [AKL84a], and Chor and Goldreich [CHGO84a] who have shown that the RSA least significant bit is $0.5 + (\ln^c N)^{-1}$ secure, for any constant $c$. This means that an adversary cannot guess the least significant bit of the message with probability better than $0.5 + (\ln^c N)^{-1}$ unless he can break the RSA scheme.

## 2.2 Complexity theory

This section is only a cursory introduction to the theory of complexity. Readers who wish to know more are urged to consult Gary and Johnson [GAJO79]. During life, people are continually engaged in solving problems. Moreover, living conditions of human beings depend on the human ability to solve everyday problems. A problem can be considered as a general task concerning a certain sphere of action. In order to carry out a task, or in other words solve a problem, people need to know the procedure which describes, step by step, all necessary subtasks. For example, assume that our task is to cook dinner. There are many different procedures (algorithms) to do this — see any cookery book. But usually people prefer the procedure which reaches the final result using the minimum time and/or money.

A similar situation arises concerning mathematical problems. A mathematical problem is understood to be a general question which consists of the two following parts:

1. a general description of the question along with all its parameters;
2. a formulation of the answer (solution) required.

For instance, consider the well-known problem of multiplying two matrices, **A** and **B**. The parameters of the problem are the coefficients of these matrices, but the solution consists of the matrix $C = A \times B$.

It is very important to be able to distinguish a problem from an instance of the problem. An instance of a problem can be generated by specifying values for all the problem parameters. Consider our problem of multiplying matrices. An instance can take on the form:

$$\text{Given matrices } A = [1,2,3] \text{ and } B = \begin{bmatrix} 2 \\ 3 \\ 4 \end{bmatrix}, \text{ find the matrix } C = A \times B.$$

An *algorithm* is a finite sequence of steps or computations which solves some problem. Of course, any algorithm deals with instances rather than with a problem itself and therefore an algorithm is said to solve a problem if that algorithm generates an answer (solution) for any instance $I$ of the problem. Going back to the problem of multiplying two matrices **A** and **B** (both matrices are of $n \times n$ dimension), we can present an algorithm which solves it by computing the product matrix **C** as follows:

```
1.   read A and B
2.   for h := 1 to n do
3.     for i := 1 to n do
4.       s := 0
5.         for j := 1 to n do s := s+A(h,j)*B(j,i){end for}
6.       C(h,i) := s
7.     end{for}
8.   end{for}
9.   output C
10.  HALT
```

The numbers on the left (1-10) are the steps or subtasks of the algorithm.

More particularly we can divide the class of all problems into two basic subclasses:

1. undecidable problems;
2. decidable problems.

A problem belongs to the class of undecidable problems if there is no algorithm which solves it. The existence of such problems was proved by A. Turing in 1936. An example of such a problem is Hilbert's tenth problem:[1]

*Instance*:  Given a polynomial equation, with integer coefficients, in an arbitrary number of unknowns.

---

1. In 1900, David Hilbert (1862-1943) presented 23 mathematical problems which had not been solved at that time. The problem in question was listed as the tenth one.

*Question*: Are there integers which are solutions of the equation?

Henceforth we are going to consider the subclass of decidable computable problems. A problem that can be solved is said to be *computable*, which is equivalent to saying that there exists an algorithm that characterizes it. Most computable problems are characterized by a class of algorithms, each of which could be used to obtain a solution to the problem. This is simply saying that there is usually more than one way a problem can be solved.

Also, we are going to describe problems in the standard way illustrated above. The first part, called '*Instance*', gives the general description of a problem. But the second part, called '*Question*', specifies the answer (solution) required — see Garey and Johnson [GAJO79].

## 2.2.1 Problems and algorithms

Assume we have a problem $\Pi$ and a suitable algorithm $\alpha$ which solves it. As we have already noticed, $\alpha$ solves the problem if it generates the solution to all instances of $\Pi$. But in order to get the solution, we must supply a sequence of all parameters that describes the instance. Usually such an input sequence is created according to a fixed encoding scheme. The input length for an instance $I$ of problem $\Pi$ is defined to be the number of elements in the input sequence created using a reasonable encoding scheme. Sometimes the name *the input length for instance I of* $\Pi$ is abbreviated to *the size of problem* $\Pi$.

Complexity theory deals with the classification of algorithms according to their *difficulty*. Difficulty in this context refers to a measure of the amount of *resources* consumed during the execution of an algorithm. The four basic resources may be identified as:

1. the number of basic operations performed when executing the algorithm;
2. the time that elapsed during the execution of the algorithm;
3. the amount of memory required to execute an algorithm;
4. the amount of hardware required to execute an algorithm.

(It is obvious that 2-4 are to some extent related and tradeoffs exist between them. 1 is commonly used because of its machine independence.)

Complexity theory quantitatively classifies *decidable* (i.e. computable) problems based on some *complexity measure* (i.e. resource usage). When (1) is used as the complexity measure, algorithms are classified according to the number of elementary operations performed as a function of the *length* or *size* of input to the problem. This is to say that if the length of the encoded input for the problem is $n$, then the number of basic operations performed during the execution of the algorithm would be some expression in $n$ such as $n^2 + 5n$, $n\log n - 1$, $n^3 + 7$, etc. The term that comes to dominate the expression when $n$ tends to infinity denotes the *asymptotic behavior* of the algorithm. The complexity of an algorithm is exactly the asymptotic behavior of the expression in $n$ that describes its resource usage with respect to some complexity measure. Recall the algorithm that was presented to multiply two $n$ by $n$ matrices. Here the basic operation is a multiplication and the length of input the dimensions of the matrices, i.e. $n$. The only place in the algorithm that a multiplication occurs is in the inner loop, where $j$ is the loop variable. Since the inner loop will iterate $n$ times, and it is nested within another loop, loop variable $i$, which is nested within another loop, loop variable $p$, both of which iterate $n$ times, the algorithm will perform $n^3$ multiplications. The asymptotic behavior of this expression is $n^3$, which is the complexity of this algorithm.

It should be stressed that the complexity of many naturally occurring problems is not known. Problems are classified in complexity theory according to the complexity of the most efficient or *optimal* algorithm for the problem. An algorithm is optimal (in the worst case, explained below) if no other algorithm from the class of algorithms that describe a problem performs fewer elementary operations than it (in the worst case), i.e. has a lower complexity. However, all the members of the class of algorithms that solve a particular problem are not known. Of the algorithms that are known, the algorithm with the lowest complexity is called the *best* algorithm for the problem. The complexity of the best algorithm for some problem should be taken as an *upper bound* on the complexity of the problem. The true complexity of the problem, i.e. the complexity of its optimal algorithm, lies between the minimal number of operations needed to solve a problem, called its *lower bound*, and the complexity of its current best algorithm.

Fundamentally, the amount of work done by an algorithm depends on the length of the input. Intuitively though, a problem may be solved easily for some instances of input, but in others may require considerably more effort to obtain a solution, even if in both cases the input was of the same length. Consider an array of $n$ integers, **A**, that is to be sorted such that the entries are arranged in non-decreasing order, using a bubblesort algorithm, whose elementary operation is a *comparison*. Given the $n$ items as input to be sorted there are $n$! distinct permutations on $n$. Thus the work done depends directly upon the number of comparisons needed to sort a particular permutation. The bubblesort algorithm[2] examines each successive pair of elements in **A**, $A(i)$ and $A(i+1)$ for $0 < i < n$, and if $A(i) > A(i+1)$, i.e. they are not in non-decreasing order, the entries are interchanged. When two elements of **A**, $A(r)$ and $A(s)$ with $r < s$, not necessarily adjacent, are out of order relative to each other, an *inversion* is said to exist on the pair $(A(r), A(s))$. The bubblesort algorithm repeatedly traverses the array until no inversions are found, implying that **A** is sorted. Each interchange removes exactly one inversion and thus if there are $i$ inversions in **A** there must be at least $i$ comparisons to sort **A**. This forms the *lower bound* on the number of operations necessary to sort **A**. Now consider the inputs $I1 = (1,2,3,4)$, $I2 = (1,2,4,3)$ and $I3 = (4,3,2,1)$. $I1$ contains no inversions and the algorithm will terminate after one traversal. $I2$ has one inversion, $(A(3)=4, A(4)=3)$, and the algorithm will terminate after two traversals. $I3$ contains six inversions and it will take the algorithm three traversals to sort the array. On the $i$th traversal there are $(n-i)$ comparisons made. Thus for differing permutations of $n$ elements the bubblesort algorithm will have differing resource usages.

A branch of computer science closely related to the study of complexity theory is *analysis of algorithms*, which concerns itself with finding more efficient algorithms for problems and the study of the resources they consume. According to this discipline each algorithm has in fact two complexities, one derived from its *average case behavior* and

---

2. As implemented by Knuth [KNUT73], p. 107.

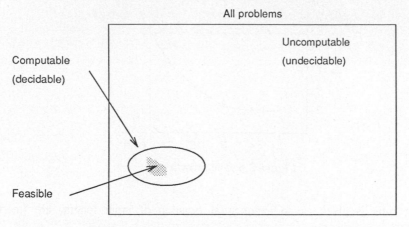

**Figure 2.5** A classification of all problems

the other from its *worst case behavior*. Using Baase's notation ([BAAS78] p. 23), let $D_n$ be the set of all input instances that are of length $n$, $P(I)$ the probability that $I \in D_n$ occurs and $t(I)$ the number of basic operations performed by the algorithm on input (instance) $I$. The average case behavior is defined as:

$$AV(n) = \sum P(I) \cdot t(I)$$

taking the average number of operations performed for each input of size $n$, and the worst case behavior is the maximum number of operations performed by an input of length $n$, defined as:

$$W(n) = \max_{I \in D_n} t(I)$$

$W(n)$ is more readily obtained than $AV(n)$ and may be considered an upper limit on the time necessary to implement any algorithm. This property is of particular interest in real-time applications. The complexity of an algorithm is taken to be the asymptotic behavior of the expression for its worst case behavior.

Unfortunately, even if a problem is computable, i.e. there exists an algorithm for it, the resources consumed during its execution may be unrealistically large (e.g. use billions of bytes of memory, take thousands of years to execute or perhaps need a hundred machines to solve the problem). Such problems are *infeasible* or *intractable*, and further reduce the domain of problems that can be solved (see Figure 2.5).

As a matter of fact, we can distinguish two kinds of intractability. The first happens when a solution of a problem takes an exponential amount of time as a function of problem size $n$. The second kind of intractability occurs when listing a solution needs an exponential number of symbols as a function of $n$.

## 2.2.2 The classes *P* and *NP*

That class of algorithms which have running time expressed in polynomial time are considered as 'good' algorithms. On the other hand, that class of algorithms, for which

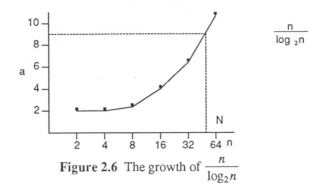

**Figure 2.6** The growth of $\dfrac{n}{\log_2 n}$

running time is given as an exponential function of input length, are 'inefficient' algorithms.

Let us consider two algorithms. The first runs in time given by the polynomial $p_1(n) = n^a$ where $n$ is an input length, and $a$ is a fixed integer. The second has a time complexity function $p_2(n) = 2^n$. Consider the following question:
Is there any integer $N \in Z^+$ such that:

$$\underset{n \geq N}{\forall} \text{ there exists } n^a \leq 2^n \text{ where } n \in Z^+?$$

In order to answer the question, take the equality,

$$n^a = 2^n$$

As $n=1, 2, 3, \ldots$, we can transform in the following way:

$$a \log_2 n = n \qquad \text{for } n=2,3, \ldots$$
$$a = \frac{n}{\log_2 n} \qquad \text{for } n=2,3, \ldots$$

The function $\dfrac{n}{\log_2 n}$ grows to infinity as $n \to \infty$ (see Figure 2.6). So there is an integer $N$ such that:

$$\forall\ n > N,\ n^a < 2^n.$$

*Example.*
Consider two algorithms. The first runs in polynomial time $p_1(n) = n^{1000}$, the second in exponential time $p_2(n)=2^{0.001n}$. Of course, the second algorithm is more efficient than the first for small $n$. But, for $n > 2^{25}$, the situation changes and the polynomial time algorithm is more efficient as it requires $\sim 2^{25000}$ steps while the exponential one needs $\sim 2^{32000}$ steps. $\qquad\qquad\qquad\qquad\qquad\qquad\qquad\qquad\qquad\qquad\qquad\square$

Algorithms that have the same complexity are grouped into equivalence classes. All the algorithms with complexity $n^3$ are said to be of the order $n^3$, written $O(n^3)$, and belong to the equivalence class that contains all algorithms of $O(n^3)$, denoted by $\Theta(n^3)$. Two broader classes will be introduced next, **P** and **NP**, that will influence the feasibility of a problem.

Algorithms that belong to the class **P** have a worst case complexity that is bounded by a *polynomial function* of the input length. More concisely, the asymptotic behavior of the expression that depicts the worst case complexity is dominated by a term of the form $n^c$, where $n$ is the length of the input and $c$ is a constant. If at each step of the computation of an algorithm the next step is *unique*, then the algorithm is said to be *deterministic*. At any point the antecedent circumstances unambiguously determine what will happen next. In the algorithm to multiply two matrices, the flow of execution is well defined and each step of the algorithm has a definite successor step. All algorithms that belong to **P** are deterministic and are *p-time bounded*, meaning that they will execute in polynomial time as their complexity is bounded by a polynomial in the input length. P-time algorithms have the property that the concatenation of two p-time algorithms is also a p-time algorithm. They also display an invariance property in that any algorithm that is a member of **P** will run in p-time on any machine or in any model.

Consider the problem of determining if a subset of the set $K$ $(i_1, \ldots, i_x)$ will sum exactly to $L$. The process of generating the possible subsets exhaustively for the case where $x = 3$ is shown as a decision tree in Figure 2.7. Each leaf represents a subset of $K$ and its path from the root has a sum associated with it (e.g. $S_1 = i_1 + i_2 + i_3$, $S_2 = i_1 + i_2$, $S_3 = i_1 + i_3$, etc.). If for some $j$, $S_j = L$ then the algorithm for the problem should halt with output 'yes', implying that there is a subset of $K$ that exactly sums to $L$. If no such $j$ exists then the algorithm should halt with output 'no', implying the converse. Known deterministic algorithms designed to solve this problem must more or less

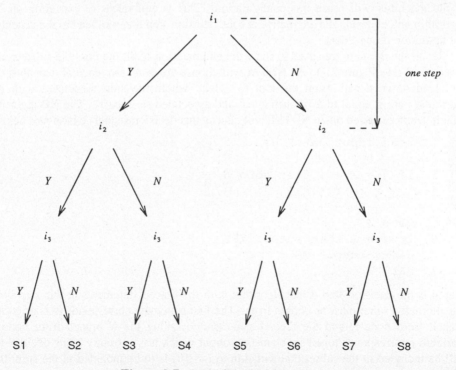

**Figure 2.7** A possible decision tree

generate all possible subsets of $K$, calculate the sum of each subset and compare this to $L$. Since there are $2^x$ possible subsets such deterministic algorithms have exponential complexity.

An algorithm that at some step of its computation must select an alternative from a finite domain, i.e. realize a decision, is called *non-deterministic* (**ND**). Examples of decisions are: *select an element from the set {A,B,C,D,E}* or *choose an element from the range (1...100)*. A machine implementing a non-deterministic algorithm could make a decision by choosing an alternative according to some criterion, e.g. randomly. Complexity theory, however, has made use of a special machine, characterized by its decision-making criterion, which albeit fictitious has important ramifications for the class **NP**. Non-determinism was first used in automata theory with respect to an abstract machine. An **ND** Turing Machine (**NDTM**) operates on **ND** algorithms and if there exists at least one sequence of decisions that can be made during the execution of the algorithm that will lead to an accepting configuration (i.e. halting with output 'yes') then the **NDTM** will choose one of these sequences. From another point of view, an **NDTM** is an infinitely parallel machine. At each decision step the **NDTM** makes as many copies of itself as there are alternatives and continues the computation independently for each alternative. Consider a problem whose possible number of computations can be described by a decision tree with $M$ branches at each node, ($M = 2$ is a binary tree). An **NDTM** would make $M$ copies of itself at each decision point, i.e. one for each alternative, and continue the computations independently. So at depth $i$ of the decision tree there are $M^i$ machines that are started to run in parallel. If a halting configuration exists, then one of the machines will reach this configuration. This is equivalent to executing an **ND** algorithm and choosing the alternative at each decision step that will lead to the accepting configuration if one exists.

Recall the decision tree used to show the enumeration of all the possible subsets of $K$ when $x = 3$ (see Figure 2.7). An **NDTM** will choose the exact sequence of decisions that will lead down a path from the root to a leaf, where the sum associated with that particular path is equal to $L$ (if such a leaf and associated sum exist). The **ND** algorithm which, when executed on an **NDTM**, will choose this decision sequence is shown below:

```
1. read input set K (i₁, ... , iₓ) , sum L
2. r := 0, j := 1
3. if j = X + 1 then goto 6
4.    { r := r + iⱼ }
      { j := j + 1 }
5. goto 3 .
6. if r = L then output YES
   else   output NO
7. HALT
```

Step 4 is the decision step of the algorithm with the braced statements at this step being the alternatives that must be chosen from. The first statement corresponds to taking the $Y$ branch from node $i_j$ and the second statement to taking the $N$ branch from node $i_j$. Variable $j$ corresponds to the set element $i_j$ about which it is currently being decided if it will be included in the subset that will sum to $L$. If $i_j$ is to be included in the sum, then the first statement is chosen (i.e. the $Y$ branch is selected), otherwise the second statement is chosen (i.e. the $N$ branch is selected). If a subset of $K$ exists that will sum to $L$, then the NDTM will choose the correct statement at step *4* that will form this subset.

Algorithms that belong to the class **NP** are non-deterministic and can be computed on an **NDTM** or a machine using infinite parallelism in p-time. Halting in p-time here can be interpreted as one of the processors of the **NDTM** reaching a halting configuration after $p(n)$ steps, where $n$ is the length of input and the step length is the depth of the tree. All problems that are members of the class **NP** have no known deterministic p-time algorithm and, in fact, the complexity of the most efficient deterministic algorithms for these problems are exponential in the worst case (i.e. complexity denoted by a term of the form $c^n$). Such problems are always phrased by asking some question that requires a *yes/no* answer and are sometimes called *decision problems*. Even though the complexity to decide an **NP** problem deterministically is exponential, the verification of a solution can be computed in p-time. The subset problem, already examined, is an **NP** problem. It is a decision problem as its solution is either *yes* or *no*, depending on whether there exists a subset of $K$ that exactly sums to $L$, and a solution can be verified (is $r = L$?) in p-time. The best algorithm for the subset problem is $O(2^n)$ and there is an **ND** algorithm for it that executes in p-time.

Let us now return to the notion of intractability. It would be convenient to say that problems that are members of **P**, deterministic algorithms which have no decision points, use a realistic amount of resources in their execution, and thus are feasible. But a term such as $n^{10000}$ is polynomial in $n$, but for any large $n$ a problem with this complexity is unfeasible. The class **P** is too broad to provide a criterion for problems with low time requirements, but it does provide a useful criterion in that problems which cannot be characterized by an algorithm in **P** are intractable in the amount of resources required to solve them. Any problem for which no deterministic p-time algorithm is known to exist is intractable in the amount of resources required to solve it.

Complexity theory still has many unresolved issues, with the most contentious being does **P** = **NP**? Trivially, **P** is a subset of **NP**, since every deterministic algorithm is equivalent to an **ND** algorithm with one alternative at each decision point. An **ND** algorithm can solve problems in p-time that deterministic algorithms take exponential time to execute. This is to say that there are problems for which there is no known deterministic p-time algorithm, but which can be solved on an **NDTM** in p-time, e.g. *traveling salesman problem, CNF satisfiability, clique cover*[3]. There has been concerted effort to find p-time algorithms for these problems and since all attempts have been fruitless it is strongly believed that in fact none do exist. It is therefore conjectured that **P** $\neq$ **NP**, but this has not yet been proved. When **P** $\neq$ **NP** is assumed then there exist algorithms within **NP** that are intractable, but since the former cannot be proved the latter cannot be shown. There is no problem that is a member of **NP** that has been proved not to be a member of **P**. Figure 2.8 shows the relationship between the two classes, assuming that **P** $\neq$ **NP**.

In his paper, Cook [COOK71] showed that a subset of **NP** problems had the following property: if there existed a deterministic p-time algorithm for one of these problems then there exists a deterministic p-time algorithm for *all* problems in **NP**, i.e.

---

3. See Karp [KARP72], pp. 94-5 for a full explanation of these problems.

NP

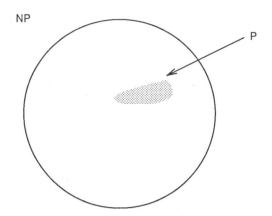

P

**Figure 2.8** The relation between **NP** and **P** problems

**P = NP.** Cook called this class of problems **NP-complete**, or **NPC** and they are considered to be the 'hardest' problems in **NP**.[4] All problems in **NP-complete** are computationally equivalent and intractable. Still this cannot be proved because of the **P = NP?** contention, but for problems that belong to **NP-complete**, it is strongly believed that no deterministic p-time algorithms exist. Another view of 'the world of **NP**' can be shown now in Figure 2.9.[5] If again it is assumed that **P ≠ NP** then there exist problems that cannot be solved in p-time and are also not members of **NP-complete**; these are called **NPI** problems.[6] Once establishing the basic tools of complexity theory, they can be used to analyze the computational difficulty of an arbitrary cipher.

## 2.3 Complexity of selected problems used in cryptology

In this section, we are going to examine several problems which create the base for many cryptographic schemes.

### 2.3.1 Factorization problems

First, consider both the Factorization (FAC) and Multiplication (MU) problems:

*Name*:    **MULTIPLICATION PROBLEM**
*Instance* :  The pair of positive integers $p$ and $q$.
*Question*:  What is the multiplication $N$ of these two integers ?

*Name*:    **FACTORIZATION PROBLEM**
*Instance*:  Positive integer $N$.
*Question*:  Are there integers $p$ and $q > 1$ such that $N = p \cdot q$ ?

---

4.  For a full list of the **NP-complete** problems see [GAJO79], p. 187.
5.  For a more precise presentation of the possible relations between the complexity classes see [DENN82], p. 32.
6.  See [GAJO79], p. 154 for a full explanation of these problems.

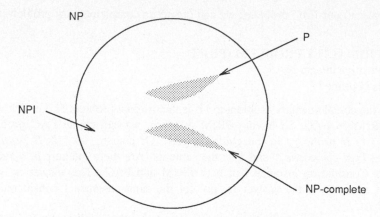

**Figure 2.9** Another view of the world of **NP**

It is easy to see that these problems are closely related. Of course, given two integers, for instance $p=3$, $q=7$, we can calculate relatively quickly their product $N=21$. On the other hand, calculation of integers $p$ and $q$ (knowing their product is $N=21$ ) is more difficult. Factorization can be carried out by trying all integers in the interval $(1,\lfloor \sqrt{N} \rfloor)$. In our case, the interval [1,4] contains the set {1,2,3,4}. As the integers {1,2,4} cannot be considered, the only possibility is 3. The second integer can be calculated by dividing 21 by 3.

In general, the MU problem belongs to the class **P** as, using the fast $Z$ transformation, we can design an algorithm which finds a product of two integers almost in linear time as the function of problem size $n$ (in this case $n$ is the number of decimal digits necessary for writing both $p$ and $q$).

On the other hand, the classification of the FAC problem is not known but there is the common consensus that the FAC does not belong to **P** and does not belong to the class **NP–complete**. In other words FAC is considered to belong to the class **NPI** (**NPI** = **NP–P–NPC**, where **NPC** = **NP–complete**). The argument that FAC does not belong to **P** results from the fact that up till now no polynomial algorithm has been found. All existing factorization algorithms run in time longer than or equal to :

$$\exp [ \sqrt{ln(n) \; ln \, ln \,(n)} \;]$$

However, the statement that FAC does not belong to **co–NP** needs a bit more justification.

Let us define the class of complementary problems as:

$$\textbf{co–NP} = \{ \; \Pi^c \; ; \; \Pi \in \textbf{NP} \; \}$$

where $\Pi^c$ means a complementary problem to $\Pi$. A complementary problem $\Pi^c$ can be easily generated from $\Pi$ as follows:

*Name*:　　**COMPLEMENTARY PROBLEM** $\Pi^c$
*Instance*:　The same description as for $\Pi$.
*Question*:　The complementary answer required.

Going back to our FAC problem, we can create its complementary problem (FAC$^c$) called as:

*Name*:     **PRIMALITY PROBLEM (PRIM)**
*Instance*:   Positive integer N.
*Question*:   Is N prime?

Clearly, the complementary problem to $\Pi^c$ is the original problem $\Pi$, i.e. $\Pi^{cc} = \Pi$. In our case, PRIM$^c$ = FAC. So having PRIM problem, we can create FAC problem by putting *not ( Is N prime? )* in the *Question* part. Of course, *not ( Is N prime? )* is equivalent to *Is N composite?* and it is the same as 'Are there integers $p$, $q$ such that: $N = p \times q$?'. Consider an instance I of both PRIM and FAC. The answer is 'yes' for I ∈ PRIM if and only if the answer is 'no' for the same instance I considered as the member of FAC.

In general, however, such an observation cannot be made for all problems of **NP** and numerous examples lead us to the conclusion that:

$$\textbf{co-NP} \neq \textbf{NP}$$

In other words, the answer 'yes' for an instance I ∈ $\Pi$ does not guarantee that the answer is 'no' for the same instance I considered as an element of $\Pi^c$. If we consider the class **P** ⊂ **NP** then it is easy to prove that:

$$\textbf{co-P} = \textbf{P}$$

that is, the class **P** is closed under complementation.

The next question concerns the interrelation between the class **NPC** and the class **co-NPC**. The answer is given in the following theorem.

**Theorem:** *If there exists an* **NP-complete** *problem* $\Pi$ *such that* $\Pi^c$ ∈ **NP**, *then* **NP** = **co-NP**.

The proof can be found in Garey and Johnson [GAJO79], p. 156. Our discussion is summarized in Figure 2.10 (assuming that **P** ≠ **NP** and **NP** ≠ **co-NP** ).

Now if we assume for the moment that FAC ∈ **NPC** and PRIM ∈ **co-NPC**, then **NPC** ∩ **co-NPC** ≠ ∅ as FAC = PRIM. But such a situation is impossible (see Figure 2.10), and we can conclude that FAC belongs to **NPI**. Of course the set **NPI** ∩ **co-NPI** is not empty as FAC and PRIM belong to it.

Factorization can be carried out using six basic algorithms. These are [POSM86]:

1. the elliptic curve algorithm of Lenstra;
2. the class-group algorithm of Schnorr-Lenstra;
3. the linear sieve algorithm of Schroeppel;
4. the quadratic sieve algorithm of Pomerance;
5. the residue list sieve algorithm of Coppersmith, Odlyzko and Schroeppel;
6. the continued fraction algorithm of Morrison–Brillhart.

All the algorithms take advantage of the observation that if we have two integers $X$ and $Y$ such that:

$$X^2 = Y^2 \ (\text{mod} \, N)$$

($N = p \cdot q$ and $p$, $q$ are primes), then the greatest common divisors,

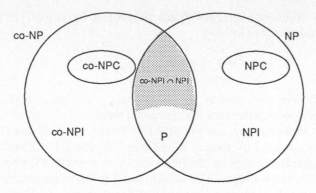

**Figure 2.10** Interrelation of classes **NP** and **co-NP** (**P** ≠ **NP** and **NP** ≠ **co-NP**)

$$(X + Y, N) \quad \text{and} \quad (X - Y, N)$$

would be either $p$ or $q$ with the probability ½. This is illustrated in the following example.

*Example*

Factorize $N = 77$. We start with the two following congruences:

$$72 = -5 \pmod{77} \quad \text{and} \quad 45 = -32 \pmod{77}$$

Multiplying the separate sides gives:

$$2^3 \times 3^4 \times 5 = (-1)^2 \times 5 \times 2^5 \pmod{77}$$

which yields upon reduction:

$$9^2 = 2^2 \pmod{77}$$

Hence the $gcd(9+2, 77)$ and $gcd(9-2, 77)$ give the primes $p = 11$ and $p = 7$. □

Readers interested in factorization algorithms are referred to the article of Pomerance, Smith and Tuler [POSM86], Caron, Silverman [CASI86].

## 2.3.2 Discrete logarithm problem

Another problem that has found great popularity in cryptography is the problem of discrete logarithms for several authentication and secrecy systems are based on it. Its definition can take the form:

*Name*: **DISCRETE LOGARITHM PROBLEM (DL PROBLEM)**
*Instance*: A pair of integers $(g, s)$ that belong to a Galois field GF($N$) determined by a prime $N$.
*Question*: Is there a positive integer $x$ ($0 \le x \le N$) such that $x = \log_g s \pmod{N}$?

It is obvious that algorithms for the DL problem run in polynomial time for infinite fields (like the field of all integers or the field of real numbers). The situation is quite different when we deal with a finite field like GF($N$) or GF($2^n$).

Very recently Wells (see [WELL84]) has shown that for any $s$ $(1 \le s \le N-1)$ the logarithm can be calculated as follows:

$$\log_g s \equiv \sum_{j=1}^{N-2} (1 - g^j)^{-1} s^j \pmod{N}$$

where $g$ is a primitive root modulo $N$. Unfortunately, the direct application of this formula creates an algorithm that runs in exponential time!

We sketch an algorithm that was published by Pohlig and Hellman [POHE78] and was independently invented by Roland Silver (see Odlyzko [ODLY84a]). The Siver-Pohlig-Hellman algorithm computes discrete logarithms over GF($N$), where $N$ is prime. Assume that $g$ is a primitive element of GF($N$) and $s$ is a non-zero element of GF($N$). We wish to calculate a non-zero element $x$ of GF($N$) such that:

$$g^x = s \pmod{N}$$

Assume the integer $N$ is a prime and the number $(N-1)$ has a non-trivial factorization of the form:

$$N - 1 = \prod_{i=1}^{n} p_i$$

where $p_i$ $(i=1, \ldots, n)$ are primes. Using the Chinese Remainder Theorem, the integer $x$ can be presented as a vector:

$$x \equiv [\, b_1 \pmod{p_1}, \ldots, b_n \pmod{p_n}\,]$$

So, the calculation of $x$ can be done by computing $b_i$ for $i=1, \ldots, n$. In order to determine $b_i$, we calculate:

$$y_i = s^{(N-1)/p_i} = \left[g^x\right]^{(N-1)/p_i} = \left[g^{(N-1)/p_i}\right]^x = \left[g^{(N-1)/p_i}\right]^{b_{i0}}$$

If we accept that:

$$h_i = g^{(N-1)/p_i}$$

then $y_i$ is an element of the following sequence:

$$h_i^0 = 1, h_i^1, h_i^2, \ldots, h_i^{p_i-1}$$

In other words, we want to find $b_i$ such that:

$$y_i = h_i^{b_i}; \quad 0 \le b_i \le p_i - 1$$

The process of searching $b_i$ can be accomplished using Shanks' 'baby steps — giant steps' technique which is described in Odlyzko's article [ODLY84a]. It takes $O(p_i^2 \log p_i)$ elementary operations.

*Example*

Take GF(31) and find the following logarithm:

$$x = \log_g s \text{ for } g=24 \text{ and } s=29$$

Note that $N-1=30$ and the factorization gives $p_1=2$, $p_2=3$, $p_3=5$. The calculations are done in three steps.

*Step* 1: $(p_1=2)$

We calculate,

$$h_1 = g^{(N-1)/p_1} = 24^{15} = -1 \ (\text{mod } 31)$$

and the sequence,

$$h_1^0 = 1, h_1^1 = -1$$

Next, we compute,

$$y_1 = s^{(N-1)/p_1} = 29^{15} = -1 \ (\text{mod } 31)$$

From the sequence $(h_1^0, h_1^1)$, we select the element that is equal to $y_1$. This is $h_1^1$ and therefore $b_1=1$.

*Step* 2: $(p_2=3)$

As before, we calculate,

$$h_2 = g^{(N-1)/p_2} = 24^{10} = 25 \ (\text{mod } 31)$$

and the sequence,

$$h_2^0=1, h_2^1=25, h_2^2=5 \ (\text{mod } 31)$$

Next, we obtain,

$$y_2 = s^{(N-1)/p_2} = 29^{10} = 1 \ (\text{mod } 31)$$

Comparing $y_2$ with the elements $h_2^i$, we obtain $b_2=0$.

*Step* 3: $(p_3=5)$

Similarly, we compute,

$$h_3 = g^{(N-1)/p_3} = 24^{6} = 4 \ (\text{mod } 31)$$

and,

$$h_3^0=1, h_3^1=4, h_3^2=16, h_3^3=2, h_3^4=8 \ (\text{mod } 31)$$

Since,

$$y_3 = s^{(N-1)/p_3} = 29^{6} = 2 \ (\text{mod } 31)$$

and,

$$h_3^3=2, \text{ then } b_3=3$$

Finally, we have the logarithm,

$$x = [1 \ (\text{mod } 2), 0 \ (\text{mod } 3), 3 \ (\text{mod } 5)] = 3 \ (\text{mod } 31) \qquad \square$$

The algorithm works differently if the factorization of $N-1$ gives $p^n$. Let us consider this case, $N-1=p^n$ where $N$, $p$ are primes. First of all, we calculate the integer,

$$h = g^{(N-1)/p} \pmod{N}$$

and the sequence,

$$h^0 = 1, \ h^1, \ h^2, \ \dots, \ h^{p-1}$$

Next, we find,

$$y_0 = s^{(N-1)/p} \pmod{N}$$

As before, we are looking for the element of sequence of $h$'s such that $h^{b_0} = y_0$. Having $b_0$, we create,

$$y_1 = \left[ s \cdot g^{-b_0} \right]^{(N-1)/p^2} \pmod{N}$$

and $b_1$ is obtained by comparing $y_1$ to elements of the sequence of $h$'s ($y_1 = h^{b_1}$). In general, knowing $y_i$ and $b_i$, we compute,

$$y_{i+1} = \left[ s \ g^{-b_0} \ g^{-b_1 p} \ \dots \ g^{-b_i p^i} \right]^{(N-1)/p^{i+2}} \pmod{N} \quad \text{for } i=1, \dots, n-2$$

Clearly, the element of the $h$'s sequence, which is equal to $y_{i+1}$, points at the integer $b_{i+1}$. Finally, the sequence $b_0, b_1, \dots, b_{n-1}$ produces the required logarithm $x$ as:

$$x = \sum_{i=0}^{n-1} b_i \, 2^i$$

*Example*
Find the logarithm,

$$x = \log_g s \pmod{N} \text{ for } g=14, \ s=5, \ N=17$$

Of course,

$$N-1 = 16 = 2^4 \text{ so } p = 2 \text{ and } n = 4$$

Let,

$$h = g^{(N-1)/p} = 14^8 = -1 \pmod{17}$$

and,

$$h^0 = 1, \ h^1 = -1 \pmod{17}$$

Next,

$$y_0 = s^{(N-1)/p} = 5^8 = -1 \pmod{17}$$

Comparing $y_0$ with $h$'s, we get $b_0 = 1$. Now,

$$y_1 = \left[ s \cdot g^{-b_0} \right]^{(N-1)/p^2} = (5 \cdot 14^{-1})^4 = 1 \pmod{17}$$

Again, $y_1 = h^0 \Rightarrow b_1 = 0$. Proceeding similarly, we get:

$$y_2 = \left[ s \cdot g^{-b_0} \cdot g^{-2b_1} \right]^{(N-1)/p^3} = (5 \cdot 14^{-1})^2 = -1 \pmod{17} \Rightarrow b_2 = 1$$

$$y_3 = \left[ s \cdot g^{-b_0} \cdot g^{-2b_1} \cdot g^{-4b_2} \right]^{(N-1)/p^4} = 5 \cdot 11 \cdot 1 \cdot 14^{-4} = -1 \ (\text{mod } 17) \ \Rightarrow \ b_3 = 1$$

So the logarithm,

$$x = \sum_{i=0}^{n-1} b_i 2^i = 13 \qquad\qquad \Box$$

In general, the Silver-Pohlig-Hellman algorithm applies the two presented methods. If $N-1 = p^n q^r$, we use the second method twice so we get two sequences:

$$b_{10}, \ b_{11}, \ \ldots, \ b_{1(n-1)} \ \text{ for } p$$

and,

$$b_{20}, \ b_{21}, \ \ldots, \ b_{2(r-1)} \ \text{ for } q$$

The final result is:

$$x = \left[ \sum_{j=0}^{n-1} b_{1j} p^j \ (\text{mod } p^n), \ \sum_{j=0}^{r-1} b_{2j} q^j \ (\text{mod } q^n) \right]$$

Calculation of logarithms in the general case is illustrated below.

*Example*

Consider the Galois field defined for $N=13$. Calculate the logarithm $x = \log_g s$ for $g = 6$ and $s = 12$.

First of all, we factorize the integer $N-1$. Now, $N-1 = 2^2 \times 3$ and $p_1 = 2$, $p_2 = 3$. As our integer $x$ can be presented as a vector,

$$x = [ b_{10} + b_{11} \cdot 2 (\text{mod } 2^2), \ b_{21} \ (\text{mod } 3) \ ]$$

we have to take into account two different cases.

*The first case*: $p_1 = 2$

We calculate,

$$h_1 = g^{(N-1)/p_1} = 6^6 = 12 (\text{mod } 13)$$

and the sequence,

$$h_1^0 = 1; \ h_1^1 = -1 (\text{mod } 13)$$

Next we compute,

$$y_1 = s^{(N-1)/p_1} = 12^6 = 1 (\text{mod } 13)$$

Now from the sequence $(h_1^0, h_1^1)$, we can select the element which is equal to $y_1$. This element is $h_1^0$ and therefore $b_{10} = 0$.

In order to find $b_{11}$, we calculate,

$$\left[ s \ g^{-b_{10}} \right]^{(N-1)/p_1^2}$$

This expression takes the value $(-1)$ for $s=12$, $g=6$. Looking at the sequence of $h$'s, we can determine $b_{11} = 1$.

*The second case*: $p_2 = 3$

As before, we calculate,

$$h_2 = g^{(N-1)/p_2} = 9 \pmod{13}$$

and the sequence,

$$h_2^0 = 1, \ h_2^1 = 9, \ h_2^2 = 3 \pmod{13}$$

Next,

$$y_2 = s^{(N-1)/p_2} = 12^4 = 1 \pmod{13}$$

Comparing $y_2$ with elements $h_2^i$ $(i=0,1,2)$, we obtain,

$$y_2 = h_2^0 \Rightarrow b_{20} = 0$$

So, $x = [0 + 1 \times 2, 0\,]$, in other words $x=6$ as:

$$6 \pmod 2 = 0 \ \Rightarrow \ b_{10} = 0$$
$$6 \pmod 4 = 2 \ \Rightarrow \ b_{11} = 1$$
$$6 \pmod 3 = 0 \ \Rightarrow \ b_{20} = 0$$

□

As has been shown, the idea of computing a discrete algorithm over GF($N$), where $N$ is prime, relies upon factoring the prime $N-1$ and then calculating components of the logarithm in suitable fields which are determined by the factorization. The Silver-Pohlig-Hellman algorithm runs in time of $\sqrt{p}$ where $p$ is the largest prime factor of $N-1$. From a cryptology point of view, we should select $N$ in such a way that $\frac{1}{2}(N-1)$ will be prime. On the other hand, calculations of algorithms in finite fields of characteristic two are usually more efficient. The reader interested in this is referred to the work of Blake et al. [BLFU84].

Suppose that we deal with the DL problem defined for an $N$ such that $\frac{1}{2}(N-1)$ is a prime. The comparison of the complexity of both DL and FAC problems has shown [ODLY84a] that the DL problem has the same asymptotic complexity as the FAC problem defined for an integer of the size of $N$. In other words the DL problem belongs to the class **NPI**.

Of course the DL problem is closely related to the following problem:

*Name*:    **EXPONENTIAL PROBLEM (EXP PROBLEM)**
*Instance*:    A pair of integers $(g, x)$ which belong to GF($N$).
*Question*:    Is there a positive integer $s$ ( $0 \le s \le N$ ) such that $s = g^x \pmod N$ ?

It is easy to show that this problem belongs to the class **P** as there is a polynomial time algorithm to solve any instance of the EXP problem (see section 2.1.1).

## 2.3.3  Knapsack problem

This problem was used as a basis by Merkle and Hellman to design their public-key cryptosystem in 1978. Despite the fact that the Merkle–Hellman cryptosystem has been broken, the knapsack problem is being applied to construction of many cryptosystems for secrecy and authenticity as well.

*Name*: **KNAPSACK PROBLEM** (KN PROBLEM)

*Instance*: A finite set $U = \{u_i\,; i=1, \ldots, n\}$, a size $s(u_i)$ of any element $u_i \in U$, and an integer $B$.

*Question*: Is there a subset $U' \subseteq U$ such that $\sum_{u_i \in U'} s(u_i) = B$ ?

As is known [GAJO79], the KN problem belongs to **NPC**. It means that, in general, there is no efficient algorithm to solve an arbitrary instance of the problem. So, the complexity of the KN problem is greater than complexities of the FAC and DL problems.

In order to illustrate this problem, take the following example of a knapsack problem instance.

*Example*

Assume that a set $U$ consists of four elements $\{u_1, u_2, u_3, u_4\}$, and their sizes are: $s(u_1) = 1$, $s(u_2) = 3$, $s(u_3) = 2$, $s(u_4) = 5$. The integer $B = 3$. As you can easily check, this instance has two different solutions. The first is characterized by $U'_1 = \{u_1, u_3\}$ as $s(u_1) + s(u_3) = 3$. The second, however, is described by the set $U'_2 = \{\,u_2\,\}$ as $s(u_2) = 3$. $\qquad\qquad\Box$

Sometimes the set $U'$ is presented as an ordered binary sequence whose elements are equal to *one* — if suitable set elements belong to $U'$ — or *zero*, if suitable elements do not belong to $U'$. In our example, we have,

$$U'_1 = \{\,u_1,\ u_3\,\} \leftrightarrow (\,1,\,0,\,1,\,0\,)$$
$$U'_2 = \{\,u_2\,\} \leftrightarrow (\,0,\,1,\,0,\,0\,)$$

Using the set representation given above, we can redefine the knapsack problem as follows:

*Name*: **KNAPSACK PROBLEM** (KN PROBLEM)

*Instance*: The $n$-dimension vector space $V$ over the binary field GF(2) with the elementary basis vectors $v_1 = (1, 0, \ldots, 0)$, $\ldots$, $v_n = (0, \ldots, 0, 1) \in V$, the vector of sizes, $S = (s(v_1), \ldots, s(v_n))$, and an integer $B$.

*Question*: Is there a binary vector $v' \in V$ such that $v' \times S = B$ ?

Of course the KN problem can be generalized by defining the vector space $V$ over an arbitrary field GF($q$) where $q$ is either a prime or a power of prime. It is obvious that the complexity of the KN problem depends upon the dimension of vector space. Moreover, Shamir [SHAM80a] has proved that the number of elements in GF($q$) is not crucial. For instance, for $n=4$, there is a polynomial time algorithm to solve any knapsack instance no matter how many elements are in GF($q$).

The statement that the KN problem belongs to **NPC** does not mean that all instances are of the same complexity. It is possible to define an easy KN problem whose instances can be solved using a linear time algorithm.

*Name*: **EASY KNAPSACK PROBLEM** (easy KN PROBLEM)

*Instance*: The $n$-dimension vector space $V$ over GF(2) with the basis

$$v_1 = (1, 0, \ldots, 0), \ldots, v_n = (0, \ldots, 0, 1) \in {}^{"} V, \text{ the vector of sizes}$$

$$S = (s(v_1), \ldots, s(v_n)) \text{ such that } s_{i+1} > \sum_{j=0}^{i} s_j$$

and an integer $B$.

*Question*:  Is there a binary vector $v' \in V$ such that $v' \times S = B$ ?

An illustration of an instance of the problem considered is given below.

*Example*

Let us consider the easy KN problem for n=6 and let:

$$s_1 = s(v_1) = 1,$$
$$s_2 = s(v_2) = 2 \quad \text{as } s_2 > s_1,$$
$$s_3 = s(v_3) = 4 \quad \text{as } s_3 > s_1 + s_2,$$
$$s_4 = s(v_4) = 8 \quad \text{as } s_4 > s_1 + s_2 + s_3,$$
$$s_5 = s(v_5) = 16 \quad \text{as } s_5 > s_1 + s_2 + s_3 + s_4,$$
$$s_6 = s(v_6) = 32 \quad \text{as } s_6 > s_1 + s_2 + s_3 + s_4 + s_5$$

Now if we have $B = 57$, then we search for $v' - (v'_1, \ldots, v'_6)$ for which,

$$v' \times (s_1, \ldots, s_6) = B = 57$$

By considering the sizes we see that:

$$v'_6 = 1 \implies B - s_6 = 57 - 32 = 25$$

Next, we can accept that:

$$v'_5 = 1 \implies B - s_6 - s_5 = 9$$

So,

$$v'_4 = 1 \implies B - s_6 - s_5 - s_4 = 1$$

and,

$$v'_3 = v'_2 = 0, \ v'_1 = 1$$

As a result, we have,

$$V' = (1, 0, 0, 1, 1, 1) \qquad \square$$

By analyzing the example, we can design an algorithm for solving the easy knapsack problem in the following way:

```
1. read   (s₁, ... ,sₙ)   and  B
2.    for i := n  to  1  do
3.    begin
4.        if B ≥ sᵢ  then  v'ᵢ := 1  and B := B − sᵢ
          else  v'ᵢ := 0
5.        {end}
6.    {end for}
7. output (v'₁,...,v'ₙ)
8. HALT
```

Usually, in cryptology, the knapsack problem should be applied in such a way that:

1. an illegal user, who does not know certain secret information, is faced with an instance of the general knapsack problem;
2. an authorized user knowing the certain secret information can convert a given instance into an instance of the easy knapsack problem.

Only feasible problems have a solution that can be computed, assuming a realistic amount of resources (time, space and hardware) are at its disposal.

## 2.4 Information theory

It would be difficult to discuss any matter concerning cryptography without referring to the fundamental precepts of *information theory*. Claude Shannon, who is seen as the father of this discipline, published in 1949 the seminal work in information theory [SHAN49], that has provided the greater portion of the theoretical foundation for modern cryptography. The principal tools of secure communications across a channel are *codes* and *ciphers*. A code is a fixed predetermined 'dictionary', where for every valid message there is an equivalent encoded message, called a *codeword*. Coding theory addresses itself to the 'noisy channel' problem, where by selecting a particular code, if a message $M$ is distorted to $M'$ during transmission, this error can be detected and hopefully corrected to the original message. On the other hand, ciphers are a more universal method of transforming messages into a format whose meaning is not apparent.

### 2.4.1 Basic notations

The *amount of information* in a message is the average number of bits needed to encode all possible messages optimally. An optimal encoding is one which minimizes the expected number of bits transmitted over a channel. More concisely, the amount of information in a message is measured by the *entropy* of the message. If $M_1, M_2, \ldots, M_n$ are $n$ possible messages and $P(M_1), P(M_2), \ldots, P(M_n)$ are their respective probabilities of occurring, then the entropy of a message is defined as:

$$H(M) = \sum_M P(M_i) \log_2 \left[ \frac{1}{P(M_i)} \right]$$

Each $\log_2(1/P(M_i))$ term represents the number of bits needed to encode the message optimally. When all the messages are equally likely, i.e. $P(M_1) = P(M_2) = \ldots = P(M_n)$ = $1/n$, then $H(M)$ is $\log_2 n$. If $n = 2^k$, then $k$ bits are needed to encode each message. The value of $H(M)$ ranges between its maximum value $\log_2 n$ and its minimum of zero when $n$ is one and $P(M) = 1$. Note that this is so because there is no information as there is no choice of messages. The entropy of a message, $H(M)$, also measures its *uncertainty*, in that it indicates the number of bits of information that must be acquired to recover a message distorted by a noisy channel or concealed through ciphers. The uncertainty of a message cannot exceed $\log_2 n$ bits, where $n$ is the possible number of messages.[7]

---

7. If a message is known to contain a marital status, either married or single, then the uncertainty is only *one* bit, since there are only two possibilities for the first character, and once this is determined the message can be recovered. If the message was a student number, say, then the uncertainty is greater than one bit but will not exceed $\log_2 n$ bits.

*Example*

Consider a random variable that takes on two values $M_1$ and $M_2$ with probabilities,

$$P(M_1) = \varepsilon \quad \text{and} \quad P(M_2) = 1 - \varepsilon$$

What is the maximum entropy of the random variable ?

First of all, we apply the definition of entropy and obtain,

$$H(M) = \sum_{i=1}^{2} P(M_i) \log_2 \frac{1}{P(M_i)} = -\varepsilon \log_2 \varepsilon - (1-\varepsilon) \log_2 (1-\varepsilon)$$

As $H(M)$ is a function of $\varepsilon$, we find its derivative:

$$\frac{d H(M)}{d\varepsilon} = -\log_2 \varepsilon + \log_2 (1-\varepsilon)$$

Clearly,

$$\frac{d H(M)}{d\varepsilon} = 0 \quad \text{for} \quad \varepsilon = \tfrac{1}{2}$$

As the second derivative,

$$\frac{d^2 H(M)}{d\varepsilon^2} = -\frac{1}{\ln 2} \left( \frac{1}{\varepsilon} + \frac{1}{1-\varepsilon} \right)$$

is negative for $\varepsilon = \tfrac{1}{2}$, $H(M)$ can have its maximum at $\varepsilon = \tfrac{1}{2}$ unless it has its maximum at for $\varepsilon = 0$ or $\varepsilon = 1$. We calculate the values of $H(M)$ at these points:

$$H(M)\,|_{\varepsilon=0} = \lim_{\varepsilon \to 0} [\, \varepsilon \log_2 \frac{1}{\varepsilon} + (1-\varepsilon) \log_2 \frac{1}{1-\varepsilon} \,]$$

and,

$$H(M)\,|_{\varepsilon=1} = \lim_{\varepsilon \to 1} [\, \varepsilon \log_2 \frac{1}{\varepsilon} + (1-\varepsilon) \log_2 \frac{1}{1-\varepsilon} \,]$$

Now,

$$\lim_{\varepsilon \to 0} (\, \varepsilon \log_2 \varepsilon) = 0, H(M)\,|_{\varepsilon=0} = H(M)\,|_{\varepsilon=1} = 0$$

In other words, the maximum entropy of the random variable with just two values is attained for the uniform distribution $P(M_1) = P(M_2) = \tfrac{1}{2}$, and then,

$$H(M) = \log_2 2 = 1 \qquad \qquad \square$$

The *rate of language* for messages of length $k$ is defined as $r = H(X)/k$, which denotes the average number of bits of information in each character. For English, when $k$ is large, $r$ has been estimated to lie between 1.0 bits/letter and 1.5 bits/letter. The *absolute rate* of a language is the maximum number of bits of information that could be encoded in each character assuming that all combinations of characters are equally likely. If there are $K$ letters in the language, then the absolute rate is given by $R = \log_2 K$, which is the maximum entropy of the individual characters. For a 26 character alphabet this is 4.7 bits/letter. The actual rate of English (3.2 bits/letter) is much less as it is highly **redundant**, like all natural languages. Redundancy stems from the underlying structure of a language, in particular certain letters and combinations of letters occur frequently, while others have a negligible likelihood of occurring (e.g. in English the letters *e*, *t* and *a* occur very frequently, as do the pairs, or *digrams*, *th* and *en*, while *z* and *x* occur less frequently).[8] The *redundancy* of a language with rate *r* is defined as $D = R - r$. When $r = 1$ and $R = 4.7$ then the ratio $D/R$ shows that English is about 79 percent redundant.

*Example*

Consider a language which consists of the 26 letters of the set $\mathbf{M} = \{A,B,C,D,E,F,G,H,I,J,K,L,M,N,O,P,Q,R,S,T,U,V,W,X,Y,Z\} = \{M_1, M_2, \ldots , M_{26}\}$. Suppose the language is characterized by the following sequence of probabilities:

$$P(M_1) = \tfrac{1}{2}; \quad P(M_2) = \tfrac{1}{4}$$

$$P(M_i) = \frac{1}{64} \quad \text{for } i=3,4,5,6,7,8,9,10$$

$$P(M_i) = \frac{1}{128} \quad \text{for } i=11, \ldots ,26$$

The entropy of our single letter language is:

$$r = H_1(M) = \sum_{i=1}^{26} P(M_i) \log_2 \frac{1}{P(M_i)}$$

$$= \frac{1}{2} \log_2 2 + \frac{1}{4} \log_2 4 + 8 \left( \frac{1}{64} \log_2 64 \right) + 16 \left( \frac{1}{128} \log_2 128 \right) = 2.625$$

Now the language has $K = 26$ letters so,

$$R = \log_2 26 \approx 4.7$$

In other words, the redundancy of the language can be calculated as:

$$D = R - r = 4.7 - 2.625 = 2.075 \qquad \qquad \square$$

   This example only applies to language structure which is described by the probability distribution of single letters only. This description should be treated as the very first approximation of language's statistical structure. As a matter of fact, a natural language's structure is far more complex and the second approximation of a language's structure can be attained using conditional probability distributions.

*Example*

Let our language be defined as in the previous example and let its conditional probability distribution be given as follows:

$$\begin{aligned} P\,(M'_{i+1}|M_i) \;&=\; P\,(M'_{i+2}|M_i) \;&=\; \tfrac{1}{2} \text{ for } i=1, \ldots ,24 \\ P\,(M'_{26}|M_{25}) \;&=\; P\,(M'_1|M_{25}) \;&=\; \tfrac{1}{2} \\ P\,(M'_1|M_{26}) \;&=\; P\,(M'_2|M_{26}) \;&=\; \tfrac{1}{2} \end{aligned}$$

where $P\,(M'_{i+1}|M_i)$ means the conditional probability that the second letter is $M_{i+1}$ provided that the first letter is $M_i$.

---

8. In coding theory, *redundancy* refers to that portion of a codeword that is used to transmit *check symbols*, so as to allow error detection and possibly correction. This portion of the codeword contains no information.

Now, we calculate the probability distribution of two letter sequences:

$$P(M_1, M'_2) = P(M'_2|M_1) P(M_1) = \frac{1}{4}$$

$$P(M_1, M'_3) = P(M'_3|M_1) P(M_1) = \frac{1}{4}$$

$$P(M_2, M'_3) = P(M'_3|M_2) P(M_2) = \frac{1}{8}$$

$$P(M_2, M'_4) = P(M'_4|M_2) P(M_2) = \frac{1}{8}$$

$$P(M_i, M'_{i+1}) = P(M'_{i+1}|M_i) P(M_i) = \frac{1}{128} \text{ for } i=3, \ldots, 10$$

$$P(M_i, M'_{i+2}) = P(M'_{i+2}|M_i) P(M_i) = \frac{1}{128} \text{ for } i=3, \ldots, 10$$

$$P(M_i, M'_{i+1}) = P(M'_{i+1}|M_i) P(M_i) = \frac{1}{256} \text{ for } i=11, \ldots, 24$$

$$P(M_i, M'_{i+2}) = P(M'_{i+2}|M_i) P(M_i) = \frac{1}{256} \text{ for } i=11, \ldots, 24$$

$$P(M_{25}, M'_{26}) = P(M_{25}, M'_1) = P(M_{26}, M'_1) = P(M_{26}, M'_2) = \frac{1}{256}$$

All other probabilities are equal zero and, in this case, the entropy of two-letter language sequences is equal to:

$$H_2(M) = \sum_{i,j=1}^{26} P(M_i, M'_j) \log_2 \frac{1}{P(M_i, M'_j)}$$

$$= 2\left(\frac{1}{4} \log_2 4\right) + 2\left(\frac{1}{8} \log_2 8\right) + 16\left(\frac{1}{128} \log_2 128\right) + 32\left(\frac{1}{256} \log_2 256\right)$$

$$= 3.625$$

Consider, for the moment, the entropy $H_1(M)$ from the previous example and compare it to $H_2(M)$. We can immediately state that $H_2(M) - H_1(M) = 1$. This equation means that, having the first letter, we can obtain the second one using the one bit only. This results from the fact that there are two equally probable possibilities, for example, if the first letter is $M_3=C$, then the second letter may be either $M_4=D$ or $M_5=E$.

Returning to our example, we calculate the rate of the language for messages of length 2, namely,

$$r = \frac{1}{2} H_2(M) = 1.8125$$

As the absolute rate of our language is fixed and depends on the number of letters only, the redundancy $D_2$ is:

$$D_2 = R - r \approx 2.9$$

We can now state that the language considered is 60 per cent redundant.     □

We note that the more redundant a language is, the stronger the statistical relations between the letters in a sequence. On the other hand, if a language has no redundancy then occurrences of subsequent letters are statistically independent.

Once we have dealt with a natural language, we can easily calculate the entropy of a single letter $H_1(M)$. Also the entropy $H_2(M)$ of two-letter words can be found relatively easily. Unfortunately, the amount of calculation for $H_n(M)$ grows exponentially as a function of *n*. So, the real redundancy of language which can be expressed as:

$$r_\infty = \lim_{n \to \infty} \frac{H_n(M)}{n}$$

is estimated using several earlier evaluated entropies.

*Equivocation*, defined as the conditional entropy of message M given that ciphertext *C* has occurred, is:

$$H_C(M) = \sum_C P(C) \sum_M P_C(M) \log_2 \left[ \frac{1}{P_C(M)} \right]$$

where $P_C(M)$ is the conditional probability of message *M* given ciphertext *C* has occurred. Shannon measured the secrecy of a cipher with respect to its *key equivocation*, $H_C(K)$; for ciphertext *C* and key *K*, it may be interpreted as the degree of uncertainty in *K* given *C*, and expressed as:

$$H_C(K) = \sum_C P(C) \sum_K P_C(K) \log_2 \left[ \frac{1}{P_C(K)} \right]$$

where $P_C(K)$ is the probability of *K* given *C*. If $H_C(K)$ is zero then there is no uncertainty in the cipher, making it breakable. The *unicity distance* of a cipher is defined as the minimum message length that forces $H_C(K)$ to be approximately zero. In another way, the unicity distance of a cipher is the amount of ciphertext needed to uniquely determine the key. Intuitively, as the length of the ciphertext increases, the equivocation of the cipher decreases.

## 2.4.2 Equivocation of a simple cryptographic system

Consider the simplest cryptographic system (see Figure 2.11) which enciphers binary messages using binary keys according to the following formula:

$$C = M \oplus K$$

where *C*, *M*, *K* are a cryptogram (ciphertext), a message, and a key, respectively ($C, M, K \in \{0,1\}$ and $\oplus$ stands for addition modulo 2). The message source is known to generate elementary messages ( bits ) with probabilities,

$$P(M=0) = s \text{ and } P(M=1) = 1 - s$$

while $0 \leq s \leq 1$. For each transmission session, a cryptographic key *K* is selected from equally probable binary elements, namely,

$$P(K=0) = P(K=1) = \tfrac{1}{2}$$

Our task is to calculate the cipher equivocation and estimate the unicity distance for $s = \tfrac{1}{2}$

Assume that our cryptosystem has generated *n* binary cryptograms so that the probability $P(A)$, where *A* stands for the statement *the ordered cryptogram sequence consists of i zeros and n−i ones*, is equal to:

$$P(A) = P[A, (K=0 \text{ or } K=1)] = P(A,K=0) + P(A,K=1)$$
$$= P(A|K=0) P(K=0) + P(A|K=1) P(K=1)$$

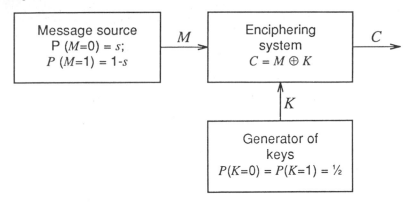

**Figure 2.11** Graphical presentation of the interrelations between messages and cryptograms in a binary cryptosystem

The conditional probability $P(A|K=0)$ is equal to the probability that the ordered message sequence consists of $i$ zeros and $n-i$ ones. On the other hand, $P(A|K=1)$ equals the probability that the ordered message sequence contains $n-i$ zeros and $i$ ones. Therefore,

$$P(A|K=0) = s^i (1-s)^{n-i} \quad \text{and} \quad P(A|K=1) = (1-s)^i s^{n-i}$$

As the result, we have:

$$P(A) = \tfrac{1}{2} [ s^i (1-s)^{n-i} + (1-s)^i s^{n-i} ]$$

Assume that $C_{i,n}$ is equivalent to the statement *the unordered cryptogram sequence contains i zeros and n−i ones* then,

$$P(C_{i,n}) = \tfrac{1}{2} \binom{n}{i} [ s^i (1-s)^{n-i} + (1-s)^i s^{n-i} ]$$

Of course, the conditional key probability is equal to:

$$P(K=0|C_{i,n}) = \frac{P(C_{i,n}|K=0) \; P(K=0)}{P(C_{i,n})}$$

The probability $P(C_{i,n} | K=0)$ is equal to the probability that the unordered message sequence contains $i$ zeros and $n-i$ ones. Substituting values, we get the following expression:

$$P(K=0|C_{i,n}) = \cfrac{1}{1 + \cfrac{s^{n-i}(1-s)^i}{s^i(1-s)^{n-i}}} = \frac{1}{1+a} \quad \text{while} \quad a = \frac{s^{n-i}(1-s)^i}{s^i(1-s)^{n-i}}$$

Considering the second conditional probability of the key, we obtain:

$$P(K=1|C_{i,n}) = \frac{a}{1+a}$$

Clearly, the conditional entropy $H_{C_{i,n}}(K)$ of the key can be calculated according to the following formula:

$$H_{C_{i,n}}(K) = \sum_K P(K \mid C_{i,n}) \log_2 \frac{1}{P(K \mid C_{i,n})}$$

$$= P(K=0 \mid C_{i,n}) \log_2 \frac{1}{P(K=0 \mid C_{i,n})} + P(K=1 \mid C_{i,n}) \log_2 \frac{1}{P(K=1 \mid C_{i,n})}$$

$$= \log_2(1+a) - \frac{a}{1+a} \log_2 a$$

So, the equivocation of the cipher (the average conditional entropy of the cryptographic key) can be presented as:

$$H_{C_n}(K) = \sum_{i=0}^{n} P(C_{i,n}) H_{C_{i,n}}(K)$$

Substituting values, we obtain:

$$H_{C_n}(K) = \frac{1}{2} \sum_{i=0}^{n} \binom{n}{i} s^i (1-s)^{n-i} (1+a) \left[ \log_2(1+a) - \frac{a}{1+a} \log_2 a \right]$$

Figure 2.12 shows the equivocation $H_{C_n}(K)$ for five different parameters of $s$, namely,

$$s = 0.5;\ 0.4;\ 0.3;\ 0.2;\ 0.1$$

*First consider the case s=0.5.* The equivocation is constant and equals 1. This means that the uncertainty in the key is fixed no matter how much cryptogram sequence is known. In other words, the key applied can be determined by selecting from two equally probable elements from all observations of cryptograms.

*The second case is for s=0.1.* More exact values of $H_{C_n}(K)$ for $n=1, \dots, 10$ are given in Table 2.4.

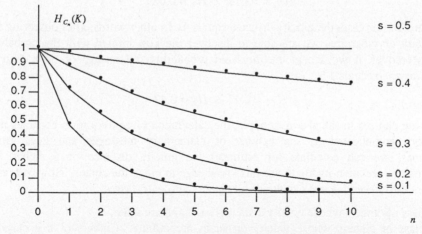

**Figure 2.12** Diagram of $H_{C_n}(K)$ for different values of $s$

**Table 2.4** The equivocation for $s=0.1$ with various numbers of observations

| Number of observations n | $H_{C_n}(K)\vert_{s=0.1}$ |
|---|---|
| 1 | 0.47 |
| 2 | 0.26 |
| 3 | 0.14 |
| 4 | 0.078 |
| 5 | 0.043 |
| 6 | 0.025 |
| 7 | 0.014 |
| 8 | 0.0081 |
| 9 | 0.0046 |
| 10 | 0.0027 |

Our equivocation is the entropy of two value random variables. Now consider such a variable which is characterized by two probabilities $p_1 = \varepsilon$, $p_2 = 1-\varepsilon$. Its entropy $H_\varepsilon$ is presented in Table 2.5.

**Table 2.5** Some probabilities and entropies

| Value of probability ε | entropy $H_\varepsilon$ |
|---|---|
| 0.5 | 1 |
| 0.4 | 0.91 |
| 0.3 | 0.88 |
| 0.2 | 0.72 |
| 0.1 | 0.47 |
| 0.05 | 0.29 |
| 0.01 | 0.081 |

From the two tables, we can state that the equivocation $H_{C_n}(K)$ for $s=0.01$ and $n=4$ is less than $H_\varepsilon$, that is:

$$H_{C_4} = 0.078 \; < \; H_\varepsilon = 0.081$$

Therefore, in this case, the unicity distance equals 4. In other words, after observing four elementary cryptograms, we are able to discover the key applied with the probability 0.99. Moreover, if we accept the threshold probability 0.9 instead of 0.99, then the unicity distance equals 1 as:

$$H_{C_1} = 0.47 \; \leq \; H_\varepsilon = 0.47$$

As you can see in the above example, the calculation of equivocation becomes more and more complicated as the number of elementary messages and keys grows. Sometimes, we can calculate (or estimate) the unicity distance of a cipher, but, unfortunately, we are not able to use this knowledge to break the cipher. However, using the unicity distance idea, we can divide all ciphers into two classes:

- the class of ciphers whose unicity distances exist and are finite;
- the class of ciphers whose unicity distances are infinite. Ciphers of this class are unbreakable (so-called *ideal ciphers*).

EXERCISES

2. 1 Calculate:
(a) $15 \times 7 \pmod{17}$;
(b) $12 \times 6 \pmod 5$.

2. 2 Find:
(a) $21 \pmod 4$;
(b) $2^{123} 3^{456} 5^{789} \pmod 4$;
(c) $4^8 \pmod{15}$;
(d) $6^8 \pmod{15}$;
(e) $1234^{567} \pmod{99}$;
(f) $3^{123} 5^{456} 7^{789} \pmod 4$;
(g) $x^{n-1} \pmod n$.

2. 3 Find $x^5 \pmod{10}$ where $x$ is an integer and (a) $0 \le x \le 9$ (b) $x \ge 10$.

2. 4 Find $x$ in the following cases:
(a) $2^x \equiv 5 \pmod{11}$;
(b) $3^x \equiv 5 \pmod{16}$;
(c) $2^x \equiv 5 \pmod{31}$;
(d) $3^x \equiv 5 \pmod{32}$.

2. 5 How many elements are there in the reduced set of residues:
(a) modulo 11;
(b) modulo 22;
(c) modulo 8;
(d) modulo 24;
(e) modulo 36;
(f) modulo 70;
(g) modulo 144.

2. 6 What is $\phi(n)$, the Euler totient function, for the following:
(a) $\phi(7)$;
(b) $\phi(14)$;
(c) $\phi(12)$;
(d) $\phi(56)$.

2. 7 Find the *gcd* in the following cases:
(a) $gcd(234, 325)$;
(b) $gcd(123, 4567)$;
(c) $gcd(123, 789456)$.

2. 8 Find the following inverses:
(a) $3^{-1} \pmod 5$;
(b) $3^{-1} \pmod{10}$;
(c) $3^{-1} \pmod{15}$;
(d) $3^{-1} \pmod{23}$;
(e) $7^{-1} \pmod{17}$;
(f) $10^{-1} \pmod{26}$;
(g) $5^{-1} \pmod{31}$;
(h) $27^{-1} \pmod{47}$;
(i) $1234^{-1} \pmod{10001}$.

2. 9   Solve:
   (a) $23x(\mod 57) \equiv 1$;
   (b) $1476x \ (\mod 13424) \equiv 1$;
   (c) $123456789x \ (\mod 10000000001) \equiv 1$.

2. 10  Solve:
   (a) $2x \ (\mod 57) \equiv 5$;
   (b) $25x \ (\mod 39) \equiv 4$.

2. 11  Write a simple factorization program in PASCAL.

2. 12  Find logarithms $x=\log_g s \ (\mod N)$ for the following cases:
   (a) $s=10, \ g=6, \ N=13$;
   (b) $s=7, \ g=6, \ N=13$;
   (c) $s=135, \ g=127, \ N=211$;
   (d) $s=116, \ g=127, \ N=211$;
   (e) $s=10, \ g=12, \ N=17$;
   (f) $s=5, \ g=12, N=17$.

2. 13  Write a PASCAL program to compute logarithms in GF(31). It should work for an arbitrary primitive root $g \in$ GF(31).

2. 14  Write a PASCAL program to compute logarithms in GF(17) for an arbitrary primitive element $g \in$ GF(17).

2. 15  Logarithms are computable if the element $g$ (the base of logarithm) is a primitive element of GF($N$). Taking advantage of the principle of the Silver-Pohlig-Hellman algorithm, design a test which decides if a given $g$ is primitive assuming that $N-p_1 p_2 ... p_n$ ($p_i$ are primes for $i=1, ..., n$). Write a PASCAL program which works in GF(31). Print out all primitive elements of GF(31).

2. 16  Write a PASCAL program to solve an easy knapsack for the vector of sizes (1,2,4,8,16,32,64,128).

2. 17  Find entropies of messages whose probabilities are given as follows:
   (a) $P(M_1) = P(M_2) = P(M_3) = P(M_4) = \frac{1}{4}$;
   (b) $P(M_1) = ... = P(M_8) = \frac{1}{8}$;
   (c) $P(M_i) = 2^{-n}$ for $i=1, ..., 2^n$;
   (d) $P(M_1)=\frac{1}{2}, P(M_2)=\frac{1}{4}, ..., P(M_i)=2^{-i}, ....$

2. 18  Calculate parameters $R$, $r$, and $D$ of the language which is defined over the alphabet $M=\{M_1, M_2, M_3, M_4\}$ and its statistical properties are described by the following probabilities:

$$P(M_1)=\frac{1}{2}, \ P(M_2)=\frac{1}{4}, \ P(M_3)=\frac{1}{8}, \ P(M_4)=\frac{1}{8}$$

Take the same language while its statistics are supplemented by conditional probabilities. Consider the following two cases:

*Case 1*:          $P(M_i|M_j)=\frac{1}{4}$ for $i,j=1,2,3,4$

*Case 2*:          $P(M_2|M_1)=P(M_3|M_1)=\frac{1}{2}$
                   $P(M_3|M_2)=P(M_4|M_2)=\frac{1}{2}$
                   $P(M_4|M_3)=P(M_1|M_3)=\frac{1}{2}$
                   $P(M_1|M_4)=P(M_2|M_4)=\frac{1}{2}$

and all other probabilities are equal zero. Compare results.

2. 19 Consider the binary cryptosystem given in section 2.4.2. Find unicity distances for three parameters $s=0.65, 0.75, 0.85$ , when $s = P\,(M = 0)$.

SOLUTIONS

2. 1   (a) 3(mod 17);
     (b) 2(mod 5).
2. 2   (a) 1;
     (b) 0;
     (c) 1;
     (d) 6;
     (e) 73(mod 99);
     (f) 1(mod 4);
     (g) 1 (*n* prime); $x$ if $x < n$; $x$(mod $n$) if $x \geq n$.
2. 3   (a) $x$(mod 10);
     (b) $x$(mod 10).
2. 4   (a) $2^4 \equiv 5$(mod 11);
     (b) no solution;
     (c) no solution;
     (d) no solution.
2. 5   (a) 10;
     (b) 10;
     (c) 4;
     (d) 8;
     (e) 12;
     (f) 24;
     (g) 48.
2. 6   (a) 6;
     (b) 6;
     (c) 4;
     (d) 24.
2. 7   (a) 13;
     (b) 1;
     (c) 3.
2. 8   (a) 2;
     (b) 7;
     (c) nonexistent;
     (d) 8;
     (e) 5;
     (f) nonexistent;
     (g) 25;
     (h) 7;
     (i) 5892.
2. 9   (a) $x = 5$;
     (b) nonexistent;
     (c) x = 2282 608 695

2. 10  (a) 31;

(b) 22.

2. 11  An example of such a program is given below:

```
program factorization (input, output);
var
  N, test, i, max, P        : integer;
begin
  write ('N=');
  read (N);
  P := N;
  max := ( trunc ( sqrt (N)));
  test := N mod 2 ;
  while test = 0   do
  begin
    writeln ('2');
    N := N div 2 ;
    test := N mod 2;
  end;
  for i:=1 to (max div 2 + 1) do
  begin
    test := N mod (1+2*i);
    if test=0 then
    begin
      N := N div (1+2*i);
      writeln ( 1+2*i );
    end;
  end;
  if P=N then write ('the integer',N,'is prime')
  else writeln (N)
end.
```

The program works well for integers which are powers of 2 and when $N$ is the product of different primes less than $N^{1/2}$.

2. 12  (a) $x=2$;

(b) $x=7$;

(c) $x=99$;

(d) $x=199$;

(e) $x=15$;

(f) $x=9$.

2. 13
```
program logarithm (input, output);
var
  s, g, y0, y1, y2, b0, b1, b2, h11, h21, h22, h23  : integer ;
  function expon (base, ep  : integer) : integer ;
  var i, max, B      : integer;
  a : array [1..100] of integer;
  c : array [1..100] of integer;
begin
  max := 1;
  B := 2;
  while ep > B do
```

```
    begin
      B := B * 2;
      max := max + 1;
    end;
    for i:=1 to max do
    begin
      a[i] := 0;
      c[i] := 0
    end;                  ,
    for i:=1 to max do
    begin
      a[i] := ep mod 2 ;
      ep := ep - a[i] ;
      ep := ep div 2
    end;
    c[1] := base ;
    for i:=2 to max do c[i] := (c[i-1] * c[i-1]) mod 31 ;
    ep := 1;
    for i:=1 to max do
    begin
      base := (a[i] * c[i]) mod 31 ;
      if base<>0 then
      begin
        ep := (ep * base) mod 31 ;
        expon := ep
      end;
    end;
  end;
begin
  write ('s=');
  read (s);
  write ('generator=');
  read (g);
  y0:= expon(s, 15);
  y1:= expon(s, 10);
  y2:= expon(s, 6);
  if y0=1 then b0:=0 else b0:=1 ;
  h11:=expon(g,10);
  if y1=1 then b1:=0 else if y1=h11 then b1:=1 else b1:=2;
  h21:=expon(g,6);
  h22:=h21*h21 mod 31;
  h23:=h22*h21 mod 31;
  if y2=1 then b2:=0 else
  if y2=h21 then b2:=1 else
  if y2=h22 then b2:=2 else
  if y2=h23 then b2:=3 else b2:=4;
  s:=(b0*15 + b1*10 + b2*6) mod 30;
  write ('the logarithm =',s);
end.
```

2. 14
```
program LOGARITHM (input, output);
var
    s, g, g2, g4, g8, b0, b1, b2, b3, y0, y1, y2, y3  : integer;
begin
  write ('s=');
  read (s);
  write ('generator =');
  read (g);
  g2:=g*g mod 17;
  g4:=g2*g2 mod 17;
  g8:=g4*g4 mod 17;
  y0 := s*s mod 17;
  y0 := y0*y0 mod 17;
  y0 := y0*y0 mod 17;
  if y0=1 then b0:=0 else b0:=1 ;
  if b0=0 then y1:=s else
  begin
     y1:=g*g2*g4*g8 mod 17;
     y1:=s*y1 mod 17;
  end;
  s:=y1;
  y1:=y1*y1*y1*y1 mod 17;
  if y1=1 then b1:=0 else b1:=1;
  if b1=0 then y2:=s else
  begin
     y2:=g2*g4*g8 mod 17;
     y2:=s*y2 mod 17;
  end;
  s:=y2;
  y2:=y2*y2 mod 17;
  if y2=1 then b2:=0 else b2:=1;
  if b2=0 then y3:=s else
  begin
     y3:=g4*g8 mod 17;
     y3:=y3*s;
  end;
  if y3=1 then b3:=0 else b3:=1;
  s:=b0+b1*2+b2*4+b3*8;
  write ('the logarithm =', s)
end.
```

2. 15  The Silver-Pohlig-Hellman algorithm works properly if the whole sequence of $h$'s can be computed. It means that $g$ is primitive if and only if:

$$g^{(N-1)/p_i} \neq 1 \pmod{N} \text{ for } i=1, \ldots, n.$$

An implementation of the test can take the form of the following program:

```
program PRIMITIVITYTEST (input, output);
var
   g, g5, test    : integer;
   result         : boolean;
```

```
      begin
        write ('g=');
        read (g);
        g5:=g*g*g mod 31;
        g5:=g5*g*g mod 31;
        test:=g5*g mod 31;
        if test=1 then result:=false else result:=true;
        test:=g5*g5 mod 31;
        if test=1 then result:=false;
        test:=test*g5 mod 31;
        if test=1 then result:=false;
        if result then
           write ('g=',g,' is primitive')
        else write ('g is not primitive')
      end.
```

After applying the program, we can obtain the set of primitive elements of GF(31) as follows:

$$\{3, 11, 12, 13, 17, 22, 24\}$$

2. 16
```
      program EASYKNAPSACK (input, output);
      const  n = 8;
      var
        s  : array[1..n] of integer;
        v  : array[1..n] of integer;
        B, i      :  integer;
      begin
        write ('B=');
        read (B);
        s[1]:=1;
        for i:=2 to n do s[i]:=s[i-1]*2;
        for i:=0 to n-1 do
        begin
          if B<s[n-i] then v[n-i]:=0 else
          begin
            v[n-i]:=1;
            B:=B-s[n-i]
          end;
        end;
        for i:=1 to n do writeln('v',i,'=',v[i])
      end.
```

2. 17 (a) $H(M)=2$; (b) $H(M)=3$; (c) $H(M)=n$; (d) $H(M)=\sum_{i=1}^{\infty}i2^{-i} = 2$.

2. 18 $R_1=2$, $r_1=H_1(M)=\sum_{i=1}^{4}P(M_i) \log_2 P^{-1}(M_i)=1.75$, $D_1=0.25$.

*Case* 1: $R_2=4$, $r_2=3.75$, $D_2=0.25$.

*Case* 2: $R_3=4$, $r_3=2.75$, $D_3=1.25$.

2. 19 For $s=0.65$, $H_{C_{12}}(K)=0.47$ and the unicity distance is equal to 12 (then the probability of guessing the key is equal to 0.9). For $s=0.75$, $H_{C_4}(K)=0.46$ (the unicity distance is equal to 4). Finally, for $s=0.85$, $H_{C_2}(K)=0.4$ but $H_{C_6}=0.081$. So, unicity distances are 2 and 6 assuming that suitable probabilities are equal 0.9 and 0.99, respectively.

# 3

# ENCRYPTION METHODS OF INFORMATION PROTECTION

## 3.1  Classical ciphers

This section gives a brief introduction to some classical ciphers. Readers who wish to discover a little more should consult Sinkov [SINK68].

Classical ciphers have been used since ancient Egypt, with Kahn's book [KAHN67] giving a fascinating tale of the long use of ciphers.

The analysis of classical ciphers is highly dependent on knowing the letter frequency distribution and the digraph distribution of the host language of the cipher. Those given in this book were compiled by Susy Deck [DECK85].

Shannon [SHAN49] observed that the English language is highly **redundant** and that many of the letters used in written English are totally unnecessary to understand the text. Some written languages such as Arabic and Hebrew recognize this by not writing down the vowel sounds but their written languages still involve redundancies.

To show that English is redundant and that not all the letters are needed for understanding, we give two following examples which illustrate this in different ways:

1. The first leaves out the vowels and yet you are still able to read the text:

th lrd s m shphrd shll nt wnt

2. The second plays on the ambiguities in written English:

> Thimble Ψ man meta Π mango ink tooth affair sed symbol
> sigh (man) <sup>Π</sup>man laird meet haste yore where sad though pimento
> seem pull siam on shawm if erst you're penny! suds in pools eye meant
> tudor pyre many endear die avaunt 10e.

Thus we separate language into two parts: the **information content** and the **redundancy**.

Shannon [SHAN49] defined the **unicity distance** of a cipher in order to be able to get some quantitative measure of:

1. the security of a cipher (if the unicity distance of a code is small then the cipher is insecure); and

2. an indication of the amount of ciphertext, $N$, needed to break the cipher.

It is given by,

$$N \approx \frac{H(K)}{D}$$

where $D$ is the redundancy of the language (3.2 bits per letter for English) and H(K) is the information content of the key.

### 3.1.1 The Caesar cipher — A monoalphabetic cipher

Julius Caesar used a cipher which moved each letter of the alphabet to the letter three to the right in the predetermined order of the letters of the alphabet, so:

$$A \to D$$
$$B \to E$$
$$C \to F$$

and so on.

Thus any cipher which moves the $i$th letter of an alphabet to the $i+j^{th}$ letter is called a *Caesar cipher.*

*Example*

$$HAL \to IBM \text{ with } j = 1$$

In Figure 3.1 we have a histogram of the percentage frequency of English characters in text. In Figure 3.2 this has been shifted using the Caesar cipher $i \to i + 3$.

L FDPH L VDZ L FRQTXHUHG $\to$ I CAME I SAW I CONQUERED with $j = 3$. $\square$

Encipherment:

$$E : i \to i+j$$

Decipherment:

$$D : i \to i-j$$

Cryptanalysis:    Uses letter frequency distributions. If encipherment is achieved by a simple letter shift then a frequency count of the letter distributions in the ciphertext will yield the same pattern as the original host language of the plaintext but shifted.

### 3.1.2 Modular arithmetic — A monoalphabetic cipher

This is a variant of the Caesar cipher obtained by numbering the letters of the alphabet and then multiplying the number of the letter to be enciphered by $a$ where $gcd(a,26) = 1$ and adding a constant $b$. The answer is then reduced modulo 26. Figure 3.3 shows what happens to the histogram of Figure 3.1 when the modular arithmetic cipher $i \to 5i + 7$ is applied.

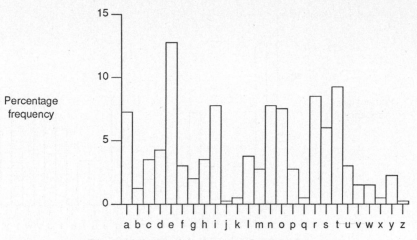

**Figure 3.1** English character frequencies

*Example*

Suppose we have to decipher:

WZDUY ZZYQB OTHTX ZDNZD KWQHI BYQBP WZDUY ZXZDSS

We note that:

Z occurs 8 times
D occurs 5 times
Y occurs 4 times
W,Q,B occurs 3 times each

Presuming the language is English, we note that the most frequently occurring letters in English text (see Appendix A) are, in order,

E,T,R,I,N,O,A

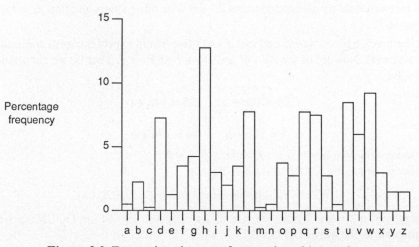

**Figure 3.2** Encryption character frequencies with $i \rightarrow i+3$

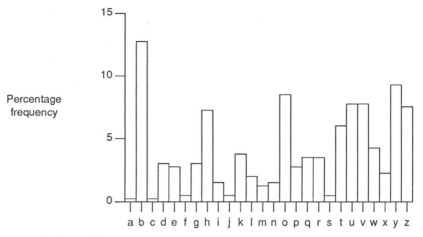

**Figure 3.3** Encryption character frequencies with $i \rightarrow 5i+7$

This leads us to try $Z \rightarrow E$ and $D \rightarrow T$ or $Y \rightarrow T$. That is, we try to simultaneously solve,

$$25 = 4a + b \qquad 25 = 4a + b$$
$$\text{or}$$
$$3 = 19a + b \qquad 24 = 19a + b$$

which have as solution $a = 2$, $b = 17$ in the first case (we reject it as $a^{-1}$ does not exist) and $a = 19$, $b = 1$ in the second.

If we try to decipher the letters WZDUY (the numerical string 22, 25, 3, 20, 24) using $(y - b) \cdot a^{-1}$, which, in this case, is $(y - 1) \cdot 19^{-1}$ or $(y - 1) \cdot 11 = (y - 20) \cdot 21$, we first note the second decipherment yields,

$$23,4,22,1,7 \text{ or XEWBH}$$

which is not a part of any recognizable English expression or word.

In fact we could try all combinations $Z \rightarrow E$ with other letters and find $Z$, in fact, does not map to $E$.

After much trial we would find that $Z \rightarrow O$ (we would expect the most common letter to be a vowel). Now let us try $Z \rightarrow O$ and $D \rightarrow T$ or $Y \rightarrow T$. That is, we simultaneously try to solve,

$$25 = 14a + b \qquad 25 = 14a + b$$
$$\text{or}$$
$$3 = 19a + b \qquad 24 = 19a + b$$

which have solutions $a = 6$, $b = 19$, and $a = 5$, $b = 7$.

Now if we use the second of these to decode,

$$\text{WZDUYZ (the numerical string 22,25,3,20,24)}$$

using $(y - b) \cdot a^{-1} = (y - 7) \cdot 21$, we get 3, 14, 20, 13, 19, 14 or DOUNTO which is recognizable as the words DO UNTO.

We leave the reader to decipher the remainder of the message.    □

## 3.1.3  Mixed alphabets — General monoalphabets

This is when a random letter of the alphabet is assigned randomly to another letter of the alphabet.

Encipherment:

$$E : x \rightarrow y$$

Decipherment:

$$D : y \rightarrow x$$

Cryptanalysis: Use frequency analysis on the letters of the alphabet.

Short amounts of ciphertext can readily be attacked by computer search but even reasonable amounts of ciphertext are easy to decipher by hand.

*Example*

Decipher:

BRYH DRL R ITEEIA IRBS TEF CIAAXA NFR NDTEA RF FGKN RGL AOAYJNDAYA EDRE BRYH NAGE EDA IRBS NRF FMYA EK ZK TE CKIIKNAL DAY EK FXDKKI KGA LRH NDTXD NRF RZRTGFE EDA YMIAF.

We do a frequency analysis and note the following distribution of letters:

| A | B | C | D | E | F | G | H | I | J | K | L | M | N | O | P | Q | R | S | T | U | V | W | X | Y | Z |
|---|---|---|---|---|---|---|---|---|---|---|---|---|---|---|---|---|---|---|---|---|---|---|---|---|---|
| 17 | 4 | 2 | 10 | 13 | 10 | 5 | 3 | 9 | 1 | 9 | 4 | 2 | 9 | 1 | | | 15 | 2 | 6 | | | | 3 | 6 | 2 |

So the most frequent letters are:

A, R, E, D or F, I or K or N

There is a one letter word so *R* is *I* or *A*.

The two most common three letter words in English are *THE* and *AND*.  So we guess *EDA* is one of these.

Since the most common letters in English are:

E, T, ...

we will guess *EDA* is *THE* and that *R* is *A* so our message becomes:

BaYH HaL a ITttIe IaBS TtF CIeeXe NaF NhDte aF FGKN aGL eOeYJNheYe that BaYH NeGt the IaBS NaF FMYe tK ZK Tt CKIIKNeL heY tK FXhKKI KGe LaH NhTXh NaF aZaTGFt the YMIeF.

Which resolves to:

mary had a little lamb its fleece was white as snow and everywhere that mary went the lamb was sure to go it followed her to school one day which was against the rules.

## 3.1.4  General monoalphabetic ciphers

It is a common practice to use a secret word or words, not repeating letters, and write them in a rectangle to use as a mnemonic for changing between plaintext and ciphertext.

Suppose the secret words were 'star wars'. We note that 'star wars' has the letters a, r and s repeated so we use only the letters s, t, a, r, w. We write these first and then fill out the rectangle with the unused letters of the alphabet:

```
STARW
BCDEF
GHIJK
LMNOP
QUVXY
Z
```

Columns are then read off to give us the following plaintext to ciphertext transformation:

| 0 | 1 | 2 | 3 | 4 | 5 | 6 | 7 | 8 | 9 | 10 | 11 | 12 | 13 | 14 | 15 | 16 | 17 | 18 | 19 | 20 | 21 | 22 | 23 | 24 | 25 |
|---|---|---|---|---|---|---|---|---|---|----|----|----|----|----|----|----|----|----|----|----|----|----|----|----|----|
| A | B | C | D | E | F | G | H | I | J | K | L | M | N | O | P | Q | R | S | T | U | V | W | X | Y | Z |
| S | B | G | L | Q | Z | T | C | H | M | U | A | D | I | N | V | R | E | J | O | X | W | F | K | P | Y |

Thus,

I KNOW ONLY THAT I KNOW NOTHING

becomes,

H UINF NIAP OCSO H UINF INOCHIT          □

This method is subject to easy attack just as in section 3.1.3.

*Remarks*

1. For substitution ciphers with alphabets of size $n$ the number of possible keys is $n!$, the number of ways of arranging the $n$ letters of the alphabet. If all keys are equally likely, the amount of text needed to break the cipher is the Shannon unicity distance,

$$N = H(K)/D = \log_2 n!/D$$

where $D$ is the redundancy of the language (3.2 bits/letter for English). So,

$$N = \log_2 26!/3.2$$

Using Sterling's approximation we have,

$$N = 26 \log_2(26/e)/3.2 = 27.6$$

hence **27 or 28 letters** are enough to break these codes by frequency analysis.

2. For polynomial based ciphers such as that used for the modular arithmetic transformation, the amount of text required is:

$$N = \log_2 26/3.2 = 1.5$$

Hence **2 letters** are enough to break these codes by frequency analysis.

## 3.1.5 Monoalphabetic transposition ciphers

The other principal technique for use on alphabets is transposition of characters. Thus,

plaintext → rearrange characters → ciphertext

*Example*

Write the plaintext CRYPTANALYST as a $3 \times 4$ matrix:

```
1 2 3 4
C R Y P
T A N A
L Y S T
```

and read off the columns in the order 2, 4, 1, 3 to get,

RAYPATCTLYNS

This technique can also be used for $n$-dimensional arrays.

Transposition ciphers often use a **fixed period**, $d$. Let $Z_d$ be the integers 1 to $d$, and $f : Z_d \to Z_d$ be a permutation. Then the **key** is the pair $K = (d, f)$ and blocks of $d$ characters are enciphered at a time. Thus,

$$M = m_1 \ldots m_d \ m_{d+1} \ldots m_{2d} \ldots$$

is enciphered to,

$$E_K(M) = m_{f(1)} \ldots m_{f(d)} \ m_{d+f(1)} \ldots m_{d+f(d)} \ldots$$

*Example*

Suppose $d = 4$ and $f = (2\ 3\ 4\ 1)$. Then the following shows a message broken into blocks and enciphered:

|  |  |
|---|---|
| Plaintext: | CRYP TOGR APHY |
| Ciphertext: | PCRY RTOG YAPH. |

## How to identify?

The frequency distribution of the characters of the ciphertext is exactly the same as for the plaintext.

## How to decipher?

A knowledge of the most frequent **pairs** and **triples** in a language is used with **anagraming**. The tables given here in Appendix A were prepared by Susy Deck from text gathered from around the world [DECK85].

The most frequent pairs of letters in English, on a relative scale from 1 to 10, are:

| | | | | | |
|---|---|---|---|---|---|
| TH | 10.00 | ED | 4.12 | OF | 3.38 |
| HE | 9.50 | TE | 4.04 | IT | 3.26 |
| IN | 7.17 | TI | 4.00 | AL | 3.15 |
| ER | 6.65 | OR | 3.98 | AS | 3.00 |
| RE | 5.92 | ST | 3.81 | HA | 3.00 |
| ON | 5.70 | AR | 3.54 | NG | 2.92 |
| AN | 5.63 | ND | 3.52 | CO | 2.80 |
| EN | 4.76 | TO | 3.50 | SE | 2.75 |
| AT | 4.72 | NT | 3.44 | ME | 2.65 |
| ES | 4.24 | IS | 3.43 | DE | 2.65 |

We note some other salient features of English:

1. The vowel-consonant pair is most common — no high frequency pair has two vowels.
2. Letters that occur in many different pairs are probably vowels.
3. Consonants, except for N and T, occur most frequently with vowels.
4. If XY and YX both occur, one letter is likely to be a vowel.

The most frequent three letter combinations, on a scale of 1 to 10, are:

| | | | | | |
|---|---|---|---|---|---|
| THE | 10.00 | FOR | 1.65 | ERE | 1.24 |
| AND | 2.81 | THA | 1.49 | CON | 1.20 |
| TIO | 2.24 | TER | 1.35 | TED | 1.09 |
| ATI | 1.67 | RES | 1.26 | COM | 1.08 |

*Example*

Decipher:

We start by looking at blocks of various lengths by dividing up the text:

LD WE OH ET TH SE ST RU HT EL OB SE DE FE IV NT.

Is $d = 2$? The pairs LD WE, which can only be permuted to DL EW, tell us no.

LDW EOH ETT HSE STR UHT ELO BSE DEF EIV NT

Is $d = 3$? The triple LDW in any permutation tells us no.

LDWE OHET THSE STRU HTEL OBSE DEFE IVNT

Is $d = 4$? This case is a bit harder because we have to try 16 permutations on the first two groups of four letters but we become convinced that none of these make sense.

LDWEO HETTH SESTR UHTEL OBSED EFEIV NT

Is $d = 5$? A bit harder because we have to try 5! permutations on the first two groups of five letters but become convinced that none of these make sense.

LDWEOH ETTHSE STRUHT ELOBSE DEFEIV NT

Is $d = 6$? The second group of six letters suggests,

THESET or TTHESE

That means we try the following permutations for deciphering,

(316245), (361245), (516243), (561243)
(612354), (412356), (621354), (421356)

When we try (561243) on the other blocks we recover the following message:

WE HOLD THESE TRUTIIS TO BE SELF EVIDENT

*Remarks*

To determine the expected number of characters required to break a permutation cipher with period $d$, we have to consider $d!$ permutations of the $d$ characters. Assuming all

**Table 3.1** The period and associated unicity distance

| $d$ | $N = 0.3d \log_2(d/e)$ | $N$ |
|---|---|---|
| 3 | $0.9\log_2(3/e)$ | 0.12804 |
| 4 | $1.2\log_2(4/e)$ | 0.66877 |
| 5 | $1.5\log_2(5/e)$ | 1.31885 |
| 6 | $1.8\log_2(6/e)$ | 2.05608 |
| 7 | $2.1\log_2(7/e)$ | 2.86579 |

**keys** (arrangements) are equally likely, the entropy of the key is thus:

$$H(K) = \log_2 d!$$

Thus the amount of text needed to break the cipher, the **unicity** distance, is:

$$N = \frac{H(K)}{D} = \frac{\log_2 d!}{D}$$

where $D$ is the redundancy of the language being used (about 3.2 bits per letter in English).

We use Sterling's approximation for $d!$ to get,

$$N \approx \frac{d \log_2(d/e)}{3.2} = 0.3d \log_2(d/e)$$

*Example*

For $d = 27$, $d/e \approx 10$ and $\log_2(d/e) \approx 3.2$. So $N = 27$. This is summarized in Table 3.1.

## 3.1.6 Homophonic substitution ciphers

Letters which occur frequently may be mapped into more than one letter in the ciphertext to flatten the frequency distribution. The number of cipher letters for a given character is determined by its frequency in the original language.

*Example*

Suppose the alphabet is mapped into the numbers 1 to 99 then,

> map E to 17, 19, 23, 47, and 64
> map A to 8, 20, 25, and 49
> map R to 1, 29, 65
> map T to 16, 31, and 85

but otherwise the $i$th letter maps to the $3i$th letter.
Then the plaintext,

> MANY A SLIP TWIXT THE CUP AND THE LIP

will become,

```
  08     20          16        3185  17        25      16   47
360839722054332445166624693185211706604525390916214733244 5
```

We now study some other methods devised to hide the frequency distribution.

### 3.1.7 Polyalphabetic substitution ciphers

Whereas homophonic substitution ciphers hide the distribution via the use of homomorphisms, **polyalphabetic substitution ciphers** hide it by making multiple substitutions, that is, using many alphabets.

Alberti, in 1568 (see [KAHN67]) , used two discs which were rotated after use. In effect this gave, for a period $d$, $d$ cipher alphabets $C_1, C_2, \ldots, C_d$. Hence, with a plaintext alphabet $A$,

$$f_i: A \rightarrow C_i$$

and the message,

$$M = m_1 m_2 \ldots m_d m_{d+1} m_{d+2} \ldots m_{2d}$$

becomes,

$$E_k(M) = f_1(m_1)f_2(m_2) \ldots f_d(m_d)f_1(m_{d+1}) \ldots f_d(m_{2d})$$

If $d = 1$ we get back the monoalphabetic cipher.
We now give a few methods for obtaining polyalphabetic ciphers.

**The Vigenere cipher.**  The key is specified by a sequence of letters:

$$K = k_1 \cdots k_d$$

where $k_i$, $(i = 1, \ldots, d)$ gives the amount of shift in the $i$th alphabet, that is:

$$f_i(a) = a + k_i \pmod{n}$$

*Example*
Encipher the message INDIVIDUAL CHARACTER with the key HOST,

$$M = \text{INDI VIDU ALCH ARAC TER}$$
$$K = \text{HOST HOST HOST HOST HOS}$$
$$E_K(M) = \text{PBVB CWVN HZUA HFSV ASJ}$$

**Beauford cipher.**  We proceed similarly but use,

$$f_i(a) = (k_i - a) \pmod{n}$$

Note that in this case the same function can be used for describing the procedure to get the ciphertext,

$$f_i^{-1} = (k_i - c) \bmod n$$

Hence this cipher actually reverses the letters of the alphabet and then shifts them to the right by $(k_i + 1)$ positions.  This can be seen by rewriting $f_i$ as follows:

$$f_i(a) = [(n-1) - a + (k_i + 1)] \bmod n$$

*Example*

Suppose that $k_i$ = D then $f_i(a) = (D - a)$ mod 26, then noting that D is the third letter of the alphabet and noting that $(3 - 0) = 3$, $(3 - 1) = 2$, $(3 - 2) = 1$, ... we see that:

*Plaintext*:     A B C D E F G H I J K L M ...
*Ciphertext*:    D C B A Z Y X W V U T S R ...

which follows because A is the zeroth, B is the first, C is the second, ... letter of the alphabet.

**Variant Beauford cipher.** Here we use:

$$f_i(a) = (a - k_i) \pmod{n}$$

Since $a - k_i = a + (n - k_i) \pmod{n}$ the Variant Beauford cipher is equivalent to the Vigenere cipher with the key character $n - k_i$.

The Variant Beauford cipher is, in fact, the inverse of the Vigenere cipher since if one is used to encipher the other is used to decipher.

The unicity distance for a periodic substitution cipher is easily calculated. If the cipher has $s$ possible keys for each simple substitution, then there are $s^d$ possible keys if $d$ substitutions are made. Thus the unicity distance is:

$$N \approx \frac{H(K)}{D} = \frac{\log_2 s^d}{D} = \frac{d \log_2 s}{D}$$

Now if $N$ ciphertext characters are needed to break each individual substitution cipher, then $dN$ characters are required to break the complete cipher.

For a Vigenere cipher with period $d$, $s = 26$ giving,

$$N \approx \frac{d \log_2 26}{3.2} = 1.5d$$

To break a periodic substitution cipher, the cryptanalyst must first determine the period of the cipher. This is done using two main tools: the **index of coincidence** and the **Kasiski** method.

**The Kasiski method** uses repetitions in the ciphertext to give clues to the cryptanalyst of the period. For example, suppose the plaintext TO BE OR NOT TO BE had been enciphered using the key NOW then we have:

Plaintext:       M = TOBEO RNOTT OBE
Key:             K = NOWNO WNOWN OWN
Ciphertext:      $E_k$(M) = **GCXRC NACPG CXR**

Since the characters that are repeated, GCXR, start nine letters apart we conclude that the period is probably 3 or 9.

**The index of coincidence** (IC), introduced in the 1920s by William Friedman [FRIE22] (see also [KAHN67]), measures the variation in the frequencies of the letters in a ciphertext. If the period of the cipher is one (1), that is simple substitution has been used, there will be considerable variation in the letter frequencies and the *IC* will be high. As the period increases, the variation is gradually eliminated (due to diffusion) and the *IC* is low (Table 3.2).

**Table 3.2** Languages and their indices of coincidence

| Language | IC |
|---|---|
| Arabic | 0.075889 |
| Danish | 0.070731 |
| Dutch | 0.079805 |
| English | 0.066895 |
| Finnish | 0.073796 |
| French | 0.074604 |
| German | 0.076667 |
| Greek | 0.069165 |
| Hebrew | 0.076844 |
| Italian | 0.073294 |
| Japanese | 0.077236 |
| Malay | 0.085286 |
| Norwegian | 0.069428 |
| Portuguese | 0.074528 |
| Russian | 0.056074 |
| Serbo Croatian | 0.064363 |
| Spanish | 0.076613 |
| Swedish | 0.064489 |

Following Sinkov [SINK68], we shall derive the *IC* by first defining a **measure of roughness**, (MR), which gives the variation of the frequencies of individual characters relative to a uniform distribution,

$$MR = \sum_{i=0}^{n-1} (p_i - \frac{1}{n})^2$$

where $p_i$ is the probability that an arbitrary character in a random ciphertext is the *i*th character $a_i$ in the alphabet ($i = 0, \ldots, n-1$) and,

$$\sum_{i=0}^{n-1} p_i = 1$$

For English letters we have:

$$MR = \sum_{i=0}^{25} (p_i - \frac{1}{26})^2 = \sum_{i=0}^{25} p_i^2 - \frac{2}{26} \sum_{i=0}^{25} p_i + 26(\frac{1}{26})^2 = \sum_{i=0}^{n-1} p_i^2 - 0.038$$

Because the period and the probability are both unknown, we cannot compute MR. But, we can estimate the MR using the distribution of letter frequencies in the ciphertext. Then we have,

$$MR + 0.038 = \sum_{i=0}^{25} p_i^2$$

is the probability two arbitrary letters in random ciphertext are the same. Now the total number of pairs of letters that can be chosen from a given ciphertext of length $N$ is

$\binom{N}{2} = \frac{1}{2}N\,(N-1)$. Now let $F_i$ be the frequency of the $i$th letter of English in the ciphertext. Then,

$$\sum_{i=0}^{25} F_i = 1$$

The number of pairs containing just the $i$th letter is:

$$\frac{F_i(F_i - 1)}{2}$$

So the *IC* defined as:

$$IC = \sum_{i=0}^{25} \frac{F_i(F_i - 1)}{N\,(N - 1)}$$

is the probability two (2) letters at random from a given ciphertext are, in fact, the same. Now we use the *IC* estimate as follows:

$$\sum_{i=0}^{25} p_i{}^2 = MR + 0.038$$

Thus we can use the ciphertext to calculate *MR*.

For plain language distribution, *MR* can be calculated by summing the squares of the characteristic frequencies of the letters and subtracting 0.038. We know the characteristic frequencies for English (and many other languages — see Appendix A). If we sum their squares we get 0.066. Thus the *MR* for plaintext English is $0.066 - 0.038 = 0.028$.

For a flat distribution of a 26 character alphabet, all letters have the same frequency, 1/26, and the sum of the squares is $(1/26)^2 \times 26$. Hence the *MR* for a flat distribution is $1/26 - 1/26 = 0$.

When the *MR* is 0, corresponding to a flat distribution, we say it has infinite period (period ∞). At the other extreme we have period one (period 1) for simple substitution. We have just seen that English with period one has $MR = 0.028$. Thus we have:

$$0.038 \quad < \quad IC \quad < \quad 0.066$$
$$\text{(period ∞)} \qquad\qquad\qquad \text{(period 1)}$$

For a cipher of period $d$, the expected value or *IC* is given by:

$$exp\,(IC) = \frac{1}{d}\frac{N-d}{N-1}(0.066) + \left[\frac{d-1}{d}\right]\frac{N}{N-1}(0.038)$$

Thus, while we can get an estimate of $d$ from the ciphertext, it is not exact but statistical in nature and a particular ciphertext might give misleading results. Table 3.2 gives the index of coincidence for some other languages.

We give tables of $d$ and *IC* in Table 3.3. See Figure 3.4 for a program that might help calculate the index of coincidence.

*Example*

Decrypt the following ciphertext which was produced using the Vigenere cipher:

```
TSMVM MPPCW CZUGX HPECP RFAUE IOBQW PPIMS
```

```
FXIPC TSQPK SZNUL OPACR DDPKT SLVFW ELTKR

GHIZS FNIDF ARMUE NOSKR GDIPH WSGVL EDMCM

SMWKP IYOJS TLVFA HPBJI RAQIW HLDGA IYOU
```

Given that the cipher was produced using a Vigenere cipher, we would first like to determine the period that has been used.

Kasiski's method allows us to do that, assuming the repetitions are not coincidental. Examining the trigraphs we find two occurrences of IYO and LVF. The IYO's are 25

Table 3.3 Periods and associated indices of coincidence

| $d$ | IC |
|-----|--------|
| 1 | 0.0066 |
| 2 | 0.0520 |
| 3 | 0.0473 |
| 4 | 0.0450 |
| 5 | 0.0436 |
| 6 | 0.0427 |
| 7 | 0.0420 |
| 8 | 0.0415 |
| 9 | 0.0411 |
| 10 | 0.0408 |
| 11 | 0.0405 |
| 12 | 0.0403 |
| 13 | 0.0402 |
| 14 | 0.0400 |
| 15 | 0.0399 |
| 16 | 0.0397 |
| 17 | 0.0396 |
| 18 | 0.0396 |
| 19 | 0.0395 |
| 20 | 0.0394 |

```
program IC (input, output);
const
  N = 100000;
  high =0.066;
  low = 0.038;
var
  d : integer;
  ic : real;
begin
  writeln('         d                      IC');
  writeln('    =======================');
  for d := 1 to 20 do
  begin
    ic := (1/d)*(N-d)/(N-1)*high+((d-1)/d)*(N/(N-1))*low;
    writeln(d:6, '             ',ic:1:4);
  end;
end.
```

Figure 3.4 A program which might help calculate the index of coincidence

letters apart and the LVF's are 55 apart. The common factors are 1 and 5.

Let us now examine the IC. The frequency count gives us:

$$
\begin{array}{lllll}
a \rightarrow 6 & g \rightarrow 5 & l \rightarrow 6 & q \rightarrow 3 & v \rightarrow 4 \\
b \rightarrow 2 & h \rightarrow 5 & m \rightarrow 8 & r \rightarrow 6 & w \rightarrow 6 \\
c \rightarrow 6 & i \rightarrow 10 & n \rightarrow 3 & s \rightarrow 10 & x \rightarrow 2 \\
d \rightarrow 6 & j \rightarrow 2 & o \rightarrow 5 & t \rightarrow 5 & y \rightarrow 2 \\
e \rightarrow 5 & k \rightarrow 5 & p \rightarrow 13 & u \rightarrow 5 & z \rightarrow 3 \\
f \rightarrow 6 & & & &
\end{array}
$$

Thus the IC = 0.04066 .

From the table of IC's it appears more likely that 10 alphabets were used than 5, but we will proceed with an assumption of 5.

We split the cipher text into five sections getting:

```
TMCHRIPFTSODSEGFANGWESITHRHI from text positions 5i,   i = 0,1,...,27.
SPZPFOPXSZPDLLHNRODSDMYLPALY  from text positions 5i+1, i = 0,1,...,27.
MPUEABIIQNAPVTIIMSIGMWOVBQDO  from text positions 5i+2, i = 0,1,...,27.
VCGCUQMPPUCKFKZDUKPVCKJFJIGU  from text positions 5i+3, i = 0,1,...,27.
MWXPEWSCKLRTWRSFERHLMPSAIWA   from text positions 5i+4, i = 0,1,...,27.
```

In Table 3.4, the frequency distribution for each of these five sections is shown.

**Table 3.4** Frequency distribution for the five sections of the cipher text

| text | 5i | 5i+1 | 5i+2 | 5i+3 | 5i+4 |
|------|------|------|------|------|------|
| a → | 1 | 1 | 2 | 0 | 2 |
| b → | 0 | 0 | 2 | 0 | 0 |
| c → | 1 | 0 | 0 | 4 | 1 |
| d → | 1 | 3 | 1 | 1 | 0 |
| e → | 2 | 0 | 1 | 0 | 2 |
| f → | 2 | 1 | 0 | 2 | 1 |
| g → | 2 | 0 | 1 | 2 | 0 |
| h → | 3 | 1 | 0 | 0 | 1 |
| i → | 3 | 0 | 5 | 1 | 1 |
| j → | 0 | 0 | 0 | 2 | 0 |
| k → | 0 | 0 | 0 | 4 | 1 |
| l → | 0 | 4 | 0 | 0 | 2 |
| m → | 1 | 1 | 3 | 1 | 2 |
| n → | 1 | 1 | 1 | 0 | 0 |
| o → | 1 | 2 | 2 | 0 | 0 |
| p → | 1 | 5 | 2 | 3 | 2 |
| q → | 0 | 0 | 2 | 1 | 0 |
| r → | 2 | 1 | 0 | 0 | 3 |
| s → | 3 | 3 | 1 | 0 | 3 |
| t → | 3 | 0 | 1 | 0 | 1 |
| u → | 0 | 0 | 1 | 4 | 0 |
| v → | 0 | 0 | 2 | 2 | 0 |
| w → | 1 | 0 | 1 | 0 | 4 |
| x → | 0 | 1 | 0 | 0 | 1 |
| y → | 0 | 2 | 0 | 0 | 0 |
| z → | 0 | 2 | 0 | 1 | 0 |
| IC | 0.04233 | 0.06614 | 0.05026 | 0.06614 | 0.04843 |

Each column of Table 3.4 corresponds to the frequency distribution of the section indicated by the text position in the heading. Thus column 4, headed by $5i+3$ corresponds to the fourth section which gave text positions $5i+3$.

It would be best to consider columns 2 and 4 as their IC is 0.06614 which corresponds most closely to 'English'. In the second column of Table 3.4 we see L and P occur frequently, suggesting that they might be A and E respectively. In the fourth column we are more uncertain what initial guess to try for A so we will try the three most frequent values as guesses for A: i.e. U, C, K.

The second section is:

$$SPZPFOPXSZPDLLHNRODSDMYLPALY$$

Since P is the most common letter we are going to replace P $\rightarrow$ E, Q $\rightarrow$ F, ... getting:

$$HEOEUDEMHOESAAWCGDSHSBNAEPAN$$

The fourth section is:

$$VCGCUQMPPUCKFKZDUKPVCKJFJIGU$$

Hence replacing U $\rightarrow$ A, V $\rightarrow$ B, ... we get:

$$BIMIAWSVVAIQLQFJAQVBIQPLFOMA$$

which we quickly decide is unlikely to be English because of the number of Qs. The other choices for A, from the frequency distribution are C $\rightarrow$ A or K $\rightarrow$ A. Trying these gives respectively:

$$TAEASOKNNSAIDIXBSINTAIHDHGES$$

$$CGCEGCFFECAFAJDEAFFCADFDCGE$$

Of these two the first looks the most promising so we look at what we have for our five sections as rows:

```
.   .   .   .   .   .   .   .   .   .   .   .   .   .
H   E   O   E   U   D   E   M   H   O   E   S   A   A   W   C   G   D   S   H   S   B   N   A   E   P   A   N
.   .   .   .   .   .   .   .   .   .   .   .   .   .   .   .
T   A   E   A   S   O   K   N   N   S   A   I   D   I   X   B   S   I   N   T   A   I   H   D   H   G   E   S
.   .   .   .   .   .   .   .   .   .   .   .   .   .   .   .
```

Neither row is part of a sentence so we look down the first column and decide that since the most common first word in English is THE we will start by leaving the first row as it is and replacing M $\rightarrow$ E, N $\rightarrow$ F, ... in the third row giving:

```
T   M   C   H   R   I   P   F   T   S   O   D   S   E   G   F   A   N   G   W   E   S   I   T   H   R   H   I
H   E   O   E   U   D   E   M   H   O   E   S   A   A   W   C   G   D   S   H   S   B   N   A   E   P   A   N
E   H   M   W   S   T   A   A   I   F   S   H   N   L   A   A   E   K   A   Y   E   O   G   N   T   I   V   G
T   A   E   A   S   O   K   N   N   S   A   I   D   I   X   B   S   I   N   T   A   I   H   D   H   G   E   S
.   .   .   .   .   .   .   .   .   .   .   .   .   .   .   .
```

Hence we decide that the plaintext is:

THE TIME HAS COME THE WALRUS SAID TO SPEAK OF MANY THINGS OF

SHOES AND SHIPS AND SEALING WAX OF CABBAGES AND KINGS AND WHY THE SEA IS BOILING HOT AND WHETHER PIGS HAVE WINGS.

Looking at the character which gave *A* in each of the five alphabets gives us the key ALICE.     □

## 3.2 Symmetric algorithms and DES

A **product cipher** $E$ is the composition of $t$ functions (ciphers) $F_1, \ldots, F_t$ where each $F_i$ may be a substitution or a transposition. Rotor machines are product ciphers, where $F_i$ is implemented by rotor $R_i$, $1 \leq i \leq t$.

The famous ENIGMA machine used by Germany, Japan and their allies were of multiple rotor type. A variation, the Hagelin machine, of Swedish origin, was used extensively by diplomatic posts for many years. The reader is referred to Kahn [KAHN67] for fascinating reading of the history and use of these devices.

These machines use *symmetric algorithms* — the same secret key must be known to both sender and receiver.

### 3.2.1 Substitution — Permutation ciphers

Shannon [SHAN49] proposed composing different kinds of functions to create 'mixing transformations', which randomly distribute the meaningful messages uniformly over the set of all possible cipher text messages. Mixing transformations could be created, for example, by applying a transposition followed by an alternating sequence of substitutions and simple linear operations. This approach is embodied in the LUCIFER cipher, designed at IBM by Feistel [FEIS70,73]. LUCIFER uses a transformation that alternately applies substitutions and transpositions. Figure 3.5 illustrates how the basic principle is applied to small blocks (in practice, longer blocks should be used). The cipher alternatively applies substitutions and permutations.

Figure 3.5 gives a small illustration of how substitution and then permutation may be used to encipher using involutions only. The first three letters are substituted by removing

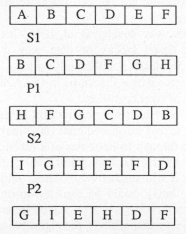

**Figure 3.5** An illustration of the text

one to the right in the alphabet and the second three letters are moved two to the right. The first permutation, P1, (and its inverse) is (16)(24)(35). The second permutation, P2, (and its inverse) is (12)(34)(56).

Clearly this can be deciphered by reversing the order of the operations and applying the inverse of each substitution and permutation.

## 3.2.2 The Data Encryption Standard (DES)

In 1977, the National Bureau of Standards announced a Data Encryption Standard to be used in unclassified United States Government applications [NBS77].

The algorithm specified in the Australian Standard AS2805.5-1985 is based on the algorithm specified in the American National Standard ANSI X3.92-1981, American National Standards Data Encryption Algorithm, © American National Standards Institute, 1981.

The two modes of operation specified in this standard are based on two modes of operation given in ANSI X3.106-1983, the American National Standard for Information Systems-Data Encryption Algorithm-Modes of Operation, © American National Standards Institute, 1983.

The same standard or part thereof was adopted by Australia [SAA2805.5] and almost all governments in the world with the intention that the *Data Encryption Algorithm* (DEA) should be available to the worldwide banking and commercial networks as an ISO standard. However, this was not to be. Diffie and Hellman [DIHE77] had predicted that the DEA algorithm would be vulnerable to attack by a special purpose machine with one million chips which could be built for around $20 million and which would break any code by searching the complete key space in around one day. They also predicted that by 1990 hardware speeds would have improved so much that a 56-bit key would no longer be secure.

As predicted, machine hardware has caught up with practice and the key length is now almost certainly too short.

Nevertheless, we describe the DEA algorithm in detail, as it is heavily used in today's technology and its overall structure has resisted intensive study and attack by a large number of research workers.

The encryption algorithm was developed at IBM, and was the outgrowth of LUCIFER. DES enciphers 64-bit blocks of data with a 56-bit key. There was disagreement over whether a 56-bit key is sufficiently strong.

The description we now give is that described in [SAA2805.5], but does not differ materially from the standards of other countries.

The algorithm, which is used both to encipher and to decipher, is summarised in Figure 3.6. An input block $T$ is first transposed under an initial permutation IP, giving $T_0$ = IP($T$). After it has passed through 16 iterations of a function $f$, it is transposed under the inverse permutation $IP^{-1}$ to give the final result. The permutations IP and $IP^{-1}$ are given in Tables 3.5(a) and 3.5(b) respectively. These tables (as well as the other permutation tables described later) should be read left-to-right, top-to-bottom (e.g. IP transposes $T = t_1 t_2 \ldots t_{64}$ into $T_0 = t_{58} t_{50} \ldots t_7$). All tables are fixed.

Between the initial and final transpositions, the algorithm performs 16 iterations of a function $f$ that combines substitution and transposition. Let $T_i$ denote the result of the $i$th

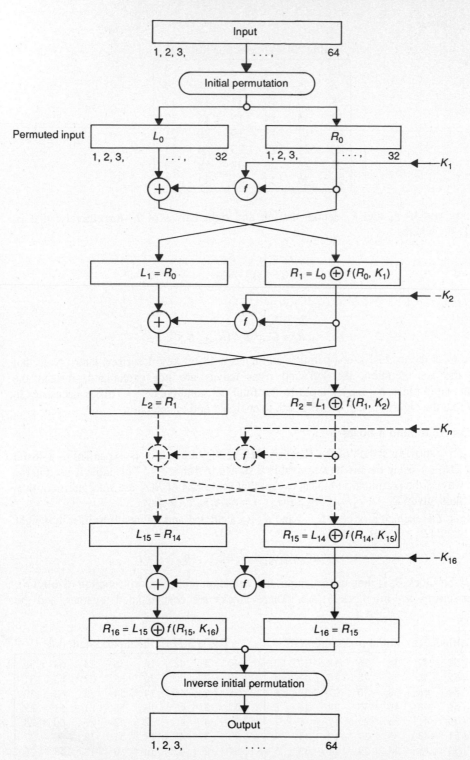

**Figure 3.6** Encrypting computation (from AS 2805.S, 1985)

**Table 3.4** Bit-selection Table E

| 32 | 1 | 2 | 3 | 4 | 5 |
|----|----|----|----|----|----|
| 4 | 5 | 6 | 7 | 8 | 9 |
| 8 | 9 | 10 | 11 | 12 | 13 |
| 12 | 13 | 14 | 15 | 16 | 17 |
| 16 | 17 | 18 | 19 | 20 | 21 |
| 20 | 21 | 22 | 23 | 24 | 25 |
| 24 | 25 | 26 | 27 | 28 | 29 |
| 28 | 29 | 30 | 31 | 32 | 1 |

iteration and let $L_i$ and $R_i$ denote the left and right halves of $T_i$ respectively; that is, $T_i = L_i R_i$, where,

$$L_i = t_1 \ldots t_{32}$$
$$R_i = t_{33} \ldots t_{64}$$

Then,

$$L_i = R_{i-1}$$
$$R_i = L_{i-1} \oplus f(R_{i-1}, K_i)$$

where $\oplus$ is the exclusive-or operation and $K_i$ is a 48-bit key described later. Note that after the last iteration, the left and right halves are not exchanged; instead the concatenated block $R_{16}L_{16}$ is input to the final permutation $\text{IP}^{-1}$. This is necessary in order that the algorithm can be used both to encipher and to decipher.

**The function f and S-boxes**

Figure 3.7 shows a sketch of the function $f(R_{i-1}, K_i)$. First $R_{i-1}$ is expanded to a 48-bit block $E(R_{i-1})$ using the bit-selection table E shown in Table 3.4. This table is used in the same way as the permutation tables, except that some bits of $R_{i-1}$ are selected more than once; thus, given $R_{i-1} = r_1 r_2 \ldots r_{32}$, $E(R_{i-1}) = r_{32} r_1 r_2 \ldots r_{32} r_1$.

Next, the exclusive-or of $E(R_{i-1})$ and $K_i$ is calculated and the result broken into eight 6-bit blocks $B_1, \ldots, B_8$, where,

$$E(R_{i-1}) \oplus K_i = B_1 B_2 \ldots B_8$$

Each 6-bit block $B_j$ is then used as input to a selection (substitution) function (**S-box**) $S_j$, which returns a 4-bit block $S_j(B_j)$. These blocks are concatenated together, and the

**Table 3.5(a)** Initial permutation IP

| 58 | 50 | 42 | 34 | 26 | 18 | 10 | 2 |
|----|----|----|----|----|----|----|----|
| 60 | 52 | 44 | 36 | 28 | 20 | 12 | 4 |
| 62 | 54 | 46 | 38 | 30 | 22 | 14 | 6 |
| 64 | 56 | 48 | 40 | 32 | 24 | 16 | 8 |
| 57 | 49 | 41 | 33 | 25 | 17 | 9 | 1 |
| 59 | 51 | 43 | 35 | 27 | 19 | 11 | 3 |
| 61 | 53 | 45 | 37 | 29 | 21 | 13 | 5 |
| 63 | 55 | 47 | 39 | 31 | 23 | 15 | 7 |

**Table 3.5(b)** Final permutation $\text{IP}^{-1}$

| 40 | 8 | 48 | 16 | 56 | 24 | 64 | 32 |
|----|----|----|----|----|----|----|----|
| 39 | 7 | 47 | 15 | 55 | 23 | 63 | 31 |
| 38 | 6 | 46 | 14 | 54 | 22 | 62 | 30 |
| 37 | 5 | 45 | 13 | 53 | 21 | 61 | 29 |
| 36 | 4 | 44 | 12 | 52 | 20 | 60 | 28 |
| 35 | 3 | 43 | 11 | 51 | 19 | 59 | 27 |
| 34 | 2 | 42 | 10 | 50 | 18 | 58 | 26 |
| 33 | 1 | 41 | 9 | 49 | 17 | 57 | 25 |

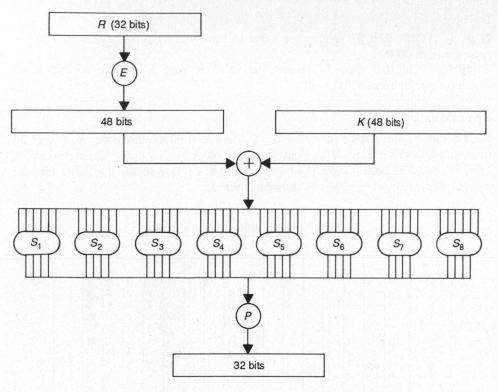

**Figure 3.7** Calculation of $f(R,K)$ (from AS 2805.S, 1985)

resulting 32-bit block is transposed by the permutation P shown in Table 3.6. Thus, the block returned by $f(R_{i-1}, K_i)$ is:

$$P\ (S_1(B_1) \dots S_8(B_8))$$

Each S-box $S_j$ maps a 6 bit block $B_j = b_1b_2b_3b_4b_6$ into a 4-bit block as defined in Table 3.7. This is done as follows: The integer corresponding to $b_1b_6$ selects a row in the table, while the integer corresponding to $b_2b_3b_4b_5$ selects a column. The value of $S_j(B_j)$ is then the 4-bit representation of the integer in that row and column.

**Table 3.6** Permutation P

| 16 | 7 | 20 | 21 |
|---|---|---|---|
| 29 | 12 | 28 | 17 |
| 1 | 15 | 23 | 26 |
| 5 | 18 | 31 | 10 |
| 2 | 8 | 24 | 14 |
| 32 | 27 | 3 | 9 |
| 19 | 13 | 30 | 6 |
| 22 | 11 | 4 | 25 |

*Example*

If $B_1 = 011100$, then $S_1$ returns the value in row 0, column 14; this is 0, which is represented as 0000.

If $B_7 = 100101$, then $S_7$ returns the value in row 3, column 2; this is 13, which is represented as 1101.    □

## Key calculation

Each iteration $i$ uses a different 48-bit key $K_1$ derived from the initial key $K$. Figure 3.8 illustrates how this is done. $K$ is input as a 64-bit block, with 8 parity bits in positions 8, 16, ... , 64. The permutation PC-1 (permuted choice 1) discards the parity bits and transposes the remaining 56 bits as shown in Table 3.8.

### Table 3.7 Selection functions (S-boxes)

| Row | Column 0 | 1 | 2 | 3 | 4 | 5 | 6 | 7 | 8 | 9 | 10 | 11 | 12 | 13 | 14 | 15 | Box |
|---|---|---|---|---|---|---|---|---|---|---|---|---|---|---|---|---|---|
| 0 | 14 | 4 | 13 | 1 | 2 | 15 | 11 | 8 | 3 | 10 | 6 | 12 | 5 | 9 | 0 | 7 | |
| 1 | 0 | 15 | 7 | 4 | 14 | 2 | 13 | 1 | 10 | 6 | 12 | 11 | 9 | 5 | 3 | 8 | |
| 2 | 4 | 1 | 14 | 8 | 13 | 6 | 2 | 11 | 15 | 12 | 9 | 7 | 3 | 10 | 5 | 0 | $S_1$ |
| 3 | 15 | 12 | 8 | 2 | 4 | 9 | 1 | 7 | 5 | 11 | 3 | 14 | 10 | 0 | 6 | 13 | |
| 0 | 15 | 1 | 8 | 14 | 6 | 11 | 3 | 4 | 9 | 7 | 2 | 13 | 12 | 0 | 5 | 10 | |
| 1 | 3 | 13 | 4 | 7 | 15 | 2 | 8 | 14 | 12 | 0 | 1 | 10 | 6 | 9 | 11 | 5 | |
| 2 | 0 | 14 | 7 | 11 | 10 | 4 | 13 | 1 | 5 | 8 | 12 | 6 | 9 | 3 | 2 | 15 | $S_2$ |
| 3 | 13 | 8 | 10 | 1 | 3 | 15 | 4 | 2 | 11 | 6 | 7 | 12 | 0 | 5 | 14 | 9 | |
| 0 | 10 | 0 | 9 | 14 | 6 | 3 | 15 | 5 | 1 | 13 | 12 | 7 | 11 | 4 | 2 | 8 | |
| 1 | 13 | 7 | 0 | 9 | 3 | 4 | 6 | 10 | 2 | 8 | 5 | 14 | 12 | 11 | 15 | 1 | |
| 2 | 13 | 6 | 4 | 9 | 8 | 15 | 3 | 0 | 11 | 1 | 2 | 12 | 5 | 10 | 14 | 7 | $S_3$ |
| 3 | 1 | 10 | 13 | 0 | 6 | 9 | 8 | 7 | 4 | 15 | 14 | 3 | 11 | 5 | 2 | 12 | |
| 0 | 7 | 13 | 14 | 3 | 0 | 6 | 9 | 10 | 1 | 2 | 8 | 5 | 11 | 12 | 4 | 15 | |
| 1 | 13 | 8 | 11 | 5 | 6 | 15 | 0 | 3 | 4 | 7 | 2 | 12 | 1 | 10 | 14 | 9 | |
| 2 | 10 | 6 | 9 | 0 | 12 | 11 | 7 | 13 | 15 | 1 | 3 | 14 | 5 | 2 | 8 | 4 | $S_4$ |
| 3 | 3 | 15 | 0 | 6 | 10 | 1 | 13 | 8 | 9 | 4 | 5 | 11 | 12 | 7 | 2 | 14 | |
| 0 | 2 | 12 | 4 | 1 | 7 | 10 | 11 | 6 | 8 | 5 | 3 | 15 | 13 | 0 | 14 | 9 | |
| 1 | 14 | 11 | 2 | 12 | 4 | 7 | 13 | 1 | 5 | 0 | 15 | 10 | 3 | 9 | 8 | 6 | |
| 2 | 4 | 2 | 1 | 11 | 10 | 13 | 7 | 8 | 15 | 9 | 12 | 5 | 6 | 3 | 0 | 14 | $S_5$ |
| 3 | 11 | 8 | 12 | 7 | 1 | 14 | 2 | 13 | 6 | 15 | 0 | 9 | 10 | 4 | 5 | 3 | |
| 0 | 12 | 1 | 10 | 15 | 9 | 2 | 6 | 8 | 0 | 13 | 3 | 4 | 14 | 7 | 5 | 11 | |
| 1 | 10 | 15 | 4 | 2 | 7 | 12 | 9 | 5 | 6 | 1 | 13 | 14 | 0 | 11 | 3 | 8 | |
| 2 | 9 | 14 | 15 | 5 | 2 | 8 | 12 | 3 | 7 | 0 | 4 | 10 | 1 | 13 | 11 | 6 | $S_6$ |
| 3 | 4 | 3 | 2 | 12 | 9 | 5 | 15 | 10 | 11 | 14 | 1 | 7 | 6 | 0 | 8 | 13 | |
| 0 | 4 | 11 | 2 | 14 | 15 | 0 | 8 | 13 | 3 | 12 | 9 | 7 | 5 | 10 | 6 | 1 | |
| 1 | 13 | 0 | 11 | 7 | 4 | 9 | 1 | 10 | 14 | 3 | 5 | 12 | 2 | 15 | 8 | 6 | |
| 2 | 1 | 4 | 11 | 13 | 12 | 3 | 7 | 14 | 10 | 15 | 6 | 8 | 0 | 5 | 9 | 2 | $S_7$ |
| 3 | 6 | 11 | 13 | 8 | 1 | 4 | 10 | 7 | 9 | 5 | 0 | 15 | 14 | 2 | 3 | 12 | |
| 0 | 13 | 2 | 8 | 4 | 6 | 15 | 11 | 1 | 10 | 9 | 3 | 14 | 5 | 0 | 12 | 7 | |
| 1 | 1 | 15 | 13 | 8 | 10 | 3 | 7 | 4 | 12 | 5 | 6 | 11 | 0 | 14 | 9 | 2 | |
| 2 | 7 | 11 | 4 | 1 | 9 | 12 | 14 | 2 | 0 | 6 | 10 | 13 | 15 | 3 | 5 | 8 | $S_8$ |
| 3 | 2 | 1 | 14 | 7 | 4 | 10 | 8 | 13 | 15 | 12 | 9 | 0 | 3 | 5 | 6 | 11 | |

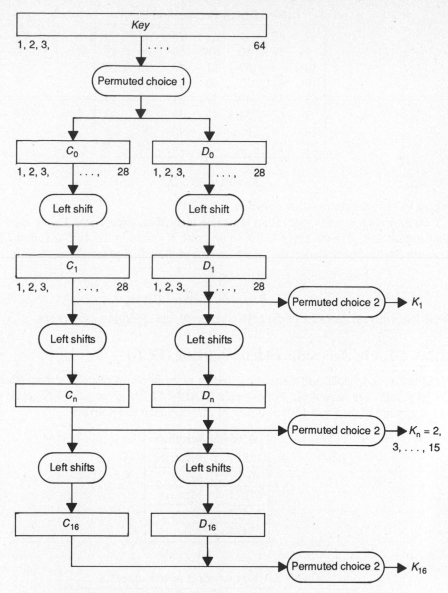

**Figure 3.8**  Key Schedule Calculation (From AS 2805.S, 1985)

The result, PC-1($K$), is then split into two halves $C$ and $D$ used to derive each key $K_i$. Letting $C_i$ and $D_i$ denote the values of C and D used to derive $K_i$, we have,

$$C_i = LS_i(C_{i-1}),$$
$$D_i = LS_i(D_{i-1}),$$

where $LS_i$ is a left circular shift by the number of positions shown in Table 3.9, and $C_0$ and $D_0$, are the initial values of $C$ and $D$. Key $K_i$ is then given by,

**Table 3.8** Key Permutation PC–1

| | | | | | | |
|---|---|---|---|---|---|---|
| 57 | 49 | 41 | 33 | 25 | 17 | 9 |
| 1 | 58 | 50 | 42 | 34 | 26 | 18 |
| 10 | 2 | 59 | 51 | 43 | 35 | 27 |
| 19 | 11 | 3 | 60 | 52 | 44 | 36 |
| 63 | 55 | 47 | 39 | 31 | 23 | 15 |
| 7 | 62 | 54 | 46 | 38 | 30 | 22 |
| 14 | 6 | 61 | 53 | 45 | 37 | 29 |
| 21 | 13 | 5 | 28 | 20 | 12 | 4 |

$$K_i = PC-2(C_i \, D_i)$$

where PC-2 is the permutation shown in Table 3.10.

*Deciphering* is performed using the same algorithm, except that $K_{16}$ is used in the first iteration, $K_{15}$ in the second, and so on, with $K_1$ used in the 16th iteration. This is because the final permutation $IP^{-1}$ is the inverse of the initial permutation IP, and,

$$R_{i-1} = L_i$$
$$L_{i-1} = R_i \oplus f(L_i, K_i)$$

Note that whereas the order of the keys is reversed, the algorithm itself is not.

### 3.2.3 DEA in electronic codebook mode (ECB)

Traditional codebooks substitute some letters or symbols in place of other, often quite lengthy, letters or sentences. For example [KAHN67] 295 gives part of Nigel de Grey's transcryption of the Code 13040 version of Zimmermann telegram as:

| | |
|---|---|
| 6706 | reichlich |
| 13850 | finanziell |
| 6929 | und |
| 67893 | Mexico |
| 36477 | Texas |
| 5454 | AR |

**Table 3.9** Key schedule of left shifts LS

| Iteration | Number of i | Iteration | Number of i |
|---|---|---|---|
| 1 | 1 | 9 | 1 |
| 2 | 1 | 10 | 2 |
| 3 | 2 | 11 | 2 |
| 4 | 2 | 12 | 2 |
| 5 | 2 | 13 | 2 |
| 6 | 2 | 14 | 2 |
| 7 | 2 | 15 | 2 |
| 8 | 2 | 16 | 1 |

**Table 3.10** Key Permutation PC-2

| 14 | 17 | 11 | 24 | 1  | 5  |
|----|----|----|----|----|----|
| 3  | 28 | 15 | 6  | 21 | 10 |
| 23 | 19 | 12 | 4  | 26 | 8  |
| 16 | 7  | 27 | 20 | 13 | 2  |
| 41 | 52 | 31 | 37 | 47 | 55 |
| 30 | 40 | 51 | 45 | 33 | 48 |
| 44 | 49 | 39 | 56 | 34 | 53 |
| 46 | 42 | 50 | 36 | 29 | 32 |

So the ECB mode may be used as in Figure 3.9 to change,

| clear text | → | input block | → | DEA | → | output block | → | ciphertext |

The cleartext datablocks are used as DEA input blocks. The resultant DEA output blocks are used as ciphertext blocks, possibly for other applications.

## 3.2.4 DEA in cipher block chaining mode(CBC)

The data to be encrypted is divided into blocks $B1, B2, \ldots, Bn$ each of 64 bits. A 64 bit initialization vector IV is chosen.

(i)  IV $\oplus$ B1 is encrypted to get C1 (see Figure 3.10),
(ii) C1 $\oplus$ B2 is encrypted to get C2,

.
.
.

(n) Cn-1 $\oplus$ Bn is encrypted to get Cn,

where $\oplus$ is addition modulo 2.

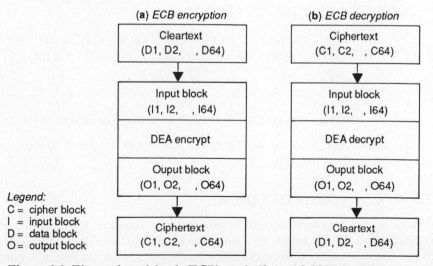

**Figure 3.9** Electronic codebook (ECB) mode (from AS 2805.S, 1985)

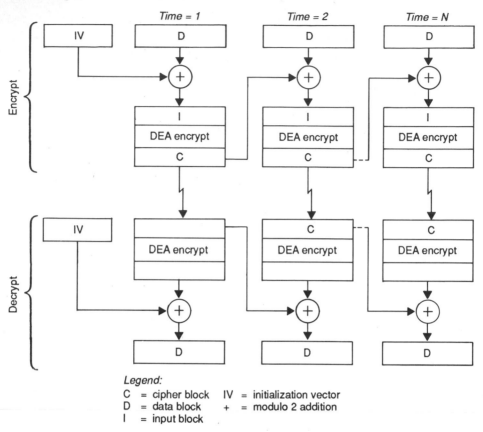

Figure 3.10  Cipher block chaining (CBC) mode (from AS 2805.S, 1985)

To decrypt we again use IV:

(i) decrypt C1 to get IV $\oplus$ B1 then form (IV$\oplus$ B1) $\oplus$ IV = B1,

(ii) decrypt C2 to get C1 $\oplus$ B2 then form (C1 $\oplus$ B2) $\oplus$ C1 = B2,

.

.

.

(n) decrypt Cn to get Cn-1 $\oplus$ Bn then form (Cn-1 $\oplus$ Bn) $\oplus$ Cn-1 = Bn.

This method has a crucial deficiency in that errors anywhere in the chain are propagated throughout the chain.

## 3.2.5  A 'C' version of DES (DEA)

For those of you who have studied the programming language 'C' we give a software implementation of DES written by Laurie Brown at the University College, Australian Defence Force Academy, University of New South Wales' Pyramid 90X in Appendix B.1
In Appendix B.2 we give data on weak keys for the users guidance.

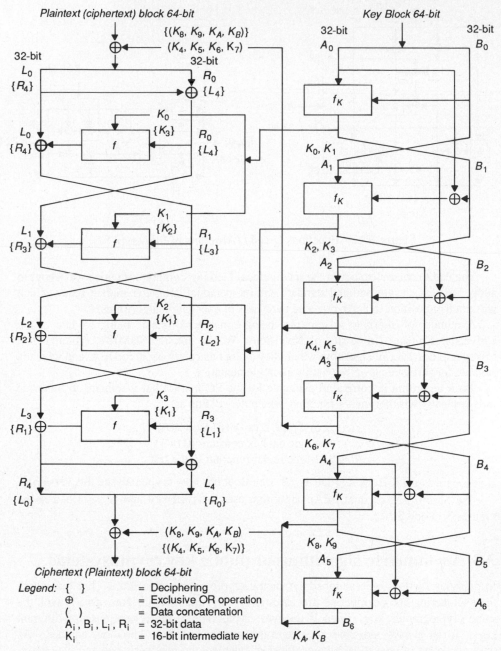

**Figure 3.11** FEAL algorithm (Abstracts of Eurocrypt 87)

## 3.2.6 The Fast Data Encipherment Algorithm (FEAL).

In the middle of 1986 the National Security Agency of the United States of America announced it would no longer certify the DEA algorithm for non-classified security use.

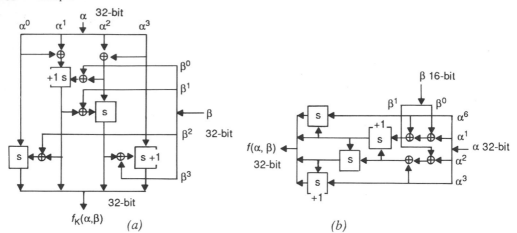

**Figure 3.12**   Functions $f_K$ and $f$ (Abstracts of Eurocrypt 87)

This led to some disquiet in the international banking community which was about to adopt DEA as an international standard and the personal computer market sector which was not in a position to make repeated purchases of encryption algorithms.

A number of alternate systems are being considered, one is being studied at the University College, University of New South Wales, and in [SHMI87], Shimizu and Miyaguchi describe an algorithm which they claim has safety equal to DEA, and which is suitable for software as well as hardware implementation.

Their algorithm is particularly suitable for the PC market but it remains to be tested independently whether their s-function, which they define as,

$$s(x, y, \delta) = ROL\,2((x+y+\delta) \bmod 256)$$
$$x, y: \text{one byte data}; \delta: \text{constant (0 or 1)}$$
$$ROL\,2: \text{2-bit circular function to the left}$$

is as secure as the S-BOX's of DEA.  (B. Den Boer has now cryptanalysed this version.)

The Shimizu-Miyaguchi FEAL algorithm uses a 64 bit key and is described in the Figures 3.11 and 3.12.

## 3.3  Asymmetric algorithms or public key cryptosystems

In previous sections we examined symmetric cryptographic algorithms.  For these both the enciphering and deciphering processes run using suitable algorithms usually with the same cryptographic key.  Even if the two cryptographic transformations use different keys, it is always possible to determine easily one key knowing another.  As the knowledge of the sender's key suffices to calculate the receiver's one and vice versa, both keys must be kept secret.  In other words, symmetric algorithms (symmetric cryptosystems) do not ensure protection if there is a high probability of the sender's key being disclosed.

Imagine that an ambassador is representing his government in an enemy state.  He/she knows that all communication means — mail, telephone lines, radio channels, messengers, etc. — are under the enemy's control, but he/she wants to use them to communicate with the government whose interests he/she represents. Moreover, he/she is sure that there is a spy among the embassy staff and all secret cryptographic keys prepared in advance, either have been, or will be, compromized so he/she cannot use them. Is it possible to arrange a secure communication channel between the ambassador and his/her government using accessible insecure channels? The answer to the question is *yes*.

In the next section, we are going to examine the idea of asymmetric algorithms which constitute the general solution to the question given above. Later on, we will describe several, selected, practical cryptographic asymmetric schemes. In particular, we shall consider three of the earliest asymmetric algorithms, namely the system invented by Rivest, Shamir and Adleman, the system designed by Merkle and Hellman, and the system proposed by McEliece.

## 3.3.1 General description of asymmetric algorithms

The solution to our question was first formulated by Diffie and Hellman [DIHE76a]. They defined an asymmetric cryptosystem (they called it a public key cryptosystem) and specified conditions which must be fulfilled. An asymmetric cryptosystem is depicted in Figure 3.13. Unlike the symmetric cryptosystem, the asymmetric one applies two different keys. The sender's key $K_B$ is public, but the receiver's key $k_B$ is secret. If the receiver's key is secret, the key generator must remain at the receiver's end. In general, the pair of keys used depends upon the initial condition of the generator. The disclosure of the secret receiver's key and/or the initial condition compromises the system.

Obviously, the public key has to differ from the secret one. Discovering the secret key, given the public one, should constitute an intractable numerical problem. Therefore, following Simmons [SIMM79b], we prefer to use the name[1] *asymmetric cryptosystems* (or *asymmetric algorithms*) instead of *public-key cryptosystems* (or *public-key algorithms*). We note there is a fine distinction in meaning between a cryptosystem and a cryptographic algorithm. Although their meanings are somewhat similar, and in many situations they may be used synonymously, their precise definitions are different. A cryptosystem is considered to be the collection of enciphering and deciphering systems, and the key generator along with the protocols for of key transmission. On the other hand, a cryptographic algorithm is defined to be the mathematical description of the enciphering and deciphering processes together with the interrelation between the enciphering and deciphering keys. Cryptosystem has a more hardware flavour, while cryptographic algorithm is more software oriented.

The characteristic feature of asymmetric cryptosystems is that both the public key and the cryptogram may be sent via insecure communication channels so the opponent knows both the cryptogram and the public key — see Figure 3.13. Furthermore, we assume that both the enciphering and the deciphering algorithms,

$$E_{B:}\ M \to C$$
$$D_{B:}\ C \to M$$

---

1. Nevertheless, later on we are going to use both names as synonyms.

are publicly known. These assumptions results from practical protection requirements. If we relied for protection upon keeping the algorithm secret, any disclosure of the algorithm would lead to the necessity to redesign the algorithm used. This is time-consuming and inefficient. In practice, however, protection relies on secrecy of cryptographic keys. Thus, after the protection of the cryptosystem has been broken, it can easily be re-established by replacing the broken key with a new one.

There are several conditions which have to be fulfilled so that an asymmetric cryptosystem can work properly. They were first formulated by Diffie and Hellman [DIHE76a], and they are given below as follows (see Figure 3.13):

Condition 1:    Calculation of the pair (the public key $K_B$, the secret key $k_B$) on the basis of the initial condition should be easy, that is, it can be done by the receiver $B$ in polynomial time.

Condition 2:    The sender $A$, knowing the public key $K_B$ and his/her message $M$, can easily determine the suitable cryptogram,

$$C = E_{K_B}(M) = E_B(M),  \tag{3.1}$$

That is, in polynomial time.

Condition 3:    The receiver $B$, using the cryptogram $C$ and his/her secret key $k_B$, can recreate the original form of $M$,

$$M = D_{k_B}(C) = D_B(C) = D_B[E_B(M)]  \tag{3.2}$$

in polynomial time.

Condition 4:    If the opponent, knowing the public key $K_B$, tries to compute the secret key and/or the initial condition, then he/she faces an instance of an intractable numerical problem, that is, solution of the instance requires so many steps that it is infeasible.

Condition 5:    If the opponent, knowing the pair $(K_B, C)$, searches for the message $M$, then he/she also faces an instance of a suitable problem which must be intractable for all instances.

In practice, the designer of asymmetric algorithms (asymmetric cryptosystems) faces five different numerical problems. The first three — corresponding to Condition 1, Condition 2, Condition 3 — must belong to the class **P**. The next two problems (see Condition 4 and Condition 5) must not belong to **P**. It means that they must belong to either the class **NPC** or **NPI**. It is very important to understand that the Conditions 4 and 5 are far more strict than the requirement that suitable problems are to be in **NPC** or **NPI**. It is known that a problem belongs to the class **NPC** if there is at least one instance of the problem which is not solvable in polynomial time. The Conditions 4 and 5 require that any instance which can appear during the enciphering process must be intractable!

Assume that problems corresponding to the Conditions 4 and 5 are solvable using suitable algorithms. Both algorithms are described by their time complexity functions.[2] Conditions 4 and 5 also require that input lengths of instances of both problems have to

---

2. Recall that the time complexity function gives the maximum number of steps required to solve each possible instance of the given input length (the input size).

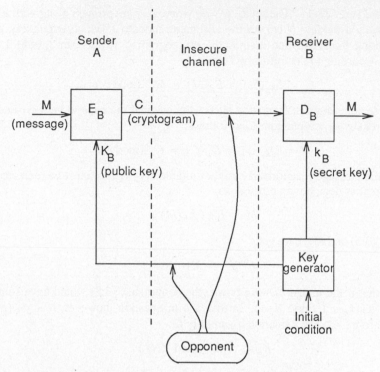

**Figure 3.13** A schematic for an asymmetric cryptosystem

have certain values for which the time complexity functions of both algorithms (these algorithms solve instances of the numerical problems given in Condition 4 and Condition 5) exceed a given bound. This bound cannot be evaluated precisely as it reflects the current progress in the computer industry. Sometimes, we can accept the number $10^{23}$ as a safe bound imposed on the time complexity functions. On the other hand, Hellman [HELL80a] has suggested choosing $10^{40}$ as an absolute safe bound.

Now consider the conditions Condition 2 and Condition 5. They define so-called one-way functions. This means that the enciphering transformation $E_B(M)$ should be one-way, i.e., computation of the cryptogram $C$, knowing the pair $(K_B, M)$, is easy but calculation of the message $M$, provided the pair $(C, K_B)$ is given, is intractable,

$$( K_B, M ) \to^{easy} \to C \tag{3.3}$$
$$( K_B, C ) \to^{hard} \to M \tag{3.4}$$

We now describe some practical asymmetric algorithms.

## 3.3.2 Rivest-Shamir-Adleman cryptosystem

The RSA system was invented by Rivest, Shamir, and Adleman [RISH78]. It is defined applying two numerical problems, namely the discrete logarithm problem and the factorization problem. A description of both problems can be found in Chapter 2. In the RSA system, messages, cryptograms and keys (public and secret) belong to the set of integers $Z_N = \{1, \ldots, N-1\}$. The set $Z_N$ ($N=pq$ where $p$, $q$ are primes) along with addition and multiplication modulo $N$ creates the arithmetic modulo $N$ which is publicly known. The enciphering transformation assigns the cryptogram $C$ to the pair (public key $K_B$, message $M$) according to the following formula:

$$C = E_{K_B}(M) = E_B(M) = M^{K_B}(\text{mod } N) \tag{3.5}$$

In turn, the deciphering transformation allows the original message to be recreated using the pair, secret key $k_B$, cryptogram $C$, as follows:

$$M = D_{k_B}(C) = D_B(C) = C^{k_B}(\text{mod } N) \tag{3.6}$$

Obviously, the message transformed into the suitable cryptogram must be recreated in its original form after deciphering process, so,

$$M = D_B(E_B(M)) \tag{3.7}$$

Substituting (3.5) and (3.6), we get:

$$(M^{K_B})^{k_B} = M(\text{mod } N) \tag{3.8}$$

It is known that if the integer $N$ were prime, the congruence (3.8) would have solution if and only if, $K_B\, k_B \equiv 1 \pmod{N-1}$. In the case in question, however, $N = pq$ ($p$, $q$ are primes) therefore (3.8) has a solution if and only if,

$$K_B\, k_B \equiv 1 \pmod{\gamma(N)} \tag{3.9}$$

where $\gamma(N) = lcm\ (p-1, q-1)$ and $lcm$ stands for the least common multiple. In other words, the receiver $B$ selects the public key $K_B$ at random while the secret key $k_B$ is calculated by him/her using (3.9). This is possible as $B$ knows the pair $(p, q)$ and can easily compute $\gamma(N)$.

Justification of the congruence (3.9) is as follows. It is known (see Chapter 2) that, in any arithmetic modulo $p$ ($p$ is prime), each element $a \in Z_p$ raised to the power $p-1$ gives 1, that is,

$$a^{p-1} = 1\ (\text{mod } p) \tag{3.10}$$

Of course, in arithmetic modulo $N=pq$ ($p$, $q$ are prime), the situation is different. If we take advantage of the Chinese Remainder Theorem, each element $a \in Z_N$ can be uniquely presented as the vector,

$$a\ (\text{mod } N) = [\,a\ (\text{mod } p),\ a\ (\text{mod } q)\,] \tag{3.11}$$

and $a^\alpha = 1 \pmod{N}$ if and only if $a^\alpha \equiv 1 \pmod{p}$ and $a^\alpha \equiv 1 \pmod{q}$. Using (3.10), we conclude that $\alpha = lcm(p-1, q-1)$ as the congruences are fulfilled simultaneously.

To find the pair of keys, the receiver, knowing the factorization of $N$, can use the extented Euclidean algorithm. We briefly reiterate the technique — see Chapter 2. To find the greatest common divisor of integers $a$ and $b$, set,

$$s_{-1} = 1,\ t_{-1} = 0,\ r_{-1} = a$$
$$s_0 = 0,\ t_0 = 1,\ r_0 = b$$

and recursively compute,

$$s_i = s_{i-2} - q_{i-1}s_{i-1}$$
$$t_i = t_{i-2} - q_{i-1}t_{i-1}$$
$$r_i = r_{i-2} - q_{i-1}r_{i-1} \qquad (3.12)$$

where $q_{i-1} = \lfloor \dfrac{r_{i-2}}{r_{i-1}} \rfloor$. Clearly, the $r_i$ form the remainder sequence for the *gcd* computation. The last non-zero remainder is the *gcd*. Now,

$$s_i r_{-1} + t_i r_0 = r_i \quad \text{for } i = 0, 1, \ldots \qquad (3.13)$$

This follows by induction since,

$$r_{i+1} = r_{i-1} - q_i r_i = s_{i-1}r_{i-1} + t_{i-1}r_0 - q_i(s_i r_{-1} + t_i r_0)$$
$$= (s_{i-1} - q_i s_i)r_{-1} + (t_{i-1} - q_i t_i)r_0 = s_{i+1}r_{-1} + t_{i+1}r_0$$

In other words, given $K_B$ and $\gamma(N)$, the receiver computes $gcd(K_B, \gamma(N))$. If $r_{i+1}=1$, he/she gets,

$$s_{i+1}K_B + t_{i+1}\gamma(N) = r_{i+1} = 1$$

So the second key is equal to $k_B = s_{i+1}$.

*Example*

Assume $K_B$ has been selected at random and is equal to 21 while $\gamma(N)=34$. To find the secret key $k_B$, we follow the algorithm,

$$s_{-1}, t_{-1}, r_{-1} \rightarrow 1, 0, 34 = \gamma(N)$$
$$s_0, t_0, r_0 \rightarrow 0, 1, 21 =, K_B$$
$$s_1, t_1, r_1 \rightarrow 1, -1, 13$$
$$s_2, t_2, r_2 \rightarrow -1, 2, 8$$
$$s_3, t_3, r_3 \rightarrow 2, -3, 5$$
$$s_4, t_4, r_4 \rightarrow -3, 5, 3$$
$$s_5, t_5, r_5 \rightarrow 5, -8, 2$$
$$s_6, t_6, r_6 \rightarrow -8, 13, 1$$

The last row generates the following equation:

$$(-8)(34) + (13)(21) = 1$$

and it can be rewritten as:

$$(13)(21) = 1 \ (\text{mod } 34)$$

The second key $k_B$ is equal to 13. □

Summing up, we observe that the receiver $B$, who creates the system, protects both:

- the secret key $k_B$; and
- the pair $(p, q)$ whose product gives $N$.

On the other hand, $B$ publishes :

- the integer $N$; and
- the public key $K_B$.

The enciphering and deciphering processes are illustrated in the example given below.

*Example*

Assume that the receiver $B$ intends to create his/her cryptosystem. First of all, $B$ selects the initial condition, that is, integers $p=5$ and $q=7$. Next, he/she calculates $\gamma(N) = lcm$ (4, 6) = 12, and randomly selects the public key $K_B$ = 17. Subsequently, $B$ finds the secret key by solving the congruence (3.9), so,

$$17\, k_B = 1(\bmod\ 12) \Rightarrow k_B = 5$$

The pair $(N=35,\ K_B=17)$ is sent to the sender via an insecure channel. If the sender now wants to transmit the message $M=33$, he/she calculates the suitable cryptogram,

$$C = M^{K_B} = 33^{17} = 3\ (\bmod\ 35)$$

and forwards it to the receiver. Having $C$ and the secret key $k_B$, $B$ recreates the message according to the following congruence:

$$M = C^{k_B} = 3^5 = 33\ (\bmod\ 35) \qquad\qquad \square$$

**Security of the RSA algorithm**

Consider an opponent who knows the modulus $N$ and the public key $K_B$ and intends to recreate the clear message from the cryptogram $C$. To carry out his/her plan, he/she may apply two attacks on the system.

The first relies on factorization of the modulus $N$. After the opponent has found primes $p$ and $q$, he/she can calculate $\gamma(N)$ and the secret key $k_B$. A careful reader may ask why the modulus $N$ is the product of two primes only. Notice that if $N$ is the product of two primes, the simple factoring algorithm needs at most $\sqrt{N}$ steps as there is a prime that is less than $\sqrt{N}$. On the other hand, if $N$ is the product of $n$ primes, the simple factoring algorithm needs at most $N^{1/n}$ steps. A more sophisticated factoring algorithm, which behaves similarly, has been worked out by Pollard [POLL75]. It allows factorization of an integer $N$ in $O(\sqrt{p})$ steps, where $p$ is the least divisor of $N$. Choosing two primes only makes Pollard's algorithm ineffective.

The second attack on the RSA system may be launched by solving a suitable instance of the discrete logarithm problem. The instance is determined by the pair $(K_B,\ C)$. Both attacks need the same number of elementary steps, namely,

$$O\ (\ \exp \sqrt{\ln N\ \ln(\ln N)}\ ) \qquad\qquad (3.14)$$

where $N$ is the modulus. For instance, if $N$ is 200-bits long, both the factoring algorithm and the discrete logarithm algorithm need $2.7\times10^{11}$ steps. However, if $N$ is 664-bits long, both algorithms need $1.2\times10^{23}$ steps [DENN82].

While at first it seems that there are only two possible kinds of attack on the system, this is not true. Simmons and Norris [SINO77] have shown that the RSA system may be compromised using their iteration attack. They have observed that the opponent, knowing the triple $(N,\ K_B,\ C)$, may generate the following sequence:

$$C_1 = C^{K_B}\ (\bmod\ N)$$

$$\vdots$$

$$C_i = C_{i-1}^{K_B} \ (\text{mod} \, N)$$     (3.15)

$$\vdots$$

If there is an element $C_j$ in the sequence $C_1, \ \ldots \ , C_i, \ \ldots$ such that:

$$C = C_j$$     (3.16)

then the message the opponent is looking for is $C_{j-1}$, i.e. $M = C_{j-1}$ as $C_{j-1}^{K_B} = C_j = C$. Clearly, such a cryptogram must always exist but the integer $j$ (for which $C_j = C$) should be large enough that the iteration attack is intractable.

Rivest [RIVE78] showed that if integers $(p-1)$ and $(q-1)$ contain large primes as factors (for instance $p-1=2p'$ and $q-1=2q'$, where $p'$, $q'$ are primes), then the probability of successful iteration attack is close to zero for large $N$. For example, if $p'$ and $q'$ are $\geq 10^{90}$, then for $0 \leq M \leq N\text{-}1$, the probability of successful iteration attack is close to $10^{-90}$.

The iteration attack is illustrated below.

*Example*

Consider our previous example and assume that the opponent knows the triple $(N, K_B, C)$ = (35, 17, 3). In the iteration attack, he/she calculates,

$$C_1 = C^{K_B} \ (\text{mod} \, N) = 3^{17} = 33 \ (\text{mod} \, 35)$$

$$C_2 = C_1^{K_B} \ (\text{mod} \, N) = 33^{17} = 3 \ (\text{mod} \, 35)$$

As $C_2 = C = 3 \ (\text{mod} \, 35)$, the message $M = C_1 = 33 \ (\text{mod} \, 35)$. □

**Concealment of messages in the RSA system**

The RSA system has a characteristic feature, pointed out by Blakley and Borosh [BLBO79], that it does not always hide the message. Assume that the sender has the public key $K_B = 17$ and the modulus $N = 35$. If he/she intends to send any message from the following set:

$$\{ \ 1, 6, 7, 8, 13, 14, 15, 20, 21, 22, 27, 28, 29, 34 \ \}$$

then all cryptograms are equal to the original messages, that is $6^{17} = 6 \ (\text{mod} \, 35)$, $7^{17} = 7 \ (\text{mod} \, 35)$, and so on. A far more dramatic situation appears when $p = 97$, $q = 109$, and $K_B = 865$. We then find that this cryptosystem provides no concealment, since $M^{865} = M \ (\text{mod} \, 97 \times 109)$ for all $M$. Changing the public key to 169 provides concealment of about 96 percent of all possible messages [BLBO79].

Observe that any arithmetic modulo $N = pq$ ($p$, $q$ are primes) always comprises at least nine messages which when raised to a positive odd integer $K_B$ do not change their form, that is,

$$M^{K_B} = M \ (\text{mod} \, N)$$     (3.17)

As $N = pq$, (3.17) can be rewritten as a pair of congruences as follows:

$$M^{K_B} = M \ (\bmod \ p)$$
$$M^{K_B} = M \ (\bmod \ q) \qquad\qquad (3.18)$$

For any $K_B$, both the congruences (3.18) have at least three solutions which yield the set $\{0,1,-1\}$. That is three integers in $Z_p$ yield the set for the first congruence, and three integers in $Z_q$ yield the set for the second congruence. The set of all messages which satisfy (3.17) is equal to,

$$\{M = [M \ (\bmod \ p), \ M \ (\bmod \ q)] \mid M \ (\bmod \ p), M \ (\bmod \ q) \in \{0,1,-1\} \} \qquad (3.19)$$

Elements of the set (3.19) can easily be presented as integers of $Z_N$ using the Chinese Remainder Theorem.

*Example*

Consider arithmetic modulo $N = 35$ ($p = 5$, $q = 7$). The congruence $M^{K_B} = M \ (\bmod \ 5)$ has three solutions, 0, 1, 4. The second congruence $M^{K_B} = M \ (\bmod \ 7)$ has also three solutions, 0, 1, 6. The set of all messages which are not altered is:

$$0 = [0 \ (\bmod \ 5), \ 0 \ (\bmod \ 7)]$$
$$1 = [1 \ (\bmod \ 5), \ 1 \ (\bmod \ 7)]$$
$$-1 = [-1 \ (\bmod \ 5), \ -1 \ (\bmod \ 7)]$$
$$15 = [0 \ (\bmod \ 5), \ 1 \ (\bmod \ 7)]$$
$$21 = [1 \ (\bmod \ 5), \ 0 \ (\bmod \ 7)]$$
$$20 = [0 \ (\bmod \ 5), \ -1 \ (\bmod \ 7)]$$
$$14 = [-1 \ (\bmod \ 5), \ 0 \ (\bmod \ 7)]$$
$$29 = [-1 \ (\bmod \ 5), \ 1 \ (\bmod \ 7)]$$
$$9 = [1 \ (\bmod \ 5), \ -1 \ (\bmod \ 7)]$$

$\square$

The exact number of unconcealable messages is given in the following theorem.

**Theorem:** *If messages are encrypted using the* RSA *system, determined for the modulus $N = pq$ (p, q are primes), and the public key $K_B$, then there are:*

$$\sigma_u = [1 + gcd(K_B-1, p-1)][1 + gcd(K_B-1, q-1)] \qquad (3.20)$$

*messages which are unconcealable.*

**Proof:** A message is unconcealable if and only if $M^{K_B} = M \ (\bmod \ N)$. The congruence is equivalent to the pair,

$$M^{K_B} = M \ (\bmod \ p)$$
$$M^{K_B} = M \ (\bmod \ q)$$

These can be rewritten as:

$$M^{K_B-1} = 1 \ (\bmod \ p) \quad or \quad M^{K_B-1} = 0 \ (\bmod \ p)$$
$$M^{K_B-1} = 1 \ (\bmod \ q) \quad or \quad M^{K_B-1} = 0 \ (\bmod \ q)$$

As the congruence $M^{K_B-1} = 1 \ (\bmod \ p)$ has $gcd(K_B-1, \ p-1)$ solutions, the result follows.

$\square$

*Example*

Let $p = 5$, $q = 7$ ($N = 35$). Consider the following cases:

If $K_B = 2$, then $\sigma_u = 4$ and the unconcealed messages are { 0, 1, 15, 21 }

If $K_B = 3$, then $\sigma_u = 9$ and the set of unconcealable messages is:

$$\{ 0, 1, 6, 14, 15, 20, 21, 29, 34 \}$$

If $K_B = 5$, then $\sigma_u = 15$ and the required set is:

$$\{ 0, 1, 6, 7, 8, 13, 14, 15, 20, 21, 22, 27, 28, 29, 34 \}$$

If $K_B = 7$, then $\sigma_u = 21$ and the required set is:

$$\{ 0, 1, 4, 5, 6, 9, 10, 11, 14, 15, 16, 19, 20, 21, 24, 25, 26, 29, 30, 31, 34 \}$$

We note that the intersection of all these sets is $\{0, 1, 15, 21\}$. This set contains idempotent elements only (recall that an element $x \in Z_N$ is idempotent if and only if $x^2 \equiv x$ (mod $N$)).    □

Thus the following general observations can be made:

- There are four unconcealable messages if $gcd(K_B-1, p-1) = gcd(K_B-1, q-1) = 1$
- There are nine unconcealable messages if $gcd(K_B-1, p-1) = gcd(K_B-1, q-1) = 2$
- If $K_B = 3$ (mod $\gamma(N)$), then $gcd(2, p-1) = gcd(2, q-1) = 2$, and the number $\sigma_u$ is equal to 9 regardless of the choice $p$ and $q$.

Observe that if the public key is selected carelessly, the congruence (3.17) may be valid for more than 50 percent of message space. As the receiver does not know the sender's messages in advance, he/she has to avoid keys which do not generate real cryptograms. The situation becomes worse once we realize that the opponent can easily discover such a lack of protection. It suffices that he/she applies the iteration attack. If we assume that :

$$\begin{aligned} p &= 2p' + 1 \\ q &= 2q' + 1 \end{aligned}$$    (3.21)

where $p'$, $q'$ are primes, then $gcd(K_B-1, p-1) = gcd(K_B-1, 2p')$ can take on three values, namely 1, 2, and $p'$. When $gcd(K_B-1, 2p')$ is equal 1 or 2, there are four or nine unconcealable messages, respectively. However, when $gcd(K_B-1, 2p') = p'$, there are at least $2(p'+1)$ unconcealable messages. Fortunately, the probability of the last case is approximately $1/p$.

Obviously, the selection of both the primes $p$ and $q$ which create the initial condition is crucial for the security of the RSA system. Thus we observe that both primes should be of about the same length (both should be expressible using about 100-digit decimal integers) and they ought to be selected at random. Simultaneously, the following conditions should be fulfilled:

- The integers $p-1$, $q-1$ should contain large factors.
- The greatest common divisor of $p-1$ and $q-1$ should be a small number.

In practical implementations of the RSA algorithm, the receiver faces the problem of testing if a randomly selected integer is prime. There are, of course, several primality testing algorithms which will to be examined in a later section.

**Cryptosystems with public key distribution**

Diffie and Hellman [DIHE76a] invented a cryptosystem (DH system) which is defined using the discrete logarithm problem only. It is similar to the RSA cryptosystem as it uses the same encryption and decryption algorithms. However, the Diffie and Hellman system is not an asymmetric cryptosystem as it does not satisfy the definition given in section 3.3.1. But, at the same time, it does not belong to the class of symmetric cryptosystems, although knowledge of the enciphering key does allow the deciphering one to be calculated, and vice versa.

Assume two parties $A$ and $B$ want to establish a secure communication channel. Both sides agree in advance upon the modulus $N$ (in this case $N$ is prime), and a primitive element, $g \in Z_N$, which generates all the nonzero elements of $Z_N$, i.e., $\{g, g^2, \ldots, g^{N-1}=1\} = Z_N-\{0\}$. Both $N$ and $g$ are public. Next, $A$ and $B$ independently select their own secret keys $k_A$ and $k_B$, respectively (see Figure 3.14). $A$ calculates $y_A=g^{k_A}$ (mod $N$) but $B$ uses $y_B=g^{k_B}$ (mod $N$). The parties $A$ and $B$ exchange their partial keys, $y_A$ and $y_B$, and they then compute a common secret key $K$ using the following congruences:

$$K = (y_B)^{k_A} = (g^{k_B})^{k_A} \pmod N \qquad (3.22)$$
$$K = (y_A)^{k_B} = (g^{k_A})^{k_B} \pmod N \qquad (3.23)$$

Clearly, $A$ applies the congruence (3.22) while $B$ uses (3.23).

Both parties $A$ and $B$ can encrypt messages using the folowing encryption transformation,

$$C = E_K(M) = M^K \pmod N \qquad (3.24)$$

In order to decrypt, the receiver first finds the deciphering key $K'$ via the congruence,

$$K \cdot K' = 1 \ (\text{mod } \gamma(N)) = 1 \ (\text{mod } N-1) \qquad (3.25)$$

and then calculates the message,

$$M = D_K(C) = C^{K'} \pmod N \qquad (3.26)$$

We illustrate the Diffie-Hellman system in the example given below.

*Example*

Assume the modulus $N=47$ and the primitive element $g=23$. Suppose that $A$ and $B$ have selected their secret keys $k_A=12$ (mod 47) and $k_B=33$ (mod 47). In order to fix the common secret key $K$, they calculate their partial keys:

$$y_A = g^{k_A} = 23^{12} = 27 \ (\text{mod } 47)$$
$$y_B = g^{k_B} = 23^{33} = 33 \ (\text{mod } 47)$$

After they exchange their partial keys, $A$ and $B$ compute the common secret key,

$$K = (y_B)^{k_A} = (y_A)^{k_B} = 27^{33} = 25 (\text{mod } 47)$$

They also find the secret deciphering key $K'$ using the following congruence:

$$KK' = 1(\text{mod } N-1) \rightarrow K' = 35(\text{mod } 46)$$

Now, if the message is $M=16$, then the cryptogram is:

$$C = M^K = 16^{25} = 21 \ (\text{mod } 47)$$

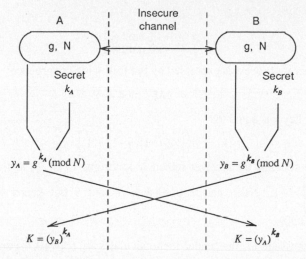

**Figure 3.14** A model for key information using exponentiation

The receiver recreates the message as follows:

$$M = C^{K'} = 21^{35} = 16 \ (\mathrm{mod}\ 47) \qquad \Box$$

We note that $A$ and $B$ share the same secret key which has been generated using partial keys $k_A$ and $k_B$. Of course, an opponent having access to the channel knows the partial keys, but recreation of any secret key is equivalent to solving an instance of the discrete logarithm problem. As both the enciphering and deciphering keys are no longer public, the modulus $N$ does not need to be composite.

**Modifications of the RSA cryptosystem**
Rabin [RABI79] suggested producing cryptograms using the fixed public key $K = 2$, and then,

$$C = M^2 \ (\mathrm{mod}\ N) \qquad\qquad (3.27)$$

where $N$ as before is the product of two primes $p$ and $q$. The legitimate receiver, who knows the proper factorizing of $N$, can decrypt by solving two suitable congruences, the first in $Z_p$ and the second in $Z_q$ using the Chinese Remainder Theorem. However Rabin's cryptosystem has the drawback that its encryption transformation is not one-to-one for all messages — there is 4:1 ambiguity in the decrypted message.

Williams [WILL80] showed how to redefine Rabin's scheme to remove most shortcomings. He has proved that the decryption process can be simplified for all messages $M$ whose Jacobi symbol[3] is $\left[\dfrac{M}{N}\right] = 1$ where primes are selected in such a way

---

3. Recall the Jacobi symbol $\left[\dfrac{a}{b}\right]$ is defined by $\left[\dfrac{a}{b}\right] = \left[\dfrac{a}{b_1}\right] \ \ldots \ \left[\dfrac{a}{b_n}\right]$, where $b = b_1 \ \ldots \ b_n$ is decomposition of $b$ into primes, $\left[\dfrac{a}{b_i}\right] = a^{\frac{1}{2}(b_i - 1)} \ (\mathrm{mod}\ b_i)$ is the Legendre symbol for $i = 1, \ \ldots \ , n.$

that,

$$p = -1 \ (\text{mod } 4)$$
$$q = -1 \ (\text{mod } 4)$$
$$(3.28)$$

Then the deciphering process is expressed by the following congruence:

$$C^k = \pm M \ (\text{mod } N)$$
$$(3.29)$$

where the secret key $k$ is equal to:

$$k = \tfrac{1}{2} \left[ \tfrac{1}{4}(p-1)(q-1) + 1 \right]$$
$$(3.30)$$

In Williams' scheme, the receiver selects $N$ according to (3.28) and a small integer $S$ such that $\left[ \dfrac{S}{N} \right] = -1$. Next, he/she publishes $N$ and $S$ but keeps secret the key $k$ determined by (3.30).

For his/her message $M$, the sender then calculates $c_1$ ($c_1 \in \{0,1\}$) such that $\left[ \dfrac{M}{N} \right] = (-1)^{c_1}$ and creates the message,

$$M' = S^{c_1} \cdot M \ (\text{mod } N) \ ; \ M' \in Z_N$$
$$(3.31)$$

Finally, the cryptogram is computed for $M'$ according to (3.27), and the sender forwards the triple $(C, c_1, c_2)$, where $c_2 = M' \ (\text{mod } 2)$.

To recover the clear message, the receiver considers (3.29) and obtains $M_t = C^k \ (\text{mod } N)$. The proper sign of $M_t$ is given by $c_2$. It is easy to verify that the original message $M$ is equal to:

$$M = S^{-c_1}(-1)^{c_1} M_t \ (\text{mod } N) \ .$$
$$(3.32)$$

as the message $M'$ is even. The enciphering and deciphering processes described above are illustrated in the following example.

*Example*

Assume that the communicating parties have agreed to apply Williams scheme to create a secure channel. Suppose the receiver $B$ has selected $p = 7$, $q = 11$ (note $p = -1 \ (\text{mod } 4)$, and $q = -1 \ (\text{mod } 4)$). $B$ next chooses the small integer $S=2$ for which the Jacobi symbol is $\left[ \dfrac{S}{N} \right] = \left[ \dfrac{2}{77} \right] = -1$. The values ($N=77$, $S=2$) are sent to the sender $A$ while the key $k=8$ is kept secret.

If $A$ wishes to transmit the message $M=54$, he/she first calculates the Jacobi symbol $\left[ \dfrac{M}{N} \right] = \left[ \dfrac{2}{77} \right] = 1$. It implies that the binary number $c_1 = 0$. According to (3.31), the message $M'=M=54$, and the cryptogram $C$ is equal to:

$$C = M^2 = 54^2 = 67 \ (\text{mod } 77)$$

Finally, $A$ forwards the triple $(C, c_1, c_2) = (67, 0, 0)$, where $c_2 = 0$, as the message.
After obtaining the triple, $B$ computes:

$$M_t = C^k = 67^8 = 23 \; (\text{mod } 77)$$

As $c_2=0$, the message $M$ must be even so $M=N-M_t=54$.     □

Williams [WILL85] considered the cryptosystem for which the public key is fixed and equal to 3 ($K = 3$). He showed its construction and proved that it is as difficult to break as it is to factor $N$. Another modification of the basic RSA system for $K \equiv 3$ (*modulo* 18) has been presented by Khoo, Bird and Seberry [KHBI85] who recommend it should be used for those $K$ whose binary representation has many zeros. Their cryptosystem is defined in the ring $Z[\omega]$, where $\omega$ is a primitive cube root. They also showed that their system is as difficult to break as it is to factor $N$.

## Primality testing algorithms

An important difference between algorithms for primality testing and ones for factorization is that primality testing algorithms can tell if a given integer is composite or prime. Factoring algorithms, however, give the actual factors when the integer is composite. Needless to say primality testing algorithms must run in polynomial time in order for the receiver to find primes $p$ and $q$ effectively. Later we assume that the receiver has selected an integer $p$ and tries to determine if it is composite or prime.

Note that if $p$ is prime, then *Fermat's Little Theorem* asserts that

$$\beta^{p-1} = 1 \; (\text{mod } p); \quad \beta \neq 0 \qquad (3.33)$$

for all $\beta \in Z_p$. Unfortunately, the converse is not true. For each $\beta \neq 0$, there are infinitely many composite $p$ for which (3.33) holds. Such a composite $p$ is called *a pseudoprime* to the base $\beta$. For example each of the Fermat numbers $F_n = 2^{2^n}+1$ satisfies (3.33) but not all these are primes.

For a fixed $\beta > 1$, the observed number of pseudoprimes to a base $\beta$ is very small compared with the number of actual primes [POME81]. Thus, the rarity of pseudoprimes combined with the ease of checking (3.33) suggests that the congruence (3.33) can be used as a primality test provided we eliminate pseudoprimes. We use the test (3.33) for different values of $\beta$. But even then, there are composite $p$ which are pseudoprimes for every $\beta$ where $gcd(\beta, p) = 1$. These are the Carmichael Numbers [LEHM76]. In other words, we need a stronger primality test.

Before we pass to the next primality test, let us consider the following example. Assume that $p$ is prime and equals 13. Any non-zero element $g$ of $Z_p$ generates its cyclic group $CG(g)$. If $g = 7$, the corresponding group is:

$$
\begin{array}{lll}
7^1 = 7 & 7^5 = 11 & 7^9 = 8 \\
7^2 = 10 & 7^6 = 12 & 7^{10} = 4 \\
7^3 = 5 & 7^7 = 6 & 7^{11} = 2 \\
7^4 = 9 & 7^8 = 3 & 7^{12} = 1
\end{array}
$$

The integer $g = 7$ generates all the non-zero elements of $Z_{13}$, and as it produces 12 different integers, we say that $g$ is of order 12. Any integer $p-1$ can be presented as the product $p-1=2^\zeta \eta$, where $\eta$ is odd, and $\zeta \geq 1$. In our case, $p-1 = 12 = 2^2 \cdot 3$, so $\zeta = 2$ and $\eta = 3$. Note that if we take $g^\eta$, then elements,

$$g^\eta, \; g^{2\eta}, \; \ldots, \; g^{2^\zeta \eta}$$

create a subgroup of $CG(g)$. In the case in question, we have,

$$7^3 = 5$$
$$7^6 = 5^2 = 12 = -1$$
$$7^9 = 5^3 = 8$$
$$7^{12} = 5^4 = 1$$

In general, if we take an arbitrary element $x = g^r$, then,

$$x^\eta = g^{r\eta} = 1 \quad \text{for } r = 2^\zeta$$

or,

$$x^{2^i\eta} = g^{r2^i\eta} = -1$$

for some $i = 1, 2, \ldots , \zeta-1$, and the second element generates the two element group $\{-1, 1\}$.

Therefore, if $gcd(p, \beta)=1$ and either

$$\beta^\eta = 1 \ (\bmod\ p) \quad or \quad \beta^{2^i\eta} = -1 \ (\bmod\ p) \qquad (3.34)$$

for some $i=1, \ldots , \zeta-1$, where $p-1=2^\zeta\cdot\eta$, then $p$ passes the second test. When (3.33) and (3.34) hold for $p$, we say that $p$ passes the strong pseudoprime test for base $\beta$ and, if $p$ is composite, then $p$ is a strong pseudoprime for base $\beta$. This test was originally proposed by G.L. Miller [MILL75b] and subsequently discussed by H.C. Williams [WILL78].

The practical significance of the test (3.34) is stated in the theorem given below (see [RABI80]).

**Theorem:** *If $p$ is composite, then (3.34) fails for at least one quarter of the integers $\beta$, where $1 \le \beta \le p-1$.*

The theorem above shows that if $\beta$ is randomly chosen such that $1 \le \beta \le p-1$, then the probability that the composite $p$ will pass the strong pseudoprime test for the base $\beta$ is at most ¼. We now have the following probabilistic algorithm. Perform the strong pseudoprime tests on $p$ for randomly chosen $\beta$ such that $\beta = 1, \ldots , p-1$. If $p$ fails on any of the bases, then $p$ is composite. Of course, if $p$ is composite the algorithm will terminate after at most $n$ steps with probability at least $1-(¼)^n$. The algorithm runs for ever if $p$ is prime.

Recently, a new primality test has been invented that represents a major breakthrough in the field of primality testing [ADPO83]. The test considered by Adleman, Pomerance and Rumley extracts information from a series of pseudoprime tests and proves that $p$ is prime, if indeed it is. Pomerance and Odlyzko [ADPO83] showed that the running time to test the primality of $p$ is $O((\log p)^{\lambda \log \log \log p})$, where $\lambda$ is a suitable constant. Thus we have a nearly polynomial time primality testing algorithm. The algorithm has been programmed and reports say that proofs of primality of numbers with more than 200 digits have been provided in less than 10 minutes [LENS80, COLE84].

### 3.3.3 Knapsack cryptosystems

Now (see Chapter 2) the knapsack problem belongs to the class **NPC**. Thus this problem seems to be very attractive for cryptography. If we have two vectors $M = (m_1, \ldots , m_n)$

and $K = (K_1, \ldots , K_n)$, it is very easy to find their product $K \times M = \sum_{i=1}^{n} k_i m_i$. On the other hand, knowing the pair $(M \times K, K)$, it is difficult to recreate the vector $M$. Notice that any knapsack is linear. This means that $(M_1 + M_2) \times K = M_1 \times K + M_2 \times K$ for all $M_1$, $M_2$, $K$. Usually, this property is undesirable in cryptography, as any linearity can potentially produce a suitable scenario for attack on cryptographic systems.

## Merkle-Hellman cryptosystem

The first asymmetric cryptosystem based on the knapsack problem was invented by Merkle and Hellman [MEHE78]. The Merkle-Hellman cryptosystem (MH system) allows $n$-bit messages to be enciphered,

$$M = (m_1, m_2, \ldots , m_n) \tag{3.35}$$

where $m_i \in 0,1$ for $i = 1, \ldots , n$, using the public key $K$,

$$K = (k_1, k_2, \ldots , k_n) \tag{3.36}$$

where $k_i \in Z_q = \{1, 2, \ldots , q-1\}$ for $i = 1, \ldots , n$, and the integer $q$ is prime. Using the pair $(M, K)$, the sender $A$ creates the cryptogram $C$ according to the following formula:

$$C = \sum_{i=1}^{n} m_i k_i \tag{3.37}$$

The enciphering process is extremely simple for it runs in linear time. To continue the description, we now consider the receiver $B$ who always initiates the algorithm (the system).

The receiver first chooses the initial condition which is a sequence of superincreasing integers,

$$W = (w_1, w_2, \ldots , w_n) \tag{3.38}$$

where $w_i; i = 1, \ldots , n$, are integers which satisfy an inequality in the form,

$$w_i > \sum_{j=1}^{i-1} w_j \tag{3.39}$$

Note that the initial condition $W$ defines the instance of the easy knapsack problem which is solvable in linear time (see Chapter 2). Now the designer $B$ transforms the instance into an instance of the knapsack problem. To do this, $B$ first determines a suitable field $Z_q$ ($q$ must be prime) and a multiplier $r \in Z_q$. Both $q$ and $r$ are usually chosen at random provided that,

$$q > \sum_{i=1}^{n} w_i \tag{3.40}$$

Next, he/she injects the vector $W$ into the field $Z_q$ according to the following congruence:

$$k_i = w_i r \pmod{q}; \quad i = 1, \ldots , n \tag{3.41}$$

The vector $K = (k_1, \ldots , k_n)$ is sent to the sender $A$ via an insecure channel while the triple (the initial condition $W$, the integer $r$, the modulus $q$) is kept secret by the receiver.

Assume now that the receiver $A$ has obtained the cryptogram generated using (3.37). First of all, $B$ transforms the cryptogram as follows:

$$C' = C\,r^{-1} \pmod{q} \tag{3.42}$$

From (3.37) and (3.41), we have:

$$C' = C\,r^{-1} = \sum_{i=1}^{n} k_i\, m_i\, r^{-1} = \sum_{i=1}^{n} w_i\, m_i \pmod{q} \tag{3.43}$$

As $w_i$ fulfills (3.39), the receiver easily finds components $m_i$ of the message $M$.

*Example*

To illustrate the Merkle-Hellman system, assume that 5-bit messages are to be transmitted. The receiver initiates the algorithm by choosing the vector,

$$W = (w_1, w_2, w_3, w_4, w_5) = (2, 3, 6, 12, 25)$$

Note that:

$$w_2 > w_1$$
$$w_3 > w_1 + w_2$$
$$w_4 > w_1 + w_2 + w_3$$

and,

$$w_5 > w_1 + w_2 + w_3 + w_4$$

Next he/she chooses the pair $(r, q)$ at random provided that $q$ is prime and $q > \sum_{i=1}^{5} w_i = 48$.

Let $q=53$ and $r=46$. It is easy to check that $r^{-1}=15 \pmod{53}$. Subsequently, the receiver calculates the public key using (3.41), namely,

$$k_1 = w_1 r \pmod{q} = 39 \pmod{53}$$
$$k_2 = w_2 r \pmod{q} = 32 \pmod{53}$$
$$k_3 = w_3 r \pmod{q} = 11 \pmod{53}$$
$$k_4 = w_4 r \pmod{q} = 22 \pmod{53}$$
$$k_5 = w_5 r \pmod{q} = 37 \pmod{53}$$

So, the public key $K = (k_1, k_2, k_3, k_4, k_5) = (39,32,11,22,37)$ is sent to the sender. Suppose now that the receiver has obtained the cryptogram $C=119$. To decrypt it, he/she first transforms it as follows:

$$C' = Cr^{-1} = 119 \cdot 15 = 36 \pmod{53}$$

and next solves the simple knapsack problem:

$$\text{as } C' = 36 > w_5 = 25 \Rightarrow m_5 = 1,$$
$$\text{as } C' - w_5 = 11 < w_4 \Rightarrow m_4 = 0,$$
$$\text{as } C' - w_5 = 11 > w_3 = 6 \Rightarrow m_3 = 1,$$
$$\text{as } C' - w_5 - w_3 = 5 > w_2 = 3 \Rightarrow m_2 = 1,$$
$$\text{as } C' - w_5 - w_3 - w_2 = 2 = w_1 \Rightarrow m_1 = 1.$$

In other words, the receiver has recreated the message $M = (1,1,1,0,1)$.     □

Shamir and Zippel [SHZI78] showed that, if the modulus $q$ is compromized, the multiplier $r$ can be readily calculated from the public key $K$. The obvious remedy is multiple applications of the initial condition in several different fields, that is, $W$ is injected into $Z_{q_1}$, $Z_{q_2}$, ... using multipliers $r_1$, $r_2$, ... , and primes $q_i$ satisfying the inequality $q_1 < q_2 < \ldots$ . The resulting cryptosystem is called the multiply iterated knapsack system.

### Cryptosystem based on idempotent elements

There are many modifications of the Merkle-Hellman system. We consider one of them described in [PIEP85]. In this modification called the IE system, the simple knapsack is defined differently using idempotent elements. As before the system encrypts $n$-bit messages. The initial condition, however, consists of $n$ different primes $p_1$, ... , $p_n$. If we accept that $N = p_1 \ldots p_n$, then the set $Z_N = \{1, \ldots, N-1\}$, along with addition and multiplication modulo $N$ defines a suitable arithmetic. The Chinese Remainder Theorem says that any integer $a \in Z_N$ can be uniquely presented in the form of the vector:

$$[a_1, \ldots, a_n] = [a \ (\mathrm{mod}\ p_1), \ldots, a \ (\mathrm{mod}\ p_n)]$$

Now there are $n$ elementary idempotent elements of the following form:

$$
\begin{aligned}
e_1 &= [1 \ (\mathrm{mod}\ p_1), 0 \ (\mathrm{mod}\ p_2), \ldots, 0 \ (\mathrm{mod}\ p_n)] = [1,0,\ldots,0] \\
e_2 &= [0 \ (\mathrm{mod}\ p_1), 1 \ (\mathrm{mod}\ p_2), \ldots, 0 \ (\mathrm{mod}\ p_n)] = [0,1,\ldots,0] \\
&\ \ \vdots \\
e_n &= [0 \ (\mathrm{mod}\ p_1), 0 \ (\mathrm{mod}\ p_2), \ldots, 1 \ (\mathrm{mod}\ p_n)] = [0,0,\ldots,1]
\end{aligned}
\tag{3.44}
$$

The elements create an algebraic space and they can be used as basis vectors, to hide the vectors and simultaneously create the public key. The idempotent elements are transformed using the random integer $r$ and the modulus $q$ as before, namely,

$$k_i = r\,e_i \ (\mathrm{mod}\ q) ; \quad i=1, \ldots, n \tag{3.45}$$

while $q > \sum_{i=1}^{n} e_i$ and $q$ is prime. Using the public key $K = (k_1, \ldots, k_n)$, the sender creates the cryptogram $C$ for the message $M = (m_1, \ldots, m_n)$ according to the following formula:

$$C = \left| \sum_{i=1}^{u} k_{j_i} m_{j_i} - \sum_{i=u+1}^{n} k_{j_i} m_{j_i} \right| \tag{3.46}$$

where both subsets of binary elementary messages $M^+ \sim = \sim \{m_{j_1}, \ldots, m_{j_u}\}$ and $M^- \sim = \sim \{m_{j_{u+1}}, \ldots, m_{j_n}\}$ are selected arbitrarily, provided that $M^+ \cup M^-$ contains all the binary elements $m_i; i = 1, \ldots, n$, and $M^+ \cap M^- = \varnothing$.

In turn, the receiver, having the cryptogram $C$, transforms it using the inverse $r^{-1}$ as follows:

$$C' = C\,r^{-1} \ (\mathrm{mod}\ q) \tag{3.47}$$

Again, he/she calculates $C'' = N-C'$. As only one element of the pair $(C',C'')$ conveys the message, the receiver presents them as vectors of the form:

$$
\begin{aligned}
C' &= [C' \bmod p_1, \ldots, C' \bmod p_n] \\
C'' &= [C'' \bmod p_1, \ldots, C'' \bmod p_n]
\end{aligned}
\tag{3.48}
$$

and selects the vector all of whose components are either $-1$ (mod $p_i$) or 1 (mod $p_i$) for $i = 1, \ldots, n$. Now if the cryptogram is generated by (3.46) and there is a vector, say $C'$, all of whose components are from the set $\{0, 1, -1\}$, then the second one, $C''$, must contain at least one component ($C''$ mod $p_j$) different from $0, 1, -1$ (mod $p_j$). To illustrate the enciphering and deciphering processes in IE system, consider the following example.

*Example*

Assume that the communicating parties have agreed to transmit 5-bit messages and the receiver has already selected the initial condition $(p_1, p_2, p_3, p_4, p_5) = (2, 3, 5, 7, 11)$. Now $N = p_1 p_2 p_3 p_4 p_5 = 2310$ and,

$$e_1 = [1 \bmod p_1, 0 \bmod p_2, 0 \bmod p_3, 0 \bmod p_4, 0 \bmod p_5] = 1155 \ (\mathrm{mod}\ 2310)$$
$$e_2 = [0 \bmod p_1, 1 \bmod p_2, 0 \bmod p_3, 0 \bmod p_4, 0 \bmod p_5] = 1540 \ (\mathrm{mod}\ 2310)$$
$$e_3 = [0 \bmod p_1, 0 \bmod p_2, 1 \bmod p_3, 0 \bmod p_4, 0 \bmod p_5] = 1389 \ (\mathrm{mod}\ 2310)$$
$$e_4 = [0 \bmod p_1, 0 \bmod p_2, 0 \bmod p_3, 1 \bmod p_4, 0 \bmod p_5] = 330 \ (\mathrm{mod}\ 2310)$$
$$e_5 = [0 \bmod p_1, 0 \bmod p_2, 0 \bmod p_3, 0 \bmod p_4, 1 \bmod p_5] = 210 \ (\mathrm{mod}\ 2310)$$

If the receiver now selects the modulus $q = 4637 > \sum_{i=1}^{5} e_i = 4621$ ($q$ is prime) and picks $r = 3475$ at random ($r^{-1} = 3372$), then components of the public key are:

$$k_1 = e_1 r \ (\mathrm{mod}\ q) = 1155 \cdot 3475 = 2620 \ (\mathrm{mod}\ 4637)$$
$$k_2 = e_2 r \ (\mathrm{mod}\ q) = 1540 \cdot 3475 = 402 \ (\mathrm{mod}\ 4637)$$
$$k_3 = e_3 r \ (\mathrm{mod}\ q) = 1386 \cdot 3475 = 3144 \ (\mathrm{mod}\ 4637)$$
$$k_4 = e_4 r \ (\mathrm{mod}\ q) = 330 \cdot 3475 = 1411 \ (\mathrm{mod}\ 4637)$$
$$k_5 = e_5 r \ (\mathrm{mod}\ q) = 210 \cdot 3475 = 1741 \ (\mathrm{mod}\ 4637)$$

In other words the public key is $K = (2620, 402, 3144, 1411, 1741)$. Here, both the initial condition and the pair $(r, q)$ are kept secret. Using $K$, the sender can encipher his/her message $M = (1, 0, 1, 1, 1)$. First, he/she constructs two subsets $M^+$ and $M^-$. Let them be $M^+ = \{m_1, m_2, m_4\}$ and $M^- = \{m_3, m_5\}$. Next he/she computes the cryptogram:

$$C = |\ (k_1 + k_4) - (k_3 + k_5)\ | = |\ 4031 - 4885\ | = 854$$

Finally, the cryptogram is forwarded to the receiver. In turn, the receiver, knowing the inverse element $r^{-1}$, transforms the cryptogram:

$$C' = C\ r^{-1} \ (\mathrm{mod}\ q) = 854 \cdot 3372 = 111 \ (\mathrm{mod}\ 4637)$$

Now, one element of the pair ($C' = 111$, $C'' = N - C' = 1199$) conveys the message. To find this element, the receiver converts the pair into vectors:

$$C' = [111 \ (\mathrm{mod}\ 2), 111 \ (\mathrm{mod}\ 3), 111 \ (\mathrm{mod}\ 5), 111 \ (\mathrm{mod}\ 7), 111 \ (\mathrm{mod}\ 11)]$$
$$= [1, 0, 1, 6, 1] = [1, 0, 1, -1, 1]$$
$$C'' = [1199 \ (\mathrm{mod}\ 2), 1199 \ (\mathrm{mod}\ 3), 1199 \ (\mathrm{mod}\ 5), 1199 \ (\mathrm{mod}\ 7), 1199 \ (\mathrm{mod}\ 11)]$$
$$= [1, 2, 4, 2, 0]$$

The first vector indicates the message $M = [1, 0, 1, 1, 1]$.     □

**Graham-Shamir cryptosystem**

Graham and Shamir [LEMP79] independently discovered a way of obscuring the superincreasing property of initial conditions. A Graham-Shamir initial condition vector

$W = (w_1, \ldots, w_n)$ has the property that each $w_j$ has the following binary representation:

$$w_j = R_j I_j S_j \tag{3.49}$$

where $R_j$ and $S_j$ are long random bit strings, and $I_j$ is a bit string of length $n$ such that $j$th high-order bit is 1 and the remaining $n-1$ bits are 0's. Each random bit string $S_j$ has $\log_2 n$ zeros in its high-order bit positions so that summing them does not cause them to overflow into the area of the $I_j$'s. Thus, $D = W \times M$ has the binary representation,

$$D = (R, M, S)$$

where $R = \sum_{j=1}^{n} R_j m_j$ and $S = \sum_{j=1}^{n} S_j m_j$. Now the vector of bit strings $((I_n, S_n), \ldots, (I_1, S_1))$ is an easy knapsack vector. The $R_j$'s are added to obscure the superincreasing property. These knapsacks are even easier to solve than Merkle-Hellman trapdoor knapsacks because $M$ can be extracted from the binary representation of $D$.

*Example*

Let $n = 5$ when $W$ is given by:

$$(R_1 \; I_1 \; S_1) = (011010 \; 10000 \; 000101) = w_1$$
$$(R_2 \; I_2 \; S_2) = (001001 \; 01000 \; 000011) = w_2$$
$$(R_3 \; I_3 \; S_3) = (010010 \; 00100 \; 000100) = w_3$$
$$(R_4 \; I_4 \; S_4) = (011000 \; 00010 \; 000111) = w_4$$
$$(R_5 \; I_5 \; S_5) = (000110 \; 00001 \; 000001) = w_5$$

Let the message be $M = (0,1,0,0,1)$. Then,

$$D = W \times M = w_2 + w_5 =$$
$$= (R_2 + R_5; I_2 + I_5; S_2 + S_5) = (001111 \; 01001 \; 000100) \qquad \square$$

The initial condition $W$ is converted to a hard knapsack vector $K$ as in the Merkle-Hellman scheme, by picking $q$ and $r$ and computing $K = rW \pmod{q}$. Similarly, a message $M$ is enciphered as in the Merkle-Hellman system, whence $C = \sum_{i=1}^{n} k_i m_i$. At the receiver's end, $C$ is deciphered by computing $D = C \, r^{-1} \pmod{q}$ and extracting from $D$ the bits representing $M$.

Shamir and Graham believed this variant was safer, faster and simpler to implement than the original scheme proposed by Merkle and Hellman.

## Security of the Merkle-Hellman system

Merkle and Hellman originally suggested using knapsacks of approximate size $n=100$. However, Schroeppel and Shamir [SCSH79] developed an algorithm to solve knapsacks of this size. By trading time and space their method can solve the knapsack problem in time $T = O(2^{\frac{1}{2}n})$ and space $O(2^{\frac{1}{4}n})$. For $n = 100$, $T = 2^{50} \approx 10^{15}$. Thus a single processor can find a solution in 11 574 days. But for $n = 200$, assuming $8.64 \times 10^{10}$ instructions per day, the algorithm is computationally infeasible.

The Merkle-Hellman system has two drawbacks which arise from its construction. They are the high cryptogram redundancy and the huge public key length. For $n=200$, every key component is 400-bit sequence, so the public key has 80 k-bits length.

Once Merkle and Hellman had announced their cryptosystem, many scientists tried to break it. Merkle promised a prize of $1000 to the first person to successfully crack his system. There are basically two attacks on the Merkle-Hellman system. The first relies upon finding an efficient algorithm to solve knapsacks defined in the form required by the system. While there is no efficient algorithm to solve the general knapsack, as it belongs to the class **NPC**, the knapsacks in question are only a small subset of all knapsacks.

The second attack is based on the knowledge of the public key only. The public key creates the hard knapsack. A number of articles addressed the following question: Is there a polynomial time algorithm to calculate easy knapsacks (initial conditions) knowing the hard ones (public keys)? Subsequently, an algorithm was invented by Shamir [SHAM82a]. Shamir's algorithm works for the basic Merkle-Hellman system only and not for all hard knapsacks vectors. At the same time Adleman [ADLE83a, ADLE83b] examined the iterated Merkle-Hellman system and showed that even this system is insecure. Some comments on his attack can be found in [BRIC83]. Next, Brickell [BRIC83] and Lagarias et al. [LAOD83] proved that any cryptosystem based on low density knapsacks (the Merkle-Hellman system is one such knapsack) is breakable in polynomial time. Subsequently, Lagarias [LAGA82, LAGA83] examined applications of simultaneous diophantine approximation problems (see [CASS65]) to design a polynomial time algorithm for breaking knapsack cryptosystems.

The Merkle-Hellman system was finally shown to be insecure by Brickell [BRIC84a, BRIC85] who invented a polynomial time algorithm which allowed the easy knapsack vectors to be recreated from the hard knapsack vectors. Brickell's algorithm was based upon the recently published algorithm for factoring polynomials with rational coefficients, due to Lenstra, Lenstra and Lovasz [LELE82, LENS83]. Needless to say that Brickell won Merkle's prize of $1000. Readers interested in details of breaking the Merkle-Hellman system are referred to two papers of Brickell et al. [BRIC84a, BRIC85] or the book by O Connor and Seberry [OCSE88].

### 3.3.4  McEliece's algebraic codes cryptosystem

McEliece suggested in 1978 [MCEL78] that error correcting codes are excellent candidates for providing public-key cryptosystems. His work has not received the prominence or detailed study it deserves, because error correcting codes are effective by virtue of their redundancy, which leads to data expansion, which has not usually been considered desirable in cryptography.

The authors believe that when security is required on noisy channels, such as satellite communications, mobile radios or car telephones, error correction incorporated with security is the wisest course to take. It may be that encryption should be applied first and then error correction via, say, convolutional codes is most appropriate. Nevertheless, the combined area of encryption and error correction is valuable to study for both digital and analog systems.

McEliece based his cryptosystem on the **Goppa codes**, a superset of the **BCH** or the **Hamming** polynomial codes, because they are easy to implement in hardware and a fast decoding algorithm exists for the general Goppa codes while no such fast decoding algorithm exists for a general linear code.

Corresponding to each irreducible polynomial,

$$p(x) = x^t + p_{t-1}x^{t-1} + \ldots + p_1x + 1, \qquad p_i \in \{0,1\}$$

of degree $t$ over GF($2^m$), there exists a binary irreducible Goppa code of length $n = 2^m$, dimension $k \geq n - tm$, capable of correcting any pattern of $t$ or fewer errors.

Patterson has given a fast algorithm, with running time, $O(nt)$, for decoding these codes (see [MCEL78, problem 8.18]).

The cryptosystem designer now chooses a desirable value of $n$ and $t$ and then randomly picks an irreducible polynomial of degree $t$ over GF($2^m$). The probability that a randomly selected polynomial of degree $t$ is irreducible is about $1/t$ and Berlekamp [BERL68, Chapter 8] describes a fast algorithm for testing irreducibility so this is a reasonable step. Next the system designer produces a $k \times n$ generator matrix G for the code, which could be in canonical form, that is:

$$G = [\, I_k \ \ F_{k \times (n-k)} \,]$$

The usual error correction method would now multiply a message vector $\mathbf{a} = (a_1, a_2, \ldots, a_k)$ onto G to form the codeword $\mathbf{b} = (b_1, b_2, \ldots, b_n)$ which is transmitted via a channel which usually corrupts the codeword to **b'** which must then be corrected and then the message recovered.

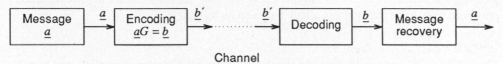

Channel

**Figure 3.15** A binary symmetric channel with error correction

If **a** were multiplied onto G in the canonical form, **b** would be:

$$\mathbf{b} = (a_1, a_2, \ldots, a_k, f_1(a_i), f_2(a_i), \ldots, f_{n-k}(a_i))$$

and if there was no corruption, the message is trivially recovered as the first $k$ bits of **b** .

Thus McEliece 'scrambles' G by selecting a random dense $k \times k$ non-singular matrix S, and a random $n \times n$ permutation matrix P. He then computes,

$$G' = SGP$$

which generates a linear code with the same rate and minimum distance as the code generated by G. G' is called **the public generator matrix**.

Sloane [SLOA79] has written an excellent article describing how the random matrices S and P can be obtained.

Thus the algorithm can be described as follows:

*Encryption:*     Divide the data to be encrypted into $k$-bit blocks. If **M** is such a block, transmit,

$$\mathbf{C} = \mathbf{M}G' + \mathbf{Z}$$

where $G'$ is the public generator matrix and **Z** is a locally generated random vector of length $n$ and weight $t$.

*Decryption:*     On receipt of **C** the receiver computes,

$$\mathbf{C'} = \mathbf{C}P^{-1}$$

where $P^{-1}$ is the inverse of the permutation matrix $P$. $\mathbf{C'}$ will then be a codeword of the Goppa code previously chosen.

The decoding algorithm is then used to find $\mathbf{M} = \mathbf{M'}S^{-1}$.

### Security of McEliece's cryptosystem

The encryption and decryption algorithms can be implemented quite simply. We need to determine the security of the system. If an opponent knows $G'$ and intercepts $\mathbf{C}$, can he/she recover $\mathbf{M}$?

There are two possible attacks:

1. to try to recover $G$ from $G'$ and so be able to use the decoding algorithm;
2. to attempt to recover $\mathbf{M}$ from $\mathbf{C}$ without knowing $G$.

The first attack appears hopeless if $n$ and $t$ are large enough because there are so many possibilities for $G$, not to mention the possibilities for $S$ and $P$.

The second attack seems more promising but the basic problem to be solved is that of decoding a more or less arbitrary $(n, k)$ linear code in the presence of up to $t$ errors. Berlckamp, McEliece and van Tilborg [BEMC78] have proved that the general coding problem for linear codes is **NP–complete**, so one can certainly expect that, if the code parameters are large enough, this attack will also be infeasible.

### *Example*

If $n = 1024 = 2^{10}$ and $t = 50$ there are about $10^{149}$ possible Goppa polynomials and a vast number of choices for $S$ and $P$. The dimension of the code will be about 524. Hence, a brute-force approach to decoding based on comparing $\mathbf{C}$ to each codeword has a work factor of about $2^{524} = 10^{158}$; and a brute-force approach based on coset leaders has a work factor of about $2^{500} = 10^{151}$.

A more promising attack is to select $k$ of the co-ordinates randomly and hope none are in error and then calculate $\mathbf{M}$. The probability of no error, however, is about $(1-t/n)^k$, and the amount of work involved in solving $k$ simultaneous equations in $k$ unknowns is about $k^3$. Hence before finding $\mathbf{M}$ using this attack one expects a work factor of $k^3(1-t/n)^{-k}$. For $n = 1024$, $k = 524$, $t = 50$ this is about $10^{19} \approx 2^{65}$.

### *Remark*

This algorithm would have a communication rate of about $10^6$ bits/sec. Thus, it would have quite viable implementation speeds.

On the other hand this cryptosystem is not suitable for producing 'signatures' as the algorithm is truly asymmetric and not one to one.

Other authors, e.g. Subash C. Kak [KAK83], have discussed joint encryption and error-correction coding and suggested further avenues for research.

More recently, Adams and Meijer [ADME87] have computed optimal values for McEliece's public key cryptosystem, which improves the cryptanalytic complexity of the system and decreases its data expansion. They show that using a $k{\times}n$ generator matrix for the McEliece code correcting $t$ errors gives a factor of:

$$w = k^a \begin{bmatrix} n \\ k \end{bmatrix} / \begin{bmatrix} n-t \\ k \end{bmatrix}$$

steps to break the code using the least complex method. This means for $n = 1024$ suggested by McEliece $k = 1024 - 10t = 2^i - it$ and searching in the range $2 \leq a \leq 3$ gives a maximal work factor of $2^{84.1}$ when $t = 37$.

They show that the likelihood of there being more than one trapdoor in the system is $\ll 1$ and a Brickell-like attack will be unsuccessful.

The analysis of Adams and Meijer shows that the work factor to break the system is significantly higher than DEA (DES) and compares favorably with the RSA cryptosystem.

EXERCISES

3. 1   Solve:

(a)   wkh hylo wkdw phq gr olyhv diwhu wkhp;
(b)   gxurr otmyz utkmg znkxy tusuyy.

3. 2   Solve the following cryptograms:

(a)   r fx sno fgyfrq ng onxnyynz gny r wfel tlls pltolyqfp fsq r cnel onqfp;
(b)   vny byrveiwr blydylq vnev owrqolsbvswrq talsri vny rypv vnlyy mwrvnq jy mety sr vny eiy jleocyvq rsry vw vkyrvu wry.

3. 3   Decipher the following ciphertext:
        wklv lv d vhfuhw

3. 4   Decipher the following Caesar ciphers:

(a)   fev gfleu fw cvriezex ivhlzivj kve gfleuj fw tfddfe jvejv kf rggcp zk;
(b)   kbsbo pxvvl rhklt xjxkq fiivl rexsb afsfa baxkf kebof qxkzb tfqee fj;
(c)   xlivi mwrsw yglxl mrkew ewyvi xlmrk.

Decipher the following general monoalphabetic ciphers:

(a)   vy iuoz idzjvqh sqn zqjl dztiuy juodhzfzi flz myvwztiz;
(b)   ob gqx tqfm gqxfrhwb uqtd rwhhy gqxfrhwb xy;
(c)   dnwwk tawvi letle tocti uvqie wj.

3. 5   Decode the following transposition ciphers:

(a)   LWLII EERBF E;
(b)   GOLIC IILST EKSEH ROWHT DESOO HWPPA LAEIO THSTL LAREP HSIIY BT;
(c)   RAEWL OCEOO TDREH TLNOS EHWYA EWNUD ERNIL LSRUO EVLES;
(d)   INAMO NTAPM ISIWT NEICS IHHTO TIDER SR;
(e)   WIEHT OEDES ONTAS HAWEC EFHTT DOLOO TLASE TSA.

3. 6   Decode the following transposition ciphers:

(a)   TLOIP SENSE ETSHI FTROA SOHOC MGNAI NGNOO ARSEE UHTOL SHGT;
(b)   ATPEI CENSI USSAT NEICD UROGA E;

(c) OHCELT OETSTS CEFREP PINOAT EROSNE MECROV HSSIWE INEHFE TLOSUL PJBOAA TLCIAP ROFNOI M.

3.7 Decrypt the following ciphertext which was produced using the Beaufort cipher with key SKATEBOARD:

KXFPM IGURK KWNBW OVMYW OFJPO HKNPF EFHPN

PGNRS HCNPL BZLJQ MDAYA MXMWV PGXTK IHMAV

ZCWBI TVTAZ SSMGL NNWGV OPWAX BVLNM AWNTT

ZANWZ BSAAW NBIRQ PSWGM TVSWZ PKHTS BQTRI

OJWPR HBXNM YXAZL UAJJL OHIRN HVSEF ARGQA

OVIVZ BGETN OKXYP RGETN X

3.8 Calculate the index of coincidence for the following ciphertext. What can you say about how it may have been encrypted?

APWVC DKPAK BCECY WXBBK CYVSE FVTLV MXGRG

KKGFD LRLZK TFVKH SAGUK YEXSR SIQTW JXVFL

LALUI KYABZ XGRKL BAFSG CCMJT ZDGST AHBJM

MLGEZ RPZIJ XPVGU OJXHL PUMVM CKYEX SRSIQ

KCWMC KFLQJ FWJRH SWLOX YPVKM HYCTA WEJVQ

DPAVV KFLKG FDLRL ZKIWT IBXSG RTPLL AMHFR

OMEMV ZQZGK MSDFH ATXSE ELVWK OCJFQ FLHRJ

SMVMV IMBOZ HIKRO MUNIE RYG

3.9 Decrypt the following ciphertext:

LIBRX DUHOR RNLQJ IRUWK HZURQ JWKLQ JFDHV

DUVFL SKHUP DBWUL FNBRX ZLWKL WVVLP SOLFL

WB

3.10 Decipher the following ciphertext using a Playfair cipher with key:

|   |   |   |   |   |
|---|---|---|---|---|
| J/I | E | N | S | B |
| R | Y | T | O | K |
| C | P | G | A | H |
| D | F | L | M | Q |
| U | V | W | X | Z |

Ciphertext: TKC XJY MRE SAT K.

3.11 What is the unicity distance of the Playfair cipher?

3.12 If you are given two Playfair ciphers $P_1$ and $P_2$ which are applied one after the other to a string of text $T$, i.e., $P_2(P_1(T))$, do you have a cipher which is more secure than using $P_1$ or $P_2$?

3.13 Determine the expected number of characters required to break a permutation cipher with period $d$. What is the unicity distance for $d = 7$?

3. 14 Decipher the following ciphertext which has been enciphered using a Variant Beauford cipher with key MES:

WPQ GWE CJI SNN IHL OU

3. 15 Determine the unicity distance of ciphers based on the affine transformation,

$$f(x) = (ax + b) \text{ modulo } 26$$

Assume the keys $a$ and $b$ both generate complete sets of residues and that all such keys are equally likely.

3. 16 Consider an affine transformation substitution cipher using the transformation,

$$f(x) = (ax + b) \text{ modulo } 26$$

Suppose it is suspected that the plaintext letter $P(15)$ (this notation means $P$ is the 15 *th* letter of the alphabet) corresponds to the ciphertext letter $R(17)$ and that the plaintext letter $G(16)$ corresponds to the ciphertext letter $Z(25)$. Break the cipher by solving for $a$ and $b$.

3. 17 Note that any asymmetric cryptosystem provides a one-way secure channel from the sender $A$ to the receiver $B$ only. Design a two-way secure channel using asymmetric cryptosystems.

3. 18 When using the Extended Euclidean Algorithm, we obtain the following two sequences of calculations (any row contains the triple $(s_i, t_i, r_i)$ for $i = -1, 0, 1, \dots$):

$$1, 0, 679 = \gamma(N)$$
$$0, 1, 234 = K_B$$
$$1, -2, 211$$
$$-1, 3, 23$$
$$10, -29, 4$$
$$-51, 148, 3$$
$$61, -177, 1$$

and,

$$1, 0, 679 = \gamma(N)$$
$$0, 1, 238 = K_B$$
$$1, -2, 203$$
$$-1, 3, 35$$
$$6, -17, 28$$
$$-7, 20, 7$$
$$34, -97, 0$$

What are the inverses in these two cases ? Discuss the results.

3. 19 Given a modulus $\gamma(N)$ and a public key $K_B$, write a Pascal program which calculates a secret key $k_B$ for the RSA system.

3. 20 Determine the time complexity function of the Extended Euclidean Algorithm.

3. 21 Assume that $p = 467$ and $q = 479$. Calculate the secret key in the RSA system, knowing that the public key is equal to $K_B = 73443$.

3. 22 Suppose you want to design an RSA system in which the modulus $N = p_1 \cdot p_2 \cdot p_3$

($p_i$ is prime for $i = 1,2,3$). Is it possible? If so, what is the main difference between this modification and the original RSA system?

3. 23 Assume you are an cryptanalyst. You know that the RSA system you want to break uses $N = 20,716,247$, and the public key is $K_B = 1,219,751$ . What is the secret key?

3. 24 In the RSA cryptosystem, the exponential function is used to encipher and decipher. Write a program for a fast exponential function.

3. 25 Given the modulus $N = 29893$, the public key $K = 12335$, and the message $M = 25776$, compute the cryptogram in the RSA cryptosystem.

3. 26 The RSA system is vulnerable to iteration attack. Design a suitable Pascal program to be able to compromise the system knowing a modulus, a public key, and a cryptogram.

3. 27 Apply the iteration attack to recreate the original message for six different pairs (cryptogram, public key) while the RSA system uses the modulus $N = 2773$. The pairs are as follows:

(a)  $C = 1561$,    $K = 573$;
(b)  $C = 1931$,    $K = 861$;
(c)  $C = 2701$,    $K = 983$;
(d)  $C = 67$,       $K = 1013$;
(e)  $C = 178$,      $K = 1579$;
(f)  $C = 2233$,    $K = 791$.

3. 28 Given the RSA cryptosystem for $p = 37$ and $q = 41$, calculate the set of all messages whose form does not change under any odd public key.

3. 29 Consider the RSA system for $N = 2773$ ($p = 47$, $q = 59$). Compute numbers of unconcealable messages while applying the following public keys:

(a)  $K = 668$,
(b)  $K = 1174$,
(c)  $K = 1043$,
(d)  $K = 878$.

3. 30 The Diffie-Hellman system is designed for $N = 4079$ and a primitive element $g = 1709$. What are the partial keys $y_A$, $y_B$, and the common secret key $K$ when the secret keys are $k_A = 2344$, $k_B = 3420$? Also calculate the deciphering key $K'$.

3. 31 Consider the Diffie-Hellman system defined for $N = 4073$ and $g = 4021$. Assume that the communicating parties have already selected their secret keys $k_A - 2331$ and $k_B = 1872$. What are the enciphering and deciphering keys ? Discuss the results and give the conditions which ensure that any pair ($k_A$, $k_B$) points to the deciphering key.

3. 32 Consider the Williams scheme for $p = 179$ and $q = 191$ and compute the deciphering key. What are cryptograms for two messages $M_1 - 33001$ and $M_2 = 18344$?

3. 33 Write a primality testing algorithm which incorporates both the test based on the Fermat Theorem 3.33 and the strong test 3.34. Select testing numbers from the interval ($\beta$, $\beta$ + trial).

3. 34 Find all primes from the interval (45700, 45750) using the PRIMALITY TEST 3.1

3. 35 Design the Merkle-Hellman system which allows to transmit 7-bit messages. Suppose that $W = (w_1, \ldots, w_7) = (2,3,6,12,24,49,100)$, $q$ is the smallest integer which satisfies 3.40 and $r = 119$. What is the cryptogram for the message $M = 1011011$ ? Show the deciphering process.

3. 36 Consider the easy knapsack vector $W$ = (1,2,4,8,16,32,64,128,256,512). Produce the public key using four iterations for pairs $(q_1, r_1)$, $(q_2, r_2)$, $(q_3, r_3)$, $(q_4, r_4)$ while primes $q_i$; $i$ = 1,2,3,4 , are kept as small as possible. Accept $(r_1, r_2, r_3, r_4) = (233, 671, 322, 157)$.

3. 37 Design a Pascal program which calculates idempotent elements in $Z_N$ while $N = p_1 \ldots p_n$.

3. 38 Design the IE system to encrypt the 5-bit message $M=(m_1, \ldots, m_5) = 11101$. Take $(p_1, \ldots, p_5)=(3, 5, 7, 11, 13)$. Choose the smallest possible integer $q$ while $r=17831$.

3. 39 The IE system can be applied to encipher messages $M = (m_1, \ldots, m_n)$, where elementary messages $m_i$; $i = 1, \ldots, n$ , are integers less than $p_i$. Consider such a modification and assume that cryptograms are calculated according to $\sum_{i=0}^{n} m_i k_i$. Design such a system for $p_1 = 11$, $p_2 = 13$, $p_3 = 17$, and $M = (m_1, m_2, m_3)$ where elementary messages are numbers of the set $\{0,1, \ldots, 9\}$.

3. 40 Modify the IE system to encipher messages whose elements are integers (see the previous problem) where cryptograms are calculated according to 3.46. What restrictions must be imposed in order to be able to recreate messages in their original form? Use $p_1 = 13, p_2 = 17, p_3 = 19$.


SOLUTIONS

3. 1   (a)   the evil that men do lives after them
       (b)   a rolling stone gathers no moss

3. 2   (a)   i am not afraid of tomorrow for i have seen yesterday and i love today
       (b)   the pentagon prefers that conscriptions during the next three months be made in the age brackets nine to twenty one

3. 3   this is a secret

3. 4   Solution to Caesar ciphers:

       (a)   one pound of learning requires ten pounds of common sense to apply it
       (b)   never say you know a man till you have divided an inheritance with him
       (c)   there is no such thing as a sure thing

       Solutions to general monoalphabetic cipher:

       (a)   in some special way each person completes the universe
       (b)   if you work yourself down sleep yourself up
       (c)   a fools mouth is his destruction

3. 5   (a)   Consideration of the first 5 letters points to block lengths of 4 or 5. A block length of 4 and permutation (3142) leads to:

                        WILL ERIE  FBE

while a block length of 5 and permutation (52413) leads to:

IWILL BEFRE E

or

I WILL BE FREE

(b)   Break into blocks of size 3 and use the permutation (13) to get:

LOGIC IS LIKE THE SWORD THOSE WHO APPEAL TO IT SHALL
PERISH BY IT

(c)   Break into blocks of size 4 and use the permutation (14)(23):

WE ARE COLD TO OTHERS ONLY WHEN WE ARE
DULL IN OURSELVES

(d)   Break into blocks of size 6 and use the permutation (16)(25)(34) to get

NO MAN IS IMPATIENT WITH HIS CREDITORS

(e)   Leave in blocks of size 5 and use the permutation (1425) to get:

THE WISE DO AT ONCE WHAT THE FOOL DOES AT LAST

3.6   Transposition:

(a)   POLITENESS IS THE ART OF CHOOSING AMONG ONES REAL THOUGHTS
(b)   PATIENCE IS SUSTAINED COURAGE
(c)   THE CLOSEST TO PERFECTION A PERSON EVER COMES IS WHEN HE
      FILLS OUT A JOB APPLICATION FORM

(The transforms are: (a) (5 3 2 4 1) (b) (2 3 1 5 4) (c) (6 2 4 3 5 1))

3.7   INVESTIGATIONS INTO THE FREQUENCY OF TERMINAL LINE TAPPING
HAVE PROVIDED AUTHORITIES WITH REASON TO BELIEVE THAT PERSONAL
CONVERSATIONS AND SENSITIVE DATA MAY HAVE BEEN UNAUTHORIZED
SCRUTINY STUDENTS WERE WARNED TO BEWARE

3.8   The results of the frequency program for the given ciphertext is found using:

```
program freq (input,output);
const
        alpha = 26;
type
        language = set of char;
var
        F : array[1..alpha] of integer;
        total : integer;
        letters : integer;
        c : char;
        ordA : integer;
        i : integer;
        IC : real;
        english : language;
begin
        english := ['a'..'z','A'..'Z'];
        for i := 1 to alpha do
          F[i] := 0;
        total := 0;
        IC := 0;
```

```
        while not eof do
        begin
                while not eoln do
                begin
                        read(c);
                        write(c);
                        if c in english then
                        begin
                                if ord(c) < ord('a') then
                                  ordA := ord ('A')
                                else
                                  ordA := ord('a');
                                F[ord(c)-ordA+1] := F[ord(c)-ordA+1) +
1;
                                letters := letters + 1;
                        end;
                end;
                readln;
                writeln;
        end;
        writeln;
        writeln('Frequency counts ...');
        writeln;
        for i := 1 to alpha do
          begin
                writeln(chr(ord('a')+i-1),' --> ',F[i]:1];
                total := total + (F[i]*(F[i]-1));
          end;
        writeln;
        IC := total/(letters*(letters-1));
        writeln('IC = ',IC:6:5);
end.
```

Giving:

```
Frequency counts ...
```

| | | | |
|---|---|---|---|
| a → 9 | b → 8 | c → 9 | d → 5 |
| e → 9 | f → 11 | g → 13 | h → 7 |
| i → 9 | j → 7 | k → 18 | l → 16 |
| m → 15 | n → 1 | o → 5 | p → 6 |
| q → 4 | r → 12 | s → 12 | t → 8 |
| u → 5 | v → 13 | w → 6 | x → 10 |
| y → 6 | z → 9 | | |

and thus the index of coincidence is 0.04162.

This IC tells us that the ciphertext is probably not the result of monoalphabetic substitution. It is more likely to be polyalphabetic with period approximately 8. (See the table of ICs in the text.) It *must* be remembered that this number, 8, is a statistical quantity which is dependent not only on the number of alphabets used, but also on the actual plaintext. Thus, if the plaintext were unusual (e.g. no *e*'s) then the value of the IC would be indicative only.

Note we are looking for IC = 0.066 for English, which is based on the 'normal' distribution for English of about 13 percent *e*'s.

3.9   We do a frequency analysis and find the following distribution for the characters:

A B C D E F G H I J K L M N O P Q R S T U V W X Y Z
0 4 0 4 0 4 0 4 2 3 4 10 0 2 2 2 3 6 2 0 6 4 6 2 0 2

Calculating the IC we find it is .05438. This indicates that perhaps two alphabets were used. We can look at the ICs that result from such a split but first we consider the (trigraphs/)digraphs that are present in the ciphertext.

A:
B:    RX    RX    WU    *
C:
D:    HV    UH    UV
E:
F:    DH    LS    LW    NB
G:
H:    OR    UP    VD    ZU
I:    BR    RU
J:    FD    IR    WK
K:    HU    HZ    LQ    LW
L:    FL    FN    IB    PS    QJ    Qj    SK    WB    WK    WV
M:
N:    BR    LQ
O:    LF    RR
P:    DB    SO
Q:    JF    JI    JW
R:    NL    QJ    RN    UW    XD    XZ
S:    KH    OL
T:
U:    HO    LF    PD    RG    VF    WK
V:    DU    FL    LP    VL
W:    B*    KH    KL    KL    UL    VV
X:    DU    ZL
Y:
Z:    LW    UR
*:    LI    *I

We are now certain that L is a vowel and it appears from the distribution that we probably have a monoalphabet as so many letters do not occur at all and the peak is relatively high.

The occurrences of R, U, V and W suggest that they might be O, R, S and T (considering the pattern). Deciphering gives

```
IF YOU ARE LOOKING FOR THE WRONG THING CAESARS CIPHER MAY
TRICK YOU WITH ITS SIMPLICITY
```

3.10  YOU ARE DOING OK.

3.11  $\dfrac{\log_2 25!}{3.2} = 26.15.$

3.12  No, for each two letter combination to be enciphered there are still the same number of 2 letter encipherments.

3. 13  We are considering a permutation cipher with period $d$. There exists $d!$ permutations of $d$ characters. Assuming all keys are equally likely the entropy of the key is:

$$H(K) = \log_2 d!$$

The amount of text needed to break the cipher is the unicity distance given by:

$$N = \frac{H(K)}{D} = \log_2 \frac{d!}{D}$$

where $D$ is the redundancy of the language being used (about 3.2 bits/letter for English). Using Stirling's approximation for $d!$

$$N = d \log_2 (d/e)/3.2$$
$$= 0.3d \log_2 (d/e).$$

For $d = 7$, $N = 0.3 \times 7 \times \log_2(7/e) = 2.87$. So 2 or 3 letters is enough to break these ciphers.

3. 14  The Variant Beauford cipher with key MES = (12, 4, 18) was used. We solve by adding the key modulo 26.

| W | P | Q | | G | W | E | | C | J | I | | S | N | N | | I | H | L | | O | U |
|---|---|---|---|---|---|---|---|---|---|---|---|---|---|---|---|---|---|---|---|---|
| 22 | 15 | 16 | | 6 | 22 | 4 | | 2 | 9 | 8 | | 18 | 13 | 13 | | 8 | 7 | 11 | | 14 | 20 |
| 12 | 4 | 18 | | 12 | 4 | 18 | | 12 | 4 | 18 | | 12 | 4 | 18 | | 12 | 4 | 18 | | 12 | 4 |
| 8 | 19 | 8 | | 18 | 0 | 22 | | 14 | 13 | 0 | | 4 | 17 | 5 | | 20 | 11 | 3 | | 0 | 24 |
| I | T | I | | S | A | W | | O | N | D | | E | R | F | | U | L | D | | A | Y |

The plaintext is:

IT IS A WONDERFUL DAY.

3. 15  $\phi(26) = (2 - 1)(13 - 1) = 12$ so there are only 12 possible values that the keys $a$ and $b$ can assume, that is,

$$a,b \; \varepsilon \; \{1, 3, 5, 7, 9, 11, 15, 17, 19, 21, 23, 25\}$$

as these are the only numbers that generate a complete set of residues.
Now the unicity distance

$$N = \frac{H(K)}{D} = \frac{entropy \; of \; key}{redundancy \; of \; the \; language}$$
$$= \frac{\log_2 12^2}{3.2}$$
$$\approx 2.24$$

Thus knowing 2 or 3 ciphertext characters is enough to break the cipher.

3. 16  Now,

$$17 \equiv (15a + b) \; \text{modulo} \; 26$$
$$25 \equiv (6a + b) \; \text{modulo} \; 26$$

So,

$$-8 \equiv 9a \text{ modulo } 26$$

Thus $a = 2$ and solving for $b$ gives $b = 13$.

Note that in the last question $a$ was required to generate a complete set of residues, but in general there are 26 choices for $b$ so the unicity distance in this question is:

$$\frac{\log_2 12{\times}26}{3.2} < 3$$

So two or three characters of ciphertext were still sufficient.

3. 17 To create a secure two-way channel, both $A$ and $B$ define their own cryptosystems. They next exchange their public keys $K_A$ and $K_B$. So, $A$ sends messages $M$ as cryptograms $E_B(M)$ under the key $K_B$. On the other hand, $B$ transmits $M$ as $E_A(M)$ using the key $K_A$.

3. 18 Consider the first sequence. Looking at both the formula 3.13 and the last row of the sequence, we get the equation,

$$t_5 K_B + s_5 \gamma(N) = (-177) K_B + 61 \gamma(N) = 1$$

This can be rewritten as:

$$t_5 K_B = (-177) K_B = 1 \ (\text{mod } \gamma(N))$$

This equation implies that the inverse of $K_B$ is equal to:

$$\gamma(N) + t_5 = 679 - 177 = 502$$

The second sequence produces the equation (3.13) in the form,

$$20 K_B + (-7) \gamma(N) = 7 \rightarrow 20 K_B = 7 \ (\text{mod } \gamma(N))$$

But 7 does not have an inverse in $Z_{679}$ as $679 = 97{\cdot}7$. In general, if $\gamma(N)$ is composite, then any integer $b$ for which $gcd(b, \gamma(N)) \neq 1$ does not have an inverse. In our case $gcd(238, 679)=7$.

3. 19 This program is an implementation of the Extended Euclidean Algorithm and it can take the following form:

```
program INVERSE (input, output);
label 1, 2 ;
var
        gammaN, publickey  : integer;
        S : array [-1..100] of integer;
        T : array [-1..100] of integer;
        R : array [-1..100] of integer;
begin
        read (gammaN);
        read (publickey);
        S[-1] := 1;
        T[-1] := 0;
        R[-1] := gammaN;
        S[0] := 0;
        T[0] := 1;
        R[0] := publickey;
        for gammaN := 1 to 100 do
```

```
begin
    S[gammaN]:= S[gammaN-2] - (R[gammaN-2] div R[gammaN-1])
                             * S[gammaN-1];
    T[gammaN]:= T[gammaN-2] - (R[gammaN-2] div R[gammaN-1])
                             * T[gammaN-1];
    R[gammaN]:= R[gammaN-2] - (R[gammaN-2] div R[gammaN-1])
                             * R[gammaN-1];
    if R[gammaN]=1 then goto 1 else
    if R[gammaN]=0 then
            begin
            write ('the secret key does not exist');
            goto 2
            end;
    end;
1 : if T[gammaN]>0 then write ('the secret key is =', T[gammaN])
    else write ('the secret key is =', R[-1]+T[gammaN] );
2 : end.
```

3. 20  Notice that the algorithm terminates when either $r_i=1$ or $r_i=0$. Having both $r_{i-2}$ and $r_{i-1}$, we can calculate $r_i$ as:

$$r_i = r_{i-2} - q_{i-1}r_{i-1} \quad - \text{see (3.12)}$$

In the worst case, $q_i=1$ for all $i=1, \ldots$ . Therefore, $r_i = r_{i-2} - r_{i-1}$. It means that $r_{i-2} = r_i + r_{i-1}$. So, if we start with $r_i = 1$ and $r_{i-1} = 2$, we get

$$r_{i-2} = 3 > 2$$
$$r_{i-3} = 5$$
$$r_{i-4} = 8 > 4$$
$$r_{i-5} = 13$$
$$r_{i-6} = 21 > 8$$

and so on. If we have $r_{-2} = x$, we must carry out at most $2 \log_2 x$ steps. It means that the time complexity function of the algorithm is $O(\log_2 x)$.

3. 21  First of all, we calculate $\gamma(N) = lcm(p-1, q-1) = lcm\ (466, 478) = 111374$. Next using the extended Euclidean algorithm, we get $k_B = 70167$ in the thirteenth iteration.

3. 22  Of course, it is possible. The only difference is that the function $\gamma(N)$ is expressible as follows:

$$\gamma(N) = lcm\ (p_1 - 1, p_2 - 1, p_3 - 1)$$

The justification for this fact is simple. According to the Chinese Remainder Theorem, any integer $x \in Z_N$ can be presented as the vector:

$$x = [\ x\ (\bmod p_1),\ x\ (\bmod p_2),\ x\ (\bmod p_3)\ ] = [\ x_1, x_2, x_3\ ]$$

where $x_i \in Z_{p_i}$ for $i = 1,2,3$. Note that any $x_i^\alpha = 1$ if $\alpha$ is a multiple of $p_i-1$. So $x^\alpha = 1$ if all $x_i^\alpha = 1$ ($i = 1,2,3$). This means that $\alpha = lcm(\ p_1-1, p_2-1, p_3-1)$.

3. 23  First of all, if we design a simple factorization algorithm, we can obtain three primes $p_1 = 227, p_2 = 263$, and $p_3 = 347$. The function $\gamma(N) = lcm(226, 262, 346)$ $= 5,121,838$ . Therefore, the secret key $k_B = 4,444,555$ .

3. 24  To design the program which generates $base^{exp} \pmod{N}$, note that it is easy to produce the sequence,

$$base, \ base^2, \ base^{2^2}, \ \dots, \ base^{2^i}, \ \dots$$

All the above integers belong to $Z_q$. Next consider exp when represented in binary form, e.g. 19 becomes 10011. The result $base^{\exp}$ is computed by multiplication of all elements from the base sequence for which suitable elements of exp are 1's. The program is as follows:

```
program FASTEXPONENTIAL (input, output);
var
        base, exp, N, i, max, result     : integer;
        a : array [1..100] of integer;
        b : array [1..100] of integer;
begin
        read (base, exp, N);
        for i:=1 to 100 do
        begin
              a[i] := exp mod 2 ;
              exp := exp - a[i] ;
              exp := exp div 2
        end;
        for i:=1 to 100 do if a[i] <>0 then max := i ;
        b[1] := base ;
        for i:=2 to max do b[i] := (b[i-1] * b[i-1]) mod N ;
        result := 1;
        for i:=1 to max do
        begin
              base := (a[i] * b[i]) mod N ;
              if base <> 0 then result:= (result * base ) mod N
        end;
        write (result)
end.
```

3. 25  The cryptogram $C=M^K \pmod{N}$ is equal to 15215. The message can be recovered using the secret key $k=12769$.

3. 26

```
program ITERATIONATTACK (input, output);
var
        cryptogram, publickey, iteration, message, modulus  : integer;
        function expon (base, ep, N : integer) : integer;
              var i, max, B    : integer;
              a : array [1..100] of integer;
              b : array [1..100] of integer;
        begin
        max := 1;
        B := 2;
        while ep > B do
              begin
              B := B * 2;
              max := max + 1
              end;
        for i:=1 to max do
              begin
              a[i] := 0;
              b[i] := 0
              end;
```

```
for i:=1 to max do
    begin
    a[i] := ep mod 2 ;
    ep := ep - a[i] ;
    ep := ep div 2
    end;
b[1] := base ;
for i:=2 to max do b[i] := (b[i-1] * b[i-1]) mod N ;
ep := 1;
for i:=1 to max do
    begin
    base := (a[i] * b[i]) mod N ;
    if base<>0 then
            begin
            ep := (ep * base) mod N ;
            expon := ep
            end;
    end;
end;

begin
read (cryptogram, publickey, modulus);
iteration := expon(cryptogram, publickey , modulus);
while iteration <> cryptogram do
    begin
    message := iteration;
    iteration := expon(iteration , publickey , modulus);
    end;
write ('the message =', message)
end.
```

3. 27 Using the ITERATIONATTACK program, we get the following solutions:

(a)   $M = 1385$ after 153 iterations.
(b)   $M = 2237$ after 153 iterations.
(c)   $M = 41$  after 307 iterations.
(d)   $M = 1289$ after 27 iterations.
(e)   $M = 1240$ after 21 iterations.
(f)   $M = 2758$ after 307 iterations.

3. 28 If the public key is odd, all messages $[M_1 \ (\text{mod } p), M_2 \ (\text{mod } q)]$, where $M_1 \in \{-1, 0, 1\} \subseteq Z_p, M_2 \in \{-1, 0, 1\} \subseteq Z_q$, do not change their form.  They are:

$$
\begin{aligned}
[0, 0] &= 0 \\
[1, 1] &= 1 \\
[36, 0] &= 369 \\
[0, 1] &= 370 \\
[36, 1] &= 739 \\
[1, 40] &= 778, \\
[0, 40] &= 1147 \\
[1, 0] &= 1148 \\
[36, 40] &= 1516
\end{aligned}
$$

3. 29  Using the formula 3.20, we get $\sigma_1 = 720$, $\sigma_2 = 24$, $\sigma_3 = 9$, $\sigma_4 = 4$, for (a), (b), (c), (d) respectively.

3. 30  The partial keys are:

$$y_A = g^{k_A} = 1709^{2344} = 3225 \ (\text{mod } 4079)$$
$$y_B = g^{k_B} = 1709^{3420} = 927 \ (\text{mod } 4079)$$

The common key is equal to

$$K = 927^{2344} = 3225^{3420} = 2539 \ (\text{mod } 4079)$$

The deciphering key $K' = 575 \ (\text{mod } 4079)$.

3. 31  The enciphering key $K = (g^{k_A})^{k_B} \equiv 2042 \ (\text{mod } 4073)$. The deciphering key $K'$ must satisfy the congruence

$$K\,K' = 1 \ (\text{mod } \gamma(N)) \ \text{where} \ \gamma(N) = N - 1 = 4072$$

$K$ does not have an inverse since $gcd(K, \gamma(N)) \neq 1$.

Note that $\gamma(N) = N - 1$ is even. If $N$ is selected in such a way that $\gamma(N) = N - 1 = 2p$ where $p$ is a prime, then $gcd(K, \gamma(N))$ can be either 2 or $p$. So, any odd common key different from $p$ has its inverse. However, keys $k_A$ and $k_B$ are selected independently so communicating parties have almost a 50 percent chance of selecting their keys properly using a one trial only.

3. 32  Obviously, $N = pq = 34189$. It is possible to select an integer $S = 2$ as the Jacobi symbol $\left[\dfrac{S}{N}\right] = \left[\dfrac{2}{N}\right] = (-1)^{(N^2-1)/8} = (-1)$. The secret key

$k = \frac{1}{2}[\frac{1}{4}(p-1)(q-1)+1] = 4228$.

Take the first message. The Jacobi symbol $\left[\dfrac{M_1}{N}\right] = \left[\dfrac{33001}{34189}\right] = 1$, so $c_1 = 0$.

Now we can calculate the cryptogram

$$C = M_1^2 \ (\text{mod } N) = 33001^2 = 9595 \ (\text{mod } 34189)$$

The sender forwards the triple $(C, c_1, c_2) = (9595, 0, 1)$. The receiver computes,

$$M_t = C^k \ (\text{mod } N) = 9595^{4228} = 33001 \ (\text{mod } 43189)$$

As $c_1 = 0$ and $M_t$ is odd, it is the final message $M_1$.

For the second message the cryptographic operations are similar. The Jacobi symbol $\left[\dfrac{M_2}{N}\right] = \left[\dfrac{18344}{34189}\right] = -1$, so $c_1 = 1$. The message,

$$M'_2 = S^{c_1} M_2 = 2\,M_2 = 2 \cdot 18344 = 2499 \ (\text{mod } 34189)$$

is enciphered and $C = M'^2_2 = 2499^2 = 22603 \ (\text{mod } 34189)$. Finally, the sender creates the triple $(C, c_1, c_2) = (22603, 1, 0)$. At the receiver's side,

$$M_t = C^k = 22603^{4223} = 2499 \ (\text{mod } 34189)$$

As $c_2 = 0$, the form of the message is $M_t = 31690$. Knowing $c_1 = 1$, the receiver can recreate the original message.

$$M_2 = S^{-1} (-1)^1 M_t = 18344 \pmod{34189}$$

3. 33  An example of such a program is given as follows:

```
program PRIMALITYTEST(input, output);
var
        p, zeta, eta, beta, trial, r, a, j, k    : integer;
        prime, pointer                           : boolean;
function expon (base, ep, N  : integer) : integer ;
var
            i, max, B     : integer;
            a : array [1..100] of integer;
            b : array [1..100] of integer;
        begin
        max := 1;
        B := 2;
        while ep > B do
            begin
            B := B * 2;
            max := max + 1;
            end;
        for i:=1 to max do
            begin
            a[i] := 0;
            b[i] := 0
            end;
        for i:=1 to max do
            begin
            a[i] := ep mod 2 ;
            ep := ep - a[i] ;
            ep := ep div 2
            end;
        b[1] := base ;
        for i:=2 to max do b[i] := (b[i-1] * b[i-1]) mod N ;
        ep := 1;
        for i:=1 to max do
            begin
            base := (a[i] * b[i]) mod N ;
            if base<>0 then
                    begin
                    ep := (ep * base) mod N ;
                    expon := ep
                    end;
            end;
        end;
begin
read (p, beta, trial);
zeta := 0;
eta := p-1;
r := 0;
while r=0 do
        begin
        zeta := zeta + 1;
        eta := eta div 2;
        r := eta mod 2;
        end;
```

```
prime := true;
pointer := true;
for j:=beta to beta + trial do
      begin
      if prime and pointer then
      begin
      a:= expon(j,p-1,p);
      if a<>1 then prime:=false;
      a:=expon(j,eta,p);
      if (a<>1) and prime then
          begin
          pointer:=false;
          for k:=1 to zeta do
                begin
                a:=(a*a) mod p;
                if (a=1) or (a=p-1) then pointer:=true
                end;
          end;
      end;
      end;
if pointer and prime then
      write('the integer is probably prime') else
      write('the integer is composite')
end.
```

Integers $\beta$ are selected deterministically. Of course, the number of trials determines the correctness of the algorithm. Note that the algorithm always correctly determines that an integer is composite. The probability that the integer is prime depends upon the number of trials and is equal to $1-(\frac{1}{4})^{trial}$.

3. 34  There are only two integers 45707 and 45737 which successfully pass the tests.

3. 35  As $\sum_{i=1}^{7} w_i = 196$, we use $q=197$. In the field $GF(197)$, the integer $r=119$ has as its inverse $r^{-1} = 149$. The components of the public key are:

$$k_1 = w_1 \quad r = 41 \text{ (mod 197)}$$
$$k_2 = w_2 \quad r = 160 \text{ (mod 197)}$$
$$k_3 = w_3 \quad r = 123 \text{ (mod 197)}$$
$$k_4 = w_4 \quad r = 49 \text{ (mod 197)}$$
$$k_5 = w_5 \quad r = 98 \text{ (mod 197)}$$
$$k_6 = w_6 \quad r = 118 \text{ (mod 197)}$$
$$k_7 = w_7 \quad r = 80 \text{ (mod 197)}$$

The public key $K = (41,160,123,49,98,118,80)$ is sent to the sender. Therefore, the cryptogram for the message $M=1011011$ is equal to:

$$C = 41 + 123 + 49 + 118 + 80 = 411$$

The deciphering process proceeds as follows. The hard knapsack is converted into the easy one by,

$$C\, r^{-1} = 169 \text{ (mod 197)}$$

Next,

$$169 > w_7 \rightarrow m_7 = 1$$
$$169 - w_7 = 69 > w_6 \rightarrow m_6 = 1$$
$$69 - w_6 = 20 < w_5 \rightarrow m_5 = 0$$
$$69 - w_6 = 20 > w_4 \rightarrow m_4 = 1$$
$$20 - w_4 = 8 > w_3 \rightarrow m_3 = 1$$
$$8 - w_3 = 2 < w_2 \rightarrow m_2 = 0 \text{ and } m_1 = 1$$

3. 36 The sum of all the easy knapsack components is equal to 1023. Therefore, we are looking for primes which are greater than 1023. They are (1031, 1033, 1039, 1049). If we apply the pair ($q_1 = 1031$, $r_1 = 233$) to the easy knapsack vector, we get:

$$(233, 466, 932, 833, 635, 239, 478, 956, 881, 731)$$

The second iteration for ($q_2 = 1033$, $r_1 = 671$) produces,

$$(360, 720, 407, 90, 489, 254, 508, 1016, 275, 859)$$

The third one for ($q_3 = 1039$, $r_1 = 322$) yields,

$$(591, 143, 140, 927, 569, 746, 453, 906, 235, 224)$$

And lastly, the fourth iteration ($q_4 = 1049$, $r_1 = 157$) gives the public key vector,

$$(475, 422, 1000, 777, 168, 683, 838, 627, 180, 551)$$

3. 37 An example of such a program is given below. It uses the function *inv* which produces inverses in the field $GF(p_i)$.

```
program IDEMPOTENTELEMENTS (input, output);
const n=6;
var
      N,a,i : integer;
      p, e :   array [1..n] of integer;

function inv( gammaN, x : integer): integer;
label 1 ;
var
      j : integer;
      S : array [-1..100] of integer;
      R : array [-1..100] of integer;
      T : array [-1..100] of integer;
      begin
      S[-1] :=1;
      T[-1] :=0;
      R[-1] := gammaN;
      S[0] :=0;
      T[0] :=1;
      R[0]:= x;
      for j:=1 to 100 do
            begin S[j]:=0;
            R[j]:=0;
            T[j]:=0
            end;
      for j := 1 to 100 do
```

```
            begin
            S[j]:= S[j-2]  -  (R[j-2] div R[j-1])*S[j-1];
            T[j]:= T[j-2]  -  (R[j-2] div R[j-1])*T[j-1];
            R[j]:= R[j-2]  -  (R[j-2] div R[j-1])*R[j-1];
            if R[j]=1 then goto 1
            end;
1 :    if T[j]>0 then inv:= T[j] else inv :=R[-1]+T[j] ;
end;

begin
for i:=1 to n do
        begin
        write ('prime p[', i ,'] is equal to ');
        read (p[i])
        end;
N:=1;
for i:=1 to n do N := N * p[i];
writeln ('N=',N);
for i:=1 to n do
        begin
        d := 0;
        e[i] := N div p[i];
        a := e[i] mod p[i];
        if a=1 then writeln ( 'idempotent element e[', i ,'] =',e[i])
else
                begin
                a := inv(p[i],a);
                e[i] := (e[i] * a ) mod N;
                writeln ('idempotent element e[', i ,'] =',e[i])
                end;
        end;
end.
```

Note that any idempotent element $e_i$ is the product of all primes except $p_i$. So to get the integer $e_i$, we first compute the integer $a = Np_i^{-1}$. Next, if $a \pmod{p_i}$ is equal to 1, then it is the number required otherwise we apply the function *inv* to find $a^{-1}$ in $GF(p_i)$. Then the idempotent element is equal to $aa^{-1} \pmod N$.

3. 38   The modulus $N = 15015$ and idempotent elements are:

$$e_1 = 5005$$
$$e_2 = 6006$$
$$e_3 = 10725$$
$$e_4 = 1365$$
$$e_5 = 6930$$

Selecting the smallest prime $q = 30047$, we get public key components as follows:

$$k_1 = 4565$$
$$k_2 = 5478$$
$$k_3 = 18367$$
$$k_4 = 1245$$
$$k_5 = 15566$$

for $r = 17831$. We compute cryptogram

$$C = |\ 4565 + 5478 - 18367 + 15566\ | = 7242$$

At the receiver's end, the cryptogram is transformed using the inverse element $r^{-1}$ in $GF(q)$, so,

$$C' = C\,r^{-1} = 7216$$

Next, the second element is calculated:

$$C'' = q - C' = 22831$$

$C'$ and $C''$ are now presented as vectors $[1,1,6,0,1]$ and $[1,1,4,7,3]$. Clearly, the first vector conveys the message 11101.

3. 39 First we calculate the modulus $N=2431$ and the idempotent elements:

$$e_1 = 221$$
$$e_2 = 1496$$
$$e_3 = 715$$

Next, we select a prime $q$ such that,

$$q > \max_{\mathbf{M}} \sum_{i=0}^{3} e_i m_i = 21888$$

Let $q = 21893$ and $r = 17321$ ($r^{-1} = 8241$). Components of the public key are equal to:

$$k_1 = e_1 r = 18559\ (\text{mod } 21893)$$
$$k_2 = e_2 r = 12797\ (\text{mod } 21893)$$
$$k_3 = e_3 r = 14970\ (\text{mod } 21893)$$

For example, for $M = (3,9,7)$, we get the cryptogram $C = 3\,k_1 + 9\,k_2 + 7\,k_3 = 275640$. The receiver transforms the cryptogram using $r^{-1}$ in $GF(q)$:

$$C\,r^{-1} = 19132\ (\text{mod } 21893)$$

The result is projected into three primes as follows:

$$19132\ (\text{mod } 11) = 3$$
$$19132\ (\text{mod } 13) = 9$$
$$19132\ (\text{mod } 17) = 7$$

and the message (3,9,7) is recovered at the sender's end.

3. 40 The modulus $N=4199$ and thus the idempotent elements equal:

$$e_1 = 1938$$
$$e_2 = 494$$
$$e_3 = 1768$$

To be able to recreate the message, we assume that elementary messages belong to $\{0,1,\ldots,\frac{1}{2}(p_i-1)\}$ where $p_i$ is the smallest integer. In the case in question $p_i = 11$. The set of elementary messages is $\{0,1,2,3,4,5,6\}$. The integer $q$ is chosen such that,

$$q > \sum_{i=1}^{3} 6 \cdot e_i = 25200$$

Let $q$ be 25219 and the random integer $r = 12357$ ($r^{-1} = 11386$). Components of the public key are equal to:

$$k_1 = e_1 \, r = 1938 \; 12357 = 15035 \; (\text{mod } 25219)$$
$$k_2 = e_2 \, r = 494 \; 12357 = 1360 \; (\text{mod } 25219)$$
$$k_3 = e_3 \, r = 1768 \; 12357 = 7522 \; (\text{mod } 25219)$$

For message $M = (6,5,2)$, we calculate:

$$m_1 \, k_1 = 6 \; 15035 = 90210$$
$$m_2 \, k_2 = 5 \; 1360 = 6800$$
$$m_3 \, k_3 = 2 \; 7522 = 15044$$

To minimize the cryptogram length, we determine it as:

$$C = 90210 - 6800 - 15044 = 68366$$

At the receiver end, we compute two candidates:

$$C' = C \, r^{-1} \; (\text{mod } q) = 68366 \; 11386 = 5622 \; (\text{mod } 25219),$$
$$C'' = q - C' = 19597.$$

The first gives:

$$C' \; (\text{mod } 13) = 5622 \; (\text{mod } 13) = 6$$
$$C' \; (\text{mod } 17) = 5622 \; (\text{mod } 17) = 12 = -5$$
$$C' \; (\text{mod } 19) = 5622 \; (\text{mod } 19) = 17 = -2$$

The second generates the triple $(6,13,8) = (6,4,11)$. The second candidate must be rejected as it does not convey the message – the third coordinate is greater than 6. So, the message is equal $(6,5,2)$ as all components are less than 6.

# 4

# AUTHENTICATION METHODS

As computer networks spread worldwide with network access via thousands of different terminals, protection requirements become more and more substantial. The challenge of providing adequate protection is closely related to both secrecy and authentication methods. Secrecy methods have been considered in the previous chapter. Now we are going to focus our attention on authentication methods. The need for providing authenticity arises in many different situations and it is especially crucial when a user operates from a remote terminal. Two different cases can be distinguished: user authentication and message authentication. User authentication can be made either directly when a user's specific characteristics (e.g. finger prints, voice frequency spectrum, retina patterns, digital signature flow, etc.) are checked, or indirectly when a unique secret piece of information is proved to be in the user's possession. As a matter of fact, the indirect user authentication is equivalent to the message authentication. Message authentication relies upon imposing a prearranged structure for the message.

Similar to the need for varying degrees and types of secrecy, there are many different levels and types of authentication. Some environments require simply message authentication, with no need for secrecy, while in others, both authentication and secrecy will be required. This chapter deals with a variety of authentication problems. It consists of four sections. The first section is devoted to elementary authentication schemes built using both classical and public-key ciphers. Having developed such elementary schemes, we can apply them to solve more complex authentication problems. In the second section, subliminal channels are considered. Several practical solutions for such channels are given. The third section examines authentication schemes which can be used for digital signatures generation. The last part of the chapter is devoted to other authentication techniques which are applied while designing computer protection.

## 4.1 Elementary methods of message authentication

Take a look at Figure 4.1 and assume that the sender forwards information to the receiver while the channel is under the opponent's control. The opponent's activity can take on many different forms but, in general, he/she can:

- block an information flow;
- record information and repeat it later during a spurious transmission session;

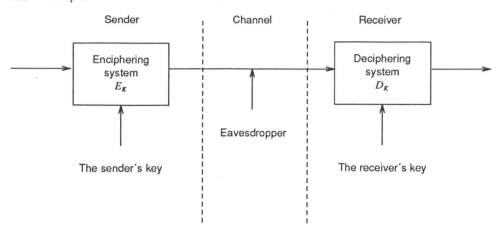

**Figure 4.1** An eavesdropper's access to an unprotected channel

- change the information content by removing, inserting, and/or rearranging several pieces of information.

Keeping in mind these attacks, we note that the receiver needs to be able to determine that:

- the message has in fact been forwarded by the alleged sender;
- the contents of the message have not been changed while transmitting via the channel.

Generally, also, the sender wants to know if the message he/she has forwarded has reached the intended destination. In order to fulfill this requirement, the receiver usually sends confirmation of any message he/she has received.

In this section we confine our attention to the simplest case of authentication where a single elementary message is sent and its receiver wishes to be able to determine its authenticity. In this case, the message authenticity relies upon fixing the set of so-called valid messages at both ends of the channel. In other words, any message is considered to be valid if it has the predetermined structure.

The general idea of elementary message authentication using classical cryptographic transformation is shown in Figure 4.2. The subset M (M ⊆ **M**) stands for the set of valid messages. This subset, whose security is not crucial, must be known to both communicating sides. The authentication process, in this case, runs as follows. The sender, having the message $M \in$ **M** creates the cryptogram $E_K(M)$, where $K$ is the key shared by both the sender and the receiver, and dispatches it. After receiving the cryptogram, the receiver decrypts it and checks the structure of the message obtained. If the message belongs to the set M, it is considered as original; otherwise it is rejected. Clearly, the correctness of this authentication scheme relies on the secrecy of the key.

Public-key cryptosystems can also be used to build an elementary authentication scheme. This second possibility is presented in Figure 4.3. Unlike public-key cryptosystems for secrecy, the sender generates the pair $(k, K)$. The key $k$ is kept secret while the key $K$ is sent via an insecure channel to the receiver. Having obtained the cryptogram $C = D_K(M)$, the receiver applies the public key $K$ and recreates the message

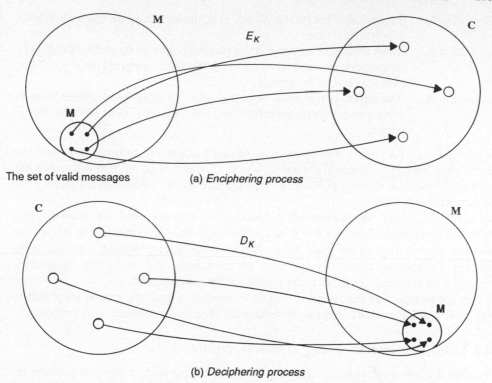

The set of valid messages    (a) *Enciphering process*

(b) *Deciphering process*

**Figure 4.2** The elementary authentication scheme based on a symmetric cryptosystem

$M = E_K(C)$ which is, from now on, considered to be original. However, to assume the authentication schemes work properly, the following conditions must be fulfilled:

Condition 1:    Calculation of both the cryptogram $C = D_K(M)$ (having the message $M$ and the secret key $k$) and the message $M = E_K(C)$, provided the cryptogram and the public key are known, must be easy, i.e. must run in polynomial time.

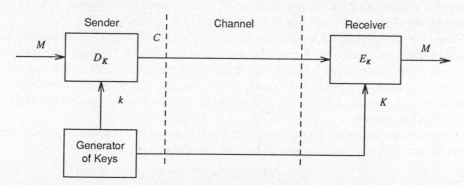

**Figure 4.3** An elementary authentication scheme based on an asymmetric cryptosystem with $k$ and $K$ secret and public keys, respectively

Condition 2:    Generation of the pair $(k, K)$ has to be dependent on the calculation being in polynomial time.

Condition 3:    Given the pair (a message and a suitable cryptogram) and the public key, computation of both the secret key $k$ and the cryptogram for any different message must be intractable.

Condition 4:    The public key $K$ must be authentic — in other words, there must be some way to establish whether the public key originated with the alleged sender.

Recall the RSA system. This system can be easily adapted to authentication purposes by shifting the key generator to the sender's side. The rest of the system is not changed. The RSA system is the only public-key cryptosystem which can be used for secrecy and authentication as well.

Generally, while using asymmetric (public-key) cryptosystems for authentication, both the cryptogram $C$ and the key $K$ are publicly known. This implies that anyone can recreate the message in the clear form. So, asymmetric cryptosystems deliver either secrecy or authentication. If you want to have both, you must use asymmetric cryptosystems twice    once for secrecy and then for authentication.

In the next section our attention will be focused on examining natural properties of symmetric and asymmetric cryptosystems that can be used for authentication purposes.

### 4.1.1 Authentication using classical ciphers

Assume that the authentication scheme is based on a symmetric cryptosystem where the same key is applied at both the sender's and the receiver's end. Clearly, the proper operation of this scheme depends on the secrecy of the key. The simplest elementary authentication scheme relies upon imposing a special message structure. For instance, the authentication process may consist in fixing beforehand a subsidiary message $M_s$ and sending cryptograms of the shape,

$$C = E_K (M, M_s)$$

where $M$ is the message whose authenticity is required to be verified, and the pair $(M, M_s)$ creates the single message which is encrypted. At the receiver's end, the cryptogram is decrypted and the extracted piece of message $M_s$ is compared to the original. If those two messages are the same, the message $M$ is considered to be authentic.

Now we assume that we would like to transmit messages without prearranging the message structure. Naturally, if messages are words of a natural language, the message structure is very well defined. Therefore, we can apply the obvious rule: If the decrypted message is a word (or a piece of the word) of the language, it is accepted as the original; otherwise it is rejected. Later on we will evaluate the effectiveness (quality) of such an authentication scheme.

Suppose that we are sending cryptograms $E_K(M)$, where $M$ is a sequence of $n$ letters. Then the set of all possible messages $\mathbf{M}$ has $26^n$ members,

$$|\mathbf{M}| = 26^n = 2^{nR}$$

where $R = \log_2 26 = 4.7$ . On the other hand, the set of acceptable messages $\mathsf{M}$ (which make sense in English) consists of $2^{nr}$, where $r$ is the rate of English language ($r = 1$).

So,

$$|M| = 2^{nr}$$

Now, assume that an opponent tries to substitute a false cryptogram for the original one. Not knowing the key, the opponent has to select the cryptogram at random and the chance of success is equal to:

$$P_e = \frac{2^{nr}}{2^{nR}} = 2^{-n(R-r)} \tag{4.1}$$

Clearly, the probability that the authentication process is carried out correctly is:

$$P_A = \frac{2^{nR} - 2^{nr}}{2^{nR}} = 1 - 2^{-n(R-r)} \tag{4.2}$$

The probability $P_A$ grows as the number of letters in the message increases. Intuitively, as the size of the message lengthens, the probability of finding a sensible English sequence drops due to the statistical interrelations between the letters in the language. For example, for $n = 5$ ($R = 4.7$ and $r = 1$), the probability of an erroneous authentication is $P_e = 2^{-18.5}$.

These results can be regarded as an estimate of the authentication effectiveness (quality). Greater $n$ corresponds to better effectiveness. Conversely, the results for $n = 1$ are totally unreliable since any single letter message is acceptable!

Formulae (4.1) and (4.2), lead to the important conclusion that:

> If the message source has no redundancy, that is, $D = R - r = 0$, then any simple authentication process, based on a symmetric cryptosystem, is useless.

Let us consider the following authentication problem. An enemy cryptanalyst observes both the message input and the cryptogram output, but he/she does not know the key (see Figure 4.4). How many observations of pairs (message, cryptogram) must the cryptanalyst obtain to determine the key correctly? Obviously, once the key has been discovered, the enemy crytanalyst can substitute any message and send it to the receiver

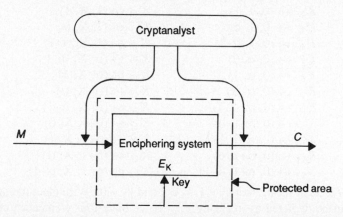

**Figure 4.4** The access available to an opponent cryptanalyst trying to determine a cryptographic key

| + | 0 | 1 | α | α+1 |
|---|---|---|---|-----|
| 0 | 0 | 1 | α | α+1 |
| 1 | 1 | 0 | α+1 | α |
| α | α | α+1 | 0 | 1 |
| α+1 | α+1 | α | 1 | 0 |

| · | 1 | α | α+1 |
|---|---|---|-----|
| 1 | 1 | α | α+1 |
| α | α | α+1 | 1 |
| α+1 | α+1 | 1 | α |

**Figure 4.5** Addition and multiplication tables for $GF(4)$

as a message generated by the genuine sender. The receiver would not be able to discover the substitution, assuming that no other measures are undertaken (the message source has no redundancy), due to the fact that the correctness of the authentication process depends upon the secrecy of keys used.

Consider the simplest case where the set of message **M**, the set of cryptograms **C**, and the set of keys **K** are the same, that is, $\mathbf{M} = \mathbf{C} = \mathbf{K} = \{0,1,\alpha,\alpha+1\}$. The set $\mathbf{X} = \{0,1,\alpha,\alpha+1\}$ along with addition and multiplication defined in Figure 4.5 creates the four element field GF(4). If our cryptosystem generates cryptograms according to the following formula:

$$C = M + K$$

where $C \in \mathbf{C}$, $M \in \mathbf{M}$, $K \in \mathbf{K}$, then the cipher takes on the form given in Figure 4.6. Our enemy cryptanalyst, knowing one pair (message, cryptogram), can determine the key applied. For example, if the observation consists of ($M = \alpha$ and $C = 1$) , then the key $K = \alpha+1$ .

A different situation arises when we deal with the cryptosystem whose operation is described by the following formula:

$$C = k_1 M^2 + (1 + k_1^3) k_2 M + k_3 \tag{4.3}$$

where $C, M, k_1, k_2, k_3$ belong to GF(4). Addition and multiplication are given in Figure 4.5. Suppose elements $k_1, k_2, k_3$ describe the key in the way shown below:

| | |
|---|---|
| $K_1 \leftrightarrow (k_1{=}0,\ k_2{=}1,\ k_3{=}0)$ | $K_{13} \leftrightarrow (1, \mathbf{X}, 0)$ |
| $K_2 \leftrightarrow (0, 1, 1)$ | $K_{14} \leftrightarrow (1, \mathbf{X}, 1)$ |
| $K_3 \leftrightarrow (0, 1, \alpha)$ | $K_{15} \leftrightarrow (1, \mathbf{X}, \alpha)$ |
| $K_4 \leftrightarrow (0, 1, \alpha+1)$ | $K_{16} \leftrightarrow (1, \mathbf{X}, \alpha+1)$ |
| $K_5 \leftrightarrow (0, \alpha, 0)$ | $K_{17} \leftrightarrow (\alpha, \mathbf{X}, 0)$ |
| $K_6 \leftrightarrow (0, \alpha, 1)$ | $K_{18} \leftrightarrow (\alpha, \mathbf{X}, 1)$ |
| $K_7 \leftrightarrow (0, \alpha, \alpha)$ | $K_{19} \leftrightarrow (\alpha, \mathbf{X}, \alpha)$ |
| $K_8 \leftrightarrow (0, \alpha, \alpha+1)$ | $K_{20} \leftrightarrow (\alpha, \mathbf{X}, \alpha+1)$ |
| $K_9 \leftrightarrow (0, \alpha+1, 0)$ | $K_{21} \leftrightarrow (\alpha+1, \mathbf{X}, 0)$ |
| $K_{10} \leftrightarrow (0, \alpha+1, 1)$ | $K_{22} \leftrightarrow (\alpha+1, \mathbf{X}, 1)$ |
| $K_{11} \leftrightarrow (0, \alpha+1, \alpha)$ | $K_{23} \leftrightarrow (\alpha+1, \mathbf{X}, \alpha)$ |
| $K_{12} \leftrightarrow (0, \alpha+1, \alpha+1)$ | $K_{24} \leftrightarrow (\alpha+1, \mathbf{X}, \alpha+1)$ |

The notation (1, **X**, 0) means that $k_1 = 1$, $k_2 \in \mathbf{X}$ and $k_3 = 0$. With the notation introduced, the cipher can be depicted as in Figure 4.7. If we have four elementary messages, the number of all possible one-to-one permutations is equal 4! = 24. So, any key points out exactly one permutation from the set of all possible permutations.

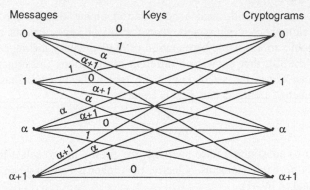

**Figure 4.6** Graph representing a simple cipher defined on *GF*(4)

Suppose now, that the key is fixed and equals $K_{17}$ (the key 17 in Figure 4.7) and our cryptanalyst knows a pair ($M = \alpha$, $C = 1$). Looking at Figure 4.7, he/she can state that the key applied must belong to the set {4,7,9,15,17,24}. In order to substitute the cryptogram for his/her false message $M_f = 1$, the enemy faces the choice of choosing the correct key from the set of six equally probable elements. Suitable cryptograms for the false message are:

$$E_{K_4}(M_f = 1) = E_{K_{17}}(M_f = 1) = \alpha$$
$$E_{K_7}(M_f = 1) = E_{K_{24}}(M_f = 1) = 0$$
$$E_{K_9}(M_f = 1) = E_{K_{15}}(M_f = 1) = \alpha+1$$

As you can see the cryptanalyst has to choose the cryptogram for the false message from all remaining elements !

A second observation ($M=\alpha+1$, $C=\alpha+1$) causes the cryptanalyst to modify the key set from which the used key belongs. This modified set equals {7,17}. Moreover, the cryptogram for $M_f=1$ can be either 0 or $\alpha$. This observation increases the chance of guessing both the correct value of the key and the cryptogram for a false message, but the enemy still does not know the key for sure! Clearly, a third observation breaks the cipher.

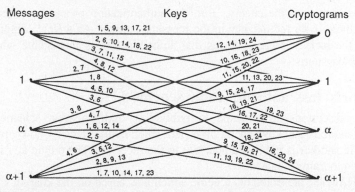

**Figure 4.7** Graph of a cipher which is broken after any three observations of (message, cryptogram)

In general, if we deal with such a permutation cipher defined for $N$ elementary messages and $N$ elementary cryptograms, then the set of keys consists of $N!$ different keys. Each key points to a suitable permutation of $N$ elementary messages. It is easy to prove [PIEP79, PIEP80], that knowing $r$ different observations (message, cryptogram), the cryptanalyst can create the set of keys from which the key that has been applied belongs. The number of elements in the set is equal to:

$$\frac{N!}{(N-r)!} \tag{4.4}$$

Similarly, in order to substitute a false message, the enemy has to select the cryptogram from $(N-r)$ equally probable elements. Clearly, the cipher is broken when the number of observations is equal to $(N-1)$.

From the point of view of authentication, the last cipher considered above has the advantage that the cryptanalyst always faces the decision of selecting the correct key or cryptogram. Unfortunately, designing such a permutation cipher is relatively easy for $N=3$ or 4 but as the number $N$ grows, the number of keys increases very rapidly ($|\mathbf{K}| = N!$). This explosion of keys causes expansion of the key length. In our case, in order to input a key, we need $\log_2 24 = 4.6$ bit sequence. Generally, the practical application of these ciphers is limited.

On the other hand, if the enemy selects a cryptogram at random (he/she is not interested in substituting a prearranged message) and forwards it supposedly from the sender, to cause confusion to the receiver, then the receiver cannot discover the substitution (assuming that the message source has no redundancy).

Summing up, symmetric cryptosystems can be used for authentication purposes when the message source has inherent redundancy. However, if the authentication procedure is very crucial and we are striving to increase the probability of discovery of illegitimate cryptograms, then we must add extra redundancy to the message source. On the other hand, assuming that the enemy cryptanalyst has access to both the message input and the cryptogram output, and has access to unlimited computation power, we can design a cipher so that the enemy cannot calculate the cryptogram for his/her prearranged message. In other words, we are saying that he/she faces a choice for the key used from a set of $\dfrac{N!}{(N-r)!}$ keys, where N is the number of messages in the cipher and $r$ is the number of observations known to the enemy. But, the authentication procedure based on this cipher fails if there is no redundancy in the message source. As a final conclusion, we can state that the lack of secrecy means that authentication is impossible while using symmetric cryptosystems.

## 4.1.2 Shamir's fast authentication scheme

All the next subsections are devoted to public-key authentication schemes. Their characteristic feature is that key generation is performed by the sender who keeps one key in secrecy while another is published and sent to the receiver. The public key is used to authenticate cryptograms obtained.

Shamir [SHAM78] presented his scheme which was based on the knapsack problem. It should be pointed out at once that the system has been broken by Odlyzko [ODLY84b]. We intend to discuss it as it is an excellent illustration of the general rule that even **NPC** problems do not always generate strong authentication schemes. Nevertheless, the system is very fast, even when implemented in software, and recreating the clear messages can be done immediately by the receiver.

The system, as first proposed by Shamir, was questioned with regard to security, and it was later improved by him. We shall follow its development. Under the original system, the sender creates a $n \times 2n$ binary matrix $K = [k_{ij}]$ whose elements are chosen at random. $K$ can be treated as a secret key known to the sender only. Next, he/she fixes a prime $p$ where $p \geq 2^n$ and calculates the vector $A = (a_1, \ldots, a_{2n})$ by solving the following congruence:

$$K \times A = \begin{bmatrix} 1 \\ 2 \\ \cdot \\ \cdot \\ \cdot \\ 2^{n-1} \end{bmatrix} \pmod p \tag{4.5}$$

where $a_i$; $i = 1, \ldots, 2n$, are integers of the GF($p$). As the sender has $n$ elementary congruences in $2n$ unknowns, he/she chooses at random $n$ elements of $A$ and computes the rest using (4.5). The pair $(A, p)$ can be treated as the public key. For a given message $M \in GF(p)$, he/she converts it to binary sequence $M = (m_1, \ldots, m_n)$ where $m_i \in \{0,1\}$ for $i = 1, \ldots, n$. The cryptogram (the authenticator) of $M$ is determined as follows:

$$C = \dot{M} \times K \tag{4.6}$$

where $\dot{M} = (m_n, \ldots, m_1)$ is the binary representation of $M$ written backwards.

Upon reception, the receiver calculates the message:

$$M = C \times A \pmod p \tag{4.7}$$

using the cryptogram $C$ and the public key $(A,p)$. The system works as:

$$E_K(C) = C \times A = \sum_{j=0}^{2n} c_j \, a_j = \sum_{j=1}^{2n} \left( \sum_{i=1}^{n} m_{n-i+1} \, k_{ij} \right) a_j = \sum_{i=1}^{n} m_{n-i+1} \sum_{j=1}^{2n} k_{ij} \, a_j =$$

$$\sum_{i=1}^{n} m_{n-i+1} \, 2^{i-1} = m_n 2^0 + m_{n-1} 2^1 + \ldots + m_2 2^{n-1} + m_1 2^n = M \pmod p$$

where $C = (c_1, \ldots, c_{2n})$ and $A = (a_1, \ldots, a_{2n})$. It is, however, very insecure, as opponents can deduce the structure of the secret matrix $K$. Each message sent yields a set of $2n$ linear equations, which lead to the discovery of some elements of $K$. On the average, it will only take $n$ messages before the whole of $K$ can be deduced.

In order to prevent this type of analysis, Shamir proposed adding a random factor with each message. In this more secure version, each message has associated with it some random vector $R = (r_1, \ldots, r_{2n})$ where $r_i \in \{0,1\}$ for $i = 1, \ldots, 2n$. The cryptogram $C$ is then formed in the following way. First of all, the sender forms the modified message:

$$\underline{M} = M - R \times A \pmod p \tag{4.8}$$

using the vector $R$ and produces the initial cryptogram:

$$\underline{C} = \underline{M} \times K \pmod p$$

The final cryptogram takes on the following form:

$$C = \underline{C} + R \qquad\qquad (4.9)$$

and is forwarded to the receiver. Once again, authentication is performed by checking that $C \times A = M \pmod{p}$. In this case, this works because,

$$C \times A = (\underline{C} + R)\,A = \underline{C} \times A + R \times A = M \pmod{p}$$

The method is illustrated as follows.

*Example*

Suppose that we are to design Shamir's system for authenticating messages of the set GF(7), that is, $p = 7$. Of course, the number $n$ should be chosen in such a way that any message can be presented in the binary form so, in this case, $n = 3$. Accept that the secret key is the matrix,

$$K = \begin{bmatrix} 0 & 0 & 1 & 1 & 0 & 0 \\ 1 & 1 & 1 & 0 & 1 & 0 \\ 1 & 0 & 0 & 0 & 1 & 1 \end{bmatrix}$$

and $a_1$, $a_2$, $a_3$ have been selected at random and $a_1 = 1$, $a_2 = 3$, $a_3 = 4$ ($a_1, a_2, a_3 \in$ GF(7)). The rest of $A$ is determined by solving the following congruence system:

$$\begin{bmatrix} 0 & 0 & 1 & 1 & 0 & 0 \\ 1 & 1 & 1 & 0 & 1 & 0 \\ 1 & 0 & 0 & 0 & 1 & 1 \end{bmatrix} \times \begin{bmatrix} 1 \\ 3 \\ 4 \\ a_4 \\ a_5 \\ a_6 \end{bmatrix} = \begin{bmatrix} 1 \\ 2 \\ 4 \end{bmatrix} \pmod 7$$

as a result, the vector $A$ (the public key) takes on the form $A = (1,3,4,4,1,2)$. Consider two cases, namely:

*Case 1*: The first version of the system without randomization. It is easy to see that, for the message $M = 3$, we get:

$$C = \dot{M} \times K = [\,1,\,1,\,0\,] \times \begin{bmatrix} 0 & 0 & 1 & 1 & 0 & 0 \\ 1 & 1 & 1 & 0 & 1 & 0 \\ 1 & 0 & 0 & 0 & 1 & 1 \end{bmatrix} = [\,1,\,1,\,2,\,1,\,1,\,0\,]$$

On receipt of the cryptogram, the receiver recreates the message using the public key $(A, p)$ as:

$$M = C \times A = [\,1,\,1,\,2,\,1,\,1,\,0\,] \times \begin{bmatrix} 1 \\ 3 \\ 4 \\ 4 \\ 1 \\ 2 \end{bmatrix} = 17 = 3 \pmod 7$$

*Case 2*: The second version of the system with randomization. Let $R = (0,1,1,1,0,1)$ and then the modified message is equal to:

$$\underline{M} = M - R \times A = 3 - [\,0,\ 1,\ 1,\ 1,\ 0,\ 1\,] \times \begin{bmatrix} 1 \\ 3 \\ 4 \\ 4 \\ 1 \\ 2 \end{bmatrix} = 3 - 13 = 4 \ (\mathrm{mod}\ 7)$$

The message $M = 4$ is converted into the binary sequence $(1,0,0)$ and then $\dot{M} = (0,0,1)$. The initial cryptogram takes the form:

$$\underline{C} = \dot{M} \times K = [\,0,\ 0,1\,] \times \begin{bmatrix} 0 & 0 & 1 & 1 & 0 & 0 \\ 1 & 1 & 1 & 0 & 1 & 0 \\ 1 & 0 & 0 & 0 & 1 & 1 \end{bmatrix} = [\,1,\ 0,\ 0,\ 0,\ 1,\ 1\,]$$

and the final cryptogram is:

$$C = \underline{C} + R = [1,0,0,0,1,1] + [0,1,1,1,0,1] = [1,1,1,1,1,2]$$

Authentication process relies upon multiplying $C$ and $A$, thus:

$$M = C \times A = [1,1,1,1,1,2] \times \begin{bmatrix} 1 \\ 3 \\ 4 \\ 4 \\ 1 \\ 2 \end{bmatrix} = 17 = 3 \ (\mathrm{mod}\ 7)$$

Notice that the generation of cryptograms is done by using binary representation of messages while, in the authentication process, messages are obtained as elements of $GF(p)$.    □

With the addition of the random vector $R$, intruders are prevented from performing the simple linear analysis which was possible originally. It is suggested by Shamir that $n$ be about one hundred.

Despite the improvement presented above, the system is still insecure as Odlyzko has shown [ODLY84b] how to cryptanalyse it. Unlike the straightforward attack on the basic system (thwarted by introducing the random vector), Odlyzko does not try to deduce the secret matrix $K$. Instead, another matrix is constructed which allows intruders to generate some cryptogram (authenticator) $C'$ for messages so that the original message can be recreated using both the original cryptogram $C$ and the forged one $C'$, that is,

$$C \times A = C' \times A = M \ (\mathrm{mod}\ p)$$

Odlyzko has shown how to find, for each integer $M \in GF(p)$, some integers $k'_1, k'_2, \ldots, k'_{2n}$ such that:

$$M = \sum_{i=1}^{2n} k'_i a_i \ (\mathrm{mod}\ p)$$

where $k'_i \in GF(p)$ for all $i$. This cryptanalysis is essentially dependent upon the secret matrix $K$ being a 0–1 matrix. However, if $K$ is not binary, attention can be restricted to matrices $K$ in which all column sums are less than or equal to $m$, for some $m < n$, so that valid cryptograms have $0 \le k'_i \le m$. But if $m$ is small, say $m < \sqrt{n}$, then this attack is expected to fail, even though individual messages could still be attacked and each of these messages would reveal information about $K$.

## 4.1.3 Ong-Schnorr-Shamir authentication scheme

Ong, Schnorr and Shamir [ONG84] presented an authentication scheme based on the factorization problem and the quadratic congruence problem.[1] The system is outlined briefly below.

The sender chooses a large integer $N$ which is known to be composite, although its factorization need not be known. The integer $N$ defines a suitable arithmetic with addition and multiplication modulo $N$. It is therefore published, creating the first part of the public key. Next, a random integer $k$ is picked such that $gcd(k,N) = 1$, and $k$ is kept secret. The second part of public key is calculated as:

$$K = -k^{-2} \pmod{N} \tag{4.10}$$

The pair $(K, N)$ constitutes the public key. To authenticate a message $M$, where $gcd(M,N) = 1$, the sender selects another random number $R$ such that $gcd(R,N) = 1$ and computes :

$$C_1 = \tfrac{1}{2}\left[\frac{M}{R} + R\right] \pmod{N} \quad \text{and} \quad C_2 = \tfrac{1}{2}k\left[\frac{M}{R} - R\right] \pmod{N} \tag{4.11}$$

The cryptogram (authenticator) $C = (C_1, C_2)$ is transmitted to the receiver.

The receiver recreates the message using the following equation:

$$M = C_1^2 + K\,C_2^2 \pmod{N} \tag{4.12}$$

The reason this works can be seen by simply substituting $C_1$ and $C_2$ back into the last equation, whence,

$$C_1^2 + K\,C_2^2 = \tfrac{1}{4}\left[\frac{M}{R} + R\right]^2 - \frac{1}{k^2}\tfrac{1}{4}k^2\left[\frac{M}{R} - R\right]^2 = \tfrac{1}{4}\,4M = M \pmod{N}$$

To illustrate the operation of the system, consider the following example.

*Example*

Suppose the sender has chosen $N=15$ and $k=2$ $(gcd(N,k) = 1)$. Knowing the secret key $k$, he/she finds that:

$$K = -k^{-2} = -(k^{-1})^2 = -8 \cdot 8 = -64 = 11 \pmod{15}$$

while $k=2 \pmod{15}$ has its inverse $k^{-1}=8 \pmod{15}$. The pair $(K, N)=(11,15)$ is published. Now, if the sender intends to send the message $M=13$ $(gcd(M, N) = 1)$, he/she first picks a random integer $R$ — let it be 4, $(R^{-1} = 4)$ — then calculates a suitable pair:

$$C_1 = \tfrac{1}{2}(MR^{-1} + R) = 8(13 \cdot 4 + 4) = 13 \pmod{15}$$
$$C_2 = \tfrac{1}{2}k(MR^{-1} - R) = (13 \cdot 4 - 4) = 3 \pmod{15},$$

---

1.  The Quadratic Congruence Problem is defined as follows:
    *Instance*: Positive integers $a$, $b$, and $c$.
    *Question*: Is there a positive integer $x<c$ such that $x^2 = a \pmod{b}$?
    This problem is **NP-complete** - see [GAJO79] p. 249.

and forwards the pair (13,3) to the receiver. In turn, the receiver recreates the message using the public key as follows:

$$M = C_1^2 + K\ C_2^2 = 13^2 + 11 \cdot 9 = 13 \ (\text{mod } 15)$$    □

Summing up, the system expands the length of cryptograms twice compared to the length of messages. Unfortunately, the system has been broken by J. M. Pollard.

## 4.1.4 El Gamal's authentication scheme

The next authentication scheme that we are going to describe is due to El Gamal [ELGA85]. Under this scheme, based on the difficulty of solving the discrete logarithm problem (see section 2.2.3), the sender chooses a finite field $GF(p)$, $p$ a prime, and a primitive element $g \in GF(p)$. He/she also selects a random integer $r \in GF(p)$ and calculates,

$$K = g^r \ (\text{mod } p) \tag{4.13}$$

$K$ along with $g$ and $p$ is published as the public key.

To authenticate a message $M$ ($M \in GF(p)$), the sender chooses the second random integer $R$ ($R \in GF(p)$) such that $gcd(R, p-1)=1$ and computes,

$$X = g^R \ (\text{mod } p) \tag{4.14}$$

The sender then uses the Euclidean Algorithm to solve the congruence,

$$M = r \cdot X + R \cdot Y \ (\text{mod } p-1) \tag{4.15}$$

for $Y$. The triple $(M,X,Y)$ is transmitted to the receiver while the pair $(r,R)$ is being kept secret.

Upon reception of $(M,X,Y)$, the receiver forms,

$$A = K^X X^Y \ (\text{mod } p) \tag{4.16}$$

and accepts the message $M$ as authentic if and only if,

$$A = g^M \ (\text{mod } p) \tag{4.17}$$

It is worth noting that possessing the pair $(X, Y)$, does not permit the message $M$ to be recreated. Instead, the sender can check if the pair $(X, Y)$ matches the message $M$. That is why $(X, Y)$ is usually called an authenticator (instead of a cryptogram).

The justification that the system works is straightforward. First notice that any primitive element $g$ of $GF(p)$ generates all non-zero elements of the field, that is,

$$g^0 = 1, \ g^1, \ g^2, \dots, \ g^{p-2}, \ g^{p-1} = 1$$

Therefore, $g^\alpha = g^\beta$ if and only if $\alpha = \beta$ (mod $p-1$). So, starting with (4.15) and (4.17), we have:

$$A = g^M = g^{rX} g^{RY}$$

Substituting $K = g^r$ and $X = g^R$, we get (4.16).

The scheme is illustrated below.

*Example*

Take the finite field $GF(11)$ and its primitive element $g = 2$. It is easy to generate all non-zero elements of $GF(11)$, namely:

$$2^0 = 1 \ (\text{mod}11)$$
$$2^1 = 2 \ (\text{mod}11)$$
$$2^2 = 4 \ (\text{mod}11)$$
$$2^3 = 8 \ (\text{mod}11)$$
$$2^4 = 5 \ (\text{mod}11)$$
$$2^5 = 10 \ (\text{mod}11)$$
$$2^6 = 9 \ (\text{mod}11)$$
$$2^7 = 7 \ (\text{mod}11)$$
$$2^8 = 3 \ (\text{mod}11)$$
$$2^9 = 6 \ (\text{mod}11)$$
$$2^{10} = 1 \ (\text{mod}11)$$

Let the sender select $r = 8$ and produce $K = g^r = 2^8 = 3 \ (\text{mod } 11)$. Then the public key $(K, g, p) = (3, 2, 11)$. Given the message $M=5$, he/she chooses the second random integer, $R = 9$ say, such that $gcd(R, p-1) = gcd(9,10) = 1$, and computes $X = g^R = 2^9 = 6 \ (\text{mod } 11)$. Next, the sender solves the congruence (4.15) for $M = 5$, $r = 8$, $X = 6$, $R = 9$ and gets $Y = 3$. The sender now forwards the triple $(M, X, Y)$, in our case $(5, 6, 3)$, to the receiver.

Having obtained the triple and public key $(K, g, p) = (3, 2, 11)$, the receiver produces two numbers:

1. $K^X X^Y \ (\text{mod p}) = 3^6 \ 6^3 = 10 \ (\text{mod } 11)$;
2. $g^M \ (\text{mod p}) = 2^5 = 10 \ (\text{mod } 11)$.

As these two integers are equal, the message $M = 5$ is accepted as authentic. ☐

El Gamal's scheme is the first example of the common technique which relies upon sending messages in the clear form along with an attached authenticator. In these cases, the authentication process consists in checking whether the authenticator fits the message.

## 4.1.5 Rivest-Shamir-Adleman authentication scheme

The RSA authentication scheme uses a sender $A$ who selects an appropriate arithmetic modulo $N_A = p_A \times q_A$, where $p_A$ and $q_A$ are primes. Subsequently, $A$ calculates,

$$\gamma (N_A) = lcm \ (p_A - 1, \ q_A - 1)$$

while $lcm$ stands for the least common multiple. The sender selects his/her pair of keys $(k_A, K_A)$ such that,

$$k_A \times K_A = 1 \ (\text{mod } \gamma(N_A))$$

The modulus $N_A$ and the key, $K_A$, are published. Finally, the sender calculates the cryptogram $C$ for the message $M$ according to the following congruence:

$$C = D_A (M) = M^{k_A} \ (\text{mod } N_A)$$

and sends it to the receiver. On the other hand, anyone who knows the triple $(C, K_A, N_A)$ can recreate the message as:

$$M = E_A(C) = C^{K_A} \pmod{N_A}$$

The RSA authentication scheme is vulnerable to so-called 'chosen cryptogram attack'. Assume that an opponent chooses at random an integer $C_f < N_A$ and computes:

$$C_f^{K_A} = M_f \pmod{N_A}$$

As a result, the opponent can claim that the message $M_f$ has been authenticated by user $A$.

This kind of attack can be applied to authentication of unpredictable messages only — the forger is forced to select cryptograms at random! To thwart the chosen-cryptogram attack, it is necessary to have redundancy in the message source. So, all integers from 0 to $N_A-1$ are messages, but only a small portion of these are valid messages.

The only known cryptosystem which can be adapted for both authentication and secrecy at the same time is the RSA system. Assume that the RSA system has been applied twice in the way shown in Figure 4.8. The system $A$ created by the sender $A$ authenticates messages while the system $B$ defined by the receiver $B$ introduces the secrecy. The key pairs $(k_A, K_A)$ and $(k_B, K_B)$ are independently calculated at the sender's and the receiver's ends, respectively (see Chapter 3). Of course, the public keys $K_A$ and $K_B$ along with the pair $(N_A, N_B)$ are interchanged between both parties, where integers $N_A, N_B$ define suitable arithmetics modulo $N_A$ and $N_B$. The moduli in question are chosen independently.

Suppose for the moment that $N_B > N_A$, then the cryptogram $C = E_B(M)$ can be greater than $N_A$ and the next operation $D_A(C)$ causes a loss of accuracy so the message cannot be recreated by the receiver. Thus the integer $N_A$ must be greater than $N_B$ to ensure the proper working of the system of Figure 4.8.

In ensuring that $N_A > N_B$ in every case, both sides should agree beforehand to a threshold integer $t$. The sender then selects his/her modulus $N_A > t$ but the receiver chooses $N_B < t$. This ensures that $N_A > N_B$ all the time.

The second solution to the problem has been suggested by Kohnfelder [KOHN78a]. In his solution, both the sender and the receiver have full freedom in choosing their moduli $N_A$ and $N_B$. However, after having published them, they calculate cryptograms according to:

$$C = \begin{cases} D_A(E_B(M)) & \text{if } N_A > N_B \\ E_B(D_A(M)) & \text{if } N_A < N_B \end{cases} \tag{4.18}$$

In other words, if $N_A > N_B$, the first cryptographic operation ensures the secrecy but the second one provides the authentication (see Figure 4.8). Otherwise $(N_A > N_B)$, the secrecy process follows the authentication one. Clearly, these observations are valid for the sender.

## 4.2 Subliminal channel

The notion of *subliminal channel* was introduced by Simmons [SIMM84a] while considering his 'Prisoners' Problem'. In order to explain the notion in question, let us present the problem in full.

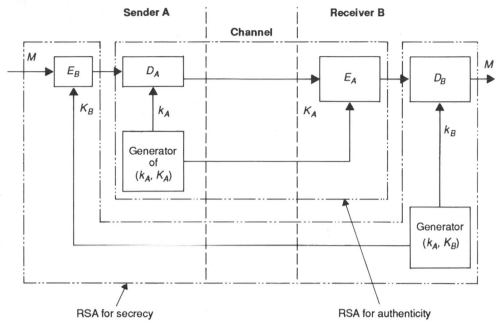

**Sender A**                              **Receiver B**

Channel

**Figure 4.8** Application of RSA cryptosystems for secrecy and authenticity

## PRISONERS' PROBLEM

*Two accomplices in a crime have been arrested and are about to be locked in widely separated cells. Their only means of communication after they are locked up will be by way of messages conveyed for them by trustees who are known to be agents of the warden. The warden is willing to allow the prisoners to exchange messages in the hope that he can deceive at least one of them into accepting as a genuine communication from the other either a fraudulent message created by the warden himself or else a modification by him of a genuine message.*

*However, since he has every reason to suspect that the prisoners want to coordinate an escape plan, the warden will only permit the exchanges to occur if the information contained in the message is completely open to him — and presumably innocuous.*

*The prisoners, on the other hand, are willing to accept these conditions, that is, to accept some risk of deception in order to be able to communicate at all, since they need to coordinate their plans. To do this they will have to deceive the warden by finding a way of communicating secretly in the exchanges, that is, of establishing a 'subliminal channel' between them in full view of the warden, even though the messages themselves contain no secret (to the warden) information. Since they anticipate that the warden will try to deceive them by introducing fraudulent messages, they will only exchange messages if they are permitted to authenticate them.*

The subliminal channel is thus a covert communication channel that cannot be read by those for whom it is not intended. Some simple examples occur in everyday life when we, for instance, give a certain look to a certain person, or wink, or raise an eyebrow perhaps. Here, some form of communication is occurring between two (or more) parties, and those who listen to the conversation but do not observe the communicants will not see the subliminal channel. This is, of course, a very simple example but should serve to illustrate the concept.

This section is intended to present different solutions of the Prisoners' Problem. In other words, we are going to describe different subliminal channels.

## 4.2.1 Elementary subliminal channel

Let us start with an elementary subliminal channel which allows the transmission of one-bit messages. In order to do this, the concept of redundancy of transmitting information must be introduced. Assume that the prisoners and the warden agree to the transmission of a three bit cryptogram. This cryptogram can be seen as a carrier of one-bit overt messages which are intended to be sent to the receiving prisoner in the presence of the warden. The set of all possible cryptograms is divided into two subsets: the first $\{000, 011, 101, 110\} = C_0$ and the second $\{111, 100, 010, 001\} = C_1$. The set $C_0$ of even parity sequences is assigned to the message "0" and the set $C_1$ of odd parity sequences corresponds to the message "1".

The prisoners agree beforehand on two patterns (one of $C_0$ and one of $C_1$) which will be accepted as sequences that transmit "0" and ".1", respectively. This agreement can be treated as a secret key shared by the prisoners only. For instance, let the prisoners fix that the sequence 011 corresponds to the message "0" but the sequence 010 stands for the message "1" (see Figure 4.9). Let the sequence (100, 010, 000, 011, 101) generated by

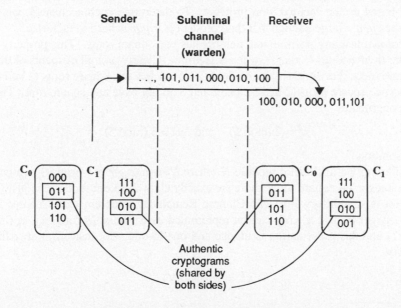

**Figure 4.9** Binary subliminal channel

the sender be transmitted via the subliminal channel to the receiver. The wardens know that the cryptogram sequence is equivalent to the message sequence (1,1,0,0,0) but they do not know which messages are meaningful. The receiver, however, having the list of authentic cryptograms, can easily decide that the first, the third, and the fifth cryptograms carry spurious messages while the second and the fourth contain meaningful ones.

The wardens, therefore if they attempt impersonation and send a message of their own construction have a probability of one-quarter of successfully deceiving the receiving prisoner. If the wardens attempt substitution, by modifying a sent cryptogram, that is, by choosing a sequence from the opposite set to the actual cryptogram given to them by the sender, then they have the same probability of successful deception.

A modification of the presented subliminal channel can rely on allowing the prisoners to agree to use more than one cryptogram from each parity set. For example, let 000, 011 $\in C_0$ and 100, 010 $\in C_1$ create two pairs of cryptograms. A cryptogram of the first pair will be sent to indicate a message "0" (a subliminal 0) and the other for a message "1" (a subliminal 1). The receiving prisoner will now accept any of four messages (i.e. 000, 011, 100, 010) as authentic, and thus the wardens' probability of successful deception rises to one-half under either the impersonation or substitution strategy.

The channel we have considered is designed to transmit one-bit messages using three-bit cryptograms. So, any cryptogram imposes two redundant bits that are applied for authentication purposes while only one bit carries the message. This kind of transmission provides authentication but no secrecy — the wardens know the parity sets $C_0$, $C_1$ and their correspondence to messages.

### 4.2.2 Simmons subliminal channel

The following method of subliminal channel construction is due to Simmons [SIMM84a], and it is based on the factorization problem. To determine such a channel, we choose three primes $p$, $q$, $r$ large enough that their product $N = pqr$ is hard to factorize.[2]

It is known that any positive real number has two square roots. This property is also held in the field modulo $N$, that is, when $N$ is prime. Clearly, not all elements of that field have square roots. For instance, in the field $GF(5)$, 1 has two square roots (1 and 4), and 4 has also two square roots (2 and 3), but 2 and 3 do not have any square root. That is to say, the congruences

$$x^2 = 2 \;(\text{mod } 5) \quad \text{and} \quad x^2 = 3 \;(\text{mod } 5)$$

have no solution.

Considering the arithmetic modulo $N$ where $N=pqr$ ($p,q,r$ are primes), we can state that if an integer has square roots, there are exactly eight different roots. The justification of this fact is straightforward. The Chinese Remainder Theorem (see Chapter 2) says that any integer $a$ $(0 < a < N)$ can be represented as a vector [$a \;(\text{mod } p)$, $a \;(\text{mod } q)$, $a \;(\text{mod } r)$] and this presentation is unique and one-to-one. So, instead of searching the congruence,

$$x^2 = a \;(\text{mod } N), \tag{4.19}$$

---

2.  Usually these primes should satisfy additional restrictions to make their product infeasible to factor.

we can solve three congruences,

$$x^2 = a_1 \ (\mathrm{mod}\ p)$$
$$x^2 = a_2 \ (\mathrm{mod}\ q) \qquad\qquad (4.20)$$
$$x^2 = a_3 \ (\mathrm{mod}\ r)$$

where $a = [a \ (\mathrm{mod}\ p), \ a \ (\mathrm{mod}\ q), \ a \ (\mathrm{mod}\ r)] = [a_1, \ a_2, \ a_3]$. The triple $[x_1, x_2, x_3] = [x \ (\mathrm{mod}\ p), \ x \ (\mathrm{mod}\ q), \ x \ (\mathrm{mod}\ r)]$ creates the solution required.

*Example*

Take the integer $N = 105$ whose factorization is $p = 3$, $q = 5$, $r = 7$ and consider the congruence:

$$x^2 = 64 \ (\mathrm{mod}\ 105) \quad \text{where} \quad gcd(64, 105) = 1$$

If we consider the congruence itself, we deal with an instance of the quadratic congruence problem (see subsection 4.1.3) which is known to be **NPC**. But knowing the factorization of $N$, we can solve three simpler congruences of the form (4.20), namely:

$$x^2 = 64 = 1 \ (\mathrm{mod}\ 3)$$
$$x^2 = 64 = 4 \ (\mathrm{mod}\ 5)$$
$$x^2 = 64 = 1 \ (\mathrm{mod}\ 7)$$

Solutions of these congruences are as follows:

$x_{10} = 1 \ (\mathrm{mod}\ 3)$, $x_{11} = 2 \ (\mathrm{mod}\ 3)$ — the first congruence
$x_{20} = 2 \ (\mathrm{mod}\ 5)$, $x_{21} = 3 \ (\mathrm{mod}\ 5)$ — the second congruence
$x_{30} = 1 \ (\mathrm{mod}\ 7)$, $x_{31} = 6 \ (\mathrm{mod}\ 7)$ — the third congruence

So, they produce eight final solutions of our basic congruence

$$x_{10}, x_{20}, x_{30} \rightarrow [1, 2, 1] = 22 \ (\mathrm{mod}\ 105)$$
$$x_{10}, x_{20}, x_{31} \rightarrow [1, 2, 6] = 97 \ (\mathrm{mod}\ 105)$$
$$x_{10}, x_{21}, x_{30} \rightarrow [1, 3, 1] = 43 \ (\mathrm{mod}\ 105)$$
$$x_{10}, x_{21}, x_{31} \rightarrow [1, 3, 6] = 13 \ (\mathrm{mod}\ 105)$$
$$x_{11}, x_{20}, x_{30} \rightarrow [2, 2, 1] = 92 \ (\mathrm{mod}\ 105)$$
$$x_{11}, x_{20}, x_{31} \rightarrow [2, 2, 6] = 62 \ (\mathrm{mod}\ 105)$$
$$x_{11}, x_{21}, x_{30} \rightarrow [2, 3, 1] = \ 8 \ (\mathrm{mod}\ 105)$$
$$x_{11}, x_{21}, x_{31} \rightarrow [2, 3, 6] = 83 \ (\mathrm{mod}\ 105)$$
□

Prisoners, knowing the factorization of $N$, solve three simple congruences (4.20), while the wardens face the basic congruence (4.19) which is computationally infeasible. The sending prisoner forwards a cryptogram $C$ $(0 < C < N)$ along with one of its square roots $(\sqrt{C})_i$; $i = 1, \ldots, 8$. The root is used to authenticate or reject the cryptogram.

The subliminal information is transmitted as the choice of the root sent, from the particular pair of square roots that is chosen for use. That is, for any $C$ (where $gcd(C, N) = 1$), there will be eight square roots $(\sqrt{C})_1, \ldots, (\sqrt{C})_8$, divided into four pairs. One pair will be chosen as being the acceptable authenticators for the cryptogram $C$. Of that pair, if the smaller root is received, then the subliminal message is a '0' $(M = 0)$, or if the larger is received, a '1' $(M = 1)$. If any of the other six square roots, or any other integer is received, the cryptogram $C$ is rejected as not authentic.

*Example*

Assume that the subliminal channel is built for $N = 105$. Prisoners have agreed in advance that the set of roots for cryptograms will be arranged considering their size, that is, for $C = 64$, this set is equal $\{8, 13, 22, 43, 62, 83, 92, 97\}$, and the first and the fourth roots will convey a one-bit message. That is, the pair $(C, (\sqrt{C})_1)$ corresponds to $M = 0$ — in our case $(64,8) \rightarrow M = 0$, but the pair $(C, (\sqrt{C})_4)$ points at $M = 1$ — in our case $(64,43) \rightarrow M = 1$. The other pairs, that is, $(64,13)$, $(64,22)$, $(64,62)$, $(64,83)$, $(64,92)$ and $(64,97)$ are being rejected by the receiving prisoner as not authentic.     $\square$

The warden, however, can produce valid cryptogram/authenticator pairs by choosing a random $X$ and squaring it modulo $N$. This will result in an acceptable cryptogram/authenticator pair, conveying a random subliminal message. To prevent this 'forward search' attack, Simmons [SIM84a] shows how to introduce cryptogram redundancy, so that the wardens have a low probability of choosing one. This, of course, reduces the number of cryptograms that can actually be sent, and an acceptable tradeoff would be sought here in a practical implementation.

### 4.2.3 Ong-Schnorr-Shamir subliminal channel

This scheme of sending subliminal messages has been designed by Simmons [SIM84b] using the Ong-Schnorr-Shamir authentication scheme — see section 4.1.3. As in the original scheme, the sender chooses the secret key $k$ such that $gcd\,(k, N) = 1$ where $N$ defines a suitable arithmetic with addition and multiplication modulo $N$. Unlike the original scheme, the sender communicates $k$ to the intended receiver of the subliminal message. The key $k$ is kept secret by both sides.

If the sender now intends to transmit the subliminal message $M$ by means of a cryptogram $C$, while $gcd\,(M, N) = 1$ $(M = 1, ..., N-1)$ and $gcd\,(C, N) = 1$ $(C = 1, ..., N-1)$, then he/she calculates two authenticators (see formula 4.11):

$$C_1 = \tfrac{1}{2}\,(\frac{C}{M} + M)\,(\mathrm{mod}\,N)$$
$$C_2 = \tfrac{1}{2}\,k\,(\frac{C}{M} - M)\,(\mathrm{mod}\,N) \qquad (4.21)$$

and transmits the triple $(\,C, C_1, C_2\,)$.

After having obtained the triple, the receiver authenticates it by computing,

$$C' = C_1^2 - \frac{C_2^2}{k^2}\,(\mathrm{mod}\,N) \qquad (4.22)$$

and comparing it to $C$. If $C' = C$, the triple is considered to be authentic. Otherwise, the triple is rejected. Once the triple has been accepted, the receiver can recover the subliminal message (see formula 4.12) as:

$$M = \frac{C}{C_1 + C_2\,k^{-1}}\,(\mathrm{mod}\,N) \qquad (4.23)$$

The considerations given above are illustrated by the following example of a simple subliminal channel.

*Example*

Assume that the channel is being designed for $N = 15$ and both communicating sides have agreed upon the secret key $k = 2$ while $gcd(k, N) = 1$ and $k^{-1} = 8 \pmod{15}$. In order to send the message $M = 4$ ($M^{-1} = 4 \bmod 15$) using the cryptogram $C = 13$ (of course $gcd\ (C, N) = 1$), the sender calculates authenticators $C_1 = 13$ and $C_2 = 3$ according to (4.21). He/she next forwards the triple, $(C, C_1, C_2)$ to the receiver.

After having received the triple, the receiver first authenticates it and then computes the subliminal message. Thus the sequence of two triples, (7,2,4) and (13,13,3), are used to calculate $C'$ for both triples. For the first triple $C' = 8$. Comparing $C' = 8$ to $C = 7$, he/she rejects the first triple.

For the second triple, the receiver finds $C' = 13$ and, as $C' = C$, he/she accepts it and recovers the subliminal message applying formula (4.23).      ☐

## 4.2.4 El Gamal subliminal channel

In the El Gamal system (see section 4.1.4), the sender chooses a finite field $GF(p)$; $p$ is prime, and a primitive element $g \in GF(p)$. Both $p$ and $g$ are publicly known. Unlike the original scheme, however, the random integer $r$ is selected by the sender and communicated to the receiver. The integer $r$ is kept secret by both parties and means the secret key.

To send a subliminal message $M$, where $gcd\ (M, p) = 1$, using a cryptogram $C$, with $gcd\ (C, p) = 1$, the sender forms:

$$X = g^M \tag{4.24}$$

and solves the congruence:

$$C = r X + M Y \pmod{p-1} \tag{4.25}$$

for $Y$ using the Euclidean algorithm as before. Next, the triple $(C, X, Y)$ is transmitted to the receiver.

On receipt of the triple, the receiver first computes:

$$
\begin{aligned}
A &= (g^r)^X X^Y \pmod{p} \\
&= g^{C-MY}(g^M)^Y \pmod{p} \\
&= g^C \pmod{p}
\end{aligned}
\tag{4.26}
$$

and accepts the cryptogram $C$ as authentic if $A = g^C \pmod{p}$. Once the cryptogram has been accepted, the subliminal message is recovered by transforming (4.25) to the form:

$$M = Y^{-1}(C - r X) \pmod{p-1} \tag{4.27}$$

A practical example of a very simple subliminal channel is given below.

*Example*

Take the finite field $GF(11)$ and its primitive element $g = 2$ (see section 4.1.4). Two integers, $p = 11$ and $g$ are published. Next, both the sender and the receiver agree and share the secret integer $r = 8$.

If the sender now wants to send the subliminal message $M = 9$ ($gcd\ (M, p) = 1$) by means of the cryptogram $C = 5$ (where we also have $gcd(C, p) = 1$, he/she forms:

$$X = g^M = 2^9 = 6 \pmod{11}$$

and next solves the congruence (4.25) for $Y$ substituting $C = 5$, $r = 8$, $X = 6$, $M = 9$. He/she obtains $Y = 3$. Finally, the sender forwards the triple $(C, X, Y)=(5, 6, 3)$ to the sender.

In turn, the receiver computes both,

$$A = (g^r)^X \, X^Y = (2^8)^6 \, 6^3 = 10 \pmod{11}$$

and,

$$g^C = 2^5 = 10 \pmod{11}$$

As $A = g^C$, the triple is accepted and the subliminal message is recovered using (4.27). So,

$$M = Y^{-1} \, (C - rX) \pmod{p-1} = 3^{-1} \, (5 - 8 \cdot 6) = 9 \pmod{10} \qquad \square$$

### 4.2.5 Seberry-Jones subliminal channel

Seberry [SEBE85] has shown how to obtain a subliminal channel in Shamir's fast authentication scheme (see section 4.1.2). However, we are going to describe a modification of Seberry's idea described by Jones and Seberry [JOSE85]. As in Shamir's original scheme, the sender creates a $n \times 2n$ matrix $K$ of elements of $GF(p)$. Also he/she finds a vector $A = (a_1, \ldots, a_{2n})$ using the formula (4.5) while choosing at random its $n$ elements. Next, according to Seberry's idea, he/she calculates the secret vector $B = (b_1, \ldots, b_n)$, using the following congruence:

$$K \times B = 0 \pmod{p} \tag{4.28}$$

$B$ is communicated to the receiver before any transmission and plays the role of the secret key known to both parties only.

If the sender intends to send a subliminal message $M^* \in GF(p)$, he/she first calculates the vector $R = (r_1, \ldots, r_{2n})$ such that,

$$M^* = R \times B \pmod{p} \tag{4.29}$$

while $r_i \in \{0,1\}$ for $i=1, \ldots, 2n$. Next the sender generates the vector $M = (m_1, \ldots, m_n)$ at random and creates for it the cryptogram $C$ via formulae (4.8) and (4.9)[3], the pair $(M,C)$ being directed to the receiver.

On receipt, the receiver computes $C \times A \pmod{p}$. If $C \times A$ is equal to M, the pair is considered to be authentic, otherwise it is rejected (the vector $A$ and the prime $p$ are public). Finally, the subliminal message is recovered, solving the congruence,

$$M^* = C \times B \pmod{p} \tag{4.30}$$

This equality holds as:

$$C \times B = (\dot{C} + R) B = (\dot{M} \times K + R) B = \dot{M} \times K \times B + R \times B \pmod{p}$$

(Where $\dot{M}$ and $\dot{C}$ are given in 4.1.2.) Thus using (4.28) and (4.29), we get (4.30).

---

3.  To avoid confusion, we use the notation of section 4.1.2.

Let us consider the following example to see how the channel operates.

*Example*

Assume that communicating parties want to send subliminal messages of $GF(5)$ — $p$ is equal 5. In order to present elements of $GF(5)$ in binary form, three bits are needed, so $n = 3$. The sender chooses the matrix $K$ at random and let,

$$K = \begin{bmatrix} 2 & 2 & 4 & 1 & 3 & 1 \\ 4 & 4 & 1 & 1 & 0 & 2 \\ 4 & 3 & 4 & 2 & 2 & 0 \end{bmatrix}$$

As in Shamir's scheme, the sender calculates a vector $A = (a_1, \ldots, a_{2n}) = (a_1, \ldots, a_6)$ using the formula (4.5). So,

$$K \times A = \begin{bmatrix} 2 & 2 & 4 & 1 & 3 & 1 \\ 4 & 4 & 1 & 1 & 0 & 2 \\ 4 & 3 & 4 & 2 & 2 & 0 \end{bmatrix} \begin{bmatrix} 2 \\ 2 \\ 2 \\ a_4 \\ a_5 \\ a_6 \end{bmatrix} = \begin{bmatrix} 1 \\ 2 \\ 4 \end{bmatrix} \pmod{p}$$

while $a_1$, $a_2$, $a_3$ are selected at random (in this case, $a_1 = a_2 = a_3 = 2$). He/she gets $A = [2, 2, 2, 2, 4, 1]$ as the result. Now, the secret vector $B$ is calculated using (4.28). Thus,

$$K \times B = \begin{bmatrix} 2 & 2 & 4 & 1 & 3 & 1 \\ 4 & 4 & 1 & 1 & 0 & 2 \\ 4 & 3 & 4 & 2 & 2 & 0 \end{bmatrix} \begin{bmatrix} b_1 \\ b_2 \\ b_3 \\ b_4 \\ b_5 \\ b_6 \end{bmatrix} = 0 \pmod{p}$$

As the sender has three congruences and six unknowns, he/she fixes three of them. Let $b_1 = 1$, $b_2 = 2$, $b_3 = 4$. Then the remaining elements can be computed and $b_4 = 4$, $b_5 = 3$, $b_6 = 0$. Thence, the secret key $B = [1, 2, 4, 4, 3, 0]$.

If the sender now wants to send the subliminal message $M^* = 4 \in GF(p)$, he/she first computes the vector $R$ such that:

$$M^* = R \times B = [r_1, r_2, r_3, r_4, r_5, r_6] \begin{bmatrix} 1 \\ 2 \\ 4 \\ 4 \\ 3 \\ 0 \end{bmatrix} = 4 \pmod 5$$

Assume the sender chooses

$$R = [1, 0, 1, 1, 0, 0]$$

as a carrier of the subliminal message. Of course, it is easy to see that there are many different binary sequences which can convey the same subliminal message. Accepting $M = 3 \pmod 5$, the sender gets the sequence of authenticators (see section 4.1.2) as follows:

$$\underline{M} = M - R \times A = 3 - [\,1, 0, 1, 1, 0, 0\,] \begin{bmatrix} 2 \\ 2 \\ 2 \\ 2 \\ 4 \\ 1 \end{bmatrix} = 2 \ (\text{mod } 5)$$

$$\underline{C} = \dot{M} \times K = [\,0, 1, 0\,] \begin{bmatrix} 2\ 2\ 4\ 1\ 3\ 1 \\ 4\ 4\ 1\ 1\ 0\ 2 \\ 4\ 3\ 4\ 2\ 2\ 0 \end{bmatrix} = [\,4, 4, 1, 1, 0, 2\,]$$

$$C = \underline{C} + R = [\,4, 4, 1, 1, 0, 2\,] + [\,1, 0, 1, 1, 0, 0\,] = [\,0, 4, 2, 2, 0, 2\,]$$

The pair $(M,C) = (\,3, [0,4,2,2,0,2]\,)$ is dispatched to the receiver.

The receiver now performs the following multiplication:

$$C \times A = [\,0,4,2,2,0,2\,] \begin{bmatrix} 2 \\ 2 \\ 2 \\ 2 \\ 4 \\ 1 \end{bmatrix} = 3 \ (\text{mod } 5)$$

As $M = 3$ is equal $C \times A$, the subliminal message can be recreated using (4.30), and so,

$$M^* = C \times B = [\,0,4,2,2,0,2\,] \begin{bmatrix} 1 \\ 2 \\ 4 \\ 4 \\ 3 \\ 0 \end{bmatrix} = 4 \ (\text{mod } 5) \qquad \square$$

We sum up our observations. Let us recall the last three subliminal channels. As has been mentioned in section 4.1, both Shamir's and Ong-Shnorr-Shamir's authentication schemes have been broken. As a result, subliminal channels based on these two schemes are not secure and therefore they cannot be acceptable as a practical solutions of the Prisoners' Problem. Instead, that of El Gamal would be preferred.

Again, all subliminal channels presented have been intended to show a variety of different approaches which can be used to design a subliminal channel applying an authentication scheme. Moreover, as illustrations of the general rule that any authentication scheme can be converted into a suitable subliminal channel, all channels fulfill their task very well!

## 4.3 Digital signatures

As the development of processing and transmission of information in both computer systems and computer networks proliferates, new needs arise. For instance, the application of computer techniques in banking business has produced the need to translate all banking operations into a form accepted by computers. At present most banking operations or transactions become legally valid only after the involved parties have signed suitable paper documents.

Parties having a computer network often, however, desire to be able to sign documents using their local computers or terminals. So, the following problem arises:

How can signatures be created in a computer environment? As computers accept information in digital form only, any signatures in question must also be digital.

However, digital signatures should have the same properties as written ones. Digital signatures should, therefore be:

1. *unique* — a given digital signature can be generated only by the user;
2. *unforgeable* — generation of authentic signatures by other users, who want to forge signatures, should be impossible, that is, illegal users must face intractable numerical problems while trying to forge signatures;
3. *easy to authenticate* — any receiver of a signature and a referee (who solves possible disputes) should be able to state its authorship even after a long time;
4. *impossible to deny* — any author of digital signatures should not be able to reject his/her true signature as a forgery;
5. *cheap and easy to generate*.

It is noteworthy to observe the difference between handwritten and digital signatures. A written signature is physically appended to a given document by means of a piece of paper that contains both a message (the text of a document) and a signature. Such a relation between messages and signatures is not possible in a computer environment. Of course, it is still possible to print messages along with suitable signatures, but, before printing, they are stored and sent via communication channels where their contents can be changed by enemy users.

The characteristic attribute of written signatures is that they are the same no matter what document is being authenticated. But with digital signatures, this attribute can no longer be valid as the form of signatures must depend upon both the text of a document (message) and the signer.

Before the law, digital signatures fulfill an important role as they confirm mutual commitments of contracting parties. So, methods of digital signature generation should allow any dispute to be solved as to the authenticity of signed documents (messages). With this requirement in mind, these methods can be divided into the two following classes:

1. methods of direct signature authentication;
2. methods of indirect signature authentication.

In the first class, authentication processes are performed by receivers only. However, in the second class, besides senders and receivers, there are third parties who solve possible disputes and are called referees or arbiters.

In this section, we are going to examine different methods of signature generation using either symmetric or asymmetric cryptosystems.

## 4.3.1 Compressing methods

The simplest way to obtain digital signatures is to apply the elementary authentication schemes of section 4.1 based on asymmetric cryptosystems. But in this case, signatures are as long as the messages themselves. It is a little embarrassing to handle documents which consist of several pages of clear text and the same number of pages of signatures. However, if data compression methods are applied, shorter signatures are possible. In

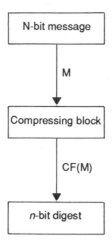

**Figure 4.10** Use of a compressing block to obtain a digest of the message M

general, any compressing method transforms $N$-bit messages $M$ into $n$-bit sequences $CF(M)$ which are called message digests $(N > n)$ (Figure 4.10). Compressing methods should be designed in such a way that computing identical digests for two different messages is intractable.

Assume that the length of sequences representing digests is 64 bits. Suppose also that an opponent intends to match his/her own false message $M'$ with the original one $M$ so that their digests are the same, that is, $CF(M') = GF(M)$ while $M' \neq M$. To do this, the opponent determines variants of $M'$ in the way illustrated below.

*Example*

Assume that an opponent would like to produce variants of the following message:

> *I state that Mr. Brown has borrowed from me 100*
> *— one hundred dollars — on 1 January 1987*

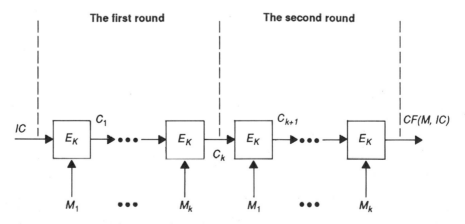

**Figure 4.11** The simple compressing system

Select pairs of words in the form:

$$\left\{\begin{array}{c} We \\ I \end{array}\right\} \left\{\begin{array}{c} note \\ state \end{array}\right\} that \left\{\begin{array}{c} Dr. \\ Mr. \end{array}\right\} Brown \left\{\begin{array}{c} obtained \\ borrowed \end{array}\right\} from \ me \left\{\begin{array}{c} 100.00 \\ 100 \end{array}\right\}$$

$$- \left\{\begin{array}{c} a \\ one \end{array}\right\} hundred \ dollars \ - \ on \left\{\begin{array}{c} January \ 1 \\ 1 \ January \end{array}\right\}, \ 1987.$$

It is easy to see that there are $2^7 = 128$ different variants of the message. Of course, two variants,

> *We state that Dr. Brown borrowed from me 100.00*
> *— one hundred dollars — on January 1 1987*

and

> *I note that Dr. Brown obtained from me 100.00*
> *— a hundred dollars — on 1st January 1987*

convey the same information. ☐

In order to have a high probability of success, the opponent must determine as many variants as there are different possible digests — in our case $\approx 2^{64}$ variants. Obviously, this kind of attack is inefficient in the case considered.

There is, however, another far more efficient attack which we are going to describe here. Suppose, as before, that an opponent wants to create a false 64-bit message $M'$ whose digest is equal to the digest of the original 64-bit message $M$. First of all, the opponent generates a feasible number of variants of both $M'$ and $M$. Let it equal $2^{32}$. He/she next calculates digests for all variants of both messages $M'$ and $M$. As a result, the opponent deals with two sets of digests: the first of $M'$ and the second of $M$. Finally, the opponent is looking for two identical elements, one from each set. If there is such an element, messages $M$ and $M'$ (being precise, their variants) have the same digest. The probability of opponent's success is high enough and equals 0.5. This kind of attack is based on the so-called birthday paradox [DAPR84].

The attack works in the general case and it does not depend on the length of messages. Its efficiency depends, however, on the length of digests. If the digest length is equal to $n$ bits, the opponent must create two sets of $2^{\frac{1}{2}n}$ digests each. This guarantees that he/she has a high probability of finding two identical digests for two different messages.

In order to protect messages against their digests being forged using the birthday-problem attack, we can use two countermeasures. The first relies on applying, if possible, a compressing function twice. The second, however, is based on introducing an additional random parameter that creates an initial condition for the compressing system.

Consider a simple solution of such a system using a symmetric cryptosystem described by its encryption function $E_K$ (Figure 4.11). A message $M$ is divided into elementary 64-bit messages $(M_1, \ldots, M_k)$ and they are next input to successive cryptosystems using their key inputs. The parameter $k$ is usually variable. A sequence $IC$ (i.e. input to the first cryptosystem) defines the initial condition of the system. $IC$ is enciphered under the message $M_1$. As the result, we obtain the cryptogram $C_1$. In general, the cryptogram $C_i$ is enciphered under the message $M_{i+1}$ and the result — the

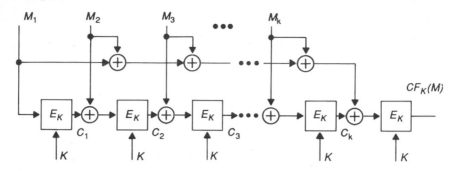

**Figure 4.12** Compressing system with a single round

cryptogram $C_{i+1}$ — is given to the $(i+2)$-th cryptosystem, and so on. In order to protect this system from the birthday-problem attack, the enciphering process is performed twice. Finally, we get the 64-bit digest $CF(M, IC)$ which depends upon all the elementary messages and $IC$.

The second system that compresses a sequence of $k$ elementary messages, using symmetric cryptosystems described by $E_K$, is shown in Figure 4.12. In this case every key input is the same, namely $K$. It can be considered an initial condition of the system. The sequence of successive cryptograms generated in the system is described as follows:

$$
\begin{cases}
C_1 = E_K(M_1) \\
C_2 = E_K(M_2 \oplus C_1) \\
\quad . \\
\quad . \\
\quad . \\
C_k = E_K(M_k \oplus C_{k-1}) \\
CF_K(M) = E_K(M_1 \oplus M_2 \oplus \ldots \oplus M_k \oplus C_k)
\end{cases}
\tag{4.31}
$$

An arbitrarily long message $M$ is divided into $k$ elementary messages (blocks of the length determined by the cryptosystems used) $M_i$; $i = 1, \ldots, k$, which is transformed by applying $K$. Of course, a digest $CF_K(M)$ depends on all elementary messages. To protect the system against the birthday-problem attack, the message input of the last cryptosystem is given all elementary messages along with the cryptogram $C_k$.

Other compressing systems can be obtained using public-key cryptosystems.

## 4.3.2 Diffie-Lamport signature scheme

This scheme due to Diffie and Lamport [MEMA84, LAMP79] is intended to generate signatures for $n$-bit messages without applying any compression. All cryptographic operations used in the scheme are based on a symmetric cryptographic transformation. Now, if a sender (also called an author of signatures) wants to sign $n$-bit messages, he/she first chooses at random $n$ key pairs, namely,

$$
(K_{10}, K_{11}), (K_{20}, K_{21}), \ldots, (K_{n0}, K_{n1})
\tag{4.32}
$$

They are kept secret and are known to the sender only. Next, the sender creates two sequences, $S$ and $R$, where,

$$S = [\, (S_{10}, S_{11}), (S_{20}, S_{21}), \ldots, (S_{n0}, S_{n1}) \,]$$
$$R = [\, (R_{10}, R_{11}), (R_{20}, R_{21}), \ldots, (R_{n0}, R_{n1}) \,] \qquad (4.33)$$

These sequences are being used to authenticate signatures. Elements of $S$ are selected at random while elements of $R$ are cryptograms of $S$ and,

$$R_{ij} = E_{K_{ij}}(S_{ij}) \quad \text{for } i = 1, \ldots, n \quad \text{and} \quad j = 0, 1 \qquad (4.34)$$

$E_K$ describes the symmetric cryptosystem used. Clearly, the structure of the cryptosystem determines the length of both $S$ and $R$. Now, $S$ and $R$ are public and known to receivers. They are stored in a public register that is, however, protected in such a way that, although anyone can read it, only authorized persons can write into it.

The signature of a $n$-bit message $M = (m_1, \ldots, m_n)$, $m_i \in \{0,1\}$ for $i = 1, \ldots, n$, is a sequence of cryptographic keys:

$$SG(M) = (K_{1i_1}, K_{2i_2}, \ldots, K_{ni_n}) \qquad (4.35)$$

where $i_j = 0$ if $m_j = 0$ otherwise $i_j = 1$; $j = 1, \ldots, n$. For example, for the 6-bit message $M = (1, 0, 1, 1, 0, 0)$, the signature takes on the form of:

$$SG(M) = (K_{11}, K_{20}, K_{31}, K_{41}, K_{50}, K_{60})$$

A receiver validates the signature $SG(M)$ by verifying whether suitable pairs of $S$ and $R$ match each other for keys known. In our example, having known keys $(K_{11}, K_{20}, K_{31}, K_{41}, K_{50}, K_{60})$, the receiver reads $S$ suitable elements from the public register and produces their cryptograms:

$$E_{K_{11}}(S_{11})$$

$$E_{K_{20}}(S_{20})$$

$$E_{K_{31}}(S_{31})$$

$$E_{K_{41}}(S_{41})$$

$$E_{K_{50}}(S_{50})$$

$$E_{K_{60}}(S_{60})$$

If they are equal to $(R_{11}, R_{20}, R_{31}, R_{41}, R_{50}, R_{60})$, the receiver accepts the signature as genuine.

The essential drawback of the scheme is the length of the signatures. If the cryptosystem used to generate $R$ transforms N-bit messages into N-bit cryptograms under N-bit keys, then the length of signatures is equal $N \cdot n$.

To overcome this shortcoming, compression can be used. If we have an $r$-bit digest $CF(M)$ of a message $M$, we can apply the Diffie-Lamport scheme directly to the digest only, instead of to the whole message $M$ (see Figure 4.13). For the receiver the validation process takes several steps. First, the receiver generates a suitable digest — this is possible as the compressing method is public. Next, he/she fetches $r$ suitable elements of $S$ and enciphers them using keys included in the signature $SG(M)$ (Figure 4.14). The resulting cryptograms are compared to $r$ elements of $R$. If they are equal, the signature is accepted.

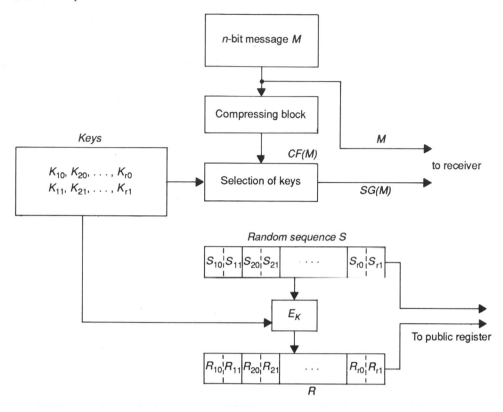

**Figure 4.13** Signature procedure in the Diffie-Lamport scheme (the sender's end)

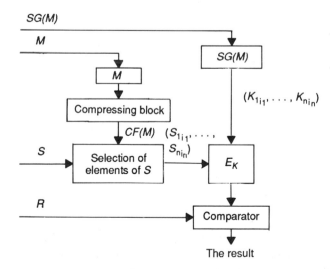

**Figure 4.14** The validation procedure in the Diffie-Lamport scheme (the receiver's end)

In this scheme, the signature is the set of $r$ keys while the second set of $r$ keys is still kept secret. Each repeated application of the scheme would cause the disclosure of other keys — in the worst case, all keys would be revealed and the security of the scheme would be compromized. To exclude such a possibility, the scheme should be applied one time only.

## 4.3.3 Rabin signature scheme

The Rabin scheme [RABI78], as before, is defined using symmetric cryptographic transformations. A sender starts constructing the signature by generating $2r$ keys at random. The parameter $r$ is determined by security requirements. Assume that the keys are:

$$K_1, K_2, \ldots, K_{2r} \tag{4.36}$$

They are secret and known to the sender only. Next, the sender creates two sequences which are necessary for the receivers to validate. The first sequence,

$$S = (S_1, S_2, \ldots, S_{2r})$$

consists of binary blocks chosen at random by the sender. The second,

$$R = (R_1, R_2, \ldots, R_{2r})$$

is created using the sequence $S$ where,

$$R_i = E_{K_i}(S_i) \quad \text{for } i = 1, \ldots, 2r \tag{4.37}$$

The sequences $S$ and $R$ are stored in a read-only public register and their lengths depend upon the cryptographic algorithm used.

In the Rabin scheme, the signature is generated according to the following steps (Figure 4.15). First of all, a message $M$ is compressed. The resulting digest $CF(M)$ is enciphered under keys $K_1, \ldots, K_{2r}$. The cryptograms,

$$E_{K_1}[CF(M)], \ldots, E_{K_{2r}}[CF(M)] \tag{4.38}$$

form the signature $SG(M)$ of the message $M$. $SG(M)$, along with $M$, is sent to the receivers.

To validate the signature, a receiver selects (mostly at random) a $2r$-bit sequence of $r$ ones and $r$ zeros. A copy of the binary sequence is forwarded to the sender. Using this $2r$-bit sequence, the sender forms an $r$-element subset of the keys. $K_i$ belongs to the subset if and only if the $i$-th element of the $2r$-bit sequence is '1'; $i = 1, \ldots, 2r$. The subset of keys is then communicated to the receiver. To authenticate the key subset the receiver generates and compares suitable $r$ cryptograms of $S$ to the originals kept in the public register (see Figure 4.16).

If the key subset is authentic, the receiver produces the digest $CF(M)$ of $M$ and calculates cryptograms as follows:

$$E_{K_{i1}}[CF(M)], \ldots, E_{K_{ir}}[CF(M)] \tag{4.39}$$

where $\{K_{i1}, \ldots, K_{ir}\}$ is the key subset known to the receiver. The elements of (4.39) are compared to the suitable subset of (4.38). If these two subsets are equal, the receiver declares the authenticity of the signature. As before, signatures in the Rabin scheme are necessarily one-time.

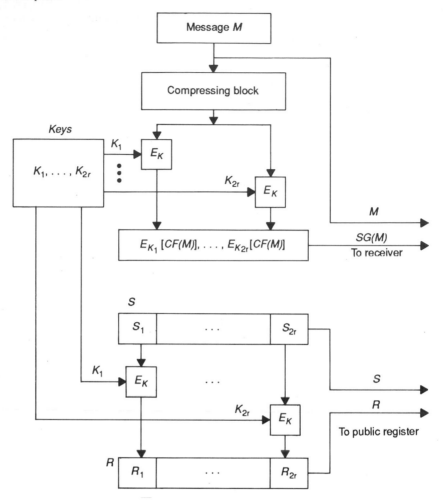

**Figure 4.15** Creation of signatures in the Rabin scheme (the sender's end)

### 4.3.4 Matyas-Meyer signature scheme

In 1981 Matyas and Meyer [MAME81] published their signature scheme based on the DES algorithm. To allow receivers to validate signatures, the sender determines appropriate parameters. To do so, the sender generates a matrix:

$$U = [u(i,j)] \quad \text{for} \quad i = 1, \ldots, 30; \quad j = 1, \ldots, 31$$

using pseudorandom generators. The elements of $U$ are 64-bit sequences. The sender next creates a secret key matrix:

$$K = [K(i,j)] \quad \text{for} \quad i, j = 1, \ldots, 31$$

while the first row of $K$, that is, $K(1,1), \ldots, K(1,31)$, is formed applying pseudorandom generators. Other rows, however, are calculated according to the following equations:

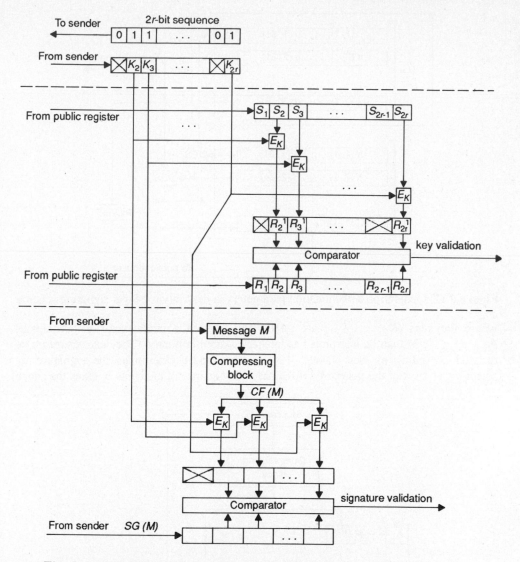

**Figure 4.16** Validation of signatures in the Rabin scheme (the receiver's end)

$$K(i+1, j) = E_{K(i,j)} [u(i,j)] \quad \text{for} \quad i = 1, \dots, 30 \quad \text{and} \quad j = 1, \dots, 31 \quad (4.40)$$

where $E_K$ stands for the encryption transformation of DES (Figure 4.17). After having calculated $K$, the sender delivers all elements of $U$ along with the last row of the matrix $K$, that is, elements $K(31,1), \dots, K(31,31)$, to both a public register and the receiver.

Once the initial steps have been completed the sender can generate his/her signature for a message $M$. First of all, he/she compresses the message in the manner described by (4.31). On obtaining the digest $CF(M)$ of $M$, the sender calculates sequences:

$$b_i = E_{K_i}(CF(M)) \quad \text{for} \quad i = 1, \dots, 31$$

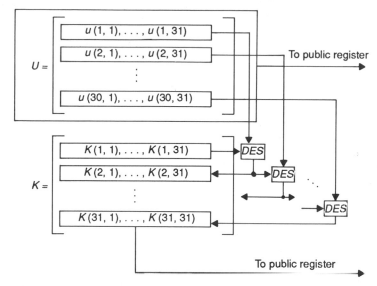

**Figure 4.17** Generation authentication parameters in the Matyas-Meyer signature scheme

where the keys $(K_1, \ldots, K_{31})$ are public and kept in a public register. Sequences $b_i$, $i = 1, \ldots, 31$, can be interpreted as integers written in binary. They can, therefore be ordered according to their values. Finally, the sender determines the signature by selecting 31 keys of the matrix $K$. If the ordered sequence of elements $b_i$ takes the shape

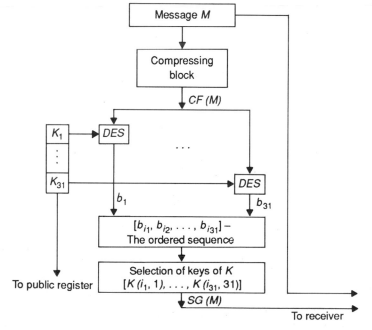

**Figure 4.18** Signature generation in the Matyas-Meyer scheme

$(b_{i_1}, \ldots, b_{i_{31}})$, then the signature has the form (see Figure 4.18):

$$[K\,(i_1,\,1),\,K\,(i_2,\,2),\,\ldots,\,K\,(i_{31},\,31)]$$

The receiver authenticates the signature by repeating the sender's steps. First, the receiver creates the message digest $CF\,(M)$, calculates sequences $b_i$ for $i=1,...,31$, and orders them according to increasing value. He/she next puts keys of the signature in the 'empty' matrix $K$ in the places indicated by the ordered sequence $(b_{i_1}, \ldots, b_{i_{31}})$. Knowing the properties of the matrix $K$ (see (4.40)), the receiver computes, for each column, all keys below the key of the signature. He/she accepts the signature as authentic if the last row of $K$ is identical to the row stored in the public register.

The schemes presented in sections 4.3.2-4 generate signatures using symmetric cryptosystems. In general, to be able to validate signatures, some portion of the secret information must be revealed. As the disclosure of secret keys compromises all these schemes, appropriate cryptograms along with messages are published. This procedure, however, requires a public register to be set up. It preserves information needed for authentication previously deposited by senders and receivers. Thus, the public register plays the role of a third party who settles disputes between the senders and the receivers. The schemes work well if both senders and receivers trust each other.

The most evident shortcoming of all signature schemes considered is that they may be used one-time only. For any signature, senders must generate separate validation parameters which must be stored in public registers.

## 4.3.5 RSA signature schemes

Let us recall section 4.1, devoted to message authentication. We note that any public-key authentication scheme can be used immediately to produce signatures because cryptograms may be seen as special kinds of signatures which reflect both the message and the unique–user feature. There is, however, another approach which involves compressing methods. The general idea of generation of signatures applying asymmetric cryptosystems and compressing blocks is illustrated in Figure 4.19.

Assume that the author (the sender $A$) of a message $M$ wants to sign it. First, he/she shortens it using the compressing block. Next, the author enciphers the resulting digest $CF\,(M)$ by means of the secret cryptographic transformation $D_A$ and obtains the signature:

$$SG\,(M)\,=\,D_A\,[\,CF\,(M\,)\,]$$

Finally, the author forwards the pair, the message $M$ and the signature $SG(M)$, to the intended receiver.

On receipt of the pair, the receiver produces the message digests in two different ways. First of all, he/she recreates the digest from the signature applying the public cryptographic transformation $E_A$, that is,

$$CF\,(M\,)\,=\,E_A\,[\,SG\,(M\,)\,]$$

Also, the receiver produces his/her digests of $M$ using the compressing block (which structure is public). He/she accepts the pair $[M, SG\,(M)]$ if the two digests are equal.

The validity of this general scheme drastically depends upon authenticity of public keys. It is conceivable that an opponent, instead of trying to break an asymmetric algorithm used, can define his/her own public-key system while claiming that his/her system has been designed by another person. To thwart this masquerade attack, a trusted third party must be appointed. This party, also called the public register or arbiter, keeps all authentic public keys.

As we have noticed in section 4.1.5, the RSA signature scheme (designed by the sender *A*) can be used in its elementary form if the message *M* is equal to or less than *N*, where *N* is the integer which defines suitable arithmetic and $N = p\,q$ (*p*,*q* are primes).

If messages are greater than *N*, compression must be applied. Of course, there are many different methods of compressing. Several of them have already been described in section 4.3.1. But now we are going to examine a compressing method which is based on RSA system.

Following Jonge and Chaum [JOCH86], we are going to consider several variations of signature generation in the case when messages are greater than modulus *N* (of course *N* defines a suitable arithmetic).

Assume that the sender has defined his/her pair $(k, K)$, where *k* and *K* are secret and public keys, respectively, and he/she creates the signature for the message *M* as follows:

$$SG\,(M) \;=\; M^{Mk} \;(\bmod\,N)\qquad\qquad(4.41)$$

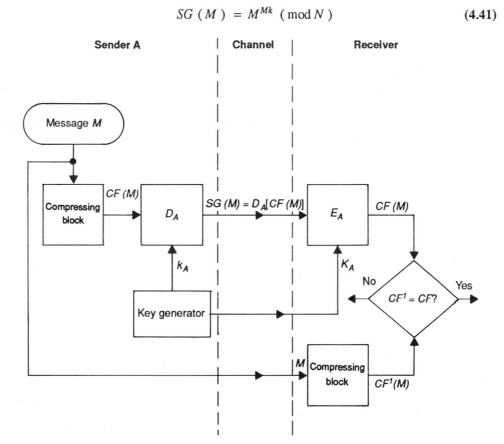

**Figure 4.19** General RSA signature scheme

In other words, compression relies on presentation of message $M$ ($M >> N$) as an integer $M$ (mod $N$). Finally, the sender forms the pair ($M, SG(M)$). Unfortunately, this kind of signature is vulnerable to so-called multiplicative attack. This is illustrated in the following example.

*Example*

Suppose that an opponent is able to construct three valid messages, $M_1$, $M_2$, and $M_3$, such that:

$$M_3 = M_1 \cdot M_2 \ (\text{mod}\,N)$$

then the signatures are $SG\,(M_i) = M_i^k \ (\text{mod}\,N)$. Now, if he/she succeeds in getting,

$$SG\,(M_1) = M_1^k \ (\text{mod}\,N)$$
$$SG\,(M_2) = M_2^k \ (\text{mod}\,N)$$

Then he/she can form the signature for $M_3$, since,

$$SG\,(M_3) = SG\,(M_1)\ SG\,(M_2) \ (\text{mod}\,N)$$

Also knowing the signature $SG\,(M)$ for $M$, the opponent can calculate signatures for $M^{-1}$ and $-M$ as:

$$SG\,(M^{-1}) = (M^{-1})^k = (M^k)^{-1} = [\,SG\,(M)\,]^{-1} \ (\text{mod}\,N)$$

and,

$$SG\,(-M) = (-M)^k = (-1)^k\,M^k = -M^k = -SG\,(M) \ (\text{mod}\,N)$$

The equation $(-1)^k = -1$ holds as the secret key $k$ is odd!                     □

Thus, having signatures of the shape (4.41) for two valid messages $M_1$, $M_2$, the opponent can calculate the signature for $M_3 = M_1\,M_2$, since:

$$SG(M_3) = (M_3)^{M_3 k} = (M_1 M_2)^{M_1 M_2 k} = [SG(M_1)]^{M_2}\,[SG(M_2)]^{M_1} \ (\text{mod}\,N) \qquad \textbf{(4.42)}$$

claiming simultaneously that $M_3$ has been signed by the author of messages $M_1$ and $M_2$.

There is also another possibility for defining the signature scheme by mapping a constant integer $I$ using the signed message $M$ as follows:

$$SG\,(M) = I^{M^{-1}\,\text{mod}\,\gamma(N)} \ (\text{mod}\,N) \qquad \textbf{(4.43)}$$

whereas $\gamma(N) = LCM\,(p-1,\,q-1)$, and $p$, $q$ are primes ($N = pq$). The message $M^{-1}$ is the inverse of $M$ such that $M\,M^{-1} = 1\ \text{mod}\ \gamma(N)$. Although this scheme is resistant to the multiplicative attack, it is open to the attack presented below.

Suppose the author has generated the signature using (4.43) and has published it along with the corresponding message. If an opponent can now factor the message $M$, that is,

$$M = m_1 \times \ldots \times m_t$$

where $m_i$ ($i = 1, \ldots, t$) do not need to be primes, then the message,

$$M_1 = m_2 \times \ldots \times m_t = \frac{M}{m_1}$$

can be signed by the opponent who uses the original signature $SG(M)$ and the factor $m_1$ as follows:

$$SG(M_1) = [SG(M)]^{m_1} \pmod{N} \tag{4.44}$$

It works as the sequence of the following equations holds:

$$[SG(M)]^{m_1} = (I^{M^{-1}})^{m_1} = I^{\left[\frac{M}{m_1}\right]^{-1}} = SG(M_1)$$

In addition, there is the added difficulty of how to guarantee existence of the inverse $M^{-1}$ mod $\gamma(N)$. It is known that such an inverse exists if $gcd(M, \gamma(N)) = 1$.

In order to eliminate the weakness (4.44) and to ensure the existence of the inverse $M^{-1}$, Jonge and Chaum [JOCH86] have suggested using the signature scheme described by,

$$SG(M) = I^{(2M+1)^{-1} \bmod \gamma(N)} \pmod{N} \tag{4.45}$$

instead of the scheme of (4.43).

Different approach to signature design has been presented by Davies and Price [DAPR80]. Let us consider the example of their proposals depicted in Figure 4.20. In this solution the message $M$ is cut by the sender $A$ into blocks, that is, $M = (M_1, \ldots, M_n)$ where any block represents an integer less than the modulus $N$. Next $A$ selects at random the initial condition $I$ ( an integer $I < N$ ). The first block $M_1$ and the initial condition $I$ are added bitwise and the result is transformed according to the secret cryptographic transformation $D_A(I \oplus M_1)$. This process is repeated $(n+1)$ times. To protect the signature against the birthday-problem attack, the last round of the process is carried out using the first block again. Finally, the sender $A$ forwards the triple: the message $M$, the signature $SG(M)$, and the cryptogram of the initial condition $D_A(I)$.

The receiver, having the authentic public key $K_A$, repeats the sender's procedure in reverse sequence. Applying the compressing procedure to the message $M$, he/she obtains the initial condition $I'$. The same condition should be recreated after decrypting the cryptogram $D_A(I)$. If $I$ and $I'$ are equal, the signature is considered to be authentic; otherwise it is rejected.

### 4.3.6 Signatures with the arbiter presence

As you have noticed, schemes considered above engage two parties: senders and receivers only. However, in schemes based on symmetric cryptosystems, there is a third party (the public register or arbiter) who keeps public data generated by senders and used by receivers to validate signatures. Unfortunately, all previous schemes do not allow disputes to be settled between senders and receivers. It is possible that a sender, after revealing his/her secret key, could not only repudiate authorship of genuine signatures generated before but seek to invalidate them as well.

To exclude this possibility, we introduce an active third party[4] called *an arbiter*. The arbiter will be able to settle disputes between senders and receivers. The necessity for the

---

4. Public registers constitute passive third parties.

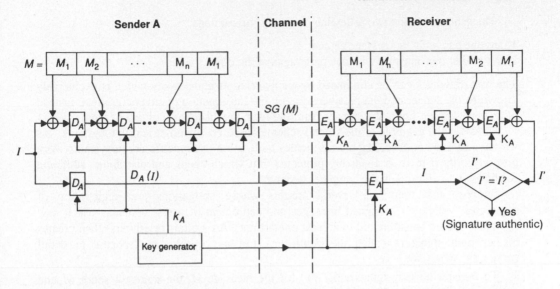

**Figure 4.20** Generation and validation of signature using RSA system and bitwise modulo-2 addition

existence of such a third party is especially urgent when a signature scheme is being designed for a computer network which is dedicated to notarial purposes. Signature schemes with an arbiter's presence have, however, a characteristic feature — the correctness of the signature validation processes depends upon the arbiter's honesty. From now on, we assume that arbiters are separate and honest network units (persons) which (who) play the same role as notaries or justices of the peace in some countries. Let us consider two examples of signature generation in computer networks using symmetric and asymmetric cryptographic algorithms.

Assume that the first scheme uses symmetric cryptosystems and that any user of the network shares with the arbiter the unique secret key. Let both the sender $A$ and the receiver $B$ have such keys $K_A$ and $K_B$ respectively. Suppose also that $A$ wishes to sign his/her message $M$ which consists of four components: the sender's *identification* (name), the receiver's *identification*, the serial number and the message contents. Thus,

$$M = (ID_A, ID_B, No, TEXT)$$

First, the sender $A$ compresses $M$ to obtain its digest $CF(M)$ and then forwards the pair (the message $M$ and the signature $E_{K_A}[CF(M)]$) to the arbiter. Knowing the sender's *identification*, the arbiter looks for the suitable key and authenticates the signature by repeating the sender's operations. If the signature is valid, the arbiter expands the message $M$ by adding his/her serial number ($SN$) and the time stamp ($TS$). Therefore,

$$M' = (M, SN, TS)$$

Next the message $M'$ is enciphered using the key $K_B$ and the cryptogram $E_{K_B}(M')$ is directed to the receiver $B$ (see Figure 4.21). At the receiver's end, the cryptogram $E_{K_B}(M')$ is deciphered and if the pattern of the message $M'$ is correct, it is accepted.

The scheme has the two following obvious shortcomings:

1. anyone can read the message signed;
2. the arbiter can conspire with one party against the other.

The first drawback can be eliminated by enciphering $M$ under a key which is exclusively known to the sender and the receiver. Again, the introduction of several arbiters, instead of a single arbiter, limits the damage resulting from the dishonesty of one of them.

Consider the example of the second scheme based on asymmetric cryptosystems. As we have already noticed, signature schemes built using asymmetric cryptosystems work properly only if there is a suitably protected unit which keeps and distributes authentic public keys to all users in the computer network.

Suppose that there are several arbiters whose obligations are: registration of signatures, validation of signed messages and settlement of users' disputes. Each new signature should be submitted to at least one arbiter. An arbiter (or arbiters) then creates his/her own signature called the certificate. Let us consider the scheme in detail [POKL78, POKL79].

To register his/her signature $SG(M)$ for the message $M$, the sender $A$ sends $M$, the signature $SG(M) = D_A[CF(M)]$ along with his/her identification $ID_A$ to the arbiter, while $CF(M)$ is the digest for $M$. Both the message $M$ and $ID_A$ are sent in clear form but the signature is forwarded as $SG(M) = D_A[CF(M)]$. Knowing $ID_A$, the arbiter takes the public key $K_A$ and recreates the clear form of $CF(M)$. To validate the signature, the arbiter checks if the message and the digest match. It is worth emphasizing that the arbiter can validate the signature and the digest but the arbiter can produce neither of them as he/she does not know the secret key of $A$. If the triple $[M, CF(M), SG(M)]$ turns out to be authentic, the arbiter generates an appropriate certificate $CR$, or in other words, his/her own signature. It takes the form,

$$CR = D_{AR}(ID_A, CF(M), TS)$$

where $D_{AR}$ is the arbiter's secret cryptographic transformation and $TS$ is a time stamp which consists of the current date and the exact time of the day. This certificate is stored

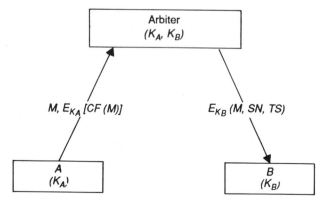

**Figure 4.21** Information flow in signature scheme with an arbiter (symmetric cryptosystem case)

by the arbiter and is supplied to the receiver on demand.

Knowing the certificate and the arbiter's public key, the receiver recovers the author's identificator $ID_A$, the digest of the message and the time stamp. On the other hand, $B$ can recreate the digest using the pair $[M, SG(M)]$ of $A$ (see Figure 4.22). If both digests are equal and they simultaneously match the message, then the signature $SG(M) = D_A[CF(M)]$ is validated.

The same validation process can be adopted while using several arbiters instead of one. Receivers can then choose at least two different strategies. The first is that the only signatures accepted are those for which all certificates convey the same digests which are equal to digests supplied by sender. In the second strategy, receivers validate signatures only if the majority of arbiters give consistent certificates (consistent means here that they generate the same digests).

As we have seen, there are two general signature schemes. The first is based on symmetric cryptographic algorithms. The second is built using asymmetric algorithms. The first general scheme works properly if senders keep their keys in secrecy and there are protected public registers which store data needed during signature authentication processes. To validate signatures, some portions of their keys have to be revealed. In the second general scheme, there is still the necessity for a separate unit. This time this unit is responsible for distributing authentic users' public keys — this is the crucial point of all public-key applications.

## 4.4  Other authentication techniques

Up until now we have hardly considered basic authentication methods. They of course supply basic tools that can be used to meet other user authentication requirements. These requirements vary from user to user and are concerned with different aspects of authentication. For example, user authentication must be designed differently depending on user accessibility. If a user resides in a computing centre, then visual authentication (direct authentication) can be used. If, however, a user works via a remote terminal, the authentication must rely on checking the user's password and/or user's key – user

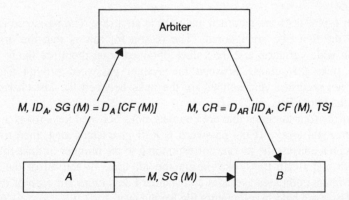

**Figure 4.22** Signature scheme with presence of an arbiter (asymmetric cryptosystem case)

authentication is carried out by means of password and/or key authentication.

In this section we are going to examine different aspects of authentication and mutual interrelations.

## 4.4.1 User authentication

In general, there are two main user authentication methods. The first is based on verifying something the user has — the indirect user authentication. The second method relies on checking something the user is — the direct user authentication. This point is devoted to the second method.

Clearly, there are many human features which can be used to establish user authenticity. For instance, Simmons et al. [SIST72] describe a system of personal verification designed at Sandia Laboratories wherein personal features such as palmprint and retinal prints are measured. Meyer and Matyas [MEMA84] describe research being done at IBM which quantifies the way in which a hand signature is actually written, using special pressure and speed sensitive pen and accelerometry. Other such research has been carried out, using such improbable methods as lip prints, smell detectors and measuring the shape of the user's head [MART73]. These measurements have the advantages that they are unique and non-transferable, but implementation has usually been at considerable expense.

Consider the solution in which the quantity being measured is the way in which an individual actually types at the keyboard. The system relies on the usual method of password entry and verification but additionally checks to see that the typing style of the user was the same as that used for initial password registration [JONE85]. This method — called the type-signature — is based solely on a statistic calculated from the time that the user takes between keystrokes during password entry. Keystroke intervals are obtained as the number of ticks of the system clock that elapse. This is not taken to be a measure of real time; the number of ticks is treated simply as a number. In systems with terminal handlers and I/O buffering, it will be necessary to take precautions that characters are processed as they are typed. This would probably mean that for inter-network authentication, this time–sensitive processing would have to be done at the originating node.

As the user types, ticks are recorded and held in an array. The password is requested six times and the first two are ignored. The reason for this is that the first attempts usually contain wide variation and the values obtained from them are likely to become outliers. The ticks that elapse between the system password prompt and the first keystroke are not recorded, and neither are the ticks between the last character of the password and the return key.

For each of the four attempts that are counted, ticks between keystrokes are recorded in a two dimensional array. If the password is $n+1$ characters long, then row $j$ of the array will contain $n$ entries, the $i$th one corresponding to the number of ticks that occurred between the $i$th and $i+1$th keystroke during the $j$th trial. When all of the copies are entered, the program computes averages and standard deviations for each of the columns of the array. These are held in a signature file for the user.

The signature of the password is checked in a simple way. The entered password is compared with the stored averages under a chi-squared test.

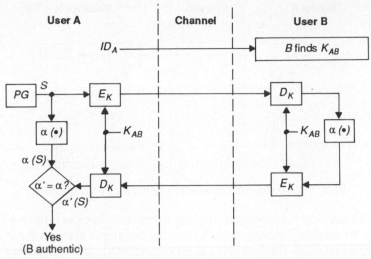

**Figure 4.23** Handshaking procedure (A authenticates B)

The implementation of the type-signature shows that the log-in probability for the true user is high enough and equal to 0.97 while the same probability for the imposter is 0.06.

## 4.4.2 User mutual authentication

Usually communicating parties require to authenticate each other. Ordinarily, the authentication process takes place at the initiation stage of the communication session. It is called the handshaking procedure. This procedure consists in mutual verification of keys used by parties — checking something the party has (the indirect authentication). In other words, parties accept each other as legitimate if they prove that they have correct keys. The handshaking procedure is commonly being used in computer networks between: users, user and host computer, host computers, etc.

Let us consider an example of a handshaking procedure for two users $A$ and $B$. This assumption has no influence on the generality of our considerations.[5] Those users share the same secret cryptographic key — it means that they use a symmetric cryptosystem.[6] The whole procedure has been depicted in Figure 4.23.

Assume that the user $A$ initiates the handshaking procedure by sending his/her identification (or name) in the clear form to the user $B$. Knowing the identificator $ID_A$, $B$ finds the secret key $K_{AB}$ and inputs it to his/her cryptographic system. In the meantime, $A$ produces a sequence $S$ by means of the pseudorandom generator PG and sends it as the cryptogram $E_{K_{AB}}(S)$ to $B$. Next, $B$ decrypts the cryptogram and recovers the clear form of the sequence $S$. Now both the users $A$ and $B$ transform the sequence $S$ according to the

---

5. There is the same procedure when communicating parties are not users.

6. In other words, we are going to present the handshaking procedure while symmetric cryptographic algorithm (e.g. DES) is applied. Fortunately, its modification for asymmetric algorithm (e.g. RSA) is straightforward.

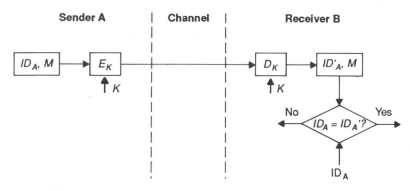

**Figure 4.24** Continuous sender's authenticity verification

publicly known one-way function $\alpha(\cdot)$. The user $B$, however, enciphers the message $\alpha(S)$ and forwards the resulting cryptogram to $A$. Finally, the user $A$ decrypts the cryptogram and compares the resulting message $\alpha'(S)$ to the original $\alpha(S)$. If these two messages are equal, the user $A$ accepts $B$ as genuine.

Clearly, $B$ authenticates $A$ in the same way. Both these procedures create the handshaking procedure which is usually carried out at the beginning of any communication session between any two parties in either time-sharing computer systems or computer networks.

Sometimes users want the continuous verification of authenticity of senders during whole communication sessions. One of the simplest methods of the continuous verification is depicted in Figure 4.24. Any transmitted cryptogram has the shape,

$$E_K(ID_A, M)$$

where $ID_A$ is an identificator of the sender $A$ and $M$ is the message. Therefore, the receiver $B$, obtaining the cryptogram, deciphers it and recovers the pair $(ID_A, M)$. If the identificator $ID_A$ matches the sender, he/she accepts the cryptogram.

Another method for continuous authentication engages a secret password of the sender instead of the sender's identificator. Prearranged passwords are known to both parties. Assume that $P_A$ and $P_B$ are passwords of users $A$ and $B$, respectively. User $A$ then creates cryptograms of the form,

$$E_K(P_A, M)$$

The receiver of the cryptogram decrypts it and compares the password recovered from the cryptogram to the original. If they are equal, he/she accepts the cryptogram.

These two methods of continuous authentication have, however, the same shortcoming: cryptograms containing the same message are used during whole sessions. This can sometimes facilitate recovery of the clear message by opponents.

### 4.4.3 Message stream authentication

Let us turn our attention to protection of the message stream integrity. This protection should allow discovery of:

- substitution of one or more elementary messages of the stream by false ones;
- cancellation of any fragment of the transmitted stream;
- rearrangement of the original sequence of messages in the stream;
- repetition of any portion of the stream.

In order to achieve this goal, we must design an appropriate authentication scheme.

Consider the simple one based on the so-called authentication code ($AC$). $AC$ reflects the message stream structure and is generated according to the publicly known procedure. Its length is usually equal to the length of the elementary message. Now $AC$ can be treated as the digest of the message stream $M = (M_1, \ldots, M_n)$, where $M_i$; $i = 1, \ldots, n$, are elementary messages defined by the cryptosystem used. The message stream authentication scheme is presented in Figure 4.25. This scheme uses an $AC$ which is generated by compressing blocks (structures of these blocks have been described in section 4.3). As you can see, the stream $M$ is transmitted in the right succession from $A$ to $B$. In the meantime, the user $A$ inputs the stream $M$ to the compressing block $CF(M)$. The resulting $AC$ (also called digest) is sent in the last cryptogram $E_K(AC)$.

On $B$'s side, all cryptograms are deciphered and stored in the original order. Finally, the receiver $B$ computes the authentication code $AC'$ using the stream $M$ and compares it to $AC$ obtained from $A$. If they are equal, the stream $M$ is accepted as genuine.

Needless to say, the quality of the scheme drastically depends on the quality of compressing blocks used. In other words, compressing functions representing these blocks should be designed in such a way that finding two different message streams of the same digest (the same $AC$) creates an intractable numerical problem.

It is possible to design message stream authentication schemes using cryptosystems whose natures allow creation of suitable cryptogram streams which are very sensitive to any change. Such a change causes the cryptogram stream to produce an unreadable

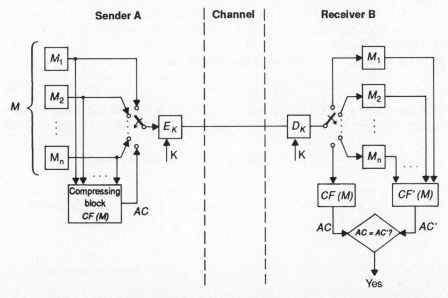

**Figure 4.25** Stream authentication scheme based on compressing blocks

sequence of messages if, of course, the message source has the redundancy. An example of a cryptosystem which can be used is the stream cryptosystem with message feedback [MEMA84].

However, the simplest authentication scheme can be built applying the well-known chaining method [FEIS70]. In this scheme, each elementary message $M_i$; $i = 1, \ldots, n$, is divided into halves ($M_i^0$, $M_i^1$) and the cryptogram stream is as follows:

$$
\begin{aligned}
C_1 &= E_K (M_1) \\
C_2 &= E_K (M_1^1, M_2^0) \\
C_3 &= E_K (M_2) \\
C_4 &= E_K (M_2^1, M_3^0) \\
&\quad \cdot \\
&\quad \cdot \\
&\quad \cdot \\
C_{2n-1} &= E_K (M_n)
\end{aligned}
$$

The obvious drawback of the scheme is that it doubles the length of cryptogram streams.

## 4.4.4 Password authentication

Special care must be taken with passwords as their secrecy is crucial to any cryptographic protection. They are usually used at the beginning of any communication session.

The simplest method of password authentication relies upon comparing the newly presented password $P_A$ with the original $P'_A$ stored in the computer center (Figure 4.26). As passwords are secret, they must be enciphered before sending via insecure transmission channels.

Sometimes the clear form of passwords must not be revealed to the receiver. In this case, instead of the clear form, the sender must supply the password image obtained using the non–invertible function $\alpha(\cdot)$ of the password. The transformation should guarantee that the opponent, knowing the image, cannot recover the password — he/she faces an intractable numerical problem.

For instance, the function $\alpha(\cdot)$ can be defined as follows:

$$
\alpha (P) = E_P (ID) \tag{4.46}
$$

where $ID$ is the sender's identificator (name), $P$ is his/her password, and $E_P$ means that the encryption process is carried out while the password is being keyed in. Such

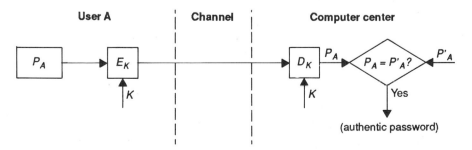

**Figure 4.26** A simple password authentication

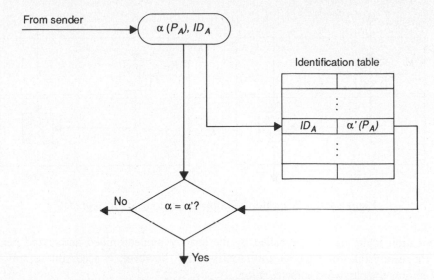

**Figure 4.27** Password authentication using identification table

functions are especially convenient when the lengths of a password and a key are the same. The password authentication, in this case, consists of sending $\alpha(P)$ to the receiver and comparing it to the precomputed and stored equivalent $\alpha'(P)$.

In practice, however, passwords consist of several letters only, to enable users to remember them. Short passwords are vulnerable to brute force attack. In order to thwart such an attack, the function $\alpha(\cdot)$ is defined differently, namely:

$$\alpha(P) = E_{P \oplus K}(ID) \qquad (4.47)$$

where $K$ and $ID$ are the key and the identificator of the sender, respectively. Obviously, $\alpha(P)$ is precomputed and stored in the receiver's identification table (Figure 4.27). The password authentication consists of comparing two images of the password and accepting the password if these images are equal.

Of course, anyone who gains access to the identification table may illegally modify its contents without such activity being detected. The next method of password authentication we give works properly even if the opponent has illegal access to the table. The method is due to Meyer and Matyas [MEMA84] and is based on two cryptographic operations defined by means of the DES. It is designed to authenticate passwords by computer centers while senders reside at terminals. The operations are:

$$OC \ : \{X, \mathbf{a}\} \to \mathbf{b}$$
$$\overline{OC} \ : \{X, \mathbf{b}\} \to \mathbf{a} \qquad (4.48)$$

where $X$ is the sequence representing the image of password, that is, $X = \alpha(P)$, $\mathbf{a}$ is the sequence associated with the password and $\mathbf{b}$ is the verification sequence. An example of their application is given in Figure 4.28. Operations $OC$ and $\overline{OC}$ are being carried out by the computer system to which the sender requires access. The key $K_0$ is generated and stored in an isolated and protected area of the computer system to which no user has access. The operation $\overline{OC}$ is used exclusively while creating a suitable row in the

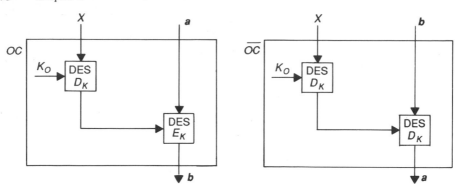

**Figure 4.28** Illustration of implementations of $OC$ and $\overline{OC}$

identification table. It may be called by the strictly predetermined authorized persons who are responsible for integrity and security. $OC$, however, is accessible to any user who requires the password authentication.

The authentication process based on $OC$ and $\overline{OC}$ is illustrated in Figure 4.29 and runs as follows. The user gives his/her identificator $ID$ and the sequence $X = \alpha(P)$ representing the password transformation. The authentication process starts with verification of the identificator format and searching for an appropriate row in the table. Both the user's $X$ and **a** from the table are transformed according to $OC$. The result **b** is compared to the sequence **b'** which is the transformation of the user's $ID$, that is, **b'** =

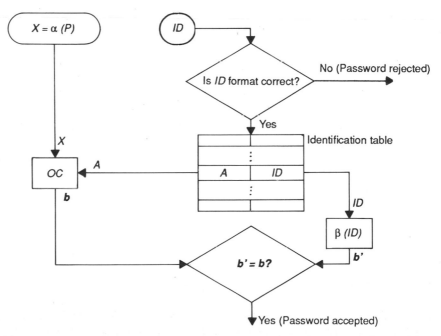

**Figure 4.29** Password authentication scheme using cryptographic operations $OC$ and $\overline{OC}$

$\beta(ID)$. If **b** and **b'** are equal, the password is accepted.

The function $\beta(\cdot)$ ought to be such that, knowing **b'**, no one is able to calculate *ID*. For example, the function $\beta(\cdot)$ can be defined according to the following formula:

$$\beta(ID) = E_{ID}(R) \qquad (4.49)$$

where $R$ is a public and fixed sequence selected at the computer end. Let us further consider the function $\beta(\cdot)$. Assume first that $ID = \mathbf{b}$. If that is true, the opponent may authenticate his/her password, acting as follows. He/she selects a password $P$ and calculates $\alpha(P)$. Next, he/she arbitrarily chooses **a** and uses the nonprotected operation $OC$ — he/she obtains **b**. The sequence **b** is accepted as the opponent's identificator *ID*. Finally, he/she writes the pair $(ID,\mathbf{a})$ into the nonprotected identification table. It is easy to check that the opponent sending $(\alpha(P), ID)$ always succeeds. There is, therefore, necessity to apply the one-way function $\beta(\cdot)$.

# 4.5 Summary

The first section was devoted to different authentication problems which appear while designing computer protection. Actually, authentication processes are performed by receivers only and they allow receivers to determine the origin of messages. All authentication schemes described above are based on cryptography. However, even the strongest cryptographic algorithm does not guarantee that the correct authentication will be possible. The simplest and simultaneously the most powerful method to introduce the authentication capability for cryptographic algorithms is the appropriate construction of the message source. In this construction, message sequences are divided into two classes. The first one corresponds to valid messages which are generated by the source. The second, however, consists of all other sequences which cannot be obtained by the source. In other words, the introduction of redundancy into the message source is the necessary condition for any efficient authentication scheme.

Redundancy ensures that any opponent who wants to substitute a cryptogram for a false message faces an intractable numerical problem or is forced to choose such a cryptogram at random (and then it may not convey any valid message). The opponent's chance of success decreases as the redundancy grows.

Any authentication scheme, however, fails if the opponent replays and retransmits original cryptograms. To exclude such a possibility, the common countermeasure is the time-stamping procedure. In general, it means that message source structure depends upon the time.

If we apply symmetric cryptography, both the sender and receiver must share the same key. This key can be considered as an identificator of the message source and, therefore, must be kept secret by both parties. Messages are usually sent in enciphered form. It is, however, possible to send messages in clear form (authentication without secrecy) but simultaneously an extra piece of information, called authenticator, must be attached. The authenticator can be seen as a unique 'fingerprint' of the current message and it must be recoverable at the receiver's end.

Clearly, any symmetric cryptosystem can be used for authentication without any structural change. This property does not hold any longer if an asymmetric cryptosystem is used.  Although the only difference between asymmetric cryptosystems used for secrecy and authenticity relies on the place the key was generated, the difference has important implications as most asymmetric cryptosystems designed for secrecy cannot be immediately used for authenticity, and vice versa.  The only exception is the RSA system which can be used for both secrecy and authenticity without any structural change.

The next section examined several solutions to the Prisoners' Problem.  It has been shown that the problem can be solved, with slight modifications, using public-key authentication schemes.  Such schemes (called subliminal channels) provide covert communication channels.  Such a channel can be in two 'states'.  The first one corresponds to the case when meaningless messages are transmitted — the receiver rejects them.  The second state corresponds to meaningful messages being sent — the receiver accepts them.  Obviously, the receiver's activity consists of two steps.  In the first step, he/she examines the current state of the channel and next, if a meaningful message is being transmitted, the receiver recovers the message.

Different authentication problems appear when one requires the possession of a digital equivalent of the handwritten signature.  Such a digital signature has to have the same properties as the handwritten one.  Clearly, it ought to ensure that either the unique user (signature author) feature — in this case usually his/her unique secret cryptographic key — or the message contents are reflected in it.  If the message consists of an elementary block, a public-key cryptosystem can be used for signature generation without any change.  If, however, the message is longer than the elementary block, then the common method is to produce the signature on the basis of the message digest.  A compressing method that yields a suitable digest should be designed in such a way that the probability of obtaining two equal digests from two different messages is less than some fixed value (e.g. less than $2^{-64}$).

In applying digital signatures, both the sender and the receiver should be aware that they cannot settle disputes regarding the signature authenticity.  In any case where the parties do not trust each other implicitly, but agree to accept judgements of a third party, the simple signature scheme can be upgraded by introducing an arbiter who plays the role of a notary or justice of the peace.  In practice, arbiters register messages along with appropriate signatures and authenticate them by producing their own signatures (also called certificates).  Any arbiter's signature (the certificate) reflects the message digest, the name of the message author, and the time stamp.

The last section was devoted to authentication techniques which are especially important at the beginning of communication sessions.  The importance of user authentication cannot be overestimated.  An efficient user authentication procedure blocks any enemy activity originating in a remote terminal at the initial stage of transmission.  A well-designed user authentication procedure excludes, with high probability, all persons who are not legitimate users of the computer system; simultaneously the probability of denying access to a legitimate user is acceptably small.

Once a user has successfully logged in, his/her authenticity is verified by the computer system using the handshaking procedure.  It relies upon the mutual checking of cryptographic keys applied by both sides.  To do this, both parties dispatch random sequences which are transformed according to the publicly known mapping at the opposite end and sent back to the sender.  This procedure illustrates the common method of authenticating without revealing the element being authenticated.

EXERCISES

4. 1    Assuming that messages are English words, calculate the length of cryptograms which ensure that the probability of false message substitutions is less than $2^{-60}$.

4. 2    Suppose that the source of equally probable messages generates $s$-bit sequences. Assume also that redundancy has been introduced by attaching an extra parity bit. Determine the length of cryptograms for which the probability of successful authentication is greater than $1-2^{-32}$. How does $s$ influence the probability?

4. 3    Take the cipher described by the formula 4.3 and simplify it by substituting $k_1 = 0$. How many different observations (message, cryptogram) are necessary to determine the key applied?

4. 4    Consider two different ciphers defined over the set { 0, 1, 2 } with addition and multiplication modulo 3. The first cipher is described by the formula,

$$C = M + K \qquad\qquad (*)$$

where $M,C,K \in \{0,1,2\}$. The second cipher is described by,

$$C = k_1 M + k_2 \qquad\qquad (**)$$

where $k_1,k_2,M,C \in \{0,1,2\}$. Draw suitable diagrams for these ciphers that reflect their operation and discuss their usability for authentication purposes.

4. 5    Given that messages belong to the set $\{0,1,2\}$, create Shamir's authentication scheme with randomization.

4. 6    Design an Ong-Schnorr-Shamir scheme for authentication of messages. Assume that the number of elementary messages is equal to 6. Take the smallest number $N$ and use the random integer $R=5$. Find cryptograms for all messages.

4. 7    Suppose that authentication is being carried out using the Ong-Schnorr-Shamir scheme and the pair ($N=15$, $K=11$) has been published. What is the secret key $k$ ?

4. 8    Design the simple El Gamal authentication scheme for $p=7$. Compute authenticators for all possible messages assuming that the primitive element is $g=3$ and integers $r$ and $R$ have been chosen to be 3 and 5, respectively.

4. 9    Define the RSA authentication scheme for primes $p_A=3$, $q_A=11$. Assuming that the secret key has been already chosen, calculate the public key and cryptograms for first seven messages.

4. 10   Compare the authentication processes of the El Gamal and the RSA schemes. Is the El Gamal scheme vulnerable to the chosen cryptogram attack?

4. 11   Suppose that the RSA system is applied for both secrecy and authenticity. Further, suppose that the sender $A$ designs his/her system for authenticity, and the receiver $B$ for secrecy. Assume also that they have exchanged their public keys along with suitable moduli $N_A$, $N_B$. What is the configuration of the system when $N_A < N_B$ ?

4. 12   Compare the DH system to the RSA complex system used for secrecy and authenticity.

4. 13   Design a subliminal channel which allows transmisssion of one-bit messages using two-bit cryptograms.

4. 14   Suppose that a subliminal channel is defined as follows. The set of cryptograms is divided into two subsets $\mathbf{C_0} = \{ (a_1,a_2,a_3,a_4); a_1 \oplus a_2 \oplus a_3 \oplus a_4 = 0\}$ and $\mathbf{C_1} = \{ (a_1,a_2,a_3,a_4); a_1 \oplus a_2 \oplus a_3 \oplus a_4 = 1\}$. Let the communicating parties agree in

advance that the message '0' $\leftrightarrow$ {0011, 1100} $\subseteq C_0$ and the message '1' $\leftrightarrow$ {0001} $\subseteq C_1$. What is the best strategy of the warden who wants to substitute his/her own messages?

4. 15  Assume that two parties intend to communicate with each other using the Simmons subliminal channel. Suppose also that they agree on three primes $p=5$, $q=7$, $r=11$ and the common receipt strategy. This strategy relies upon the first and the fifth roots to carry the messages '0' and '1', respectively. Calculate authenticators for both binary messages while applying the cryptogram $C=256$.

4. 16  Consider the Ong-Schnorr-Shamir subliminal channel which has been designed for $N=21$ while the secret key $k=5$. Determine if the triples $(C, C_1, C_2)$ from the set $\{(14,12,11), (11,1,5), (8,18,5)\}$ transmit subliminal messages. If so, calculate them.

4. 17  You are given the El Gamal subliminal channel for the prime $p=13$, with $g=6$. Assuming that the message $M=9$ is to be sent by means of the cryptogram $C=11$, calculate the parameters $X$ and $Y$. Use the secret key $r = 10$.

4. 18  Using the parameters from the previous problem, check whether the triple $(C, X, Y) = (11, 5, 1)$ conveys a subliminal message. If so, compute its clear form.

4. 19  It is known that the El Gamal scheme is defined over the field $GF(p)$ which is generated by a primitive element $g$. Assume that the element $g$ is not primitive. What is the influence of such a choice on the enciphering and deciphering processes ?

4. 20  Construct the Seberry-Jones channel for transmitting subliminal messages of the set $\{0,1,2,3,4,5,6\}$. Is it possible to use the matrix $K$ and the vector $A$ from the example of section 4.2.5? If so, present the enciphering and deciphering processes for the subliminal message $M^* = 3$.

4. 21  Suggest a digital signature scheme for the case when the lengths of messages are less than the lengths of messages of the authentication scheme used for signature generation.

4. 22  Draw the general signature scheme. Describe the role of a compressing block used.

4. 23  Assuming that the DES algorithm is being used for the Diffie-Lamport signature scheme, calculate the signature length and lengths of both vectors $S$ and $R$ (the compressing block is not used).

4. 24  Describe the Rabin signature scheme for the parameter $r = 1$.

4. 25  Consider a simplified version of the Matyas-Meyer signature scheme for which the matrix $U$ has four rows and five columns. Describe the signature generation process, and the signature validation process supposing that $b_i$; $i = 1,2,3,4,5$ , are ordered as follows:

$$b_4 > b_3 > b_2 > b_5 > b_1$$

4. 26  Use the RSA authentication scheme to generate signatures according to the following formula:

$$SG\ (M) = I^{Mk}\ (\mathrm{mod}\ N)$$

where $M, I, k$ stand for the message ($M \gg N$), the constant integer and the author's secret key, respectively. The integer $N$ defines the arithmetic modulo $N$ ($N = pq$; $p$ and $q$ are primes). Analyze the signature scheme.

4. 27   Suppose that the signature scheme is described by formula 4.43. Is it possible to calculate the signature for $M^{-1}$ knowing the signature of $M$?

4. 28   Let us define a signature scheme as follows. A message $M$ is divided into elementary messages $(M_1, \ldots, M_n)$ where $M_i < N$ for $i = 1, \ldots, n$ — $N$ defines the modulo $N$ arithmetics and the signature is:

$$SG(M) = \sum_{i=1}^{n} M_i^k \pmod{N}$$

where $k$ is the author's secret key. Discuss the quality of this signature scheme.

4. 29   Consider the signature scheme given in problem 4.28. How can this signature be improved?

4. 30   Modify the signature scheme illustrated in Figure 4.21 in order that the arbiter will not be able to read the message.

4. 31   Modify the handshaking procedure while using an asymmetric cryptographic algorithm. Compare the result to the procedure given in Figure 4.23.


SOLUTIONS

4. 1   The solution relies upon finding the length of messages $n$ ($n$ expresses the number of letters in message) for which the proportion of elements of the set of meaningful words to elements of the set of all possible words of length $n$ is less than $2^{-60}$. Taking advantage of formula 4.1, we get:

$$P_e = 2^{-n(R-r)} < 2^{-60}$$

Using $R = \log_2 26 = 4.7$ and $r = 1$, we obtain $n > 16$.

4. 2   Clearly, if messages consist of $t$ elementary sequences, that is, any message comprises $t(s+1)$ bits, then the set of all possible messages has $2^{t(s+1)}$ elements but the set of meaningful messages possesses $2^{ts}$ elements. Therefore, the probability of successful substitution of false message is:

$$\frac{2^{ts}}{2^{t(s+1)}} = 2^{-t}$$

In other words, the cryptogram must be composed of at least 32 elementary sequences. As you can see, the probability does not depend on $s$.

4. 3   Substituting $k_1$ in formula 4.3 we get:

$$C = k_2 M + k_3$$

This cipher has exactly 12 different keys. In Figure 4.7, they are numbered $K_1, \ldots, K_{12}$ — the rest of the keys are removed (as they correspond to keys for which $k_1 = 1$). The result is given in Figure 4.30.

Assume that the first observation is $(M = 0, C = 1)$. The opponent then knows that the key belongs to the set $\{2, 6, 10\}$. Let the second opponent's observation be $(M = 1, C = 1)$. Then the key used is revealed as:

$$\{2, 6, 10\} \cap \{2, 7, 12\} = \{2\}$$

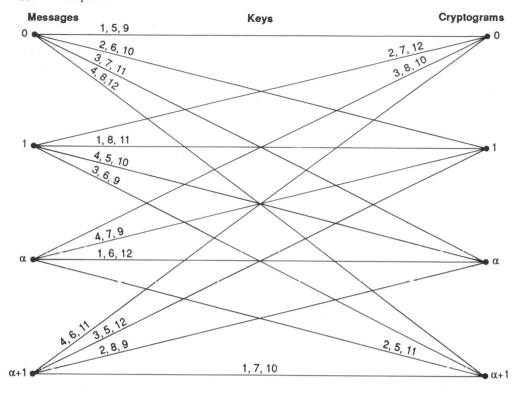

**Figure 4.30** Cipher considered in problem 4.3

This example illustrates the general rule that any two different observations break the cipher.

4. 4    The simple cipher given by (*) can be presented by Figure 4.31. For example, $M = 2$ and $K = 2$ give the cryptogram $C = 1$ (mod 3). Obviously, any single observation allows us to determine the key applied.

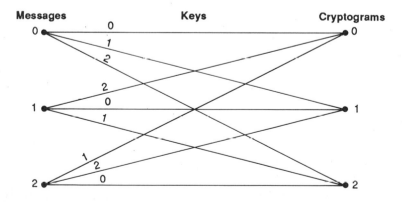

**Figure 4.31** A simple cipher defined on a three element field

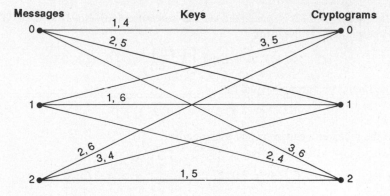

**Figure 4.32** A cipher with three messages and six keys for problem 4.4

The second cipher (**) is well defined for $k_1 \neq 0$. Using:

$$
\begin{aligned}
K_1 &= (k_1 = 1, \ k_2 = 0) \\
K_2 &= (k_1 = 1, \ k_2 = 1) \\
K_3 &= (k_1 = 1, \ k_2 = 2) \\
K_4 &= (k_1 = 2, \ k_2 = 0) \\
K_5 &= (k_1 = 2, \ k_2 = 1) \\
K_6 &= (k_1 = 2, \ k_2 = 2)
\end{aligned}
$$

we can draw the diagram of the cipher (see Figure 4.32). Any simple observation does not disclose the key used, any two different observations point at the key applied.

4. 5   As the message set is $\mathbf{M} = \{0,1,2\}$, we can use arithmetic modulo 3. On the other hand, to represent numbers of the set $\mathbf{M}$ in the form of binary sequences, we only require two bits, so $n = 2$. The secret key is an $n \times 2n$ matrix $K$. Let this matrix be:

$$
K = \begin{bmatrix} 1 & 1 & 0 & 1 \\ 0 & 1 & 1 & 0 \end{bmatrix}
$$

Next we calculate the public key $A = [a_1, a_2, a_3, a_4]$. Let the first components be equal to $a_1 = 1$ and $a_2 = 2$. The rest of the components of $A$ are calculated using the following congruence:

$$
K \times \begin{bmatrix} 1 \\ 2 \\ a_3 \\ a_4 \end{bmatrix} = \begin{bmatrix} 1 & 1 & 0 & 1 \\ 0 & 1 & 1 & 0 \end{bmatrix} \times \begin{bmatrix} 1 \\ 2 \\ a_3 \\ a_4 \end{bmatrix} = \begin{bmatrix} 1 \\ 2 \end{bmatrix} \pmod 3
$$

Thus we obtain $A = [1,2,0,1]$. To randomize the system, we select the binary vector $R = [0,1,0,1]$. If we have the message $M = 2$, we first calculate its modified form $\underline{M}$ as follows:

$$
\underline{M} = M - R \times A = 2 - [0, 1, 0, 1] \begin{bmatrix} 1 \\ 2 \\ 0 \\ 1 \end{bmatrix} = 2 \pmod 3
$$

The message $\underline{M}=2$ is presented as the sequence $[1,0]$ so $\underline{M} = [0,1]$. The initial cryptogram takes the form:

$$\underline{C} = \underline{\dot{M}} \times K = [0, 1] \begin{bmatrix} 1 & 1 & 0 & 1 \\ 0 & 1 & 1 & 0 \end{bmatrix} = [0, 1, 1, 0]$$

The final cryptogram is equal to:

$$C = \underline{C} + R = [0, 2, 1, 1]$$

At the receiver's end, the clear message is:

$$M = C \times A = [0, 2, 1, 1] \begin{bmatrix} 1 \\ 2 \\ 0 \\ 1 \end{bmatrix} = 5 = 2 \ (\text{mod } 3)$$

4. 6   To select $N$, first observe that all messages are integers $M$ for which $gcd(M,N) = 1$. The smallest integer which satisfies the requirement is $N = 14$. Thus the set $\mathbf{M} = \{1,3,5,9,11,13\}$. The secret key $k$ is selected at random where $gcd(N,k) = 1$. Let $k = 9$. Note that $k^{-1} = 11 \ (\text{mod } 14)$. We next calculate:

$$K = -k^{-2} = 5 \ (\text{mod } 14)$$

The pair $(N = 14, K = 5)$ is published as the public key. Substituting values in formula 4.11, we get:

$$
\begin{aligned}
M &= 1 &\rightarrow&\quad C_1 = 4, C_2 = 5 \\
M &= 3 &\rightarrow&\quad C_1 = 7, C_2 = 4 \\
M &= 5 &\rightarrow&\quad C_1 = 3, C_2 = 10 \\
M &= 9 &\rightarrow&\quad C_1 = 9, C_2 = 8 \\
M &= 11 &\rightarrow&\quad C_1 = 5, C_2 = 0 \\
M &= 13 &\rightarrow&\quad C_1 = 8, C_2 = 13
\end{aligned}
$$

4. 7   To answer the question, consider arithmetic modulo 15 and compute squares for all integers, namely:

$$
\begin{aligned}
x &= 1 &\rightarrow&\quad x^2 = 1 \\
x &= 2 &\rightarrow&\quad x^2 = 4 \\
x &= 3 &\rightarrow&\quad x^2 = 9 \\
x &= 4 &\rightarrow&\quad x^2 = 1 \\
x &= 5 &\rightarrow&\quad x^2 = 10 \\
x &= 6 &\rightarrow&\quad x^2 = 6 \\
x &= 7 &\rightarrow&\quad x^2 = 4 \\
x &= 8 &\rightarrow&\quad x^2 = 4 \\
x &= 9 &\rightarrow&\quad x^2 = 6 \\
x &= 10 &\rightarrow&\quad x^2 = 10 \\
x &= 11 &\rightarrow&\quad x^2 = 1 \\
x &= 12 &\rightarrow&\quad x^2 = 9 \\
x &= 13 &\rightarrow&\quad x^2 = 4 \\
x &= 14 &\rightarrow&\quad x^2 = 1
\end{aligned}
$$

Now using 4.10, it is obvious that:

$$K = -(k^{-1})^2 \pmod{N}$$

In our case, the congruence takes on the form:

$$(k^{-1})^2 = 4 \pmod{15}$$

In other words, we are looking for $x$ where $x^2 = 4$. Using the above, we can see that there are four different integers whose squares are equal 4, namely 2, 7, 8, 13. Even if we observe that $gcd(N,k) = 1$, the number of candidates does not diminish.

4. 8   First of all, we calculate all powers of our primitive element $g = 3$, namely:

$$3^1 = 3 \pmod{7}$$
$$3^2 = 2 \pmod{7}$$
$$3^3 = 6 \pmod{7}$$
$$3^4 = 4 \pmod{7}$$
$$3^5 = 5 \pmod{7}$$
$$3^6 = 1 \pmod{7}$$

The public key $K$ is calculated using the random integer $r$, that is:

$$K = g^3 = 6 \pmod{7}$$

Next we calculate:

$$X = g^R = 3^5 = 5 \pmod{7}$$

Having the message $M$, we solve the congruence 4.15 and obtain the following sequence of authenticators:

$$M = 1 \quad \rightarrow \quad (X, Y) = (5, 2)$$
$$M = 2 \quad \rightarrow \quad (X, Y) = (5, 1)$$
$$M = 3 \quad \rightarrow \quad (X, Y) = (5, 0)$$
$$M = 4 \quad \rightarrow \quad (X, Y) = (5, 5)$$
$$M = 5 \quad \rightarrow \quad (X, Y) = (5, 4)$$
$$M = 6 \quad \rightarrow \quad (X, Y) = (5, 3)$$

The authentication process relies upon matching the message to the pair $(X, Y)$. For instance, for $M = 1$, we first calculate:

$$A = K^X X^Y = 6^5 \, 5^2 = 3 \pmod{7},$$

and next,

$$A' = g^M = 3 \pmod{7}$$

If both $A$'s are equal, the message is accepted.

4. 9   First we determine,

$$\gamma = lcm(p_A - 1, q_A - 1) = lcm(2, 10) = 10$$

The public key must obey the congruence $k_A K_A = 1 \pmod{\gamma}$. Substituting values, we get:

$$k_A K_A = 1 \pmod{10}$$

For $k_A = 7$, the public key $K_A = 3$. As the cryptograms are equal to $C = M^{k_A}$ (mod $p_A q_A$), we obtain the following results:

$$
\begin{array}{ccc}
M = 1 & \rightarrow & C = 1 \\
M = 2 & \rightarrow & C = 29 \\
M = 3 & \rightarrow & C = 9 \\
M = 4 & \rightarrow & C = 16 \\
M = 5 & \rightarrow & C = 14 \\
M = 6 & \rightarrow & C = 30 \\
M = 7 & \rightarrow & C = 28 \\
\end{array}
$$

4. 10  In the El Gamal scheme, the receiver is given the triple: the message $M$ and the pair of authenticators $(X, Y)$. The authentication process relies upon calculation of two numbers $A = K^X X^Y$ (mod $p$) and $A' = g^M$, where $K$, $p$, $g$ are known to the receiver. If they are equal then the message $M$ is accepted.

In the RSA scheme, the cryptogram is given and the message is recreated using the public key $K$ as follows:

$$
M = C^K \ (\text{mod } N)
$$

where $N = pq$ is known to the receiver (of course, $p$ and $q$ are secret). Therefore, there is the essential difference between the two schemes. In the first, the clear message must be given to the receiver. In the second, however, it is not necessary. In conclusion, we observe that the El Gamal is not vulnerable to the chosen cryptogram attack as such a cryptogram does not exist. Even if the opponent selects his/her own pair $(X, Y)$, the opponent is not able to determine the required message $M$ (both the message and the pair of authenticators must produce the same value of $A$). In other words, the opponent, knowing $g$ and $A$ and wanting to calculate $M$, faces an instance of the discrete logarithm problem.

4. 11  As the modulus $N_A$ is less than $N_B$, the first operation must be carried out using the sender's authentication scheme. It guarantees that resulting cryptograms are less than $N_B$ and the cascade of cryptographic transformations is invertible. So, the sender first applies $D_A$ and next $E_B$.

4. 12  First of all, we observe that the RSA system is based on two numerical problems, namely the factorization and the discrete logarithm problems. The second system is based on the discrete logarithm problem only. As a matter of fact, both systems use secret keys which are created by applying the public key of the second party and his/her own secret key. The resulting enciphering key is different from the deciphering key for both cases. There is, however, an essential difference. Disclosure of the enciphering key in the RSA system causes authenticity to be compromised. On the other hand, revealing the deciphering key compromises the secrecy of RSA system. The system is broken when both keys are compromised. In the second system, however, disclosure of either key compromises the system totally.

4. 13  Such a subliminal channel is a simplification of the channel considered in section 4.2.1. Assume that the set of all possible cryptograms is divided into two subsets $\mathbf{C_0} = \{ 00, 11 \}$ and $\mathbf{C_1} = \{ 01, 10 \}$. The subset $\mathbf{C_0}$ corresponds to the message '0', and $\mathbf{C_1}$ to the message '1'. Both the sender and the receiver must agree

beforehand on the secret key which points out cryptograms which carry meaningful messages. Suppose that cryptograms 11 and 01 carry meaningful messages 0 and 1, repectively. For instance, if the sender transmits the sequence 00, 11, 01, 00, 11, 01, 10, ... , the receiver recreates the corresponding message sequence 0, 1, 0, 0, 1, 1, ... . Deleting spurious messages using the secret key, the receiver obtains the sequence 0, 1, 0, 1, ... . The channel is, however, vulnerable to the following attack. Assume that the opponent (warden) intends to send on behalf of the sender his/her own sequence of messages, (e.g. (0, 1, 1, 0, 0)). In order to do this, the opponent can transmit the following sequence of cryptograms: 00, 11, 01, 10, 01, 10, 00, 11, 00, 11.

4.14 Consider the first case when the warden intends to send the message '0'. The warden then faces the problem of selecting one or more cryptograms from the set $C_0$. If he/she selects one cryptogram only, the probability of his/her success is equal to ¼. If, however, the warden chooses two cryptograms to transmitt '0', the probability is equal to $\frac{3}{7}$. In general, if the warden decides to use $n$ different cryptograms to send '0' ($n \leq 6$), then there are $\begin{bmatrix} 8 \\ n \end{bmatrix}$ different possibilities, but 2 $\begin{bmatrix} 6 \\ n-1 \end{bmatrix}$ are favorable. Thus, for $n=3$, the probability of the warden's success is maximum and amounts to 0.536.

Summing up, we observe that the warden's best strategy is as follows. If the warden wants to substitute '0', he/she selects at random three different cryptograms from the set $C_0$. In the second case, if he/she intends to send '1', he/she generates all cryptograms of the set $C_1$ as he/she knows that is the only cryptogram which carries the meaningful message '1'.

4.15 Knowing the primes, both parties first solve three congruences as follows:

$$x^2 = 256 = 1 \, (\text{mod } 5)$$
$$x^2 = 256 = 4 \, (\text{mod } 7)$$
$$x^2 = 256 = 3 \, (\text{mod } 11)$$

The first congruence produces two solutions:

$$x_{10} = 1 \, (\text{mod } 5)$$
$$x_{11} = 4 \, (\text{mod } 5)$$

the second:

$$x_{20} = 2 \, (\text{mod } 7)$$
$$x_{21} = 5 \, (\text{mod } 7)$$

and the third:

$$x_{30} = 5 \, (\text{mod } 11)$$
$$x_{31} = 7 \, (\text{mod } 11)$$

In general, 256 has eight different square roots, namely:

$$x_{10}, x_{20}, x_{30} \; \rightarrow \; [1, 2, 5] = 16 \, (\text{mod } 385)$$
$$x_{10}, x_{20}, x_{31} \; \rightarrow \; [1, 2, 7] = 51 \, (\text{mod } 385)$$
$$x_{10}, x_{21}, x_{30} \; \rightarrow \; [1, 5, 5] = 236 \, (\text{mod } 385)$$

$$x_{10}, x_{21}, x_{31} \;\rightarrow\; [1, 5, 7] = 271 \;(\text{mod } 385)$$
$$x_{11}, x_{20}, x_{30} \;\rightarrow\; [4, 2, 5] = 324 \;(\text{mod } 385)$$
$$x_{11}, x_{20}, x_{31} \;\rightarrow\; [4, 2, 7] = 359 \;(\text{mod } 385)$$
$$x_{11}, x_{21}, x_{30} \;\rightarrow\; [4, 5, 5] = 159 \;(\text{mod } 385)$$
$$x_{11}, x_{21}, x_{31} \;\rightarrow\; [4, 5, 7] = 194 \;(\text{mod } 385)$$

According to the prearranged strategy, if the sender intends to send the message '0', he/she picks the pair (256,16). On the other hand, for the message '1', the sender dispatches the pair (256,324). Other pairs — (256, 51), (256, 236), (256, 271), (256, 359), (256, 159), (256, 194) — convey no subliminal message.

4. 16 Take the first triple (14,12,11). Of course, the cryptogram $C$ must be relatively prime to $N$, that is, $gcd(C, N) = 1$. We can see that the cryptogram $C = 14$ does not meet the requirements, so we reject it. By the way, we could use the fact that the cryptogram $C'$ calculated using formula 4.22 is equal to $C$ so it would be acceptable if $gcd(C, N) = 1$.

The second triple $(11, 1, 5)$ is also rejected. This time, however, $C' = C_1^2 - \dfrac{C_2^2}{k^2} = 0 \neq 11$. Finally, the third triple is acceptable as $C' = C$. The cryptogram produces the message:

$$M \;=\; \frac{C}{C_1 + C_2 k^{-1}} \;(\text{mod } N) \;=\; 17 \;(\text{mod } 21)$$

4. 17 First of all, compute all powers of the primitive element:

$$
\begin{aligned}
g^1 &= 6 \;(\text{mod } 13) \\
g^2 &= 10 \;(\text{mod } 13) \\
g^3 &= 8 \;(\text{mod } 13) \\
g^4 &= 9 \;(\text{mod } 13) \\
g^5 &= 2 \;(\text{mod } 13) \\
g^6 &= 12 \;(\text{mod } 13) \\
g^7 &= 7 \;(\text{mod } 13) \\
g^8 &= 3 \;(\text{mod } 13) \\
g^9 &= 5 \;(\text{mod } 13) \\
g^{10} &= 4 \;(\text{mod } 13) \\
g^{11} &= 11 \;(\text{mod } 13) \\
g^{12} &= 1 \;(\text{mod } 13)
\end{aligned}
$$

We next solve the congruence:

$$C = r X + M Y \;(\text{mod } p-1)$$

for $C = 11$, $r = 10$, $X = g^M = g^9 = 5$, and $M = 9$. After substituting all values, we get $Y \equiv 1 \;(\text{mod } 12)$. So, if the sender wants to send the message $M = 9$ using the cryptogram $C = 11$, he/she has to dispatch the triple $(C, X, Y) = (11, 5, 1)$.

4. 18 In order to do this, we first compute:

$$A \;=\; (g^r)^X X^Y \;(\text{mod } p) \;=\; 11 \;(\text{mod } 13)$$

and $A' = g^C = 6^{11} = 11$. As $A = A'$, the triple contains a subliminal message. To recover it, we calculate:

$$M = Y^{-1}(C - rX) \pmod{p-1} = 9 \pmod{12}$$

4. 19 Consider the simplest case when $g$ is an idempotent element, that is, $g^2 = 1$ (mod p). Therefore, $X = g^M$ is equal to either $g$ or 1. Thus, if $M \pmod 2 = 0$, then $X = 1$. However, if $M \pmod 2 = 1$, then $X = g$. As the number of different elements generated by $g$ is equal to 2, formulae 4.25 and 4.27 are congruences modulo 2 instead of modulo $p-1$. In other words, having the triple $(C, X, Y)$, we cannot recreate the message $M$ unless it belongs to the set $\{0,1\}$.

In general, if $g^1, g^2, \ldots, g^\alpha = 1$ and $\alpha \neq p-1$ (of course, $\alpha < p-1$), then the congruences 4.25 and 4.27 take the following forms:

$$C = rX + MY \pmod{\alpha}$$
$$M = Y^{-1}(C - rX) \pmod{\alpha}$$

respectively. The message $M$ can be recovered if and only if $M < \alpha$. If, however, $M > \alpha$, then the receiver can recreate $M \pmod{\alpha}$.

4. 20 As any elements of the set can be represented as a 3-bit sequence, we can use the matrix $K$. The vector $A$, however, must be recalculated according to the congruence given below:

$$K \times A = \begin{bmatrix} 2 & 2 & 4 & 1 & 3 & 1 \\ 4 & 4 & 1 & 1 & 0 & 2 \\ 4 & 3 & 4 & 2 & 2 & 0 \end{bmatrix} \begin{bmatrix} 2 \\ 2 \\ 2 \\ a_4 \\ a_5 \\ a_6 \end{bmatrix} = \begin{bmatrix} 1 \\ 2 \\ 4 \end{bmatrix} \pmod 7$$

while $a_1, a_2, a_3$ are selected at random. Let them be the same as in the example, that is, $a_1 = a_2 = a_3 = 2$. After simple calculations, we get $a_4 = 6 \pmod 7$, $a_5 = 6 \pmod 7$, $a_6 = 3 \pmod 7$. The vector $A$ and the prime $p$ are public. Next, we calculate the secret vector $B$ as follows:

$$K \times B = \begin{bmatrix} 2 & 2 & 4 & 1 & 3 & 1 \\ 4 & 4 & 1 & 1 & 0 & 2 \\ 4 & 3 & 4 & 2 & 2 & 0 \end{bmatrix} \begin{bmatrix} b_1 \\ b_2 \\ b_3 \\ b_4 \\ b_5 \\ b_6 \end{bmatrix} = 0 \pmod 7$$

Assuming that $b_1 = 1$, $b_2 = 2$, $b_3 = 4$, we obtain that $b_4 = 4 \pmod 7$, $b_5 = 4 \pmod 7$, $b_6 = 4 \pmod 7$. Of course, the vector $B = [1,2,4,4,4,4]$ plays the role of the secret key therefore it is shared by the sender and the receiver only.

The enciphering process for $M^* = 3$ consists of several steps. First we determine the vector $R$ such that:

$$M^* = R \times B = [r_1, r_2, r_3, r_3, r_4, r_5, r_6] \begin{bmatrix} 1 \\ 2 \\ 4 \\ 4 \\ 4 \\ 4 \end{bmatrix} = 3 \pmod 7$$

Let us take $R = [0,1,0,0,1,1]$. Next we choose the parameter $M = 5 \pmod 7$, and we calculate:

$$\underline{M} = M - R \times A = 5 - [0,1,0,0,1,1] \begin{bmatrix} 2 \\ 2 \\ 2 \\ 6 \\ 6 \\ 3 \end{bmatrix} = 1 \pmod 7$$

$$\underline{C} = \dot{M} \times K = [1,0,0] \begin{bmatrix} 2 & 2 & 4 & 1 & 3 & 1 \\ 4 & 4 & 1 & 1 & 0 & 2 \\ 4 & 3 & 4 & 2 & 2 & 0 \end{bmatrix} = [2,2,4,1,3,1]$$

$$C = \underline{C} + R = [2,2,4,1,3,1] + [0,1,0,0,1,1] = [2,3,4,1,4,2]$$

The pair $(M, C) = (5, [2,3,4,1,4,2])$ is sent to the receiver.

The deciphering process starts with computing $C \times A = 5 \pmod 7$. If $C \times A$ is equal to $M$, then the cryptogram conveys the subliminal message. As there is such a case in our example, we recreate the clear form of the message as follows:

$$M^* = C \times B = [2,3,4,1,4,2] \begin{bmatrix} 1 \\ 2 \\ 4 \\ 4 \\ 4 \\ 4 \end{bmatrix} = 3 \pmod 7$$

In other words, the clear form of the subliminal message is equal to 3.

4. 21 In this case message-compressing techniques are needless. So we can produce signatures like those in section 4.3, while the compressing block is omitted. Thus, to obtain digital signatures in this case, we can use any authentication scheme described in section 4.1.

4. 22 The general signature scheme consists of two main blocks. The first – the compressing block – reduces the message length such that an authentication scheme – the second block – can produce a suitable cryptogram which is considered to be the signature. Therefore, the compressing block adapts the message size to the authentication scheme.

4. 23 It is known that the DES algorithm operates on 64-bit messages and produces 64-bit cryptograms. Suppose that the message contains $n$ bits. Looking at formula 4.33, we can see that the lengths of $S$ and $R$ are the same and equal $128n$ bits. On the other hand, as the signature consists of $n$ cryptographic keys (see formula 4.35), its length is to equal $64n$.

4. 24 The set of keys generated by the sender is equal to $K_1$ and $K_2$. Next the sequence $S = (S_1, S_2)$ is selected at random and enciphered. Suitable cryptograms $R_i = E_{K_i}(S_i);\ i = 1, 2$ , create the sequence $R = (R_1, R_2)$. Similarly, the signature consists of two elements, namely $E_{K_1}(CF(M))$ and $E_{K_2}(CF(M))$.

To verify the signature, the receiver selects a 2-bit vector, either $(0,1)$ or $(1,0)$ and sends it to the sender. He/she responds by sending suitable subset of keys, that is,

$(0, K_2)$ if he/she has obtained $(0,1)$

$(K_1, 0)$ if he/she has obtained $(1,0)$

In turn, the receiver first validates the key obtained using sequences $S$ and $R$ from the public register, and next states authenticity of the signature.

4.25   The first row of the matrix $K$ is yielded using a pseudorandom generator. The rest of the rows are calculated applying the previous row and the corresponding row of the matrix $U$. So,

$$K_{i+1,j} = E_{K_{i,j}}[u_{i,j}] \quad \text{for } i = 1,2,3,4 \quad j = 1,2,3,4,5$$

As result we have:

$$K = \begin{bmatrix} K_{1,1} & K_{1,2} & K_{1,3} & K_{1,4} & K_{1,5} \\ K_{2,1} & K_{2,2} & K_{2,3} & K_{2,4} & K_{2,5} \\ K_{3,1} & K_{3,2} & K_{3,3} & K_{3,4} & K_{3,5} \\ K_{4,1} & K_{4,2} & K_{4,3} & K_{4,4} & K_{4,5} \\ K_{5,1} & K_{5,2} & K_{5,3} & K_{5,4} & K_{5,5} \end{bmatrix}$$

The first row constitutes the initial condition. The last one, however, is being sent to the public register while others are kept secret. To sign the message $M$, the sender computes:

$$b_i = E_{K_{5,i}}(CF(M)) \quad \text{for } i = 1,2,3,4,5$$

As $b_4 > b_3 > b_2 > b_5 > b_1$, the signature is :

$$[K_{4,1}, K_{3,2}, K_{2,3}, K_{5,4}, K_{1,5}]$$

Having the message $M$, the receiver first calculates the digest $CF(M)$, next determines the sequence $b_i$; $i = 1, 2, 3, 4, 5$, and orders them according to increasing values. As $b_4 > b_3 > b_2 > b_5 > b_1$, the receiver puts them into the empty matrix $K$ as follows:

$$K = \begin{bmatrix} \times & \times & \times & \times & K_{1,5} \\ \times & \times & K_{2,3} & \times & \square \\ \times & K_{3,2} & \square & \times & \square \\ K_{4,1} & \square & \square & \times & \square \\ \square & \square & \square & K_{5,4} & \square \end{bmatrix}$$

whereas $\times$ stands for keys which are unknown to the receiver, and $\square$ points at those elements which are calculated by the receiver using equation (4.40) — he/she knows the matrix $U$, as it is accessible in the public register. Once the receiver has obtained the last row of the matrix $K$, he/she compares it to the row stored in the public register.

4.26   Assume that the author has signed two different messages $M_1$ and $M_2$. The signatures are equal:

$$SG(M_1) = I^{M_1 k} \pmod{N}$$
$$SG(M_2) = I^{M_2 k} \pmod{N}$$

An opponent, who knows these two pairs $[M_1, SG(M_1)]$ and $[M_2, SG(M_2)]$, can produce the signature,

$$SG(M_3) = SG(M_1)\, SG(M_2) = I^{M_1 k} I^{M_2 k} = I^{(M_1 + M_2) k} \pmod{N}$$

for the message $M_3 = M_1 + M_2$. Applying the same procedure, the opponent can produce any signature for $M_3 = aM_1$ as:

$$SG(M_3) = I^{M_3 k} = I^{aM_1 k} = (I^{M_1 k})^a = [SG(M_1)]^a \pmod{N}$$

Concluding, we can state that the opponent, knowing the original signature along with the message $M$, is able to sign any message of the form $aM$, where $a$ is an arbitrary integer.

4.27 Use the following congruence:

$$SG(1) = SG(M \cdot M^{-1}) = I^{M \cdot M^{-1} \bmod \gamma(N)} \pmod{N}$$

Transforming it, we get:

$$\left[ I^{M^{-1} \bmod \gamma(N)} \right]^M = I \pmod{N}$$

and therefore:

$$[SG(M)]^M = [SG(M^{-1})]^{M^{-1}} = I \pmod{N}$$

In other words, if the opponent knows the pair $[SG(M), M]$, he/she may calculate the integer $I$ but may not compute $SG(M^{-1})$ as he/she needs to know $M^{-1} \pmod{\gamma(N)}$. Computing $M^{-1}$ is intractable as long as the factorization of $N$ is kept secret.

4.28 Assume that the author has signed two messages:

$$M_1 = (M_{11}, M_{12}, \ldots, M_{1n})$$
$$M_2 = (M_{21}, M_{22}, \ldots, M_{2m})$$

whose signatures are:

$$SG(M_1) = \sum_{i+1}^{n} M_{1i}^k \pmod{N}$$
$$SG(M_2) = \sum_{i+1}^{m} M_{2i}^k \pmod{N}$$

We note that the opponent may produce the new message $M_3 = (M_1, M_2)$ whose signature is equal to:

$$SG(M_3) = SG(M_1) + SG(M_2)$$

In general, as the scheme is additive, any two messages which contain the same set of elementary messages have the same signature, that is, the shape of signature does not depend upon the order of elementary messages.

4.29 The main drawback of the scheme considered is that the signature does not depend on the order of the elementary messages. So, to improve it, we insert any elementary message to its position in the form of the following recurrent congruences:

$$C_1 = (M_1 + I)^k \pmod{N}$$
$$C_2 = (M_2 + C_1)^k \pmod{N}$$
$$\bullet$$
$$\bullet$$
$$\bullet$$
$$C_n = (M_n + C_{n-1})^k \pmod{N}$$

where $I$ is the initial condition and $k$ the secret key. The resulting scheme is similar to that given in Figure 4.20.

4. 30 Assume that the user A wants to sign the message which consists of ($ID_A$, $ID_B$, $No$, $TEXT$), where $ID_A$, $ID_B$ are identificators of the sender and the receiver, respectively, $No$ is the current message number, and $TEXT$ is the actual message. Suppose that the sender and the receiver also share the common key $K_{AB}$ which is known to them exclusively. The arbiter, however, communicates to both the sender and the receiver using keys $K_A$ and $K_B$, respectively.

Firstly, the sender prepares the message $M = [ID_A, ID_B, No, E_{K_{AB}}(TEXT)]$ and generates its digest $CF(M)$. Second, he/she forwards the pair $[M, E_{K_A}(CF(M))]$ to the arbiter. Knowing $ID_A$ and $ID_B$, the arbiter finds suitable keys $K_A$ and $K_B$. Next, the arbiter validates the pair $[M, CF(M)]$ by repeating the sender's operations. If the pair is valid, the arbiter creates the following new message:

$$M' = [M, SN, TS]$$

(where $SN$, $TS$ stand for the serial number and the time stamp, respectively) and sends it to the receiver as the cryptogram $E_{K_B}(M')$. In turn, the receiver decrypts it and checks its pattern. If the pattern is acceptable, he/she recovers $TEXT$ by using $K_{AB}$.

4. 31 We only need to consider the case when the sender $A$ authenticates the receiver $B$. Assume that both $A$ and $B$ know suitable public keys $K_B$ and $K_A$, respectively. Firstly, $A$ sends his/her identificator $ID_A$ to $B$ in clear form. Second, $A$ generates, using a pseudorandom generator, the secret sequence $S$ and encrypts it using the $B$'s public key. Next, the cryptogram $E_B(S)$ is sent to $B$. At the receiver's end, $B$ decrypts $E_B(S)$ and transforms $S$ using the known one-way function $\alpha(\cdot)$. The resulting message $\alpha(S)$ is encrypted by applying the public key $K_A$. The cryptogram $E_A[\alpha(S)]$ is forwarded to the sender $A$ who, after decryption, compares $\alpha(S)$ obtained from $B$ to $\alpha(S)$ generated by himself/herself. If both sequences are equal, $A$ accepts $B$.

The procedure given above is similar to the one in Figure 4.23. The only difference results from the principle of asymmetric cryptosystem. Therefore, both $A$ and $B$ use different public keys if they want to communicate with each other.

# 5

# CRYPTOGRAPHY IN COMPUTER NETWORK SECURITY

A computer network can be regarded as a single 'super computer', whose hardware and software resources are distributed over a given geographic area. An especially important component of this super computer is the communication network (Figure 5.1) that connects computers together. It is susceptible to illegal activity by unfriendly users. The large physical dimensions of the network make it impossible to protect the network resources by physical security measures (see [SEID83], [TANE81a], [TANE81b]). The application of operating methods of protection in the computer network has obvious limitations, for example, they cannot be used to protect information that is being sent through the communication network. The only class of protection methods which can be applied is the class of cryptographic methods. It is worth noting that cryptographic protection does not exclude all illegal user activity. Its main benefit is the protection of the computer network against the effects of such activity.

In the first section of this chapter we look in detail at the problems and methods for protection of information in computer networks. The discussion of the first section raises further questions about how to manage and distribute keys in a cryptographically protected network. This is discussed more fully in section 5.2. The third section is devoted to the Electronic Funds Transfer (EFT) and the security problems involved. We described the importance of the Personal Identification Number (PIN) in EFT systems. Finally we discuss both PIN oriented and PIN/personal key oriented EFT systems.

## 5.1 Information protection in computer networks

Historically, cryptography was exclusively applied in order to hide the clear form of text by making it unreadable. The second aim of enciphering is the detection of illegally injected, removed or changed information. Cryptographic methods can be used to protect the following types of transmission channels:

- channels that connect terminals with their host computers (or nodes);
- channels that create the communication network.

The level and quality of security obtained by cryptographic methods of protection depend

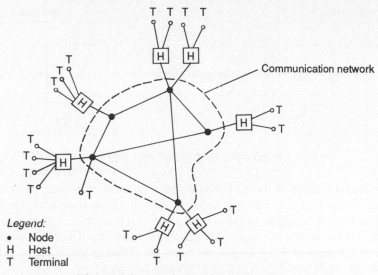

**Figure 5.1** A typical computer network

ultimately on channel capacity. Especially high enciphering quality requirements are formulated when transmitting information via satellite channels.

In this section we present the main problems which arise while introducing cryptographic methods to computer network protection ([DAPR84], [MEMA84]). First we show how cryptographic keys can be distributed between nodes where information is being enciphered and deciphered. Next we present enciphering protocols which must be incorporated into the network management system as tools for carrying out the necessary cryptographic operations such as enciphering, deciphering and re-enciphering. Last we analyse the generation and storage methods for keys.

## 5.1.1 Distribution of cryptographic keys

The computer network, from the point of view two communicating users *A* and *B*, is simply a transmission channel (Figure 5.2). Usually users want their information protected against unfriendly activity. When discussing the user's activity, we mean either

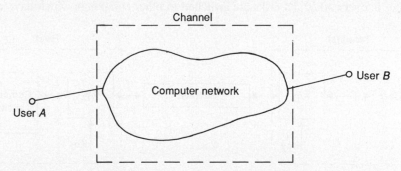

**Figure 5.2** A computer network from the user's point of view

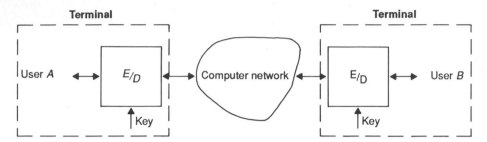

**Figure 5.3** End-to-end encryption

a single person or a group of users. For example, a group of unfriendly users could gain control over a large part of a computer network. The designers of information protection systems must build the security shield in such a way that protection measures overlap and take into account a variety of possible illegal access methods. Therefore, cryptographic protection of information is applied many times on different levels of the information flow organization ([POKL78], [POKL79]). We can deal with:

- end-to-end encryption (terminal to terminal communication);
- terminal-to-host computer encryption; and
- host-to-host encryption.

The end-to-end encryption ensures that all information sent throughout a network is unreadable as long as it is within the computer network. Simply, a computer network, from the point of view of users $A$ and $B$, is treated as a single channel (see Figure 5.3). In other words, such a protection may be used if users do not want to process their data. However, if the user wishes to take advantage of a variety of the computer network resources, the terminal-to-host encryption is applied in order to protect user data transmitted to/from the host computer. Of course, in this case, a terminal and a host computer must share a suitable key (Figure 5.4). Sometimes a user resides in the terminal of a foreign host computer and wishes to carry out a processing task in his/her own host computer. This situation, depicted in Figure 5.5, is somewhat similar to that of Figure 5.4.

Since the concept of computer networks arises from the desire for uniform usage of computer resources, there is information flow between host computers. If one host computer is overworked, its tasks are switched to other computers which have a surplus

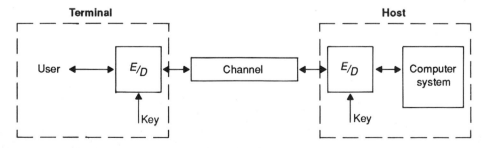

**Figure 5.4** Terminal-to-host encryption

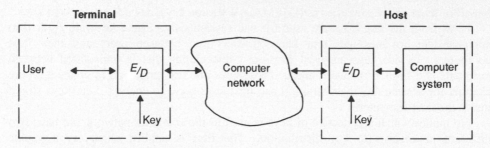

**Figure 5.5** Terminal-to-host encryption via a foreign terminal

of computing capacity. In order to allow for flexible working arrangements within the computer network, without endangering information protection when transmitting, the problem of key management must be solved properly with account taken of all possible places where shared keys are needed.

The first problem is key distribution between two communicating parties. This distribution must be carried out by means of secure channels. Historically, secure channels were created by messengers who used to physically carry letters containing written keys. Such a channel introduces considerable delays and cannot be applied in computer networks for key distribution.

There are two approaches to key distribution. The first relies on the use of a separate communication network for key distribution only. The second approach consists of using the same communication network for both information and key transmission: the secure channel is created by means of cryptography. In other words, cryptographic keys are enciphered and sent to suitable parties in the form of cryptograms; for example, see Figure 5.6.

Now consider the situation where a user resides in a foreign terminal and requires to share a key with his/her own host computer $j$. The requirement is accepted by host $i$ and the host generates a suitable key $K_S$. Afterwards, $K_S$ is sent to both the user and the host computer $j$ by means of two prearranged secure channels. We suppose keys $K_T$ and $K_H$ were used to create these channels.

There are many different keys which are used simultaneously for different purposes

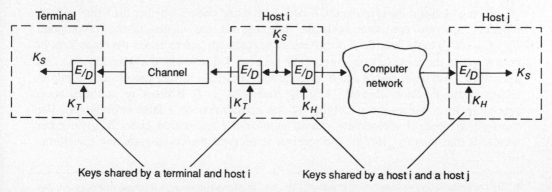

**Figure 5.6** An example of key distribution between a terminal and a host

but all of them can be classified as ([MEMA84]) session keys, device keys, or host keys.

Keys from the first class are used for one session only. These keys are applied to encipher/decipher messages sent between users and between users and their host computers. Device keys are used to protect information that is transmitted between terminals and hosts or between hosts. These keys are also employed to create a secure channel for session key distribution. Last, host keys serve to encrypt other keys stored inside the host computer.

No matter which architecture of keys is used in the computer network, we have two different approaches to key distribution. The first is applied when cryptographic protection is based on symmetric algorithms and the second approach when asymmetric algorithms are used. Let us consider these two approaches in turn (see [POKL79]).

## 5.1.2 Key distribution for symmetric cryptographic algorithms

Assume that key distribution is performed using the same communication network and that keys are being sent in the shape of suitable cryptograms. The distribution of keys in the computer network is controlled by either a single host computer, which has been selected from all other computers of the network (the so-called centralized key distribution system), or a group of host computers (the so-called decentralized key distribution). In decentralized key distribution, each host with a center of key distribution (CKD) responsibility is responsible for correct and safe key delivery among entities[1] that are subject to it.

First, we consider the case where there exists only one key distribution center in a network. Assume that each user shares with the CKD a prearranged pair of unique keys. Suppose further that a user $A$ requires protection for information while sending it to user $B$. First, the user $A$ transmits a suitable requirement along with an identification name to CKD (see Figure 5.7) in clear form. Responding, CKD sends $A$ a cryptogram of the message that consists of:

- a key $K_{AB}$ that will be used to protect transmission between users $A$ and $B$;
- the identification name of $A$ ($ID_A$);
- a copy of $A$'s request ($R_A$);
- a cryptogram of the pair ($K_{AB}, ID_A$) obtained for a key $K_B$ shared between B and CKD namely, $E_{K_B}(K_{AB}, ID_A)$.

Having obtained the cryptogram, $A$ deciphers it and checks whether the name and the request copy are consistent with the original. If so, $A$ directs the cryptogram $E_{K_B}(K_{AB}, ID_A)$ to the user $B$. $B$ deciphers the cryptogram and recreates the clear form of both $K_{AB}$ and the name $ID_A$ (this is possible because $B$ shares with CKD the key $K_B$). As a result of these steps, both $A$ and $B$ have the same key $K_{AB}$, so they can create a common secure communication channel. Usually having $K_{AB}$, $B$ initiates an authentication procedure to eliminate the possibility of the substitution of a false cryptogram. For example, $B$ sends $A$ a randomly chosen number $RN$ enciphered under $K_{AB}$ (in other words, $B$ transmits $E_{K_{AB}}(RN)$). The receiver $A$ decrypts the cryptogram and transforms

---

1. By computer entity, we mean users, terminals, files, etc. In general, an entity is anything within a computer system that requires a secure transmission channel.

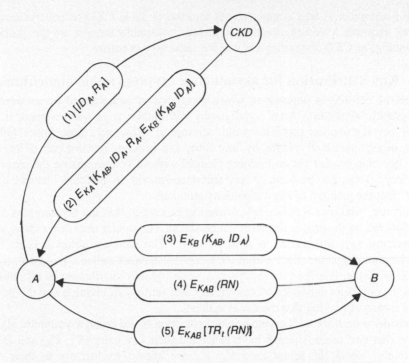

(1) [$ID_A$, $R_A$]

(2) $E_{KA}$ [$K_{AB}$, $ID_A$, $R_A$, $E_{KB}$ ($K_{AB}$, $ID_A$)]

(3) $E_{KB}$ ($K_{AB}$, $ID_A$)

(4) $E_{KAB}$ (RN)

(5) $E_{KAB}$ [$TR_t$ (RN)]

**Figure 5.7** A scheme for key distribution in a network with a CKD

*RN* according to a previously defined function $TR_t(RN)$ which depends on the time. The sequence $TR_t(RN)$ is encrypted under $K_{AB}$, and the cryptogram obtained is dispatched to the user *B*. This procedure may be simplified if users who communicate often store several successive keys in their private files.

Quite the opposite solution consists of giving key distribution rights to every host computer of the network. In this case each host has to store as many keys as there are other hosts. If the network contains *n* hosts (*n* nodes) each host keeps $n-1$ keys which are exclusively used to communicate with the appropriate host. Thus $\frac{1}{2}n(n-1)$ different keys must be stored in the network and they should be changed from time to time, using, for example, registered mail (the lifetime of these keys is measured in weeks). If we do not want to use separate channels for host key distribution, a hierarchical key distribution system may be applied.

Such an organization is a compromise between centralized and decentralized key distribution. Usually hosts are divided into three classes of hosts:

1. global CKD;
2. regional CKD;
3. local CKD.

A local CKD is responsible for key distribution among all the entities of a suitable host computer. Hosts with local CKDs situated within a region are subject to a corresponding host with regional CKD responsibilities. Next, all hosts with regional CKD responsibilities are subject to a host with global CKD. So, if any entity (the entity can be a computer, a host computer with regional or local CKD responsibilities) of the network requires a secure channel, it directs a suitable request to the proper host. Responding, its CKD dispatches a key in the same way as before.

### 5.1.3 Key distribution for asymmetric cryptographic algorithms

Now let us consider a network in which protection is being based on an asymmetric cryptographic algorithm. After cryptography with public keys was invented, it seemed that all key distribution problems would disappear. However, these hopes failed. Of course, in asymmetric cryptography, any entity can generate its own pair of keys, and a public key may be sent via an insecure channel without compromising the security of a secret key. Thus, the problem of key transmission via an insecure channel has been solved. But the problem of key authenticity remains!

A sender, who uses a public key, wishes to be certain that the cryptograms sent will be deciphered by the proper receiver. To do this in a computer network with asymmetric cryptography key, authentication must be used. The simplest solution is to keep all public keys in a separate place within the computer network called a key directory (KD). The KD is responsible for the maintenance, updating and distribution of all public keys used in the computer network. Moreover, any user (entity) receiving a key should also be given a means of proving that the key is authentic.

Consider a network with cryptographic protection based on an asymmetric algorithm. Assume that two users $A$ and $B$ have generated their key pairs $(K_A, k'_A)$ and $(K_B, k'_B)$, respectively, where the secret keys $k'_A$, $k'_B$ are known exclusively to their owners. Suppose also, that KD has revealed its public key $K_{KD}$ (e.g. in the local press, as a way of key authentication). Now, if a user $A$ wants to send information to a user $B$, a suitable request is first directed by $RQ_A$ to KD along with the time $T$ (see Figure 5.8). In response, KD dispatches to $A$ a message (the public key of the user $B$ - $K_B$, a copy of A's request $RQ_A$, and the time $T$) enciphered under a secret key of KD. Notice that KD uses cryptography for authentication only — anyone can read the messages but nobody can change the contents of the messages. Knowing $K_{KD}$, $A$ deciphers the cryptogram $D_{KD}(K_B, RQ_A, T)$ and recreates an authentic public key $K_B$, a copy of the request $RQ_A$, and the time $T$. Now, having the public key $K_B$, $A$ sends $B$ a cryptogram $E_B(N_A, RS)$ where $N_A$ is the name of A, and $RS$ is a random sequence chosen by $A$.

Subsequently, in order to get the authentic public key for $A$, the user $B$ directs a suitable request $RQ_B$ along with the current time $T'$ in clear form. The key directory KD responds by sending a cryptogram $D_{KD}(K_A, RQ_B, T')$, where $K_A$ is the public key of user $A$. After deciphering the cryptogram, $B$ has the authentic public key of $A$. Next, $B$ creates a pair: the sequence $RS$ obtained from user $A$ and a random sequence $RS'$ which is self generated. The pair $(RS, RS')$ is enciphered under A's public key and sent to $A$ in the shape of cryptogram $E_A(RS, RS')$. The cryptogram is decrypted by $A$ who compares the original sequence $RS$ with that obtained from the cryptogram. If these sequences are the same, $A$ is sure that the user $B$ is authentic. Finally, $A$ retransmits $RS'$ in the form of cryptogram $E_B(RS')$. After decrypting, $B$ also compares the original $RS'$ with that recreated from the cryptogram. If they match, $B$ confirms the authenticity of $A$. We note that the authentication procedure presented above is not the only one possible. There are many other procedures which, for example, do not require the distribution of keys by the KD. In those cases, the KD verifies the authenticity of the keys used by users and then

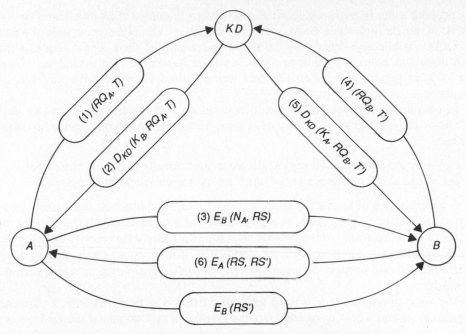

**Figure 5.8** A scheme for key distribution in a network with KD

sends the users the result of the verification process. For other solutions, see Meyer and Matyas [MEMA84] and Davies and Price [DAPR84].

Thus we conclude that either of these two solutions (based on symmetric and asymmetric cryptographic algorithms) require existing control centers that verify the authenticity of keys and initiate communication between network entities. In order to perform these functions, the same amount of software, hardware, and time is needed by control centers for either solution [POKL79]. Moreover, in either case, the crucial question is the protection of all keys that create secure channels between an entity and a center. It would appear that a center of a network, with protection based on a symmetric cryptographic algorithm, is more sensitive to illegal activity as all cryptographic keys are stored there and their security plays a vital role. On the other hand, in a network with protection based on an asymmetric algorithm, we know that a center distributes public keys whose protection is not needed. However, in a network with symmetric algorithm protection, all keys are stored in the form of cryptograms which have been obtained using the main key of the host (the so-called master key). So, we observe that the two solutions are similar as in a network with an asymmetric algorithm protection the entire cryptographic protection depends upon the security of the secret key of the center. Comparing other properties of the two solutions considered, we assert the conclusion that these two solutions are equivalent.

### 5.1.4 Generation and storage of cryptographic keys

Up till now, we have assumed that keys are generated and stored in some suitable place in the network. If we consider protection based on an asymmetric cryptographic algorithm, any network entity is responsible for the generation and storage of its own secret key — that is, we are dealing with a distributed key management. Of course, generation of a pair (secret key, public key) depends on the asymmetric algorithm used. For example, in the RSA algorithm, either the public or secret key is an integer selected at random. If one pair of keys (public and secret) has been compromised, then the other pair can be calculated.

In considering networks with protection based on a symmetric algorithm, we deal with many different kinds of cryptographic keys. However, we can distinguish two main classes:

1.  the first class consists of all keys which are applied directly to encipher messages;
2.  the second class comprises all keys which are used to encipher other keys.

Among all keys of the second class, we specify keys called a host master key and a terminal master key. They reside at a given host and a given terminal, respectively, in clear form. So, disclosure of their values compromises entirely the security of either the host or the terminal. On the other hand, destruction of their values means that all other enciphered keys are wrongly deciphered, and, thus, that all enciphered messages become unreadable.

The value of a master key is fixed for a longer period of time. Usually, its lifetime amounts to several weeks or months. So, the generation and storage of master keys are crucial issues in cryptographic protection. In practice, a host master key is created by truly random selection among all possible key values (e.g. by tossing a coin). After being chosen in this way, a key is put into a protected write-only cryptographic system. This system should be designed in such a way that, after a key has been put into a cryptographic system, disclosure of the key is impossible, but still there must be a way to check if a key value is correct. This problem (authentication of keys) can be solved in different ways. One is shown in Figure 5.9. An administrator, having changed a host

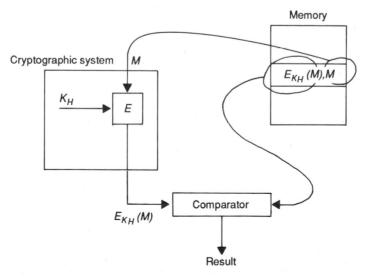

**Figure 5.9** Authentication of a host master key

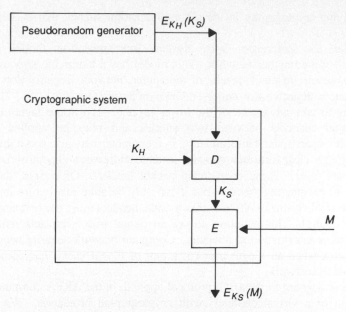

**Figure 5.10** A method for key protection

master key, enciphers a given message $M$ under $K_H$. The pair (cryptogram $E_{K_H}(M)$, message $M$) is stored in a memory. Whenever an authentication of a host master key is required, the message $M$ is brought from memory and put into the cryptographic system. A cryptogram is obtained and compared with the cryptogram stored in memory. If they match, the key is considered to be correct.

Other subsidiary keys are usually created by means of a pseudorandom generator and they can be stored in an unprotected place. This is possible since all subsidiary keys are generated in the form of suitable cryptograms, that is a generator yields, instead of a key $K_S$, its cryptogram $E_{K_H}(K_S)$ obtained using a host master key $K_H$. Deciphering the cryptogram is carried out just before the key $K_S$ is to be used. Such a solution is given in Figure 5.10. If we want to encipher a message $M$ under a key $K_S$, we put both the cryptogram $E_{K_H}(K_S)$ and the message $M$ into suitable inputs of the cryptographic system. First, $K_S$ is recreated and, next, $M$ is enciphered using the clear form of $K_S$.

As we see, protection of subsidiary keys depends on the security of the cryptographic system. A cryptographic system should be designed as a one LSI circuit and enclosed in a physically protected place.

## 5.1.5 Cryptographic protocols

Up till now we have considered the protection of information between different entities of the computer network like terminals, hosts, user programs, supervisor programs, etc. The communication subnet has been treated as a single channel whose role is to supply the transmission medium. However, cryptographic protection may also be introduced into the communication subnet between suitable nodes. We describe problems that appear while applying cryptography inside a communication subnet, that is, between network nodes.

Consider the Reference Open System Interconnection model (OSI model)[2] [TANE81a] of a computer network. This model has a hierarchic structure and we can distinguish seven different layers of computer network organization. In order to communicate with each other, entities defined on layer $j$ ($j = 2,3, \cdots , 7$) create suitable connections to take advantage of the lower layer $(j-1)$. Some layers can be used to create virtual channels between two entities and may be applied for supplying cryptographic operations. Unfortunately, in a computer network, some information must be transmitted in clear form as it contains suitable addresses and control data that are used by the lower layer. These data create packet headers. Of course, there is still the possibility of enciphering headers but it can only be done just before inputting packets into the physical channel. While within a node, headers must not be enciphered because of routing control. This situation allows an illegal user, who acts within a node, to substitute some information in a header. Computer network security becomes more and more complex when an illegal user (or group of illegal users) has complete access to some part of the network.

We are now going to present a protocol applied, in the ARPA computer network, for the creation of a virtual channel[3] with cryptographic protection. We deal with the network layer of OSI ISO model. The general scheme of information exchange for this protocol [POKL79] is given in Figure 5.11. Shown there is the network management system (NMS) responsible for:

1. channel allocation;
2. information flow control;
3. retransmission of information that has been destroyed and which cannot be recreated in its correct form.

Of course, the quality of the cryptographic protection depends on the correctness of the operating systems that supervise the operation of the cryptographic transformations. From now on we assume that the operating systems work correctly and that they are enriched by adding two cryptographic subroutines, ENCRYPT (channel name, data) and DECRYPT(channel name, address of destination node). Suppose a certain program $A$ of node $N_1$ requires a data file to be transmitted to another program $B$ of a distant node $N_2$. First of all, it calls the operating system (OS) of node $N_1$. OS takes the data file and transforms it using the ENCRYPT subroutine. After doing this, ENCRYPT notifies its local NMS which, in turn, reads in suitable cryptograms. These are organized in packets. Next, a header is attached to any packet and this collection of packets is sent via the communication subnet using a prearranged routing algorithm. The headers, which are in clear form, make it possible to recreate the right sequence of packets in the destination node $N_2$. At this node, after checking the addresses in the headers, NMS of $N_2$ advises

---

2.  This model is due to the International Standards Organization (ISO).
3.  The concept of a virtual channel is especially useful in a computer network with packet switching. Messages are divided into transmission units called packets. Packets of the message can be sent through different routes. The correct sequence of the packets is recreated at the destination node from the information in the headers. To both the sender and the receiver, it appears that the message has been sent via a single virtual channel.

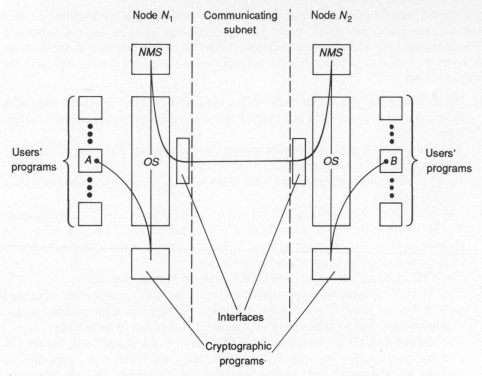

**Figure 5.11** Information exchange between two users' programs A and B

the program *B* that the data file has arrived and it is stored in a suitable buffer of $N_1$. *B* calls its local OS using the subroutine DECRYPT. OS, using a prearranged cryptographic key, deciphers the resultant file. The clear form of file is then sent to the program *B*.

When considering a method of key distribution between two communicating nodes, we assume that we are dealing with a computer network with decentralized key distribution and where the enciphering transformation is carried out by a symmetric cryptographic algorithm. Now suppose also that a key table resides in each node of the network. The table, which is accessible only to a suitable local OS, contains descriptions of all the currently existing virtual channels which either originate in or terminate at that node. Consider the table in node $N_1$. The description of a single virtual channel which connects two programs *A* and *B* of nodes $N_1$ and $N_2$, respectively, consists of:

- the name of the outer node $N_2$ along with the name of the program *B*;
- the name of the local program *A*;
- the name of the virtual channel;
- the value of the cryptographic key.

Clearly the OS of any node should be enriched by adding two subroutines which perform two operations over the key table contents. The first subroutine CREATE (name of outer program, name of local program, channel name, additional data) can be called by a local program and it writes suitable data into the key table. The second subroutine CANCEL (name of channel) causes erasure of all information concerning a given virtual channel and simultaneously, any node, where this operation has been carried out, advises a corresponding outer node about cancellation. Therefore, if two programs $A$ and $B$ reside in nodes $N_1$ and $N_2$, respectively, then information exchange between nodes takes the following form:

1.  Program $A$ of $N_1$ sends to its local NMS a request to establish communication with the program $B$ of $N_2$ via a virtual channel called $X$. This message is delivered in clear form.
2.  The NMS of $N_1$ transmits a control message to the NMS of $N_2$ using the message exchange protocol via a prearranged virtual channel.
3.  In order to read the message in, the NMS of $N_2$ calls an input/output subroutine via a suitable interrupt.
4.  The NMS of $N_2$ carries out step (2) and initiates step (3) to be carried out within node $N_1$. This leads to the virtual channel called $X$ being established if this is possible. The channel connects the operating systems of the appropriate nodes and is intended to enable communication between programs $A$ and $B$.
5.  The NMS of $N_1$ calls the subroutine CREATE $(B, A, X,$ additional data).
6.  The OS of $N_1$ generates a cryptographic key and puts it along with other additional data in the key table. Next it sends a suitable message via a prearranged secure channel to the OS of $N_2$ which passes the triple $(B, A, X)$ on to its local NMS.
7.  The NMS of $N_2$ calls the subroutine CREATE $(A, B, X,$ additional data), and the OS puts the cryptographic key into the key table. Next, the NMS of $N_2$ generates an interrupt of program $B$ and advises the NMS of $N_1$ which, in turn, interrupts program $A$.
8.  Programs $A$ and $B$ communicate with each other via the virtual channel $X$ using cryptographic protection.

The procedure just outlined for information exchange may fail if either the virtual channel is engaged or the key table does not have a space for a new entry. Also the procedure for information exchange should be modified slightly if the cryptographic protection is based on an asymmetric algorithm. However, whichever cryptographic protection method we apply, the design of cryptographic protocols is both burdensome and time-consuming as it is necessary to give consideration to both the network architecture and the need for protection.

## 5.2  Key management issues

It has been shown that to use cryptography to encrypt data and PINs and to authenticate messages it is vitally important to manage a large set of cryptographic keys. Not only are different keys needed on each different link but there should also be different keys for each different function or activity.

The function of key management is to securely distribute and update keys whenever required in the network.

There are a number of contenders for key management in a symmetric environment including *transaction keys* and *session keys*.

Any solution to the problem of key management for cryptographic protection in a computer network depends on:

• the type of cryptographic transformation (cryptographic algorithm) used;
• the protection requirements when the cryptographic protection is to be applied to data transmission and/or file protection (database protection);
• the network architecture.

We will now describe three key management ideas.

## 5.2.1  Example of key management using DES

Suppose that the whole cryptographic protection is based on the DES algorithm. Assume also that we want to protect information which is transmitted between terminals and hosts or between hosts. We make the following assumptions about the cryptographic architecture:

(A1)  There is only one key (in any host) and it is stored in clear form. It is called the *host master key* $(K_H)$.

(A2)  There is only one key (in any terminal) and it is stored in clear form. It is called the *terminal master key* $(K_T)$.

(A3)  All other keys are stored as suitable cryptograms (they are enciphered under the corresponding master keys).

(A4)  The generation of master keys is made by a truly random generator (in clear form).

(A5)  The generation of other keys is performed by a pseudorandom generator and output sequences are considered as suitable key cryptograms.

We must also take into consideration the following security requirements:

(R1)  The master keys must be kept in secure places.

(R2)  Under no circumstances must the disclosure of other keys be possible.

(R3)  Cryptographic instructions, that are needed to handle cryptographic operations for both information and keys, should be non-privileged and their execution be carried out by the operating system of the corresponding host computer.

(R4)  The application of any subset of the cryptographic instructions should not allow an illegal user to obtain protected information (either keys or messages).

Our project consists of two stages. The first concerns cryptographic protection of transmissions between a terminal and a host. The second applies to transmissions between hosts. The project is based on the key management scheme designed by W. Ehrasm et al. [EHMA78] and given in [MEMA84] and [KONH81].

### Cryptographic protection of transmissions between terminal and host

We assume that there are prearranged keys in both the host computer and its terminal. These are $K_H$ and $K_T$ respectively. Before any session, a suitable session key must be generated and sent to the terminal. Suppose that such a key has been obtained and, according to assumption A3, it has the form $E_{K_H}(K_S) = E_H(K_S)$. As $K_T$ exists only at the terminal, $E_H(K_S)$ must be reenciphered into $E_{K_T}(K_S) = E_T(K_S)$. In order to do this, we define the first cryptographic instruction *reencipher* from host master key as follows:

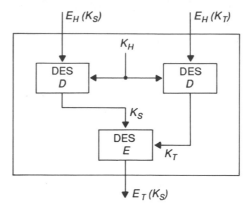

**Figure 5.12**  Implementation of the RHMK instruction

$$RHMK[\, E_H\,(K_S)\,,\; E_H\,(K_T)\,] = E_T\,(K_S)$$

Cryptographic transformations involving the *RHMK* instruction are presented in Figure 5.12.  As soon as $E_T(K_S)$ has been obtained and stored at the terminal, transmission can take place between the terminal and its host.  If a host wants to encrypt data, it now uses the non-priviledged cryptographic instruction *encipher data* which has the form:

$$ENCH\;[\,message\;M,\;E_H(K_S)\,] = E_{K_S}(M) = E_S(M)$$

The hardware realization of the *ENCH* instruction is given in Figure 5.13.  The cryptogram obtained is transmitted to the terminal.  At the terminal, the cryptogram is decrypted by applying the instruction *decipher message at terminal* in the form (see Figure 5.14):

$$DECT\;[\,E_S(M),\,E_T(K_S)\,] = M$$

In turn, if the terminal wishes to send information, a second instruction *encryption of data at terminal* must be defined as follows:

$$ENCT\;[\,message\;M,\;E_T(K_S)\,] = E_S(M)$$

The hardware implementation of the *ENCT* instruction is the same as in Figure 5.13.  The only difference is that *ENCT* engages $K_T$ but *ENCH* uses $K_H$.

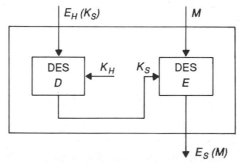

**Figure 5.13**  Scheme of the ENCH instruction

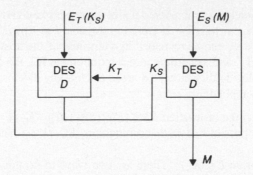

**Figure 5.14** Schematic diagram of the DECT instruction

To decrypt cryptograms sent from the terminal, a third cryptographic instruction has to be defined. It is called *decryption of data* and can be written as:

$$DECH\ [\ E_S(M),\ E_H(K_S)\ ] = M$$

Both *DECT* and *DECH* need the same kind of hardware (see Figure 5.14) as before. The only difference is that they use different keys.

Let us further consider the instruction *RHMK*. As all instructions are non-privileged, any user, who resides at the host, can change the sequence of the *RHMK* input. The user then gets $E_S(K_T)$ instead of $E_T(K_S)$. When the instruction $DECH[E_S(K_T),E_H(K_S)]$ is next applied, the user obtains the clear form of $K_T$. This contradicts the requirement R2.

Thus, it is desirable to destroy the symmetry of the *RHMK* instruction. To do this we can introduce two variants of the master key, namely $K_{H0}$ and $K_{H1}$. The key $K_{H1}$ is created by permutation of the bits of $K_{H0}$. The first variant is used to protect session keys. In other words, session keys are stored as cryptograms $E_{H0}(K_S)$. The second variant is applied to encipher terminal master keys $E_H(K_T)$. So, the revised cryptographic instruction *RHMK* has the form:

$$RMK\ [\ E_{H0}(K_S),\ E_{H1}(K_T)\ ] = E_T(K_S)$$

Summing up, we have defined two cryptographic operations at a terminal. The first, *ENCT* generates cryptograms for messages. The second, *DECT* allows us to recreate the clear form of messages. On the other hand, at the host, we have defined suitable encryption, *ENCH*, and decryption, *DECH*, instructions and also the *RMK* instruction that reenciphers session keys.

### Cryptographic protection of transmission between hosts

Consider two hosts who have their own terminals and communication between terminals and hosts is protected using cryptography. Suppose we want to enrich our cryptographic protection in order to allow secure transmission between hosts $i$ and $j$. To design a secure communication channel between the two hosts, a suitable session key should be distributed between them. Suppose that, in hosts $i$ and $j$, there is a prearranged key $K_{SC}^{ij}$ which is called a secondary communication key and is applied to create a secure channel for session keys between hosts $i$ and $j$.

Using our assumption A3, we observe that the secondary communication key has to be stored in the host $i$ as a cryptogram either $E_{H0}^i(K_{SC}^{ij})$ or $E_{H1}^i(K_{SC}^{ij})$, where $E_{H0}^i$ means that, in the host $i$, a given key is enciphered under the master key variant $K_{H0}$.

Assume for the moment that $K^{ij}_{SC}$ is stored in the host $i$ as $E^i_{H0}(K^{ij}_{SC})$. Then the clear form of the session key $K_S$ can be recreated in a terminal of the host $i$. Now this key $K_S$ is shared by hosts $i$ and $j$, and, according to our requirement R2, the clear form of keys is never to be revealed outside of a protected area. Such a key disclosure is possible if the following procedure is applied:

1. Apply (in the host $i$) the instruction $RMK[E^i_{H0}(K^{ij}_{SC}), E^i_{H1}(K_T)]$. As a result $E^i_T(K^{ij}_{SC})$ is obtained. It is possible as both cryptograms $E^i_{H0}(K^{ij}_{SC})$ and $E^i_{H1}(K_T)$ are not protected.
2. Intercept a cryptogram $E^{ij}_{SC}(K_S)$. There are two ways to do this. The first one relies upon penetrating an unprotected memory where cryptograms of keys are stored. The second one consists in eavesdropping on a channel which connects the two hosts.
3. Having obtained both $E^i_T(K^{ij}_{SC})$ and $E^{ij}_{SC}(K_S)$, the instruction $DECT[E^{ij}_{SC}(K_S), E^i_T(K^{ij}_{SC})]$ is carried out. Thus, the clear form of the session key $K_S$ is recreated.

In other words, secondary communication keys must not be enciphered using the variant $K^i_{H0}$ of the master key. The second possibility is to store secondary communication keys under the encipherment of the master key variant $K^i_{H1}$. Hence we suppose that a secondary communication key is stored as a cryptogram $E^i_{H1}(K^{ij}_{SC})$ and $E^j_{H1}(K^{ij}_{SC})$ in host $i$ and host $j$, respectively.

Assume that host $i$ wants to transmit messages to host $j$. The initial step relies on the session key generation. In host $i$, the session key is produced as a cryptogram $E^i_{H0}(K_S)$. Before sending this key to the host $j$, we have to reencipher it. Fortunately, in host $i$, we can use the instruction $RMK$ as follows:

$$RMK \, [\, E^i_{H0}(K_S), \, E^i_{H1}(K^{ij}_{SC}) \,] \rightarrow E^{ij}_{SC}(K_S)$$

Next, a cryptogram $E^{ij}_{SC}(K_S)$ is sent via an insecure channel to the host $j$. The host $j$ has

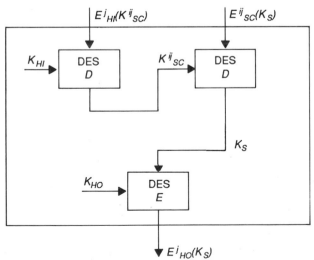

**Figure 5.15** Reenciphering session keys via the RSK instruction

to have the key $K_{SC}^{ij}$. Assume that this key is stored there as a cryptogram $E_{H1}^{j}(K_{SC}^{ij})$, and the session key $K_S$ is kept in the form $E_{H0}^{j}(K_S)$. In order to get this, we define a new cryptographic instruction called *reenciphering session keys* in the form:

$$RSK\ [\ E_{H1}^{j}(K_{SC}^{ij}),\ E_{SC}^{ij}(K_S)\ ] = E_{H0}^{j}(K_S)$$

A diagram of the instruction scheme is given in Figure 5.15. Of course, the *RSK*

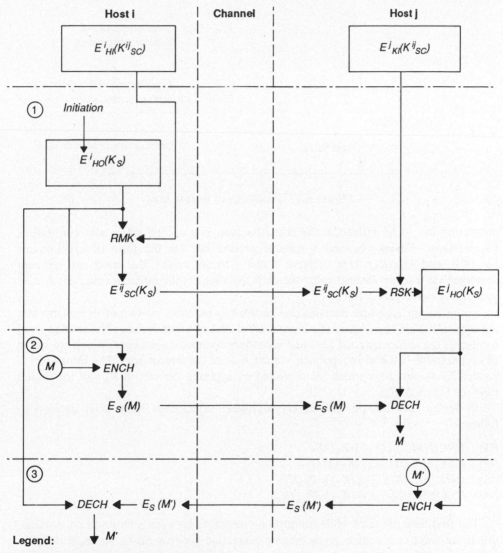

**Legend:**

1. initiation stage (session key exchange);
2. transmission of a message from host i to host j;
3. transmission of a message from host j to host i.

**Figure 5.16** A schematic for key management during transmission of information between hosts i and j

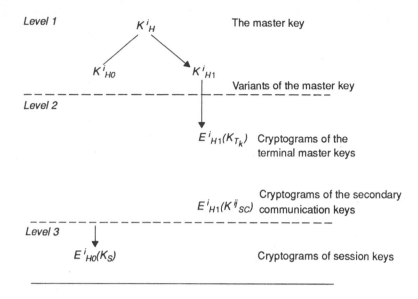

**Figure 5.17** Hierarchy of keys in host $i$

instruction has to be defined in the host $i$ because it is needed when host $j$ initializes transmission. Having obtained a suitable session key (in the form of cryptograms $E_{H0}^i(K_S)$ and $E_{H0}^j(K_S)$ kept in hosts $i$ and $j$, respectively), the hosts can transmit messages via a secure channel using the corresponding cryptographic instructions *ENCH* and *DECH* (see Figure 5.16).

Summing up, each host contains one master key but there are two of its variants that are applied. This key creates the highest level of key organization. The second level comprises the master terminal keys and secondary communication keys, which are stored as cryptograms obtained by applying variant $K_{H1}$ of the master key. The third level is created by session keys which are protected by applying the variant $K_{H0}$ of the master key (see Figure 5.17).

In hosts, four non-priviledged cryptographic instructions have been defined as follows:

(I1)    $ENCH[M,E_{H0}^i(K_S)]=E_S(M)$
(I2)    $DECH[E_S(M),E_{H0}^i(K_S)]=M$
(I3)    $RMK[E_{H0}^i(K_S),E_{H1}^i(K_T)]=E_T(K_S)$
(I4)    $RSK[E_{H1}^i(K_{SC}^{ij}),E_{SC}^{ij}(K_S)]=E_{H0}^i(K_S)$

The first three are used while transmitting messages between a host and its terminal. But if we want to introduce cryptographic protection between hosts, we must define a fourth instruction *RSK*. As has been shown, all four cryptographic instructions are applied during message transmission between two hosts. Of course, such transmission is only possible if both hosts share a prearranged secondary communication key. It is worth noting that both communicating hosts have the same access to the channel. By this we mean that both hosts can send and receive messages through the channel.

## 5.2.2  Transaction keys

This concept was proposed by Becker, Friend and Halliden [BEFR83].

As the name implies, a transaction key is used for only a single transaction. Transaction keys are mainly applicable between a terminal and a node and are not a realistic alternative for managing keys between nodes. However, if transaction keys are used at the terminal, then end to end protection of the PIN over session key protected node to node links is possible.

Transaction keys are working keys, but instead of being transported to the other end of a link, they are generated separately at each end, and preferably not transmitted.

A new set of transaction keys is generated for each transaction for the different types if function. The inputs used to derive the new transaction keys are based on data read from the customer's plastic card (Track 2) and from a terminal register stored in the terminal which is also updated after each transaction.

Different keys are generated for authentication, PIN encryption and Privacy (data encryption) by different manipulations and permutations of the available data.

### Terminal key update

One of the inputs is a terminal key register. A terminal must maintain one register for each acquirer with which it can communicate. The system uses as inputs the old terminal key and the so-called Message Authentication Code (MAC) residues which are described more fully in section 5.3.4.

When a MAC is calculated for a message a 64–bit value results. However only half of this (32 bits) is transmitted with the message. The remainder, which is never transmitted, is termed the MAC residue. The use of MAC residues to both update terminal registers and chain messages together was first suggested by Chris Reilly of EFTEL Pty. Ltd.

### Other keys

A number of other keys are derived from the available data in addition to the PIN encrypting key and the MAC key mentioned above:

*Card key.* The card key is based only on data input from the customer's card. This key is also known as the personal key.

*Decoupling key.* The decoupling key is calculated from the card key plus the transaction amount and the system trace audit number and is thus specifically related to a particular transaction. If two identical transactions were done using the same card then the card key would stay the same but the decoupling key would change.

*Privacy key.* The privacy key is derived from the key register, the terminal identifier and the system trace audit number and may be used to provide privacy (encryption) of all or part of a message. This key is thus based only on the terminal and transaction data.

### Transaction key advantages

The advantages of the transaction key system are as follows:

*End to end possible.* It is possible using this scheme to provide end to end protection of the PIN even though some intermediate links were of the session key type.

*Message chaining.* Message chaining using the MAC residue method provides increased security in the selection of missing and inserted messages and the guarantee of correct receipt of the previous message in a transaction by the other party.

*More security for terminal to node.* Transaction keys provide a more secure environment between a terminal and a node because backtracking is not possible and keys are changed at each transaction.

*Future smart card transition.* Transaction keys are ideally suited to provide transition to future smart card technology. The transaction key scheme itself will become more secure with integrated circuit cards because the length of the other card data (OCD) portion that is not transmitted can be much larger.

*No key change transactions required.* There is no overhead for the key change transaction on either the network or the node.

### Transaction key disadvantages

The disadvantages of the transaction key system are as follows:

*Some card data should NOT be transmitted.* For maximum security, some Track 2 data from which the transaction keys are calculated should not be transmitted on the network. The problem is that there are few spare positions on the Track 2 data that are not already used by someone. It is difficult to get universal agreement on what data not to transmit. The longer the field that is not transmitted, the greater the security afforded by the scheme. The number of bytes currently available for non transmission purposes is generally considered too few to provide a large enough key space.

*Varying requirements to issuers.* These requirements pertain to the interchange situation, where a single acquirer will handle cards for multiple issuers. Different issuers have different requirements about how much of the other card data (OCD) they require to be transmitted. The terminal either requires a list of requirements for each issuer or an indicator on the card regarding which data is not required to be transmitted.

*Initialization.* Initialization is as much a problem for transaction keys as it is for session keys. An initial piece of secret data must be inserted in the terminal to start the chain. Logistical problems increase if the terminal is to communicate with multiple acquirers.

*New generation terminals.* The transaction key system requires the development of a new generation of terminals. Some pilot schemes are now in operation in the United Kingdom and have proven to present few problems.

*Node to node.* This system has not been used for node to node communications. It is thought that MAC residue chaining could present problems for high volume links.

*Transition from existing schemes.* Most existing schemes in Australia do not use the transaction key scheme. Currently installed terminals need to come to the end of their useful life before large scale replacements could be considered. There will need to be a period of overlap between different systems, which would mean that two systems would need to be supported in parallel by acquirers.

## 5.2.3  Session keys

A session key is a working key used to protect data. In this system these keys are used in a symmetric algorithm (i.e. DEA) and are therefore secret keys. These keys may be used for one or more transactions and are themselves changed by a key change transaction.

The keys are generated by a pseudo random process at one end of a link and must then be securely transported to the other end of the link.

The essential difference between session keys and transaction keys is that session keys are used for multiple transactions and are transported by being encrypted under key encrypting keys, whilst transaction keys are used for only one transaction and are derived independently at each end of the link.

The use of session keys varies slightly between node to node and node to terminal links. In node to node links, the process is symmetrical and each node creates its own send keys and receives receive keys from the other end of the link. However, in terminal to node links the process is usually, but not necessarily, asymmetric. The acquirer usually generates all the keys and transmits and/or installs them to/in the terminal.

## Key hierarchy (layers)

The need to transmit keys encrypted under other keys leads to the concept of a hierarchy of keys. This can also be referred to as key layers. Starting at the lowest layer, are the working or session keys, which are used to encrypt data and PINs and authenticate messages and any other as yet defined cryptographic functions. When these keys are encrypted for transmission or storage requirements they are encrypted under the next layer, the *key encrypting keys*.

Key encrypting keys must never be used as working keys and vice versa. For maximum security this separation of function must always be maintained. In fact the standard specifies that different types of working keys (e.g. data encryption, authentication etc.) must always be encrypted under different versions of the keys encrypting key.

The key encrypting keys used to transport keys between two nodes are also known as *cross domain keys*. It is usual for there to be two cross domain keys per link, one for each direction. Therefore each node will have a *cross domain send key* and a *cross domain receive key* for each link maintained with another node.

At the top layer of the hierarchy is the *master key*. This key is used to encrypt key encrypting keys when these are required to be stored outside a secure cryptographic facility, such as on disk. There is generally only one master key (sometimes called a *domain master key*) at each computer site.

## Session key advantages

The advantages of the session key scheme are as follows:

*Node to node operations.* Session keys are ideally suited for mode to node operations and are at present being used for this purpose.

*Can be mixed in network.* The two methods can be mixed in the network. The terminal to node links could use the transaction key system, whilst the node to node links could use the session key system.

*Existing proven technology.* The session key system has been largely in use up till now and presents few problems.

## Session key disadvantages

The disadvantages of the session key scheme are as follows:

*KEK security in EFTPOS terminal.* The key encrypting key(s) used to transport the session keys to the terminal must be securely stored in the terminal. If the key encrypting key can be extracted from the terminal by an intruder, then he/she can decode all traffic on the line by intercepting it.

*End to end.* By using the session key system, it is impossible to have end to end protection on a message. The session keys are only exchanged between adjacent nodes and therefore the message requires translation from being encrypted under one key to being encrypted with another key, at each node it traverses. Unless this translation process is carried out in a secure facility, such as a security control module, there are security exposures at each node.

*Backtracking to last KEK change.* Backtracking can be carried out back to the previous key encrypting key change.

*Initialization.* Initialization involves the installation in a terminal of the initial key encrypting key. This must be a secret process and involves considerable logistical problems for acquiring institutions. If the terminal can communicate with multiple acquirers then problems are magnified. Initialization may also be required after servicing or when a terminal has lost synchronization through malfunction or network problems.

*Key change transactions.* A separate transaction is required to cause the working keys to be changed. If this is done fairly frequently, then it will impose an overhead on the network and may increase response time at the terminal.

*Maybe less secure in some cases.* Although the session key system is adequate for node to node links, because nodes are generally located in secure areas, in the terminal to node case not all conditions specified in AS 2805, Part 6.1 are met. These conditions relate to the backtracking capability and the capability of the EFTPOS terminal to protect its master key. However the security is still considered to be adequate in many cases for the forseeable future.

*Multiple acquirers.* If a terminal is to communicate with multiple acquirers, then extra logistical problems arise with relation to loading the secret data in the terminal and keeping the secret data of the different acquirers partitioned from each other. This does not present a problem in node to node links.

*Requires security hardware at nodes.* In order to provide acceptable security at intermediate nodes, expensive security hardware must be installed at each to provide translation functions.

## 5.3  Electronic funds transfer (EFT)

In today's competitive world, every financial institution tries to improve its services by applying contemporary technology in order to attract new customers. A good example of such institutions is the banking community. At the beginning of the 1970s, banks started examining solutions to the remote access to funds by means of terminals. Now, many financial institutions offer both distant access — so-called Electronic Funds Transfer (EFT) — and the traditional paper-based funds transfer. EFT can be implemented using the bank's own computer network (or computer system). Every customer can theoretically access his/her funds via the terminals of the bank's network. On the other hand, there are more and more financial institutions which have agreed to integrate their own networks into one large network which serves customers of many banks and financial institutions.

Although the computer network is capable of providing every service available from a bank, terminals are usually purpose oriented. Their abilities are limited to strictly predetermined transactions. Thus, terminals can provide withdrawal of cash, selling traveller's cheques, paying bills, booking flights, etc.

There are, of course, many security problems which have to be solved before the EFT network is installed, for instance, how customers can be identified before transactions, how the authenticity and integrity of transactions can be ensured, etc. There is, however, common consensus that a good way of customer identification is to use secret Personal Identification Numbers (*PINs*) along with bank cards that carry other information needed to initiate transactions. Obviously, *PINs* have to be kept secret, all the time, everywhere, within the EFT network (or system).

As *PINs* are closely connected to the relevant bank cards, they can be treated as signatures of the cardholders. Usually, to initiate a transaction, cardholders who use the EFT terminal put their cards into a special slot and enter their *PINs* using the keyboard of the terminal. If the pair, *PIN* and the account number imprinted on the magnetic stripe of the card, matches, the transaction is initiated and the cardholder can proceed.

In this section, we intend to give a general outlook on the security problems that appear while designing an EFT system. We are especially going to examine the application of cryptography to ensure the protection of transactions. Information about EFTPOS in Australia can be found in Gyoery[GYOE86] or Gyoery and Seberry [GYSE87]. Much of this information can be directly applied in other countries.

## 5.3.1 Personal identification number (PIN)

The protection of both the *Personal Identification Number* or *PIN* and the bank card is crucial for the entire EFT security. Bank cards may be lost, stolen or forged. In such cases, the only existing countermeasure against an unauthorized access is the secret *PIN*. This is why the clear form of the *PIN* should be known only to the legitimate cardholder. It should never be stored or transmitted within the EFT system.

The length of *PINs* should be large enough so that the probability of guessing the correct value by a brute force attack is acceptably small. On the other hand, *PINs* should be short to allow cardholders to memorize them. The recommended length of *PINs* is from four to eight decimal digits. Assuming that the *PIN* is four digits long, an enemy who tries to match the *PIN* to a forged bank card, faces the problem of choosing one out of ten thousand possibilities. If the number of incorrect *PIN* entry attempts is limited to five per card per day, the enemy has a chance of less than 1:2000 of success. But the next day, the enemy can try again and his/her chance has increased to 1:1000. Every following day the probability of the enemy's success increases. Therefore, many banks introduce an absolute limit on the number of incorrect trials per card to exclude this kind of attack. If the limit is exceeded, the card is considered to be invalid and is retained.

Clearly, the method of *PIN* generation has a considerable influence on EFT security. In general, *PINs* can be selected by either the bank or cardholders. If the bank chooses the *PINs*, it adopts usually one of two procedures. In the first procedure, the *PINs* are generated cryptographically from cardholders' account numbers. The apparent advantage of this procedure is that *PIN* records need not be stored inside the EFT system. But the disadvantage is that changing the *PIN* requires selecting either a new customer account number or a new cryptographic key. Banks, however, prefer account numbers to be fixed once and for all. On the other hand, as all *PIN*s are calculated using the same cryptographic key, changing a single *PIN* necessitates changing all *PIN*s. In the second procedure, the bank picks a *PIN* at random and simultaneously keeps a record of the *PIN* in the form of a suitable cryptogram (the clear form of *PIN* should never be exposed within the EFT system). Next, selected *PIN*s are sent to cardholders by the registered mail.

PINs can also be selected by cardholders. It is important to stress that the best cardholder procedure is the selection of the *PIN* at random. Once the *PIN* has been chosen, it should be notified to the bank. *PIN*s can be sent to the bank by registered mail or transmitted via a secure terminal (located at the bank office) that encrypts the *PIN* immediately.

The main requirement for security is that *PIN*s should be memorized by their holders and should never be stored in any readable form. But humans are imperfect and quite frequently *PIN*s are forgotten. Therefore, banks should prearrange special procedures to deal with such cases. In general, the procedure can adopt one of two different approaches. The first relies on recovering the forgotten *PIN* and sending it back to the holder. The second, however, generates a new *PIN*.

## 5.3.2  PIN oriented EFT system

Consider an example of a simple transaction session. A customer approaches a suitable EFT terminal and wishes to transfer $50.00 from his/her account to another one. First, the customer inserts his/her bank card into a special terminal device which reads the primary account number (*PAN*) written on it. The *PAN* not only provides the customer's account number but also identifies the financial institution if the customer is a client of another bank. Next, the customer inputs his/her *PIN* via a keyboard and gives the transaction details such as the type of transaction, the amount of money involved, etc. All this information is transmitted to the issuer's host computer (a bank which in regard to its own customers is also called the issuer). If the *PIN* corresponds to the customer's *PAN*, the host computer authenticates the transaction message and verifies the correctness of the transaction (e.g. a transaction is incorrect if the customer's account balance is less than the proposed withdrawal). If the transaction is authentic and valid, the host computer accepts the transaction, sends a positive response back to the customer via the terminal, and reduces his/her account balance by $50.

From a security point of view, any transaction session consists of two stages: the customer's identification and the transaction message authentication. In this simple case, the customer's identification relies upon examining the correspondence between the *PIN* given by the customer and the *PAN* written on the card. The transaction message authentication, however, is carried out using a *message authentication code* (*MAC*). The *MAC* can be treated as the digest of a message and it is attached to the transaction message. The issuer knowing the pair (a message, the corresponding *MAC*) and the way of *MAC* generation, can validate the transaction.

In general, any transaction can proceed at either a local or a remote host. A local transaction takes place if a cardholder acts via his/her issuer's terminals. Otherwise, we are dealing with a remote host transaction. As the terminal, in this case, does not belong to the issuer, all the information involved during a session must flow through the foreign host computer (called an acquirer).

Let us consider a transaction session for both local and remote host mode in detail. Suppose that the EFT computer network uses cryptographic protection (see the previous section). Any terminal has the unique prearranged terminal master key $(K_T)$ which is stored inside the tamper-proof security module [MEMA84]. As soon as a cardholder has activated the terminal, the issuer's host computer provides a successive session key $K_S$ as the cryptogram $K_T(K_S)$ (see Figure 5.18). The cardholder next inserts his card and inputs his *PIN*. The security module having $(K_T, E_T(K_S), PIN, PAN)$, produces cryptograms $E_S(PIN)$ and $E_S(PAN)$ applying appropriate cryptographic instructions.

The pair $[E_S(PIN), E_S(PAN)]$ is transmitted to the issuer's host. As *PIN*s cannot be stored in the clear form anywhere, the host keeps all *PIN*s as $E_{K_p}(PIN) = E_P(PIN)$, where $K_P$ is the *PIN* master key (all *PIN*s are stored using a single *PIN* master key). The quadruple $[E_S(PIN), E_S(PAN), E_P(PIN), E_T(K_S)]$ is input to the host security module. Knowing the terminal master key $K_T$, and the *PIN* master key $K_P$, the module decrypts the required cryptograms and compares the *PIN*s. If they do not match or the *PIN* does not correspond to the *PAN*, the cardholder is identified negatively.

A transaction request message can be protected using the same session key and then a *MAC* is not needed. But if the message is transmitted as plaintext, its *MAC* must be enciphered in order that the issuer's host will be able to authenticate the message.

A session in the remote host mode of transactions looks similar. Its initial stage is depicted in Figure 5.19. We assume that there is a secure channel, created by the

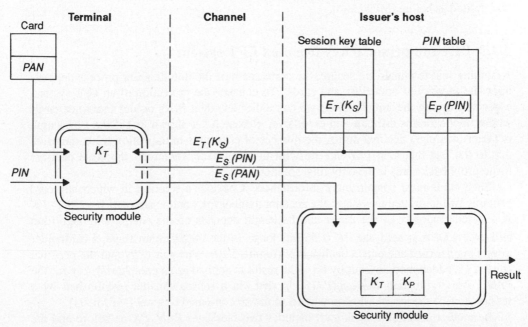

**Figure 5.18** Processing of the PIN and PAN during a local transmission session

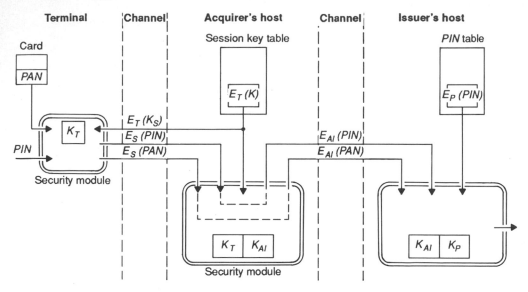

**Figure 5.19** Processing of the PIN and PAN during the transmission interchange session

interhost key $K_{AI}$, between the acquirer and the issuer. The process is the same until cryptograms $E_S(PIN)$, $E_S(PAN)$, $E_T(K_S)$ reach the acquirer's security module. The *PAN* indicates the issuer so the module re-enciphers *PIN* and *PAN* into $E_{AI}(PIN)$, $E_{AI}(PAN)$ using the interhost key $K_{AI}$. After the cryptograms have been inserted into the issuer's security module, it works out its final decision. The transaction request message is transmitted as before [MEMA84].

### 5.3.3  PIN and personal key oriented EFT system

Assuming that terminals are secure, the correctness of the initialization process depends upon the security of both *PINs* and cards. To enhance the protection of an EFT system, especially during the initialization, we can either lengthen *PINs* or/and introduce cards whose duplication is difficult and expensive. Research has shown that if the *PIN* length is larger than eight decimal digits, the number of erroneous initialization trials increases due to the fact that long *PINs* are difficult to memorize. Therefore, the issue of more forge-proof bank cards is the only final solution.

Such cards must contain more information. Consider a solution in which any card contains two imprinted messages: the account number *PAN* and a *personal key* (*PK*). *PK* is selected randomly by the issuer and its length depends on the enciphering algorithm utilized. If DEA is used, the *PK* is 56 bits long. In the initialization stage, a cardholder inserts his/her card and enters his/her *PIN* (Figure 5.20). The pair (*PIN* and the personal key *PK*) is added modulo 2 bit by bit. The result is applied as an enciphering key for the *PAN*. The cryptogram $E_{PK \oplus PIN}(PAN)$ is sent via a secure channel (established by a session key) to the issuer who compares it to the precomputed original [MEMA84].

In another solution, a bank card includes two messages *PAN*, *PK* as before and the third one called a *personal authentication code PAC*. The interrelation between these

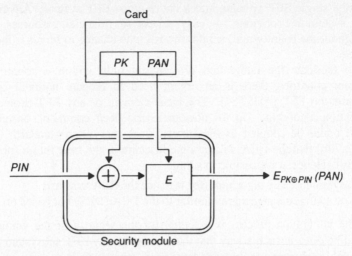

**Figure 5.20** Processing of the PIN and card message during the initialization stage

elements is shown in Figure 5.21. While a card is being issued, a *PAC* is created as:

$$PAC = E_{IK} [ E_{PK \oplus PIN}(PAN) ]$$

where *IK* is the secret *issuer's key*. In the initialization stage, after a cardholder has provided a *PIN* and entered his/her card, the pair $(E_{PK \oplus PIN}(PAN)$, and *PAC*) is transmitted via a secure channel to the issuer. The issuer then uses the secret key, *IK*, to calculate the reference $PAC^*$. If $PAC = PAC^*$, the cardholder is accepted as genuine.

Compared to the first, the second solution has the advantage that, to verify a cardholder, the issuer applies the unique secret key, *IK*, for all sessions. In the first solution, however, the issuer must keep a record of cryptograms $E_{PK \oplus PIN}(PAN)$ for all customers.

## 5.3.4 Protection requirements in EFT systems

At the early stage of the EFT development, financial institutions introduced security measures based on widely different standards. However, there is a natural trend to

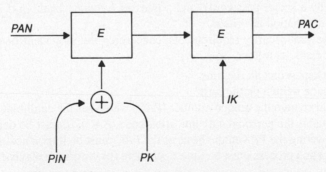

**Figure 5.21** A schematic of the PAC generation

integrate single EFT systems into a nation-wide EFT system. Advantages of a nation-wide system are obvious — easy access to financial resources for any customer throughout the country and, simultaneously, the chance to increase the range of banking services.

To facilitate the integration process not only within a country but also among different countries, there is an urgent need to prepare national or/and international standards on EFT [AUST84]. The basic element of any EFT protection system is the encryption algorithm. Up till now there has been common consensus that the DEA (DES) could be adopted as the international encryption standard. It is now obvious [HELL79b] that the DEA will become insecure in the near future (perhaps it is insecure already). Hence, it is possible to adopt:

- an asymmetric key algorithm (for instance the RSA system);
- a new symmetric algorithm (similar to the DEA (DES) but based on 128-bit keys).

The integration process is essential for the security of the whole EFT system and should be done in such a way that the security of any EFT subsystem (owned by a single financial institution) is independent from protection measures undertaken by other institutions in their EFT subsystems. At the same time, any integrated EFT system terminal — either an *automatic teller machine* (ATM) or a *point-of-sale terminal* (POS terminal) — should be able to be used by customers of different financial institutions (banks, building societies, credit unions, etc.).

The most vulnerable points of any EFT system are its entry points or terminals. Terminals must be accessible to all persons and at the same time they must be able to distinguish a legitimate user from an intruder. The user identification in the EFT system should be reliable, efficient, and cheap. Identification is reliable if the probabilities of both refusing the service for a legitimate customer and granting the service for an intruder are less than thresholds assumed by the designer of the EFT system. Efficient identification can be accomplished by means of a minimum number of references to the issuer.

Any identification can be carried out by checking either something an individual user knows or/and something an individual user has. All possible identification solutions which recognize a user's personal features (such as fingerprints, voice, face, ears, etc.) are very expensive and sometimes unreliable. This is why they cannot be applied in any terminal as a standard. In practice, however, it is possible to obtain a trade-off between reliability and cost when the customer knows his/her secret *PIN* (sometimes supplemented by a secret password), and possesses a unique bank card in which other identification information is written.

There are several security requirements, concerning the user identification, based on *PIN*s and bank cards, as follow:

- *PIN* must be kept secret all the time.
- *PIN* must not be written on the card.
- A card should contain the unique number (*PAN*) which fits the cardholder's *PIN*.
- If a card contains the personal authentication code (*PAC*), it must be dependent on the *PIN* but recovering the *PIN* on the basis of the *PAC* must be impractical.
- The identification process must be time-dependent (to thwart the playback attack).

The next set of protection requirements refers to the second part of a communication session which involves a message authentication code (*MAC*). The requirements are as follows:

- A *MAC* must contain a transaction description (a transaction request message), a cardholder's *PIN*, and the current data and time.
- The calculation of the *PIN* must be intractable on the basis of the *MAC*.
- The time reference of the *MAC* must be possible to be determined independently by the issuer.
- a message (messages) involved during the cardholder's identification stage must be cryptographically associated with the message (messages) generated in the second stage of a communication session.

Let us return to the security of the terminal. We should emphasize the necessity for its physical security. Such security must be provided as every terminal contains its security module within which its terminal master key and session (transaction) keys are kept. The terminal master key is stored in clear form. However, session keys $K_S$ is transmitted from the terminal's host and stored in the form of cryptograms, $E_{K_T}(K_S)$, enciphered under the terminal master key $K_T$ [BEKE84, REIL84]. As all cryptographic operations are performed just inside of the security module, all information generated by the set (keyboard - *PIN*, card reader — *PAN*, *PK*, or/and *PAC*) are transmitted as plaintext to it. Needless to say the information flow between input/output devices of the terminal and the secure module must be carefully designed and protected.

A further step to enhance the security of EFT systems has been made by introducing the so-called *smart card* (also referred to as intelligent card, secure card and chip card). Application of this card has virtually eliminated the unprotected information flow between a card reader and the security module in the identification stage. All needed enciphering transformations are carried out by the smart card itself as it contains a built-in microprocessor. Further information on smart cards is given in Chapter 7.

# 5.4 Summary

The problems considered in this chapter constitute only a small part of the cryptographic techniques used in computer networks. Of course, the solutions to these problems depend on the kind of environment in which the cryptographic protection is to be applied. Although there are many possible environments, we have concentrated on computer networks as it was in fact the extensive use of computer networks which pushed the development of modern cryptography. Moreover, all aspects of cryptographic engineering, together with their mutual connections, are illustrated within the framework of computer networks. Among other issues, we note that special attention should be paid to the following problems:

- the generation, distribution and storage of cryptographic keys;
- the choice of the set of cryptographic operations needed in hosts and terminals to ensure cryptographic protection;
- the incorporation of cryptographic operations into network protocol systems;
- the design of suitable authentication procedures to initiate sessions between different network entities;

- the application of cryptography in order to enrich a range of computer network services (e.g. electronic funds transfer, digital signatures, notary services, etc.).

There is a wide variety of articles on and references to this subject. However, the first book entirely devoted to the application of cryptography in computer networks was written by Meyer and Matyas in 1982 [MEMA84] and it covers a large range of the problems which appear in computer networks. Also, Davies and Price [DAPR84], in their book, have surveyed solutions to many cryptographic problems which appear in computer networks. These books can be treated as guides to different cryptographic applications. But there is still a need for a unified approach to cryptography in computer networks. Such an approach would take into account the connections between the hardware and the software, on one hand, and the quality of the cryptographic protection on the other hand. Moreover, it would present methods of design of cryptographic security vis à vis the architecture properties and parameters of the computer network.

## EXERCISES

5. 1  Describe a key distribution procedure for a network which has one regional CKD and several local CKDs. Assume that cryptographic protection is based on a symmetric cryptographic algorithm and there are prearranged keys to create secure channels between regional CKD and local CKDs, and local CKDs and their users.
    Consider the key distribution for two cases:

(a)  when two users A and B belong to the same local CKD;
(b)  when two users A and B belong to different local CKDs.

In your procedures use the time-stamping technique in order to protect the message exchange from replying.[4]

5. 2  Suppose a computer network utilizes an asymmetric cryptographic algorithm. Assume that there are two different levels of key directories. The global KD keeps all the public keys of all the local KD and its public key is known to them. Each local KD, however, serves its own set of users who know its authentic public key (foreign users do not have the public key of a foreign KD). Design a key distribution scheme when:

(a)  two users of the same local KD want to know each other's authentic public keys;
(b)  two users of different KDs want to know each other's authentic public keys.

In both cases, use the time-stamping technique.

5. 3  Authentication techniques may also be introduced in order to protect cryptographic keys against errors which may arise during transmission between components of a computer system (or computer network). Create such an authentication technique

---

4. Any transmission can be endangered by an illegal user who records it and then, at a later time, masquerades as a legal user replying by replaying prerecorded parts of the transmission. In order to protect against such an activity time-stamping technique is used. This relies on appending the exact time (i.e. time of day and date) of transmission to every message sent.

for 64-bit keys by adding an additional bit which checks the parity of all bits of the key. Calculate the failure probability of this authentication technique, that is, the probability that the authentication procedure says that the key is valid though errors have appeared.

5.4   Consider a key authentication procedure similar to that used in DES. Each 64-bit key consists of 56 independent bits and 8 bits which are used to maintain parity. The parity bits are numbered 8, 16, 24, 32, 40, 48, 56 and 64. Describe an authentication procedure and give the probability of its failure.

5.5   Consider the authentication of keys given in Figure 5.9. What is the chance of failure of this procedure?

5.6   Consider cryptographic protection for a transmission between a host and a terminal. Now all cryptographic operations are carried out independently of any user. Modify the scheme presented in section 5.4 by adding a third cryptographic operation *DMK*. This operation is to be defined at the terminal and is to produce the clear form of a session key $K_S$ as follows:

$$DMK\ [\ K_T\ ,\ E_T(K_S)\ ]\ \rightarrow\ K_S$$

What is the influence of *DMK* on the other cryptographic operations?

5.7   Design a cryptographic protection for files stored in hosts of a computer network assuming that:

- cryptographic protection of information transmitted between terminals and hosts and between hosts exists already (see section 5.2);
- the clear form of files can be recreated in hosts only.

Make suitable additional assumptions taking into account the security requirements given in section 5.2.

## SOLUTIONS

5.1   (a)   This is a similar situation to that considered in section 5.1. If two users A and B want a common secure channel (they need to share the common cryptographic key) and they are subject to the same local CKD, then the key distribution procedure can take the following form:

- User A initiates the process by sending the name $ID_A$ and the request $R_A$ in clear form to the local CKD.
- The local CKD, knowing the user's name, searches the key table for the prearranged key $K_A$ which is shared with user A. Next, on the basis of the request $R_A$, the CKD finds the key $K_B$ ($K_B$ is known to both CKD and B only) and generates a key $K_{AB}$ which will be used by A and B to establish the common, secure channel. Finally, the CKD creates the message $M_1 = (K_{AB},\ ID_A,\ R_A,\ E_B(K_{AB},ID_A,T_1),\ T_1)$ where $E_B(K_{AB},ID_A,T_1) = E_{K_B}(K_{AB},ID_A,T_1)$ which should be sent to B by user A, and $T_1$ identifies the time $K_{AB}$ was generated. The message $M_1$ is encrypted using $K_A$ and is transmitted to user A as the cryptogram $E_A(M_1)$.

- Having obtained the cryptogram from the CKD, A recreates the clear form of message $M_1$ by applying the key $K_A$. The first part of the message is stored but the second part, that is, the cryptogram $E_B(K_{AB}, ID_A, T_1)$, is directed to user B.
- After applying the key $K_B$, B reveals the triple $(K_{AB}, ID_A, T_1)$. Since B knows the name $ID_A$, B can prepare the message $M_2 = (T_1, T_2, RN)$ and send it as the cryptogram $E_{AB}(M_2)$, where $T_2$ is the current time and date, and $RN$ is a random number.
- A decrypts the cryptogram and verifies if $T_1$ is consistent with the original one obtained from the CKD. If satisfied, A sends back to B the cryptogram $E_{AB}(T_2, T_3, RN)$ where $T_3$ is the current time and date.

(b) In this case users A and B belong to different local CKDs, namely to $CKD_1$ and $CKD_2$, respectively. Now, there are two prearranged keys $K_A$ and $K_B$ which are shared between the users and their local CKDs. Assume that these two local CKDs are subject to the regional CKD, and keys $K_1$, $K_2$ create secure channels between the pairs ($CKD_1$, the regional CKD) and ($CKD_2$, the regional CKD), respectively. The procedure for fixing the common cryptographic key $K_{AB}$ between A and B can proceed as follows:

- A initiates the procedure by sending the name $ID_A$, along with a suitable request $R_A$ in clear form to $CKD_1$.
- As the request specifies the name of the user B, $CKD_1$ states that B is not one of its local users and sends its name $ID_1$ and the request $R_1$ in clear form to the regional CKD.
- On obtaining the request, the regional CKD sends back the cryptogram $E_{K_1}[K_{12}, ID_1, R_1, R_1, T_1, E_{K_2}(K_{12}, ID_1, T_1)]$, where the key $K_{12}$ is to create the secure channel between local CKDs, and $T_1$ is the time of the generation of $K_{12}$.
- $CKD_1$ decrypts the cryptogram and passes on the pair (the cryptogram $E_{K_2}$ $(K_{12}, ID_1, T_1)$, the request $R_2$) to $CKD_2$.
- $CKD_2$ recreates $(K_{12}, ID_1, T_1)$ and, knowing of the request $R_2$, generates the session key $K_{AB}$. Next, it produces the cryptogram $E_{K_{12}}[K_{AB}, ID_1, R_2, T_2, E_{K_B}(K_{AB}, ID_1, T_2)]$ and sends it to $CKD_1$, where $T_2$ is the time of the session key generation.
- At the $CKD_1$, this cryptogram is re-encrypted into the form $E_{K_A}[K_{AB}, ID_1, R_2, T_2, E_{K_B}(K_{AB}, ID_1, T_2)]$ and directed to user A.
- A decrypts the cryptogram and sends $E_{K_B}(K_{AB}, ID_1, T_2)$ to user B. User B reveals the triple $(K_{AB}, ID_1, T_2)$. Since B knows $ID_1$, B can send back the cryptogram $E_{K_{AB}}(T_2, T_3, RN)$, where $T_3$ is the current time and RN is a random number.
- A decrypts the cryptogram and verifies if $T_2$ and $T_3$ are consistent with the original obtained from the $CKD_1$. If satisfied, A sends back to B the cryptogram $E_{K_{AB}}(T_3, T_4, RN)$, where $T_4$ is the current time.

5.2 (a) If two users A and B are subject to a local KD, their public keys ($K_A$ and $K_B$) are known to the KD. In this situation the public key $K_{KD}$ of the KD is known to all its users.  The procedure for establishing a secure common channel between A and B can take the following form:

- A indicates he/she wants the public key of B by sending the pair (request $RQ_A$, the current time $T_1$) to the KD in the clear.
- In response, the KD transmits the public key $K_B$ of B, along with a copy of $(RQ_A, T_1)$, in the form of the cryptogram $D_{KD}(K_B, RQ_A, T_1)$.
- Since A knows the public key $K_{KD}$, A can decrypt the cryptogram and extract the public key $K_B$. The pair $(RQ_A, T_1)$ is then compared to the original. Next, A uses $K_B$ and creates the cryptogram $E_B(N_A, T_2, RS)$ which is directed to B ($N_A$ is A's name, $T_2$ is the current time, and $RS$ is a random sequence chosen by A).
- On receiving the cryptogram, B recreates the clear form of messages using the secret key $K'_B$. Since B knows the name $N_A$, B can ask for A's authentic public key from the KD by sending the pair (the appropriate request $RQ_B$, the current time $T_3$).
- In response, the KD transmits the triple ($K_A$, a copy of $RQ_B$, $T_3$) to B in the form of the cryptogram $D_{KD}(K_A, RQ_B, T_3)$.
- B can then recreate messages from the cryptogram. $K_A$ is stored in a suitable place but the pair $(RQ_B, T_3)$ must be compared with the original. Next, B creates the cryptogram $E_A(T_2, RS, T_4, RS')$ where $T_4$ is the current time and $RS'$ is a random sequence generated by B. Subsequently, this cryptogram is sent to A.
- After decryption, A compares $(T_2, RS)$ with the original and sends back the pair $(T_4, RS')$ as the cryptogram $E_B(T_4, RS')$.

(b)  Assume that A and B are subject to their local key directories $KD_1$ and $KD_2$, respectively.  So, if either A or B wants to establish a secure common channel, then the procedure can take the following form:

- Suppose A initiates the communication. In order to get the authentic public key of B, A sends the request $RQ_A$ and the current time $T_1$ to $CKD_1$ in clear form.
- As $KD_1$ does not know the authentic public key of $KD_2$, it transmits a suitable request $RQ_1$, along with the current time $T_2$, in clear form to the global KD.
- In response, the KD delivers to $KD_1$ the authentic public key $K_2$ of $KD_2$ by means of the cryptogram $D_{KD}(K_2, RQ_1, T_2)$.
- $KD_1$ decrypts the cryptogram (verifies if $RQ_1$, $T_2$ are consistent with the original) and creates the message $(K_2, RQ_A, T_1)$ which is sent to A as the cryptogram $D_A(K_2, RQ_A, T_1)$.
- Now, A transmits the pair $(RQ'_A, T_3)$ in clear form to $KD_2$.
- $KD_2$ sends back the cryptogram $D_2(K_B, RQ'_A, T_3)$.
- Since A knows the authentic public key $K_2$, A can decrypt the cryptogram. The authentic public key of B is stored but the pair $(RQ'_A, T_3)$ is compared with the original. Next, A directs to B the cryptogram $E_B(N_A, T_4, RS)$, where $N_A$ is A's name, $T_4$ is the current time, and $RS$ is a random sequence.
- B recreates the clear form of the triple. Since B knows A's name, B can

send the pair (the request $RQ_B$, and the current time $T_5$) in clear form to $KD_2$.

- Subsequently, as $KD_2$ requires the authentic key of $KD_1$ from the KD, it directs the pair (the request $RQ_2$, the current time $T_6$) in clear form to the KD.
- In response, the KD returns the cryptogram $D_{KD}(K_1, RQ_2, T_6)$, where $K_1$ is the authentic public key of $KD_1$.
- In turn, $KD_2$ directs to B the cryptogram $D_2(K_1, RQ_B, T_5)$.
- First, B recreates $K_1$ and verifies the pair $(RQ_B, T_5)$. Next, B sends to $KD_1$ the pair (the request $RQ'_B$, the current time $T_7$) in clear form.
- $KD_1$ transmits back the cryptogram $D_1(K_A, RQ'_B, T_7)$.
- Since B knows the authentic public key $K_1$, B can decrypt the cryptogram and recreate the authentic public key $K_A$ (and, of course, compare the remaining part with the original).
- Now B responds to A by sending the cryptogram $E_A(T_4, RS, T_8, RS')$.
- Finally, A is able to send the cryptogram $E_B(T_8, RS')$ to user B.

5. 3  Assume a key $K = (k_1, \cdots, k_{64})$ where $k_i \in \{0,1\}$ for $i = 1,...,64$. We append $k_{65} = k_1 \oplus \cdots \oplus k_{64}$ ($\oplus$ stands for the sum mod 2). In other words, $k_{65} = 0$ if the number of bits in $K$ is even, and $k_{65} = 1$ otherwise. The key $K' = (K, k_{65})$ is stored or transmitted within the computer system (or computer network).

In this case, the authentication procedure is as follows:

- From $K' = (k_1, \cdots, k_{65})$, we calculate the error syndrome $e = k_1 \oplus \cdots \oplus k_{65}$.
- If $e = 0$ then $K'$ is accepted.
- If $e = 1$ then $K'$ is rejected.

This procedure works properly when the number of errors (during transmission or storage) is odd (i.e. is equal to 1, 3, $\cdots$, 65). However, $K'$ is wrongly accepted when the number of errors is even (i.e. is equal to 2, 4, $\cdots$, 64).

Suppose that the probability of an error in one bit position is equal to $P_e$, and elementary errors appear independently in the sequence. Then, in general, the probability that $i$ different elementary errors appear is equal to:

$$\binom{65}{i} P_e^i (1-P_e)^{65-i}$$

Thus, the probability of a failure of our authentication procedure is equal to:

$$P_f = \sum_{i=2,4,\cdots,64} \binom{65}{i} P_e^i (1-P_e)^{65-i}$$

5. 4  Assume that:

$$k_8 = k_1 \oplus \cdots \oplus k_7$$
$$k_{16} = k_9 \oplus \cdots \oplus k_{15}$$

.

.

.

$$k_{64} = k_{57} \oplus \cdots \oplus k_{63}$$

where $K = (k_1, \cdots, k_{64})$. An authentication procedure for $K$ can take the following form:

- Calculate error syndromes for all the parity groups, that is:

$$e_1 = k_1 \oplus \cdots \oplus k_8$$
$$e_2 = k_9 \oplus \cdots \oplus k_{16}$$

.
.
.

$$e_8 = k_{57} \oplus \cdots \oplus k_{64}$$

- If $e_i = 0$ for all $i = 1, \cdots, 8$, then $K$ is accepted.
- If there is at least one $e_j = 1$, then $K$ is rejected.

The procedure fails when all syndromes are equal to zero even though the key is wrong. A single syndrome is equal to zero when:

- there is no error;
- there is an even number of errors (i.e. 2,4,6,8).

Assume that the probability of an elementary error is equal to $P_e$. We can calculate the probability of an even number of errors in one group as follows:

$$P_g = \sum_{i=2,4,6,8} \binom{8}{i} P_e^i (1-P_e)^{8-i}$$

The wrong key is accepted with probability $P_f = (P_g)^8$.

5. 5 The authentication procedure relies upon comparing cryptograms for a prearranged message $M$. This fails when the following equation is satisfied:

$$E_{K'}(M) = E_K(M) \quad \text{for } K' \neq K$$

We recall the definition of a cryptographic transformation is:

$$E : \mathbf{M} \times \mathbf{K} \rightarrow \mathbf{C}$$

If the key is fixed, the transformation $E_K$ is one-to-one. However, if the message is prearranged, the cryptographic transformation need not be one-to-one. Therefore, although $K$ and $K'$ $(K \neq K')$ give different one-to-one cryptographic transformations, there is a probability $2^{-64}$ that they may match, that is, $E_K(M) = E_{K'}(M)$ for $K \neq K'$.

5. 6 There are two cryptographic operations already defined at the terminal, namely:

$$ENCT\ [\ M,\ E_T(K_S)\ ] = E_S(M)$$
$$DECT\ [\ E_S(M),\ E_T(K_S)\ ] = M \cdot$$

If we also have the operation $DMK$, the clear form of the key $K_S$ can be used in these cryptographic operations. So, both $DECT$ and $ENCT$ can be revised and they may take on the form:

$$ENCT'\ [\ E_S(M),\ K_S\ ] = M$$
$$DECT'\ [\ M,\ K_S\ ] = E_S(M)$$

5. 7    Assume that a file is to be enciphered by a key $K_F$. Consider the requirement that all keys must be stored in the form of suitable cryptograms. Suppose for the present that $K_F$ is stored as the cryptogram $E_{H0}^i(K_F)$, where $i$ means that the host $i$ is being considered. Now the file can be sent to other hosts and recovery of $K_F$ is impossible unless $K_{H0}^i$ is shared with the other hosts. However, this contradicts our security requirements. Therefore, we use a secondary file key $K_{SF}$ to store the file key $K_F$ as the cryptogram $E_{K_{SF}}(K_F) = E_{SF}(K_F)$.

We have solved one problem but created another. How should $K_{SF}$ be stored? Consider the following possibilities.

- Let $K_{SF}$ be stored as the cryptogram $E_{H0}^i(K_{SF})$. Then the clear form of the file key can be reproduced by applying *DECH* operation as follows:

$$DECH\,[\,E_{SF}\,(K_F),\,E_{H0}^i(K_{SF})\,] = K_F$$

This possibility must be disallowed as it contradicts our security requirements.
- Thus we let $K_{SF}$ be stored as the cryptogram $E_{H1}^i(K_{SF})$. Consider the following scenario:

  - $RSK\,[\,E_{H1}^i\,(K_{SF}),\,E_{SF}\,(K_F)\,] = E_{H0}^i\,(K_F)$
  - $RMK\,[\,E_{H0}^i\,(K_F),\,E_{H1}^i\,(K_T)\,] = E_T\,(K_F)$
  - $DECT\,[\,E_F\,(FILE),\,E_T\,(K_F)\,] = FILE$

  Thus, the file can be recreated in clear form in any terminal of the host $I$. This also contradicts our security requirements.
- Suppose $K_{SF}$ is protected by storing it as the cryptogram $E_{H2}^i(K_{SF})$, where $K_{H2}^i$ is the variant of the master key $K_{H0}^i$. As this variant is used to protect secondary keys only and all host cryptographic operations are defined using $K_{H0}^i$ and $K_{H1}^i$, we have all security requirements fulfilled.

Finally, we assume that $K_{SF}$ is kept as the cryptogram $E_{H2}^i(K_{SF})$. In order to use the *ENCH* and *DECH* operations, we have to define a new cryptographic operation as follows:

$$RFK\,[\,E_{H2}^i\,(K_{SF}),\,E_{SF}\,(K_F)\,] = E_{H0}^i\,(K_F)$$

As we have the operation *RFK*, we can encipher and decipher files using the *ENCH* and *DECH* operations.

# 6

# APPLICATION OF CRYPTOGRAPHY IN DATABASES

A database is a collection of information sets stored in a computer system which is shared among different users. Databases, like other computer components (programs, procedures, routines, terminals, readers, discs, etc.), are subject to either intentional or accidental human alteration. This alteration may be generated by:

- an authorized user who breaks his access rights; or
- an illegal user who, by by-passing the security shell, gets through to the computer resources.

Protection of computer components against illegal human alteration or destruction relies on the running of a suitable operating system whose reliability has been extensively tested.

As it is a part of the computer, protection of the database is completely dependent on the operating system. Unfortunately, there is a great deal of evidence that even sufficiently complex operating systems, used along with other security measures, possess gaps which allow illegal information leakage.

Better protection of computer information can be obtained if several security measures are applied simultaneously whenever possible. Such an approach is especially necessary when protection of databases is concerned. The operating system supervises the user access to data in the operating memory. However, cryptography can be easily applied to protect all data sets stored in auxiliary memory.

Such a solution has the advantage that all the data sets which create a database are stored in the form of suitable cryptograms so they are non-readable to anyone who does not have the appropriate cryptographic key to apply. Thus, either stealing or illegal copying of auxiliary memory content does not compromise protection of the database. As cryptographic operations are usually carried out under the supervision of the operating system, transmission of information between the computer and the auxiliary memory is also protected (because only ciphertext is being sent instead of cleartext).

In this chapter we shall consider problems that occur while introducing cryptographic protection into a database system.

# 6.1  Database model

Consider the organization of data in a computer system. A database can be seen as either a physical database (when we think of organization of data in auxiliary memory) or a logical database (when we consider relations among data which depend on user applications and reflect the given part of the real world). In other words, the physical database is strictly connected with the organization of a storage medium. On the other hand, the logical database simply describes natural interrelations between data, with the organization of a logical database not being dependent on a type of storage medium. The presented model of databases is similar to that given by Gudes, Koch and Stahl [GUKO76].

In general, users are divided into classes. Two different users belong to the same class if they use the same part of a logical database. Then, user programs, along with their databases, create suitable user work spaces. The bottom of a multilevel database organization is a physical database. The top consists of the collection of all user work spaces. Between the bottom and the top, there can be several different levels (e.g. a database of user classes and a logical database). It is worth noting that the presented multilevel organization scheme of a database system is consistent with the relational database model. Between successive organization levels there are connections that will be considered later.

In order to define these connections, we introduce a formal description of a database. The description is based on the notion of *a data item*. Data items, which appear on different levels of the database, can have different forms although they supply the same information.

*Example*

Assume we have a data item which gives the distance between two cities. The item '160' expressed in kilometers can be transformed into '100' miles. Of course, these two different data items give the same information.    □

So, in order to have proper interpretation of a data item, it should be considered in relation to the level on which it is defined. A data item $d$ on $i$ level is denoted $d^{(i)}$. The notation $d^{(i)}$ is simplified to $d$ if the level in the database does not matter.

Now let us consider the relation of a data item to the real world. An item specifies an attribute of a given entity (e.g. the item 'GREEN' describes an attribute 'COLOR'). An individual data item does not exist independently; it is interrelated with other data items. Such an interrelated and ordered sequence of data items is called *a physical record (PR)*. Thus a physical record on level $i$ of the database is defined as:

$$PR^{(i)} = (d_1^{(i)}, \ldots, d_n^{(i)})$$

*Example*

Consider data stored in the form of database record:

| NAME | CAR | COLOR |
|---|---|---|
| Brown | Volvo | green |
| Smith | Mercedes | yellow |
| Glenn | Ford | yellow |
| Johnson | Ford | red |

This record contains 12 data items. Any row of the table creates *a single physical record*. On the other hand, columns of the table form sets of homogeneous data. These sets are called *fields*. Notice that any column describes the same attribute. For instance, data {*green, yellow*} specify the color attribute. Finally, the entire table along with the unique name creates a *logical record*.    □

Thus, we have two more definitions. *A field* $F^{(i)}$ on the $i$th level database is the set of all data items of a suitable attribute which supplies the same type of information. The notation $F^{(i)}$ is simplified to $F$ whenever the level of the database does not matter. Next, *a logical record* $LR^{(i)} = I(F_1, \ldots, F_k)$ on the $i$th level of the database is called a subset of product

$$F_1 \times \ldots \times F_k$$

together with the unique identification name $I$. Last, *a logical database* $LDB^{(i)}$ on the $i$th level consists of collection of all *logical records* along with their *interpretation*. Thus,

$$LDB^{(i)} = \{ LR_1^{(i)}, \ldots, LR_m^{(i)} \} + INTERPRETATION$$

*Example*

Suppose that our database comprises three logical records: $LR_1, LR_2, LR_3$ given in the form below.

$LR_1$

| EMPLOYEE # | EMPLOYEE NAME | POSITION | SALARY | PROJECT |
|---|---|---|---|---|
| 4129 | Green | professor | 3500 | a12 |
| 3909 | Brown | tutor | 1500 | a12 |
| 2457 | Grey | lecturer | 2200 | tr1 |
| 1234 | Smith | professor | 3100 | tr1 |
| 3467 | Jones | associate professor | 2700 | x243 |

$LR_2$

| PROJECT | SPONSOR NAME | COMPLETION DATE |
|---|---|---|
| a12 | Sydney Uni | 12.08.1985 |
| tr1 | IBM | 30.12.1986 |
| x243 | ITT | 15.10.1989 |

$LR_3$

| POSITION | MIN. SALARY | MAX. SALARY |
|---|---|---|
| Tutor | 1500 | 1800 |
| Senior Tutor | 1900 | 2100 |
| Lecturer | 2200 | 2400 |
| Senior Lecturer | 2500 | 2600 |
| Associate Professor | 2700 | 2900 |
| Professor | 3000 | 3500 |

For instance, $PR$ = (2457, Grey, lecturer, 2200, tr1) belongs to $LR_1 = I_1$ (EMPLOYEE#, EMPLOYEE NAME, POSITION, SALARY, PROJECT). The field PROJECT is = {a12, tr1, x243}.    □

## 6.2 Cryptographic transformations preserving data structure

Assume that we are going to consider two neighboring database levels:

1. level 1 (data sets are in clear form);
2. level 2 (data sets are enciphered).

In Figure 6.1 the notation $E_K ( LDB^{(1)} ) = LDB^{(2)}$ means that the database on the second level is a transformation of the database on first level, whereas $E$ is a cryptographic transformation (rather a set of suitable cryptographic transformations defined for particular database elements) and $K$ is a cryptographic key (the set of keys for corresponding cryptographic transformations).

At this point, we confine our consideration to cryptographic transformations of a specific type. Simply, we take into account transformations which preserve data structure. A *cryptographic transformation preserves data structure* if and only if cryptograms are still *elements*[1] of a database. Let us define the simplest cryptographic transformation, called *substitution of data items*.

### 6.2.1 Substitution of data items

In the transformation described either clear data elements or cryptograms are data items. Thus,

$$d^{(2)} = E_K(d^{(1)}); \quad d^{(1)} \in F^{(1)}, \ d^{(2)} \in F^{(2)}, \ K \in \mathbf{K} \qquad (6.1)$$

where $d^{(1)}$, $d^{(2)}$ are data items, $F^{(1)}$, $F^{(2)}$ are fields, and $E_K$ is a cryptographic transformation. With such a substitution defined, fields are affected as well. It is possible to distinguish two cases:

1. when both clear data items and cryptogram items belong to the same field ($F^{(1)} = F^{(2)}$);

---

1. Elements of database are: data items, physical records, fields and logical records.

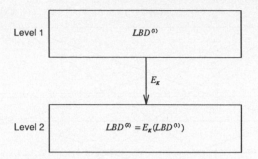

**Figure 6.1** Two neighbouring database levels

2. when clear data items and cryptogram items belong to different fields ($F^{(1)} \neq F^{(2)}$).

In the first case, forms of data items before and after encipherment do not differ, which can sometimes mislead an illegal user who does not have any chance of recognizing whether items are enciphered or not. In the second case, however, data items representing cryptograms can be alphanumerical sequences which are not necessarily readable.

*Example*

Let a logical record be of the following form:

| $LR^{(1)}$ | |
|---|---|
| EMPLOYEE NAME | SALARY |
| Green | 3500 |
| Brown | 1500 |
| Grey | 2200 |

Consider the cryptographic transformation $E_K$ defined for three cryptographic keys ($K = 0, 1, 2$). These three transformations $E_0$, $E_1$, $E_2$ are described as follows:

| $E_0$ | |
|---|---|
| d | $E_0(d)$ |
| Green | Green |
| Brown | Brown |
| Grey | Grey |

| $E_1$ | |
|---|---|
| d | $E_1(d)$ |
| Green | Brown |
| Brown | Grey |
| Grey | Green |

| $E_2$ | |
|---|---|
| d | $E_2(d)$ |
| Green | Grey |
| Brown | Green |
| Grey | Brown |

The cryptographic transformation can be presented differently (see Figure 6.2). If we assign an integer to each data item in the following way:

$$Green \leftrightarrow 0$$
$$Brown \leftrightarrow 1$$
$$Grey \leftrightarrow 2$$

then our cryptographic transformation can be redefined as:

$$E_K(d) = d + K \pmod 3$$

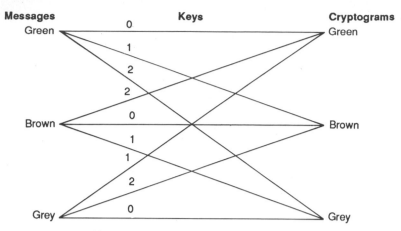

**Figure 6.2** Simple substitution cipher

For instance, $d = Brown$ ($Brown \leftrightarrow 1$), for key $K = 1$ has a cryptogram $E_1(1) = 2$ (mod 3). Looking at the assignment, we state that the cryptogram data item is *Grey*. ☐

In practice, cryptographic transformations are not determined by means of lists. Usually, suitable cryptographic algorithms are used for the encryption. However, each cryptographic algorithm produces cryptograms for messages of strictly determined length. As cryptographic transformations should preserve data structure, the length of cryptogram items cannot be larger than the original one. On the other hand, the length of cryptogram items cannot be smaller than the original one (any cryptographic transformation has to be one-to-one function while the key is fixed). The DES algorithm may be easily applied to data items broken into blocks which are a multiple of 64 bits.[2]

## 6.2.2 Transposition of data items

Consider the logical record $LR^{(1)}$ which consists of $n$ physical records, thus:

$$LR^{(1)} = \{ PR_1, \ldots, PR_n \}$$

Each physical record $PR_r^{(1)}$ is an ordered sequence:

$$PR_r^{(1)} = ( d_{r,1}^{(1)}, d_{r,2}^{(1)}, \ldots, d_{r,k}^{(1)} ) ; \quad r = 1,2,\ldots,n$$

*Transposition of data items* is a cryptographic transformation defined in the following way:

$$d_{r,l}^{(2)} = d_{r,E_K^{(r)}(l)}^{(1)} \tag{6.2}$$

where $r = 1, \ldots, n$, and $E_K^{(r)}$ is a cryptographic transformation determined for integers $l$ ($l = 0, \ldots, k$) and $K \in \mathbf{K}$. The form of cryptographic transformation depends on $r$, so each physical record can use different cryptographic transformations, fo example, the first record subjects to $E_K^{(1)}$, the second uses $E_K^{(2)}$, and so on.

---

2. Sixty-four bits are equivalent to eight letters in ASCII code.

A modification of the above given definition can take on the following form:

$$d^{(2)}_{r,l} = d^{(1)}_{r,E_{K_r}(l)} \; ; \quad K_r \in K; \quad r = 1, \ldots, n \tag{6.3}$$

where a key $K_r$ is independently selected for each physical record; however, the form of the cryptographic transformation is fixed. So, guessing the right sequence of data items in one physical record does not have any influence on the security of others.

*Example*

Let us consider the logical record $LR^{(1)}$

$$LR^{(1)}$$

| EMPLOYEE # | EMPLOYEE NAME | POSITION | SALARY | PROJECT |
|---|---|---|---|---|
| 4129 | Green | professor | 3500 | a12 |
| 3909 | Brown | tutor | 1500 | a12 |
| 2457 | Grey | lecturer | 2200 | tr1 |
| 1234 | Smith | professor | 3100 | tr1 |
| 3467 | Jones | associate professor | 2700 | x243 |

Assume that our cryptographic transformation takes the following form:

$$E_K(M) = K M + 3 \;(\text{mod } 5) ; \quad K = 1,2,3,4$$

where $M$ stands for a cleartext (in our case an integer $l$). Suppose also that the key $K = 2$ has been selected for the first physical record (the first row of table contents). First of all, we calculate $E_K(l)$ for $l = 0,1,2,3,4$, thus:

| $l$ | $E_K(l)$ for $K=2$ |
|---|---|
| 0 | 3 |
| 1 | 0 |
| 2 | 2 |
| 3 | 4 |
| 4 | 1 |

The physical record is $PR^{(2)}_1 = (d^{(2)}_{1,0}, d^{(2)}_{1,2}, d^{(2)}_{1,3}, d^{(2)}_{1,4})$ and so simultaneously,

$$d^{(2)}_{1,0} = d^{(1)}_{1,E_K(0)} = d^{(1)}_{1,3}$$
$$d^{(2)}_{1,1} = d^{(1)}_{1,E_K(1)} = d^{(1)}_{1,0}$$
$$d^{(2)}_{1,2} = d^{(1)}_{1,E_K(2)} = d^{(1)}_{1,2}$$
$$d^{(2)}_{1,3} = d^{(1)}_{1,E_K(3)} = d^{(1)}_{1,4}$$
$$d^{(2)}_{1,4} = d^{(1)}_{1,E_K(4)} = d^{(1)}_{1,1}$$

In other words, the first record $PR^{(1)}_1 = (4129,\text{ Green, professor, }3500,\text{ a12})$ is permuted to a record $PR^{(2)}_1 = (d^{(1)}_{1,3}, d^{(1)}_{1,0}, d^{(1)}_{1,2}, d^{(1)}_{1,4}, d^{(1)}_{1,1}) = (3500, 4129, \text{professor, a12, Green})$. Computing the successive physical records in the same way, we can get the new logical record whose row permutations are governed by keys 2,4,2,1,3, respectively. This logical record with enciphered data item positions has the following form:

| 3500 | 4129 | professor | a12 | | Green |
|------|------|-----------|-----|---|-------|
| 1500 | tutor | Brown | 3909 | | a12 |
| 2200 | 2457 | lecturer | tr1 | | Grey |
| 3100 | tr1 | 1234 | Smith | | professor |
| 2700 | Jones | x243 | associate professor | | 3467 |

□

It is worth noting that the transposition does not change the form of data items. It simply permutes data items in every physical record. This kind of cryptographic transformation protects databases against browsing.

## 6.2.3  Reduction of data items

A cryptographic transformation called *a reduction of data items* is defined by the following formula:

$$d^{(2)} = E_K ( d_1^{(1)} , \ldots, d_p^{(1)} ) \tag{6.4}$$

The reduction of $p$ data items on the first database level points out a single data item on the second database level and the form of the cryptogram data items depends on the cryptographic key applied.  This transformation is illustrated in the next example.

*Example*

Let us consider the logical record in the following form:

| LR$^{(1)}$ | | | | |
|---|---|---|---|---|
| EMPLOYEE # | EMPLOYEE NAME | POSITION | SALARY | PROJECT |
| 4129 | Green | professor | 3500 | a12 |
| 3909 | Brown | tutor | 1500 | a12 |
| 2457 | Grey | lecturer | 2200 | tr1 |
| 1234 | Smith | professor | 3100 | tr1 |
| 3467 | Jones | assoc. professor | 2700 | x243 |

Assume that each physical record $PR^{(1)} = (d_1,d_2,d_3,d_4,d_5)$ is divided into two parts $(d_1,d_2)$ and $(d_3,d_4,d_5)$.  Each part is subject to encryption row by row.  As a result, we obtain a new logical record $LR^{(2)}$:

| LR$^{(2)}$ | |
|---|---|
| $d_{11}^{(2)} = E_K$ (4129, Green) | $d_{12}^{(2)} = E_K$ (professor, 3500, a12) |
| $d_{21}^{(2)} = E_K$ (3909, Brown) | $d_{22}^{(2)} = E_K$ (tutor, 1500, a12) |
| $d_{31}^{(2)} = E_K$ (2457, Grey) | $d_{32}^{(2)} = E_K$ (lecturer, 2200, tr1) |
| $d_{41}^{(2)} = E_K$ (1234, Smith) | $d_{42}^{(2)} = E_K$ (professor, 3100, tr1) |
| $d_{51}^{(2)} = E_K$ (3467, Jones) | $d_{52}^{(2)} = E_K$ (associate professor, 2700, x243) |

where the key $K$ is fixed.  Of course, cryptogram data items $d_{ij}^{(2)}$ ($i = 1,2,3,4,5$ and

$j = 1,2$) have not been readable already. However, sets $\{d_{i1}^{(2)}; \ i = 1,2,3,4,5\}$ and $\{d_{i2}^{(2)}; \ i = 1,2,3,4,5\}$ create fields $F_1^{(2)}$ and $F_2^{(2)}$, respectively.     □

Reduction of data items can be carried out in two steps. The first one relies on concatenation of given data items and the second utilizes a cryptographic transformation. We observe that manipulation and retrieval of data is still possible. For each logical record, which has been created by reduction, there is a well-defined key-field. It is due to the one-to-one property of cryptographic transformations while a key is fixed. A key-field of a relation on the second database level is simply a field which comprises data items of the key-field on the first database level. A drawback of reduction, which results from the nature of cryptographic transformation, is that the access to data items on the second database level does not allow the retrieval of the original data items.

## 6.2.4  Expansion of data items

*Expansion* is defined as an opposite operation to reduction and, of course, it must be applied once *reduction* has been used to recover the original form of the data. The following formula defines this cryptographic transformation:

$$(d_1^{(2)}, d_2^{(2)}, \ldots, d_q^{(2)}) = E_K(d^{(1)}) \tag{6.5}$$

Thus, a single data item on the first level is subject to encryption and, then, the cryptogram data item is being split into $q$ different data items. Let us illustrate this operation by the example given below.

*Example*

Assume we must deal with the logical record given in the previous example and we want to protect both the SALARY and PROJECT fields. Next, suppose that each data item $d_{4i}^{(1)}$ of the SALARY field is enciphered. As a result a cryptogram data item is cut into two pieces, that is, $(d_{4i}^{(2)}, d_{6i}^{(2)}) = E_K(d_{4i}^{(1)})$. Clearly, data items $d_{5i}^{(1)}$ of the PROJECT field can be transformed in the same way, thus $(d_{5i}^{(2)}, d_{7i}^{(2)}) = E_K(d_{5i}^{(1)})$; i = 1,2,3,4,5. Finally, we get the record with expanded data items:

| LR$^{(2)}$ | | | | | | |
|---|---|---|---|---|---|---|
| EMPLOYEE# | EMPLOYEE NAME | POSITION | SAL1 | PRO1 | SAL2 | PRO2 |
| 4129 | Green | professor | $d_{41}$ | $d_{51}$ | $d_{61}$ | $d_{71}$ |
| 3909 | Brown | tutor | $d_{42}$ | $d_{52}$ | $d_{62}$ | $d_{72}$ |
| 2457 | Grey | lecturer | $d_{43}$ | $d_{53}$ | $d_{63}$ | $d_{73}$ |
| 1234 | Smith | professor | $d_{44}$ | $d_{54}$ | $d_{64}$ | $d_{74}$ |
| 3467 | Jones | associate professor | $d_{45}$ | $d_{55}$ | $d_{65}$ | $d_{75}$ |

□

The expansion operation influences a number of fields in logical records. Thus, because data items are not defined on the second database level, it protects, like reduction, data items from illegal access.

### 6.2.5 Encipherment of access address

This type of cryptographic transformation deals exclusively with logical records. If a logical record on the first database level has a form of:

$$LR^{(1)} = I(F_1, F_2, \ldots, F_n)$$

then, after applying the transformation considered, we get two logical records:

$$LR_1^{(2)} = I_1(F_1, \ldots, F_j, E_K(AD)) \quad \text{and} \quad LR_2^{(2)} = I_2(F_{j+1}, \ldots, F_n) \qquad (6.6)$$

where $AD$ is a field of addresses of the second part of physical record, and $E_K(AD)$ is the field of cryptograms of addresses.

*Example*

Consider the following logical record:

| EMPLOYEE# |
|-----------|
| 4129 |
| 3909 |
| 2457 |

| EMPLOYEE NAME |
|---------------|
| Green |
| Brown |
| Grey |

Applying encipherment to the access address, the logical record takes on the following form:

| $LR_1^{(2)}$ | |
|-----------|----------|
| EMPLOYEE# | $E_K(AD)$ |
| 4129 | $E_K(a_1)$ |
| 3909 | $E_K(a_2)$ |
| 2457 | $E_K(a_3)$ |

| EMPLOYEE NAME |
|---------------|
| Green |
| Brown |
| Grey |

where the field $AD = \{a_1, a_2, a_3\}$ shows the addresses of the second part of every physical record.  □

### 6.2.6 Cryptographic transformation versus database levels

Now we consider the application of the above cryptographic transformations to database protection [GUKO76]. First, we consider both user and user class levels (see Figure 6.3).

Of course, a user operates in his/her work space (all user work spaces create the user level) and has access to the part of the database on user class level. We assume that database elements of user class level are enciphered so users can properly manipulate data if they are granted suitable cryptographic keys. While transferring data between these two levels, three elementary cryptographic transformations may be applied:

1. substitution;
2. reduction;
3. expansion.

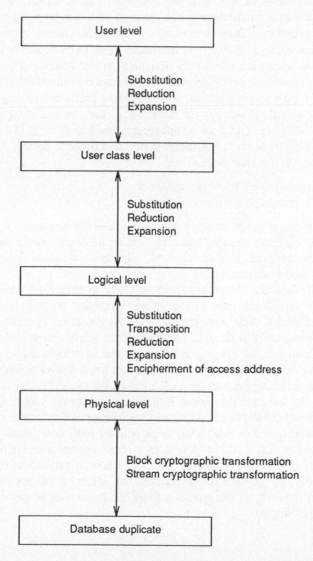

**Figure 6.3** Applications of cryptographic transformation between neighbouring DB levels

The same cryptographic transformations can be used between user class levels and logical levels. However, between logical level and physical level all cryptographic transformations (below) can be applied:

1. substitution;
2. transposition;
3. reduction;
4. expansion;
5. encipherment of access address.

Hence, data items of the same physical level can be subject to encipherment several times. All transformations preserve database structure so management and retrieval of data are possible. There are many different limitations imposed on cryptographic transformations so multilevel encipherment helps in overcoming these difficulties. The situation is somewhat similar to designing an enciphering algorithm using only two insecure elementary cryptographic transformations: substitution and permutation. In general, in order to get good quality enciphering protection in only one enciphering step, we must constrain drastically the flexibility of the physical database. However, there is one case when we apply an enciphering algorithm (like DES) to protect data items. Think of a database duplicate which is stored in order to protect the original one against destruction. In that case, we can use:

1. block cryptographic transformations; or
2. stream cryptographic transformations.

Both kinds of transformation destroy the database structure. It means that to retrieve a required database element we must first decipher the whole database. Then we can retrieve the required database element. The same situation appears when we want to update or modify the database.

Usually data in a computer system are stored in clear form which increases the risk of access by an illegal user. Even if we introduce cryptographic transformations as considered above, key management and cryptographic operations (encipherment and decipherment) are still handled by the database management system (DBMS). A better solution seems to be cryptographic protection in which cryptographic operations are handled by individual owners of data. A user must deliver a suitable cryptographic key while data are being put into the database and also while data are being retrieved from the database. In this case the user is responsible for storing a key. On the other hand, the DBMS should use the key in a way which excludes its disclosure.

The vital question, which has been omitted until now, is the problem of semantic connections which exist in databases. These connections increase considerably the probability of revealing protected data. In certain circumstances they allow discovery of data simply by deduction. Therefore, the selection of cryptographic measures of protection depends on the semantic connections existing in the database. Consider the following example.

*Example*

Let us assume that we are dealing with three logical records, $LR_1$, $LR_2$, $LR_3$ described as follows:

| $LR_1$ | |
|---|---|
| NAME | SALARY |
| Green | 3500 |
| Brown | 1500 |
| Grey | 2200 |
| Smith | 3100 |
| Jones | 2700 |

| $LR_2$ | |
|---|---|
| NAME | POSITION |
| Green | professor |
| Brown | tutor |
| Grey | lecturer |
| Smith | professor |
| Jones | associate professor |

| $LR_3$ | | |
|---|---|---|
| POSITION | MIN. SALARY | MAX. SALARY |
| Tutor | 1500 | 1800 |
| Senior Tutor | 1900 | 2100 |
| Lecturer | 2200 | 2400 |
| Senior Lecturer | 2500 | 2600 |
| Associate Professor | 2700 | 2900 |
| Professor | 3000 | 3500 |

We protect $LR_1$ from illegal access by enciphering all its data items so the logical record is unreadable. Nevertheless, an illegal user can take advantage of $LR_2$ and $LR_3$ to which he/she has access. So the illegal user knows, for example, that Green's salary must be in the interval (3000, 3500). His/her knowledge is summarized thus:

| | |
|---|---|
| Green | 3000 < Salary < 3500 |
| Brown | 1500 < Salary < 1800 |
| Grey | 2200 < Salary < 2400 |
| Smith | 3000 < Salary < 3500 |
| Jones | 2700 < Salary < 2900 |

□

Assume we have to protect the logical record $LR(F_1, \ldots, F_n)$ and $F_1$ is a key-field. First of all we should encipher all the data items of $LR$. Next we can use two approaches:

1. the first relies on enciphering logical records which comprise fields determined for the same attribute as key-field $F_1$;
2. the second approach relies on enciphering all logical records which are defined using any attributes of the $F_1, \ldots, F_n$ fields of the protected record $LR$ as required.

## 6.3  Application of cryptography to protection of information during processing

Up till now we have not considered the protection of data during processing in the computer system. In practice, such protection is supplied by a suitably designed operating system which supervises the data processing of every user. It should be designed in such a way that any unauthorized flow of data among users is impossible. However, in certain circumstances, a user can require additional protection and, instead of processing in clear form, he/she can choose to carry out the processing of programs for input data in the form of cryptograms. Such a processing method requires the user to generate, store and manage keys so the safety of the processed data does not depend on the computer security. The drawback of this way of processing is that all cryptographic operations must be carried out by the user.

Now a problem arises: How can cryptographic transformations be designed in order to ensure the correct result after processing?

The problems to be presented appear while designing cryptographic transformations for the relatively simple case of a processing program using only two elementary arithmetic operations: addition and multiplication. We assume that these operations are being carried out using integers as input data and, moreover, we suppose that cryptanalysis of those cryptographic transformations is performed using both ciphertext only attack and a known plaintext attack [PIEP86].

### 6.3.1  Specification of cryptographic transformations preserving arithmetic operations

Let us recall that a cryptographic transformation is a function $E$ of two variables $(M,K)$ having the form:

$$E_K(M) = E(M, K) ; \quad M \in \mathbf{M}, \; K \in \mathbf{K}, \; E_K(M) \in \mathbf{C}$$

where $\mathbf{M}, \mathbf{K}, \mathbf{C}$ are sets of messages, keys and cryptograms, respectively. First of all, let us start our consideration with the answer to the following question: What does it mean to say that a cryptographic transformation preserves an operation $OP$, where $OP$ stands for any operation not necessarily arithmetic? The answer is given by the following definition.

*Definition*

A cryptographic transformation preserves an operation $OP$ of $n$ variables, if,

$$\underset{K \in \mathbf{K}}{\forall} \quad E_K[OP(M_1, \dots, M_n)] = OP[E_K(M_1), \dots, E_K(M_n)] \qquad (6.7)$$

for any sequence of messages $(M_1, \dots, M_n)$. In other words, a cryptographic transformation preserves an operation $OP$ when a cryptogram of the result of an operation is the same as the result of the operation carried out on suitable cryptograms. It also means that the correct result of an operation can be obtained by deciphering the result of the operation performed on cryptograms, that is,

$$OP(M_1, \dots, M_n) = D_K[OP(E_K(M_1), \dots, E_K(M_n))] \qquad (6.8)$$

where $D$ is the corresponding decryption function (see Figure 6.4). Applying our definition to arithmetic operations, we get the following definition.

*Definition*

A cryptographic transformation $E$ preserves elementary arithmetic operations (multiplication and addition), if, for a fixed $K \in \mathbf{K}$, the following conditions are fulfilled:

$$\underset{M_1,M_2 \in \mathbf{M}}{\forall} \quad E_K(M_1 + M_2) = E_K(M_1) + E_K(M_2) \tag{6.9}$$

$$\underset{\alpha \in \mathbf{Z}}{\forall} \quad \underset{M \in \mathbf{M}}{\forall} \quad E_K(\alpha M) = \alpha \, E_K(M) \tag{6.10}$$

$$\underset{M_1,M_2 \in \mathbf{M}}{\forall} \quad E_K(M_1 \, M_2) = E_K(M_1) \, E_K(M_2) \tag{6.11}$$

where $\mathbf{Z}$ stands for a set of positive integers, $M$, $M_1$, $M_2$ are messages considered as positive integers $(\mathbf{M} = \mathbf{Z})$.

Let us consider formula (6.9). It simply tells us that $E_K$ is a linear transformation. Therefore, a cryptographic transformation preserving addition is described by a matrix $E(K)$, where,

$$E_K(M) = M \times E(K) \, ; \quad M \in \mathbf{M}, \; K \in \mathbf{K} \tag{6.12}$$

and both message and cryptogram spaces are of dimensions $n$ and $t$ respectively $(n \le t)$, a matrix $E(K)$ is of dimension $n \times t$ and its coefficients depend on the key only. Therefore,

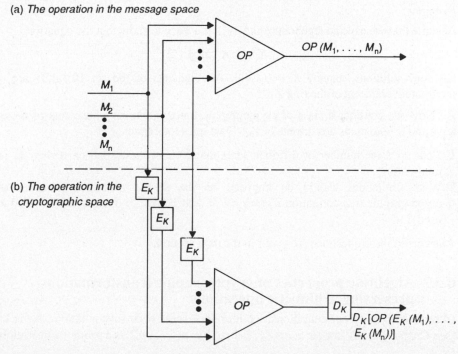

**Figure 6.4** Illustration of a cryptographic transformation which preserves an operation OP

with sets of messages and cryptograms $\mathbf{M}, \mathbf{C} \subseteq \mathbf{Z}$, a cryptographic transformation takes on the following form:

$$E_K(M) = MK \tag{6.13}$$

Of course, the transformation given by (6.13) satisfies both (6.9) and (6.10). Note the condition (6.11) is equivalent to two equations of the form:

$$E_K(M_1 M_2) = E_K(M_1) \ E_K(M_2) = M_1 M_2 K^2 \tag{6.14}$$

$$E_K(M_1 M_2) = M_1 M_2 K \tag{6.15}$$

Thus, any key of the cryptographic transformation defined by (6.9), (6.10) and (6.11) has to satisfy the equality

$$K^2 = K \tag{6.16}$$

If $K \in \mathbf{Z}$ ($\mathbf{Z}$ stands for the set of positive integers), there are two integers that satisfy (6.16), namely $K = 0$ and $K = 1$. As a cryptographic transformation is not one-to-one for $K = 0$ and, for $K = 1$, it takes a trivial form which, as a matter of fact, cannot be used to data protection, so we have the following conclusion.

**Corollary:** *If the sets* $\mathbf{M}, \mathbf{C}, \mathbf{K} = \mathbf{Z}$*, then there is no cryptographic transformation preserving arithmetic operations.*

In order to get rid of these difficulties, we use other algebraic constructions in which (6.16) has more than two solutions. Consider the following example.

*Example*

Assume that we have an algebraic ring[3] $Z_{12}$. It is easy to show that the equation

$$K^2 = K \pmod{12}$$

has four solutions, namely $K = 0,1,4,9$. All elements of the set $\{0,1,4,9\}$ are called idempotent elements of the ring $Z_{12}$. □

Now we consider a class of cryptographic transformations whose sets of messages, keys and cryptograms are subsets of $Z_N$. Two questions arise:

1. How does the number of different idempotent elements depend on a ring $Z_N$ (or on integer $N$)?
2. What limitations should be imposed on the set of messages in order that a cryptographic transformation $E_K(M) = KM$ will be one-to-one (assume a fixed key is used)?

Answers to these questions are given in the next section.

## 6.3.2  Algebraic properties of cryptographic transformations preserving arithmetic operations

In order to specify our conditions, we introduce some necessary notation. As is known (see Chapter 2), any integer $a$, $a \in Z_N$, (where $N = p_1^{\alpha_1} \ldots p_n^{\alpha_n}$ is a prime factorization of $N$

---

3.  A ring $Z_N$ is defined by the set $\{0,1,\ldots,N-1\}$ along with addition and multiplication *modulo N*.

when $p_1, \ldots, p_n$ are primes ), can be expressed as a vector $[a_1, \ldots, a_n]$, where $a_i = a$ (mod $p_i^{\alpha_i}$ ) for $i = 1, \ldots, n$. Moreover, the vector representation is one-to-one. So, having a vector $[a_1, \ldots, a_n]$, we can find the corresponding integer $a$.

Let us turn our attention to multiplication and addition of elements in the ring $Z_N$. It is easy to prove that, instead of doing arithmetic operations on integers of $Z_N$, we may carry them out using vector representation, thus:

$$[a_1, \ldots, a_n] + [b_1, \ldots, b_n] = [a_1 + b_1, \ldots, a_n + b_n] \qquad (6.17)$$

$$[a_1, \ldots, a_n] \times [b_1, \ldots, b_n] = [a_1 \times b_1, \ldots, a_n \times b_n] \qquad (6.18)$$

where $a = [a_1, \ldots, a_n]$, $b = [b_1, \ldots, b_n]$, $a, b \in Z_N$, $N = p_1^{\alpha_1}, \ldots, p_n^{\alpha_n}$. So both multiplication and addition can be done pairwise for successive components of a vector. We concentrate on the $n$ vectors with a special form:

$$e_1 = [1, 0, 0, \ldots, 0]$$
$$e_2 = [0, 1, 0, \ldots, 0]$$

$$\cdot$$
$$\cdot$$
$$\cdot$$

$$e_n = [0, 0, 0, \ldots, 1]$$

as they provide a set of basic idempotent elements $\{e_1, \ldots, e_n\}$. This set has interesting properties:

1. $e_i^2 = e_i$; $i = 1, \ldots, n$ (this is the definition of idempotent elements);
2. the sum of any subset of $\{e_1, \ldots, e_n\}$ gives an idempotent element;
3. the sum of all the elements gives $1 \in Z_N$.

These properties lead us to the following theorem and simultaneously give the answer to the first question posed above.

**Theorem:** *Given the congruence*:

$$K^2 \equiv K \ (\text{mod } N) \qquad (6.19)$$

*where* $N = p_1^{\alpha_1} \ldots p_n^{\alpha_n}$ *is a factorization of integer N, then the solutions of the congruence are expressed in the form*:

$$K \equiv [k_1 \ (\text{mod } p_1^{\alpha_1}), \ldots, k_n \ (\text{mod } p_1^{\alpha_1})]$$

*where* $k_i \in \{0,1\}$ $(i = 1, \ldots, n)$ *are solutions of congruence*:

$$k_i^2 \equiv k_i \ (\text{mod } p_i^{\alpha_i}) \qquad (6.20)$$

*and the number of nonzero solutions is equal* $(2^n - 1)$.

Note that the number of solutions does not depend on the integers $(\alpha_1, \ldots, \alpha_n)$. Furthermore, we now assume that an integer can be written $N = p_1 \ldots p_n$. Moreover, we note there is a one-to-one mapping between a key (idempotent element) and a pair $(N_1, N_0)$. Hence,

$$K \leftrightarrow (N_0, N_1)$$

where $N_1 = p_{i_1} \ldots p_{i_s}$ is a product of all primes $p_{i_j}$ for which,

$$K \equiv 1 \ (\mathrm{mod} \ p_{i_j})$$

However, the number $N_0 = p_{i_{t+1}}, \ldots, p_{i_t}$ consists of all integers of the set $\{p_1, \ldots, p_n\}$ for which,

$$K \equiv 0 \ (\mathrm{mod} \ p_{i_j})$$

Of course, $N = N_0 N_1$.

Let us consider the conditions that have to be fulfilled to ensure that cryptographic transformation will be one-to-one while fixing the key. Suppose that we are given a cryptographic transformation $E_K(M) = MK$. Suppose a key[4] $K \in Z_N$ is chosen and written in the form of a vector:

$$K \equiv [\, k_1 (\mathrm{mod} \ p_1) \,, \ldots, \, k_n \ (\mathrm{mod} \ p_n) \,]$$

where $k_i \in \{0,1\}$ ; $i = 1, \ldots, n$. Then using the equations given above, we get:

$$MK \equiv M \ (\mathrm{mod} \ N_1) \quad \text{and} \quad MK \equiv 0 \ (\mathrm{mod} \ N_0) \tag{6.21}$$

These two congruences lead us to the following conclusions:

• Decipherment of a cryptogram $C = MK$ is performed according to the congruence

$$M \equiv D_K(C) \equiv C \ (\mathrm{mod} \ N_1) \tag{6.22}$$

• The cryptographic transformation $E_K(M) = MK$ is one-to-one if and only if a message $M$ (an integer) belongs to the set $Z_{N_1}$.

These observations are illustrated in the next example.

### Example

Suppose the cryptographic transformation is given for the key $K = [1 \ (\mathrm{mod} \ 3), 0 \ (\mathrm{mod} \ 5), 1 \ (\mathrm{mod} \ 7)] = 85 \ (\mathrm{mod} \ 105)$, with $N = 105$ and $N_1 = 21$, $N_0 = 5$. The transformation $E_K = KM$ (for $K = 85$) is one-to-one for all messages $M \in Z_{21}$. Let $M = 20$, then $C = 1700$. Decipherment of the cryptogram is simple:

$$M \equiv D_K(C) \equiv 1700 \equiv 20 \ (\mathrm{mod} \ 21) \qquad \square$$

Some properties of this cryptographic transformation are given below:

• If $M \in Z_{N_1}$ and $C = MK \ (K \in Z_N)$, then there is a one-to-one correspondence between a key $K$ and a pair $(N_0, N_1)$.
• Decipherment of the cryptogram can be carried out according to the following formula.

$$M = D_K(C) = C \ (\mathrm{mod} \ N_1)$$

• For messages $M_1, M_2 \in Z_{N_1}$ and $K = Z_N$, the following equations are satisfied:

$$
\begin{aligned}
E_K(M_1 + M_2) &= E_K(M_1) + E_K(M_2) & \text{if } M_1 + M_2 < N_1 & \tag{6.23}\\
E_K(M_1 M_2) &= E_K(M_1) \ E_K(M_2) & \text{if } M_1 \ M_2 < N_1 & \tag{6.24}\\
E_K(aM_1) &= a \ E_K(M_1) & a \in Z_{N_1} \text{ and } a \ M_1 < N_1 & \tag{6.25}
\end{aligned}
$$

---

4. Keys are idempotent elements.

$$E_K(a + M_1) = a + E_K(M_1) \qquad\qquad a \in Z_{N_1} \text{ and } a + M_1 < N_1 \quad \textbf{(6.26)}$$

$$E_K(M^i) = [E_K(M)]^i \qquad\qquad\qquad \text{if } M^i < N_1 \qquad\qquad \textbf{(6.27)}$$

$$E_K\left(\sum_{i=1}^{r} a_i M^i\right) = \sum_{i=1}^{r} a_i E_K(M^i) \qquad\qquad\qquad\qquad\qquad\qquad \textbf{(6.28)}$$

In order to ensure the correctness of computations, the following conditions have to be fulfilled:

1. Computational results carried out without the application of cryptography have to belong to the set $Z_{N_1}$.
2. Calculations can use only the four elementary arithmetic operations $(+,-,\times,\div)$, and, while processing, intermediate results should take the form of either integers or fractions.
3. If input data are fractions, cryptograms of numerator and denominator ought to be kept as separate integers. On the other hand, if the final result is a fraction, the cryptograms of both numerator and denominator are sent to the user.

*Example*

Assume we wish to calculate the result of:

$$y = \frac{4+M}{2M^2-4} \qquad \text{for } M = 3$$

Now, $y = 0.5$ for $M = 3$. Let $p_1 = 3$, $p_2 = 5$, $p_3 = 7$, and therefore $N = 105$. Suppose that the key $K = (1 \ (\text{mod } 3), 1 \ (\text{mod } 5), 0 \ (\text{mod } 7)) = 91$. In order to simplify calculations, we use the cryptogram in the form:

$$C = M' + M''K = 93 \quad \text{with } M' + M'' = M$$

So, we have:

$$E_K(y) = \frac{4 + E_K(M)}{2(E_K(M))^2 - 4} = \frac{97}{17294} = \frac{E_K(y_1)}{E_K(y_2)}$$

Deciphering both the numerator and the denominator, we obtain:

$$y_1 = D_K(97) = 97 \ (\text{mod } 15) = 7$$

and,

$$y_2 = D_K(17294) = 17294 \ (\text{mod } 15) = 14$$

Therefore, $y = \frac{1}{2}$. As any fraction may be presented in many different ways, special countermeasures should be undertaken while computing fractions. In our example, we have:

$$E_K(y) = \frac{97}{17294} = \frac{(97)\,2}{(17294)\,2} = \frac{194}{34588}$$

If we now decipher suitable cryptograms, we get:

$$194 \ (\text{mod } 15) = 14 \quad \text{and} \quad 34588 \ (\text{mod } 15) = 13$$

The final result is wrong. The mistake is due to the fact that the denominator multiplied by 2 exceeds the integer $N_1$.  $\square$

### 6.3.3 Assessment of the quality of ciphers preserving arithmetic operations

We divide the quality of ciphers into two cases:

1. protection against ciphertext only attack;
2. protection against known plaintext attack.

In the first case, an illegal user has access to cryptograms only. In the second case, however, an illegal user is assumed to have access to both plaintext (messages) and ciphertext (cryptograms). Also a factor which has an important influence on encipherment quality is the method of key selection. We can use two different methods. The first relies on the selection of a key among $(2^t-1)$ different nonzero idempotent elements which are solutions of the congruence $K^2 = K \pmod{N}$, with the integer $N$ fixed. In this case it can be discovered by an illegal user. The second method consists of a random selection of two integers $N_0$ and $N_1$ (of course $N_0$, $N_1 \leftrightarrow K$ and simultaneously these integers are limited by a suitable upper bound) so that messages and results will be less than $N_1$. In this case an illegal user does not know the numbers $N_0$ and $N_1$. In the subsequent discussion, we assume that the key is generated according to the second method.

If we suppose, for the time being, that messages (input data) appear with the known probability distribution then, for a fixed key, the following equation is true:

$$\mathbf{P}(M_i) = \mathbf{P}(C_i) ; \quad M_i \in \mathbf{M}, \ C_i \in \mathbf{C}, \ \text{and} \ C_i = M_i K$$

In other words, probability distributions of both messages and cryptograms are, for a fixed key, the same. Thus, after a large enough number of observations, an illegal user can determine the clear form of messages. Fortunately, an authorized user sends only a small number of messages and individual messages usually belong to sets of different probability distributions. Therefore, it forces an illegal user to calculate a key on the basis of several cryptograms. Suppose an illegal user has access to the following cryptograms:

$$C_1 = M_1 K = p_1^{\alpha_{11}} \ \ldots \ p_u^{\alpha_{u1}} \leftrightarrow \{p_1^{\alpha_{11}}, \ldots, p_u^{\alpha_{u1}}\} = \mathbf{R}_1$$
$$C_2 = M_2 K = p_1^{\alpha_{12}} \ \ldots \ p_u^{\alpha_{u2}} \leftrightarrow \{p_1^{\alpha_{12}}, \ldots, p_u^{\alpha_{u2}}\} = \mathbf{R}_2$$
$$\vdots$$
$$C_l = M_l K = p_1^{\alpha_{1l}} \ \ldots \ p_u^{\alpha_{ul}} \leftrightarrow \{p_1^{\alpha_{1l}}, \ldots, p_u^{\alpha_{ul}}\} = \mathbf{R}_l$$

where $p_1, \ldots, p_u$ are primes and $\alpha \geq 0$ $(i = 1, \ldots, u; \ j = 1, \ldots, l)$. Then, we can determine the set $\mathbf{R} = \mathbf{R}_1 \cap \mathbf{R}_2 \cap \ldots \cap \mathbf{R}_l$. The set $\mathbf{R}$ gives the exact factorization of the key used if and only if there are at least two messages (integers) whose values are relatively prime.

This pessimistic conclusion is no longer true when we apply a different method of encipherment partially illustrated in the example given above. Namely, any message $M$ can be presented as:

$$M = (m_0 + m_1 + \ldots + m_v) ; \quad v = 0, 1, \ldots, M-1 \tag{6.29}$$

For any sum of the form (6.29), we define the polynomial:

$$p(M,K) = m_0 + m_1 K + \ldots + m_v K^v \qquad (6.30)$$

It is easy to see that $p(M,K)$, for fixed key generates a cryptogram of $M$, such as:

$$D_K(E_{K(M)}) = D_K(p(M,K)) = p(M,K) \bmod N_1 = M \qquad (6.31)$$

Thus, for a message $M$, we can define a cryptogram in the form:

$$c = E_K(M) = m_0 + m_1 K + \ldots + m_v K^v \; ; \quad \text{where } M = \sum_{i=0}^{v} m_i \qquad (6.32)$$

If the cryptosystem generating ciphertext according to (6.32) is subject to ciphertext only attack, then breaking the system is more difficult, as the system can yield different cryptograms for the same message. In this case, statistical analysis of cryptograms does not lead to a successful attack.

Now consider a known plaintext attack. In this case, a cryptanalyst knows a pair $(M,C)$, where:

$$M = m_0 + m_1 + \ldots + m_v$$
$$C = m_0 + m_1 K + \ldots + m_v K_v$$

Thus a cryptanalyst can calculate:

$$C - M = M_1(K-1) + \ldots + M_v(K^v - 1)$$

The last equation shows that the number $K-1$ divides an integer $C-M$. If our cryptanalyst knows $r$ different pairs (message $M_i$, cryptogram $C_i$; $i = 1, \ldots, r$), he/she can compute $gcd(C_1-M_1, \ldots, C_r-M_r)$, where $gcd$ stands for the *greatest common divisor*. This integer is exactly equal to $(K-1)$ if there are two relatively prime integers among $C_i-M_i$; $i = 1, \ldots, r$.

## 6.4 Privacy homomorphisms

In the previous section we observed that the class of cryptographic transformations preserving arithmetic operations is rather small, and thus its practical usage is limited. If we reject condition (6.10) and either (6.9) or (6.11), then we are dealing with a broader class of possible cryptographic transformations which will be called *privacy homomorphisms*.

The class of privacy homomorphisms was first defined by Rivest, Adleman, and Dertouzos [RIAD78] as the quadruple:

$$(E_K, D_K, OP, OP^*) \qquad (6.33)$$

such that:

$$D_K[OP^*(E_K(M_1), \ldots, E_K(M_r))] = OP(M_1, \ldots, M_r) \qquad (6.34)$$

for each cryptographic key $K \in \mathbf{K}$ and any sequence of $M_1, \ldots, M_r$ in the message space $\mathbf{M}$. $OP$ and $OP^*$ are operations that are permissible in the message and cryptogram spaces, respectively. Notice that the definition says that we get the same result either applying the operation $OP^*$ in the cryptogram space $\mathbf{C}$, or using the operation $OP$ in the message space $\mathbf{M}$ (see Figure 6.5).

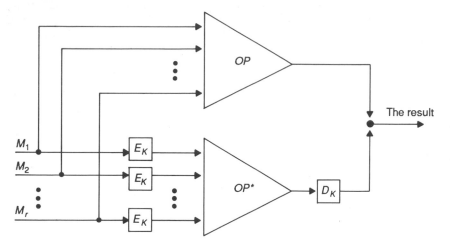

**Figure 6.5** Two ways of getting the result, the first using *OP* in the message space and the second using $OP^*$ in the cryptogram space

*Example*

Consider the cryptographic transformation for which the condition (6.9) is satisfied. If we use $OP = OP^*$ and,

$$OP(M_1, \dots, M_r) = M_1 + \dots + M_r$$

then we get privacy homomorphisms which preserve addition. Clearly, after we have swapped multiplication for addition, we get the definition of privacy homomorphisms that preserve multiplication.    □

## 6.4.1 Homomorphisms based on the RSA system

Recall that the enciphering transformation in the RSA system is $E_K = M^K$ (mod $N$), where $K$ is the enciphering key, $M$ is the message, and the modulus $N = p \cdot q$ ($p, q$ are primes). Notice that:

$$E_K(M_1 \cdot M_2) = (M_1 \cdot M_2)^K = M_1^K \cdot M_2^K = E_K(M_1) \cdot E_K(M_2) \qquad (6.35)$$

Thus, the enciphering transformation of the RSA system has the multiplication property. In other words, it is possible to define the multiplicative homomorphism [RIAD78] ($E_K$, $D_K$, $OP$, $OP^*$) for which $E_K$, $D_K$ are cryptographic transformations defined in the RSA system and $OP = OP^*$ while:

$$OP(M_1, \dots, M_r) = M_1 \dots M_r \qquad (6.36)$$

Of course the product $M_1 \dots M_r$ must be less than $N$. This privacy homomorphism is as secure as the RSA system.

*Example*

Let $r = 3$ and each integer be less than or equal to 10. The RSA system must be defined for $N > 1000$. Assume $N = 1147$ ($p = 31$, $q = 37$), the enciphering key $K = 131$ (the deciphering key $k = 11$) and $M_1 = 7$, $M_2 = 9$, $M_3 = 6$. So, instead of calculating the product $M = M_1 M_2 M_3 = 378$ in the message space, we can carry out multiplications in the cryptogram space as follows:

$$C_1 = E_K(M_1=7) = 7^{131} = 268$$
$$C_2 = E_K(M_2=9) = 9^{131} = 293$$
$$C_3 = E_K(M_3=6) = 6^{131} = 956$$
$$C = C_1 C_2 C_3 \ (\text{mod } N) = 88 \ (\text{mod } 1147)$$

We obtain the product $M$ as:

$$M = D_K(C) = 88^{11} = 378 \ (\text{mod } 1147) \qquad \square$$

## 6.4.2 Homomorphisms based on exponential function

Suppose primes $p$ and $q$ define the arithmetic modulo $N = pq$ where one prime, say $p$, is selected such that:

$$p - 1 = \prod_{i=1}^{n} p_i^{e_i} \qquad (6.37)$$

and all $p_i \leq B$ where $B$ is a small integer. Let $g$ be a generator of GF($p$), then the encryption transformation is:

$$E_K(M) = g^M \ (\text{mod } N) \qquad (6.38)$$

So, the decryption transformation is:

$$D_K(C) = \log_g C \ (\text{mod } p) \qquad (6.39)$$

As $p$ satifies (6.37), calculations of the logarithm are considerably simplified and run in time $O(B^{\frac{1}{2}})$. Notice that:

$$E_K(M_1 + M_2) = g^{M_1+M_2} = g^{M_1} \cdot g^{M_2} = E_K(M_1) \cdot E_K(M_2) \qquad (6.40)$$

Therefore, the homomorphisms are defined for $OP(M_1, \ldots, M_r) = M_1 + \ldots + M_r$ and $OP^*(M_1, \ldots, M_r) = M_1 \ldots M_r$.

*Example*

Let $p = 31$ $(p-1 = 2\cdot3\cdot5)$, $q = 37$ (so $N = 1147$), a generator $g = 17$, and $(M_1, M_2) = (12,15)$. Calculations in the cryptogram space are as follows:

$$C_1 = E_K(M_1) = 17^{12} = 1025 \ (\text{mod } 1147)$$
$$C_2 = E_K(M_2) = 17^{15} = 495 \ (\text{mod } 1147)$$
$$OP^*(C_1, C_2) = C_1 C_2 = 401 \ (\text{mod } N)$$

The result is deciphered, that is, the logarithm is calculated, in the field GF(31), so:

$$D_K(401) = \log_g 401 = \log_{17} 29 \ (\text{mod } 31)$$

Applying the Silver-Pohlig-Hellman algorithm given in section 2.3.1, we find the message $M = [-1 \ (\text{mod } 2), 0 \ (\text{mod } 3), 2 \ (\text{mod } 5)] = 27$. $\qquad \square$

Brickell and Yacobi [BRYA87] have proved that the homomorphisms in question are insecure. Before we start describing their attack, we note that $p$ is a proper divisor of,

$$gcd(a^{B!^e}-1, N) \tag{6.41}$$

where $e \geq \max\{e_i; i = 1, \ldots, n\}$ and an integer $a$ is a generator of GF($p$). This holds for any generator $a \in$ GF($p$) as:

$$a^{p-1} = 1 \pmod{p} \implies a^{\prod_{i=1}^{n} p_i^{e_i}} = 1 \pmod{p}$$

It is obvious that $\prod_{i=1}^{n} p_i^{e_i}$ divides $B!^e$ so:

$$a^{B!^e} = a^{\prod_{i=1}^{n} p_i^{e_i}} = 1 \pmod{p}$$

The last congruence says that, for any generator $a$ of GF($p$), $a^{B!^e}-1$ is multiple of $p$. Although cryptanalysts know neither $B$ nor $e$, they can select them at random ($B$ is small). If the *gcd* given by (6.41) is equal to 1 or $N$, the next $B$ is selected until the *gcd* of (6.41) is equal to $p$. The expected running time of the attack is O($eB$ log$B$ log$N$).

*Example*

The cryptanalysis of the homomorphism taken from the previous example is as follows. Knowing $N = 1147$, we pick randomly $a = 237$ while choices for $B$ will be selected one by one from the set $\{3,4,5,\ldots\}$. It is easy to see that, given $B$, $e$ must belong to the set $\{1,2,\ldots,\lfloor\log_2 B\rfloor\}$. Results of calculations are presented below.

| Value B | Value e | $\alpha = B!^e$ | $\beta = a^\alpha - 1$ | $gcd(\beta, N)$ |
|---------|---------|-----------------|------------------------|-----------------|
| 3 | 1 | 6 | 840 | 1 |
| 4 | 1 | 24 | 379 | 1 |
| 4 | 2 | 576 | 592 | 1 |
| 5 | 1 | 120 | 62 | 31 |

$\square$

## 6.4.3 R-additive homomorphisms

Homomorphisms for which $OP = OP^*$ and $OP(M_1,\ldots,M_R) = (M_1 + \ldots + M_R)$ are called R-additive. Assume that $\mathbf{M} = \{0,1,\ldots,\alpha\}$ and,

$$E_K : \mathbf{M}^n \to \mathbf{Z}^+$$

where $\mathbf{Z}^+$ is the set of all positive integers. Therefore, all intermediate results will be less than or equal to $\alpha R$. To describe R-additive homomorphisms, the following elements are defined:

- A prime $p$ ($p > \alpha R$). It can be the first integer which satisfies the inequality — it can be public.
- An $n \times n$ matrix $K$ all elements of which are chosen randomly. It is nonsingular over GF($p$) and kept secret.
- A prime $q$ ($q > Rp$) — it can be public.
- An integer $z$ which is randomly selected in the interval ($Rpq^{n-1}$, $2Rpq^{n-1}$) — it is secret.

- An integer $y$ for which $gcd(y, z) = 1$ — it is secret.

The enciphering process $E_K$ runs in the several following steps:

- A message $M = (m_1, \ldots, m_n)$, where each component $m_i \in \mathbf{M} = \{0,1,2,\ldots,\alpha\}$, is multiplied by the matrix $K$, so:

$$S = (s_1, \ldots, s_n) = K \times M \pmod{p} \qquad (6.42)$$

- Having the vector $S$, the integer $t$ is calculated as:

$$t = \sum_{i=1}^{n} s_i\, q^{i-1} \qquad (6.43)$$

- The cryptogram $C = E_K(M) = t\,y \pmod{z}$.

The deciphering process is the repetition of inverse operations in the reverse order. So, given the cryptogram $C$, the integer $t$ is calculated, that is, $t = Cy^{-1} \pmod{z}$. Having the base $q$, $t$ is decomposed into the vector $S = (s_1, \ldots, s_n)$. Finally, the message is recreated since $M = K^{-1} \times S \pmod{p}$.

To prove that the homomorphisms are additive, it is sufficient to show that:

$$E_K(M_1) + \ldots + E_K(M_R) = E_K(M_1 + \ldots + M_R) \qquad (6.44)$$

Assume that all messages $M_i = (m_{i,1}, \ldots, m_{i,n})$; $i = 1, \ldots, R$, are enciphered into cryptograms $C_i$ while $S_i = (s_{i,1}, \ldots, s_{i,R})$, and $t_i$ are obtained while enciphering. Elements $p, q, y, z$, and the matrix $K$ are fixed.

Starting with $C = C_1 + \ldots + C_R$, we get that $t = Cy^{-1} = t_1 + \ldots + t_R \pmod{p}$. Regarding (6.43), the last congruence can be rewritten as:

$$\sum_{j=1}^{R} t_j = \sum_{j=1}^{R} \sum_{i=1}^{n} s_{j,i} q^{i-1} = \sum_{i=1}^{n} \sum_{j=1}^{R} s_{j,i} q^{i-1}$$

As $\sum_{j=1}^{R} s_{j,i} < q$ for $i = 1, \ldots, n$, $\sum_{j=1}^{R} t_j < z$ and the decomposition of $t$ produces the values $\sum_{j=1}^{R} s_{j,i}$.

Let $S = (\sum_{j=1}^{R} s_{j,1}, \ldots, \sum_{j=1}^{R} s_{j,n})$, then $K^{-1} \times S = M_1 + \ldots + M_R \pmod{p}$. As $p > R\alpha$, we have proved the homomorphisms are additive.

*Example*

Construct a homomorphism for $R = 3$, $n = 2$, and $\mathbf{M} = \{1,2,3,4,5\}$. Our design begins with selecting $p = 17$ as $p > R\alpha = 15$. Next, a non-singular matrix $K$ over GF(17) is chosen and,

$$K = \begin{bmatrix} 8 & 3 \\ 11 & 1 \end{bmatrix} \quad \text{while} \quad K^{-1} = \begin{bmatrix} 2 & 11 \\ 12 & 16 \end{bmatrix}$$

Also, we choose the last three integers, namely the prime $q = 53$ ($q > Rp = 51$), $z = 3134$ ($z \in [Rpq, \ 2Rpq] = [2703, 5406]$), and $y = 1131$ where $gcd(z, y) = 1$. Notice that

$y^{-1} = 2771$ in the arithmetic modulo $z$.

    Let $M_1 = (3,5)$, $M_2 = (4,3)$, and $M_3 = (5,1)$. The cryptogram $C_1$ can be computed in three steps as follows:

$$S_1 = (s_{11}, s_{12}) = K \times M_1 = \begin{bmatrix} 8 & 3 \\ 11 & 1 \end{bmatrix} \begin{bmatrix} 3 \\ 5 \end{bmatrix} = [5,4] \ (\text{mod } 17)$$
$$t_1 = s_{11} + s_{12}q = 217$$
$$C_1 = t_1 \cdot y \ (\text{mod } z) = 975 \ (\text{mod } 3134)$$

Repeating the enciphering process twice, we get:

$$S_2 = (s_{21}, s_{22}) = K \cdot M_2 = [7,13] \ (\text{mod } 17),$$
$$t_2 = s_{21} + s_{22} \, q = 696,$$
$$C_2 = t_2 \cdot y \ (\text{mod } z) = 542 \ (\text{mod } 3134)$$

and,

$$S_3 = (s_{31}, s_{32}) = K \cdot M_3 = [9,5] \ (\text{mod } 17)$$
$$t_3 = s_{31} + s_{32}q = 274$$
$$C_3 = t_3 \cdot y \ (\text{mod } z) = 2762 \ (\text{mod } 3134)$$

The sum of cryptograms is equal to:

$$C = C_1 + C_2 + C_3 = 4279$$

To decrypt the cryptogram $C$, we proceed as follows:

$$t = Cy^{-1} \ (\text{mod } z) = 4279 \cdot 2771 = 1187 \ (\text{mod } 3134)$$
$$t = 1187 \rightarrow S = (s_1, s_2) = (21, 22) \text{ as } t = s_1 + s_2 q = 21 + 22 \cdot 53$$
$$M = K^{-1} \times S = [12, 9] \ (\text{mod } 17) \qquad \qquad \square$$

    Brickell and Yacobi [BRYA87] stated that as the homomorphisms apply modular multiplication, the cryptosystem in question can be broken (like the MII system) using the Lenstra-Lenstra-Lovasz algorithm [LELE82]. Although their attack works well for small $n$, it is inefficient for larger $n$, say $n > 30$.

## 6.5 Summary

This chapter has been devoted to protection of databases using cryptography. As has been shown, the cryptography gives a wide range of security measures which can be applied in database systems. Since the structure of database systems is very rich in semantic interconnections, any protection mechanism should be carefully designed.

    In order to get good cryptographic protection using elementary cryptographic transformations which, considered separately, are insecure, we should combine them. Having introduced the multilevel database organization, we can apply the elementary cryptographic transformations between two neighboring levels [GUKO76]. However, taking into account the point of view of a DB administrator, we have distinguished five different levels of DB organization, namely: the level of individual users (user work spaces), the level of user classes, the level of logical DB, the level of physical DB, and the level of DB duplicate.

Up till now, there has been consistency between DB organization levels and cryptographic protection levels. In general, organization levels can be divided into several levels of cryptographic protection levels. The number of cryptographic levels depends upon the required quality of cryptographic protection. Of course, the larger the number of levels, the better the quality that can be obtained. This is a variation of the classic Shannon's idea of designing a secure cryptosystem having two insecure cryptographic transformations (substitution and transposition) [SHAN49].

The second part of this chapter has been devoted to cryptographic transformations which preserve elementary arithmetic operations, namely: addition and multiplication. The observations given in the chapter can be generalized by considering other operations which are required to be preserved. It is clear that introducing any new operation imposes additional limitations on the set of allowable cryptographic transformations. For example, if you want to design a cryptographic transformation which preserves relations $=, <, >$, then there is not any 'good' transformation [DENN82].

When a cryptographic transformation preserves only the arithmetic operation, either multiplication or addition, we deal with privacy homomorphisms. The third part of Chapter 6 examines three different classes of privacy homomorphisms [RIAD78]. The first class preserves multiplication and it is based on the RSA system. The second class of homomorphisms is designed using the exponential function. In this case, addition in the message space is substituted by multiplication in the cryptogram space. Unfortunately, these privacy homomorphisms are insecure as they are subject to the Brickell-Yacobi attack [BRYA87]. The third class preserves addition. Again Brickell and Yacobi [BRYA87] launched an attack which is successful for small parameter $n$ only.

Works on the database protection are dispersed all over both the cryptographic and the database literature. The first book which partially concerns database protection was written by Hoffman in 1973 [HOFF73]. However, the multilevel database organization with application to cryptography has been introduced by Gudes et al. in 1976 [GUKO76]. Dorothy Denning has devoted a relatively large portion of her book [DENN82] to protection of statistical databases. Also Davies and Price in their book [DAPR84] have considered the subject of database security.

## EXERCISES

6. 1    The logical record, which is a part of a bank database, has the following form:

| MEMBER # | SURNAME | BALANCE |
|---|---|---|
| 11 | Green | 31 555 |
| 7 | Smith | 9 878 |
| 24 | White | 11 145 |
| 30 | Grey | 245 |

Apply a simple substitution of data items to protect data of the field BALANCE. Consider two cases:

(a)    when only the field BALANCE is enciphered;
(b)    when all fields of the logical record are enciphered.

6. 2   Consider the same logical record as in problem 6.1, and think of a cryptographic transformation which can be used to encipher data items of all fields. What shape will the logical record be after applying such a transformation (this transformation should be substitution of data items)?

6. 3   Consider the transposition of data items and suppose that a logical record consists of $n$ physical records which are defined for $l$ fields. Discuss the relation between the parameters of logical record and the form of cryptographic transformation used.

6. 4   Consider the DES algorithm. Is it possible to apply the algorithm to transposition of data items? Justify your answer.

6. 5   Consider the logical record of the following form:

| $F_1$ | $F_2$ |
|-------|-------|
| $d_{11}$ | $d_{12}$ |
| $d_{21}$ | $d_{22}$ |
| $d_{31}$ | $d_{32}$ |

Let the cryptographic transformation be defined as:

$$E_K(d_{i1}, d_{i2}) = (d'_{i1}, d'_{i2})$$

where $i = 1,2,3$ and $d'_{i1} \in F'_1$, $d'_{i2} \in F'_2$. Name the cryptographic transformation used.

6. 6   Consider a simple database system. Try to apply all cryptographic transformations (which preserve database structure) in order to protect your database. Estimate the quality of the cryptographic protection.

6. 7   Consider the algebraic ring $Z_{30}$. Calculate all idempotent elements of the ring.

6. 8   Using basic idempotent elements, find a procedure which gives the set of idempotent elements. Apply your procedure to compute idempotent elements of the ring $Z_{210}$.

6. 9   Let the ring $Z_N$ be defined by $N = 385$. Assuming that results of calculations are less than 35, determine the set of cryptographic keys for cryptographic transformation which preserve arithmetic operations.

6. 10  Consider three variations of the enciphering process defined over the ring $Z_N$:

(a)  $E_K(M) = K M$;
(b)  $E_K(M) = K M_1 + M_2$, where $M_1 + M_2 = M$;
(c)  $E_K(M) = K^2 M_1 + K M_2 + M_3$, where $M_1 + M_2 + M_3$.

Are the variations equivalent in the sense that they use the same deciphering process?

6. 11  Design a privacy homomorphism using the RSA system, which allows four integers of the set $\{0,1,...,9\}$ to be enciphered while multiplying them. Assume $M_1 = 7$, $M_2 = 8$, $M_3 = 9$, $M_4 = 6$, and use the correct value of the modulus $N$ from the set $\{6557, 7031\}$. Let the enciphering key be 2137.

6. 12  Discuss the dependence between the modulus $N$ and the maximum value of addition results for privacy homomorphisms based on the exponential function.

6. 13  Consider the privacy homomorphism determined for $p = 43$, $q = 59$, and $g = 5$ (see

formula 6.38). Show the correct decryption transformation from two possible ones given below:

$$D_K(M) = \log_g C \ (\text{mod } p)$$
$$D_K(M) = \log_g C \ (\text{mod } q)$$

and justify your answer. Find also cryptograms for two messages $M_1 = 31$, $M_2 = 10$, and for their sum. Verify if $E_K(M_1 + M_2) = E_K(M_1) E_K(M_2) \ (\text{mod } N)$.

6. 14 Consider the homomorphism of the previous problem. Decrypt the following cryptograms $C_1 \doteq 1301$ and $C_2 = 2110$. Of course $p = 43$, $q = 59$, $g = 5$ ($N = 2537$).

6. 15 Suppose the homomorphism based on exponential function is defined for $p = 43$, $q = 59$ and $g = 23$ ($N = 2537$). Is the homomorphism determined correctly? Try to decrypt two cryptograms: $C_1 = 183$ and $C_2 = 656$.

6. 16 Cryptanalyse the homomorphism using the Brickell-Yacobi attack. Suppose the homomorphism is defined for $N = 47897$ and a generator $a$ is randomly picked equal to 5.

6. 17 Design an additive homomorphism for $R = 2$, $n = 3$, $\mathbf{M} = \{1,2,3,4,5\}$. Choose $p$, $q$, $z$ as small as possible while the matrix $K$ is of the following form:

$$\begin{bmatrix} 1 & 2 & 3 \\ 0 & 1 & 2 \\ 4 & 8 & 3 \end{bmatrix}$$

Find cryptograms for $M_1 = (4,3,5)$ and $M_2 = (2,1,5)$ for $y = 47$.

## SOLUTIONS

6. 1 *Case I.* As the field BALANCE has numerical data items, we assume that our substitution is defined as follows:

$$E_K(d) = d + K \ (\text{mod } N)$$

where d, K, N stand for a clear data item, a key, and an integer (which has to be larger then the greatest data item in BALANCE), respectively. Therefore, the logical record takes on the form for $K = 12358$ and $N = 32100$:

| MEMBER # | SURNAME | BALANCE |
|----------|---------|---------|
| 11 | Green | 11 793 |
| 7 | Smith | 22 236 |
| 24 | White | 23 503 |
| 30 | Grey | 12 603 |

*Case II.* Of course between data items MEMBER # and SURNAME, there is one-to-one correspondence so we must encipher both fields simultaneously. Suppose that data items of MEMBER # are to be enciphered according to:

$$E_K(d) = K_1 d + K_2 \ (\text{mod } p)$$

where the key $K = (K_1, K_2)$ and the prime $p = 31$. However, the field SURNAME is enciphered using the following steps:

- Transforming names into numerical data items. Let f(Green) $\equiv$ 00, f(Smith) $\equiv$ 01, f(White) $\equiv$ 10, f(Grey) $\equiv$ 11.
- Applying the cryptographic transformation,

$$E_K(d) = d \oplus K$$

where the key $K \in \{00, 01, 10, 11\}$ and $\oplus$ means the mod-2 sum.
- Transforming numerical data back to names using the transformation $f$.

After having applied cryptographic transformations to MEMBER # (the key $K = (K_1, K_2) = (3,7)$ ), SURNAME (the key $K = 10$ ), and BALANCE (see Case I), we get our logical record in the following form:

| MEMBER # | SURNAME | BALANCE |
|----------|---------|---------|
| 9        | White   | 11 793  |
| 28       | Grey    | 22 236  |
| 17       | Green   | 23 503  |
| 4        | Smith   | 12 603  |

6. 2   As two fields are numerical and one contains names, we must first standardize the form of data items. Of course, there is the standard code ASCII which allows us to present both letters and numbers in the binary form. Having presented all data in a uniform way (lengths of all data are assumed to be the same), we can consider a simple cryptographic transformation of the form:

$$E_K(d) = d \oplus K$$

where $d$ is a uniform clear data item and $K$ stands for the key.

6. 3   Taking into account all the assumptions, we can see each physical record as an ordered sequence of $l$ data items. The cryptographic transformation is to change the natural order according to the cryptographic key $K_i$ ($i = 1, \ldots, n$) which is being selected independently for any physical record. Therefore, the cryptographic transformation $E_{K_i}$ ( $E_{K_i} : Z_l \rightarrow Z_l$, where $Z_l = \{1, \ldots, l\}$ ) points out a permutation of the set $Z_l$ for any $i = 1, \ldots, n$.

Summing up, we can state that:

- the number of data items in physical record determines the set $Z_l$ over which $E_{K_i}$ is defined ($i = 1, \ldots, n$);
- the number $n$ (the number of physical records in a logical record) gives the number of different cryptographic keys needed (one key per physical record).

6. 4   If a physical record consists of $l$ data items, then the transposition is defined as $E_K$: $Z_l \rightarrow Z_l$ (a cryptographic key is fixed) and the $i$th data item of the original physical record has position $E_K(i)$ in the physical record after enciphering.

As is known, the DES algorithm transforms 64-bit messages into 64-bit cryptograms, therefore:

$$DES : \{0,1\}^{64} \rightarrow \{0,1\}^{64}$$

and the message space comprises $2^{64}$ different messages. Hence, the physical record in question must have had $2^{64}$ different data items — it is impossible to have such a large record!

Another way to describe the transposition is by the application of the common mathematical notation for permutations. For instance, if we have four elements $\{1,2,3,4\}$ and their permutation $pr \equiv (3,1,4,2)$ means that:

$$pr\,(1) = 3, \quad pr\,(2) = 1, \quad pr\,(3) = 4, \quad pr\,(4) = 2$$

where $pr$: $\{1,2,3,4\} \rightarrow \{1,2,3,4\}$, so, any permutation of four elements may be presented as a sequence of 8 bits (each element from the set of four elements can be encoded using 2 bits). Similar, any permutation of eight elements may be represented as a sequence of 24 bits (each element can be encoded using 3 bits). Finally, we can summarize:

- A single cryptogram of DES can describe 64 permutations of two elements (each permutation needs one bit, that is, '0' if the order of elements is not changed and '1' otherwise).
- A single cryptogram of DES can represent 8 permutations of four elements (each permutation needs 8 bits).
- A single cryptogram of DES can define 3 permutations of eight elements (each permutation applies 21 bits assuming that the first element of the sequence, which presents the permutation, is missing).
- A single cryptogram of DES can determine a single permutation of sixteen elements.

6. 5   The first cryptographic transformation is reduction of data items as the cryptogram $c_i = E_K\,(d_{i1}, d_{i2})$; $i = 1,2,3$, and $(d_{i1}, d_{i2})$ means the concatenation of two data items. The second transformation divides data items into two parts and, of course, this transformation does not engage any cryptographic key but it can be considered as a preliminary step for extension of data items.

6. 6   This is left as a project.

6. 7   Recall that an idempotent element $e$ of $Z_{30}$ has the property that $e^2 = e$ (mod 30). The simplest way of solving is to check this property for all integers in the ring. The set of all non-zero idempotent elements is as follows: $\{1,6,10,15,16,21,25\}$.

6. 8   As the factorization of 210 gives the set of primes $\{2,3,5,7\}$, the ring $Z_{210}$ can be seen as the vector space $Z_2 \oplus Z_3 \oplus Z_5 \oplus Z_7$. So, every integer $a \in Z_{210}$ may be presented as a vector $[a$ (mod 2), $a$ (mod 3), $a$ (mod 5), $a$ (mod 7)$]$. Of course, among the idempotent elements, we can distinguish the set of basic idempotent elements $\{e_1, e_2, e_3, e_4\} = \{ [1,0,0,0], [0,1,0,0], [0,0,1,0], [0,0,0,1] \}$. Clearly, $e_1 = 105$, $e_2 = 70$, $e_3 = 126$, $e_4 = 120$. Once the basic idempotent elements have been determined, we can use them to find all the remaining ones. Thus, we get:

$$[1,0,0,0] = e_1 = 105 \text{ (mod 210)}$$
$$[0,1,0,0] = e_2 = 70 \text{ (mod 210)}$$
$$[1,1,0,0] = e_1 + e_2 = 175 \text{ (mod 210)}$$
$$[0,0,1,0] = e_3 = 126 \text{ (mod 210)}$$

$$[1,0,1,0] = e_1 + e_3 = 21 \pmod{210}$$
$$[0,1,1,0] = e_2 + e_3 = 196 \pmod{210}$$
$$[1,1,1,0] = e_1 + e_2 + e_3 = 91 \pmod{210}$$
$$[0,0,0,1] = e_4 = 120 \pmod{210}$$
$$[1,0,0,1] = e_1 + e_4 = 15 \pmod{210}$$
$$[0,1,0,1] = e_2 + e_4 = 190 \pmod{210}$$
$$[1,1,0,1] = e_1 + e_2 + e_4 = 85 \pmod{210}$$
$$[0,0,1,1] = e_3 + e_4 = 36 \pmod{210}$$
$$[1,0,1,1] = e_1 + e_3 + e_4 = 141 \pmod{210}$$
$$[0,1,1,1] = e_2 + e_3 + e_4 = 106 \pmod{210}$$
$$[1,1,1,1] = e_1 + e_2 + e_3 + e_4 = 1 \pmod{210}$$

The procedure is as follows:

- Calculate the basic idempotent elements. In general, if we deal with $Z_N$, where $N = p_1 \cdot p_2 \ldots p_n$ , and $p_i$ are primes for $i = 1, \ldots, n$, then $e_i$ must be the multiplication of $p_1, \ldots, p_{i-1}, p_{i+1}, \ldots, p_n$ so $e_i = \alpha \, p_1 \cdot p_{i-1} \cdots p_n$.
- Any idempotent element can be created as a sum of a subset of the basic idempotent elements. By considering all subsets, we get the set of all idempotent elements (it contains $2^n - 1$ different elements).

6. 9   Basic idempotent elements are:

$$e_1 = [\, 1 \bmod 5 \,, 0 \,, 0 \,] = 231$$
$$e_2 = [\, 0 \,, 1 \bmod 7 \,, 0 \,] = 330$$
$$e_3 = [\, 0 \,, 0 \,, 1 \bmod 11 \,] = 210$$

As the results of the calculations are to be less than 35, the set of cryptographic keys (set of idempotent elements) has the form:

$$\{\, e_1 + e_2, \; e_1 + e_3, \; e_2 + e_3, \; e_1 + e_2 + e_3 \,\} = \{\, 176, \; 56, \; 155 \,, 1 \,\}$$

6. 10  Each key $K$ identifies a unique integer $N_1$ for which $K \pmod{N_1} = 1$. So the first version allows us to get back the clear message by applying:

$$K\,M \, (\bmod\, N_1 \,) = M$$

The second version obtains the plaintext by applying:

$$K\,M_1 + M_2 = M_1 + M_2 = M \, (\bmod\, N_1\,)$$

as $K\,M_1 = M_1 \, (\bmod\, N_1\,)$, and the third by applying:

$$K^2\,M_1 + K\,M_1 + M_3 = K\,M_1 + K\,M_2 + M_3$$
$$= K\,(M_1 + M_2) + M_3 = M\,(\bmod\, N_1)$$

The final conclusion is that all versions are equivalent.

6. 11  As the results are less than or equal to $9^4 = 6561$, we use $N = 7031$ ($p = 79$, $q = 89$). Therefore, $\gamma(N) = 3432$ and the deciphering key is $k = 697$ for $K = 2137$. Now, we can calculate the cryptograms:

$$C_1 = E_K(M_1) = 7^{2137} = 2139 \pmod{7031}$$
$$C_2 = E_K(M_2) = 8^{2137} = 3538 \pmod{7031}$$

$$C_3 = E_K(M_3) = 9^{2137} = 1585 \pmod{7031}$$
$$C_4 = E_K(M_4) = 6^{2137} = 5030 \pmod{7031}$$

Finally, $C = C_1 C_2 C_3 C_4 = 4175 \pmod{7031}$, and $M = D_K(C) = 4175^{697} = 3024 \pmod{7031}$. It is easy to check that $C$ has generated the proper result of multiplication $7 \cdot 8 \cdot 9 \cdot 6$.

6. 12 Consider formula (6.39). Now all results must be less than the prime $p$. However, logarithms are unique if they belong to the set $\{0, 1, 2, \ldots, p-2\}$. Thus the integer $p-1$ must be excluded as $g^{p-1} = 1 \pmod{p}$ and it is equivalent to 0.

6. 13 As $p-1 = 42 = 2 \cdot 3 \cdot 7$ but $q-1 = 58 = 2 \cdot 29$ (29 is prime), the decryption must be done modulo $p$. Using $p$, the deciphering process is more efficient as all prime factors of $p$ are small. Now $N = 2537$ and:

$$C_1 = E_K(M_1) = 5^{31} = 320 \pmod{2537}$$
$$C_2 = E_K(M_2) = 5^{10} = 712 \pmod{2537}$$
$$C = E_K(M_1 + M_2) = 5^{41} = 2047 \pmod{2537}$$

On the other hand, the cryptogram $C = C_1 C_2 = 2047 \pmod{2537}$.

6. 14 To obtain the message, we solve the following congruence:

$$M_1 = \log_5 1301 \pmod{43} \to M_1 = \log_5 11 \pmod{43}$$

As $p-1 = 2 \cdot 3 \cdot 7$, we consider three cases (we use the notation of section 2.3.1). Let $p_1 = 2$, then:

$$h_1 = g^{(p-1)/p_1} = 5^{21} = 42 \pmod{43}$$

so $h_1^0 = 1$, $h_1^1 = -1$, $h_1^2 = 1$. As $y_1 = 11^{21} = 1 \pmod{43}$ and $h_1^0 = y_1$, the first component of the message is $b_{10} = 0$.
Let $p_2 = 3$, then:

$$h_2 = g^{(p-1)/p_2} = 5^{14} = 36 \pmod{43}$$

so $h_2^0 = 1$, $h_2^1 = 36$, $h_2^2 = 6$, $h_2^3 = 1$. As $y_2 = 11^{14} = 1 \pmod{43}$ and $h_2^0 = y_2$, the second component of the message is $b_{20} = 0$.
Let $p_3 = 7$, then:

$$h_3 = g^{(p-1)/p_3} = 5^6 = 16 \pmod{43}$$

so $h_3^0 = 1$, $h_3^1 = 16$, $h_3^2 = 41$, $h_3^3 = 11$, $h_3^4 = 4$, $h_3^5 = 21$, $h_3^6 = 35$, $h_3^7 = 1$. As $y_3 = 11^6 = 4 \pmod{43}$ and $h_3^4 = y_3$, the third component of the message is $b_{30} = 4$. Having obtained all the components, we are able to recreate the message $M_1 = [0 \pmod{2}, 0 \pmod{3}, 4 \pmod{7}] = 18$.

The decryption process is the same for $C_2 = 2110$. First, we find the congruence:

$$M_2 = \log_5 2110 = \log_5 3 \pmod{43}$$

Second, we calculate components of the message as follows:

$$\text{for } p_1 = 2, \ y_1 = 3^{21} = 42 \pmod{43} \to b_{10} = 1$$
$$\text{for } p_2 = 3, \ y_2 = 3^{14} = 36 \pmod{43} \to b_{20} = 1$$
$$\text{for } p_3 = 7, \ y_3 = 3^6 = 41 \pmod{43} \to b_{30} = 2$$

In other words, the message $M_2 = [1 \pmod 2), 1 \pmod 3), 2 \pmod 7)] = 37$.

6. 15 Transforming suitable congruences for these two cryptograms, we get:

$$M_1 = \log_{23} 183 = \log_{23} 11 \pmod{43}$$
$$M_2 = \log_{23} 656 = \log_{23} 11 \pmod{43}$$

So both cryptograms produce the same congruence. In other words, our homomorphism is not one-to-one. As $p$ and $q$ are primes, $g$ is not a generator of the multiplicative group of GF($p$). If $g = 23$ is a generator, the following equations must be true:

$$g^{p-1} = 1 \pmod p,$$
$$g^{(p-1)/p_i} \neq 1 \pmod p \text{ for } i = 1, \ldots, n,$$

where $p-1 = p_1, p_2 \ldots p_n$.

Let us verify these conditions:

$$23^{21} = 1 \pmod{43}$$

The first congruence shows that $g = 23$ is not the generator. Once the logarithm is computed, we obtain the message, say $M_1 = 36$. The other message $M_2 = 36-21 = 15$.

6. 16 Results of the computations are given in the following table.

| Value B | Value e | Value $\alpha = B!^e$ | $\beta = a^{\alpha}-1$ | $gcd(\beta, N)$ |
|---|---|---|---|---|
| 3 | 1 | 6 | 15624 | 1 |
| 4 | 1 | 24 | 26245 | 1 |
| 4 | 2 | 576 | 6838 | 1 |
| 5 | 1 | 120 | 29472 | 1 |
| 5 | 2 | 14400 | 22720 | 1 |
| 6 | 1 | 720 | 569 | 1 |
| 6 | 2 | 518400 | 9849 | 1 |
| 7 | 1 | 5040 | 22999 | 211 |

So, one prime is $p = 211$ and the other is $q = 227$. As $p-1 = 210 = 2\cdot3\cdot5\cdot7$ while $q-1 = 2\cdot113$, the decryption process applies $p$.

6. 17 As $R\alpha = 10$, we use $p = 11$. Therefore, the matrix $K$ over GF($p$) is non-singular and:

$$K^{-1} = \begin{bmatrix} 10 & 9 & 6 \\ 4 & 1 & 10 \\ 9 & 0 & 6 \end{bmatrix} \pmod{11}$$

The second prime $q$ should be greater than $Rp$ so let $q = 23$. Again $z \in [11638, 23276]$. Although $z$ should be selected at random, we use $z = 11638$ so as to keep $z$ as small as possible. Now the $gcd(y, z) = 1$, and $y^{-1} = 8419$. For the message $M_1$, we get the following intermediate results:

$$S_1 = K \times M_1 = [3,2,0] \text{ and } t_1 = 49$$

The cryptogram $C_1 = t_1 \, y = 2303$ (mod 11638). Similarly, for $M_2 = [2,1,5]$, we get $S_2 = [8,0,9]$, $t_2 = 4769$, and the cryptogram $C_2 = 3021$ (mod 11638).

Let us compute $C = C_1 + C_2 = 5324$. To recover the message, we find $t = Cy^{-1} = 4818$ (mod 11638), $S = [11,2,9]$, and the message $M = K^{-1} \times S = [6,4,10]$.

# 7

# OTHER CRYPTOGRAPHIC TECHNIQUES

Protection procedures fall into three classes:

1. Authentication schemes: $A$'s identity can be proven to $B$ by $A$ alone. Someone else cannot impersonate $A$.
2. Identification schemes: $A$'s identity can be proven to $B$ by $A$. $B$ cannot prove to $C$ that $A$ is indeed $A$.
3. Signature schemes: $A$'s identity can be proven to $B$ by $A$. $B$ cannot impersonate $A$ even to $B$.

In previous chapters we have discussed a number of techniques for achieving some of these levels of protection. Far more exist in the literature and we mention just a few in this chapter.

## 7.1 Linear feedback shift registers

A recursive series,

$$u_1, u_2, u_3, \ldots, u_p, \ u_{p+1} = u_1, u_{p+2} = u_2, \ldots$$

is one which, after $p$ elements (the 'period'), repeats. A series of this type is generated by using an irreducible polynomial $(n < p)$,

$$a_n x^n + a_{n-1} x^{n-1} + \ldots + a_1$$

and by setting,

$$-u_n = a_1 u_1 + a_2 u_2 + \ldots + a_{n-1} u_{n-1}$$

The series is started by choosing an arbitrary series of $n-1$ numbers (not all zero). As the series progresses, the most recent $n-1$ elements generate the next element.

*Example*

In $GF(27)$, all the series which can be generated are of length 26, 13 or 2. For instance, the primitive polynomial $x^3 = x^2 + 2x + 2$ generates a series according to the following formula:

$$2u_n + 2u_{n+1} + u_{n+2} = u_{n+3} \ (\text{mod } 3)$$

Starting with $u_1 = 0$, $u_2 = 1$, $u_3 = 2$, the series, of length 26, is:

$$0\ 1\ 2\ 1\ 1\ 1\ 2\ 0\ 0\ 1\ 1\ 0\ 1\ 0\ 2\ 1\ 2\ 2\ 2\ 1\ 0\ 0\ 2\ 2\ 0\ 2$$

If we had started with the polynomial $x^3 = x + 1$ (which is not primitive) and the recurrence relation,

$$u_n + u_{n+1} = u_{n+3} \text{ (mod 3)}$$

with $u_1 = 0$, $u_2 = 1$, $u_3 = 2$, as before, we would get the following series of length 13:

$$0\ 1\ 2\ 1\ 0\ 0\ 1\ 0\ 1\ 1\ 1\ 2\ 2$$

The period of the sequence is of maximal length, here $3^n - 1$, when the generating polynomial is *primitive* or *irreducible*, that is, it has no proper factors.

A *linear feedback shift-register* is a feedback shift-register whose feedback function is linear:

$$f(u_1, u_2, \ldots, u_n) = a_1 u_1 + a_2 u_2 + \ldots + a_n u_n$$

$a_1, a_2, \ldots a_n$ are the *feedback coefficients* and can be from any Galois Field although we restrict ourselves to $GF(2)$.

Now the output of a linear feedback shift register with $a_1 = 1$ will always be periodic. The maximum period, called *maximal*, is at most $2^n - 1$.

*Example*

Consider the field $GF(16)$ and the polynomials:

$$m_1(x) = x^2 + x + 1$$
$$m_2(x) = x^4 + x^3 + x^2 + x + 1$$
$$m_3(x) = x^4 + x + 1$$
$$m_4(x) = x^4 + x^3 + 1$$

We note in passing that:

$$x^{15} - 1 = (x - 1)\,m_1(x)\,m_2(x)\,m_3(x)\,m_4(x)$$

over $GF(2)$.

These polynomials give the *linear recurrence relations* or *difference equations*:

$$a_{n+2} = a_{n+1} + a_n$$
$$b_{n+4} = b_{n+3} + b_{n+2} + b_{n+1} + b_n$$
$$c_{n+4} = c_{n+1} + c_n$$
$$d_{n+4} = d_{n+3} + d_n$$

respectively. Starting with:

| | | |
|---|---|---|
| $a_1 = 1$, $a_2 = 0$ | we get | 1 0 1 (period 3) |
| $b_1 = 1$, $b_2 = 0$, $b_3 = 0$, $b_4 = 0$ | we get | 1 0 0 0 1 (period 5) |
| $c_1 = 1$, $c_2 = 0$, $c_3 = 0$, $c_4 = 0$ | we get | 1 0 0 0 1 0 0 1 1 0 1 0 1 1 1 (period 15) |
| $d_1 = 1$, $d_2 = 0$, $d_3 = 0$, $d_4 = 0$ | we get | 1 0 0 0 1 1 1 1 0 1 0 1 1 0 0 (period 15) |

Extensive tables of primitive polynomials are given in Peterson [PETE61].

Every possible subsequence of length $n$, except $n$ zeros, will occur in a linear recurring sequence generated by a primitive polynomial over a Galois Field $GF(p^n)$.

*Example*

Consider the primitive polynomial $p(x) = x^4 + x + 1$ over GF(16). It generates a linear recurring sequence by using the recurrence relation:

$$c_{n+4} = c_{n+1} + c_n$$

We gave the sequence above generated with $(c_1, c_2, c_3, c_4) = (1, 0, 0, 0)$. Now suppose $(c_1, c_2, c_3, c_4) = (1, 0, 1, 0)$ had been used. Then the sequence would be:

$$1\,0\,1\,0\,1\,1\,1\,1\,0\,0\,0\,1\,0\,0\,1$$

This is a permutation of the previous sequence and also contains all subsequences of length 4, except 0000.

Linear recurring sequences of maximal length have remarkable properties that lead to a suggestion of 'randomness':

- The expected number of times each symbol, $a$, from $GF(p)$ occurs is:

$$\frac{p^{n-1}}{p^n - 1}, \quad a \neq 0$$
$$\frac{p^{n-1} - 1}{p^n - 1}, \quad a = 0$$

- Each subsequence, except $p$ zeros, occurs equally often.

Thus it might be expected that such sequences, of sufficient length, might be ideal to modulo 2 add to a stream of plaintext, $M$, to produce enciphered text for systems which need stream encipherment, such as *voice*.

This suggestion would have an advantage as an error in transmission of $y_i$ would only lead to the incorrect decipherment of one symbol $x_i$.

Unfortunately the use of linear recurring sequences for such use produces weak ciphers because the system *is* linear. Another disadvantage occurs if a bit is lost in transmission as there will be *synchronization* problems, but there are ways of overcoming these.

Cryptanalysis can be carried out in three environments:

1. ciphertext only;
2. corresponding plain and ciphertext;
3. chosen plaintext and corresponding ciphertext.

The last two are equivalent for stream encipherment. A cryptographic system is not acceptable if it is feasible for an opponent to make a chosen plaintext attack and find the key. Suppose the feedback coefficients **a** form the *long term key*, and plaintext and the corresponding ciphertext are known so the opponent has some fragment of the key stream:

$$q_0, q_1, \ldots, q_{n-1}$$

Suppose the polynomial over $GF(2^n)$ which generated the linear recurring sequence was:

$$p(x) = a_0 + a_1 x + a_2 x^2 + \ldots a_r x^r$$

Let $A$ be the $r \times r$ matrix:

$$
\begin{array}{llll}
a_{r-1} & 1\ 0\ \ldots\ 0\ 0 \\
a_{r-2} & 0\ 1\ \ldots\ 0\ 0 \\
\\
& \cdot\quad\cdot\ \cdot\ \cdot\ \cdot\ \cdot\ \cdot\ \cdot \\
& \cdot\quad\cdot\ \cdot\ \cdot\ \cdot\ \cdot\ \cdot\ \cdot \\
a_2 & 0\ 0\ \ldots\ 1\ 0 \\
a_1 & 0\ 0\ \ldots\ 0\ 1 \\
a_0 & 0\ 0\ \ldots\ 0\ 0
\end{array}
$$

Note that $A$ is invertible if and only if $a_0 \neq 0$.

Now note that:

$$(q_{i+1}, q_i, \ldots, q_{i-r+2}) = (q_i, q_{i-1}, \ldots, q_{i-r+1})\ A$$

Hence, any block of $2r$ consecutive values of $q_j$ can determine the coefficient vector **a**.

Nevertheless, shift-registers are of enormous importance in the theory of error correcting codes where they are used to generate Hamming, BCH and Goppa codes. The famous Massey-Berlekamp algorithm for decoding BCH codes is used to finally cryptanalyse the sequences as initially the value of $r$ is not known to the cryptanalyst.

For more information on the mathematics behind these sequences the reader should consult [LIPI85] and for more on stream ciphers [BEPI82].

The theory of feedback shift registers in cryptography is the subject of massive research the aim of which is the introduction of non-linear and time-dependent features to ensure the safe usage of the registers. See for example [GUNT87], [SIEG84], and [VOGE84].

## 7.2  One-way ciphers and passwords

A *one-way cipher* is a function $f$ which it is computationally infeasible to invert. A comparison is made only with the enciphered plaintext, $f(M)$.

One-way ciphers are used only in situations where $M$ itself is never required, such as in passwords. An early use of one-way ciphers seems to have been in a device, due to R. M. Needham, implemented at Cambridge, England.

Purdy [PURD74] suggests using polynomials over a prime modulus for encipherment. Probably most installations would use a variant of DEA unless this proved too time-consuming.

There is an apocryphal story about a bank which let customers choose their own passwords. At a convention of bank managers, an after-dinner speaker remarked that it was well known that many customers used their car registration numbers as their passwords. The next morning bank security staff noted that 20 customers had changed their passwords at the ATM closest to the convention.

On UNIX users are encouraged to use longer passwords, ideally at least eight symbols, and to change passwords at regular intervals. Each password is concatenated with a 12-bit random number, called the *salt*, before encryption, effectively lengthening the password by 12 bits.

When a password, $P$, is first created, a salt, $S$, is generated and concatenated to $P$. Write $SP$ for the concatenation. Both $S$ and $f(SP)$ are stored in the password file along with the user's *ID*. When the user logs in, the system retrieves $S$ from the file, forms a concatenation, *SP*, with the password $P$ supplied by the user, and then checks $f(SP)$ against the password file.

What should appear on the terminal might look like (what the computer types is in bold):

> **login**  jpandjs
> **password**  <you can't see it>
> **%**

where % is the prompt.

Ideally the system should tell you before it returns the prompt:

*   how many password tries you made;
*   when you last used the system.

If either of these items is incorrect, you should alert the system's programmer.

It is also valuable to note how long the system takes to respond to your identification information, here *jpandjs*, or if your password appears on the screen. If you have any doubts, alert the system's programmer to look for a *Trojan horse attack*.

Many users when left to choose their own password will use short, common words or expressions, their own or a relative's name, or the name of their dog or cat.

The Trojan horse attack occurs when a program is inserted which pretends to be the system. It returns the word **password:** and, after you have typed in your password, the program stores your password, and then passes your password to be processed by the system as usual.

Another attack is to try to guess users' passwords, or even try all possible passwords. In an attack on UNIX, the attacker would have to try $2^{n+12}$ possibilities to match a password of $n$ bits. If the password has an alphabet of 60 possibilities of which $n$ are chosen, there are $\binom{60}{n}$ possible passwords. For $n = 4$ this is around $2^{19}$ which is not impossible to search. This is why longer passwords are desirable.

In security situations users might have more than one variant of their passwords: one to be used in normal circumstances, the other to be used if the user is under duress.

## 7.3  Smart cards and information cards

The *smart card* or *carte à memoire* is a French invention. The card appears similar to other bank cards but contains a silicon chip (see Figure 7.1). This gives the card the capacity to process information internally and to store all transactions in non-erasable memory, thus giving the smart card a high degree of security and extended performance capabilities. The smart card opens up exciting possibilities for use with electronic money and a secure means for providing identification or data storage. It opens up the areas of access control to telematic networks, portable files and privacy for an individual's transactions.

Since the end of 1982, after the successful completion of negotiations between the French Ministry of PTT and the banking sector, various electronic payment experiments have been carried out. The Groupement des Cartes Bancaires, created in 1984, which includes all French banks and financial institutions, has decided that by 1988 a mixed smart and striped (ordinary bank cards with magnetic strips) card would be progressively distributed.

The smart card is intended to be a truly multiservice card. It can be used for point of sale payment, remote telepayment and public payphones. Furthermore, its protected memory can store data other than payment transactions.

Some possible uses for the card are: restricting access to public or private databases, medical management and monitoring, social security renewable debit cards, mass transit token prepayment, token-oriented payments for taxis, parking, bridge or road tolls, after sales service or warranty tracking, premises access, control and reporting, and national security cards.

Smart cards, when used with appropriate terminals dedicated to an application, promise to vastly alter the use of paper money.

Smart card readers have been developed for professional and public use. Hardware that enables smart cards to be used to authenticate a user for access control, banking, videotex, and telephone use all exist.

David Chaum and his colleagues have been working on the exciting possibility of using smart cards instead of paper money. That means using the cards to ensure certain exchange of value, without unnecessarily revealing the identity of the payer or payee.

While smart cards have the potential to replace all magnetic stripe cards, they have yet to be justified on a cost basis.

Smart cards have been adopted recently by some Australian, United States and New Zealand banks for a trial period.

## 7.4  Unforgeable ID cards using smart cards

We outline a protocol devised by Fiat and Shamir [FISH87] to securely use smart cards.

Creating unforgeable ID cards based on the emerging technology of smart cards is an important problem with numerous commercial and military applications. The problem becomes particularly challenging when the two parties (the prover $A$ and the verifier $B$) are adversaries, and we want to make it impossible for $B$ to misrepresent himself/herself as $A$ even after he/she witnesses and verifies arbitrarily many proofs of identity generated by $A$. Typical applications include passports (which are often inspected and photocopied by hostile governments), credit cards (whose numbers can be copied to blank cards or used over the phone), computer passwords (which are vulnerable to hackers and wire tappers), and military command and control systems (whose terminals may fall into enemy hands).

Authentication schemes are useful only against external threats when $A$ and $B$ cooperate. The distinction between identification and signature schemes is subtle, and manifests itself mainly when the proof is interactive and the verifier later wants to prove its existence to a judge. In identification schemes $B$ can create a credible transcript of an imaginary communication by carefully choosing both the questions and the answers in the dialog, while in signature schemes only real communication with $A$ could generate a credible transcript. However, in many commercial and military applications the main problem is to detect forgeries in real time and to deny the service, access, or response that the forger wants.

The scheme for smart cards assumes the existence of a trusted center (a government, a credit company, a computer center, a military headquarters, etc.) which issues the smart cards to users after properly checking their physical identity. No further interaction with the center is required either to generate or to verify proofs of identity. An unlimited number of users can join the system without degrading its performance, and it is not even necessary to keep a list of all the valid users. Interaction with the smart cards will not enable verifiers to reproduce them, and even complete knowledge of the secret contents of all the cards issued by the center will not enable adversaries to create new identities or to modify existing identities. Since no information whatsoever is leaked during the interaction, the cards can last a lifetime regardless of how often they are used.

Before the center starts issuing cards, it chooses and makes public a modulus $n$ and a pseudo random function $f$ which maps arbitrary strings to the range $[0,n)$. The modulus $n$ is the product of two secret primes $p$ and $q$, but unlike the RSA scheme, only the center knows the factorization of the modulus and thus everyone can use the same $n$. The function $f$ should be indistinguishable from a truly random function by any polynomially bounded computation. Goldreich, Goldwasser, and Micali [GOGO84] describe a particular family of functions which is provably strong in this sense, but in practice one can use simpler and faster functions (e.g. multiple DES) without endangering the security of the scheme.

When an eligible user applies for a smart card, the center prepares a string $I$ which contains all the relevant information about the user (name, address, ID number, physical description, security clearance, etc.) and about the card (expiration date, limitations on validity, etc). Since this is the information verified by the scheme, it is important to make it detailed and to double check its correctness. The center then performs the following steps:

1. Compute the values $v_j = f(I, j)$ for small values of $j$.
2. Pick $k$ distinct values of $j$ for which $v_j$ is a quadratic residue (mod $n$) and compute the smallest square root $s_j$ of $v_j^{-1}$ ( mod $n$).
3. Issue a smart card which contains $I$, the $k$ $s_j$ values, and their indices.

*Remarks*

1. To simplify notation we now assume that the first $k$ indices $j = 1,2,\ldots,k$ are used.
2. For non-perfect functions $f$, it may be advisable to randomize $I$ by concatenating it with a long random string $R$ which is chosen by the center, stored in the card, and revealed along with $I$.
3. In typical implementations, $k$ is between 1 and 18, but larger values of $k$ can further reduce the time and communication complexities of the scheme.
4. $n$ should be at least 512 bits long. Factoring such moduli seems to be beyond reach with today's computers and algorithms, with adequate margins of safety against foreseeable developments.
5. The center can be eliminated if each user chooses his/her own $n$ and publishes it in a public key directory. However, this RSA-like variant makes the schemes considerably less convenient.

The verification devices are identical standalone devices which contain a microprocessor, a small memory, and I/O interface. The only information stored in them

**Figure 7.1** Two example of smart cards

are the universal modulus $n$ and function $f$. When a smart card is inserted into a verifier, it proves that it knows $s_1, \ldots, s_k$, without giving away any information about their values. The proof is based on the following protocol:

1. $A$ sends $I$ to $B$.
2. $B$ generates $v_j = f(I, j)$ for $j = 1, \ldots, k$.

Repeat steps 3 to 6 for $i = 1, \ldots, t$:

3. $A$ picks a random $r_i \in [0, n)$ and sends $x_i = r_i^2 \pmod{n}$ to $B$.
4. $B$ sends a random binary vector $(e_{i1}, \ldots, e_{ik})$ to $A$.
5. $A$ sends to $B$:

$$y_i = r_i \prod_{e_{ij} = 1} s_j \pmod{n}$$

6. $B$ checks that:

$$x_i = y_i^2 \prod_{e_{ij} = 1} v_j \pmod{n}$$

*Example*

Let $I = (1\ 0\ 1\ 1\ 1\ 1\ 1\ 0\ 1\ 0\ 0\ 0\ 1\ 1\ 1\ 0\ 0)$ say, containing (name, address, ID number, physical description, security clearance, expiration date, validity limitations, etc.).

Suppose $n = 35$. We make a random function $v_j = f(I, j)$ described in Table 7.1 along with suitable $v_j^{-1}$ and $s_j$ values.

The information,

$$\text{I } 4\ 6\ 3\ 7\ 8\ 8\ 4\ 11\ 1\ 12$$

or,

$$\text{I } s_6\ 6\ s_7\ 7\ s_8\ 8\ s_{11}\ 11\ s_{12}\ 12$$

is now recorded on the smart card.

In the present example $k = 5$.

To implement the protocol

1. $A$ send $I$ to $B$.
2. $B$ generates $v_j = f(I,\ j)$ for $j = 6, 7, 8, 11, 12$ and renames these $v_1, v_2, v_3, v_4, v_5$.

Steps 3 to 6 are repeated for $i = 1, \ldots, t$:

3. $A$ picks a random $r_1 \in [0, 35)$, say $r_1 = 6$ and sends $x_1 = 6^2 \equiv 1 \pmod{35}$ to $B$.
4. $B$ sends a random binary vector, say $(10111)$ to $A$.
5. $A$ sends to $B$:

$$y_1 = r_1 \prod_{e_{1j} = 1} s_j \pmod{35}$$

$$= 6 \cdot s_1 \cdot s_3 \cdot s_4 \cdot s_5 \pmod{35}$$

$$= 6 \cdot 4 \cdot 8 \cdot 4 \cdot 1 \pmod{35}$$

$$= 33 \pmod{35}$$

6. $B$ checks that:

$$x_1 = y_1^2 \prod_{e_{1j} = 1} v_j \pmod{35}$$

$$= 33^2 \cdot 11 \cdot 29 \cdot 11 \cdot 1 \pmod{35}$$

$$\equiv 1 \pmod{35}$$

Steps 3 to 6 are repeated until $B$ is satisfied (probabilistically) that $A$ has the claimed knowledge on the card. ☐

*Remarks*

1. The verifier $B$ accepts $A$'s proof of identity only if all the $t$ checks are successful.
2. To decrease the number of communicated bits, $A$ can hash $x_i$ by sending $B$ only the first 128 bits of $f(x_i)$ in step 3. $B$ can check the correctness of this value in step 6 by applying $f$ to the right hand side of the equation and comparing the first 128 bits of the results.
3. $A$ can authenticate a particular message $m$ (e.g. an instruction to a remote control system or a program sent to a remote computer) without having to extract new square roots by sending $B$ the first 128 bits of $f(m,\ x_i)$ in step 3. If $B$ knows $m$, this value can easily be checked in step 6. $A$ is fully protected against modifications and forgeries of his message by the pseudo random nature of $f$, but this is not a real signature scheme: without participating in the interaction, a judge cannot later decide if a message is authentic.

**Table 7.1** Sample calculations for a possible smart card

| $j$ | $v_j$ | quadratic residue modulo 35? | $v_j^{-1}$ | $s_j = \sqrt{v_j^{-1}}$ |
|---|---|---|---|---|
| 1 | 2 | NO | | |
| 2 | 3 | NO | | |
| 3 | 5 | NO | | |
| 4 | 6 | NO | | |
| 5 | 2 | NO | | |
| 6 | 11 | YES | 16 | 4 |
| 7 | 4 | YES | 9 | 3 |
| 8 | 29 | YES | 29 | 8 |
| 9 | 18 | NO | | |
| 10 | 5 | NO | | |
| 11 | 11 | YES | 16 | 4 |
| 12 | 1 | YES | 1 | 1 |
| 13 | 10 | NO | | |
| 14 | 12 | NO | | |
| 15 | 18 | NO | | |

**Lemma 7.1:** *If A and B follow the protocol, B always accepts the proof as valid.*

**Proof:** By definition

$$y_i^2 \prod_{e_{ij}=1} v_j = r_i^2 \prod_{e_{ij}=1} (s_j^2 v_j) = r_i^2 = x_i \ (\mathrm{mod}\ n) \qquad \square$$

**Lemma 7.2:** *Assume that A does not know the $s_j$ and cannot compute in polynomial time the square root of any product of the form $\prod_{j=1}^{k} v_j^{c_j}$ (mod n) ($c_j = -1$, 0 or +1, not all of them zero). If B follows the protocol (and A performs arbitrary polynomial time computations), B will accept the proof as valid with probability bounded by $2^{-kt}$.*

**Proof** (Sketch): $A$ can cheat by guessing the correct $e_{ij}$ vectors and sending:

$$x_i = r_i^2 \prod_{e_{ij}=1} v_j \ (\mathrm{mod}\ n) \quad \text{and} \quad y_i = r_i$$

However, the probability of this event is only $2^{-k}$ per iteration and $2^{-kt}$ for the whole protocol. To increase this probability, $A$ must choose the $x_i$ values in such a way that for a non-negligible fraction of them he/she can compute the square roots $y_i'$ and $y_i''$ of:

$$x_i \Big/ \prod_{e_{ij}=1} v_j \ (\mathrm{mod}\ n)$$

for two vectors $e'_{ij}$ and $e''_{ij}$. The ratio $y'_i/y''_i$ (mod $n$) is of the form $\prod_{j=1}^{k} s_j^{c_j}$ (mod $n$). This contradicts the assumption, since $A$ can simulate $B$'s random questions and thus compute in expected polynomial time a value we assumed $A$ could not compute.     $\square$

$B$'s role in the interactive identification scheme is passive but crucial: the random $e_{ij}$

matrix $B$ sends contains no information but its unpredictability prevents cheating by $A$. To turn this identification scheme into a signature scheme, we replace $B$'s role by the function $f$ and obtain the following protocol:

*To sign a message m:*

1. $A$ picks random $r_1, \ldots, r_t \in [0,n)$ and computes $x_i = r_i^2 \pmod{n}$.
2. $A$ computes $f(m, x_1, \ldots, x_t)$ and uses its first $kt$ bits as $e_{ij}$ values ($1 \leq i \leq t, 1 \leq j \leq k$).
3. $A$ computes:

$$y_i = r_i \prod_{e_{ij}=1} s_j \pmod{n} \quad \text{for } i = 1, \ldots, t$$

and sends $I$, $m$, the $e_{ij}$ matrix and all the $y_i$ to $B$.

*To verify A's signature on m:*

1. $B$ computes $v_j = f(I, j)$ for $j = 1, \ldots, k$.
2. $B$ computes:

$$z_i = y_i^2 \prod_{e_{ij}} v_j \pmod{n} \quad \text{for } i = 1, \ldots, t$$

3. $B$ verifies that the first $kt$ bits of $f(m, z_1, \ldots, z_t)$ are $e_{ij}$.

The formal proof of security assumes that $n$ is sufficiently large and that $f$ is a truly random function. Consequently, there can be no generic attack which breaks the scheme for any $n$ and $f$ unless factoring is easy. Practical implementations which use particular moduli $n_0$ and pseudo-random functions $f_0$ may still be vulnerable to specialized attacks, but they merely show that $n_0$ is too small or that $f_0$ is demonstrably non-random. When $n_0$ is at least 512 bits long and $f_0$ is sufficiently strong (e.g. multiple DES with a fixed cleartext and variable key), such attacks are quite unlikely.

**Lemma 7.3:** *If A and B follow their protocols, B always accepts the signature as valid.*

**Proof:** By definition,

$$z_i = y_i^2 \prod_{e_{ij}=1} v_j = r_i^2 \prod_{e_{ij}=1} (s_j^2 v_j) = r_i^2 = x_i \pmod{n}$$

and thus $f(m, z_1, \ldots, z_t) = f(m, x_1, \ldots, x_t)$.    □

**Lemma 7.4:** *A chooses a particular signature among all the possible signatures for the message m with uniform probability distribution.*

**Proof:** Given a signature ($e_{ij}$ matrix and $y_i$ values), it is possible to recreate $r_1^2, \ldots, r_k^2 \pmod{m}$ uniquely, and $r_1, \ldots, r_k$ in exactly $4^k$ ways. Since $A$ chooses the $r_i$ at random, the various signatures are chosen with equal probabilities.    □

**Lemma 7.5:** *Let AL be any polynomial time probabilistic algorithm which accepts n, $v_1$, ..., $v_k$ and the signatures of arbitrary messages $m_1, m_2, \ldots$ of its choice, and produces a valid signature of another message $m_0$ of its choice. If the complexity of factoring and $2^{kt}$ grow non-polynomially with the size of n, AL cannot succeed with non-negligible probability for random functions f.*

**Proof** (Sketch): By contradiction. Using a simple combinatorial argument, we can prove that a polynomial time variant $AL'$ of $AL$ can compute a square root of some product $\prod_{j=1}^{k} v_j^{c_j} \pmod{n}$ $(c_j = -1, 0, \text{ or } +1, \text{ not all of them zero})$ with a similar probability of success.

To turn $AL'$ into a factoring algorithm for $n$, pick random $s_1, \ldots, s_k$ and define $v_j = s_j^2 \pmod{n}$. Execute $AL'$ with $n$, $v_1, \ldots, v_k$ as input, and use the $s_j$ to supply the signatures of $m_1, m_2, \ldots$ requested by $AL'$. The output of $AL'$ is a square root $Q$ of $\prod_{j=1}^{k} v_j^{c_j} \pmod{n}$, but another square root $S$ $(=\prod_{j=1}^{k} s_j^{c_j} \pmod{n})$ is already known. By Lemma 7.4, $AL'$ cannot find out which one of the four possible roots is $S$ by analysing the given signatures of $m_1, m_2, \ldots$. Consequently, $gcd(Q - S, n)$ is a proper factor of $n$ with probability of $\frac{1}{2}$. By repeating this procedure several times, we can make this probability arbitrarily close to 1. $\qquad\qquad\square$

It is easy to forge signatures for arbitrary messages $m_0$ in time $T$ with probability $T \cdot 2^{-kt}$ by guessing the $e_{ij}$ matrix $T$ times. A refinement of Lemma 7.5 shows that when the complexity of factoring is considerably higher than $2^{kt}$, this attack is essentially optimal.

In the proposed signature scheme, an adversary knows in advance whether his/her signature will be accepted as valid, and thus by experimenting with $2^{kt}$ random $r_i$ values, the adversary is likely to find a signature that can be sent to $B$. Consequently, the product $kt$ must be increased from 20 to at least 72 when we replace the identification scheme by a signature scheme.

A choice of $k = 9$, $t = 8$ attains the desired $2^{-72}$ security level. The private key can be stored in a 576 byte ROM, and each signature requires 521 bytes. The average number of modular multiplications for this choice is $t(k + 2)/2 = 44$.

By doubling the key size to 1152 bytes ($k = 18$), we can reduce the size of each signature to 265 bytes ($t = 4$) without changing the $2^{-72}$ security level. By optimizing the order of the multiplications to compute the $t$ subset products simultaneously, we can reduce their average number to 32. This is only 4 percent of the number of multiplications required in the RSA signature scheme.

## 7.5 Summary

We have briefly discussed a small sample of other techniques which might be used to enhance the security of a system or network.

We have barely touched the available literature which is expanding rapidly in this important area.

# 8
# SECURITY IN OPERATING SYSTEMS

Until now we have not mentioned security issues in operating systems. This is a vital question for any computerized information system. Sometimes, the security of the operating system is of paramount importance, for instance when military information processing systems are concerned. We have already considered cryptographic protection in computer systems, computer networks and EFT systems, but we have always assumed that the operating system is secure and works properly. A secure operating system should be resistant to any illegal activity tending towards unauthorized access to computer system resources. There are, of course, a great variety of methods for illegal penetration, but all can be divided into the two following classes:

- when a legitimate user of a process violates his/her legal access rights;
- when an intruder impersonates a legitimate user to circumvent the authentication mechanism and gains access to computer components.

For example, a user can abuse his/her access rights by applying the so-called *Trojan horse attack*. In this attack, a borrowed program illegally accesses information which belongs to the borrower; for example, a penetrator 'borrows' the 'login routines' and illegally obtains the passwords of third parties or gives himself/herself privileges usually not permitted (see [MAOL87]). On the other hand, *the masquerade attack* is an example of a penetration method of the second class. An intruder, applying this attack, tries to get the password of a legitimate user (by tapping, guessing, or otherwise) to successfully log on.

To study the protection of an operating system, a proper model of access control must be given. The first section provides such a model. The second section, however, describes several practical implementations of access control.

## 8.1 Access control in computer systems

In general, all computer components can be classified into two groups. The first consists of active computer entities which usually access other computer components. The second group comprises passive computer entities to which access is controlled. Such a classification is the cornerstone of all access control models. The material in this section is, however, based on the access matrix model introduced by Lampson [LAMP71] and subsequently improved by Graham and Denning [GRDE72] and by Harrison, Ruzzo, and Ullman [HARU76].

## 8.1.1 Access matrix

The access matrix model is defined by applying the classification given above. All computer components are:

- **subjects** if they are active computer entities;
- **objects** if they are passive ones.

A subject may be considered as the pair (process, domain). The domain describes a protection environment in which the process is executing. Of course, if a protection environment changes while the process remains the same, we are dealing with a different subject. Objects are passive computer entities like files, segments, or pages of main memory, communication channels, auxiliary devices, etc. Clearly, all subjects are also objects as access to subjects must be controlled even while they are idle.

The access matrix describes the current protection state of the computer system. Its rows are assigned to subjects and its columns to objects. Any matrix entry $[S_i, O_j]$ defines the current access rights (access privileges). Take the matrix given in Table 8.1.

**Table 8.1** An example of an access matrix

|       | $O_1 = S_1$ | $O_2 = S_2$ | $O_3 = S_3$ | $O_4$ | $O_5$ |
|-------|-------------|--------------|--------------|--------|-------------|
| $S_1$ |             | wait         |              | read   | read, write |
| $S_2$ | signal      | execute      | send, receive | delete | write |
| $S_3$ | control     | signal, wait | control      | execute | read |

For instance, subject $S_1$ has wait access right to object $O_2$, read access right to $O_4$, and read and write rights to object $O_5$. Of course, access privileges depend upon the type of object. For files, privileges like read, write, create, delete, and copy are usually defined. However, wait, signal, send, receive, and execute are examples of access privileges for processes.

## 8.1.2 Dynamic access matrix

Since the contents of the access matrix reflect the current state of protection privileges in the computer system, it must be changed whenever a new privilege has been granted to a specific subject or an existing one has been withdrawn from a specific matrix entry. All changes to the matrix are controlled by an associated monitor called the **access matrix monitor**. The monitor changes the matrix contents by applying a strictly determined set of protection commands. Following Graham and Denning [GRDE72], we use eight such commands. They are:

1. *Transfer* the privilege α to another subject.
2. *Grant* the privilege α to another subject.
3. *Delete* the privilege α.
4. *Read* the contents of the access matrix.
5. *Create* an object.

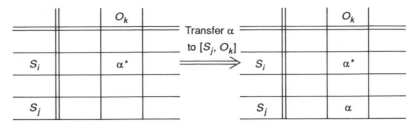

**Figure 8.1**  Alteration of the access matrix as a result of transferring $\alpha$ from $S_i$ to $S_j$

6. *Delete* an object.
7. *Create* a subject.
8. *Delete* a subject.

The *transfer* command involves two subjects: $S_i$, $S_j$ and an object $O_k$. The subject $S_i$ intends to transfer its privilege $\alpha$ (which concerns $O_k$) to the subject $S_j$. The *transfer* command will be executed only if the initiating subject $S_i$ has a *copy flag* associated with the privilege $\alpha$ (denoted by $\alpha^*$). In other words, if a matrix entry $[S_i, O_k]$ contains $\alpha^*$, the subject $S_i$ may transfer the privilege $\alpha$ to another subject (see Figure 8.1).

The *grant* command permits the owner (the subject $S_i$) of the object $O_k$ to pass on one or several privileges to another subject $S_j$. Granted privileges must be different from the *owner* privilege. Simply, the *owner* privilege is untransferable. This command is exemplified in Figure 8.2.

The third command, *delete*, may be applied in two situations. If the subject $S_i$ owns the object $O_k$, $S_i$ can delete any privilege from any entry of the access matrix column $O_k$ (Figure 8.3(a)). If the subject $S_i$, however, controls the subject $S_j$ (it means that the entry $[S_i, S_j]$ contains the *control* privilege), then $S_i$ can delete any privilege from any entry of the row $S_j$ (Figure 8.3(b)).

The subject $S_i$ can read entries of the access matrix using the *read* command. Its access is limited to all entries of its row and to columns which correspond to either its own objects or its subordinate subjects — it can read the column $O_k$ if the entry $[S_i, O_k]$ has either the *owner* or the *control* privilege.

Commands *create object* and *create subject* can be applied by any subject, say $S_i$, to create either its own object or its subordinate subject. *Create object* causes a new column $O_k$ to be added to the matrix and *owner* is written into the entry $[S_i, O_k]$. On the other hand, *create subject* affects the matrix by attaching both a new row and column

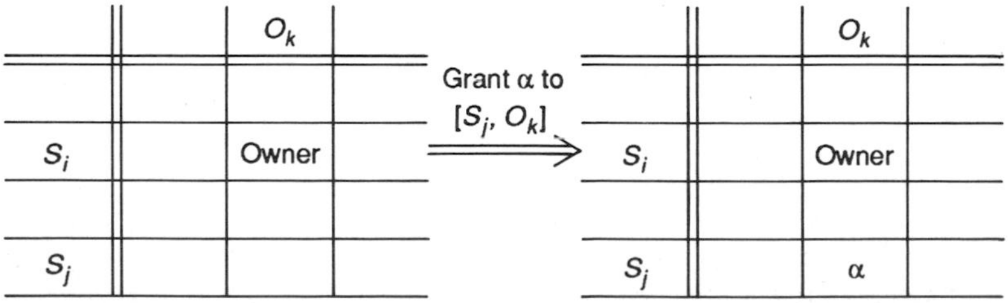

**Figure 8.2**  Access matrix before and after the execution of the grant $\alpha$ command

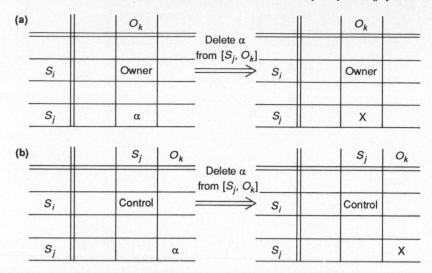

**Figure 8.3** Illustration of the delete command

(the row $S_j$ and the column $S_j$) while *owner* and *control* are input into the entries $[S_i, S_j]$ and $[S_j, S_j]$, respectively. Obviously, both commands *delete object* and *delete subject* erase all related information from the access matrix.

## 8.1.3 Sharing versus protection

Needless to say, any selection of privileges and protection commands is to some extent arbitrary. For instance, Harrison, Ruzzo, and Ullman [HARU76] assumed a different set of commands and they obtained a different protection system. There is a natural tradeoff between protection and accessibility of computer resources. If we accept a very limited set of protection commands, we will presumably get better protection but sharing computer objects will be very restricted.

Eventually, if we reject the first four protection commands (i.e. *transfer*, *grant*, *delete*, *read*) from the Graham-Denning model, we get a protection mechanism which allows us to create and destroy objects and subjects but does not allow any sharing at all. This mechanism provides complete isolation among subjects and is extremely inflexible but it is perfectly secure! So, there are different levels of sharing depending upon the choice of the protection command set. For instance, Maekawa, Oldehoeft, and Oldehoeft [MAOL87] describe five different levels of sharing. However, whatever the classification used, there are three main levels of sharing:

1. no sharing (complete isolation);
2. sharing of data objects;
3. sharing untrusted subjects.

The first and second level can be implemented using the Graham-Denning model, but the sharing on the third level requires introducing new protection commands. To illustrate difficulties which appear while designing a secure operating system on the third level, consider the following situation (see [MAOL87]). Assume there are three subjects

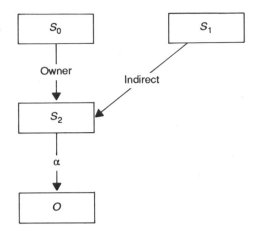

**Figure 8.4** Illustration of the indirect access privilege

$S_0, S_1, S_2$. Two $S_0$ and $S_1$ agree to share the common subject $S_2$ which is subordinate to $S_0$ (Figure 8.4). Although $S_0$ and $S_1$ trust each other, the subject $S_1$ does not trust $S_2$ and requires protection against $S_2$'s illegal access to its objects. To solve the problem, we can introduce a new access privilege *indirect*, defined as follows:

- The privilege engages three subjects: the owner $S_0$, the acquirer $S_1$, and the subordinate $S_2$.
- *Indirect* access to $S_2$ can be granted by its owner $S_0$ only.
- The acquirer $S_1$ can access all objects which are accessible on $S_2$ (in the case of Figure 8.4 it can access the object $O$ according to the privilege $\alpha$).
- A privilege can be deleted at any time by the owner $S_0$.

In general, the more flexible an access control system is intended to be, the more protection commands must be added. Unfortunately, some access control problems cannot be solved using the access matrix model. This is especially true when we deal with untrustworthy subjects. If the privilege $\alpha^*$ is transferred from one subject to another, then the second subject can propagate the privilege $\alpha$ without permission of the first one.

## 8.2 Implementations of access control systems

The direct implementation of the access matrix can take two forms:

1. capability oriented;
2. access control list oriented.

In the capability oriented implementation, any subject $S_i$ is assigned the list of pairs $\{(O_j, [S_i, O_j]; j = 1, 2, \ldots\}$, where $O_j$ is the name of subject and $[S_i, O_j]$ is a suitable entry in the access matrix. A single element of the list (the pair $O_j, [S_i, O_j]$) is called *capability*. In other words, any matrix row is attached to the corresponding subject.

In the second implementation, the list of pairs $\{(O_j, [S_i, O_j]; j = 1, 2, \ldots\}$ is attached to any object $O_i$; $i = 1, 2, \ldots$. In this case, the access matrix is split up into columns in the second one. So, in the first implementation, privileges to a single object are scattered all over capability lists, but, in the other, privileges of a single subject are placed into different access control lists. To remove this drawback, the *Lock/key mechanism* is suggested (see [MAOL87]).

## 8.2.1 Capability system

Saltzer and Schroeder [SASC75] considered an implementation of the capability oriented access control (Figure 8.5). Any user who wishes to log in sends his/her name along with his/her password. The system supervisor (part of the operating system) checks if the pair (name, password) exists in the user identification table. After positive identification, the supervisor creates a user's process using the corresponding catalog where the user's capabilities are stored. Of course, all protection commands which change the access matrix (here, catalogs) must be exclusively under the supervisor's control. Also, capabilities of any subject must be stored in the protected area accessible to the supervisors only. This area can be either the collection of distinguished registers of the processor as far the active subject is concerned or part of main memory if inactive subjects are concerned.

So there are two different processor work modes. The first, when it is under the supervisor's control, allows all areas where capabilities are stored to be accessible. In the second mode, the processor is under a user's process control and the areas are not accessible. Moreover, any processor reference to objects is controlled by protection registers where capabilities of the current active subject are stored.

An example of a system with the capability oriented access control is IBM/38. This system has a huge main memory which is uniformly addressable. Many of the supervisor functions are implemented in hardware and any single reference to a protected object is verified [MAOL87].

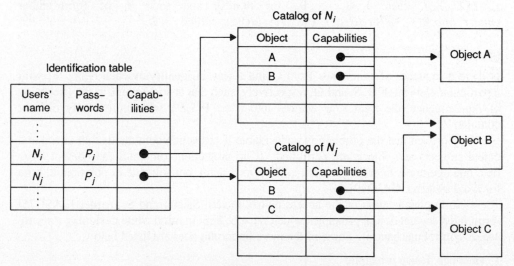

**Figure 8.5** Illustration of a capability system

## 8.2.2 Access control list system

Any object has a unique list which contains users' system names along with their privileges. Whenever a subject (which belongs to the corresponding user) requires the access $\alpha$ to an object, the supervisor looks at the appropriate access control list of the object. If the privilege $\alpha$ stands against the user's name, the access is approved.

This procedure of access control is inefficient as it is repeated whenever a new reference appears. To speed up the verification procedure, the processor is equipped with extra registers (also called *shadows registers*). When the first reference to an object takes place, a copy of the appropriate row of the access control list is input. Every further reference to the object is verified using a suitable shadow register. If the next reference, however, concerns a different object, which has not been used, then the next shadow register is loaded, and from now on each reference to this object is also via the shadow register.

MULTICS and UNIX exemplify the access control list implementation (see [MAOL87]).

## 8.2.3 An undecidable access problem

The access matrix model is commonly used to examine general properties of access control problems. For instance, Harrison, Ruzzo, and Ullman [HARU76] considered the following numerical problem known as *the security of file protection system* and defined it as follows. (See [GAJO79].)

*Instance*

Given the set $\mathbf{R}$ of *privileges*, the set $\mathbf{O}$ of objects, the set $\mathbf{S}$ of subject ($\mathbf{S} \subseteq \mathbf{O}$), the set $\mathbf{P}(S,O) \subseteq \mathbf{R}$ of privileges for each ordered pair $(S,O)$, $S \in \mathbf{S}$, $O \in \mathbf{O}$, a finite set $\mathbf{C}$ of protection commands, each having the form if $r_1 \in \mathbf{P}(X_1,Y_1)$ and $r_2 \in \mathbf{P}(X_2,Y_2)$ and ... $r_m \in \mathbf{P}(X_m,Y_m)$, then $\theta_1, \theta_2, \ldots, \theta_n$ for $m,n \geq 0$, and each $\theta_i$ of form either *enter $r_i$ into* $\mathbf{P}(X_j,Y_k)$ or *delete $r_i$* $\mathbf{P}(X_j,Y_k)$, and a specified $r' \in \mathbf{R}$.

*Question*

Is there a sequence of commands from $\mathbf{C}$ and a way of identifying each $r_i$, $X_j$, $Y_k$ with a particular element of $\mathbf{R}$, $\mathbf{S}$, and $\mathbf{O}$, respectively, such that at some point in the execution of the sequence, the right $r'$ is entered into a set $\mathbf{P}(S,O)$ which previously did not contain $r$?

They proved that the problem is undecidable if protection commands that create and delete subjects and objects are permitted. If no protection command can contain more than one operation, then the problem is **NPC** in general, but solvable in polynomial time for fixed systems [GAJO79].

As to implementation of the access matrix model, Saltzer and Schroeder [SASC75] formulated several design principles which must be kept in mind while designing a secure access control mechanism. Some of the more important ones are listed below:

1. The open design principle.
2. The complete meditation principle.

3. The least privilege principle.
4. The economy of mechanism principle.
5. The acceptability principle.

The *open design principle* says that security of the access control mechanism must not depend upon its secrecy. This principle is universal and is also valid while designing cryptographic protection. The *complete meditation principle* states that any single access to an object must be verified by access control mechanisms before it is permitted. *The least privilege principle* means that any active subject must be given the minimum set of privileges to complete its action. Also, access control mechanisms should be implemented applying *the economy of mechanism principle*. It means that mechanisms must be as simple as possible so that they can be tested thoroughly, and their correctness is verifiable. The last principle — *the acceptability principle* — states that if mechanisms are not easy to apply, then probably they may be abused to gain illegal access to objects.

Readers interested in protection in operating systems are referred to the book of Maekawa et al. [MAOL87] and articles [SASC75], [WULF76].

# 8.3  Rationale for security evaluation classes

The following information from the United States Department of Defense Document *Trusted Computer System Evaluation Criteria*, 1983 (called *The Orange Book*) gives the desired features of secure operating systems. The need to specify such desired features comes from the problems we saw arising in the access matrix model.

## 8.3.1  The reference monitor concept

In the Anderson Report [ANDE72] the concept of 'a *reference monitor* which enforces the authorized access relationships between subjects and objects of a system' was introduced. The reference monitor concept was found to be an essential element of any system that would provide multilevel secure computing facilities and controls.

The Anderson report went on to define the *reference validation mechanism* as "an implementation of the reference monitor concept ... that validates each reference to data or programs by any user (program) against a list of authorized types of reference for that user'. It then listed the three design requirements that must be met by a reference validation mechanism:

1. The reference validation mechanism must be tamper proof.
2. The reference validation mechanism must *always* be invoked.
3. The reference validation mechanism must be small enough to be subject to analysis and tests, the completeness of which can be assured.

Extensive peer review and continuing rersearch and development activities have sustained the validity of the Anderson Committee's findings. Early examples of the reference validation mechanism were known as *security kernels*. The Anderson Report described the security kernel as 'that combination of hardware and software which implements the reference monitor concept'. In this vein, it will be noted that the security kernel must support the three reference monitor requirements listed above.

## 8.3.2  A formal security policy model

Following the publication of the Anderson Report, considerable research was initiated into formal models of security policy requirements and of the mechanisms that would implement and enforce those policy models as a security kernel. Prominent among these efforts was the ESD-sponsored development of the Bell and LaPadula model, an abstract formal treatment of the United States Department of Defense security policy [BELA76]. Using mathematics and set theory, the model defines precisely the notion of secure state, fundamental modes of access, and the rules for granting subjects specific modes of access to objects. Finally, a theorem is proven to demonstrate that the rules are security-preserving operations, so that the application of any sequence of the rules to a system that is in a secure state will result in the system entering a new state that is also secure. This theorem is known as the Basic Security Theorem.

The Bell and LaPadula model defines a relationship between clearances of subjects and classifications of system objects, now referenced as the *dominance relation*. From this definition, accesses permitted between subjects and objects are explicitly defined for the fundamental modes of access, including read-only access, read/write access, and write-only access. The model defines the Simple Security Condition to control granting a subject read access to a specific object, and the *-Property (read "Star Property") to control granting a subject write access to a specific object. Both the Simple Security Condition and the *-Property include mandatory security provisions based on the dominance relation between the clearance of the subject and the classification of the object. The Discrepancy Security Property is also defined, and requires that a specified subject be authorized for the particular mode of access required for the state transition. In its treatment of subjects (processes acting on behalf of a user), the model distinguishes between trusted subjects (i.e. not constrained within the model by the *-Property) and untrusted subjects (those that are constrained by the *-Property).

From the Bell and LaPadula model there evolved a model of the method of proof required to formally demonstrate that all arbitrary sequences of state transitions are security-preserving. It was also shown that the *-Property is sufficient to prevent the compromise of information by Trojan horse attacks.

## 8.3.3  The trusted computing base

In order to encourage the widespread commercial availability of trusted computer systems, evaluation criteria have been designed to address those systems in which a security kernel is specifically implemented as well as those in which a security kernel has not been implemented. The latter case includes those systems in which objective (3) is not fully supported because of the size or complexity of the reference validation mechanism. For convenience, these evaluation criteria use the term *Trusted Computing Base* to refer to the reference validation mechanism, be it a security kernel, front-end security filter, or the entire trusted computer system.

The heart of a trusted computer system is the Trusted Computing Base (TCB) which contains all the elements of the system responsible for supporting the security policy and supporting the isolation of objects (code and data) on which the protection is based. The bounds of the TCB equate to the 'security perimeter' referenced in some computer security literature. In the interest of understandable and maintainable protection, a TCB should be as simple as possible, consistent with the function it has to perform. Thus, the TCB includes hardware, firmware, and software critical to protection and must be designed and implemented such that system elements excluded from it need not be trusted to maintain protection. Identification of the interface and elements of the TCB with their correct functionality therefore forms the basis for evaluation.

For general-purpose systems, the TCB will include key elements of the operating system and may include all the operating system. For embedded systems, the security policy may deal with objects in a way that is meaningful at the application level rather than at the operating system level. Thus, the protection policy may be enforced in the application software rather than in the underlying operating system. The TCB will necessarily include all those portions of the operating system and application software essential to the support of the policy. Note that as the amount of code in the TCB increases, it becomes harder to be confident that the TCB enforces the reference monitor under all circumstances.

## 8.3.4 Assurance

The third reference monitor design objective is currently interpreted as meaning that *the TCB must be of sufficiently simple organization and complexity to be subjected to analysis and tests, the completeness of which can be assured.*

Clearly, as the perceived degree of risk increases (e.g. the range of sensitivity of the system's protected data, along with the range of clearances held by the system's user population) for a particular system's operational application and environment, so also must the assurances be increased to substantiate the degree of trust that will be placed in the system. The hierarchy of requirements that are presented for the evaluation classes in the trusted computer system evaluation criteria reflect the need of these assurances.

The evaluation criteria must uniformly require a statement of the security policy that is enforced by each trusted computer system. In addition, it is required that a convincing argument be presented that explains why the TCB satisfies the first two design requirements for a reference monitor. It is not expected that this argument will be entirely formal. This argument is required for each candidate system in order to satisfy the assurance control objective.

The systems to which security enforcement mechanisms have been added, rather than built-in as fundamental design objectives, are not readily amenable to extensive analysis since they lack the requisite conceptual simplicity of a security kernel. This is because their TCB extends to cover much of the entire system. Hence, their degree of trustworthiness can best be ascertained only by obtaining test results. Since no test procedure for something as complex as a computer system can be truly exhaustive, there is always the possibility that a subsequent penetration attempt could succeed. It is for this reason that such systems must fall into the lower evaluation classes.

On the other hand, those systems that are designed and engineered to support the TCB concepts are more amenable to analysis and structured testing. Formal methods can be used to analyze the correctness of their reference validation mechanisms in enforcing the system's security policy. Other methods, including less-formal arguments, can be used in order to substantiate claims for the completeness of their access mediation and their degree of tamper-resistance. More confidence can be placed in the results of this analysis and in the thoroughness of the structured testing than can be placed in the results for less methodically structured systems. For these reasons, it appears reasonable to conclude that these systems could be used in higher-risk environments. Successful implementations of such systems would be placed in the higher evaluation classes.

## 8.3.5 Security evaluation classes

It is highly desirable that there be only a small number of overall evaluation classes. Three major division have been identified in the evaluation criteria with a fourth division reserved for those systems that have been evaluated and found to offer unacceptable security protection. Within each major evaluation division, it was found that 'intermediate' classes of trusted system design and development could be meaningfully defined. These intermediate classes have been designated in the criteria because they identify systems that:

- are viewed to offer significantly better protection and assurance than would systems that satisfy the basic requirements for their evaluation classes; and
- there is reason to believe that systems in the intermediate evaluation classes could eventually be evolved so that they would satisfy the requirements for the next higher evaluation class.

Except within division A it is not anticipated that additional 'intermediate' evaluation classes satisfying the two characteristics described above will be identified.

Distinctions in terms of system architecture, security policy enforcement, and evidence of credibility between evaluation classes have been defined such that the 'jump' between evaluation classes would require a considerable investment of effort on the part of implementors. Correspondingly, there are expected to be significant differentials of risk to which systems from the higher evaluation classes will be exposed.

## 8.3.6 United States trusted computer system security classifications

The criteria produced in 1983 by the United States Department of Defense for measuring a computer system technical security against standardized security evaluation classifications have four recognized classes.

The four classifications are:

D:  Minimal protection.
C:  Discretionary protection.
    C1:  Discretionary security protection
    C2:  Controlled access protection
B:  Mandatory protection.
    B1:  Loaded security protection.
    B2:  Structured protection.
    B3:  Security domains.
A:  Verified protection.
    A1:  Verified design

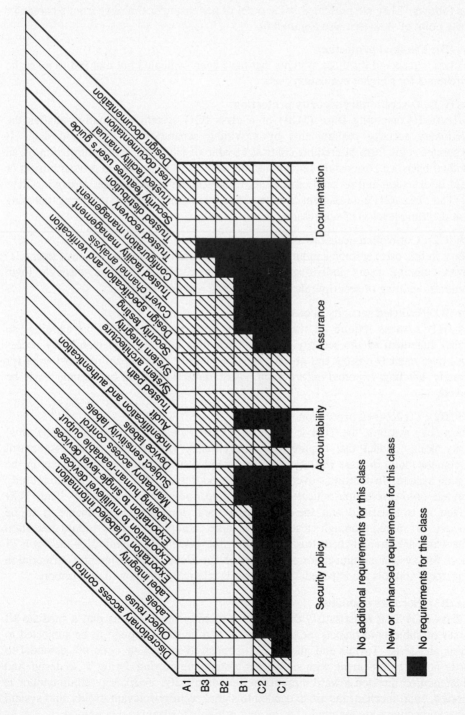

**Figure 8.6** Trusted computer system evaluation criteria summary chart

The classes of systems recognized under the trusted computer system evaluation criteria are as follows. They are presented in the order of increasing desirability from a computer security point of view (see also Figure 8.6).

### Class (D): Minimal protection
This class is reserved for those systems that have been evaluated but that fail to meet the requirements for a higher evaluation class.

### Class (C1): Discretionary security protection
The Trusted Computing Base (TCB) of a class (C1) system nominally satisfies the discretionary security requirements by providing separation of users and data. It incorporates some form of credible controls capable of enforcing access limitation on an individual basis, i.e., ostensibly suitable for allowing users to be able to protect project or private information and to keep other users from accidently reading or destroying their data. The class (C1) environment is expected to be one of cooperating users processing data at the same level(s) of sensitivity.

### Class (C2): Controlled access protection
Systems in this class enforce a more finely grained discretionary access control than (C1) systems, making users individually accountable for their actions through login procedures, auditing of security-relevant events, and resource isolation.

### Class (B1): Labeled security protection
Class (B1) systems require all the features required for class (C2). In addition, an informal statement of the security policy model, data labeling, and mandatory access control over named subjects and objects must be present. The capability must exist for accurately labeling exported information. Any flaws identified by testing must be removed.

### Class (B2): Structured protection
In class (B2) systems, the TCB is based on a clearly defined and documented formal security policy model that requires the discretionary and mandatory access control enforcement found in class (B1) systems be extended to all subjects and objects in the computer system. In addition, covert channels are addressed. The TCB must be carefully structured into protection-critical and non-protection-critical elements. The TCB interface is well-defined and the TCB design and implementation enable it to be subjected to more thorough testing and more complete review. Authentication mechanisms are strengthened, trusted facility management is provided in the form of support for system administrator and operator functions, and stringent configuration management controls are imposed. The system is relatively resistant to penetration.

### Class (B3): Security domains
The class (B3) TCB must satisfy the reference monitor requirements that it mediate all accesses of subjects to objects, be tamperproof, and be small enough to be subjected to analysis and tests. To this end, the TCB is structured to exclude code not essential to security policy enforcement, with significant system engineering during TCB design and implementation directed toward minimizing its complexity. A security administrator is supported, audit mechanisms are expanded to signal security-relevant events, and system recovery procedures are required. The system is highly resistant to penetration.

**Class (A1): Verified design**

Systems in class (A1) are functionally equivalent to those in class (B3) in that no additional architecture features or policy requirements are added. The distinguishing feature of systems in this class is the analysis derived from formal design specification and verified techniques and the resulting high degree of assurance that the TCB is correctly implemented. This assurance is developmental in nature, starting with a formal model of the security policy and a formal top-level specification (FTLS) of the design. In keeping with the extensive design and development analysis of the TCB required of systems in class (A1), more stringent configuration management is required and procedures are established for securely distributing the system to sites. A system security administrator is supported.

# 8.4 Summary

There are clearly problems in specifying access control in computer systems as tightened security restricts the range of activities and speed with which activities can be carried out.

The access matrix model gives one approach to the problem but, as is shown by Harrison, Ruzzo and Ullman [HARU76], the security cannot be assured unless the access rights are severely limited.

We have also presented the trusted computing base approach to operating system security and detailed the classification classes used by the U.S. Department of Defense certification procedures.

# 9
# MINIMUM KNOWLEDGE SYSTEMS

In the past two years interest has been excited by the new area of *minimum knowledge proofs*. These were also previously refered to as *zero-knowledge proofs*. This chapter gives a brief introduction to this fascinating new area which will be important in obtaining provably secure communications.

The following discussion is usually minimum not zero knowledge because actually physical knowledge is used in producing some part of the system.

## 9.1 An introduction to the minimum knowledge concept

**Concept**

Suppose $A$ sends $B$ a string of random bits. Then clearly $A$ has given $B$ *no* knowledge. $A$ has said nothing to $B$.

We now query whether this situation can be used to convince $B$ that $A$ knows some fact.

The first minimum knowledge identification protocol was apparently proposed by Shamir at a seminar in Marseille. It assumes that each country has a center which has on record public moduli $n_i = p_i q_i$ which are unique for each country, credit card or other required facility. Thus there needs to be about 250 different $n_i$. The center provides $A$, whose identity is required to be established, with an identification number:

$$I = (\text{name, country, physical attributes, security level, etc.})$$

$A$ wishes to prove to $B$ it is indeed $A$. So $A$ approaches the center which uses a standard one-way function to provide a passport which contains:

1. a certificate that the center has verified $I$;
2. $m = f(I,j)$ such that $m$ is a quadratic residue;
3. $j$ and $\sqrt{m}$ mod $n$ which is the $A$ identification secret.

$\sqrt{m}$ mod $n$ is the least square root of $n$.

To identify $A$ to $B$ the following protocol is followed which proves (statistically) to $B$ that $A$ knows $\sqrt{m}$ without revealing it, that is, proves using a minimum (or zero) knowledge protocol to $B$ that it is indeed $A$:

1. $A$ (prover) sends to $B$ $(I, j)$.
2. $B$ (verifier) calculates $m = f(I, j)$.
3. $B$ chooses a random string of zeros and ones, $r_1, r_2, \ldots, r_k$.

Repeat steps 4 to 7 many times.

4. $A$ chooses $\sqrt{t}$ and sends $B$ $t(\bmod n)$.
5. $B$ sends $A$ $r_i$.
6. If $r_i = 1$ $A$ sends $B$ $\sqrt{mt}$.
   Else $A$ sends $B$ $\sqrt{t}$.
7. $B$ verifies by squaring that the correct response was received from $A$.

   end

If $B$ only sends zeros to $A$ at step 5, then $B$ will not be satisfied that $A$ has $\sqrt{m}$ at all. On the other hand, if $B$ sends ones to $A$, $B$ is not sure there is any interaction with $A$.

Given time and resources $B$ could calculate $\sqrt{m}$ given that $n$ is known, but the time involved in the interaction is so short that $B$ becomes convinced after enough responses that $A$ already possesses $\sqrt{m}$ but has not told $B$ $\sqrt{m}$.

Another senario rests on the knowledge of graphs rather than number theory.

Let $G_1$ and $G_2$ be two graphs. $A$ can tell $B$ that $G_1$ is isomorphic to $G_2$. $A$ has given $B$ no knowledge except that $G_1 \approx G_2$ ($G_1$ is isomorphic to $G_2$): $B$ of course may not believe $A$.

Now if $A$ sends $B$ an isomorphism between $G_1$ and $G_2$, $B$ becomes convinced that $G_1 \approx G_2$, but *also* $B$ has learnt an isomorphism between $G_1$ and $G_2$.

This is *not* a minimum knowledge protocol given today's technology *but* if a polynomial time algorithm to prove $G_1 \approx G_2$ were discovered tomorrow, then it would not yield more knowledge.

We say $A$ tells $B$ no more than $\alpha$ if $B$, even cheating, sees a *view* when interacting with $A$, which can be efficiently generated (or approximated) just using $\alpha$, without interacting with $A$.

The view of $B$ is what $B$ sees: the random bits $B$ possesses plus $B$'s communications from $A$. (Interacting with $A$, $B$ gets a certain view, but just using $\alpha$, $B$ could generate the same view with the same probability distribution).

Shamir suggested using minimum knowledge protocols to establish identification. In essence, $A$ proves to $B$ that $A$ knows something (e.g. the square root of a number) but does not give $B$ enough information to be able to pretend to be $A$.

*Example*
Suppose $A$ gives to $B$ a minimum knowledge proof that $G_1 \approx G_2$ ($G_1$, $G_2$ graphs as before).
   The proof is as follows:

**do** many times

1. $A$ chooses a "random" H, different each time, isomorphic to $G_1$ and $G_2$;
2. $A$ sends H to $B$;
3. $A$ chooses a random $i \in \{1, 2\}$
4. $B$ sends $i$ to $A$

5. *A* sends *B* an isomorphism between H and $G_i$.

**end do**

Clearly if this is done enough times, *B* becomes convinced that *A* does know how to show $G_1 \approx G_2$ but has not revealed to *B* how to establish the isomorphism.

### Some other minimum knowledge proofs and protocols

Goldreich, Micali, Wigderson [GOMI86] have given a simple and elegant minimum knowledge interactive protocol for any *k* that a graph is *k*-colorable without revealing any information about a specific coloring (it is assumed that the prover possesses a *k*-colouring of the graph). Because *k*-colorability is **NP**-complete, this means that *any* positive instance of a problem in **NP** for which a prover holds a certificate (e.g. a satisfying assignment for a Boolean formula) can be reduced to graph colorability and shown in a minimum knowledge fashion to be a positive instance. The only assumption made is the existence of a probabilistic cryptosystem which is implied by the existence of a one-way permutation ([GOMI84], [YAO82]).

Benaloh [BENA87], Brassard and Crepeau [BRCR87], [GOMI86], and [CHAU87] have all produced similar methods to give minimum knowledge protocols to interactively prove that a given Boolean formula (or arbitrary Boolean circuit with in-degree 2) has a satisfying assignment.

Crepeau [CREP87] describes a minimum knowledge poker protocol that achieves confidentiality of the player's strategy and Chaum, Evertse, van der Graaf, and Peralta [CHEV87] show how to demonstrate possession of a discrete logarithm without revealing it.

## 9.2  More on the Fiat-Shamir smart card protocol

One valuable advantage of the protocol given in section 7.4 is that it constitutes a minimum-knowledge protocol.

**Lemma 9.1:** *For fixed k and arbitrary t, the proof of the Fiat-Shamir protocol for smart cards is a minimum-knowledge proof.*

### Proof (Sketch):

The intuitive (but non-rigorous) reason the proof reveals no information whatsoever about the $s_j$ is that the $x_i$ are random squares, and each $y_i$ contains an independent random variable which masks the values of the $s_j$. All the messages sent from *A* to *B* are thus random numbers with uniform probability distributions, and cheating by *B* cannot change this fact.

To prove this claim formally, it is necessary to exhibit a probabilistic algorithm which simulates the communication between *A* and *B* without knowing the $s_j$ with a probability distribution which is indistinguishable from the real distribution. The expected running time of this algorithm is $t \cdot 2^k$ times the sum of the expected running times of *A* and *B*. By assumption, this running time is polynomial.                           $\square$

### Remarks and assumptions in the Fiat-Shamir protocol

1. $2^{kt}$ is assumed to be much smaller than the time required to factor the modulus *n*.
2. The quadratic residuosity protocol of Fischer, Micali and Rackoff [FIMI84] is a special

case of this protocol with $k = 1$. The main practical advantage of the Fiat-Shamir protocol is that for the same security we can use only the square root of the protocol and its applications.

3. An adversary who records polynomially many proofs of identify does not obtain an increased chance of success. If a recorded $x_i$ is reused, the recorded answers can be played back only if the questions happen to be the same. Since $A$ uses each $x_i$ only once, the probability of success is still $2^{-kt}$.

4. In the parallel version of this protocol. $A$ sends all the $x_i$, then $B$ sends all the $e_{ij}$, and finally $A$ sends all the $y_i$. This version is not zero-knowledge for technical reasons, but its security can still be formally proven.

The $2^{-kt}$ probability of forgery is an absolute constant, and thus there is no need to pick large values of $k$ and $t$ as a safeguard against future technological developments. In most applications, a security level of $2^{-20}$ suffices to deter cheaters. No one will present a forged passport at an airport, give a forged driver's license to a policeman, use a forged ID badge to enter a restricted area, or use a forged credit card at a department store, if it is known the probability of success is only one in a million. In all these applications, the forged ID card (rather than the transcript of the communication) can be presented to a judge as evidence in a trial. Even if the only penalty for a failed attempt is the confiscation of the card, and smart cards cost only \$1 to manufacture, each success will cost about one million dollars. For national security applications, we can change the security level to $2^{-30}$: Even a patient adversary with an unlimited budget, who tries to misrepresent himself 1000 times each day, is expected to succeed only once every 3000 years.

To attain a $2^{-20}$ level of security, it suffices to choose $k = 5$, $t = 4$ (for $2^{-30}$, increase these values by 1). The average number of modular multiplications required to generate or verify a proof of identity in this case is $t(k + 2)/2 = 14$. The number of bytes exchanged by the parties during the proof is 323, and the secret $s_j$ values can be stored in a 320 byte ROM. Even better performance can be obtained by increasing $k$ to 18 (a 1152 byte ROM). If we use $e_{ij}$ vectors with at most three 1's in them, we have a choice of 988 possible vectors in each iteration. With $t = 2$ iterations, the security level remains about one in a million, but the number of transmitted bytes drops to 165 and the average number of modular multiplications drops to 7.6 (which is two orders of magnitude faster than the 768 multiplications required by the RSA scheme). Note that the $2 \times 18$ $e_{ij}$ matrix is so sparse that $B$ has to generate at most 6 out of the 18 $v_j$ values to verify the proof.

The time, space, communication and security of the scheme can be traded off in many possible ways, and the optimal choices of $k$, $t$ and the $e_{ij}$ matrix depends on the relative costs of these resources. Further improvements in speed can be obtained by parallelizing the operations. Unlike the RSA scheme, the two parties can pipeline their operations (with $A$ preparing $x_{i+1}$ and $y_{i+1}$ while $B$ is still checking $x_i$ and $y_i$), and use parallel multipliers to compute the product of $v_j$ or $s_j$ values in log $k$ depth. Since the protocol uses only multiplication (and no gcd or division operations which are hard to parallelize), each iteration of the protocol is in **NPC**, and thus the scheme is suitable for very high speed applications.

The sequential version of the interactive identification scheme is zero-knowledge and thus $B$ cannot deduce any information whatsoever about the $s_j$ from interaction with $A$.

The parallel identification scheme and the signature scheme, on the other hand, cannot be proven zero-knowledge for very subtle technical reasons. In fact, strong signature schemes cannot be zero-knowledge by definition: If everyone can recognize valid signatures but no one can forge them, $B$ alone cannot generate $A$'s messages with the same probability distribution. However, the information about the $s_j$'s that $B$ gets from signatures generated by $A$ is so implicit that it cannot be used to forge new signatures, and thus the signature scheme is provably secure (if factoring is difficult) even though it is not zero-knowledge.

## 9.3  Subliminal free verification using minimum knowledge protocols

This section is the result of a lecture given by Ivo Desmedt at Crypto '87.

We remember that in the Shamir protocol (see section 9.1), the interaction could be described as:

| A receives | A sends | B sends | B expects |
|:---:|:---:|:---:|:---:|
| 1 | $\sqrt{mt}$ | 1 | $\sqrt{mt}$ |
| 0 | $\sqrt{t}$ | 0 | $\sqrt{t}$ |

Since there are more than one $\sqrt{m}$ a subliminal message could be conveyed, say by an illegal or terrorist organization by utilizing the services of an active but neutral intermediary called the Active Warden.

The Active Warden (A.W.) chooses $\sqrt{t'}$ and when sent $I,j$ by $A$ calculates $m = f(I,j)$ as does $B$ to whom $I,j$ is passed. The A.W. also calculates $m^{-1}$.

All the actions of the A.W. are known in principle to $A$ and $B$ so the A.W. can be trusted as an intermediary.

As before the protocol is:

1. $A$ sends $I,j$ to A.W. and the A.W. forwards to $B$.
2. $B$ and the A.W. calculate $m = f(I,j)$. The A.W. also calculates $m^{-1}$
3. The A.W. chooses $\sqrt{t'}$ and must be trusted to have access to $\sqrt{mt'}$ (a better solution to this part of the protocol would be valuable).
4. $B$ now chooses a random string of binary bits $\underline{e} = e_1, \ldots, e_k$ and the A.W. chooses a random string of binary bits $\underline{d} = d_1, \ldots, d_k$.

Repeat steps 5 to 8 many times

5. $A$ chooses $\sqrt{t}$ and sends $t \pmod{n}$ to the A.W. who sends $tt'$ to $B$.
6. $B$ sends $e_i$ to the A.W. who sends $e_i \oplus d_i$ to $A$.
7. If $e_i \oplus d_i = 1$ $A$ sends $\sqrt{mt}$ to the A.W.
   Else $A$ sends $\sqrt{t}$ to the A.W.
8. If $d_i = 0$ the A.W. multiples the message received from $A$ by $\sqrt{t'}$ and forwards to $B$.
   If $d_i = 1$ the A.W. multiples the message received from $A$ by $\sqrt{mt'}$. If $e_i \oplus d_i = 1$ it is now further multiplied by $m^{-1}$, and in either case the new message is passed on to $B$.

end

**Table 9.1** A summary of the results of the participation of an Active Warden in preventing the passage of information using a subliminal channel

| $e$ | $d$ | $e \oplus d$ | $A$ sends | Active Warden | $B$ receives |
|---|---|---|---|---|---|
| 0 | 0 | 0 | $\sqrt{t}$ | $*\sqrt{t'}$ | $\sqrt{tt'}$ |
| 0 | 1 | 1 | $\sqrt{mt}$ | $*\dfrac{\sqrt{mt'}}{m}$ | $\sqrt{tt'}$ |
| 1 | 0 | 1 | $\sqrt{mt}$ | $*\sqrt{t'}$ | $\sqrt{mtt'}$ |
| 1 | 1 | 0 | $\sqrt{t}$ | $*\sqrt{mt'}$ | $\sqrt{mtt'}$ |

Steps 5 to 8 are summarized in Table 9.1.

This protocol eliminates the use of $t$, $m$ or $e$ for sending subliminal channel, but requires the trust of $A$ and $B$, and especially $A$ who knows that as the A.W. knows $\sqrt{t'}$ and $\sqrt{mt'}$, given sufficient time, the A.W. can recover $\sqrt{m}$ by using $1/\sqrt{t'}$.

# 9.4 Conclusion

We have opened the door to the area of minimum knowledge protocols, outlining a few of their possible uses.

This area of knowledge appears to be vital to obtaining provably secure communications.

# APPENDIX A

Appendix A.1 is frequencies of characters in alphabets (expressed as percentages).

Appendix A.2 is frequencies of characters in some natural languages (expressed as frequency per 10000 letters).

**Table A.1** Frequencies of occurrence of characters in alphabets (expressed as percentages)

| Arabic | | Danish | | Dutch | | English | | Finnish | |
|---|---|---|---|---|---|---|---|---|---|
| a | 17.75 | a | 6.50 | a | 8.25 | a | 7.25 | a | 12.50 |
| b | 3.75 | b | 1.25 | b | 1.75 | b | 1.25 | b | 0.25 |
| t | 6.00 | c | 0.25 | c | 1.00 | c | 3.50 | c | 0.25 |
| h | 9.25 | d | 5.50 | d | 5.25 | d | 4.25 | d | 0.75 |
| j | 1.25 | e | 16.00 | e | 19.00 | e | 12.75 | e | 8.25 |
| k | 3.25 | f | 3.00 | f | 1.00 | f | 3.00 | f | 0.25 |
| d | 5.00 | g | 4.50 | g | 3.00 | g | 2.00 | g | 0.50 |
| r | 5.00 | h | 1.75 | h | 2.50 | h | 3.50 | h | 2.00 |
| z | 0.75 | i | 6.50 | i | 6.50 | i | 7.75 | i | 11.00 |
| s | 5.00 | j | 0.50 | j | 1.50 | j | 0.25 | j | 1.75 |
| 9 | 4.00 | k | 3.00 | k | 2.75 | k | 0.50 | k | 5.50 |
| g | 0.75 | l | 5.00 | l | 4.00 | l | 3.75 | l | 6.00 |
| f | 2.50 | m | 4.25 | m | 2.75 | m | 2.75 | m | 3.25 |
| q | 2.00 | n | 7.00 | n | 10.25 | n | 7.75 | n | 8.75 |
| k | 0.00 | o | 5.25 | o | 6.00 | o | 7.50 | o | 6.25 |
| l | 8.75 | p | 1.50 | p | 1.75 | p | 2.75 | p | 1.75 |
| m | 5.75 | q | 0.00 | q | 0.25 | q | 0.50 | q | 0.00 |
| n | 4.50 | r | 9.50 | r | 6.25 | r | 8.50 | r | 3.00 |
| w | 6.25 | s | 6.25 | s | 4.00 | s | 6.00 | s | 7.25 |
| y | 7.25 | t | 7.25 | t | 7.25 | t | 9.25 | t | 10.75 |
| o | 3.25 | u | 1.75 | u | 2.50 | u | 3.00 | u | 5.00 |
| | | v | 2.75 | v | 2.25 | v | 1.50 | v | 2.25 |
| | | w | 0.25 | w | 2.00 | w | 1.50 | w | 0.25 |
| | | x | 0.25 | x | 0.25 | x | 0.50 | x | 0.00 |
| | | y | 0.50 | y | 0.25 | y | 2.25 | y | 2.25 |
| | | z | 0.25 | z | 1.25 | z | 0.25 | z | 0.00 |
| | | } | 1.25 | | | | | } | 2.00 |
| | | { | 1.00 | | | | | { | 1.75 |
| | | | | 0.75 | | | | | | | 0.25 |

**Table A.1** (cont'd)

| French | | German | | Greek | | Hebrew | | Italian | |
|---|---|---|---|---|---|---|---|---|---|
| a | 8.25 | a | 5.00 | a | 14.25 | b | 6.50 | a | 12.50 |
| b | 1.25 | b | 2.50 | b | 0.75 | g | 1.00 | b | 0.75 |
| c | 3.25 | c | 1.50 | g | 2.00 | d | 3.25 | c | 5.00 |
| d | 3.75 | d | 5.00 | d | 1.50 | h | 7.75 | d | 3.50 |
| é | 17.75 | e | 18.50 | e | 9.00 | z | 1.00 | e | 13.75 |
| f | 1.25 | f | 1.50 | z | 0.50 | c | 1.00 | f | 1.25 |
| g | 1.25 | g | 4.00 | h | 4.25 | y | 12.75 | g | 1.75 |
| h | 1.25 | h | 4.00 | u | 1.25 | k | 2.75 | h | 0.75 |
| i | 7.25 | i | 8.00 | i | 9.25 | l | 8.00 | i | 12.50 |
| j | 0.75 | j | 0.00 | k | 4.50 | m | 7.75 | l | 0.00 |
| k | 0.00 | k | 1.00 | l | 2.75 | n | 5.25 | m | 0.00 |
| l | 5.75 | l | 3.00 | m | 4.00 | s | 1.00 | n | 7.75 |
| m | 3.25 | m | 2.50 | n | 6.50 | p | 1.75 | o | 3.50 |
| n | 7.25 | n | 11.50 | j | 0.75 | q | 1.00 | p | 7.25 |
| o | 5.75 | o | 3.50 | o | 9.25 | w | 12.25 | q | 5.50 |
| p | 3.75 | p | 0.50 | p | 3.75 | x | 2.50 | r | 3.50 |
| q | 1.25 | q | 0.00 | r | 4.25 | t | 4.50 | s | 0.75 |
| r | 7.25 | r | 7.50 | s | 4.25 | r | 5.50 | t | 7.25 |
| s | 8.25 | s | 7.00 | w | 3.00 | $ | 4.25 | u | 5.50 |
| t | 7.25 | t | 5.00 | t | 7.75 | + | 0.50 | v | 6.75 |
| u | 6.25 | u | 5.00 | y | 4.25 | ( | 4.00 | z | 3.50 |
| v | 1.75 | v | 1.00 | f | 1.25 | ) | 7.00 | | |
| x | 0.00 | w | 1.50 | x | 1.50 | & | 1.25 | | |
| y | 0.75 | x | 0.00 | c | 0.25 | | | | |
| z | 0.00 | y | 0.00 | v | 2.25 | | | | |
| | | z | 1.50 | | | | | | |

**Table A.1** (cont'd)

| Japanese | | Latin | | Malay | | Norwegian | | Portuguese | |
|---|---|---|---|---|---|---|---|---|---|
| a | 9.00 | a | 11.00 | a | 20.25 | a | 5.75 | a | 13.50 |
| b | 1.75 | b | 1.50 | b | 3.75 | b | 1.50 | b | 0.50 |
| c | 0.75 | c | 4.00 | c | 0.50 | c | 0.25 | c | 4.00 |
| d | 1.75 | d | 3.00 | d | 3.50 | d | 4.25 | d | 5.50 |
| e | 5.75 | e | 9.75 | e | 8.00 | e | 16.25 | e | 12.50 |
| f | 0.75 | f | 0.75 | f | 0.25 | f | 1.75 | f | 1.00 |
| g | 1.75 | g | 8.50 | g | 4.50 | g | 4.50 | g | 1.00 |
| h | 5.25 | h | 0.75 | h | 2.75 | h | 1.75 | h | 1.00 |
| i | 13.00 | i | 10.50 | i | 7.25 | i | 6.25 | i | 6.00 |
| j | 1.25 | k | 0.25 | j | 1.25 | j | 1.25 | j | 0.00 |
| k | 8.50 | l | 3.50 | k | 4.75 | k | 3.75 | l | 0.00 |
| m | 0.00 | m | 5.50 | l | 4.00 | l | 5.25 | m | 2.50 |
| n | 2.25 | n | 5.50 | m | 4.50 | m | 3.50 | n | 4.50 |
| o | 7.50 | o | 5.25 | n | 10.25 | n | 7.75 | o | 5.50 |
| p | 15.75 | p | 2.50 | o | 1.00 | o | 4.50 | p | 11.50 |
| r | 0.75 | q | 1.00 | p | 2.75 | p | 1.75 | q | 3.00 |
| s | 0.00 | r | 6.00 | r | 0.00 | q | 0.00 | r | 1.00 |
| t | 4.75 | s | 6.00 | s | 4.75 | r | 9.00 | s | 8.00 |
| u | 8.00 | t | 7.75 | t | 3.25 | s | 6.25 | t | 9.00 |
| w | 5.75 | u | 7.50 | u | 5.50 | t | 8.00 | u | 4.50 |
| y | 9.00 | v | 1.75 | v | 7.50 | u | 2.00 | v | 4.00 |
| z | 0.00 | w | 0.25 | w | 0.00 | v | 3.25 | x | 1.50 |
| | | x | 0.50 | x | 0.25 | w | 0.25 | y | 0.00 |
| | | y | 0.25 | y | 0.00 | x | 0.25 | z | 0.50 |
| | | z | 0.25 | z | 2.25 | y | 0.50 | | |
| | | | | | | z | 0.00 | | |
| | | | | | | } | 2.00 | | |
| | | | | | | { | 0.50 | | |
| | | | | | | \| | 1.25 | | |

**Table A.1** (cont'd)

| Russian | | Sanskrit | | Serbo-Croatian | | Spanish | | Swedish | |
|---|---|---|---|---|---|---|---|---|---|
| a | 8.40 | a | 31.25 | a | 11.42 | a | 13.25 | a | 9.50 |
| b | 1.76 | b | 1.50 | b | 0.99 | b | 1.25 | b | 1.25 |
| c | 1.76 | c | 1.50 | c | 2.18 | c | 4.50 | c | 1.00 |
| d | 2.65 | d | 3.00 | d | 4.57 | d | 4.75 | d | 4.50 |
| e | 8.84 | e | 2.75 | e | 7.94 | e | 14.75 | e | 10.25 |
| f | 0.44 | f | 0.00 | f | 0.50 | f | 0.75 | f | 2.00 |
| g | 1.76 | g | 1.25 | g | 2.28 | g | 1.25 | g | 3.75 |
| h | 3.98 | h | 5.75 | h | 0.79 | h | 1.00 | h | 1.50 |
| i | 8.84 | i | 5.75 | i | 8.34 | i | 7.25 | i | 6.50 |
| j | 0.88 | j | 1.25 | j | 5.96 | j | 0.50 | j | 0.50 |
| k | 3.53 | k | 2.50 | k | 2.68 | l | 0.00 | k | 3.25 |
| l | 3.53 | l | 0.75 | l | 3.28 | m | 5.75 | l | 5.00 |
| m | 2.65 | m | 6.50 | m | 2.38 | n | 2.75 | m | 3.75 |
| n | 6.63 | n | 5.25 | n | 6.65 | o | 6.50 | n | 9.50 |
| o | 9.73 | o | 1.75 | o | 9.73 | p | 8.75 | o | 3.75 |
| p | 2.65 | p | 2.25 | p | 3.77 | q | 3.50 | p | 1.75 |
| r | 4.42 | r | 5.25 | r | 5.66 | r | 1.75 | q | 0.00 |
| s | 6.63 | s | 4.75 | s | 6.85 | s | 7.25 | r | 8.50 |
| t | 5.75 | t | 7.25 | t | 4.97 | t | 8.00 | s | 6.25 |
| u | 3.09 | u | 3.25 | u | 3.97 | u | 4.50 | t | 10.00 |
| v | 4.42 | v | 3.75 | v | 3.97 | v | 4.25 | u | 1.75 |
| y | 4.42 | y | 4.25 | z | 1.09 | x | 0.75 | v | 2.25 |
| z | 1.32 | z | 1.25 | | | w | 0.25 | | |
| _ | 1.76 | z | 0.25 | | | | | | |
| | | | | | | y | 0.75 | | |
| | | | | | | z | 0.25 | | |
| | | | | | | } | 1.50 | | |
| | | | | | | { | 2.00 | | |
| | | | | | | \| | 1.50 | | |

**Table A.2** Arabic (expressed as frequency per 10000 letters)

| | o | y | w | n | m | l | k | q | f | g | 9 | s | z | r | d | k | j | ḥ | t | ḅ | a |
|---|---|---|---|---|---|---|---|---|---|---|---|---|---|---|---|---|---|---|---|---|---|
| a | 75 | 103 | 103 | 12 | 12 | 89 | 89 | 72 | 72 | 46 | 46 | 43 | 43 | 115 | 115 | 92 | 92 | 59 | 59 | 46 | 46 |
| ḅ | 20 | 20 | 12 | 12 |  | 36 | 36 | 7 | 7 | 10 | 10 | 4 | 4 | 20 | 20 | 21 | 21 | 2 | 2 | 114 | 114 |
| t | 21 | 21 | 37 | 37 |  | 37 | 37 | 15 | 15 | 21 | 21 | 5 | 5 | 109 | 109 | 17 | 17 | 38 | 38 | 90 | 90 |
| ḥ | 23 | 20 | 20 | 2 | 2 | 64 | 64 | 109 | 109 | 11 | 11 | 4 | 4 | 27 | 27 | 50 | 50 | 28 | 28 | 183 | 183 |
| j |  | 1 | 1 | 2 | 2 | 8 | 8 | 8 | 8 | 12 | 12 |  |  | 1 | 1 | 1 | 1 | 2 | 2 | 37 | 37 |
| k |  | 10 | 12 | 12 | 1 | 1 | 20 | 20 | 7 | 7 | 2 | 2 | 2 | 64 | 64 | 31 | 31 | 11 | 11 | 76 | 76 |
| d | 10 | 14 | 8 | 8 |  | 7 | 7 | 7 | 7 | 18 | 18 | 4 | 4 | 141 | 141 | 14 | 14 | 20 | 20 | 86 | 86 |
| r | 14 | 12 | 12 | 18 | 18 |  |  | 21 | 21 | 34 | 34 |  |  | 23 | 23 | 17 | 17 | 28 | 28 | 105 | 105 |
| z | 1 | 1 |  |  | 1 | 1 |  | 1 | 1 | 4 | 4 | 11 | 12 | 1 | 1 | 1 | 1 | 2 | 2 | 24 | 24 |
| s | 1 | 5 | 5 | 10 | 10 |  |  |  | 4 | 4 | 11 | 10 |  | 154 | 154 | 27 | 27 | 18 | 18 | 90 | 90 |
| 9 |  | 10 | 10 |  | 14 | 14 |  | 25 | 12 | 12 | 10 |  | 1 | 12 | 25 | 25 | 11 | 11 | 93 | 9 | 9 |
| g | 2 |  |  |  |  |  | 25 | 23 |  |  |  | 1 |  |  |  | 56 | 56 |  |  | 1 | 1 |
| f |  | 4 | 5 | 5 | 8 | 25 | 25 | 8 | 8 | 1 | 1 | 5 | 5 | 8 | 8 | 12 | 12 | 5 | 5 | 34 | 34 |
| q | 4 |  | 5 | 5 | 4 | 8 |  | 11 | 11 | 24 | 24 | 18 | 18 | 1 | 1 | 24 | 24 | 5 | 5 | 38 | 38 |
| l | 4 | 92 | 92 | 4 | 4 | 17 | 17 | 38 | 38 | 43 | 43 |  |  | 25 | 25 | 98 | 98 | 38 | 38 | 167 | 167 |
| m | 40 | 36 | 36 | 4 | 4 | 30 | 30 | 10 | 10 | 24 | 24 | 10 | 10 | 37 | 37 | 44 | 44 | 8 | 8 | 63 | 63 |
| n | 24 | 18 | 18 | 1 | 1 | 2 | 2 | 20 | 20 | 25 | 25 | 8 | 8 | 21 | 21 | 21 | 21 | 15 | 15 | 115 | 115 |
| w | 27 | 40 | 40 | 17 | 17 | 46 | 46 | 44 | 44 | 25 | 25 | 1 | 1 | 37 | 37 | 18 | 18 | 24 | 24 | 151 | 151 |
| y | 31 | 36 | 36 | 11 | 11 | 50 | 50 | 51 | 51 | 12 | 12 | 1 | 1 | 34 | 34 | 64 | 64 | 17 | 17 | 134 | 134 |
| o | 14 | 14 | 5 | 5 |  | 1 | 1 | 5 | 5 | 20 | 20 | 1 | 1 | 10 | 10 | 8 | 8 | 24 | 24 | 112 | 112 |

**Table A.2** (cont'd) Danish (expressed as frequency per 10000 letters)

| | a | b | c | d | e | f | g | h | i | j | k | l | m | n | o | p | q | r | s | t | u | v | w | x | y | z | æ | ø | å |
|---|---|---|---|---|---|---|---|---|---|---|---|---|---|---|---|---|---|---|---|---|---|---|---|---|---|---|---|---|---|
| a | 2 | 2 | 10 | 10 | | 22 | 22 | 4 | 4 | 51 | 51 | 30 | 30 | 5 | 5 | 5 | 5 | | 12 | 12 | 63 | 63 | 41 | 41 | 131 | 131 | 3 | 3 | 2 |
| b | 7 | 7 | | | | 35 | 35 | | | | 9 | 9 | | 1 | | 21 | 21 | 37 | | 9 | 9 | | | 15 | 15 | | 2 | 2 | |
| c | 4 | 4 | | | | 5 | 5 | | | 2 | 2 | 5 | 1 | | | | | 23 | | | | | | | | | | | |
| d | 30 | 30 | 5 | 5 | 1 | 1 | | | | | | | 5 | | | | | | | | | | | | | | | | |
| e | 39 | 39 | 13 | 13 | 1 | 1 | 10 | 10 | 304 | 304 | 11 | 11 | 4 | 4 | 12 | 12 | 37 | | 9 | 3 | 3 | 7 | 7 | 2 | 2 | 2 | 4 | 14 | 14 |
| f | 16 | 16 | | | 4 | 4 | 95 | 95 | 33 | 33 | 56 | 56 | 38 | 38 | 20 | 20 | 23 | 1 | 8 | 9 | 29 | 29 | 101 | 101 | 64 | 4 | 258 | 258 | 29 |
| g | 22 | 22 | | | | 21 | 12 | 12 | 6 | 6 | 2 | 2 | 8 | 2 | 24 | 24 | | | 1 | 8 | 2 | 2 | 2 | 2 | 84 | 64 | | | 44 |
| h | 47 | 47 | 4 | 4 | | 33 | 21 | 151 | 151 | 10 | 10 | 8 | 7 | 14 | 14 | 24 | 24 | | | 4 | 4 | 9 | 9 | 11 | 11 | 84 | | 10 | 10 |
| i | 10 | 10 | | | | | 33 | 48 | 18 | 18 | 4 | 4 | 94 | 7 | | | | | 11 | 11 | | | 1 | 1 | | 7 | 7 | 28 | 24 |
| j | | | 2 | 2 | 4 | 4 | 48 | | | | 12 | 12 | | 94 | 5 | 5 | 7 | 7 | | 33 | 33 | | | 18 | 18 | 117 | 28 | 13 | 13 |
| k | 51 | 51 | | 2 | 2 | 15 | 15 | 120 | 120 | 4 | 17 | 17 | 7 | 27 | 27 | 1 | 1 | 4 | 4 | 1 | 1 | | | 1 | | | 117 | | |
| l | 39 | 39 | 5 | | | 82 | 82 | 119 | 119 | 12 | 4 | 2 | 2 | 5 | 5 | 12 | 12 | 1 | 1 | 7 | 7 | | | 1 | 1 | | | 22 | |
| m | 69 | 69 | 1 | | | 29 | 29 | 128 | 99 | 99 | 12 | 18 | 86 | 8 | 8 | 81 | 81 | 3 | 3 | 4 | 3 | 102 | 102 | 6 | 6 | 1 | 22 | 22 | 9 |
| n | 27 | 27 | | | | 6 | 6 | 17 | 4 | 1 | 18 | 14 | 112 | 86 | 14 | 25 | 25 | | 4 | 27 | 27 | 28 | 1 | 33 | 1 | | 22 | 17 | 5 |
| o | 1 | 1 | 7 | 7 | 2 | 4 | 128 | 29 | 178 | 4 | 14 | 2 | 2 | 112 | 5 | 14 | 39 | 39 | | 21 | 21 | 56 | 28 | 30 | 30 | 21 | 17 | 25 | 21 |
| p | 6 | 6 | 11 | 11 | | | 17 | 178 | 75 | 37 | 37 | 2 | 7 | 27 | 27 | 5 | 81 | 3 | 3 | 19 | 19 | 3 | 56 | 23 | 23 | | 21 | 17 | 25 |
| q | 102 | 102 | 4 | 4 | | 66 | 29 | 4 | 142 | 75 | | 7 | | 4 | 4 | 81 | 60 | 2 | 5 | 94 | 94 | 4 | 33 | 2 | | 1 | 17 | | |
| r | 34 | 34 | 2 | 2 | 2 | 2 | 66 | 16 | 3 | 142 | 5 | 5 | 4 | 4 | 35 | 60 | 118 | 2 | 2 | 11 | 11 | 100 | 4 | 1 | 37 | 23 | | 48 | 48 |
| s | 91 | 91 | 16 | 16 | 1 | 1 | 4 | 3 | | 1 | 22 | 22 | | 2 | 2 | 35 | 3 | 118 | 2 | 11 | 4 | 15 | 100 | 37 | 12 | 9 | 23 | 86 | 86 |
| t | 2 | 2 | 5 | 5 | 28 | 28 | 16 | 108 | 3 | 3 | 10 | 10 | 54 | 54 | | | 2 | 3 | | 1 | | 4 | 2 | 12 | 17 | 6 | 9 | 69 | 69 |
| u | 19 | 19 | 13 | 13 | 4 | 4 | 3 | | | | | | | | | | | 2 | 11 | | | 8 | 15 | 17 | | | 6 | 37 | 37 |
| v | | | | | 1 | 1 | 108 | | | | | | | | | | | | 1 | | | 4 | 4 | 59 | | | | 11 | 11 |
| w | 4 | 4 | | | | | | | | | | | | | | | | | | | | 4 | 8 | 24 | | | 2 | 2 | 2 |
| x | | | 3 | 2 | 5 | 2 | 2 | 7 | 2 | 2 | 6 | 2 | 2 | 4 | 4 | 4 | 4 | 5 | 5 | 6 | 6 | | | | 5 | 5 | 3 | 3 | 3 |
| y | | | 2 | 3 | | 20 | 20 | | 4 | 4 | 5 | | | 2 | 2 | | | 1 | 1 | 5 | 5 | | | | | 1 | 1 | 2 | 2 |
| z | 4 | 4 | | 2 | 2 | 2 | 2 | | 7 | 6 | 2 | | | | 2 | 2 | 18 | 18 | | 12 | 12 | | | | 26 | 26 | 9 | 9 | 7 |
| æ | | 2 | | | 8 | 8 | | 1 | 1 | 2 | | | 2 | 6 | 6 | | 8 | 8 | 4 | 4 | | 2 | | | 27 | 27 | 4 | 4 | 1 |

## Table A.2 (cont'd) Dutch (expressed as frequency per 10000 letters)

| | a | b | c | d | e | f | g | h | i | j | k | l | m | n | o | p | q | r | s | t | u | v | w | x | y | z |
|---|---|---|---|---|---|---|---|---|---|---|---|---|---|---|---|---|---|---|---|---|---|---|---|---|---|---|
| a | 147 | 147 | 7 | 7 | 18 | 18 | 19 | 19 | 6 | 6 | 13 | 13 | 9 | 9 | 4 | 4 | 3 | 3 | 1 | 1 | 21 | 21 | 86 | 86 | 27 | 27 |
| b | 8 | 8 | 5 | 5 | 1 | | 67 | 67 | | | | 27 | 27 | 1 | 1 | | 6 | 6 | | | 16 | 16 | | | 21 | 21 |
| c | 2 | 2 | | 1 | | | 6 | 6 | | | | 62 | 4 | 4 | | 2 | 2 | | 1 | 1 | | 4 | 4 | | | |
| d | 71 | 71 | 1 | 1 | 10 | 14 | 14 | 244 | 244 | | 62 | 4 | 6 | 6 | 59 | 53 | 4 | 4 | | 2 | 2 | 2 | 2 | 2 | 2 | 31 |
| e | 37 | 37 | 1 | 47 | | 10 | 74 | 74 | 182 | 182 | 4 | 25 | 43 | 43 | 27 | 27 | 64 | 64 | | 2 | 57 | 57 | 131 | 131 | 44 | 44 |
| f | 4 | 4 | | 3 | | | 5 | 11 | 11 | 4 | 25 | | 1 | 3 | 3 | 4 | 4 | | | | 5 | 5 | | 5 | 5 | |
| g | 17 | 17 | | | | 5 | 7 | 157 | 157 | | 8 | 8 | 2 | 2 | 16 | 16 | 2 | 1 | | 2 | 5 | 5 | 5 | 5 | 11 | 11 |
| h | 32 | 32 | 47 | | 16 | 7 | 99 | 1 | 1 | | | 29 | 29 | | | 2 | 102 | 1 | | 34 | 2 | 16 | 16 | | | 4 |
| i | 12 | 12 | | 16 | | 99 | 20 | | 115 | | 3 | 28 | 28 | | 1 | | 1 | 102 | 2 | 35 | 16 | 16 | 13 | 13 | 153 | 153 |
| j | 7 | 7 | | 1 | | 20 | 9 | 115 | 23 | | 3 | 1 | 1 | 1 | 6 | 12 | 12 | | | 14 | | 1 | 1 | 14 | 14 | |
| k | 27 | 27 | | 6 | | 9 | 7 | 23 | 58 | | 1 | 4 | 4 | 6 | 10 | 2 | 73 | | | 1 | 6 | 6 | 4 | 4 | 5 | 6 |
| l | 49 | 49 | 3 | 5 | | 7 | | 58 | 84 | 84 | 4 | 4 | 4 | 10 | 2 | 26 | 26 | | | | 5 | 5 | 34 | 34 | 2 | 5 |
| m | 33 | 33 | 16 | 3 | | 1 | 23 | 23 | 99 | 1 | 4 | 2 | 2 | 4 | 2 | 37 | 72 | 73 | 34 | | 8 | 8 | 2 | 2 | 31 | 2 |
| n | 82 | 82 | 1 | 20 | 1 | 8 | 8 | 99 | 92 | 92 | 4 | 17 | 104 | 104 | 37 | | 4 | | 35 | 3 | 23 | 23 | 11 | 11 | 35 | 31 |
| o | 20 | | 6 | 3 | | 4 | 156 | 156 | 59 | 59 | 17 | 3 | 27 | 27 | 1 | 5 | 1 | 72 | 14 | 20 | 20 | 15 | 15 | 47 | 47 | 35 |
| p | 3 | | 5 | 2 | | 4 | 13 | 13 | 29 | | 3 | | 4 | 4 | 5 | | | 4 | 1 | 3 | 14 | 14 | 1 | 1 | | 69 |
| q | 31 | 31 | 3 | | 4 | 3 | 3 | 29 | | | | 3 | | 4 | | 12 | 45 | 1 | | | 1 | 1 | | | | 12 |
| r | | | 20 | 17 | | | | | 101 | 101 | 3 | 8 | 17 | 17 | 12 | 22 | 22 | 45 | 3 | 21 | | | 11 | 25 | 25 | |
| s | 54 | 54 | 3 | 11 | 2 | 2 | 78 | 78 | 54 | 54 | | 2 | 8 | 11 | 11 | 33 | 47 | 47 | | 2 | 21 | 11 | 11 | 6 | 6 | 22 |
| t | 11 | 11 | 2 | 22 | 24 | 24 | 15 | 15 | 204 | 204 | 2 | 1 | 15 | 15 | 33 | | 9 | 9 | 3 | 5 | 2 | 21 | 21 | 4 | 16 | 9 |
| u | 54 | 54 | 17 | 4 | 3 | 3 | 37 | 37 | 2 | | 1 | 9 | | 59 | 59 | | | | 5 | 7 | 6 | 6 | 18 | 18 | 16 | 16 |
| v | 5 | 5 | | 3 | 4 | 10 | 10 | 2 | | | 9 | 1 | | | 4 | | | | 7 | 51 | 5 | 5 | 11 | 11 | 1 | 1 |
| w | 63 | 63 | | 2 | 4 | 62 | 62 | | 87 | | | | 1 | 19 | 19 | 1 | 5 | 5 | 51 | 1 | | | 17 | | | |
| x | 52 | 52 | 3 | 3 | | 1 | 1 | 87 | | | | | | | 1 | | | | 1 | 1 | 5 | 17 | 17 | 11 | 1 | 1 |
| y | | | | | 1 | 1 | | | | | | | | | | | | | | 2 | | | | | | |
| z | 11 | 11 | | | | 37 | 37 | | | | 35 | 35 | 1 | | | 1 | 5 | 5 | 21 | 21 | 2 | 17 | 17 | | | |

**Table A.2** (cont'd) English (expressed as frequency per 10000 letters)

| | a | b | c | d | e | f | g | h | i | j | k | l | m | n | o | p | q | r | s | t | u | v | w | x | y | z |
|---|---|---|---|---|---|---|---|---|---|---|---|---|---|---|---|---|---|---|---|---|---|---|---|---|---|---|
| a | 6 | 6 | 12 | 12 | 27 | 27 | 54 | 54 | 2 | 2 | 8 | 8 | 12 | 12 | 4 | 4 | 34 | 34 | 2 | 2 | 4 | 4 | 64 | 64 | 27 | 27 |
| b | 8 | 8 | | | | 36 | 36 | | | | 4 | 4 | 2 | 2 | | 12 | 12 | 2 | 2 | | 8 | 8 | | | 4 | 4 |
| c | 40 | 40 | 8 | 6 | 6 | 2 | 2 | | 64 | 2 | 2 | | 27 | 27 | 13 | 13 | | 8 | 8 | 10 | 10 | 2 | 2 | 2 | 2 | 82 |
| d | 64 | 64 | 8 | 8 | 8 | 8 | 16 | 64 | 66 | 66 | 16 | 16 | 4 | 4 | 4 | 4 | 54 | 54 | 2 | 2 | | 6 | 6 | 10 | 10 | 8 |
| e | 70 | 70 | | 4 | 64 | 64 | 120 | 16 | 84 | 84 | 36 | 36 | 8 | 8 | 13 | 13 | 54 | 54 | 2 | 2 | 2 | 58 | 58 | 27 | 27 | 222 |
| f | 10 | 10 | | 4 | 4 | | 2 | 120 | 20 | 22 | 22 | 2 | 2 | | 78 | 78 | 10 | | 4 | 4 | 4 | | | 80 | 80 | 2 |
| g | 13 | 13 | 2 | 2 | 4 | 2 | 2 | | 27 | 4 | 4 | 10 | 2 | 40 | 40 | 10 | | 2 | 2 | | 4 | 4 | 2 | | | 6 |
| h | 40 | 40 | 4 | 4 | 6 | 6 | 2 | 27 | 4 | 40 | 10 | 20 | 38 | 38 | 66 | 66 | | | 2 | 2 | 46 | 4 | 6 | 6 | 40 | 40 |
| i | 16 | 16 | | 2 | 44 | 44 | 4 | 4 | 26 | 26 | 20 | 4 | | | | | 4 | 4 | 4 | 46 | | 18 | 18 | 150 | 150 | 82 |
| j | 2 | 2 | | | 2 | 4 | 12 | 12 | | | 6 | 6 | 4 | | | | | 4 | | | | | | 4 | 4 | 2 |
| k | 55 | 55 | 6 | 6 | 6 | 6 | | 12 | | | 2 | 18 | 4 | 2 | 2 | 2 | | | | | | | | | 2 | 2 |
| l | 72 | 72 | 12 | 12 | 6 | 6 | 12 | 18 | 74 | 74 | 18 | 50 | 2 | 2 | 2 | 2 | 40 | 40 | 2 | | 54 | 54 | 4 | 4 | 2 | 16 |
| m | 52 | 52 | 4 | 4 | 38 | 38 | 18 | 2 | 52 | 52 | 50 | 4 | 54 | 54 | 8 | 18 | 18 | | | 2 | 26 | 26 | | 20 | 20 | 10 |
| n | 13 | 13 | 8 | 8 | 16 | 16 | 2 | 104 | 114 | 114 | 4 | | 4 | 4 | 6 | 8 | | | | | 4 | 4 | 10 | 10 | 10 | 50 |
| o | 27 | 27 | 2 | 2 | 2 | 2 | 104 | 24 | 6 | 6 | | 12 | 2 | 6 | 6 | 6 | 60 | 60 | 2 | | 4 | 4 | 38 | 38 | 50 | 34 |
| p | 78 | 78 | | 4 | 18 | 18 | 24 | 2 | 46 | 46 | 12 | 24 | 13 | 2 | | 12 | 10 | 10 | 2 | 2 | 26 | 8 | 8 | 2 | 2 | 18 |
| q | 48 | 48 | | 6 | 26 | 26 | 2 | | 196 | 196 | 24 | 13 | 4 | 13 | | | 12 | | | 2 | 2 | | 30 | 30 | | 8 |
| r | 55 | 55 | | 6 | 12 | 12 | 34 | 34 | 98 | 98 | 13 | 2 | | 4 | 6 | 6 | 60 | 60 | 2 | 26 | 2 | 2 | 10 | 10 | 18 | 13 |
| s | 10 | 10 | | 6 | 26 | 26 | 10 | 10 | 142 | 142 | 2 | 24 | 16 | 2 | 52 | 52 | 68 | 68 | 2 | 2 | 2 | 4 | 10 | 6 | 6 | 2 |
| t | 12 | 12 | | 6 | 12 | 12 | 12 | 12 | 22 | 22 | 24 | 26 | 26 | 16 | 156 | 156 | 89 | 89 | | 2 | 10 | 10 | 12 | 12 | 13 | 2 |
| u | 24 | 24 | | | 6 | 6 | 6 | 6 | | | 8 | | 2 | | 10 | 10 | 10 | 2 | | 2 | 12 | | | 42 | 42 | 2 |
| v | 4 | 4 | | | | 114 | 114 | | 2 | 8 | 2 | 22 | 2 | | | | | | | | 38 | 38 | | 2 | 2 | 2 |
| w | 12 | 12 | | 4 | 4 | 44 | 44 | 2 | | | | 2 | | 2 | 4 | 2 | 2 | | 2 | | 2 | 2 | 2 | | 2 | 4 |
| x | 2 | 2 | 4 | 4 | 8 | 8 | 8 | 8 | 18 | 18 | 22 | 22 | | 2 | 2 | 4 | | | 4 | 4 | | | | | | |
| y | | | | | | | 8 | 8 | 2 | 2 | 2 | 2 | | | | 2 | 2 | 6 | | | 10 | 10 | | | | 12 |
| z | 2 | 2 | | 4 | 8 | 4 | 4 | 8 | 18 | 18 | 2 | 2 | 2 | 2 | 2 | | | 6 | | | 4 | 4 | 4 | 4 | 12 | 12 |

## Table A.2 (cont'd) Finnish (expressed as frequency per 10000 letters)

| | a | b | c | d | e | f | g | h | i | j | k | l | m | n | o | p | q | r | s | t | u | v | w | x | y | z | å | ä | ö |
|---|---|---|---|---|---|---|---|---|---|---|---|---|---|---|---|---|---|---|---|---|---|---|---|---|---|---|---|---|---|
| a | 62 | 62 | | | 4 | 4 | 39 | 39 | 4 | 4 | 1 | 1 | 43 | 43 | 103 | 103 | 35 | 35 | 97 | 97 | 129 | 129 | 68 | 68 | 167 | 167 | 54 | 54 | 44 |
| b | | | | | 3 | 3 | | | | | | | | | | | | | 19 | | | | | | 2 | 2 | | | |
| d | 11 | 11 | | | | 20 | 20 | 87 | 87 | | 7 | 7 | 11 | 11 | 76 | 76 | 7 | 19 | 35 | 35 | 80 | 80 | 29 | 29 | 181 | 181 | 7 | 7 | 11 |
| e | 14 | 14 | | | 9 | 9 | | | 11 | 11 | 2 | 2 | 1 | 1 | | | | 7 | | | | | | | | | | | |
| f | | | | | | | | | | 3 | 3 | | | | | | | | | | | | | | | | | | |
| g | 1 | 1 | | | 21 | 21 | 29 | 29 | 1 | | 14 | 14 | 14 | 24 | 24 | 68 | 1 | 1 | 11 | | 1 | 1 | 3 | 3 | 3 | 14 | 14 | 31 | 31 |
| h | 31 | 31 | 1 | 1 | 17 | 17 | 51 | 51 | | | 2 | 14 | 25 | 25 | 68 | 19 | | 11 | 77 | | 4 | 4 | | | 202 | 3 | 28 | 28 | 11 |
| i | 33 | 33 | | | | 14 | 14 | | | 1 | 1 | 2 | 61 | 61 | 19 | 19 | 11 | 11 | 47 | 77 | 76 | 76 | 40 | 40 | 202 | 202 | | | |
| j | 69 | 69 | | | | 54 | 54 | | | | 1 | 65 | 65 | 2 | 2 | 1 | 19 | 11 | 47 | 132 | | | | | 7 | 7 | | | 57 |
| k | 117 | 117 | | | 5 | 87 | 87 | 75 | 75 | 4 | | 65 | 60 | 21 | 21 | 1 | | 47 | 31 | 132 | 132 | 46 | 46 | 3 | 3 | 50 | 50 | 1 | 1 | 24 |
| l | 94 | 94 | | | | 40 | 40 | 2 | | 4 | 60 | 60 | 172 | 172 | 21 | 47 | 118 | 118 | 31 | 31 | 18 | 9 | 9 | | | 3 | | | 2 | 31 |
| m | 77 | 77 | | | | 2 | 2 | | | | 4 | 5 | 5 | 53 | 53 | 9 | 9 | 23 | 23 | 26 | 18 | 18 | 20 | 29 | 29 | | 29 | 2 | 2 | 77 |
| n | 74 | 74 | 1 | 1 | 6 | 5 | 21 | 101 | 101 | 4 | 32 | 32 | 172 | 145 | 145 | 17 | 17 | 47 | 26 | 59 | 104 | 104 | 20 | 20 | 87 | 63 | 63 | 77 | 63 | 20 |
| o | 74 | 74 | | | | 5 | 21 | 21 | 21 | 4 | 26 | 26 | 53 | 3 | 3 | 28 | 27 | 27 | 59 | 104 | 25 | 25 | 87 | 2 | 2 | 10 | 12 | 12 | 5 |
| p | 13 | 13 | | | 4 | 21 | 18 | | | 3 | 3 | 3 | 145 | 145 | 3 | 24 | 14 | 10 | 10 | 10 | 25 | 1 | 2 | 2 | 5 | 1 | 1 | 20 | 20 | 2 |
| r | 34 | 34 | | | 1 | 18 | 18 | 1 | | | 3 | 3 | 89 | 89 | 3 | 2 | 28 | 14 | 14 | 3 | 7 | 2 | 13 | 1 | 5 | 2 | 2 | 5 | 5 | 8 |
| s | 91 | 91 | 3 | 3 | | 122 | 101 | 9 | 9 | | 16 | 16 | 20 | 20 | 2 | 2 | 24 | 3 | 3 | 4 | 7 | 13 | 13 | 2 | 4 | 3 | 54 | 4 | | |
| t | 91 | 91 | | | | 122 | 122 | | | | 41 | 41 | | 5 | 5 | | 35 | 5 | 5 | 4 | 4 | | | 42 | 54 | 5 | 39 | 54 | | |
| u | 270 | 270 | | | 6 | | 21 | 21 | | 7 | 14 | 14 | | 3 | 3 | 15 | | | 66 | 66 | 13 | | | 42 | 39 | 39 | 4 | 39 | 5 | |
| v | 10 | 10 | | | 4 | 6 | 11 | 11 | | | 3 | 3 | 8 | 5 | 5 | 5 | 15 | 7 | 7 | 7 | 7 | 4 | 4 | 12 | 12 | 7 | 7 | 3 | 12 | |
| y | 115 | 115 | | | 1 | 4 | 1 | 1 | | | 7 | 8 | 8 | 3 | 3 | | 13 | 14 | 14 | 11 | 11 | 4 | 7 | 7 | 63 | 63 | 27 | 27 | 3 | 20 |
| å | 9 | 9 | | | | 1 | 1 | 9 | 9 | | | 2 | 2 | 5 | | | 13 | 13 | 6 | 6 | 14 | 14 | 24 | 24 | 4 | 3 | 3 | 3 | 3 | 5 |
| ä | 3 | 3 | | | | 3 | 9 | | | | | | | | | | 1 | 1 | | | | 2 | 2 | 3 | 4 | 3 | 3 | 3 | 3 | |
| ö | 3 | 3 | | | | | 3 | | | | | 2 | 2 | 2 | | | 1 | 1 | | | | | 2 | 3 | 3 | 3 | 3 | 3 | 3 | 2 |

**Table A.2** (cont'd) French (expressed as frequency per 10000 letters)

| | a | b | c | d | e | f | g | h | i | j | k | l | m | n | o | p | q | r | s | t | u | v | x | y | z |
|---|---|---|---|---|---|---|---|---|---|---|---|---|---|---|---|---|---|---|---|---|---|---|---|---|---|
| a | 5 | 5 | 21 | 21 | 37 | 37 | 20 | 20 | 3 | 3 | 11 | 11 | 25 | 25 | 27 | 103 | 103 | 4 | 4 | 13 | 52 | 52 | 24 | 24 | 117 |
| b | 17 | 17 | 3 | 3 | | 8 | 8 | 3 | 73 | 73 | 6 | 6 | 27 | 27 | 17 | 27 | | 3 | 13 | 10 | 3 | 3 | 8 | 8 | 4 |
| c | 40 | 40 | 10 | 10 | 13 | 13 | 3 | 3 | 73 | 73 | 2 | 2 | 50 | 50 | 17 | 17 | 15 | 16 | 16 | 10 | 19 | 19 | 129 | 77 | 77 |
| d | 62 | 62 | | 10 | 4 | 4 | 236 | 236 | 70 | 70 | 34 | 34 | 17 | 17 | 13 | 13 | 15 | 1 | 3 | 6 | 129 | 129 | 24 | 117 | 17 |
| e | 55 | 55 | | 1 | 84 | 84 | 119 | 119 | 16 | 16 | 13 | 13 | 2 | 2 | 6 | 6 | | 1 | 6 | 8 | 1 | 1 | 1 | 24 | 117 |
| f | 30 | 30 | | | 1 | 1 | 1 | 1 | 86 | 86 | 1 | 1 | 2 | 2 | | | 1 | | 1 | 18 | 18 | 1 | | | |
| g | 9 | 9 | | | | 37 | 37 | 37 | | | 1 | 1 | 6 | 6 | | | | | 12 | 12 | 69 | 19 | 19 | 74 | 74 |
| h | 8 | 8 | | | 10 | 36 | 36 | 18 | | | 1 | 6 | 1 | 1 | | 2 | 2 | | 1 | | | | 1 | 1 | 1 |
| i | 12 | 12 | | | 4 | 10 | 18 | 18 | | | 6 | 1 | 23 | 23 | 1 | 32 | 12 | 12 | 12 | | | | 19 | 4 | 9 |
| j | 2 | 2 | | 6 | | 8 | 8 | 8 | 337 | 337 | | 13 | | | | | 32 | 2 | | | | | 4 | 24 | |
| k | | | | | | 4 | 1 | 119 | 119 | | | 1 | 42 | 42 | 1 | 26 | 26 | 2 | 2 | 18 | 73 | 73 | 24 | 24 | |
| l | 107 | 107 | | 1 | 54 | 1 | 1 | 8 | 183 | 183 | 13 | 13 | 6 | 6 | | | 6 | 17 | 17 | 12 | 23 | 23 | 2 | 2 | 57 |
| m | 34 | 34 | | 20 | 8 | 54 | 58 | 58 | 2 | 2 | 4 | | 48 | 48 | | 64 | 64 | 1 | 1 | | 4 | 4 | 2 | 6 | 6 |
| n | 44 | 44 | | 3 | 23 | 4 | 4 | 2 | 168 | 168 | 4 | 9 | 6 | 6 | 99 | 1 | 70 | 6 | 38 | 38 | 167 | 167 | 10 | 10 | 94 |
| o | | 8 | 2 | 8 | 40 | 46 | 46 | | 145 | 145 | 12 | 12 | 9 | | | 99 | 3 | 70 | | 44 | 54 | 54 | 20 | 94 | 10 |
| p | 48 | 48 | 4 | 2 | 6 | 1 | 1 | 168 | 140 | 140 | 2 | 2 | 1 | 1 | 4 | 66 | 3 | 3 | 2 | 2 | 44 | 51 | 51 | 10 | 12 |
| q | | | | 23 | 24 | 38 | 38 | 84 | 86 | 86 | 13 | 13 | 5 | 5 | | | 66 | 6 | 6 | | 31 | 10 | 20 | 10 | 15 |
| r | 85 | 85 | 4 | 4 | 6 | 40 | 84 | 71 | 71 | | 32 | 32 | 3 | 3 | 2 | | 1 | 32 | 32 | 31 | 31 | 25 | 51 | 12 | 55 |
| s | 58 | 58 | 4 | 6 | 24 | 24 | 71 | 12 | 8 | 8 | 32 | 13 | | | | 2 | | 8 | 8 | | 25 | 10 | 10 | 15 | |
| t | 82 | 82 | 1 | 3 | 3 | 55 | 12 | 8 | 3 | 3 | 2 | 13 | 5 | | | 2 | | 8 | 32 | 3 | 3 | 25 | 19 | 19 | 2 |
| u | 29 | 29 | | 1 | 1 | 5 | 55 | 8 | 1 | | 13 | 32 | 3 | 3 | 4 | 2 | 1 | 8 | 8 | 1 | 3 | 9 | 9 | 9 | |
| v | 34 | 34 | | | | 3 | 5 | 8 | | 3 | 32 | 5 | | | | | | 1 | 2 | 1 | 1 | 1 | 1 | 2 | |
| x | 4 | 4 | 1 | 3 | 3 | | 8 | 3 | | | | | 5 | 4 | 2 | 2 | | | 2 | 2 | 3 | | 1 | 2 | |
| y | 5 | 5 | | 1 | 1 | 3 | 3 | 1 | 1 | 3 | | | | 4 | 2 | | 1 | | | 1 | 1 | 1 | 1 | 1 | 2 |
| z | | 5 | | | | | | | | | | | | | | | | | | 2 | | | | | |

**Table A.2** (cont'd) German (expressed as frequency per 10000 letters)

| | a | b | c | d | e | f | g | h | i | j | k | l | m | n | o | p | q | r | s | t | u | v | w | x | y | z |
|---|---|---|---|---|---|---|---|---|---|---|---|---|---|---|---|---|---|---|---|---|---|---|---|---|---|---|
| a | 2 | 37 | 60 | 19 | 27 | 22 | 44 | 5 | 4 | 11 | 44 | 42 | 68 | 2 | 15 | | | 57 | 36 | 63 | 3 | 33 | 5 | | | |
| b | 2 | 37 | 60 | 19 | 27 | 22 | 44 | 5 | 4 | 11 | 44 | 42 | 68 | 2 | 15 | | | 57 | 36 | 63 | 17 | 3 | 33 | | | 5 |
| c | 36 | 4 | | 5 | 47 | 2 | 2 | 6 | 8 | | | 6 | 6 | 34 | 19 | | | 24 | 13 | 11 | 17 | | | | | 1 |
| d | 36 | 4 | | 5 | 47 | 2 | 2 | 6 | 8 | | | 6 | 6 | 34 | 19 | | | 24 | 13 | 11 | 21 | | | | | 1 |
| e | 33 | 1 | | | 21 | | | 71 | | | | 1 | | 3 | 6 | | | 15 | 68 | | 21 | | | | | 1 |
| f | 33 | 1 | 24 | 21 | 3 | 13 | 5 | 71 | 13 | 26 | | 1 | 12 | 3 | 6 | 8 | | 15 | 68 | 27 | 5 | 59 | 1 | | | 2 |
| g | 2 | 4 | 24 | 51 | 8 | 13 | 5 | 16 | 13 | 26 | 20 | 12 | | 237 | 8 | 8 | | 66 | 37 | 27 | 5 | 59 | 37 | | | 2 |
| h | 2 | 4 | 248 | 241 | 51 | 52 | 181 | 64 | 16 | | 20 | 37 | | 237 | 8 | 8 | | 66 | 37 | 223 | 22 | 37 | | | | 39 |
| i | 131 | 248 | 241 | 35 | 52 | 181 | 64 | 186 | | 2 | 75 | 37 | 122 | | 8 | | | 129 | 107 | 223 | 22 | | | | | 39 |
| j | 6 | 131 | | 4 | 35 | 11 | 4 | 2 | 186 | | 2 | 75 | 6 | 122 | 13 | | | 129 | 107 | 4 | 29 | | | | | 1 |
| k | 6 | | 4 | | 35 | 11 | 4 | 2 | 3 | | 2 | 6 | 19 | 13 | 3 | | | 23 | 4 | 4 | 29 | 11 | 1 | | | 1 |
| l | 22 | 1 | 20 | 5 | 35 | 5 | 4 | 5 | 3 | | 2 | 2 | 9 | 19 | 12 | 3 | | 23 | 4 | 21 | 18 | 11 | | | | 1 |
| m | 22 | 1 | 20 | 5 | 41 | 5 | 4 | 5 | 41 | | 2 | 8 | 3 | 102 | 12 | 10 | | 13 | 13 | 21 | 18 | 38 | | | | |
| n | 30 | 1 | 2 | 41 | 2 | 3 | 23 | 41 | 8 | | 4 | 102 | 13 | 10 | 13 | 13 | | 13 | 13 | 38 | 15 | | | | | |
| o | 30 | 1 | 2 | 40 | 2 | 3 | 23 | 10 | 4 | | 12 | 13 | | 11 | 1 | 13 | 13 | | | | | | | | | 15 |
| p | 6 | .3 | 1.5 | 40 | 6 | 8 | .5 | .0 | 6 | | 48 | 35 | .2 | 1 | | | | 11 | 1 | 34 | 3 | | | | | |
| q | 6 | 13 | 115 | 225 | 6 | 8 | 15 | | 5 | | 6 | 48 | 35 | 51 | 1 | 3 | | 54 | 46 | 34 | 3 | | | | | |
| r | 1 | | 225 | | 2 | 1 | | | 5 | | | 51 | | | 3 | | | 54 | 46 | 1 | 1 | 33 | | | | 4 |
| s | 1 | | 3 | 5 | 2 | 2 | 1 | 2 | | | 4 | 2 | 5 | 1 | | | | 3 | 5 | 1 | 1 | 33 | | | 1 | 4 |
| t | 1 | 11 | 3 | 5 | 2 | 6 | 3 | 2 | 15 | | 4 | 2 | 5 | 1 | | | | 3 | 5 | 2 | 1 | | | | 9 | 1 |
| u | 1 | 11 | 3 | 11 | 3 | 6 | 3 | 27 | 15 | 48 | 3 | 15 | 16 | 6 | 3 | | | 17 | 9 | 2 | 1 | | | | | 9 |
| v | 51 | | 3 | 11 | 3 | 16 | 30 | 27 | | 48 | 3 | 15 | 16 | 6 | 3 | | | 17 | 9 | 8 | 5 | | | | | 3 |
| w | 51 | | 2 | 91 | | 16 | 30 | 21 | | 22 | 10 | 22 | 9 | 18 | 6 | 8 | 5 | 2 | | | | | | | | 3 |
| x | 21 | 3 | 2 | 91 | 2 | 1 | 9 | 21 | 2 | 13 | 6 | 22 | 10 | 22 | 9 | 18 | 6 | 5 | 19 | 2 | 2 | | | | | |
| y | 21 | 3 | 4 | 42 | 2 | 1 | 9 | 145 | 13 | 6 | 2 | 18 | 60 | | 22 | 6 | 5 | 19 | 2 | | | | | | | |
| z | 111 | | 4 | 42 | 6 | 1 | 16 | 145 | 11 | 2 | 18 | 60 | 20 | 22 | 6 | 2 | 152 | | | | | | | | | |

**Table A.2 (cont'd) Greek (expressed as frequency per 10000 letters)**

|   | a | b | g | d | e | z | h | u | i | k | l | m | n | j | o | p | r | s | w | t | y | f | x | c | v |
|---|---|---|---|---|---|---|---|---|---|---|---|---|---|---|---|---|---|---|---|---|---|---|---|---|---|
| a | 24 | 24 | 30 | 16 | 18 | 5 | 15 | 30 | 189 | 174 | 54 | 98 | 196 | 9 | 19 | 76 | 99 | 53 | 25 | 173 | 11 | 16 | 28 | 2 | 8 |
| b | 24 | 24 | 30 | 16 | 18 | 5 | 15 | 30 | 189 | 174 | 54 | 98 | 196 | 9 | 19 | 76 | 99 | 53 | 25 | 173 | 11 | 16 | 28 | 2 | 8 |
| g | 15 |  | 12 | 2 | 6 |  | 1 | 2 | 10 |  | 1 | 1 | 2 | 5 |  |  |  |  |  |  |  |  |  |  | 4 |
| d | 15 | 3 | 6 | 12 | 2 | 6 |  | 1 | 2 | 10 |  | 1 | 1 | 2 | 5 |  |  |  |  |  |  |  |  |  | 4 |
| e | 46 | 3 | 6 | 31 | 12 | 20 |  |  |  | 5 | 18 | 7 | 11 |  |  |  | 57 | 11 | 57 | 10 | 14 |  |  |  | 4 |
| z | 46 |  | 38 | 31 | 18 |  | 20 | 36 | 43 |  | 5 | 9 | 10 |  |  |  | 6 | 8 |  | 14 |  |  |  |  |  |
| h | 26 | 4 | 30 | 38 | 9 | 18 | 30 | 34 | 116 | 7 | 23 | 1 | 7 |  |  |  | 57 | 57 | 8 | 57 |  | 10 | 35 | 5 | 2 |
| u | 26 | 4 | 30 |  | 9 |  | 34 |  | 116 |  |  | 70 | 7 |  |  |  |  | 8 |  |  |  |  |  |  | 4 |
| i | 38 |  |  | 4 | 15 | 1 | 12 | 12 | 50 | 15 | 25 |  | 99 | 5 | 18 | 14 | 42 | 27 | 144 | 26 |  | 6 | 3 |  | 4 |
| k | 38 | 4 | 9 | 4 | 15 | 1 | 12 | 12 | 50 | 15 | 25 | 17 | 99 |  | 18 | 14 | 42 | 23 | 27 | 144 | 26 | 7 | 6 | 3 |  |
| l | 20 | 4 | 9 | 1 |  | 1 | 13 |  | 17 | 1 |  | 2 |  |  | 23 | 1 |  | 1 |  | 1 |  | 1 | 4 |  |  |
| m | 20 |  | 38 | 1 | 3 |  | 6 | 13 | 78 | 31 |  | 1 | 2 | 2 | 28 | 16 | 3 | 1 | 70 | 1 | 9 | 1 | 1 | 4 | 4 |
| n | 10 | 3 | 41 | 38 | 6 | 3 | 4 | 6 | 18 | 78 | 31 |  | 45 | 42 | 6 | 28 | 16 | 3 | 8 | 70 | 7 | 9 | 10 | 1 | 5 |
| j | 10 | 3 | 41 |  | 6 |  | 4 |  | 18 | 3 |  |  | 45 | 42 | 6 |  | 6 | 31 | 8 |  | 7 |  | 10 |  | 5 |
| o | 29 |  | 8 |  | 7 |  | 12 |  | 8 | 3 | 20 |  | 11 |  | 6 | 15 | 6 | 31 | 7 |  | 7 | 2 |  |  | 1 |
| p | 29 | 6 | 8 |  | 7 |  | 12 |  | 8 | 12 | 20 |  | 11 |  | 6 | 15 | 69 | 20 | 7 |  | 7 | 2 | 1 |  | 1 |
| r | 175 | 6 | 3 |  | 180 |  | 2 |  | 2 | 12 |  | 5 | 29 |  | 51 | 69 | 20 | 3 |  | 2 |  | 1 |  |  | 6 |
| s | 175 |  | 3 |  | 180 |  | 2 |  | 2 |  | 1 | 5 | 29 |  | 51 | 4 | 4 |  | 3 |  | 2 | 2 |  |  | 6 |
| w | 95 | 7 | 7 |  | 46 | 7 | 39 | 7 | 78 |  | 1 | 4 | 24 | 2 | 46 | 4 | 4 | 19 | 42 | 220 | 21 | 2 | 4 |  | 1 |
| t | 95 | 7 | 7 |  | 46 | 7 | 39 | 7 | 78 |  |  | 4 | 24 | 2 | 46 |  |  | 19 | 42 | 220 | 21 |  | 4 |  | 1 |
| y | 71 | 8 | 4 |  | 33 |  | 8 |  | 14 | 72 | 45 |  | 3 |  | 34 | 131 | 6 |  | 3 |  | 17 | 20 |  |  | 19 |
| f | 71 | 8 | 4 | 7 | 33 |  | 8 | 7 | 14 | 72 | 45 |  | 72 |  | 34 | 131 | 6 |  | 3 | 38 | 17 | 20 | 14 |  | 19 |
| x | 84 |  | 7 | 7 | 44 | 36 | 7 | 46 |  | 1 | 72 | 15 |  |  | 60 | 1 | 8 | 24 | 22 | 38 | 28 |  | 14 |  | 37 |
| c | 84 | 7 | 14 |  | 44 | 36 |  | 46 | 25 | 1 | 22 | 15 |  |  | 60 | 1 | 8 | 24 | 22 | 14 | 28 | 4 |  |  | 37 |
| v | 178 | 7 | 14 |  | 106 | 62 |  | 81 | 25 |  | 22 | 7 |  |  | 90 | 31 | 1 | 14 | 7 | 14 | 44 | 4 | 7 |  | 3 |

**Table A.2** (cont'd) Hebrew (expressed as frequency per 10000 letters)

| | b | g | d | h | z | c | y | k | l | m | n | s | p | q | w | x | t | r | s | + | ( | ) | & |
|---|---|---|---|---|---|---|---|---|---|---|---|---|---|---|---|---|---|---|---|---|---|---|---|
| b | 19 | 19 | 5 | 5 | 25 | 25 | 12 | 12 | | 3 | 3 | 91 | 91 | 20 | 20 | 17 | 17 | 14 | 14 | 187 | 187 | 1 | 1 |
| g | 13 | 13 | | 14 | 14 | 1 | 1 | 2 | 2 | | 5 | 5 | | 9 | 9 | 4 | 4 | 9 | 9 | 1 | | 8 | 8 |
| d | 28 | 28 | 16 | 6 | 6 | 24 | 24 | 28 | 6 | 27 | 27 | 6 | 6 | 19 | 19 | 12 | 12 | 42 | 77 | 77 | 1 | 2 | 2 |
| h | 59 | 59 | | 16 | 10 | 10 | 28 | 1 | | 6 | 6 | 6 | 71 | 71 | 22 | 22 | 42 | 1 | 1 | | 20 | 20 | 10 |
| z | 11 | 11 | 10 | | 10 | 10 | 1 | | | 12 | 12 | 12 | 6 | 2 | 2 | 3 | 3 | 1 | 1 | | | 5 | 5 |
| c | 10 | 10 | | 5 | 5 | 6 | 6 | | 1 | 1 | 12 | 13 | | 7 | 7 | 2 | 2 | 43 | 219 | 219 | 1 | 1 | |
| y | 49 | 49 | 8 | 10 | 88 | 88 | 203 | 203 | 7 | 7 | 13 | 43 | 35 | 35 | 30 | 30 | 43 | 10 | 12 | 12 | 35 | 35 | 9 |
| k | 10 | 10 | 5 | 5 | 5 | 19 | 19 | | 1 | 1 | 43 | 3 | 5 | 5 | 58 | 58 | 10 | 19 | 69 | 69 | 6 | 6 | 3 |
| l | 48 | 48 | 6 | 8 | 25 | 25 | 105 | 105 | 3 | 3 | 3 | 9 | 103 | 103 | 59 | 59 | 19 | 86 | 25 | 25 | 8 | 8 | 3 |
| m | 34 | 34 | | 15 | 9 | 9 | 52 | 52 | 7 | 7 | 3 | 3 | 52 | 52 | 18 | 18 | 86 | 7 | 13 | 13 | 42 | 42 | 13 |
| n | 25 | 25 | | 6 | 8 | 8 | 43 | 43 | 3 | 3 | 3 | 1 | 180 | 180 | 4 | 4 | 4 | | | 18 | 13 | 13 | 13 |
| s | 11 | 11 | 8 | 1 | 1 | 3 | 3 | | | 5 | 5 | 3 | 3 | | 6 | 1 | 1 | 16 | 16 | 3 | 18 | | 24 |
| p | 3 | 3 | | 1 | 1 | 4 | 4 | | 11 | 17 | 17 | 10 | 6 | 19 | 19 | 2 | 2 | 7 | | 64 | 3 | 13 | 1 |
| q | 3 | 3 | | 9 | 9 | 7 | 7 | | 9 | 11 | 11 | 47 | 204 | 204 | 5 | 5 | 7 | 88 | 64 | 14 | 66 | 66 | 13 |
| w | 97 | 97 | 4 | 8 | 28 | 28 | 84 | 84 | 2 | 11 | 10 | 2 | 47 | 1 | 25 | 25 | 88 | 25 | 25 | 45 | 14 | 3 | 8 |
| x | 12 | 12 | 4 | 11 | 11 | 7 | 7 | 9 | 3 | 10 | 10 | 15 | 83 | 83 | 1 | 20 | 20 | 27 | 45 | 26 | 22 | 22 | 3 |
| t | 25 | 25 | | 4 | 4 | 4 | 44 | 44 | | 2 | 2 | 6 | 110 | 110 | 10 | 10 | 27 | 22 | 26 | | 16 | 16 | 3 |
| r | 41 | 41 | | 4 | 12 | 12 | 28 | 28 | 6 | 3 | 15 | | 5 | 50 | 15 | 15 | 22 | 23 | 23 | 10 | 13 | 13 | 5 |
| s | 32 | 32 | | 1 | 1 | 26 | 26 | | 28 | 58 | 58 | 35 | 1 | 3 | 50 | 61 | 61 | | | 7 | 10 | | |
| + | 1 | 1 | | | 7 | 7 | | | 2 | 6 | 6 | 26 | 35 | 3 | 2 | 2 | 59 | 44 | 44 | 10 | 7 | | |
| ( | 27 | 27 | | 22 | 22 | 16 | 16 | 28 | 8 | 6 | 5 | 3 | 25 | 10 | 3 | 59 | 175 | 29 | 29 | | 10 | 7 | 1 |
| ) | 57 | 57 | 1 | 12 | 12 | 25 | 25 | 2 | | 5 | 3 | | 1 | 1 | 10 | 175 | | | | | 4 | 4 | 7 |
| & | | | | | | | | | | | | | | | | | | | | | | | |

**Table A.2** (cont'd) Italian (expressed as frequency per 10000 letters)

| | a | b | c | d | e | f | g | h | i | l | m | n | o | p | q | r | s | t | u | v | z |
|---|---|---|---|---|---|---|---|---|---|---|---|---|---|---|---|---|---|---|---|---|---|
| a | 25 | 25 | 20 | 20 | 55 | 55 | 80 | 80 | 40 | 40 | 15 | 15 | 30 | 30 | 10 | 25 | 25 | 124 | 124 | 65 | 65 |
| b | 15 | 15 | 20 | 20 | | | 20 | 20 | | | | 20 | 20 | 10 | | | | 119 | 119 | | |
| c | 60 | 60 | | 20 | 20 | | 40 | 40 | | | 100 | 100 | 60 | 60 | | | 40 | 40 | | 35 | 2 |
| d | 30 | 30 | 15 | | 2 | 2 | 138 | 138 | | | | 138 | 138 | | | 50 | 50 | 148 | 148 | 10 | |
| e | 40 | 40 | | 15 | 80 | 80 | 85 | 85 | 35 | 35 | 10 | 10 | 55 | 55 | | 10 | 10 | 5 | 5 | 20 | 35 |
| f | 10 | 10 | | | | 10 | 10 | | | | 20 | 20 | | | | 40 | | | | | 10 |
| g | 15 | 15 | | | | 20 | 20 | | 20 | 20 | | 5 | 65 | 65 | 40 | 2 | 2 | 20 | 95 | 95 | 20 |
| h | 5 | 5 | | | | 70 | 70 | | | | 30 | 30 | | | | 5 | 20 | 124 | 15 | 15 | |
| i | 104 | 104 | 15 | 15 | 100 | 100 | 60 | 60 | 70 | 70 | 25 | 25 | 40 | 40 | 5 | 100 | 124 | 30 | 30 | 35 | 60 |
| l | 133 | 133 | 2 | 2 | 20 | 20 | 10 | 10 | 114 | 114 | | 10 | 10 | | 100 | 10 | | | | 5 | |
| m | 70 | 70 | 2 | 2 | | | 80 | 80 | 109 | 109 | | 25 | 25 | | 10 | 55 | 55 | 2 | 80 | 80 | 35 |
| n | 80 | 80 | 2 | 2 | 40 | | 30 | 30 | 15 | 15 | | | 15 | 15 | | 2 | 35 | 35 | 25 | | 5 |
| o | 30 | 30 | | | 40 | 40 | 70 | 70 | | | | 5 | 20 | 20 | | 70 | 70 | 25 | 55 | 55 | 30 |
| p | 60 | 60 | 10 | 10 | | 40 | 65 | | | | | 15 | | | 2 | | | | 15 | 15 | 44 |
| q | | | | | | 65 | | | | | 139 | 25 | | | | | | | | 60 | |
| r | 124 | 124 | 2 | 2 | 25 | 25 | 20 | 20 | 152 | 152 | 2 | 5 | 5 | | 89 | 89 | 15 | 15 | | 60 | 15 |
| s | 30 | 30 | | 35 | 35 | 5 | 5 | 89 | 89 | | | 139 | | 139 | 139 | | 10 | 10 | | 5 | 60 |
| t | 119 | 119 | | | | 100 | 100 | 10 | 40 | 40 | 40 | 2 | | 5 | | 114 | 114 | | | 10 | 60 |
| u | 35 | 35 | 10 | 10 | 10 | 10 | 10 | | | | 55 | 40 | | | | 20 | 20 | 20 | 20 | | 5 |
| v | 25 | 25 | | | | 44 | 44 | | | | | 55 | 5 | | | 20 | 20 | | | | 10 |
| z | 30 | 30 | | | | 5 | 5 | | | | | | | | | 2 | 2 | | | | |

**Table A.2** (cont'd) Japanese (expressed as frequency per 10000 letters)

| | a | b | c | d | e | f | g | h | i | j | k | m | n | o | p | r | s | t | u | w | y | z |
|---|---|---|---|---|---|---|---|---|---|---|---|---|---|---|---|---|---|---|---|---|---|---|
| a | 6 | 6 | 6 | 6 | 2 | 2 | 20 | 20 | 6 | 6 | 6 | 6 | 17 | 17 | 13 | 13 | 201 | 201 | 8 | 8 | 138 | 138 |
| b | 16 | 16 | | | 1 | 1 | 24 | 24 | 24 | 24 | | 32 | 32 | | | 2 | 1 | 1 | 16 | 16 | | |
| c | 1 | 1 | | | | | | | | | | 2 | | | | | 2 | 44 | 44 | | | |
| d | 43 | 43 | 3 | 3 | | 16 | 16 | | | | | 2 | 2 | 6 | 3 | 3 | 129 | 129 | 3 | 3 | | |
| e | 2 | 2 | | | 1 | 1 | 5 | 5 | 1 | 1 | | | 6 | | | | | | | | | |
| f | 1 | 1 | | 16 | 1 | 1 | 23 | 1 | 1 | 1 | 2 | 2 | 2 | | | | | 1 | 1 | | | |
| g | 58 | 58 | | | | 23 | 23 | | | | 38 | 38 | | | | | 32 | 32 | 40 | 40 | 47 | 47 |
| h | 51 | 51 | 13 | 13 | 5 | 9 | 9 | 21 | 12 | 12 | 50 | 50 | | | | | 122 | 122 | | | 1 | 1 |
| i | 8 | 8 | | | | 6 | 21 | | | | 30 | 30 | | | | | 36 | 36 | | | | |
| j | 2 | 2 | | | | 1 | 1 | | | | 46 | 46 | | | 50 | 50 | 27 | 27 | | | | |
| k | 200 | 200 | 15 | 15 | | 60 | 60 | | 20 | 20 | 89 | 89 | 54 | 54 | 43 | 50 | | 160 | 160 | 60 | 149 | 149 |
| m | 34 | 34 | 38 | 38 | | 37 | 37 | | 10 | 10 | 34 | 34 | 23 | 43 | 43 | 13 | 2 | 2 | 60 | 17 | 2 | |
| n | 94 | 94 | | | | 4 | 20 | 20 | | | 5 | 5 | 37 | 1 | 1 | 43 | 190 | 190 | 17 | 23 | 47 | 47 |
| o | 15 | 15 | | 1 | 6 | 6 | 24 | 24 | | | 10 | 10 | | 23 | 13 | 1 | 42 | 42 | 23 | 9 | 237 | 237 |
| p | | 6 | | | | 2 | 2 | | | | 2 | 2 | | 37 | 43 | 1 | 13 | 13 | 9 | | 1 | 1 |
| r | 47 | 47 | | 3 | 1 | | 42 | | 4 | 4 | 103 | 103 | 194 | 1 | 1 | | 1 | 1 | | | | |
| s | 37 | 37 | | | | 42 | 108 | 108 | | | 87 | 87 | | 194 | 1 | | 1 | 1 | | 31 | 31 | 3 |
| t | 122 | 122 | 24 | 24 | | 102 | 102 | | 1 | 1 | 52 | 52 | 33 | 33 | 13 | 1 | 1 | 155 | 155 | 57 | 57 | |
| u | 8 | 8 | 44 | 3 | 5 | 5 | 12 | 12 | | | 10 | 10 | 2 | | 25 | 25 | 25 | 25 | 12 | 12 | 130 | 130 |
| w | 102 | 102 | | 3 | | 1 | 1 | | | | 1 | 1 | | | 1 | 1 | 55 | 55 | 1 | 1 | | |
| y | 20 | 20 | | | | 4 | 4 | | | | 1 | 2 | | | | | 1 | 1 | | | 147 | 147 |
| z | 22 | 22 | | | | 29 | 29 | | | | | 1 | | | | | 8 | 8 | | | 1 | 1 |

**Table A.2 (cont'd) Latin (expressed as frequency per 10000 letters)**

| | a | b | c | d | e | f | g | h | i | k | l | m | n | o | p | q | r | s | t | u | v | w | x | y | z |
|---|---|---|---|---|---|---|---|---|---|---|---|---|---|---|---|---|---|---|---|---|---|---|---|---|---|
| a | 23 | 23 | 25 | 25 | 47 | 47 | 111 | 111 | 69 | 69 | 7 | 7 | 84 | 84 | 2 | 2 | 19 | 19 | 2 | 2 | 53 | 53 | 57 | 57 | 167 |
| b | 16 | 16 | 1 | 1 | | | 26 | 26 | | 4 | 4 | 4 | 4 | 35 | 35 | | 4 | | 1 | 1 | 8 | 9 | 9 | 1 | 1 |
| c | 104 | 104 | 2 | 2 | 4 | 4 | 5 | 5 | 42 | 42 | 1 | 1 | 7 | 7 | 4 | 4 | 50 | 50 | | 8 | 2 | 1 | 1 | 4 | 4 |
| d | 83 | 83 | 1 | 1 | | 2 | 2 | 66 | 66 | 2 | 2 | 2 | 2 | | 50 | 50 | | 1 | 1 | 2 | 28 | | 30 | 30 | 1 |
| e | 35 | 35 | 9 | 9 | 57 | 57 | 19 | 19 | 16 | 16 | 8 | 8 | 109 | 109 | 8 | 8 | 39 | 39 | 1 | 1 | 28 | 28 | 61 | 61 | 77 |
| f | 12 | 12 | | | | 21 | 21 | | | | 12 | 12 | | 1 | 1 | | | 5 | 5 | | 11 | 11 | 11 | | |
| g | 95 | 95 | 1 | 1 | 78 | 78 | 11 | 11 | 60 | 60 | 9 | 9 | 19 | 19 | | 15 | 61 | 61 | | 11 | | 214 | 214 | 33 | 33 |
| h | 12 | 12 | | | | 5 | 5 | | 14 | 14 | | 4 | 4 | | 15 | | | | 7 | 7 | 60 | 60 | | | 1 |
| i | 139 | 139 | 36 | 36 | 76 | 76 | 29 | 29 | 22 | 22 | 7 | 7 | 57 | 57 | 1 | 1 | 25 | 25 | 1 | 1 | 1 | | 43 | 43 | 123 |
| k | | | | | | | | | 5 | 5 | | 1 | 1 | | 1 | 1 | 1 | 1 | | 1 | 1 | 1 | 1 | 1 | |
| l | 56 | 56 | 1 | 1 | 2 | 2 | | 33 | 33 | | 15 | 15 | 1 | 1 | 1 | | | | 45 | 4 | 1 | 1 | 1 | 19 | 19 |
| m | 56 | 56 | 4 | 4 | 7 | 7 | 2 | 2 | 74 | 74 | 2 | 2 | 211 | 211 | | 81 | 38 | 45 | | 1 | 1 | 8 | 8 | 9 | 9 |
| n | 47 | 47 | 1 | 1 | 16 | 16 | 38 | 38 | 67 | 67 | 4 | 4 | 33 | 33 | 81 | 1 | 69 | 38 | 1 | 43 | 4 | 1 | 1 | 2 | 2 |
| o | 14 | 14 | 15 | 15 | 36 | 36 | 11 | 11 | 9 | 9 | 2 | 2 | 19 | 19 | 1 | 2 | 5 | 69 | 43 | 43 | 38 | 38 | 73 | 73 | 2 |
| p | 19 | 19 | | | | 71 | 71 | | 8 | 8 | 2 | 2 | 25 | 25 | 2 | 5 | 4 | | 5 | 5 | 26 | 26 | | 2 | |
| q | 1 | 1 | | | | | | 5 | 5 | | | | | | | 1 | 1 | | | | | | | 71 | |
| r | 102 | 102 | 12 | 12 | 14 | 14 | 9 | 9 | 85 | 85 | 11 | 11 | 22 | 22 | 4 | 4 | 123 | 91 | 1 | 21 | 21 | 8 | 8 | 47 | 47 |
| s | 73 | 73 | 4 | 4 | 21 | 21 | 15 | 15 | 80 | 80 | 5 | 5 | 29 | 29 | 1 | 1 | 91 | 164 | | 1 | 12 | 12 | 12 | 12 | 7 |
| t | 149 | 149 | 5 | 5 | 4 | 4 | 14 | 14 | 129 | 129 | 5 | 5 | 29 | 29 | 1 | 123 | 164 | 39 | 1 | 5 | 5 | 15 | 15 | 8 | 8 |
| u | 39 | 39 | 7 | 7 | 16 | 16 | 14 | 14 | 30 | 30 | 4 | 4 | 143 | 143 | 1 | 4 | 39 | 39 | 1 | 1 | 42 | 42 | 59 | 59 | 22 |
| v | 9 | 9 | | | 1 | 1 | 36 | 36 | | 2 | 2 | | 63 | 63 | 1 | 1 | 1 | 1 | 2 | 1 | | | 25 | | |
| w | | | | | | | | | 1 | 1 | | 15 | 15 | | | | | | 2 | 2 | | | | | |
| x | 2 | 2 | 1 | 1 | | | | | 8 | 8 | 7 | | 1 | 1 | | | 1 | 2 | 2 | 2 | | 2 | 2 | 4 | 4 |
| y | | | 4 | 4 | 2 | 2 | | | | 7 | | | | | | | | | | | | | | | 1 |
| z | 1 | 1 | 4 | 4 | | | | | | | 7 | | 1 | 1 | | 1 | | | | | | | | 1 | |

**Table A.2** (cont'd) Malay (expressed as frequency per 10000 letters)

| | a | b | c | d | e | f | g | h | i | j | k | l | m | n | o | p | r | s | t | u | v | w | y | z |
|---|---|---|---|---|---|---|---|---|---|---|---|---|---|---|---|---|---|---|---|---|---|---|---|---|
| a | 28 | 28 | 70 | 70 | 8 | 8 | 112 | 112 | 8 | 8 | 8 | 8 | 26 | 26 | 124 | 124 | 118 | 118 | 22 | 22 | 192 | 192 | 124 | 124 |
| b | 98 | 98 | | | | 92 | 92 | | | | 48 | 48 | | 2 | 2 | | | 2 | 2 | 18 | 18 | | | |
| c | 18 | 18 | | | 6 | 4 | 4 | 6 | 6 | | 8 | 8 | 32 | | | 6 | 6 | | | | | | 6 | 6 |
| d | 178 | 178 | | | 6 | 34 | 34 | | | 12 | 116 | 116 | | 32 | | | | | | | 70 | 116 | 12 | 12 |
| e | | 18 | | | | 8 | 8 | | | | 8 | 8 | 2 | | | | | | | | | 4 | 4 | |
| f | 4 | 4 | 16 | 6 | | | 6 | | 12 | 4 | | 2 | 38 | 14 | 14 | | | | | | | 22 | 116 | 200 |
| g | 100 | 100 | 14 | 16 | 6 | 6 | 26 | 26 | 20 | | | 38 | 2 | 30 | 30 | 62 | 62 | 2 | 2 | 24 | 24 | 22 | 4 | |
| h | 52 | 52 | 38 | 14 | | 22 | 22 | 20 | | | 4 | 2 | 2 | 10 | 10 | | 14 | 14 | 2 | 2 | 22 | 22 | 22 | 22 |
| i | 76 | 76 | | 38 | | 54 | 54 | 22 | 86 | 86 | | 22 | 22 | | | 16 | 16 | 66 | 66 | 60 | 60 | 32 | 6 | 6 |
| j | 58 | 58 | | | | 20 | 20 | 40 | 154 | | 6 | 6 | | | | | | | | | | 28 | 32 | 96 |
| k | 178 | 178 | | | | | | 154 | 20 | 20 | 2 | | | | 26 | 26 | | | 12 | 4 | 4 | | 16 | 16 |
| l | 250 | 250 | 16 | 16 | 2 | 4 | 4 | 38 | 4 | | | 340 | 340 | 24 | 2 | 8 | 8 | 2 | 2 | 2 | 6 | 2 | 2 | 12 |
| m | 90 | 90 | 2 | 2 | | 10 | 38 | 4 | | | | 2 | 340 | 8 | 2 | 2 | 2 | 20 | 20 | 6 | 8 | 24 | 2 | 4 |
| n | 140 | 140 | 90 | 90 | | 2 | 94 | 94 | | | | 22 | 2 | 14 | 14 | 32 | 32 | 2 | 2 | 2 | | 40 | 24 | 20 |
| o | 110 | 110 | 16 | 16 | 10 | 4 | 14 | 14 | 2 | 2 | | 14 | 22 | 28 | 28 | 4 | 4 | 20 | 20 | 20 | | 16 | | 4 |
| p | 114 | 114 | | 38 | 2 | | 38 | 120 | 120 | | 14 | 6 | 4 | 4 | 2 | 2 | 4 | 2 | 10 | 10 | 16 | 28 | | |
| r | 104 | 104 | | 6 | | 2 | | 6 | 64 | 2 | | 12 | 6 | 32 | 50 | 50 | 10 | 10 | 10 | 2 | 2 | | | 4 |
| s | 156 | 156 | 12 | 12 | 2 | 2 | 6 | 44 | 64 | 64 | 12 | | | 32 | 32 | 6 | 6 | 6 | 14 | 10 | 6 | 6 | 12 | 12 |
| t | 48 | 48 | 34 | 34 | 2 | 2 | 44 | 44 | | | 12 | | 28 | 90 | 90 | 26 | 16 | 14 | 14 | 88 | 32 | 32 | 56 | 56 |
| u | 16 | 16 | | | | | | | | | 6 | 6 | | 28 | 26 | 26 | 16 | 16 | 88 | 88 | 2 | 2 | | |
| w | 194 | 194 | | | | 6 | 6 | | | | 2 | 2 | | | | | | | | | | 2 | | |
| y | | | | | | | | | | | | | | | | | | | | | | | | |
| z | | | | | | | | | | | | | | | | | | | | | | | | 10 |

## Table A.2 (cont'd) Norwegian (expressed as frequency per 10000 letters)

| | a | b | c | d | e | f | g | h | i | j | k | l | m | n | o | p | q | r | s | t | u | v | w | x | y | z | æ | ø | å |
|---|---|---|---|---|---|---|---|---|---|---|---|---|---|---|---|---|---|---|---|---|---|---|---|---|---|---|---|---|---|
| a | 7 | 7 | 4 | 4 | 1 | 1 | 16 | 16 | 4 | 4 | 5 | 5 | 64 | 64 | 2 | 9 | 9 | 3 | 3 | 36 | 36 | 40 | 40 | 32 | 32 | 89 | 89 | 3 | 3 |
| b | 9 | 9 | 9 | 9 | 1 | 1 | 52 | 52 | 193 | 8 | 8 | 8 | 8 | 2 | 28 | 30 | 30 | 17 | 31 | 3 | 3 | 8 | 4 | 16 | 16 | 11 | 4 | 4 | 27 |
| c | 2 | 2 | 1 | 1 | 1 | 20 | 1 | 193 | 35 | 38 | 38 | 8 | 8 | 28 | 29 | 44 | 17 | 5 | 5 | 31 | 8 | 100 | 100 | 4 | 11 | 277 | 277 | 27 | 6 |
| d | 34 | 34 | 16 | 16 | 1 | 109 | 20 | 35 | 4 | 9 | 9 | 71 | 71 | 29 | 13 | 28 | 44 | 8 | 17 | 37 | 37 | 47 | 11 | 64 | 64 | 17 | 10 | 6 | 36 |
| e | 22 | 22 | 4 | 4 | 16 | 22 | 109 | 4 | 88 | 24 | 6 | 12 | 12 | 13 | 16 | 11 | 8 | 17 | 8 | 4 | 47 | 11 | 96 | 13 | 17 | 10 | 52 | 36 | 8 |
| f | 3 | 3 | 4 | 4 | 6 | 16 | 22 | 88 | 24 | 3 | 12 | 10 | 10 | 16 | 11 | 18 | 28 | 9 | 40 | 8 | 4 | 96 | 1 | 6 | 13 | 52 | 143 | 8 | 10 |
| g | 35 | 35 | 7 | 7 | 1 | 1 | 8 | 31 | 3 | 6 | 6 | 6 | 1 | 1 | 10 | 73 | 9 | 18 | 4 | 47 | 47 | 1 | 63 | 1 | 6 | 143 | 24 | 10 | 1 |
| h | 58 | 58 | 3 | 3 | 6 | 68 | 16 | 79 | 120 | 5 | 5 | 12 | 28 | 28 | 8 | 13 | 18 | 40 | 3 | 14 | 14 | 63 | 35 | 1 | 1 | 24 | 1 | 1 | 23 |
| i | 7 | 7 | 10 | 10 | 12 | 1 | 31 | 120 | 137 | 16 | 16 | 2 | 2 | 10 | 10 | 57 | 18 | 4 | 4 | 5 | 5 | 12 | 17 | 35 | 1 | 1 | 8 | 23 | 2 |
| j | 2 | 2 | 8 | 8 | 1 | 24 | 68 | 137 | 92 | 20 | 6 | 10 | 10 | 8 | 8 | 5 | 73 | 4 | 19 | 3 | 12 | 17 | 84 | 11 | 4 | 4 | 46 | 8 | 39 |
| k | 2 | 2 | 13 | 13 | 16 | 6 | 79 | 92 | 20 | 229 | 14 | 3 | 3 | 10 | 5 | 8 | 13 | 75 | 1 | 16 | 16 | 10 | 16 | 84 | 11 | 46 | 2 | 39 | 13 |
| l | 34 | 34 | 24 | 24 | 6 | 107 | 24 | 18 | 4 | 83 | 5 | 128 | 128 | 8 | 25 | 25 | 57 | 25 | 5 | 19 | 10 | 8 | 15 | 16 | 46 | 46 | 23 | 2 | 3 |
| m | 66 | 66 | 18 | 18 | 1 | 1 | 6 | 25 | 229 | 189 | 22 | 1 | 70 | 70 | 12 | 12 | 8 | 88 | 16 | 1 | 24 | 24 | 12 | 15 | 33 | 23 | 16 | 16 | 40 |
| n | 35 | 35 | 4 | 4 | 6 | 27 | 107 | 5 | 83 | 2 | 1 | 14 | 34 | 34 | 14 | 14 | 75 | 17 | 4 | 5 | 58 | 58 | 14 | 12 | 13 | 33 | 11 | 11 | 57 |
| o | 24 | 24 | 6 | 1 | 12 | 1 | 18 | 10 | 189 | 8 | 2 | 5 | 1 | 1 | 113 | 12 | 25 | 4 | 17 | 16 | 8 | 8 | 73 | 14 | 24 | 13 | 8 | 8 | 38 |
| p | 3 | 3 | | 6 | | 6 | 27 | 5 | 5 | 1 | 8 | 22 | 4 | 4 | 3 | 2 | 88 | 2 | 3 | 4 | 1 | 73 | 3 | 3 | 13 | 24 | 29 | 29 | 9 |
| q | 18 | 18 | | | | 1 | 25 | 79 | 10 | | | 1 | 4 | 113 | 1 | 7 | 12 | 12 | 2 | 1 | 2 | 2 | 14 | 4 | 4 | 13 | 2 | 9 | 9 |
| r | 61 | 61 | | | | 13 | 5 | 10 | 1 | | | 4 | 4 | 4 | | 1 | 2 | 12 | 2 | 3 | 8 | 14 | 9 | 5 | 5 | 2 | 4 | 14 | 14 |
| s | 50 | 50 | | | | 6 | 10 | | | | | 7 | 7 | 3 | | | 4 | | 25 | 2 | 1 | 9 | | 35 | 35 | 4 | 4 | | |
| t | 51 | 51 | | | | 12 | 13 | | | | | | 11 | 11 | | | 7 | | 12 | 8 | 2 | 1 | | | | 4 | | | |
| u | 3 | 3 | | | | 10 | 79 | | | | | | | | | | | | | 25 | | 2 | | | | | | | |
| v | 29 | 29 | | | | 10 | 10 | | | | | | | | | | | | | | | | | | | | | | |
| w | 7 | 7 | | | | 6 | 10 | | | | | | | | | | | | | | | | | | | | | | |
| x | | | | | | | 6 | | | | | | | | | | | | | | | | | | | | | | |

**Table A.2** (cont'd) Serbo-Croatian (expressed as frequency per 10000 letters)

| | a | b | c | d | e | f | g | h | i | j | k | l | m | n | o | p | r | s | t | u | v | z |
|---|---|---|---|---|---|---|---|---|---|---|---|---|---|---|---|---|---|---|---|---|---|---|
| a |  | 4 | 4 | 19 | 19 | 89 | 89 |  | 4 | 4 | 29 | 29 | 9 | 9 | 24 | 24 | 119 | 119 | 64 | 64 | 69 | 69 |
| b | 14 | 14 | 14 | 14 |  | 9 | 9 | 19 | 19 | 9 | 19 | 19 | 14 | 14 | 24 | 4 | 4 |  | 4 | 4 | 14 | 14 |
| c | 49 | 49 |  | 9 |  | 34 | 34 | 34 | 19 | 24 | 59 | 59 | 39 | 24 | 39 | 24 | 19 | 19 | 19 | 4 | 4 | 4 |
| d | 114 | 114 | 9 |  | 9 | 129 | 34 |  |  | 9 | 9 | 39 | 34 | 39 | 24 | 4 | 4 | 4 | 89 | 89 | 44 | 44 |
| e | 4 | 9 | 4 | 4 | 9 | 19 | 129 | 14 |  | 4 | 4 | 34 | 4 | 29 | 29 | 9 | 9 | 69 | 24 | 24 | 24 | 24 |
| f | 39 | 4 |  |  |  | 4 | 4 | 14 | 9 | 29 | 24 | 4 | 4 |  | 4 | 29 | 29 | 104 | 69 |  |  |  |
| g | 4 | 39 | 4 | 4 | 74 | 74 | 14 |  |  | 14 | 4 | 4 | 4 | 44 | 44 | 9 | 4 | 4 | 104 | 14 | 14 | 29 |
| h | 4 | 4 | 4 | 9 | 9 | 4 | 4 | 9 | 9 | 9 | 69 | 4 | 29 | 4 | 4 | 29 | 24 | 9 | 9 | 14 | 14 | 19 |
| i | 89 | 89 | 4 | 4 | 14 | 4 | 14 | 94 |  | 4 | 89 | 25 | 49 | 49 | 4 | 84 | 84 | 9 |  | 39 | 39 | 19 |
| j | 34 | 34 |  | 9 | 14 | 74 | 14 | 34 | 328 | 4 | 9 | 5 | 29 | 4 | 4 | 59 | 59 | 9 | 9 |  |  | 4 |
| k | 119 | 89 |  | 4 |  | 4 | 14 |  |  |  |  | 25 |  | 159 | 4 |  |  | 104 |  | 34 | 104 | 104 |
| l | 14 | 34 | 4 | 14 | 14 | 19 | 19 |  |  |  | 69 | 65 | 29 | 19 | 4 | 24 | 24 | 4 | 9 |  | 34 |  |
| m | 14 | 119 | 34 | 14 | 14 | 129 | 129 | 9 | 29 | 29 | 89 | 5 | 89 | 159 | 159 | 84 | 84 | 9 | 9 | 19 | 19 | 79 |
| n | 174 | 14 | 14 | 14 | 14 | 4 | 4 | 74 | 74 | 14 | 9 | 89 | 44 | 19 | 19 | 59 | 59 | 4 | 4 | 4 | 134 | 134 |
| o | 14 | 169 |  | 24 | 24 | 44 | 44 | 4 | 14 |  | 89 | 29 | 44 | 89 |  | 4 | 4 | 74 | 74 | 59 | 59 | 4 |
| p | 14 | 54 |  | 4 | 4 |  | 4 | 44 | 34 | 9 | 9 | 9 | 9 | 29 | 4 |  | 4 | 4 | 4 | 4 | 9 |  |
| r | 169 | 119 | 14 | 9 | 14 | 44 | 19 | 19 | 4 | 4 | 4 | 44 | 44 | 29 | 29 |  | 34 | 74 | 24 | 29 | 29 | 4 |
| s | 54 | 69 | 34 | 24 | 24 | 9 | 4 | 4 | 4 |  | 19 | 9 | 9 | 4 | 4 | 4 | 9 | 4 | 4 | 24 | 9 | 9 |
| t | 119 | 14 |  | 14 | 9 | 9 | 19 | 19 |  | 4 | 4 | 44 | 44 | 29 | 29 |  | 74 | 74 | 74 | 29 | 9 | 84 |
| u | 14 | 69 | 14 | 9 | 4 | 4 | 4 | 4 |  | 4 | 4 | 9 | 9 | 4 | 4 | 4 | 9 | 4 | 4 | 4 | 29 | 9 |
| v | 69 | 69 |  |  | 9 |  |  |  | 29 |  | 4 | 44 | 44 | 29 | 29 | 4 |  |  |  |  |  |  |
| z | 49 | 49 |  |  | 4 | 4 | 4 | 4 |  | 4 | 4 | 9 | 9 | 4 | 4 |  |  | 4 | 4 | 4 | 4 |  |

**Table A.2** (cont'd) Spanish (expressed as frequency per 10000 letters)

|   | a | b | c | d | e | f | g | h | i | j | l | m | n | o | p | q | r | s | t | u | v | x | y | z |
|---|---|---|---|---|---|---|---|---|---|---|---|---|---|---|---|---|---|---|---|---|---|---|---|---|
| a | 29 | 29 | 46 | 46 | 94 | 94 | 123 | 123 | 41 | 41 | 10 | 10 | 24 | 24 | 14 | 14 | 16 | 16 | 5 | 5 | 107 | 107 | 55 | 55 |
| b | 27 | 27 |  |  |  | 15 | 15 |  |  |  | 26 | 26 |  | 13 | 13 |  | 1 | 1 | 5 | 5 |  |  | 19 | 19 |
| c | 67 | 67 |  | 12 | 12 |  | 48 | 48 |  |  | 27 | 27 | 99 | 99 |  | 6 | 6 |  | 1 | 1 | 106 | 106 |  |  |
| d | 73 | 73 | 7 | 7 | 8 | 8 | 138 | 138 |  |  |  | 57 | 57 |  | 2 | 2 | 2 | 2 | 1 | 1 | 82 | 82 | 1 | 1 |
| e | 33 | 33 |  | 7 | 83 | 83 | 66 | 66 |  |  | 9 | 9 | 33 | 33 | 18 | 18 | 3 | 3 | 14 | 14 | 154 | 154 | 53 | 53 |
| f | 12 | 12 |  |  |  | 18 | 18 |  | 47 | 47 | 21 | 21 |  |  |  | 1 | 1 | 9 | 9 |  |  | 8 | 8 |  |
| g | 32 | 32 | 5 | 5 |  | 18 | 18 |  |  |  | 7 | 7 |  |  |  | 7 | 1 | 18 | 18 |  |  |  | 10 |  |
| h | 40 | 40 |  |  |  | 13 | 13 |  | 76 | 76 | 10 | 10 |  |  |  |  |  | 20 | 10 | 35 | 35 | 10 |  | 73 |
| i | 91 | 91 |  |  |  | 80 | 52 | 52 | 71 | 1 | 11 | 11 |  |  |  | 3 |  |  |  |  |  | 35 | 35 | 3 |
| j | 7 | 7 |  |  |  | 16 | 16 |  |  |  | 2 | 2 |  |  |  |  | 20 | 10 |  |  |  |  |  | 74 |
| l | 183 | 183 |  | 13 | 80 | 11 | 11 | 71 | 61 | 61 | 1 | 13 | 20 | 20 | 30 | 30 | 3 | 3 | 30 | 9 | 9 | 2 | 2 |  |
| m | 56 | 56 | 10 | 10 | 13 |  | 49 | 49 | 46 | 46 | 14 | 49 | 14 | 9 | 37 |  | 3 | 30 | 52 | 52 | 38 | 38 |  | 6 |
| n | 59 | 59 | 2 | 2 |  | 51 | 55 | 55 |  |  | 9 | 14 | 13 | 8 | 3 | 3 | 1 | 1 | 3 | 3 | 33 | 33 | 6 | 48 |
| o | 23 | 23 | 18 | 18 | 51 | 26 | 52 | 52 |  |  | 37 | 9 | 49 | 4 | 6 | 6 | 59 | 59 | 1 | 1 |  | 40 | 48 |  |
| p | 51 | 51 |  |  | 26 | 62 | 62 |  |  |  |  | 37 | 8 | 16 | 16 |  | 5 | 5 | 67 |  | 40 | 59 | 59 |  |
| q |  |  | 1 | 1 |  | 1 |  |  |  |  |  |  | 4 |  |  |  | 76 | 67 |  | 110 | 110 |  |  |  |
| r | 155 | 155 | 3 | 3 | 24 | 24 | 12 | 12 | 147 | 147 | 3 | 3 | 4 | 4 | 6 | 76 | 63 | 63 | 28 | 28 | 13 | 13 | 15 | 15 |
| s | 83 | 83 |  |  | 32 | 32 | 45 | 45 | 105 | 105 | 14 | 14 | 2 | 2 |  | 6 | 82 | 82 | 1 | 1 | 11 | 11 | 23 | 23 |
| t | 105 | 105 |  |  |  | 93 | 93 | 15 | 152 | 152 | 83 | 83 |  | 1 |  |  | 15 |  | 1 | 1 |  | 70 | 70 | 1 |
| u | 24 | 24 | 5 | 5 | 12 | 12 | 15 |  |  |  | 2 | 2 |  |  |  | 15 | 18 | 18 | 19 | 19 | 12 | 12 | 38 | 38 |
| v | 15 | 15 |  |  |  | 29 | 29 |  | 5 | 5 | 28 | 28 |  |  |  |  | 11 | 11 | 5 | 5 |  |  |  |  |
| x |  |  |  |  |  |  |  |  | 19 | 19 |  |  |  |  |  |  | 2 | 2 |  |  |  |  | 1 |  |
| y | 18 | 18 | 2 | 2 | 6 | 6 | 7 | 7 |  |  | 1 | 1 | 2 | 2 |  |  | 2 |  |  |  |  | 1 |  |  |
| z | 19 | 19 |  | 3 | 3 |  |  |  |  |  |  |  |  |  |  | 2 |  |  |  |  |  | 7 | 7 | 2 |

**Table A.2** (cont'd) Swedish (expressed as frequency per 10000 letters)

| | a | b | c | d | e | f | g | h | i | j | k | l | m | n | o | p | q | r | s | t | u | v | w | x | y | z | } | { | | |
|---|---|---|---|---|---|---|---|---|---|---|---|---|---|---|---|---|---|---|---|---|---|---|---|---|---|---|---|---|---|
| a | 16 | 16 | 9 | 9 | 3 | 3 | 47 | 47 | 13 | 13 | 20 | 20 | 33 | 33 | 5 | 5 | 9 | 9 | 1 | 1 | 31 | 31 | 63 | 63 | 51 | 51 | 176 | 176 | 10 |
| b | 10 | 10 | 1 | 1 | | | 35 | 35 | | | | 9 | 9 | | | 19 | 19 | | | 11 | 11 | | | 4 | 4 | 1 | 1 | | 1 |
| c | | | | | 11 | 11 | | | 43 | 43 | 4 | 4 | | 32 | 32 | | | | | | | | | | | | | | |
| d | 58 | 58 | 3 | 3 | | 10 | 10 | 193 | 193 | 5 | 5 | 1 | 1 | 1 | 1 | 23 | 23 | 1 | 1 | 3 | 3 | 11 | 11 | 4 | 4 | 36 | 36 | 15 | 15 |
| e | 10 | 10 | 14 | 14 | 5 | 5 | 57 | 57 | 9 | 9 | 20 | 20 | 16 | 16 | 13 | 13 | 7 | 7 | 1 | 1 | 21 | 21 | 87 | 87 | 28 | 28 | 239 | 239 | 11 |
| f | 15 | 15 | | | | 13 | 13 | 3 | 3 | | | 19 | 19 | | | 7 | 7 | | | 11 | 11 | | | 20 | 20 | | 16 | 16 | 4 |
| g | 63 | 63 | 1 | 1 | | 3 | 3 | 77 | 77 | 5 | 5 | 9 | 9 | 6 | 6 | 13 | 13 | 1 | 1 | 2 | 2 | 6 | 6 | 4 | 4 | 9 | 9 | 24 | 24 |
| h | 50 | 50 | | | 3 | 3 | 29 | 29 | 2 | 2 | | | 8 | 8 | 1 | 1 | 1 | 1 | 1 | 1 | 2 | 2 | | 8 | 8 | 1 | 1 | | 2 |
| i | 9 | 9 | 4 | 4 | 8 | 8 | 73 | 73 | 11 | 11 | 7 | 7 | 76 | 76 | 2 | 2 | | | 38 | 38 | 50 | 50 | 8 | 8 | 184 | 184 | 23 | 23 | 4 |
| j | 11 | 11 | | | | 7 | 7 | | | | | | | 3 | 3 | | | 3 | 3 | | | | | | 8 | 8 | | | |
| k | 73 | 73 | | | 1 | 1 | 33 | 33 | 2 | 2 | 2 | 2 | 2 | 2 | 8 | 8 | | | 16 | 16 | | 16 | 16 | 43 | 43 | | | 18 | 18 |
| l | 66 | 66 | 2 | 2 | | 14 | 14 | 60 | 60 | 4 | 4 | 8 | 8 | 2 | 2 | 88 | 88 | 8 | 8 | 8 | 8 | 88 | 88 | 8 | 8 | 6 | 6 | 8 | 8 |
| m | 59 | 59 | 4 | 4 | | 9 | 9 | 76 | 76 | 8 | 8 | 5 | 5 | 5 | 5 | 19 | 19 | | 4 | 4 | 3 | 3 | 48 | 48 | 7 | 7 | 11 | 11 | 13 |
| n | 98 | 98 | 13 | 13 | 4 | 4 | 108 | 108 | 45 | 45 | 22 | 22 | 117 | 117 | 16 | 16 | 107 | 107 | 3 | 3 | 26 | 26 | 14 | 14 | 16 | 16 | 52 | 52 | 29 |
| o | | 6 | 6 | 51 | 51 | 7 | 7 | 2 | 2 | 5 | 5 | 13 | 13 | | 1 | 1 | | 4 | 4 | 13 | 13 | 88 | 88 | 46 | 46 | | 9 | 9 | |
| p | 13 | 13 | | | | 17 | 17 | 1 | 1 | | 1 | 1 | 3 | 3 | | | 12 | 12 | 1 | 1 | 2 | 2 | 11 | 11 | 19 | 19 | | 35 | 35 |
| r | 149 | 149 | 19 | 19 | | 46 | 46 | 104 | 104 | 24 | 24 | 18 | 18 | 14 | 14 | 78 | 78 | 9 | 9 | 26 | 26 | 17 | 17 | 23 | 23 | 34 | 34 | 50 | 50 |
| s | 58 | 58 | 5 | 5 | 1 | 1 | 4 | 4 | 50 | 50 | 11 | 11 | 2 | 2 | 3 | 3 | 55 | 55 | 5 | 5 | 64 | 64 | 12 | 12 | 11 | 11 | 10 | 10 | 46 |
| t | 113 | 113 | 14 | 14 | | 18 | 18 | 155 | 155 | 30 | 30 | 12 | 12 | 13 | 13 | 139 | 139 | 2 | 2 | 15 | 15 | 15 | 15 | 25 | 25 | 18 | 18 | 37 | 37 |
| u | 2 | 2 | 3 | 3 | 1 | 1 | 9 | 9 | 3 | 3 | 1 | 1 | 1 | 1 | 2 | 2 | 1 | 1 | | 4 | 4 | 12 | 12 | 8 | 8 | 27 | 27 | | 11 |
| v | 51 | 51 | 1 | 1 | | 6 | 6 | 40 | 40 | 1 | 1 | 1 | 1 | 6 | 6 | 38 | 38 | | | 2 | 2 | 2 | 2 | 9 | 9 | 3 | 3 | 2 | 2 |
| x | 1 | 1 | | | | 5 | 5 | | | | 1 | 1 | | | | | | | 1 | 1 | | | | 11 | 11 | | | | |
| y | 3 | 3 | | 10 | 10 | 3 | 3 | | 1 | 1 | 4 | 4 | 3 | 3 | | | | 1 | 1 | 1 | 1 | 2 | 2 | 1 | 1 | | | 4 | 4 |
| z | | | | | | | | | 1 | 1 | | | | | | | | | | | | | | | | | | | |
| } | 9 | 9 | 1 | 1 | | 8 | 8 | 11 | 11 | 5 | 5 | 16 | 16 | 1 | 1 | | | 8 | 8 | 12 | 12 | 4 | 4 | 18 | 18 | 1 | 1 | 1 | 1 |
| { | | | 3 | 3 | 3 | 3 | | | 7 | 7 | | | | 4 | 4 | 16 | 16 | 10 | 10 | 34 | 34 | | | | 71 | 71 | 11 | 11 | 19 |
| | | | | | 3 | 3 | | 1 | 1 | 1 | 1 | | | 3 | 3 | 5 | 5 | 3 | 3 | 2 | 2 | 3 | 3 | | | | 88 | 88 | 3 |

# APPENDIX B

## B1 DES code

```
/*
 *  des.h - specifies the interface to the DES encryption library.
 *          This library provides routines to install a key, encrypt and
 *          decrypt 64-bit data blocks.  The DES Data Encryption Algorithm
 *          is a block cipher which ensures that its output is a complex
 *          function of its input and the key.  A description of the
 *          algorithm may be found in:
 *
 *              Australian Standard AS2805.5-1985 Data Encryption Algorithm
 *
 *
 *  Author:     Lawrence Brown <lpb@csadfa.oz>         Dec 1987
 *              Computer Science, UC UNSW, Australian Defence Force Academy,
 *                  Canberra, ACT 2600, Australia.
 *
 *          The user interface and some code has been inspired by the PD
 *          programs of:    Phil Karn, KA9Q <karn@flash.bellcore.com> 1986
 *          and             Jim Gillogly 1977.
 *
 *  Description:
 *      The routines provided by the library are:
 *
 *      desinit()           - perform any data structure initialization needed.
 *                            Must be called before any other functions.
 *
 *      keyinit(key)        - installs key for use in subsequent encryptions and
 *          Long  key[2];     decryptions. A key must be installed before encryption
 *                            or decryption may be done.
 *
 *      endes(b)            - main DES encryption routine, this routine encrypts
 *          Long  b[2];       one 64-bit block b with the current key
 *
 *      dedes(b)            - main DES decryption routine, this routine decrypts
 *          Long  b[2];       one 64-bit block b with the current key
 *
 *
 *      The 64-bit data blocks used in the algorithm are specified in two
 *              unsigned longwords (see the Long type specification below).
```

321

```
*               For the purposes of implementing the DES algorithm, the bits
*               are numbered as follows:
*                   [1 2 3 ... 32] [33 34 35 ... 64]
*                  in    b[0]              b[1]
*
*               The L (left) half is b[0], the R (right) half is b[1]
*
*       The key is passed as a 64-bit value, of which the 56 non-parity
*               bits are used. The parity bits are in DES bits
*               8, 16, 24, 32, 40, 48, 56, 64 (nb: these do NOT correspond to
*               the parity bits in ascii chars when packed in the usual way).
*/

typedef    unsigned long       Long;   /* type specification used for DES data */

extern desinit();               /* DES library initialization        */
extern keyinit();               /* DES key installation              */
extern endes();                 /* DES Encryption                    */
extern dedes();                 /* DES Decryption                    */



/*
*       des64.i - contains the fixed permutation and substitution tables
*                    for a 64 bit DES implementation
*          see "AS2805.5-1985 DEA" for table definitions and explanations
*
*       Notes: Lawrence Brown <lpb@csadfa.oz>    12/87
*/

char IP[64]                             /* initial permutation P         */
= {     58, 50, 42, 34, 26, 18, 10,  2,
        60, 52, 44, 36, 28, 20, 12,  4,
        62, 54, 46, 38, 30, 22, 14,  6,
        64, 56, 48, 40, 32, 24, 16,  8,
        57, 49, 41, 33, 25, 17,  9,  1,
        59, 51, 43, 35, 27, 19, 11,  3,
        61, 53, 45, 37, 29, 21, 13,  5,
        63, 55, 47, 39, 31, 23, 15,  7 };

char FP[64]                             /* final permutation F     */
= {     40,  8, 48, 16, 56, 24, 64, 32,
        39,  7, 47, 15, 55, 23, 63, 31,
        38,  6, 46, 14, 54, 22, 62, 30,
        37,  5, 45, 13, 53, 21, 61, 29,
        36,  4, 44, 12, 52, 20, 60, 28,
        35,  3, 43, 11, 51, 19, 59, 27,
        34,  2, 42, 10, 50, 18, 58, 26,
        33,  1, 41,  9, 49, 17, 57, 25 };

char E[48] = { 32,  1,  2,  3,  4,  5,      /* expansion operation matrix */
                4,  5,  6,  7,  8,  9,      /*   nb: NOT USED             */
                8,  9, 10, 11, 12, 13,      /*     expand() does this fn  */
               12, 13, 14, 15, 16, 17,
               16, 17, 18, 19, 20, 21,
```

```
                    20, 21, 22, 23, 24, 25,
                    24, 25, 26, 27, 28, 29,
                    28, 29, 30, 31, 32,  1  };


char PC1[64]        /* permuted choice table (key)  */
                    /* Rewritten as a 64 bit permutation, where 4 parity bits are */
                    /*   permuted to DES bits 29-32 in each 32 bit longword        */
                    /*   and subsequently ignored                                  */
= {     57, 49, 41, 33, 25, 17,  9,
         1, 58, 50, 42, 34, 26, 18,
        10,  2, 59, 51, 43, 35, 27,
        19, 11,  3, 60, 52, 44, 36,
         8, 16, 24, 32,                            /* <- these are parity bits  */
        63, 55, 47, 39, 31, 23, 15,
         7, 62, 54, 46, 38, 30, 22,
        14,  6, 61, 53, 45, 37, 29,
        21, 13,  5, 28, 20, 12,  4,
        40, 48, 56, 64};                           /* <- these are parity bits  */


char keyrot[16]                                    /* key rotation schedule      */
= {     1,1,2,2,2,2,2,2,1,2,2,2,2,2,2,1 };


char PC2[48]                                       /* permuted choice key (table)*/
= {     14, 17, 11, 24,  1,  5,
         3, 28, 15,  6, 21, 10,
        23, 19, 12,  4, 26,  8,
        16,  7, 27, 20, 13,  2,
        41, 52, 31, 37, 47, 55,
        30, 40, 51, 45, 33, 48,
        44, 49, 39, 56, 34, 53,
        46, 42, 50, 36, 29, 32  };


char S[8][64]                  /* S-Boxes: 48->32 bit compression tables      */
                               /* nb: DES bits (16) select row in each table  */
                               /*     DES bits (2345) select column in row    */
= {                                    /* S[1]                     */
        14,  4, 13,  1,  2, 15, 11,  8,  3, 10,  6, 12,  5,  9,  0,  7,
         0, 15,  7,  4, 14,  2, 13,  1, 10,  6, 12, 11,  9,  5,  3,  8,
         4,  1, 14,  8, 13,  6,  2, 11, 15, 12,  9,  7,  3, 10,  5,  0,
        15, 12,  8,  2,  4,  9,  1,  7,  5, 11,  3, 14, 10,  0,  6, 13,
                                       /* S[2]                     */
        15,  1,  8, 14,  6, 11,  3,  4,  9,  7,  2, 13, 12,  0,  5, 10,
         3, 13,  4,  7, 15,  2,  8, 14, 12,  0,  1, 10,  6,  9, 11,  5,
         0, 14,  7, 11, 10,  4, 13,  1,  5,  8, 12,  6,  9,  3,  2, 15,
        13,  8, 10,  1,  3, 15,  4,  2, 11,  6,  7, 12,  0,  5, 14,  9,
                                       /* S[3]                     */
        10,  0,  9, 14,  6,  3, 15,  5,  1, 13, 12,  7, 11,  4,  2,  8,
        13,  7,  0,  9,  3,  4,  6, 10,  2,  8,  5, 14, 12, 11, 15,  1,
        13,  6,  4,  9,  8, 15,  3,  0, 11,  1,  2, 12,  5, 10, 14,  7,
         1, 10, 13,  0,  6,  9,  8,  7,  4, 15, 14,  3, 11,  5,  2, 12,
                                       /* S[4]                     */
         7, 13, 14,  3,  0,  6,  9, 10,  1,  2,  8,  5, 11, 12,  4, 15,
        13,  8, 11,  5,  6, 15,  0,  3,  4,  7,  2, 12,  1, 10, 14,  9,
        10,  6,  9,  0, 12, 11,  7, 13, 15,  1,  3, 14,  5,  2,  8,  4,
         3, 15,  0,  6, 10,  1, 13,  8,  9,  4,  5, 11, 12,  7,  2, 14,
```

```
                                        /* S[5]                        */
        2, 12,   4,   1,   7, 10, 11,   6,   8,   5,   3, 15, 13,   0, 14,   9,
       14, 11,   2, 12,   4,   7, 13,   1,   5,   0, 15, 10,   3,   9,   8,   6,
        4,  2,   1, 11, 10, 13,   7,   8, 15,   9, 12,   5,   6,   3,   0, 14,
       11,  8, 12,   7,   1, 14,   2, 13,   6, 15,   0,   9, 10,   4,   5,   3,
                                        /* S[6]                        */
       12,  1, 10, 15,   9,   2,   6,   8,   0, 13,   3,   4, 14,   7,   5, 11,
       10, 15,   4,   2,   7, 12,   9,   5,   6,   1, 13, 14,   0, 11,   3,   8,
        9, 14, 15,   5,   2,   8, 12,   3,   7,   0,   4, 10,   1, 13, 11,   6,
        4,  3,   2, 12,   9,   5, 15, 10, 11, 14,   1,   7,   6,   0,   8, 13,
                                        /* S[7]                        */
        4, 11,   2, 14, 15,   0,   8, 13,   3, 12,   9,   7,   5, 10,   6,   1,
       13,  0, 11,   7,   4,   9,   1, 10, 14,   3,   5, 12,   2, 15,   8,   6,
        1,  4, 11, 13, 12,   3,   7, 14, 10, 15,   6,   8,   0,   5,   9,   2,
        6, 11, 13,   8,   1,   4, 10,   7,   9,   5,   0, 15, 14,   2,   3, 12,
                                        /* S[8]                        */
       13,  2,   8,   4,   6, 15, 11,   1, 10,   9,   3, 14,   5,   0, 12,   7,
        1, 15, 13,   8, 10,   3,   7,   4, 12,   5,   6, 11,   0, 14,   9,   2,
        7, 11,   4,   1,   9, 12, 14,   2,   0,   6, 10, 13, 15,   3,   5,   8,
        2,  1, 14,   7,   4, 10,   8, 13, 15, 12,   9,   0,   3,   5,   6, 11  };

char P[32]                              /* 32-bit permutation function P */
= {       16,   7, 20, 21,
          29, 12, 28, 17,
           1, 15, 23, 26,
           5, 18, 31, 10,
           2,  8, 24, 14,
          32, 27,  3,  9,
          19, 13, 30,  6,
          22, 11,  4, 25  };




/*
 *      des64.c - contains routines to perform encryption/decryption of 64-bit
 *              datablocks using the DES Data Encryption Algorithm.
 *              A description of the algorithm may be found in:
 *                  Australian Standard AS2805.5-1985 Data Encryption Algorithm
 *
 *      Author: Lawrence Brown <lpb@csadfa.oz>          Dec 1987
 *              Computer Science, UC UNSW, Australian Defence Force Academy,
 *                      Canberra, ACT 2600, Australia.
 *
 */


#include "des.h"         /* include Interface Specification header file      */
#include "des64.i"       /* include DES Substitution and Permutation tables  */
#include <stdio.h>

/*
 *      Define global data structures used by DES routines
 */
```

```
char      subkey[16][8];  /* Storage for the 16 sub-keys used in the DES rounds */
          /*   each 48-bit subkey is saved as eight 6-bit values, in each byte  */




/*
 *        endes(b) - main DES encryption routine, this routine encrypts one 64-bit
 *                   block b using the DES algorithm with the current key
 *
 *              The encryption operation involves permuting the input block
 *              using permutation IP, applying a DES round sixteen times
 *              (which ensures the output is a complex function of the input,
 *              and the key), and finally applying permutation FP (inverse IP).
 *
 *              nb: The 64-bit block is passed as two longwords. For the
 *                  purposes of the DES algorithm, the bits are numbered:
 *                      [1 2 3 ... 32] [33 34 35 ... 64] in thew two halves.
 *                  The L (left) half is b[0], the R (right) half is b[1]
 */
endes(b)
Long      b[2];
{
          Long      work[2];                      /* 64-bit working store      */
          register int    i;

          perm64(work, b, IP);                    /* Apply IP to input block   */

          for (i=0; i<=15; i++)                    /* Perform the 16 rounds     */
                  round(work, subkey[i]);          /*    on the data            */
          swap(work);                              /* Unswap after final round  */

          perm64(b, work, FP);                     /* Perform Inverse IP        */
}


/*
 *        dedes(b) - main DES decryption routine, this routine decrypts one 64-bit
 *                   block b using the DES algorithm with the current key
 *
 *              Decryption uses the same algorithm as encryption, except that
 *              the subkeys are used in reverse order.
 */
dedes(b)
Long      b[2];
{
          Long      work[2];
          register int    i;

          perm64(work, b, IP);                    /* Apply IP to input block   */

          for (i=15; i>=0; i--)                    /* Perform the 16 rounds     */
                  round(work, subkey[i]);
          swap(work);                              /* Unswap after final round  */

          perm64(b, work, FP);                     /* Perform Inverse IP        */
}
```

```
/*
 *      desinit() - perform any data structure initialization needed
 */
desinit()
{                               /* No preinitialized tables used here      */
}


/*
 *      round(d, k) - implements a single DES round on 64-bit block d, using
 *              48-bit subkey k. Each round performs the following calculation:
 *                      L(i) = R(i-1)
 *                      R(i) = L(i-1) XOR f(R(i-1), K(i))
 *
 *              nb: L (left) component is in d[0], R (right) component in d[1]
 */
round(d, k)
Long    d[2];
char    *k;
{
        Long    t;
        extern Long    f();

        t = d[0] ^ f(d[1], k);   /* Calc complex fn  t = f(R(i-1), K(i))   */
                                 /*    and XOR with L(i-1)                  */
        d[0] = d[1];             /* L(i) = R(i-1)                          */
        d[1] = t;                /* R(i) = L(i-1) XOR f(R(i-1), K(i))      */
}


/*
 *      f(r, k) - is the complex non-linear DES function, whose output
 *              is a complex function of both input data and sub-key
 *              The input data R(i-1) is expanded to 48-bits via expansion fn E,
 *              is XOR'd with the subkey K(i), substituted into the S-boxes,
 *              and finally permuted by P. ie the calculation is:
 *                      A = E(R(i-1)) XOR K(i)          (a 48-bit value)
 *                      B = S(A)                        (a 32-bit value)
 *                      f = P(B)                        (a 32-bit value)
 *
 *      nb: the 48-bit values are stored as eight 6-bit values.
 *              In each byte, the bits are numbered  [x x 1 2 3 4 5 6]
 *              Overall the bit numbering is:
 *          [x x 1 2 3 4 5 6] [x x 7 8 9 10 11 12] ... [x x 43 44 45 46 47 48]
 *      nb: the 6-bit S-box input value [x x 1 2 3 4 5 6] is interpreted as:
 *              bits [1 6] select a row within each box,
 *              bits [2 3 4 5] then select a column within that row
 *              hence the input value is reordered to [x x 1 6 2 3 4 5] before
 *              indexing into the S-box tables.
 */

Long
f(r, k)
Long    r;      /* Data value R(i-1) */
char    *k;     /* Subkey    K(i)    */
{
        Long    b = 0,    /* 32 bit S-box output block                    */
                out = 0; /* 32-bit output value                          */
```

```
        char    a[8];      /* store expanded input data as eight 6-bit values */
        register Long    s;       /* an S-box output                          */
        register Long   rc;    /* an S-box row-col index                  */
        register int    j;

        expand(a, r);    /* expand input data R(i) to 48 bits using fn E    */

        for (j=0; j<8; j++) {          /* Lookup S-boxes to get B = S(A)   */
            rc = a[j] ^ k[j];          /* A = E(R(i-1)) XOR K(i)            */
            rc =    (rc & 0x20)  |           /* reorder S-box index so   */
                   ((rc << 4) & 0x10)  |  /*   bits 1,6 form the row */
                   ((rc >> 1) & 0x0F);     /*   bits 2-5 form the col */
            s = S[j][rc];              /* S-box j output                   */
            b = (b << 4) | s;          /* Concatenate S-box output to b    */
        }

        perm32(&out, &b, P);              /* Apply 32-bit permutation P to B */

#ifdef  TRACE
                /* If Tracing, dump R(i-1), K(i), and f(R(i-1),K(i))      */
        fprintf(stderr," f(%08lx, %02x %02x %02x %02x %02x %02x %02x %02x) = %08lx  ",
                r, k[0], k[1], k[2], k[3], k[4], k[5], k[6], k[7], out);
#endif  TRACE

        return(out);                     /* f returns the result of P(B)    */
}

/*
 *      keyinit(key) - installs key for use in subsequent encryptions and
 *              decryptions. A key must be installed before endes/dedes can
 *              be called.
 *
 *              The key is passed as a 64-bit value, of which the 56 non
 *              parity bits are used. The parity bits are in DES bits
 *              8, 16, 24, 32, 40, 48, 56, 64 (nb: these do NOT correspond to
 *              the parity bits in ascii chars when packed in the usual way).
 *              The function performs the key scheduling calculation, saving
 *              the resulting sixteen 48-bit sub-keys for use in subsequent
 *              encryption/decryption calculations. These 48-bit values are
 *              saved as eight 6-bit values, as detailed previously.
 *
 *              The key scheduling calculation involves
 *                      permuting the input key by PC1 which selects 56-bits
 *                      dividing the 56-bit value into two halves C, D
 *                      sixteen times
 *                        rotates each half left by 1 or 2 places according
 *                          to schedule in keyrot
 *                        concatenates the two 28-bit values, and permutes with
 *                          PC2 which selects 48-bits to become the subkey
 *
 *      nb: the two 28-bit halves are stored in two longwords, with bits
 *              numbered as [1 2 ... 27 28 x x x x] ... [29 30 ... 48 x x x x]
 *              in Longs              n[0]                 n[1]    (MSB to LSB)
 *              the bottom 4 bits in each longword are ignored
 *              This scheme is used in keyinit(), keysched(), and rotl28()
 */
```

```
#define MASK28   0xFFFFFFF0L              /* Mask DES key bits 1 to 28      */


keyinit(key)
Long    key[2];          /* Key to use, stored as an array of Longs        */
{

        Long    cd[2];   /* Storage for the two 28-bit key halves C and D  */
        register int    i;

        perm64(cd, key, PC1);            /* Permute key with PC1           */

        cd[0] &= MASK28; /* form 28-bit value C by dropping 4 parity bits */
        cd[1] &= MASK28; /* form 28-bit value D by dropping 4 parity bits */

        for (i=0; i<16; i++) {           /* Form sixteen subkeys           */
                rotl28(&cd[0], (int)keyrot[i]); /* Rotate by 1 or 2 bits   */
                rotl28(&cd[1], (int)keyrot[i]); /*   according to schedule*/
                keyperm(cd, i);          /* Apply PC2 to form subkey i     */
        }.
}


/*
 *      keyperm(cd, i) - takes the two key halves in cd, permutes them
 *              according to PC2, and generates a 48-bit output value,
 *              which is stored as eight 6-bit values
 *
 *      nb: to set bits in the output word, as mask with a single 1 in it is
 *              used. On each step, the 1 is shifted into the next location
 */

#define KEYBIT1 0x20                     /* bit 1 of a 6-bit value         */


keyperm(cd, i)
Long    cd[2]; /* The two 28-bit key halves                               */
int     i;     /*    subkey number i                                      */
{
        register int    j, k;
        register char   mask;            /* mask used to set bit in output  */
        register char   *perm = PC2;     /* used to step through perm PC2   */


                                         /* Process half C */
        for (j=0; j<4; j++) {                    /* For each S-box input      */
            subkey[i][j] = 0;                    /* Clear output word         */
            mask = KEYBIT1;                      /* Reset mask to bit 1       */
            for (k=0; k<6; k++) {                /* For each S-box input bit  */
                if (keybit(cd, (int)*perm++) == 1) /* If input bit permuted   */
                    subkey[i][j] |= mask;        /* to this loc is 1, set it  */
                mask >>= 1;                      /* Shift mask to next bit    */
            }
        }

                                         /* Process half D */
        for (j=4; j<8; j++) {                    /* For each S-box input      */
```

```
            subkey[i][j] = 0;                      /* Clear output word       */
            mask = KEYBIT1;                         /* Reset mask to bit 1     */
            for (k=0; k<6; k++) {                   /* For each S-box input bit */
                if (keybit(cd, (int)*perm++) == 1) /* If input bit permuted   */
                        subkey[i][j] |= mask;       /* to this loc is 1, set it */
                mask >>= 1;                         /* Shift mask to next bit  */
            }
        }
}


/*
 *      keybit(n, pos) - return bit at position pos in n (1 <= pos <= 48)
 *          when n is the two 24-bit halves used in the key scheduling
 *          bits are numbered [1 2 ... 27 28 x x x x]  [29 30 ... 48 x x x x]
 *              in Longs              n[0]                         n[1]
 *          nb: bottom 4 bits in each longword are ignored
 */
int
keybit(n, pos)
Long    n[2];
int     pos;
{
        register int    b, d, o;

        d = (pos - 1) / 28;             /* calculate which half bit is in  */
        o = 31 - ((pos - 1) % 28);      /* calculate offset within half    */
        b = ((n[d] >> o) & 01);         /* shift wanted bit to LSB, mask it */
        return (b);                     /* and return wanted wbit          */
}


/*
 *      rotl28(b, pos) - rotate block b (where b is a 28-bit key half)
 *              left by pos bits, (0 <= pos <= 32)
 */
rotl28(b, pos)
Long    *b;     /* Block to rotate left          */
int     pos;    /* Number of bits to rotate left */
{
        *b = ((*b << pos) | (*b >> (28-pos)) ) & MASK28;
}


/*
 *      perm64(out, in, perm) is the general permutation of a 64-bit input
 *          block to a 64-bit output block, under the control of a
 *          permutation array perm. Each element of perm specifies which
 *          input bit is to be permuted to the output bit with the same
 *          index as the array element.
 *
 *      nb: to set bits in the output word, a mask with a single 1 in it is
 *          used. On each step, the 1 is shifted into the next location
 */
```

```
#define DESBIT1 0x80000000L              /* DES bit 1, MSB of 32-bit word */

perm64(out, in , perm)
Long    out[2];          /* Output 64-bit block to be permuted            */
Long    in[2];           /* Input  64-bit block after permutation         */
char    perm[64];        /* Permutation array                             */
{
        Long    mask = DESBIT1;          /* mask used to set bit in output    */
        register int    i;

                         /* Process left half out[0]                        */
        out[0] = 0L;                          /* Clear output word         */
        for (i=0; i<32; i++) {                /* For each bit position     */
                if (bit(in, (int)*perm++) == 1) /* If the input bit permuted */
                        out[0] |= mask;       /*  to this loc is 1, set it */
                mask >>= 1;                   /* Shift mask to next bit     */
        }
                         /* Process right half out[1]                       */
        out[1] = 0L;                          /* Clear output word         */
        mask = DESBIT1;
        for (i=0; i<32; i++) {                /* For each bit position     */
                if (bit(in, (int)*perm++) == 1) /* If the input bit permuted */
                        out[1] |= mask;       /*  to this loc is 1, set it */
                mask >>= 1;                   /* Shift mask to next bit     */
        }
}


/*
 *      perm32(out, in, perm) is the general permutation of a 32-bit input
 *              block to a 32-bit output block, under the control of a
 *              permutation array perm. Each element of perm specifies which
 *              input bit is to be permuted to the output bit with the same
 *              index as the array element.
 *
 *      nb: to set bits in the output word, as mask with a single 1 in it is
 *              used. On each step, the 1 is shifted into the next location
 */
perm32(out, in , perm)
Long    *out;            /* Output 32-bit block to be permuted            */
Long    *in;             /* Input  32-bit block after permutation         */
char    perm[32];        /* Permutation array                             */
{
        Long    mask = DESBIT1;          /* mask used to set bit in output    */
        register int    i;

        for (i=0; i<32; i++) {                /* For each bit position     */
                if (bit(in, (int)*perm++) == 1) /* If the input bit permuted */
                        *out |= mask;         /*  to this loc is 1, set it */
                mask >>= 1;                   /* Shift mask to next bit     */
        }
}


/*
 *      expand(a, r) - expands the 32 bit value r into a 48-bit value a
 *              stored as eight 6-bit values in a char array, with bits
 *              numbered as specified previously.
```

```
*
*                Due to the regular nature of the expansion matrix E,
*                this function implements it directly for efficiency reasons
*                It takes each 4-bit nybble of the input word, and concatenates
*                it with the adjacent bit on either side to form a 6-bit value.
*                (nb: bit 32 is assumed to be adjacent to bit 1)
*/


#define MASK6    0x3f                      /* mask out all bar lower 6-bits       */

expand(a, r)
char     *a;        /* output array to store the 48-bit value in               */
Long     r;         /* 32-bit input data block                                  */
{
         register Long    t;              /* temporary storage for values       */

         t = (r<<5) | (r>>27);   a[0] = t & MASK6;   /* bits 32  1  2  3  4  5 */
         t = r >> 23;            a[1] = t & MASK6;   /* bits  4  5  6  7  8  9 */
         t = r >> 19;            a[2] = t & MASK6;   /* bits  8  9 10 11 12 13 */
         t = r >> 15;            a[3] = t & MASK6;   /* bits 12 13 14 15 16 17 */
         t = r >> 11;            a[4] = t & MASK6;   /* bits 16 17 18 19 20 21 */
         t = r >> 07;            a[5] = t & MASK6;   /* bits 20 21 22 23 24 25 */
         t = r >> 03;            a[6] = t & MASK6;   /* bits 24 25 26 27 28 29 */
         t = (r<<1) | (r>>31);   a[7] = t & MASK6;   /* bits 28 29 30 31 32  1 */
}



/*
 *      bit(n, pos) return bit at position pos in n (1 <= pos <= 64)
 *              bits are numbered [1 2 ... 31 32]   [33 34 ... 64]
 *              in Longs            n[0]                  n[1]
 */
int
bit(n, pos)
Long     n[2];
int      pos;
{
         register int      b, d, o;

         d = (pos - 1) / 32;              /* calculate which half the bit is in */
         o = 32 - (pos % 32);             /* calculate offset within the half   */
         b = ((n[d] >> o) & 01);          /* shift wanted bit to LSB, mask it   */
         return (b);                      /* and return it                      */
}



/*
 *      swap(b) - exchange the two 32-bit halves of the 64-bit block b
 */
swap(b)
Long     b[2];   /* data block */
{
         Long     tmp;
         tmp = b[0]; b[0] = b[1]; b[1] = tmp;     /* Swap halves of b           */
}
```

```
/*
 *      des.c - DES file encryption/decryption program.
 *
 *              This program reads its stdin, and encrypts/decrypts using the
 *      DES Data Encryption Algorithm in either Cipher Block Chaining (CBC), or
 *      Electronic Codebook (ECB) Mode.  In ECB mode, each block is treated
 *      separately, is encrypted and the ciphertext output. In CBC mode, the
 *      plaintext input is XOR'd with the ciphertext output from the previous
 *      block (or an initialization vector on the first block). Thus each
 *      block depends on all previous blocks. The DES encryption/decryption is
 *      performed by calling DES library routines. For a detailed description
 *      of the DES encryption/decryption and modes of use see:
 *
 *          Australian Standard AS2805.5-1985   The Data Encryption Algorithm
 *
 *
 *      Usage:  des -e|-d [-h] -k key [-b]
 *              Flags:
 *                  -e              encrypt input (default)
 *                  -d              decrypt input
 *                  -h              specify that key is supplied in hex
 *                  -k key          specifies key as 8 ascii chars, or 16 hex digits
 *                  -b              use ECB mode, otherwise CBC mode is used
 *
 *      Author: Lawrence Brown <lpb@csadfa.oz>          Dec 1987
 *              Computer Science, UC UNSW, Australian Defence Force Academy,
 *                      Canberra, ACT 2600, Australia.
 *
 *              The user interface and some code has been inspired by the PD
 *              programs of:    Phil Karn, KA9Q <karn@flash.bellcore.com> 1986
 *              and             Jim Gillogly 1977.
 *
 *
 *      nb: if this program is compiled on a little-endian machine (eg Vax)
 *                      #define LITTLE_ENDIAN
 *              in order to enable the byte swapping  routines
 */

#include "des.h"         /* include DES Interface Specification header file   */
#include <stdio.h>
#include <strings.h>

/*
 *      Define global data structures used by DES routines
 */

Long    iv[2]  = {0, 0};          /* Initialization Vector & previous block   */
Long    key[2] = {0, 0};          /* DES key                                  */
char    *usage = "des -e|-d [-h] -k key [-b]";  /* Program usage statement    */
char    *Name  = 0;               /* name of this program                     */
int     ecb    = 0;               /* use ECB mode flag (default false)        */
int     encrypting = 1;           /* Encrypt input flag (default true)        */
int     hexkey = 0;               /* Key supplied in hex (default false)      */

main(argc, argv)
int     argc;
```

```
char      **argv;
{
        int       errflag = 0;      /* Error detected in command line flags ?  */
        int       c;                /* current flag found                       */
        char      *keyinp = 0;      /* acsii key supplied                       */
        extern char   *optarg;          /* current getopt argument pointer    */

        Name = argv[0];             /* save name of program for error messages  */
                                    /* scan command line flags                  */
        while ((c = getopt(argc, argv, "edhk:b")) != EOF) {
                switch (c) {
                        case 'e':    encrypting = 1;          break;
                        case 'd':    encrypting = 0;          break;
                        case 'h':    hexkey = 1;              break;
                        case 'k':    keyinp = optarg;         break;
                        case 'b':    ecb = 1;                 break;
                        default:     errflag++;               break;
                }
        }

        if (errflag || keyinp == 0) {   /* error in flags, or no key given   */
                fprintf(stderr, "%s0, usage);
                exit(1);
        }

        if (hexkey)                        /* convert key from ascii to long    */
                gethex(keyinp, key);       /*    specified in hex               */
        else
                getkey(keyinp, key);       /*    specified in ascii             */

        desinit();                         /* initialize des library routines   */

        keyinit(key);                      /* specify key to use                */

        if (encrypting)                    /* Encrypt/decrypt input as specified*/
                do_encrypt();
        else
                do_decrypt();

}

/*
 *      do_encrypt() - the main encryption routine. This procedure reads 64-bit
 *              (8 byte) blocks of input, XOR's with chain vector if in CBC mode
 *              encrypts the block, and writes it out, saving the output as the
 *              next chain vector. It swaps bytes around if necessary on a
 *              little-endian machine. The last byte of the last block contains
 *              the number of valid characters in that block (the remaining
 *              chars are garbage).
 */

do_encrypt()
{
        int       cnt = 0;         /* count of characters read in last read   */
        Long      work[2];         /* 64-bit work value used by DES routines  */
```

```
            do {                        /* read next 8 byte block, if the last one   */
                if ((cnt = fread((char *)work, 1, 8, stdin)) != 8)
                        ((char *)work)[7] = cnt; /* save cnt of valid bytes   */

#ifdef LITTLE_ENDIAN
                swap((char *)work);        /* swap bytes round if little-endian */
#endif LITTLE_ENDIAN

                if (!ecb) {       /* if in CBC mode, chain previous ciphertext */
                        work[0] ^= iv[0];          /* work = work XOR iv          */
                        work[1] ^= iv[1];
                }

                endes(work);     /* encrypt data block                        */

                if (!ecb) {       /* if in CBC mode, save ciphertext as next iv*/
                        iv[0] = work[0];
                        iv[1] = work[1];
                }

#ifdef LITTLE_ENDIAN
                swap((char *)work);        /* swap bytes round if little-endian */
#endif LITTLE_ENDIAN

                fwrite((char *)work, 1, 8, stdout);     /* write ciphertext   */

        } while (cnt == 8);      /* loop back until last block has been read   */
}

/*
 *      do_decrypt() - the main decryption routine. This procedure reads 64-bit
 *              (8 byte) blocks of input, XOR's with chain vector if in CBC mode
 *              decrypts the block, and writes it out, saving the output as the
 *              next chain vector. It swaps bytes around if necessary on a
 *              little-endian machine. The last byte of the last block contains
 *              the number of valid characters in that block. Hence must delay
 *              writing the plaintext out until have checked to see that it
 *              wasn't the last block.
 */

do_decrypt()
{
        int     cnt = 0;           /* count of characters read in last read    */
        Long    work[2];           /* 64-bit work value used by DES routines   */
        Long    prev[2];           /* previous 64-bit plaintext saved          */
        Long    nextiv[2];         /* each 64-bit ciphertext block is next iv   */

        cnt = fread((char *)work, 1, 8, stdin); /* read the first 8 bytes      */
        do {
#ifdef LITTLE_ENDIAN
                swap((char *)work);        /* swap bytes round if little-endian */
#endif LITTLE_ENDIAN

                if (!ecb) {       /* if in CBC mode, save cipher as next iv     */
                        nextiv[0] = work[0];
                        nextiv[1] = work[1];
```

```
                }

                dedes(work);      /* decrypt data block                       */

                if (!ecb) {       /* if in CBC mode, chain previous iv to work */
                        work[0] ^= iv[0];        /* work = work XOR iv          */
                        work[1] ^= iv[1];
                        iv[0] = nextiv[0];       /* & move next iv to current   */
                        iv[1] = nextiv[1];
                }

#ifdef LITTLE_ENDIAN
                swap((char *)work);      /* swap bytes round if little-endian  */
#endif LITTLE_ENDIAN

                prev[0] = work[0];       /* save plaintext while do EOF check   */
                prev[1] = work[1];
                                 /* read next 8 byte block, if the last one     */
                if ((cnt = fread((char *)work, 1, 8, stdin)) != 8) {
                        cnt = ((char *)prev)[7]; /* extract no valid bytes       */
                        if (cnt<0 || cnt >7) {   /* aaargh - bad file            */
                                fprintf(stderr, "%s: Corrupted ciphertext0, Name);
                                exit(-1);
                        } else if (cnt > 0)      /* last block has valid chars*/
                                fwrite((char *)prev, 1, cnt, stdout);
                } else {          /* normal case - in middle of file            */
                        fwrite((char *)prev, 1, 8, stdout);
                }
        } while (cnt == 8);      /* loop back until last block has been read    */
}


/*
 *      gethex(kin, k)  and  getkey(kin, k)  convert the string supplied for
 *              the key into a 64-bit block, assuming the string is hex chars,
 *              or standard 7-bit ascii chars respectively. getkey will
 *              provide odd parity for each byte (to overcome differing systems
 *              default values). This is compatible with the SUN des(1) command
 */

gethex(kin, k)
char    *kin;                    /* input string supplied for key              */
Long    k[2];                    /* output 64-bit key value                    */
{
        if ((strlen(kin) != 16) ||       /* check for valid length key         */
            (sscanf(kin, "%81x%81x", &k[0], &k[1]) != 2)) {
                fprintf(stderr, "%s: Bad key specification0, Name);
                exit(-1);
        }
}


getkey(kin, k)
char    *kin;                    /* input string supplied for key              */
Long    k[2];                    /* output 64-bit key value                    */
{
        char    *lk = (char *)k;         /* char pointer to 64-bit value       */
```

```c
        int     i, j, p;


        if (strlen(kin) < 8) {              /* check for valid length key      */
                fprintf(stderr, "%s: Bad key specification0, Name);
                exit(-1);
        }
                                /* Calculate parity bit for each key byte  */
        for (i=0; i<8; i++) {   /* for each key char                        */
                lk[i] = kin[i]; /* copy it into 64-bit block                */
                for (p=0, j=0; j<7; j++)         /* calculate parity & set it */
                        if ( lk[i] & (1 << j))   /* count number of 1's       */
                                p++;
                if ((p & 1) == 0)                /* if even            */
                        lk[i] |= 0x80;           /* set parity bit     */
                else                             /* otherwise          */
                        lk[i] &= 0x7f;           /* clear parity bit   */
        }

#ifdef LITTLE_ENDIAN
        swap(k);                        /* swap bytes round if little-endian          */
#endif LITTLE_ENDIAN
}


#ifdef LITTLE_ENDIAN
/*
 *      swap(b) - exchanged bytes in each longword of a 64-bit data block
 *                      on little-endian machines where byte order is reversed
 */

swap(b)
Long    b[2];
{
        register char   *cb = (char *)b;        /* get char ptr to block      */
        register char   c;

        c = cb[0]; cb[0] = cb[3]; cb[3] = c;
        c = cb[1]; cb[1] = cb[2]; cb[2] = c;
        c = cb[4]; cb[4] = cb[7]; cb[7] = c;
        c = cb[5]; cb[5] = cb[6]; cb[6] = c;
}
#endif LITTLE_ENDIAN
```

# B2 Key representation for DES

We reproduce the following from the Standard AS2805.5–1985 for the benefit of the user:

## B1 Introduction

DEA keys, while used in 56-bit form, will be stored in 64-bit form that includes a parity bit on each byte (8 bits). The bits are numbered left to right (i.e. 1, 2, ... 63, 64).

When keys are written, the 64 bits shall be represented as sixteen hexadecimal characters (0-9, A-F) with a space between each pair of characters. Thus a valid DEA key is 01 23 45 67 89 AB CD EF. In the following example, there is an odd number of bits in each character pair (i.e. the parity of every 8-bit byte is odd).

Valid DEA keys range from:

| | | | | | | | | |
|---|---|---|---|---|---|---|---|---|
| 01 | 01 | 01 | 01 | 01 | 01 | 01 | 01 | to |
| FE | FE | FE | FE | FE | FE | FE | FE | |

## B2 Weak keys

It must be realized that the mathematical complexity of the DEA algorithm, and hence its cryptographic strength, would be reduced if the internal keys generated were the same. For this reason, the condition $K(1) = K(2) \ldots = K(16)$ should be avoided.

There is however, a set of weak keys within the DEA which satisfies the above condition. This occurs whenever the bits of permuted choice 1, as specified in Clause 3.5 of AS2805.5–1985, are all ones or zeros.

Thus there are four weak keys altogether and they are represented as (parity-adjusted) external keys:

| | | | | | | | |
|---|---|---|---|---|---|---|---|
| 01 | 01 | 01 | 01 | 01 | 01 | 01 | 01 |
| 1F | 1F | 1F | 1F | 0E | 0E | 0E | 0E |
| E0 | E0 | E0 | E0 | F1 | F1 | F1 | F1 |
| FE | FE | FE | FE | FE | FE | FE | FE |

Weak keys also have the property that there is no difference between the operations of enciphering and deciphering.

## B3 Semi-weak keys

There is another set of keys that may be defined as semi-weak. These have the property that only two different internal keys are produced, with each occurring eight times. These keys may be grouped as pairs which exhibit the property of having some identical internal keys.

List of pairs of semi-weak represented as (parity-adjusted) external keys:

| | | | | | | | |
|---|---|---|---|---|---|---|---|
| E0 | FE | E0 | FE | F1 | FE | F1 | FE |
| FE | E0 | FE | E0 | FE | F1 | FE | F1 |
| | | | | | | | |
| 1F | FE | 1F | FE | 0E | FE | 0E | FE |
| FE | 1F | FE | 1F | FE | 0E | FE | 0E |

| 01 | FE | 01 | FE | 01 | FE | 01 | FE |
|----|----|----|----|----|----|----|----|
| FE | 01 | FE | 01 | FE | 01 | FE | 01 |

| 1F | E0 | 1F | E0 | 0E | F1 | 0E | F1 |
|----|----|----|----|----|----|----|----|
| E0 | 1F | E0 | 1F | F1 | 0E | F1 | 0E |

| 01 | E0 | 01 | E0 | 01 | F1 | 01 | F1 |
|----|----|----|----|----|----|----|----|
| E0 | 01 | E0 | 01 | F1 | 01 | F1 | 01 |

| 01 | 1F | 01 | 1F | 01 | 0E | 01 | 0E |
|----|----|----|----|----|----|----|----|
| 1F | 01 | 1F | 01 | 0E | 01 | 0E | 01 |

## B4  Other keys

Certain other keys display the property of producing only four internal keys, each occurring four times. Moreover, the pattern of recurrence is such that the same internal key never occurs twice in succession, although it will occur alternately.

These keys are listed as follows:

| 1F | 1F | 01 | 01 | 0E | 0E | 01 | 01 |
|----|----|----|----|----|----|----|----|
| 01 | 1F | 1F | 01 | 01 | 0E | 0E | 01 |
| 1F | 01 | 01 | 1F | 0E | 01 | 01 | 0E |
| 01 | 01 | 1F | 1F | 01 | 01 | 0E | 0E |

| E0 | E0 | 01 | 01 | F1 | F1 | 01 | 01 |
|----|----|----|----|----|----|----|----|
| FE | FE | 01 | 01 | FE | FE | 01 | 01 |
| FE | E0 | 1F | 01 | FE | F1 | 0E | 01 |
| E0 | FE | 1F | 01 | F1 | FE | 0E | 01 |
| FE | E0 | 01 | 1F | FE | F1 | 01 | 0E |
| E0 | FE | 01 | 1F | F1 | FE | 01 | 0E |
| E0 | E0 | 1F | 1F | F1 | F1 | 0E | 0E |
| FE | FE | 1F | 1F | FE | FE | 0E | 0E |

| FE | 1F | E0 | 01 | FE | 0E | F1 | 01 |
|----|----|----|----|----|----|----|----|
| E0 | 1F | FE | 01 | F1 | 0E | FE | 01 |
| FE | 01 | E0 | 1F | FE | 01 | F1 | 0E |
| E0 | 01 | FE | 1F | F1 | 01 | FE | 0E |

| 01 | E0 | E0 | 01 | 01 | F1 | F1 | 01 |
|----|----|----|----|----|----|----|----|
| 1F | FE | E0 | 01 | 0E | FE | F1 | 01 |
| 1F | E0 | FE | 01 | 0E | F1 | FE | 01 |
| 01 | FE | FE | 01 | 01 | FE | FE | 01 |
| 1F | E0 | E0 | 1F | 0E | F1 | F1 | 0E |
| 01 | FE | E0 | 1F | 01 | FE | F1 | 0E |
| 01 | E0 | FE | 1F | 01 | F1 | FE | 0E |
| 1F | FE | FE | 1F | 0E | FE | FE | 0E |

| E0 | 01 | 01 | E0 | F1 | 01 | 01 | F1 |
|----|----|----|----|----|----|----|----|
| FE | 1F | 01 | E0 | FE | 0E | 01 | F1 |
| FE | 01 | 1F | E0 | FE | 01 | 0E | F1 |
| E0 | 1F | 1F | E0 | F1 | 0E | 0E | F1 |
| FE | 01 | 01 | FE | FE | 01 | 01 | FE |
| E0 | 1F | 01 | FE | F1 | 0E | 01 | FE |
| E0 | 01 | 1F | FE | F1 | 01 | 0E | FE |
| FE | 1F | 1F | FE | FE | 0E | 0E | FE |

| 1F | FE | 01 | E0 | 0E | FE | 01 | F1 |
|----|----|----|----|----|----|----|----|
| 01 | FE | 1F | E0 | 01 | FE | 0E | F1 |
| 1F | E0 | 01 | FE | 0E | F1 | 01 | FE |
| 01 | E0 | 1F | FE | 01 | F1 | 0E | FE |

| 01 | 01 | E0 | E0 | 01 | 01 | F1 | F1 |
|----|----|----|----|----|----|----|----|
| 1F | 1F | E0 | E0 | 0E | 0E | F1 | F1 |
| 1F | 01 | FE | E0 | 0E | 01 | FE | F1 |
| 01 | 1F | FE | E0 | 01 | 0E | FE | F1 |
| 1F | 01 | E0 | FE | 0E | 01 | F1 | FE |
| 01 | 1F | E0 | FE | 01 | 0E | F1 | FE |
| 01 | 01 | FE | FE | 01 | 01 | FE | FE |
| 1F | 1F | FE | FE | 0E | 0E | FE | FE |

| FE | FE | E0 | E0 | FE | FE | F1 | F1 |
|----|----|----|----|----|----|----|----|
| E0 | FE | FE | E0 | F1 | FE | FE | F1 |
| FE | E0 | E0 | FE | FE | FE | F1 | F1 |
| E0 | E0 | FE | FE | F1 | F1 | FE | FE |

## B5 Conclusion

Finally, it should be realized that the described set of keys (weak, semi-weak, etc.) pose no threat to the algorithm's security. This is because the number of such keys is small in comparison to the total set of 72057594037927936 ($2^{56}$) possible different keys. Provided that keys are randomly selected, the likelihood of selecting such a key is therefore small. These keys could easily be avoided during key generation (if they were intended to be installed in a system for relatively long period of time).

The user of this algorithm should be aware of any potentially weak keys that may be applicable to a specific hardware/software implementation.

# APPENDIX C
# VIGENERE, BEAUFORD OR VARIANT BEAUFORD CODE

```
program enc(input,output);
{
      This program encrypts files using one of Vigenere Cipher,
      Beauford Cipher or Variant Beauford Cipher (the inverse of Vigenere).

      *********************************************************************
      ** Author: Leisa Condie <phoenix@csadfa.oz> June 24, 1987       **
      ** Dept. of Computer Science, University College, UNSW,         **
      ** Australian Defence Force Academy, Canberra, 2600, Australia. **
      *********************************************************************

      Input files are of the form:
          cipher type
          key
          the message in free format

      Output is of the form:
          theen crypt edmes sage

      The cipher type is one of 'V' for Vigenere, 'B' for Beauford and
      'A' for Variant Beauford. If any other character is used an /
      error message will be printed and the Vigenere cipher will be used
      to encrypt the file.

      Note that both upper and lower case characters are encrypted and
      that the output is in lower case only.

      The alphabet length can be adjusted (it is currently 26).

      The output is in 5 letter chunks (this can also be simply changed) to
      confuse the word lengths being encrypted.

      Another thing easily changed is the possible key length (currently 10).
      If the key entered is longer than MAXKEYLENGTH then it is truncated to
      this length.

      An example:
      V
      orbit
      An ambassador is an Honest man sent to Lie and Intrigue abroad for the
      benefit of his Country

      produces:
```

```
oebuu ojtiw cijat bypvx gknig gvobm ccjmt bujvm fzhcx osswt rwpzm vvcmg
swjbh tyjav clobk m
}


{
 *  Author:      Leisa Condie <phoenix@csadfa.oz>         1987
 *               Computer Science, UC UNSW, Australian Defence Force Academy,
 *                      Canberra, ACT 2600, Australia.
 *
}

const
    ALPHA = 26;        {Number of characters in alphabet used}
    MAXKEYLENGTH = 10;  {Maximum characters allowable in key}
    BLOCKLENGTH = 5;  {Number of letters per chunk}

var
    ch : char;         {Character read in}
    key : array[1..MAXKEYLENGTH] of char; {Array containing the key}
    i   : integer;
    count  : integer;   {Counts off the BLOCKLENGTH letter chunks}
    kcount : integer;    {Holds the length of the key read in}
    num : integer;
    newline   : boolean;    {Set true when a carriage return detected.
                  The program finishes the 5 letter chunk it
                  was printing then prints a carriage return.
                  Newline then set false}
    vigenere: boolean;  {Set true when Vigenere cipher mode chosen}
    varbeau   : boolean;    {Set truw when Variant Beauford mode chosen}
    beauford: boolean;  {Set true when Beauford mode chosen}

begin
    {Initialise}

    count  := 0;
    i    := 1;
    kcount := 0;
    newline   := false;
    vigenere:= false;
    varbeau   := false;
    beauford:= false;

    {Read in type of encipherment}

    readln(ch);

    if ch = 'V' then
        vigenere := true
    else if ch = 'B' then
        beauford := true
    else if ch = 'A' then
        varbeau := true
    else
    begin
        writeln('Invalid cipher type: Vigenere will be assumed');
        write('Valid cipher types are V for Vigenere, ');
```

```pascal
    writeln('B for Beauford and A for Variant Beauford');
    vigenere := true;
end;

{Read in key}

while not eoln do
begin
    kcount := kcount + 1;
    if kcount <= MAXKEYLENGTH then
        read(key[kcount])
end;
readln;

{If key given too long print message and use part of the given key}

if kcount > MAXKEYLENGTH then
begin
    writeln('Key length exceeded the limit of', MAXKEYLENGTH:2);
    write('Only the first', MAXKEYLENGTH:2);
    writeln('letters will be used as the key');
    kcount := MAXKEYLENGTH;
end;

{Read and encrypt message}

while not eof do
begin
    while not eoln do
    begin
        read(ch);
        if ch in ['a'..'z','A'..'Z'] then
        begin
        {Convert upper case to lower}

        if ch in ['A'..'Z'] then
            ch := chr((ord(ch) - ord('A')) + ord('a'));

        if vigenere then
            num := (ord(ch)+ord(key[i])-2*ord('a')) mod ALPHA
        else if beauford then
            num := (ord(key[i])-ord(ch)) mod ALPHA
        else
            num := (ord(ch)-ord(key[i])) mod ALPHA;

        if num < 0 then
            num := num + ALPHA;

        {Count through the key}

        if i = kcount then
            i := 1
        else
            i := i + 1;

        {Check if 5 letter chunk finished}
```

```pascal
        if count = BLOCKLENGTH then
        begin
            write(' ');
            count := 0;
            if newline then
            writeln;
            newline := false;
        end;

        {Write encrypted letter}

        write(chr(num + ord('a')));
        count := count +1;
         end;
    end;
    readln;
    newline := true; {A writeln will be performed as soon
                as the current 5 letter chunk
                is finished}
    end;
    writeln;
end.
```

# BIBLIOGRAPHY

[ABRA64] M. Abramowitz, *Handbook of Mathematical Functions with Formulas, Graphs And Mathematical Tables*, National Bureau of Standards, Applied Mathematics Series 55, June 1964.

[ADLE79] L. Adleman, 'A Subexponential Algorithm for the Discrete Logarithm Problem with Applications to Cryptography', *Proc. IEEE, 20th Annual Symposium of Foundations of Computer Science*, (29-31 Oct. 1979), pp. 55-60.

[ADLE83a] Leonard Adleman, 'On breaking the iterated Merkle-Hellman knapsack public key cryptosystem', (preprint).

[ADLE83b] Leonard Adleman, 'On Breaking Generalized Knapsack Public Key Cryptosystems', *Proc. 15th ACM Symposium on Theory of Computing*, 1983, pp. 402-412.

[ADMA76] L. Adleman, K. Manders and G. Miller, 'On Taking Roots in Finite Fields', *Proceedings of IEEE Conference on Switching and Automata Theory*, 1976.

[ADME86] Carslisle M. Adams and Henk Meijer, 'Security-related comments regarding McEliece's public-key cryptostem', preprint, Queen's University, Kingston.

[ADPO83] L. M. Adleman, C. Pomerance, and R. S. Rumley, 'On distinguishing prime numbers from composite numbers', *Annals of Mathematics*, Vol. 117, No. 1, 1983, pp. 173-206.

[ADRI79] L. M. Adelman and R. L. Rivest, 'How to Break the Lu-Lee (COMSAT) Public-key Cryptosystem', preprint, 1979.

[ADSH82] W. Adams and D. Shanks, 'Strong Primality Tests That Are Not Sufficient', *Math. Comp.*, Vol. 39, 1982, pp. 255-300.

[AHHO74] A. V. Aho, J. E. Hopcroft, and J. D. Ullman, *The Design and Analysis of Computer Algorithms*, Addison-Wesley, Reading, Mass., 1974.

[AKL83] S. G. Akl, 'Digital signatures: a tutorial survey', *IEEE Computer*, Vol. 16, 2 Feb., 1983, pp. 15-24.

[AKL84] S. G. Akl, 'On the security of compressed encodings', *Advances in Cryptology: Proceedings of CRYPTO 83*, (ed. D. Chaum), Plenum, New York, 1984, pp. 209-30.

[AKME84] S. G. Akl and H. Meijer, 'A fast pseudo random permutation generator with applications to Cryptology', *Advances in Cryptology: Proceedings of CRYPTO '84*, (eds G. R. Blakely and D. Chaum), 1985, pp. 269-75.

[ANDE72] James P. Anderson & Co., 'Computer security technology planning study', *ESD-TR-73-51*, Vol. 1, AD-758 206, ESD/AFSC, Hanscom AFB, Belford, Mass., 1972.

[ANDE79] D. Andelman, 'Maximum Likeihood Estimation Applied To Cryptanalysis', Information Systems Laboratory, Stanford University Department, of Electrical Engineering, Stanford, Dec. 1979.

[ARAZ80a] B. Arazi, 'Maximizing the Domain of Messages to be Signed Digitally', preprint 1980.

[ARAZ80b] B. Arazi, 'A trapdoor multiple mapping', *IEEE Trans. Inform. Theory*, Vol. IT-26, No. 1, Jan. 1980, pp. 100-102.

[ARUL85] A. A. Aruliah, 'Pascal Implementation of the RSA Algorithm', *NPL-DITC-66/85*, National Physical Laboratory, Teddington, England, Sep. 1985.

[ATMA76] C. R. Attansio, P. W. Markstein and R. J. Phillips, 'Penetrating an operating system: a study of VM/370 integrity', *IBM Systems Journal*, Vol. 15, No. 1, 1976, pp. 102-16.

[AUST84] *Proceedings of Public Seminars on EFT*, Standards Association of Australia, Sydney, 1984.

[BAAS78] Sara Baase, *Computer Algorithms: Introduction to Design and Analysis*, Addison-Wesley, Reading, Mass., 1978.

[BARK75] W. G. Barker, *Cryptanalysis of the Simple Substitution Cipher with Word Divisions Using Non-pattern Word Lists*, reprinted by Aegean Park Press, Laguna Hills, Ca., 1975.

[BARK77] W. G. Barker, *Cryptanalysis of the Haegelin Cryptograph*, reprinted by Aegean Park Press, Laguna Hills, Ca., 1977.

[BEFR83] H. J. Beker, J. M. K. Friend and P. W. Halliden, 'Simplifying key management in electronic funds transfer point of sale systems', *Electronic Letters*, Vol. 12, No. 19, 1983, pp. 442-4.

[BEHE83] T. Beth, P. Heß and K. Wirl, *Kryptographie*, Teubner, Stuttgart, 1983.

[BEKE84] H. Beker, 'Security of Keys and Transaction Keys', *Proceedings of Public Seminar on EFT*, Melbourne, July 1984, pp. 47-52.

[BELA76] D. E. Bell and L. J. La Padula, 'Secure computer systems: Unified exposition and multics interpretation', *MTR-2997 Rev. 1*, MITRE Corp., Bedford, Mass., 1976.

[BELL57] R. Bellman, *Dynamic Programming*, Princeton University Press, Princeton, 1957.

[BEMC78] E. R. Berlekamp, R. J. McEliece and H. Van Tilborg, 'On the inherent intractibility of certain coding problems', *IEEE Trans. Inform. Theory.*, IT-24, 1978, pp. 384-6.

[BEPI82] H. Beker and F. Piper, *Cipher Systems: The Protection of Communications*, Northwood Books, London, 1982.

[BEPI83] H. Beker and F. Piper, 'Cryptography for beginners', *New Scientist*, Vol. 221, July. 1983, pp. 17-19.

[BERK79] S. Berkovits, J. Kowalchuk and B. Schanning, 'Implementing public-key scheme', *IEEE Comm. Mag.*, Vol. 17, 1979, pp. 2-3.

[BERL68] E. R. Berlekamp, *Algebraic Coding Theory*, McGraw-Hill, New York, 1968.

[BERL70] E. R. Berlekamp, 'Factoring polynomials over large finite fields', *Math. Comp.*, 24, No. 111, July 1970, pp. 713-35.

[BERL73] E. R. Berlekamp, 'Goppa codes', *IEEE Trans. Inform. Theory*, IT-19, Sep. 1973, pp. 590-2.

[BLAK79] G. R. Blakley, 'Safeguarding cryptographic keys', *Proc. AFIPS 1979: National Computer Conference*, Vol. 48, Arlington, Va., June 1979, pp. 313-17.

[BLBL78] B. Blakley and G. R. Blakley, 'Security of number theoretic public-key cryptosystems against random attack', I, *Cryptologia*, Vol. 2, Oct. 1978, pp. 305-21.

[BLBL79a] B. Blakley and G. R. Blakley, 'Security of number theoretic public-key cryptosystems against random attack', II, *Cryptologia*, Vol. 3, Jan. 1979, pp. 29-49.

[BLBL79b] B. Blakley and G. R. Blakley, 'Security of number theoretic public-key cryptosystems against random attack', III, *Cryptologia*, Vol. 3, April 1979, pp. 105-18.

[BLBO79] G. R. Blakley and I. Borosh, 'Rivest-Shamir-Adleman public-key cryptosystems do not always conceal messages', *Comp. and Maths. with Appls*, Vol. 5, 1979, pp. 169-78.

[BLFU84] I. F. Blake, R. Fuji-Hara, R. C. Mullin and S. A. Vanstone, 'Computing logarithms in finite fields of characteristic two', *SIAM J. Alg. Disc. Meth.*, No. 5, 1984, pp. 276-85.

[BLOM82] R. Blom, 'Nonpublic key distribution', *Advances in Cryptology: Proceedings of CRYPTO '82'* (eds D. Chaum, R.L. Rivest, and A.T. Sherman), Plenum, New York–London, 1983, pp. 231-6.

[BLUM83] M. Blum, 'How to exchange (secret) keys', *ACM Trans. on Comp. Syst.*, Vol. 1, 1983, pp. 175-8.

[BOOT81] K. S. Booth, 'Authentication of signatures using public-key encryption', *CACM*, Vol. 24, No. 11, Nov., 1981, pp. 772-4.

[BOND84] D. J. Bond, 'Practical primality testing, *Proceedings of International Conference on Secure Communictions Systems, IEE*, 22-23 Feb. 1984, pp. 50-53.

[BOWE60] W. M. Bowers, 'Practical cryptanalysis — Volume 1', *Digraphic Substitution*, The American Cryptogram Ass., 1960.

[BOWE60a] W. M. Bowers, 'Practical Cryptanalysis — Volume II', *The BIFID Cipher*, The American Cryptogram Ass., 1960.

[BOWE61] W. M. Bowers, 'Practical Cryptanalysis — Volume III', *The TRIFID Cipher*, The American Cryptogram Ass., 1961.

[BRAN73] D. K. Branstad, 'Security aspects of computer networks', *AIAA Computer Network Systems Conference*, Paper 73-427, April 1973.

[BRAS79a] G. Brassard, 'A note on the complexity of cryptography', *IEEE Trans. Inform. Theory*, IT-25, 1979, pp. 232-3.

[BRAS79b] Gilles Brassard, 'Relativized cryptography', *IEEE Trans. Inform. Theory*, Vol. IT-25, No. 2, March 1979, pp. 877-94.

[BRAS83] Gilles Brassard, 'A note on the complexity of cryptography', *IEEE Trans. Inform. Theory*, Vol. IT-29, No. 6, Nov. 1983, pp. 232-3.

[BRCR87a] G. Brassard and C. Crepeau, 'Zero-knowledge simulation of Boolean circuits', *Advances in Cryptology: Proceedings of CRYPTO '86*, (ed. A. M. Odlyzko), Vol. 263, Lecture Notes in Computer Science, Springer-Verlag, Berlin, 1987, pp. 223-34.

[BRCR87b] G. Brassard, C. Crepeau and J. M. Robert, 'All-or-nothing disclosure of secrets', *Advances in Cryptology: Proceedings of CRYPTO '86*, (ed. A. M. Odlyzko), Vol. 263, Lecture Notes in Computer Science, Springer-Verlag, Berlin, 1987, pp. 234-8.

[BRDA84] Ernest F. Brickell, J. A. Davis and Gustavus J. Simmons, 'A preliminary report on the cryptanalysis of the Merkle-Hellman knapsack Cryptosystem', *Advances in Cryptology: Proceedings of CRYPTO 82*, (eds D. Chaum, R. Rivest, A. T. Sherman), Plenum, New York-London, 1983, pp. 289-301.

[BREN80] R. P. Brent, 'An improved monte carlo factorization algorithm', *BIT*, Vol. 20, 1980, pp. 176-84.

[BRGA77] D. K. Branstad, J. Gait and S. Katzke, 'Report of the workshop on cryptography in support of computer security', *NBSIR 77-1291*, National Bureau of Standards, 21-22 Sep., 1976, Sep. 1977.

[BRGE66] R. Brooks and A. Geoffrion, 'Finding Evertt's Lagrange multipliers by linear programming', *Operations Research*, Vol. 14, 1966, pp. 1149-53.

[BRIC83] Ernest F. Brickell, 'Solving low density knapsacks', *Advances in Cryptology: Proceedings of CRYPTO 83*, (ed. D. Chaum), Plenum, New York, 1984, pp. 25-37.

[BRIC84] Ernest F. Brickell, 'A New Knapsack Based Cryptosystem', Internal report, Sandia National Laboratories, Albuquerque, NM, 1984.

[BRIC84a] E. F. Brickell, 'Breaking iterated knapsacks', *Advances in Cryptology: Proceedings of CRYPTO 84*, (eds G.R. Blakely and D. Chaum), Vol. 196, Lecture Notes in Computer Science, Springer-Verlag, Plenum, New York, 1984, pp. 342-358.

[BRIC84b] E. F. Brickell, 'A Few Results in Message Authentication', Internal paper, Sandia National Laboratories, Albuquerque, NM, 1984.

[BRIC85] Ernest F. Brickell, 'Attacks on Generalized Knapsack Schemes', *EUROCRYPT '85 Abstracts*, Linz, Austria, 9-11 April, 1985.

[BRLA83] Ernest F. Brickell, J. C. Lagarias and Andrew M. Odlyzko, 'Evaluation of the Adleman attack on the multiply iterated knapsack cryptosystems', *Advances in Cryptology: Proceedings of CRYPTO 83*, (ed. D. Chaum), Plenum, New York, 1984, pp. 39-42.

[BRSI83d] Ernest F. Brickell and Gustavus J. Simmons, 'A Status Report on Knapsack Based Public Key Cryptosystems', *Sandia Report*, Sandia National Laboratories, 1983 and *Congressus Numeratum*, Vol. 37, 1983, pp. 3-72.

[BRYA67a] W. G. Bryan, *Cryptographic ABC's — Volume 1: Substitution and Transposition Ciphers*, The American Cryptogram Ass., 1967.

[BRYA67b] W. G. Bryan, *Cryptographic ABC's, Volume II*, The American Cryptogram Association, 1967. Vol. 5, pp. 169-78.

[BRYA87] Ernest F. Brickell and Yacov Yacobi, 'On privacy homomorphisms', *EUROCRYPT 87 Abstracts*, Amsterdam, 13-15 April, 1987, pp. IV7-14.

[BUHO74] J. Bunch and J. E. Hopcroft, 'Triangular factorization and inversion by fast matrix multiplication', *Math. Comp.*, Vol. 28, pp. 125ff.

[CABO70] V. A. Cabot, 'An enumeration algorithm for knapsack problems', *Operations Research*, Vol. 18, 1970, pp. 306-11.

[CAHU68] V. A. Cabot and A. P. Hunter, Jr, 'The Application of an Approach to Zero-one Programming to Knapsack Problems', presented at the joint ORAS/TIMS meeting in San Francisco, 1968.

[CASI86] T. R. Caron and R. D. Silverman, 'Parallel Implementation of the Quadratic Sieve', *Abstracts of CRYPTO '86*, Santa Barbara, Ca., 1986, pp. 4.1-4.17.

[CASS59] J. W. S. Cassels, *Geometry of Numbers*, Springer-Verlag, Berlin, 1959.

[CASS65] J. Cassels, *An Introduction to Diophantine Approximation*, Cambridge University, Cambridge, 1965.

[CASS78] J. Cassels, *Rational Quadratic Forms*, Academic Press, New York, 1978.

[CHAU81] D. L. Chaum, 'Untraceable electronic mail, return addresses, and digital pseudonyms', *CACM*, Vol. 24, No. 2, Feb 1981, pp. 84-8.

[CHAU84] D. L. Chaum, 'Design concepts for tamper responding systems', *Advances in Cryptology: Proceedings of CRYPTO 83*, (ed. D. Chaum), Plenum, New York, 1984, pp. 387-92.

[CHAU87] D. L. Chaum, 'Demonstrating that a public predicate can be satisfied without revealing any information how', *Advances in Cryptology: Proceedings of CRYPTO 86*, (ed. A. M. Odlyzko), Vol. 263, Lecture Notes in Computer Science, Springer-Verlag, Berlin-New York, 1987, pp. 195-99.

[CHEV87] D. L. Chaum, J. H. Evertse, J. Van de Graaf and R. Peralta, 'Demonstrating possession of a discrete logaritm without revealing it', *Advances in Cryptology: Proceedings of CRYPTO 86*, (ed. A. M. Odlyzko), Vol. 263, Lecture Notes in Computer Science, Springer-Verlag, New York, 1987, pp. 200-212.

[CHPA82] B. J. Chorley and G. I. Parkin, 'A Revised Definition of a Secure Communication Protocol and Its Implementation', *NPL Report DITC 5/82*, April 1982.

[CHRI84] Benny Chor and Ronald L. Rivest, 'A knapsack type public key cryptosystem based on arithmetic in finite fields', *Advances in Cryptography: Proceedings of CRYPTO 84*, Lecture Notes in Computer Science, Vol. 196, (eds G. R. Blakely and David Chaum), Springer-Verlag, Berlin, 1984, pp. 54-65.

[CHEV86] D. Chaum and J. H. Evertse, 'Cryptanalysis of DES with a reduced number of rounds; sequences of linear factors in block ciphers', *Advances in Cryptography: Proceedings of CRYPTO 85*, (ed. H.C.Williams), Lecture Notes in Computer Science, Vol. 218, Springer-Verlag, New York, 1986, pp. 192-212.

[CHGO84] B. Chor and O. Goldreich, 'RSA/Rabin least significant bits are $\frac{1}{2}$ $+1/\text{poly}(\log N)$ secure, *Advances in Cryptology: Proceedings of CRYPTO 84*, 1985, pp. 303-13.

[COGR75] Don Coppersmith and Edna Grossman, 'Generators for certain alternating groups with applications to cryptography', *SIAM J. on Appl. Math.*, Vol. 29, No 4, Dec. 1975, pp. 624-7.

[COHE79] Jacques Cohen, 'ND algorithms', *Computing Surveys*, Vol. 11, No. 2, June 1979.

[COHE79] J. Cohen Benaloh, 'Cryptographic capsules: a disjunctive primitive for interactive protocols', *Advances in Cryptology: Proceedings of CRYPTO 86*, (ed. A. M. Odlyzko), Lecture Notes in Computer Science, Vol. 263, Springer-Verlag, Berlin-New York, 1987, pp. 213-22.

[COLE84] H. Cohen and II. W. Lenstra, Jr., 'Primality testing and Jacobi sums, *Math. Comp.*, Vol. 42, 1984, pp. 297-330.

[COOK71] Stephen Cook, 'The complexity of theorem proving procedures', *Procs. 3rd ACM Symposium on the Theory of Computation*, 1971, pp. 151-8.

[COPA85] Rodney H. Cooper and Wayne Patterson, 'Eliminating data expansion in the Chor-Rivest algorithm', *EUROCRYPT '85 Abstracts*, Linz, Austria, 9-11 April,

1985.

[COPP84] Don Coppersmith, 'Fast evaluation of logarithms in fields of characteristic two', *IEEE Trans. Inform. Theory*, IT-30, 1984, pp. 587-94.

[COQU82] C. Couvreur, J. J. Quisquater, 'An introduction to fast generation of large prime numbers', *Philips Journal Research*, Vol. 37, No. 5–6, 1982, pp. 231–64.

[CREP87] C. Crepeau, 'A zero-knowledge poker protocol that achieves confidentiality of the players' strategy or how to achieve an electronic poker face', *Advances in Cryptology: Proceedings of CRYPTO 86*, (ed. A. M. Odlyzko), Lecture Notes in Computer Science, Vol. 263, Springer-Verlag, New York, 1987, pp. 239-50.

[CRYP85] *Crypto '85 Abstracts and Papers*, Santa Barbara, Ca., Aug. 1985.

[CRYP86] *Crypto '86 Abstracts and Papers*, Santa Barbara, Ca., Aug. 1986.


[DADE84] M. Davio, Y. Desmedt, M. Fosseprez, R. Govaerts, J. Hulsbosch, P. Neutjens, P. Piret, J. J. Quisquater, J. Vandewalle and P. Wouters, 'Analytical characteristics of the DES', *Advances in Cryptology: Proceedings of CRYPTO 83*, (ed. D. Chaum), Plenum, New York, 1984, pp. 171-202.

[DAHO84] J. A. Davis, D. B. Holdrige and G. J. Simmons, 'Status report on factoring', Sandia National Laboratories, preprint, 1984.

[DAPR80] D. W. Davies and W. L. Price, 'The application of digital signature based on public key signatures', *NPL Report*, DNACS 39/80, 1980.

[DAPR84] D. W. Davies and W. L. Price, *Security for Computer Networks: An Introduction to Data Security in Teleprocessing and Electronic Funds Transfer*, Wiley and Sons, New York, 1984.

[DAVI78] R. Davis, 'Remedies sought to defeat Soviet eavesdropping on microwave links', *Microwave Syst.*, Vol. 8, No. 6, June 1978, pp. 17-20.

[DAVI83] D. W. Davies, 'Applying the RSA digital signature to electronic mail', *Computer*, Vol. 16, No. 2, Feb. 1983, pp. 55-62.

[DAVI84] D. W. Davies, 'Use of the 'signature token' to create a negotiable document', *Advances in Cryptology: Proceedings of CRYPTO 83*, (ed. D. Chaum), Plenum, New York, 1984, pp. 377-82.

[DAVI87] R. E. Davids, 'Australian EFTPOS security standards', *IEEE Secure Communications Workshop*, Melbourne, July 1987.

[DAWE81] G. I. Davida, D. L. Wells and J. B. Kam, 'A database encryption system with subkeys', *ACS Trans. on Database Systems*, Vol. 6, 2 June, 1981.

[DEIT84] H. M. Deitel, *An Introduction to Operating Systems*, Addison-Wesley, Reading, Mass., 1984, pp. 458-68.

[DECK85] Susy Deck, *Computational Methods for Foreign Language Identification with Application to Cryptography*, Honours Thesis, Basser Deptartment of Computer Science, The University of Sydney, 1985.

[DENN81] P. J. Denning, 'Report of the public cryptography study group', *CACM*, Vol. 24, 1981, pp. 434.

[DENN82] Dorothy Robling Denning, *Cryptography and Data Security*, Addison-Wesley, 1982.

[DENN86] Dorothy E. Denning, 'An Intrusion-Detection Model', *Proc. IEEE Symposium on Security and Privacy*, Oakland, Ca., 1986, pp. 118-31.

[DERE77] C. A. Deavours and J. Reeds, 'The enigma, part I, historical perspectives',

*Cryptologia*, Vol. 1, Oct. 1977, pp. 381-91.

[DES77] *Data Encryption Standard*, Federal Information Processing Standard (FIPS), Publication 46, National Bureau of Standards, US Department of Commerce, Jan. 1977.

[DES80] *Data Encryption Standard*, Federal Information Processing Standards Publication 81, National Bureau of Standards, Washington, DC, 25 Sep. 1980.

[DEVA82a] Yvo G. Desmedt, Joos P. Vandewalle and Rene J. M. Govaerts, 'A highly secure cryptographic algorithm for high speed transmission', *Globecom '82, IEEE Global Telecommunications Conference*, Vol. 1, 1982, pp. 180-4.

[DEVA82b] Yvo G. Desmedt, Joos P. Vandewalle and Rene J. M. Govaerts, 'How iterative transformations can help to crack the Merkle-Hellman cryptographic scheme', *Electronic Letters*, Vol. 18, 14 Oct. 1982, pp. 910-11.

[DEVA83a] Yvo G. Desmedt, Joos P. Vandewalle and Rene J. M. Govaerts, 'A general public key cryptographic knapsack algorithm based on linear algebra', *Proc. IEEE Int. Symp. Inform. Theory, Abstract of papers*, St Jovite, Quebec, 26 Scp. 1983, pp. 129-30.

[DEVA83b] Yvo G. Desmedt, Joos P. Vandewalle and Rene J. M. Govaerts, 'Does Public-Key Cryptography Provide a Practical and Secure Protection of Data Storage and Transmission?', *Proc. of the International Carnahan Conf. on Security Technology*, 1983, pp. 133-9.

[DEVA84] Yvo G. Desmedt, Joos P. Vandewalle and Rene J. M. Govaerts, 'A critical analysis of the security of knapsack public-key algorithms', *IEEE Trans. Inform. Theory*, Vol. IT-30, No. 4, July 1984, pp. 601-11.

[DIET75] U. Dieter, 'How to calculate shortest vectors in a lattice', *Math. Comp.*, Vol. 29, 1975, pp. 827-33.

[DIFF82] Whitfield Diffie, 'Cryptographic technology: 15 year forecast', *Secure Communications and Asymmetric Cryptosystem AAAS Selected Symposium 69*, (ed. Gustavius J. Simmons 1982), pp. 301-27.

[DIHE76a] W. Diffie and M. E. Hellman, 'New directions in cryptography', *IEEE Trans. Inform. Theory*, IT-22, Vol. 6, Nov. 1976, pp. 644-54.

[DIHE76b] W. Diffie and M. E. Hellman, 'Multiuser Cryptographic Techniques', *Proceedings of National Computer Conference*, New York, 7-10 June 1976.

[DIHE77] W. Diffie and M. Hellman, 'Exhaustive cryptanalysis of the NBS data encryption standard', *Computer*, Vol. 10, June 1977, pp. 74-84.

[DIHE79] W. Diffie and M. E. Hellman, 'Privacy and authentication: An introduction to cryptography', *Proc. IEEE*, Vol. 67, No. 3, March 1979, pp. 397-427.

[DIPO85] Adina di Porto, 'A public-key cryptosystem based on a generalization of the knapsack problem', *EUROCRYPT 85 Abstracts*, Linz, Austria, 9-11 April, 1985.

[DIXO81] J. D. Dixon, 'Asymptotically fast factorization of integers', *Math. Comp.*, Vol. 36, 1981, pp. 255-60.

[DIXO84] J. D. Dixon, 'Factorization and primality tests', *Amer. Math. Monthly*, Vol. 91, No. 6, June-July 1984, pp. 333-52.

[DURH83] T. Durham, 'The software pirates' boats are scuppered', *Computing*, 17 Nov. 1983, p. 36.

[EHMA78] W. F. Ehrasm, S. M. Matyas, C. H. Meyer and W. L. Tuchman, 'A cryptographic key management scheme for implementing the data encryption standard', *IBM Systems J.*, Vol. 17, No. 2, 1978, pp. 106-25.

[EIER82] R. Eier and H. Logger, 'Trapdoors in knapsack cryptosystems', *Cryptography Proceedings*, Burg Feuerstein, Lecture Notes in Computer Science, Vol. 149, Springer-Verlag, Berlin-New York, 1982, pp. 316-22.

[ELAL83] A. El-Kateeb and S. Al-Khayatt, 'Public-key cryptosystems', *Information Age* (G. Br.), Vol. 5, No. 4, Oct. 1983, pp. 232-7.

[ELGA85] T. El Gamal, 'A public key cryptosystem and signature scheme based on discrete logarithms', *IEEE Trans. on Inform. Theory*, Vol. IT-31, No. 4, July 1985, pp. 469-72.

[ELGA84a] Taher El Gamal, 'A subexponential-time algorithm for computing Discrete logarithms over GF($p^2$)', *Advances in Cryptology: Proceedings of CRYPTO 83*, (ed. D. Chaum), Plenum, New York, 1984, pp. 275-92.

[EURO86] *EUROCRYPT 86 Abstracts*, Linkoping, Sweden, 20-22 May, 1986.

[EVER63] H. Everett, 'Generalised lagrange multiplier methods for solving problems of optimum allocation of resources', *Operations Research*, Vol. 11, 1963, p. 399.

[EVER78] J. K. Everton, 'A hierarchical basis for encryption key management in a computer communications network', *Proceedings ICC'78*, Toronto, 1978.

[EVKA74] A. Evans, W. Kantrowitz and E. Weiss, 'A User authentication scheme not requiring secrecy in the computer', *CACM*, Vol. 17, Aug. 1974, pp. 437-42.

[EVYA79a] S. Even and Y. Yacobi, 'On the cryptocomplexity of a public-key system', preprint, 1979.

[EVYA79b] S. Even and Y. Yacobi, 'Cryptosystems which are NP-hard to break', preprint, Computer Science Department, The Technion, Haifa, Israel, July 1979.

[FAFL82] P. Faflick, 'Opening the trapdoor knapsack', *Time*, Vol. 25, Oct. 1982.

[FARA67] L. Farago, *The Broken Seal*, Random House, New York, 1967.

[FEFO82] H. R. P. Ferguson and R. W. Forcade, 'Multidimensional Euclidean algorithms', *J. Reine Angew. Math.*, Vol. 344, 1982, pp. 171-81.

[FEIS70] H. Feistel, 'Cryptographic coding for data-bank privacy', *IBM Research Report*, RC 2827, 18 March 1970.

[FEIS73] H. Feistel, 'Cryptography and computer privacy', *Sci. Amer.*, Vol. 228, No. 5, May 1973, pp. 15-23.

[FELL57] W. Feller, *An Introduction to Probability Theory and Its Applications*, Vol. 1 and 2, Wiley, New York, 1957, 1966.

[FENO75] Horst Feistel, William A. Notz and J. Lynn Smith, 'Some cryptographic techniques for machine-to-machine data communications', *Proc. IEEE*, Vol. 63, No. 11, Nov. 1975, pp. 1545-54.

[FIMI84] M. Fischer, S. Micali and C. Rackoff, 'A secure protocol for the obvious transfer', *Advances in Cryptology: Proceedings of EUROCRYPT 84*, presented at *EUROCRYPT 84*, April 1984.

[FIPS77] *Data Encryption Standard*, National Bureau of Standards, Federal Information Processing Standards, Publication 46, 15 Jan. 1977.

[FISH87] A. Fiat and A. Shamir, 'How to prove yourself: Practical solutions to identification and signature problems', *Advances in Cryptology: Proceedings of CRYPTO 86*, (ed. A. M. Odlyzko), Lecture Notes in Computer Science, Vol. 263,

Springer-Verlag, New York, 1987, pp. 186-94.

[FLIC67] W. F. Flicke, *War Secrets In The Ether*, Vols 1 and 2, Aegean Park Press, Laguna Hills, Ca., 1967.

[FRIE17] W. F. Friedman, *A Method of Reconstructing the Primary Alphabet from a Single One of the Series of Secondary Alphabets*, Riverbank Laboratories, Publication 15, 1917.

[FRIE18a] W. F. Friedman, *Methods for the Solution of Running-Key Ciphers*, Riverbank Laboratories Publication 16, 1918.

[FRIE18b] W. F. Friedman, *Formula for the Solution of Geometrical Transposition Ciphers*, Riverbank Laboratories, Publication 19, 1918.

[FRIE18c] W. F. Friedman, *Several Machine Ciphers and Methods for Their Solutions*, Riverbank Laboratories, Publication 20, 1918.

[FRIE18d] W. F. Friedman, *Methods for the Reconstruction of Primary Alphabets*, Riverbank Laboratories, Publication 21, 1918.

[FRIE22] W. F. Friedman, *The Index of Coincidence and Its Applications in Cryptography*, Riverbank Laboratories, Publication 22, 1922.

[FRIE76] W. F. Friedman, *The Classic Element of Cryptanalysis*, Reprinted by Aegean Park Press, Laguna Hills, Ca., 1976.

[FUMA85] M. Fugini and G. Martella, 'Criteria for the design of cryptographic systems', *Sist. and Autom.* (Italy), Vol. 31, No. 265, Dec. 1985, pp. 1319-32.


[GAIN56] H. F. Gaines, *Cryptanalysis: A Study of Ciphers and Their Solutions*, Dover, New York, 1956.

[GAJO79] M. R. Garey and D. S. Johnson, *Computers and Intractibility: A Guide to the Theory of NP – Completeness*, W. H. Freeman and Co., San Francisco, 1979.

[GILM66] P. C. Gilmore and R. E. Gomory, 'The theory and computation of knapsack functions', *Operations Research 14*, 1966, pp. 1045-74.

[GLMI72] V. Glee and G. Minty, 'How good is simplex algorithm', (ed. O. Shisha), *Inequalities 3*, NY Academic Press, New York, 1972, pp. 159-75.

[GOCO80a] J. M. Goethals and C. Couvreur, 'A cyptoanalytic attack on the Lu-Lee public key cryptosystem', *Philips J. Res.*, Vol. 35, 1980, pp. 301-306.

[GOGO84] O. Goldreich, S. Goldwasser and S. Micali, 'How to Construct Random Functions', *25th Symposium on Foundations of Computer Science*, Oct. 1984.

[GOMC84] R. M. F. Goodman and A. J. McAuley, 'A new trapdoor knapsack public-key cryptosystem', Advances in Cryptography: Proceedings of Eurocrpyt 84, Lecture Notes in Computer Scicnce, (eds T. Beth, N. Cot and I. Ingemarsson), 1984, pp. 150-8.

[GOMI86] O. Goldreich, S. Micali and A. Wigderson, 'Proofs that Yield Nothing but the Validity of the Assertion and the Methodology of Cryptographic Protocol Design', *27th Symposium on Foundations of Computer Science*, Nov. 1986.

[GOMI86] O. Goldreich, S. Micali and A. Wigderson, 'How to prove all NP-statements in zero-knowledge, and a methodology of cryptographic protocol design' (Extended Abstract), *Advances in Cryptology: Proceedings of CRYPTO '86*, (ed. A. M. Odlyzko), Lecture Notes in Computer Science, Vol. 263, Springer-Verlag, Berlin-New York, 1987, pp. 171-85.

[GOULD] 'Secure UNIX® System white paper', AT & T, Gould Computer Systems,

Distributed at the 20 Jan. 1987 meeting of the /usr/group subcommittee on Security, Washington, DC.

[GRDE72] G. S. Graham and P. J. Denning, 'Protection: Principles and Practices', *Proceedings of the AFIPS Spring Joint Computer Conference*, 1972, pp. 417-29.

[GRHE70] H. Greenberg and R. L. Hegerich, 'A branch search algorithm for the knapsack problem', *Management Sci.*, Vol. 16, 1970, pp. 159-62.

[GRMO84] F. T. Grampp and R. H. Morris, 'UNIX operating system security', AT&T Bell Syst. Tech. J., Vol. 63, No. 8, 1984, pp. 1651-71.

[GROS74] E. K. Grossman, 'Group theoretic remarks on cryptographic systems based on two types of addition', *IBM Research Report*, RC 4742, 26 Feb. 1974.

[GRTU77] E. K. Grossman and B. Tuckerman, 'Analysis of a Feistel-like cipher weakened by having no rotating key', *IBM Research Report*, RC 6375, 31 Jan. 1977; also *Proceedings ICC'78*.

[GUKO76] E. Gudes, H. S. Koch and F. A. Stahl, 'The application of cryptography for data base security', *Proc. NCC*, AFIPS Press, 1976, pp. 97-107.

[GUY76] R. K. Guy, 'How to factor a number', *Congressus Numerantium XVI: Proceedings Fifth Manitoba Conference on Numerical Math.*, Winnipeg, 1976, pp. 49-89.

[GYOE86] Ralph Gyoery, *Electronic Funds Transfer Point of Sale*, Honours Thesis, Basser Department of Computer Science, The University of Sydney, Sydney, 1986.

[GYSE87] Ralph Gyoery and Jennifer Seberry, 'EFTPOS in Australia', *Advances in Cryptology: Proceedings of CRYPTO 86*, (ed. A. M. Odlyzko), Lecture Notes in Computer Science, Vol. 263, Springer-Verlag, Berlin-New York, 1987, pp. 347-80.


[HALBE70] H. Halberstam, 'On integers all of whose prime factors are small', *Proceedings of the London Mathematical Society*, Vol. 3, No. 21, 1970, pp. 102-107.

[HARR59] F. A. Harris, *Solving Simple Substitution Ciphers*, The American Cryptogram Ass., 1959.

[HARU76] M. A. Harrison, W. L. Ruzzo and J. D. Ullman, 'Protection in operating systems', *CACM*, Vol. 19, No. 8, pp. 461-71.

[HAU78] Dirk Hausmann (ed.), *Integer Programming and Related Areas, A Classified Bibliography 1976-1978*, Springer-Verlag, 1978.

[HEJO81] T. Herlestam and R. Johannesson, 'On computing logarithms over $GF(2^p)$', *BIT*, Vol. 21, 1981, pp. 326-34.

[HELL77] M. E. Hellman, 'An extension of the Shannon theory approach to cryptography', *IEEE Trans. Inform. Theory*, IT-23, May 1977, pp. 289-94.

[HELL79a] Martin Hellman, 'The mathematics of public key cryptography', *Sci. Amer.*, Vol. 241, No. 3, Aug. 1979, pp. 130-9.

[HELL79b] Martin Hellman, 'DES will be totally insecure within ten years', *IEEE Spectrum*, Vol. 16, No. 7, July 1979, pp. 32-9. With rebuttals from George I. Davida, Walter Tuchman and Denis Branstad.

[HELL80] M. E. Hellman, 'A cryptanalytic time-memory trade off', *IEEE Trans. Inform. Theory*, Vol. IT-26, No. 4, July 1980, pp. 401-406.

[HEME76] M. E. Hellman, R. Merkle, R. Schroeppel, L. Washington, W. Diffie, S. Pohlig and P. Schweitzer, 'Results of an initial attempt to cryptanalyze the NBS Encryption Standard', *Stanford University Systems Laboratory Report*, No. 9, Sep. 1976.

[HEN82] P. S. Henry, 'Fast decryption algorithm for the knapsack cipher', *Comp. Security* (Neth.), Vol. 1, No. 1, Jan. 1982, pp. 80-3.

[HENR81] P. S. Henry, 'Fast decryption algorithm for the knapsack cryptographic system', *Bell Syst. Tech. J.*, Vol. 60, No. 5, May-June 1981, pp. 767-73.

[HERE83] M. E. Hellman, and J. M. Reyneri, 'Fast computation of discrete logarithms in $GF(q)$', *Advances in Cryptology: Proceedings of CRYPTO 82*, (eds D. Chaum, R. Rivest, A. T. Sherman), Plenum, New York-London, 1983, pp. 3-13.

[HERL78] T. Herlestam, 'Critical remarks on some public-key cryptosystems', *BIT*, Vol. 18, 1978, pp. 493-6.

[HIGE73] F. Higenbottam, *Codes and Ciphers*, St Paul's House, London, 1973.

[HIN81a] H. J. Hindin, 'Bell algorithm speeds decryption of public key coding schemes', *Electron*, Vol. 54, No. 16, 11 Aug., 1981, pp. 39-40.

[HIN81b] H. J. Hindin, 'Communications', *Electron*, Vol. 54, No. 21, 20 Oct. 1981, pp. 217-21.

[HOFF73] Lance J. Hoffman, *Security and Privacy in Computer Systems*, Melville, Los Angeles, 1973.

[HOSA74] E. Horowitz and S. Sahni, 'Computing partitions with applications to the knapsack problem', *JACM*, Vol. 21, No. 2, April 1974, pp. 277-92.

[IBAR78] T. Ibaraki, 'Approximate algorithms for the multiple choice continuous Knapsack problem', unpublished manuscript.

[IBKI75] O. H. Ibarra and C. E. Kim, 'Fast approximation algorithms for knapsack problems and sum of subset problems', *JACM*, Vol. 22, No. 2, Oct. 1975, pp. 463-8.

[IBM-a] IBM 3848 Cryptographic Unit Product Description And Operating Procedures, IBM Systems Library, Order No. GA22-7073-0.

[IBM-b] OS/VS2 MVS Cryptographic Unit Support: General Information Manual, IBM Systems Library, Order No. GC28-1015-1.

[IBM-c] OS/VSI And OS/VS2 MVS Access Method Services Cryptographic Options, IBM Systems Library, Order No. SC26-3916.

[IBM-d] Programmed Cryptographic Facility Program Product – General Information Manual, IBM Systems Library, Order No. GC28-0942.

[INBL74] I. Ingemarsson, R. Blom and R. Forchheimer, 'A System for Data Security Based on Data Encryption', Department of Electrical Engineering, Linkoeping University, 1974.

[INGE81] I. Ingemarsson, 'Knapsacks which are not partly solvable after multiplication modulo q', *Proceedings of the IEEE International Symposium on Information Theory*, Abstract of papers, 1981, p. 45.

[INGE82] I. Ingemarsson, 'A new algorithm for the solution of the knapsack problem', *Cryptography Proceedings*, Burg Feuerstein, Lecture Notes in Computer Science, Vol. 149, 1982, pp. 309-15.

[JOCH86] W. de Jonge and D. Chaum, 'Some variations on RSA signatures and their security', *Crypto 86: Abstracts*, 1986, pp. 49-59.

[JONE85] T. Jones, *Secrecy and Authentication*, Honours Thesis, Basser Department of Computer Science, The University of Sydney, 1985.

[JOSE85] T. C. Jones and J. Seberry, 'Authentication without secrecy', *Ars Combinatoria*, Vol. 21A, 1986, pp. 115-21.


[KAHN67] D. Kahn, *The Code Breakers, the Story of Secret Writing*, MacMillan, New York, 1967.

[KAHN80] D. Kahn, 'Cryptology goes public', *IEEE Comm. Mag.*, Vol. 18, No. 1, Jan. 1980, pp. 19-28. See also *Foreign Affairs*, Fall 1979, pp. 141-59.

[KAHN81] D. Kahn, 'The public's secret', *Cryptologia*, Vol. 5, No. 1, Jan. 1981, pp. 20-6.

[KAK83] Subash C. Kak, 'Joint encryption and error correction coding', *IEEE Conference on Security and Privacy*, 1983, pp. 55-60.

[KALT83] E. Kaltofen, 'On the complexity of finding short vectors in integer lattices', *Computer Algebra*, (ed. J. A. van Hulzen), Lecture Notes in Computer Science, Vol. 162. Springer-Verlag, New York, 1983, pp. 236-44.

[KARN84] E. D. Karnin, 'A parallel algorithm for the knapsack problem', *IEEE Trans. Comp.* (USA), Vol. C-33, No. 5, May 1984, pp. 404-408.

[KARP72] R. M. Karp, 'Reducibility among combinatorial problems', *Complexity of Computer Computations.* (eds R. E. Miller and J. W. Thatcher), 1972, pp. 85-104.

[KENT78] S. T. Kent, 'Network security: a top-down view shows problem', *Data Communications*, June 1978, pp. 57-75.

[KHBI85] D. S. P. Khoo, G. J. Bird and J. Seberry, 'Encryption exponent 3 and the security of RSA', Technical Report 275, Basser Department of Computer Science, The University of Sydney, 1985.

[KHBI86] D. Khoo, G. Bird, J. Seberry, 'RSA and encryption exponents e ≡ 3 (mod 18)', *Abstracts of EUROCRYPT 86.*

[KLPO79] C. S. Kline and G. J. Popek, 'Public key vs conventional key encryption'fP, *Proceedings of National Computer Conference 1979.*

[KNUT68] Donald Knuth, *The Art of Computer Programming, Vol. 1, Fundamental Algorithms*, Addison-Wesley, Reading, Mass., 1968.

[KNUT69] D. Knuth, *The Art of Computer Programming, Vol. 2, Semi-Numerical Algorithms*, Addison-Wesley, Reading, Mass., 1969.

[KNUT73] Donald Knuth, *The Art of Computer Programming, Vol. 3, Sorting and Searching*, Addison-Wesley, Reading, Mass., 1973.

[KOHN78a] L. M. Kohnfelder, 'On the signature reblocking problem in public-key cryptosystems', *CACM*, Vol. 21, No. 2, Feb. 1978, p. 179.

[KOHN78b] L. M. Kohnfelder, 'Toward a practical public key cryptosystem', *MIT Lab. for Comp. Sci.*, June 1978.

[KOLA84] S. Kothari and S. Lakshmivarahan, 'On the concealability of messages by the Williams public-key encryption scheme', *Comp. and Maths. with Appls.*, Vol. 10, No. 1, pp. 15-24.

[KOLE67] P. J. Kolesar, 'A branch and bound algorithm for the knapsack problem', *Management Science*, Vol. 13, No. 9, May 1967.

[KONH81] Alan G. Konheim, *Cryptography: A Primer*, John Wiley, 1981.

[KULL38] S. Kullback, *Statistical Methods in Cryptanalysis*, War Department, Office of Chief Signal Officer, United States Government Printing Office, 1938. (Reprinted by Aegean Park Press, Laguna Hills, Ca., 1981.)

[KUSH86] G. C. Kurtz, D. Shanks and H. C. Williams, 'Fast primality tests for numbers less than $50 \times 10^9$', *Math. Comp.*, Vol. 46, No. 174, April 1986, pp. 691–701.

[LAGA82] J. C. Lagarias, 'The computational complexity of simultaneous diophantine approximation problems', *Procs. IEEE Sym. Founds. Com. Sci.*, 1982, pp. 32-9.

[LAGA83] J. C. Lagarias, 'Knapsack public key cryptosystems and diophantine approximation', *Advances in Cryptology: Proceedings of CRYPTO 83*, (ed. D. Chaum), Plenum, New York, 1984, pp. 4-23.

[LAKS83] S. Lakshmivarahan, 'Algorithms for public key cryptosystems: theory and application', *Advances in Computers*, (ed. Marshall Yovits), Vol. 22, Academic Press, 1983, pp. 45-108.

[LAMP71] B. W. Lampson, 'Protection', *5th Princeton Conference on Information and System Sciences*, 1971, pp. 437-43.

[LAMP78] L. Lamport, 'Time, clocks, and the ordering of events in a distributed system', *CACM*, Vol. 21, No. 7 July 1978, pp. 558-65.

[LAMP79] L. Lamport, 'Constructing digital signatures from a one way function', *SRI International Computer Science Laboratory Report No. CSL-98*, 18 Oct. 1979.

[LAOD83] J. C. Lagarias and A. M. Odlyzko, 'Solving low-density subset sum problems', *Procs. IEEE Sym. Founds. Com. Sci.*, 1983, pp. 1-10.

[LAWL76] E. L. Lawler, *Combinatorial Optimisation: Networks and Matroids*, Holt, Rinehart and Winston, 1976.

[LAWL77] E. L. Lawler, 'Fast approximation algorithms for knapsack problems', *Procs. IEEE Sym. Founds. Com. Sci.*, 1977, pp. 206-13.

[LEBR66] J. Levine and J. V. Brawley, Jr, 'Involutory commutants with some applications to algebraic cryptography I', *J. Reine Angew. Math.*, Vol. 224, 1966, pp. 20-43.

[LEBR67] J. Levine and J. V. Brawley, Jr, 'Involutory commutants with some applications to algebraic cryptography II', *J. Reine Angew. Math.*, Vol. 227, 1967, pp. 1-24.

[LEBR77] J. Levine and J. V. Brawley, Jr, 'Some cryptographic applications of permutation polynomials', *Cryptologia*, Vol. 1, Jan. 1977, pp. 76-92.

[LEHM76] D. H. Lehmer, 'Strong carmichael numbers', *J. Australian Math. Soc. Ser. A.*, 1976, pp. 508-10.

[LELE82] H. W. Lenstra, A. K. Lenstra and L. Lovasv, 'Factoring polynomials with rational coefficients', *Math. Operations Research*, Vol. 8, No. 4, Math. Annalen 261, 1982, pp. 515-34.

[LEMP79] A. Lempel, 'Cryptology in transition: A survey', *Computing Surveys*, Vol. 11, No. 4, 1979, pp. 285-304.

[LENA62] Jack Levine and H. M. Nahikian, 'On the construction of involutory matrices', *Amer. Math. Monthly*, Vol. 69, 1962, pp. 267-72.

[LENN78] R. E. Lennon, 'Cryptography architecture for information security', *IBM Systems J.*, Vol. 17, No. 2, 1978, pp. 138-50.

[LENS80] H. W. Lenstra, Jr, 'Primality testing algorithms', *Seminaire Bourbaki*, Lecture Notes in Mathematics, 1980.

[LENS83] H. W. Lenstra, Jr, 'Integer programming with a fixed number of variables', *Math. of Operations Research*, Vol. 8, No. 4, 1983, pp. 538-47.

[LENS84] H. W. Lenstra, Jr, 'Integer programming and cryptography', *The Math. Intelligencier*, Vol. 6, No. 4, 1984, pp. 14-9.

[LEVA79] S. K. Leung and G. Vacon, 'A Method for Private Communication Over a Public Channel', preprint, 1979.

[LEVE62] W. J. LeVeque, *Elementary Theory of Numbers*, Addison-Wesley, Reading, Mass., 1962.

[LEVE77] W. LeVeque, *Fundamentals of Number Theory*, Addison-Wesley, Reading, Mass., 1977.

[LEVI58a] Jack Levine, 'Variable matrix substitution in algebraic cryptography', *Amer. Math. Monthly*, Vol. 65, 1958, pp. 170-79.

[LEVI58b] Jack Levine, 'Some further methods in algebraic cryptography', *Journal Elisha Mitchell Science Society*, Vol. 74, 1958, pp. 110-13.

[LEVI61a] Jack Levine, 'Some elementary cryptanalysis of algebraic cryptography', *Amer. Math. Monthly*, Vol. 68, 1961, pp. 411-18.

[LEVI61b] Jack Levine, 'Some applications of high-speed computers to the case N = 2 of algebraic cryptography', *Math. Comp.*, Vol. 15, 1961, pp. 254-60.

[LEVI63] Jack Levine, 'Analysis of the case N = 3 in algebraic cryptography with involutory key-matrix and known alphabet', *J. Reine Agnew. Math.*, Vol. 213, 1963, pp. 1-30.

[LEXR76] Lexar Corporation, 'An Evaluation of the NBS Data Encryption Standard', Sep. 1976.

[LIMA78] S. M. Lipton and S. M. Matyas, 'Making the digital signature legal – and safeguarded', *Data Comm.*, Feb. 1978, pp. 41-52.

[LOVA80] L. Lovasv, 'A new linear programming algorithm – better or worse than the simplex method', *Math. Intelligencier*, Vol. 2, No. 3, 1980, pp. 141-6.

[LUEK75] G. S. Lueker and K. S. Booth, 'Linear algorithms to recognise interval graphs, graph planarity using PQ-tree algorithms', *Procs. 7th ACM Sym. Theory Comp. Sci.*, 1975, pp. 254-65.

[LULE79] S. C. Lu and L. N. Lee, 'A simple and effective public key cryptosystem', *Comsat Tech. Rev.*, Vol. 9, Spring 1979, pp. 15-24.


[MACK82] C. A. Mackenzie, *Modern Cryptographic Techniques and Communication Protocols*, Honours Thesis, Department Applied Mathematics, The University of Sydney, Sydney, 1982.

[MAME78] S. M. Matyas, C. H. Meyer and 'Generating distribution, and installation of cryptographic keys', *IBM Systems J.*, Vol. 17, No. 2, 1978, pp. 126-37.

[MAME81] S. M. Matyas and C. H. Meyer, 'Electronic signature for Data Encryption Standard', *IBM Tech. Disc. Bull.*, Vol. 24, No. 5, 1981, pp. 2332-24.

[MAOL87] Mamoru Maekawa, Arthur E. Oldehoeft and Rodney R. Oldehoeft, *Operating Systems*, The Benjamin/Cummings Publishing Company, Menlo Park, Ca., 1987.

[MAOS83] S. M. Matyas and J. Oseas, 'Decipher operation for public-key algorithm', *IBM Tech. Disc. Bull.* (USA), Vol. 26, No. 7a, Dec. 1983, pp. 3289-91.

[MART73] J. Martin, *Security, Accuracy and Privacy in Computer Systems*, Prentice Hall, Englewood Cliffs, NJ, 1973.

[MCEL78] R. J. McEliece, 'A public-key cryptosystem based on algebraic coding theory', *Deep Space Network Progress Report*, Nos. 42-44, Jet Propulsion Labs, Pasadena, Ca. 1978, pp. 114-6.

[MCGO83] A. J. McAuley and R. M. F. Goodman, 'Modifications to the trapdoor-knapsack public key cryptosystem', *1983 IEEE International Symposium in Information Theory, Abstracts of papers*, p. 130.

[MCTU76] R. K. McNeill, B. Tuckerman, 'User's Guide to the IPS cryptographic programs for the OS and OS/VS/TSO systems', *IBM Research Report*, RC 5942, 13 April 1976.

[MEHE78] R. C. Merkle and M. E. Hellman, 'Hiding information and signatures in trap door knapsacks', *Stanford University Report*; also *1977 IEEE International Symposium on Information Theory*, Ithaca, New York, Oct. 1977; also *IEEE Trans. Inform. Theory*, Vol. 24, No. 5, Sep. 1978, pp. 525-30.

[MEMA81] Carl H. Meyer, Stephen H. Matyas and R. E. Lennon, 'Required cryptographic authentication criteria for EFT systems', *Symposium on Security and Privacy*, 1981, pp. 89-98.

[MEMA84] Carl H. Meyer, Stephen M. Matyas and *Cryptography: A New Dimension in Computer Data Security*, John Wiley & Sons, New York, 1982.

[MERE] R. Merkle and J. Reeds, unpublished work.

[MERI79] P. D. Merillat, 'Secure stand alone positive personnel identity verification system (SSA-PPIV)', *Technical Report SAND79-0070*, Sandia National Laboratories, Albuquerque, NM, March 1979.

[MERK78] R. Merkle, 'Secure communications over insecure channels', *CACM*, Vol. 21, No. 4, April 1978, pp. 294-9.

[MERK79a] R. C. Merkle, 'Secrecy, authentication, and public-key systems', *Technical Report No. 1979-1*, Information Systems Library, Stanford Electronics Laboratories, Stanford, Ca., 1979.

[MERK79b] R. C. Merkle, 'A Certified Digital Signature', preprint, 1979.

[METU72] C. H. Meyer and W. L. Tuchman, 'Breaking a Cryptographic Scheme Employing a Linear Shift Register with Feedback I, *IBM Systems Product Division, TR 21.506*, Nov. 1972.

[METU73] C. H. Meyer and W. L. Tuchman, 'Breaking a Cryptographic Scheme Employing a Linear Shift Register with Feedback II, *IBM Systems Product Division, TR 27.101*, May 1973.

[MILL75a] J. C. P. Miller, 'On factorization, with a suggested new approach', *Math. Comp.*, Vol. 29, 1975, pp. 155-72.

[MILL75b] G. L. Miller, 'Riemann's hypothesis and tests for primality'. *Proceedings of the Seventh Annual ACM Symposium on the Theory of Computing*. Albuquerque, NM, May 1975, pp. 234-9; extended version available as *Res. Rep. CS-75-27*, Department of Computer Science, University of Waterloo, Waterloo, Ont., Canada, Oct. 1975.

[MISU__] G. Miller, S. Sutton, M. Mattthews, J. Yip and T. Thomas, 'Integrity mechanisms in secure UNIX', *Gould UTX/32S*, preprint.

[MOBR75] M. N. Morrison and J. Brillhart, 'A method of factoring and the factorization of $F_7$', *Math. Comp.*, Vol. 29, 1975, pp. 183-205.

[MORR78] R. Morris, 'The Data Encryption Standard-retrospective and prospect', *IEEE Comms*, Vol. 16, No. 6, Nov. 1978, pp. 11-14.

[MOSI86] J. H. Moore and G. J. Simmons, 'Cycle structure of the DES with weak and semiweak keys', *Advances in Cryptology: Proceedings of CRYPTO '86*, (ed. A. M. Odlyzko), Lecture Notes in Computer Science, Vol. 263, Springer-Verlag, New York, 1987, pp. 187-205.

[MOSL77] R. Morris, N. J. A. Sloane and A. D. Wyner, 'Assessment of the National Bureau of Standards proposed Federal Data Encryption Standard', *Cryptologia*, Vol. 1, No. 3, 1977, pp. 181-91.

[MOTH79] R. Morris and K. Thompson, 'Password security : A case history', *CACM*, Vol. 22, No. 11, Nov. 1979, pp. 594-7.

[MULL83] C. Muller-Schloer, 'A microprocessor-based cryptoprocessor', *IEEE Micro*, Oct. 1983, pp. 5-15.

[MUNE84] R. C. Mullin, E. Nemeth and N. Weidenhofer, 'Will public key cryptosystems live up to their expectations?', *HEP Implementation of the Discrete Log Codebreaker*, ICPP 84, pp. 193-6.

[NBS77] National Bureau of Standards, *Report of the Workshop on Cryptography in Support of Computer Security*, 21-22 Sep. 1976, NBSIR77-1291, Sep. 1977.

[NEED00] R. M. Needham, referred to in [WILK68] op cit.

[NESC78] R. M. Needham and M. D. Schroeder, 'Using encryption for authentication in large networks of computers', *CACM*, Vol. 21, No. 12 Dec. 1978, pp. 993-9.

[NEUM78] P. G. Neumann, 'Computer system security evaluation', *AFIPS Conference Proceedings 47*, June 1978, pp. 1087-95.

[NIED85] Harold Niederreiter, 'A public-key cryptosystem based on shift register sequences', *EUROCRYPT 85 Abstracts*, Linz, Austria, 9-11 April 1985, pp. 35-9.

[NIZU72] I. Niven and H. S. Zuckerman, *An Introduction to the Theory of Numbers*, Wiley, New York, 1972.

[NOBA__] R. Nobauer, 'Redei-Funktionen und ihre Anwendung in der Kryptographie', *Acta Sci. Math. Szeged*, to appear.

[OCSE87] L. J. OConnor and J. Seberry, *The Cryptographic Significance of the Knapsack Problem*, Aegean Park Press, Ca., 1987.

[ODLY84a] A. M. Odlyzko, 'Discrete logarithms in finite fields and their cryptographic significance', *Advances in Cryptography: Proceedings of EUROCRYPT 84*, pp. 224-314.

[ODLY84b] A. M. Odlyzko, 'Cryptanalytic attacks on the multiplicative knapsack cryptosystem and on Shamir's fast signature scheme', *IEEE Trans. on Inform. Theory*, Vol. IT30, No. 4, July 1984, pp. 594-601.

[ONG84] H. Ong, C. P. Schnorr and A. Shamir, 'An efficient signature scheme based on quadratic equations', *Proceedings of the 16th Symposium on the Theory of Computing*, Washington DC, April 1984.

[ONSC84] H. Ong and C. P. Schnorr, 'Signatures through approximate representations by quadratic forms', *Advances in Cryptology: Proceedings of CRYPTO 83*, (ed. D. Chaum), Plenum, New York, 1984, pp. 117-32.

[ORRO86] G. A. Orton, M. P. Roy and P. A. Scott, 'VLSI implementation of public-key encryption algorithms', *CRYPTO '86: Abstracts*, 1986, pp. 277-301

[PAWI79] E. S. Page and L. B. Wilson, *An Introduction to Combinatorics*, Cambridge University Press, Cambridge, 1979.

[PEAR1900] K. Pearson, 'On the criteria that a given system of deviations from the probable in the case of *s* correlated system of variables is such that it can be reasonably supposed to have arisen from random sampling', *Philosphical Magazine*, Series 5, No. 50, 1900, pp. 157-72.

[PETE61] W. W. Peterson, *Error-Correcting Codes*, MIT Press, Cambridge and Mass., John Wiley, New York, 1961.

[PIEP79] J. P. Pieprzyk, 'Generalization of Vigenere ciphers', *Archiwum Automatyki i Telemechaniki*, No. 4, 1979, pp. 453-68.

[PIEP80] J. P. Pieprzyk, 'Random Vigenere ciphers and their application in computer systems', *Archiwum Automatyki i Telemechaniki*, No. 2, 1980, pp. 419-36.

[PIEP85] J. P. Pieprzyk and D. A. Rutkowski, 'Design of public key cryptosystems using idempotent elements', *Computers and Security*, No. 4, 1985, pp. 297-308.

[PIEP86] Josef P. Pieprzyk, 'On some cryptographic morphisms', *Rozprawy Elektrotechniczne*, No. 1, 1986, pp. 297-308.

[POET85] Ron Poet, 'The design of special purpose hardware to factor large integers', *Computer Physics Communications*, Vol. 37, 1985, pp. 337–41.

[POHE78] S. C. Pohlig and M. E Hellman, 'An improved algorithm for computing logarithms in GF(p) and its cryptographic significance', *IEEE Trans. on Inform. Theory*, Vol. IT-24, Jan. 1978, pp. 106-11.

[POHL77] S. C. Pohlig, *Algebraic and Combinatorial Aspects of Cryptography*, Ph.D. Thesis, Stanford University; Technical Report 6602-1, Oct. 1977.

[POHS81] M. Pohst, 'On the computation of lattice vectors of minimal length, successive minima and reduced bases with applications', *Assoc. Comput. Mach. SIGSAM Bull.*, Vol. 15, 1981, pp. 37-44.

[POKL78] G. J. Popek and C. S. Kline, 'Encryption protocols, public key algorithms, and digital signatures in computer networks', *in Foundations of Secure Computation*, (eds R. A. Demillo, et al.) , Academic Press, New York, 1978, pp. 133-53.

[POKL79] G. J. Popek and C. S. Kline, 'Encryption and secure computer networks', *Computing Surveys*, Vol. 11, No. 4, Dec. 1979, pp. 331-56.

[POLL74] J. M. Pollard, 'Theorems on factorization and primality testing', *Proc. Camb. Phil. Soc.*, Vol. 76, 1974, pp. 521-28.

[POLL75] J. M. Pollard, 'A monte carlo method for factorization', *BIT*, Vol. 15, 1975, pp. 331-34.

[POME81] C. Pomerance, 'Recent developments in primality testing', *Math. Intelligencer*, Vol. 3 , 1981, pp. 97-105.

[POME84] Carl Pomerance, 'The quadratic sieve factoring algorithm', *Proc. EUROCRYPT 84: Advances in Cryptology*, New York-London, pp. 169-82.

[POSM86] Carl Pomerance, J. W. Smith and Randy Tuler, 'A pipe-line architecture for factoring large integers with quadratic sieve algorithm', *Abstracts of CRYPTO 86*, Santa Barbara, Ca., 1986, pp. 3.1-3.20.

[POTT77] R. J. Potter, 'Electronic mail', *Science*, Vol. 195, 1977, pp. 1160-4.

[PRIC82] W. L. Price, 'Public-key cryptosystems, authentication and signatures', *New Advances in Distributed Computer Systems: Proc. of the NATO Advanced Study Inst.*, 1982, pp. 327-40.

[PURD74] G. Purdy, 'A high security log-in-procedure', *CACM*, Vol. 17, Aug. 1974, pp. 442-5.

[QUCO82] J. J. Quisquater and C. Couvreur, 'Fast decipherment algorithm for RSA public-key crytosytem', *Electronic Letters*, Vol. 18, No. 21, Oct. 1982, pp. 905–907.

[RABI76] M. O. Rabin, 'Probabilistic algorithms' in *Algorithms and Complexity*, (ed. J. F. Traub), Academic Press, New York, 1976, pp. 21-40.

[RABI78a] M. O. Rabin, 'Digitalized signatures' in *Foundations of Secure Computation*, R. Lipton and R. DeMillo (eds), Academic Press, New York, 1978, pp. 155-66.

[RABI78b] M. O. Rabin, 'Signature and certification by coding', *IBM Tech. Disc. Bull.*, Vol. 20, No. 8, Jan. 1978, pp. 3337-38.

[RABI79] M. O. Rabin, 'Digitalized signatures and public-key functions as intractable as factorization', *Techical Report*, MIT/LCS/TR212, MIT Lab., Computer Science, Cambridge, Mass. Jan. 1979.

[RABI80] M. O. Rabin, 'Probabilistic algorithms for primality testing', *Journal Number Theory*, No. 12, 1980, pp. 128-38.

[REIL84] C. Reilly, 'Authentication, encryption and key security', *Proceedings of Public Seminar on EFT*, Melbourne, July 1984, pp. 39-46.

[RIAD78] Ronald L. Rivest, Len Adleman and Michael L. Dertouzos, 'On data banks and privacy homomorphisms', *Foundation of Secure Computations*, Academic Press, New York, 1978.

[RISH78] R. Rivest, A. Shamir and L. Adleman, 'A method for obtaining digital signatures and public-key cryptosystems', *CACM*, Vol. 21, No. 2, Feb. 1978, pp. 120-8.

[RITH74] D. M. Ritchie and K. Thompson, 'The UNIX time-sharing system', *CACM*, Vol. 17, No. 7, July 1974, pp. 365-75.

[RIVE78] R. Rivest, 'Remarks on a proposed cryptanalytic attack on the MIT public-key cryptosystem', *Cryptologia*, No. 2, 1978, pp. 62-5.

[RIVE79] R. L. Rivest, 'Critical remarks on "Critical remarks on some public-key cryptosystems"' by T. Herlestam, *BIT*, Vol. 19, April 1979, pp. 274-5.

[ROHR48] H. Rohrbach, 'Mathematical and mechanical methods in cryptography', *FIAT Review of German Science, Applied Mathematics*, Part I, Wiesbaden, 1948, pp. 233-57.

[SAA2805.5] Australian Standard®, 2805.5 -1985, *Electronic Funds Transfer- Requirements for Interfaces, Data Encryption Algorithm*, Part 5, Standards Association of Australia, Sydney, N.S.W.

[SACC36] L. Sacco, *Manual Of Cryptography*, Reprinted by Aegean Park Press, Laguna Hills, Ca. (translation of 'Manuale di cripttografia', Roma, 1936).

[SALK75] Harvey M. Salkin, 'The knapsack problem: A survey', *Naval Research Logistics Quarterly*, Vol. 22, 1975, pp. 127-44.

[SALO85] A. Salomaa, 'Cryptography from Caesar to DES and RSA', *Bull. Eur. Assoc. Th. Comp. Sci.* (Austria), No. 26, pp. 101-20, June 1985.

[SALT78] J. Saltzer, 'On digital signatures', *Operating Systems Review*, special interest group of ACM, Vol. 12, 1978, pp. 12-14.

[SANT76] L. A. Santalo, *Integral Geometry and Geometric Probability*, Addison-Wesley, 1976.

[SASC75] J. H. Saltzer and M. D. Schroeder, 'Protection of information in computer systems', *Proc. IEEE*, Vol. 63, No. 9, 1975, pp. 1278-1308.

[SCHO83] P. Schobi and J. L. Massey, 'Fast authentification in a trapdoor-knapsack public key cryptosystem', *Cryptography*, (ed. T. Beth), Lecture Notes in Computer Science, Vol. 149, Springer-Verlag, New York, 1983, pp. 289-306.

[SCSH79] R. Schroeppel and A. Shamir, 'A $T.A^2 = O(2^n)$ time/space tradeoff for certain NP-complete problems', *Proc. IEEE 20th Annual Symposium on the Foundations of Computer Science*, Oct. 1979.

[SEBE85] J. Seberry, 'A subliminal channel in codes for authentication without secrecy', *Ars Combinatoria*, Vol. 19A, 1985, pp. 337-42.

[SEID83] Jerzy Seidler, *Principles of Computer Communication Network Design*, Chichester, West Sussex, England, 1983.

[SHAM78] A. Shamir, 'A fast signature scheme', *MIT Laboratory for Computer Science*, Tech. Memo. 107, July 1978.

[SHAM79] Adi Shamir, 'On the cryptocomplexity of knapsack systems', *Proceedings of the 11th ACM Symposium Theory of Computers*, pp. 118-29, May 1979.

[SHAM79a] A. Shamir, 'A Fast Signature Scheme', *Tech Rpt. MIT/LCS/TM-107*, MIT Laboratory for Computer Science, Cambridge, Mass., 1979.

[SHAM79b] A. Shamir, 'How to Share a Secret', *Tech. Memo. 134*, MIT Laboratory for Computer Science, May 1979.

[SHAM80a] Adi Shamir, 'The cryptographic security of compact knapsacks', *Proceedings of the Symposium on Privacy and Security*, 1980, pp. 94-9.

[SHAM82a] Adi Shamir, 'A polynomial time algorithm for breaking the basic Merkle-Hellman cryptosystem', *Proceedings of the 23rd IEEE Symposium on Founds. Computer Science*, 1982, pp. 145-52.

[SHAM82b] Adi Shamir, 'The Strongest Knapsack-based Algorithm?', *Absracts: CRYPTO '82*, Santa Barbara, Ca., Aug. 1982.

[SHAM83] Adi Shamir, 'Embedding cryptographic trapdoors in arbitrary knapsack systems', *Inf. Proc. Lett.* (Nether.), Vol. 17, No. 2, 24 Aug. 1983, pp. 77-9.

[SHAM85a] A. Shamir, 'Identity-based cryptosystems and signature schemes', *Advances in Cryptology: Proc. of CRYPTO '84*, Lecture Notes in Computer Science, No. 196, Springer-Verlag, 1985, pp. 47-53.

[SHAM85b] A. Shamir, 'On the security of DES', *Advances in Cryptology: CRYPTO '85*, Lecture Notes in Computer Science, No. 218, (ed. H.C. Williams), Springer-Verlag, Berlin, Aug. 1985, pp. 280-1.

[SHAN49] C. E. Shannon, 'Communication theory of secrecy systems', *Bell Syst. Tech. J.*, Vol. 28, 1949, pp. 656-715.

[SHAN51] C. E. Shannon, 'Prediction and entropy of printed English', *Bell Syst. Tech. J.*, Vol. 30, 1951, pp. 50-64.

[SHAN79] B. Shanning, 'Data encryption with public key distribution', *Proc. EASCON*,

1979.

[SHAP71] G. F. Shapiro, 'Generalised lagrange multipliers in integer programming', *Operations Research*, Vol. 19, 1971, pp. 68-77.

[SHMI87] Akihiro Shimizu, Shoji Miyaguchi, 'Fast Data Encipherment Algorithm FEAL', *Abstracts of EUROCRYPT 87*, Amsterdam, 13-15 April 1987, pp. VII-11.

[SHUL76] D. Shulman, *An Annotated Bibliography of Cryptography*, Garland Publishing, New York-London, 1976.

[SHZI78] A. Shamir and R. E. Zippel, 'On the Security of the Merkle-Hellman Cryptographic Scheme', *Tech. Rpt. MIT/LCS/TM-119*, MIT Laboratory for Computer Science, Cambridge, Mass., 1978.

[SIMM00] G. J. Simmons, 'Authentication Theory/Coding Theory', Internal paper, Sandia Labs, preprint.

[SIMM79a] G. J. Simmons, 'Cryptology: The mathematics of secure communication', *The Mathematical Intelligencer*, Vol. 1, No. 4, pp. 233-46.

[SIMM79b] G. J. Simmons, 'Symmetric and asymmetric encryption', *Computing Surveys*, Vol. 11, No. 4, Dec. 1979, pp. 305-30.

[SIMM80] G. J. Simmons, 'Secure communications in the presence of pervasive deceit', *Proceeding of the 1980 Symposium on Security and Privacy*, April 1980, pp. 84-93.

[SIMM82a] G. J. Simmons, *Secure Communications and Asymmetric Cryptosystems*, AAAS Selected Symposia Series, Westview Press, Boulder, Col., 1982.

[SIMM82b] G. J. Simmons, 'Message authentication without secrecy', in *Secure Communications and Asymmetric Cryptosystems*, (ed. G. J. Simmons), AAAS Selected Symposia Series, Westview Press, Boulder, Col., 1982, pp. 105-39.

[SIMM83] G. J. Simmons, 'Verification of treaty compliance revisited', *Proceedings of the 1983 Symposium on Security and Privacy*, Oakland, Ca., 25-27 April 1983.

[SIMM84a] G. J. Simmons, 'The prisoners' problem and the subliminal channel', *Advances in Cryptology: Proceedings of CRYPTO 83*, (ed. D. Chaum), Plenum, New York, 1984, pp. 51-67.

[SIMM84b] G. J. Simmons, 'The Subliminal Channel and Digital Signatures', Sandia National Laboratory, preprint, 1984.

[SIMM84c] G. J. Simmons, 'A system for verifying user identity and authorization at the point-of sale or access', *Cryptologia*, Vol. 8, No. 1, 1984.

[SINK68] A. Sinkov, *Elementary Cryptanalysis*, Mathematical Association of America, a mathematical approach, Random House, New York, 1968.

[SINO77] G. J. Simmons and M. J. Norris, 'Preliminary comments on the MIT public-key cryptosystem', *Cryptologia*, Vol. 1, 1977, pp. 406-14.

[SIST72] G. J. Simmons, R. E. Steward and P. A. Stokes, *Digital Data Authenticator*, Patent Application SD2654, S42640, June 1972.

[SLOA81] N. J. A. Sloane, 'Error-correcting codes and cryptography', *The Mathematical Gardner*, Wadsworth, Belmont, Ca., 1981, pp. 346-82, (reprinted in *Cryptologia*), Vol. 6, 1982, pp. 128-53 and pp. 258-78.

[SLOA83] N. J. A. Sloane, 'Encrypting by random rotations', Lecture Notes in Computer Science, Vol. 149, (ed. T. Beth), Springer-Verlag, Berlin-New York, 1983, pp. 71-128.

[SMIT55] L. D. Smith, *Cryptography – The Science of Secret Writing*, Dover

Publications, New York, 1955.

[SOST77] R. Solovay and V. Strassen, 'A fast Monte-Carlo test for primality'. *SIAM J. Comput.*, Vol. 6, March 1977, pp. 84-5, (erratum, ibid, 7, 1978, p. 118).

[SQUI75] J. Squires, 'Russ monitor of U. S phones', *Chicago Tribune*, June 25 1975, p. 123.

[STEV76] W. Stevenson, *A Man Called Intrepid*, Ballantine, New York, 1976.

[STST87] Anne P. Street and Deborah J. Street, *Combinatorics of Experimental Design*, Oxford University Press, 1987.

[SWAR72] W. W. Swart, 'A Multi-compartment Knapsack Problem', presented at the Joint National Meeting of AIIE, ORSA, and TIMS, Atlantic City, NJ, Nov. 1972.

[SZE70] G. Szekeres, 'Multidimensional continued fractions', *Ann. Univ. Sci. Budapest, Sect. Math.*, Vol. 13, 1970, pp. 113-40.


[TANE81a] Andrew S. Tanenbaum, *Computer Networks*, Prentice Hall, NJ, 1981.

[TANE81b] Andrew S. Tanenbaum, 'Network protocols', *Computing Surveys*, Vol. 13, No. 4, Dec. 1981, pp. 453-89.

[TUCK70] L. Tuckerman, 'A Study of the Vigenere-Vernam single and multiple enciphering loop systems', *IBM Research Report*, RC. 2879, 14 May 1970.

[TUCK73] L. Tuckerman, 'Solution of a fractionation-transposition cipher', *IBM Research Report*, RC. 4537, 21 Sep. 1973.


[VAND78] E. Van der Rhoer, *Deadly Magic*, Robert Hale, London, 1978.

[VANL83] J. H. van Lint, 'Cryptography', *Informatie* (Nether.), Vol. 25, No. 9, Sep. 1983, pp. 47-51.

[VAVA84a] U. Vazirani and V. Vazirani, 'Efficient and secure pseudo-random number generation', *Proceedings of the $25^{th}$ FOCS*, 1984.

[VAVA84b] U. Vazirani and V. Vazirani, 'RSA bits are .732+ε secure', *Advances in Cryptology: Proceedings of CRYPTO 83*, (ed. D. Chaum), Plenum, New York, 1984, pp. 369-75.

[VEIK69] E. Veikko, 'On numbers with small prime divisors', *Ann. Acad. Sci. Fenn Series A I*, 440, 1969.

[VINO61] I. M. Vinogradov, *Elementary Number Theory*, Dover, New York, 1961.


[WAER53] Van der Waerden, Frederick Ungar *Modern Algebra*, (Vol. 1 and 2), New York, 1953.

[WAGN84] Neal R. Wagner, 'Searching for public key cryptosystems', *Proceedings of Symposium on Privacy and Security*, pp. 91-8, 1984.

[WELL84] A. L. Wells, Jr, 'A polynomial form for logarithms modulo a prime', *IEEE Trans. Inform. Theory*, Nov. 1984, pp. 845-6.

[WEST68] A. E. Western and J. C. P. Miller, 'Tables of indices and primitive roots', *Royal Soc. Math. Tables*, Vol. 9, Cambridge University Press, England, 1968.

[WILK72] M. V. Wilkes, *Time Sharing Computer Systems*, Elsevier, New York, 1972.

[WILL78] H. C. Williams, 'Primality testing on a computer', *Ars Combinatoria*, No. 5, 1978, pp. 127-85.

[WILL80] H. C. Williams, 'A modification of the RSA public-key encryption procedure', *IEEE Trans. Inform. Theory*, IT-26, 1980, pp. 726-9.

[WILL82] H. C. Williams, 'Computationally "hard" problems', *Secure Communications and Asymmetric Cryptosystem AAAS Selected Symposium*, Vol. 69, (ed. Gustavius J. Simmons), 1982, pp. 11-39.

[WILL83] H. C. Williams, 'Encryption Exponents', presented at CRYPTO '85, Santa Barbara, Ca., 1985.

[WILL84] H. C. Williams, 'An overview of factoring', *Advances in Cryptology: Proceedings of CRYPTO 83*, (ed. D. Chaum), Plenum, New York, 1984, pp. 71-80.

[WILL85] H. C. Williams, 'An $M^3$ public-key encryption scheme', *Advances in Cryptography: Proceedings of CRYPTO 85*, (ed. H.C.Williams), Lecture Notes in Computer Science, Vol. 218, Springer-Verlag, New York, 1986, pp. 358-68.

[WINT74] F. W. Winterbotham *The Ultra Secret*, Dell, New York, 1974.

[WISC79] H. C. Williams and B. K. Schmid, 'Some remarks concerning the MIT public-key cryptosystem', *BIT*, Vol. 19, 1979, pp. 525-38.

[WOHL62] R. Wohlstetter, *Pearl Harbor: Warning And Decision*, Stanford University Press, Stanford, Ca., 1962.

[WOLF70] J. R. Wolfe, *Secret Writing-The Craft of the Cryptographer*, McGraw-Hill, New York, 1970.

[WULF75] W. A. Wulf, 'Reliable hardware/software architecture', *IEEE Transactions on Software Engineering*, Vol. SE-1, No. 2, June 1975, pp. 233-40.

[WUWI86] M. C. Wunderlich and H. C. Williams, 'A parallel version of the continued fraction integer algorithm', *Abstracts of CRYPTO '86: Santa Barbara*, Ca., 1986, pp. 5.1-5.16.

[WYN75] A. D. Wyner, 'The wire tap channel', *Bell Syst. Tech. J.*, Vol. 54, No. 8, Oct. 1975, pp. 1355-87.


[YIPE82] K. Yiu and K. Peterson, 'A single-chip VLSI implementation of the discrete exponential public-key distribution system', *Proc. GLOBCOM-82, IEEE 1982*, pp. 173-9. *IBM Systems J.*, Vol. 15, No. 1, 1976, pp. 102-16.

[YUVA79] G. Yuval, 'How to swindle Rabin', *Cryptologia*, Vol. 3, No. 3, July 1979, pp. 187-9.

## ADDENDA

[GUNT87] C.G. Gunter, 'Altering step generators controlled by De Bruijn Sequences', *Advances in Cryptology, EUROCRYPT'87*, (eds. D. Chaum and W.L. Price), Lecture Notes In Computer Science, Vol. 304, Springer-Verlag, Berlin-New York, 1987, pp. 5-14.

[SIEG84] T. Siegenthaler, Applications', *IEEE Transactions on Inf. Theory*, Vol. IT-30, No. 5, September 1984, pp. 776-780.

[VOGE84] R. Vogel, *Advances in Cryptology, Proceedings EUROCRYPT '84*, (eds. T. Beth, N. Cot and I. Ingemarsson), Lecture Notes In Computer Science, Vol. 209, Springer-Verlag, Berlin-New York, 1985, pp. 99-109.

# INDEX